TEST-ITEM FILE

Gleitman   Fridlund   Reisberg

Psychology

FIFTH EDITION

TEST-ITEM FILE

Gleitman   Fridlund   Reisberg

Psychology

FIFTH EDITION

Su Boatright-Horowitz
Susan Rakowitz
Paul Cornwell
Richard Day
John Jonides

 W • W • NORTON & COMPANY • NEW YORK • LONDON

Printed in the United States of America

Composition and layout by Roberta Flechner Graphics

Cover illustrations: (*Left*) Michelangelo Buonarroti, *David,* detail of head
in profile. Accademia, Florence, Italy. Photograph courtesy Scala/Art
Resource, NY. (*Right*) Michelangelo Buonarroti, *Studies for the Libyan
Sybil* (copy). Uffizi Gallery, Florence, Italy.

ISBN 0-393-97375-1 (pbk.)

W. W. Norton & Company, Inc., 500 Fifth Avenue, New York, NY 10110
http://www.wwnorton.com

W. W. Norton & Company Ltd., 10 Coptic Street, London WC1A 1PU

1 2 3 4 5 6 7 8 9 0

CONTENTS

Gleitman   Fridlund   Reisberg

Psychology

FIFTH EDITION

CHAPTER 1 | Introduction

Answer: d
The scope of psychology
p. 1

1. The subject matter of psychology:
   a. may include biological analyses of the behavior of organisms.
   b. includes an analysis of organisms in isolation and in groups.
   c. may include an analysis of organisms other than humans.
   d. all of the above

Answer: c
The scope of psychology
p. 1

2. Electrical stimulation of the brain is:
   a. exceedingly painful.
   b. only done with the patient fully anesthetized.
   c. done in locally anesthetized patients undergoing neurosurgery.
   d. almost certain to cause the patient to lose consciousness.

Answer: b
The scope of psychology
p. 1

3. Studies of the rate at which blood flows through the brain show that:
   a. blood flow is uniform.
   b. the rate depends on physiological function.
   c. reading silently and aloud produce the same pattern.
   d. blood flows away from active areas of the brain to allow them to function.

Answer: a
The scope of psychology
p. 1

4. Cerebral blood flow studies indicate:
   a. which areas of the brain are active.
   b. that blood flow to certain areas of the brain produces auditory experiences such as hearing clicks.
   c. that blood flow to certain areas of the brain produces involuntary movements.
   d. that blood flow to certain areas of the brain produces visual experiences such as seeing lights.

Answer: a
The scope of psychology
p. 2

5. An ambiguous figure:
   a. is one that can be interpreted in more than one way.
   b. is one that is blurry and difficult to discern.
   c. is perceived in a particular way regardless of the viewer's prior experiences.
   d. is one that is too dark to discern.

Answer: b
The scope of psychology
p. 2

6. The way an ambiguous figure is perceived:
   a. depends solely on characteristics of the figure.
   b. can be influenced by the perceiver's prior experiences.
   c. is invariably unpredictable.
   d. is based primarily on the colors in the figure.

Answer: c
The scope of psychology
p. 2

7. The way an ambiguous sentence is understood:
   a. depends solely on characteristics of the sentence.
   b. is invariably unpredictable.
   c. can be influenced by the perceiver's prior experiences.
   d. depends on a careful grammatical analysis.

Answer: b
The scope of psychology
p. 2

8. Alex sees a number of pictures of old women and is then shown an ambiguous figure that could be either an old or a young woman. He is:
   a. most likely to see the figure as a young woman because old women have become too familiar and his brain is looking for novel stimulation.
   b. most likely to see the figure as an old woman because of the context.
   c. equally likely to perceive it either as an old or young woman because the pictures he saw previously are irrelevant.
   d. more likely to see the picture one way than the other, but there's no basis for predicting which way is more likely.

Answer: d
The scope of psychology
p. 2

9. The sentence "visiting relatives can be a nuisance":
   a. is ambiguous.
   b. may require context to help interpret.
   c. is an example of perceptual bias.
   d. a and b

Answer: d
The scope of psychology
p. 2

10. "Riding horses can be dangerous." Knowing whether this sentence means "A few riding horses aren't safe to be around" or "One must watch out while riding a horse" depends upon:
    a. what we heard just before.
    b. a thorough grammatical analysis.
    c. context.
    d. a and c

Answer: a
The scope of psychology
p. 2

11. Which of the following statements is true?
    a. Ambiguity occurs both in visual patterns and in language.
    b. The sentence "Jill got a *B* in calculus" is ambiguous.
    c. The sentence "Visiting relatives is always a nuisance" is ambiguous.
    d. all of the above

Answer: c
The scope of psychology
p. 2

12. Which of the following statements is false?
    a. Ambiguity occurs both in visual patterns and in language.
    b. How an ambiguous sentence is interpreted depends on the context of prior discussion.
    c. The sentence "Jim never drinks gin" is ambiguous.
    d. The sentence "Visiting relatives can be a nuisance" is ambiguous.

Answer: b
The scope of psychology
p. 2

13. The visual cliff is used to study:
    a. courtship displays in animals.
    b. the perceptual world of infants.
    c. ambiguous sights and sounds.
    d. visual images produced through electrical stimulation of the brain.

Answer: c
The scope of psychology
p. 3

14. Experiments with the visual cliff show that:
    a. infants are more sensitive to depth than adults.
    b. adults are more sensitive to depth than infants.
    c. perception of depth may be innate.
    d. perception of depth depends heavily on prior experiences.

Answer: a
The scope of psychology
p. 3

15. In animals, many social interactions depend largely on _____ forms of communication.
    a. innate
    b. learned
    c. complex
    d. verbal

Answer: d
The scope of psychology
p. 3

16. Displays in different species:
    a. are a form of social communication.
    b. may serve as courtship rituals.
    c. are largely innate.
    d. all of the above

Answer: b
The scope of psychology
p. 4

17. In panicky situations, people in crowds behave:
    a. more logically than if they were alone.
    b. differently than if they were alone.
    c. the same as if they were alone.
    d. differently depending on whether they're toward the rear or the side of the crowd.

Answer: d
A science of many faces
p. 5

18. The discipline of psychology has some overlap with which of the following fields?
    a. sociology
    b. biology
    c. ethology (the study of animal behavior in the wild)
    d. all of the above

19. Dreams:
    a. are never repetitious of sights and sounds that occurred during the dreamer's waking hours.
    b. are never stressful in content.
    c. sometimes are influenced by events in the environment.
    d. are not experienced as real.

20. Some investigators have found that:
    a. external events are never incorporated into dreams.
    b. external events occurring in the present supplement dream images.
    c. external stimulation has no effect on dreaming.
    d. external stimulation causes dreamers to forget their dreams.

21. Dreams are likely to occur:
    a. when the sleeper's eyes are motionless.
    b. when the sleeper's breathing and heart rate are slow and regular.
    c. during slow-wave sleep.
    d. during REM sleep.

22. Dreams are likely to occur:
    a. when the sleeper's eyes move back and forth behind closed
    b. when the sleeper's breathing and heart rate accelerate.
    c. during REM sleep.
    d. all of the above

23. During REM sleep:
    a. breathing rate is depressed.
    b. one observes a decrease in the number of spontaneous eye movements.
    c. heart rate accelerates.
    d. an individual is in the stage of sleep immediately preceding a dream.

24. One characteristic of slow-wave sleep is that:
    a. breathing is fast.
    b. the eyes move in quick irregular darts.
    c. the heart rate is slow and regular.
    d. it produces intense dreaming.

25. Which of the following statements is true?
    a. It's fairly easy to determine when a sleeper is likely to be dreaming.
    b. Dreams have no observable manifestations.
    c. The only way to study dreaming is to ask people what they remember about their dreams.
    d. b and c

Answer: c
A science of many faces
p. 6

26. As sleep becomes deeper the brain waves become:
    a. unpredictable.
    b. smaller.
    c. slower.
    d. irregular.

Answer: b
A science of many faces
p. 6

27. EEG patterns during REM sleep:
    a. predict the content of the dream.
    b. resemble the awake pattern.
    c. are highly regular.
    d. are slow and large.

Answer: a
A science of many faces
p. 6

28. During REM sleep the EEG shows waves that are:
    a. rapid, small, and irregular.
    b. relatively slow, large, and regular.
    c. rapid, large, and regular.
    d. relatively slow, small, and regular.

Answer: a
A science of many faces
p. 6

29. During dreaming, the EEG most resembles that:
    a. of when you are attentively listening to a fascinating introductory psychology lecture.
    b. of when you are awake, but relaxed and have your eyes closed.
    c. of the deepest stages of slow-wave sleep.
    d. of when you are close to death in a coma.

Answer: a
A science of many faces
p. 7

30. Which of the following is likely to have the best dream recall?
    a. someone with vivid visual imagery in waking life
    b. someone who wakes up to a radio news program
    c. someone who wakes up to a child complaining of not feeling well
    d. someone who is not getting enough visual stimulation during the day

Answer: a
A science of many faces
p. 7

31. Research using the comparative approach has revealed that:
    a. many, but not all, types of animals have REM sleep.
    b. many, but not all, types of animals have dreams.
    c. all types of animals have REM sleep.
    d. all types of animals have dreams.
    e. a and b

Answer: a
A science of many faces
p. 7

32. The content of dreams:
    a. often revolves around people or one's association with people.
    b. is universally the same in all cultures.
    c. is a direct representation of one's thoughts and desires, according to Freud.
    d. is the same in all individuals within a culture.

Answer: c
A science of many faces
p. 7

33. Most of our dreams involve:
    a. aggression.
    b. sex.
    c. other people.
    d. premonitions about the future.
    e. all of the above

Answer: a
A science of many faces
p. 7

34. A glimpse into Cheryl's dreams is likely to tell you something about
    a. Cheryl's daily experiences.
    b. Cheryl's future.
    c. Cheryl's personal, but not her professional, life.
    d. Cheryl's professional, but not her personal, life.

Answer: d
A science of many faces
p. 8

35. In some societies, dreams are:
    a. dismissed as fantasies.
    b. revered as supernatural visions.
    c. seen as giving guidance regarding future behavior.
    d. all of the above

Answer: d
A science of many faces
p. 8

36. According to Freud, one's dreams:
    a. may reflect one's inner desires.
    b. are unaffected by societal constraints.
    c. often involve some sexual or aggressive theme.
    d. a and c

Answer: d
A science of many faces
p. 8

37. According to Freud, dreams:
    a. allow us to express our undisguised primitive impulses with none of the shame or guilt we would experience during waking life.
    b. are often senseless because they represent experiences during an early period of childhood when we could not yet make sense of the world.
    c. are often senseless because the intellect is dulled during sleep.
    d. allow us to indulge in unacceptable wishes in disguised form.

Answer: a
A science of many faces
p. 8

38. According to Freud, dreams are
    a. a compromise between forbidden impulses and social constraints.
    b. the result of random activity in certain areas of the brain.
    c. a direct expression of forbidden impulses.
    d. the brain's attempt to understand sensory experiences (e.g., noises) that the sleeper is unaware of.

Answer: b
A science of many faces
p. 9

39. Analysis of the dreams of young children suggests that:
    a. in children, dreams are not associated with REM sleep.
    b. children may have difficulty differentiating between dreams and events that actually occurred.
    c. the content of children's dreams is completely different from that of adults' dreams.
    d. all of the above

40. The idea that dreams are processes that go on inside the head:
    a. arises from feedback from the rapid eye movements combined with information about the relaxed postural muscles.
    b. leads to them being dismissed by most cultures as relatively unimportant events.
    c. takes most children several years to acquire.
    d. implies that it is almost impossible to study them.
    e. helps many people to learn the general rules by which their brains operate.

41. The idea that dreams are processes that go on inside the head:
    a. suggests that neurological techniques are needed to study their content.
    b. isn't common among preschoolers.
    c. is an outgrowth of the psychoanalytic methods of Freud.
    d. suggests they are not influenced by external events prior to, or during, the dream itself.
    e. all of the above

42. In the mind of a two- or three-year-old-child, dreams are:
    a. made up of experiences encoded in the DNA rather than the child's own experiences.
    b. very real.
    c. the reenactment of what actually happened the previous day.
    d. the means by which the culture enters the child's own thought processes.

43. Dreams are:
    a. fairly similar across people within the same culture.
    b. fairly similar across people in diverse cultures.
    c. typically more bizarre and morbid in schizophrenics than in normals.
    d. typically less bizarre and morbid in schizophrenics than in normals.

44. Dreams have been studied as:
    a. mental experiences.
    b. cognition.
    c. behavior.
    d. all of the above

45. Sally tells her husband at breakfast that she dreamt of walking to the very top of the Washington Monument, being breathless, and collapsing in a bed of straw at the very top. Who of the following is likely to be most interested in her dream?
    a. a development psychologist, like Jean Piaget, who theorizes an orderly progression in the development of both locomotion and subjective events like dreams
    b. a neurological psychologist who studies the relation between eye movements and dreaming
    c. an expert on schizophrenia who studies extremely bizarre dreams
    d. a psychoanalyst, like Freud, who thinks dream content often represents disguised sexual motives

Answer: d
The task of psychology
p. 10

46. Which two fields were most important as the early roots for psychology?
    a. physiology and economics
    b. literature and chemistry
    c. engineering and art
    d. philosophy and medicine

Answer: a
A science of many faces
p. 10

47. The discipline of psychology:
    a. was strongly influenced by philosophy.
    b. arose independently of other disciplines.
    c. is unrelated to newer fields like computer science.
    d. is constantly at odds with biology and medicine.

Answer: b
The task of psychology
p. 11

48. The major goal of contemporary psychology is to:
    a. understand the causes of deviant behavior.
    b. elucidate general principles of behavior.
    c. produce therapies for mental illness.
    d. understand the biological mediators of behavior.

Answer: c
The task of psychology
p. 11

49. The major goal of psychology is to:
    a. cure mental illness.
    b. understand the underlying causes of abnormal behavior.
    c. understand the general principles of behavior.
    d. control human behavior.

Answer: e
The task of psychology
p. 11

50. Psychology is
    a. an art.
    b. a science.
    c. the study of individuals.
    d. the study of behavior.
    e. b and d

Answer: d
The task of psychology
p. 11

51. The major goal of contemporary psychology is to:
    a. collaborate with physicians to cure mental illness.
    b. understand the underlying causes of abnormal behavior.
    c. discover ways to help employers control the behavior of employees.
    d. understand the general principles of behavior.

Answer: b
The task of psychology
p. 11

52. A focus on a particular instance or case and its use to gain insight into what is common to all people is most characteristic of:
    a. management.
    b. the arts and humanities.
    c. the biological sciences.
    d. the social sciences.

Answer: b
The task of psychology
p. 11

53. Psychology and literature
    a. are unrelated.
    b. address many of the same issues, but with different methods.
    c. use the same methods, but apply them to different issues.
    d. typically make contradictory claims.

CHAPTER 2 | Biological Bases of Behavior

Answer: c
Biological bases of behavior
p. 15

1. Animistic explanations of animal behavior involve the postulations of:
   a. free will.
   b. tropisms.
   c. inner spirits.
   d. reflexes.

Answer: d
The organism as machine
p. 15

2. Rene Descartes made his speculations about relexes shortly after:
   a. Darwin published his own speculations about the origin of species, and the U.S. Civil War (1850s).
   b. Freud had popularized his ideas about the unconscious, and the time of World War I (1910s).
   c. Marco Polo traveled to China (about 1300).
   d. Kepler and Galileo developed ideas about movements of planets (1600s).

Answer: d
The organism as machine
p. 16

3. Descartes' early forerunner of the reflex differed from our modern concept because Descartes:
   a. distinguished between sensory and motor nerves.
   b. posited the existence of the synapse.
   c. said that nerve impulses are electrochemical events.
   d. none of the above

Answer: c
The organism as machine
p. 16

4. The word *reflex* has its origin in:
   a. Sherrington's work on synapses.
   b. Sherrington's studies of scratching in dogs.
   c. Descartes' belief that the energy from the outside is reflected back by the nervous system to an animal's muscles.
   d. Descartes' belief that animals act as automatons but people are rational and have souls.

Answer: a
The organism as machine
p. 16

5. The word *reflex* has its origin in:
    a. Descartes' belief that the energy from the outside is reflected back by the nervous system to an animal's muscles.
    b. Descartes' belief that animals act as automatons but people are rational and have souls.
    c. Descartes' desire to explain coughing and sneezing without reference to the soul.
    d. Descartes' idea that the pineal gland mediates the relationship between the nonmaterial mind and the material brain.

Answer: a
The organism as machine
p. 16

6. The word *reflex* has its origin in:
    a. Descartes' belief that the nervous system is analogous to a mirror; stimuli come in and are reflected out by nerves to the muscles.
    b. Descartes' belief that animals act as automatons but people are rational and have souls.
    c. Freud's idea that mechanisms in the spinal cord do not involve symbolism, while mechanisms in the upper reaches of the brain involve substantial symbolism.
    d. Freud's early work on aphasia and the fact that some speech seems to be almost automatic.

Answer: c
The organism as machine
p. 16

7. The word *reflex* has its origin in:
    a. Descartes' idea that animals, but not humans, act automatically.
    b. Descartes' desire to explain such acts as sneezing without reference to the soul.
    c. Descartes' belief that the energy from the outside is reflected back by the nervous system to the animal's muscles.
    d. none of the above

Answer: d
The organism as machine
p. 16

8. Descartes' conceptualization of the reflex differs most from the contemporary viewpoint in which of the following respects?
    a. the idea that some initial event triggers behavior
    b. the involvement of nerves in reflexive movement
    c. the use of contemporary technology as a basis for analogy
    d. the view that the human soul serves as a central switching mechanism

Answer: b
The organism as machine
p. 16

9. Which of the following commonly observed characteristics of human or animal behavior is inconsistent with Descartes' view on reflexes?
    a. the withdrawal response upon touching a hot object
    b. behavior (e.g., running) in the absence of any obvious stimulus
    c. the existence of nerves that connect receptors and effectors to the brain
    d. the fact that the same stimulus usually produces the same response

Answer: c
The organism as machine
p. 16

10. Galileo had to recant his suggestions that the earth orbits around the sun. Similarly, Descartes would probably have had trouble with the Christian Church if he had:
    a. suggested that people have reflexes.
    b. continued his study of evolution.
    c. not put a "ghost" in his machine.
    d. pursued his work in analytic geometry.

Answer: a
The organism as machine
p. 16

11. To Descartes, nonhuman animals were machines but humans were not because humans, and only humans:
    a. possessed souls.
    b. had complex enough nervous systems to make it obvious that their actions were not governed only by reflexes.
    c. possessed senses, nerves, and animal spirits.
    d. had a central switching mechanism.
    e. all of the above

Answer: b
How the nervous system is studied
p. 18

12. Which of the following is false regarding the use of clinical observation in psychology?
    a. It was probably the first technique used to study the relationships between physical brain abnormalities and behavior.
    b. It is a noninvasive technique that provides dynamic images of the brain as an individual moves freely in the environment.
    c. It may require waiting until an individual dies in order to identify the site of physical brain damage.
    d. It is problematic because the results may not generalize to other individuals with similar types of brain damage.

Answer: d
How the nervous system is studied
p. 19

13. Which of the following is an invasive technique for studying brain functioning?
    a. lesioning
    b. ablation
    c. electrical stimulation
    d. all of the above

Answer: a
How the nervous system is studied
p. 19

14. A scientist wants to identify the function(s) of a specific site in a rat's brain. If she uses intracranial recording as an investigative technique, what is she most likely to do?
    a. anesthetize the animal and place a cannula in the brain site to be studied
    b. train the rat to run through a maze for food and then lesion the brain site to be studied
    c. place electrodes on the rat's scalp in the location of the brain site to be studied
    d. expose the rat to x-rays that will damage the site to be studied

Answer: b
How the nervous system is studied
p. 19

15. A CT scan shows:
    a. which areas of the brain are abnormally active or inactive.
    b. a computer-generated picture of the brain's structure.
    c. the electrical activity of various brain regions.
    d. the reaction of parts of neurons to the introduction of magnetic fields.

Answer: d
How the nervous system is studied
p. 20

16. Powerful electromagnets are essential for making a detailed image of the brain in the technique known as:
    a. EEGs.
    b. CT scans.
    c. PET scans.
    d. MRI.

Answer: c
How the nervous system is studied
p. 20

17. Which of the following investigative techniques provide static images of the brain, showing its anatomy, but not its neural activity?
    a. CT scans and PET scans
    b. PET scans and MRI
    c. CT scans and MRI
    d. none of the above

Answer: a
How the nervous system is studied
p. 20

18. Which of the following investigative techniques allows scientists to study active representations of ongoing neural activity of brain structures rather than only static images?
    a. EEGs
    b. CT scans
    c. MRI
    d. all of the above

Answer: c
The nervous system is studied
p. 20

19. Low doses of radioactive substances are used in the brain-imaging technique of:
    a. EEG.
    b. CT scans.
    c. PET scans.
    d. MRI.

Answer: c
The architecture of the nervous system
p. 22

20. In invertebrates like worms, the "brain" is composed of centralized:
    a. cerebral hemispheres.
    b. reflexes.
    c. ganglia.
    d. neurons.

Answer: c
The architecture of the nervous system
p. 23

21. Hierarchical control in nervous systems means that:
    a. some parts are contained within other parts, like synaptic vesicles within neurons.
    b. some parts send messages to other parts, as in afferents and efferents of reflex pathways.
    c. some parts are orchestrated by other parts, like command cells in cardiac ganglia of snails.
    d. some parts control some processes (like vision) and other parts control other processes (like taste).

Answer: d
The architecture of the nervous system
p. 24

22. The two parts of the central nervous system are the brain and the:
    a. brainstem.
    b. nerves.
    c. autonomic nervous system.
    d. spinal cord.

Answer: b
The architecture of the nervous system
p. 24

23. A patient sustains a head injury which results in loss of ability to breathe. Upon autopsy, neural damage will most likely be found in the:
    a. hypothalamus.
    b. medulla.
    c. cerebellum.
    d. midbrain.

24. The parts of the hindbrain can be diagrammed as:

                        medulla
    hindbrain   pons
                  _____

    This missing part is the:
       a.   midbrain.
       b.   thalamus and hypothalamus.
       c.   spinal cord.
       d.   brainstem.
       e.   cerebellum.

25. The cerebellum is part of the:
       a.   brainstem.
       b.   hindbrain.
       c.   midbrain.
       d.   forebrain.

26. The forebrain's parts can be diagrammed as:

                   ─── cortex
                   ─── basal ganglia
    forebrain ───── thalamus
                   ─── hypothalamus
                       _____

    This missing part is the:
       a.   limbic system.
       b.   cerebellum.
       c.   midbrain.
       d.   reticular formation.

27. The limbic system:
       a.   is involved in the control of sensory functions.
       b.   is involved in the control of the skeletal musculature.
       c.   is involved in the control of such higher mental processes as
             thinking and language.
       d.   is involved in the control of emotional and motivational
             activities.

28. Chopin, the quintessential Romantic, had his heart buried in Warsaw.
    From what we now know about emotions, what else should he have had
    returned to his emotional home?
       a.   his limbic system and his ANS
       b.   his reticular formation
       c.   his left hemisphere
       d.   his corpus callosum

Answer: b
The architecture of the nervous system
p. 27

29. Which of the following has the closest functional ties with the hypothalamus?
    a. thalamus
    b. limbic system
    c. cerebellum
    d. reticular system

Answer: b
The architecture of the nervous system
p. 27

30. A rat can walk, chew, swallow, and track moving objects with its eyes, but it cannot find food or water for itself. These observations most suggest that:
    a. the limbic system and lower regions are intact, but the cerebral cortex is damaged.
    b. the midbrain and lower regions are intact, but the forebrain is damaged.
    c. the medulla and cerebellum are intact, but the midbrain is damaged.
    d. the spinal cord is intact, but the medulla and cerebellum are damaged.

Answer: d
The architecture of the nervous system
p. 27

31. A cat with the limbic system intact but with massive damage to the cerebral cortex would most likely be:
    a. unable to walk or regulate its body temperature.
    b. unmotivated to eat or drink, but be able to swallow if food or water was placed in its mouth.
    c. able to walk, chew, swallow, and track moving objects with its eyes but be unable to coordinate these activities into acts.
    d. able to do all of the above things, but be inept when faced with a tactical challenge such as a fight with another cat.

Answer: c
The architecture of the nervous system
p. 28

32. _____ are bundles of neurons that lead from the central nervous system to the muscles.
    a. Receptors
    b. Effectors
    c. Efferent nerves
    d. Afferent nerves

Answer: d
The architecture of the nervous system
p. 28

33. _____ are bundles of neurons that conduct excitation toward the brain or spinal cord.
    a. Receptors
    b. Effectors
    c. Efferent nerves
    d. Afferent nerves

Answer: b
The architecture of the nervous system
p. 28

34. Afferent is to efferent as:
    a. up is to down.
    b. sensory is to motor.
    c. reflex is to decision.
    d. integration is to reaction.
    e. discrimination is to generalization.

Answer: d
The architecture of the nervous system
p. 28

35. Afferent is to efferent as:
    a. under is to over.
    b. central is to peripheral.
    c. voluntary is to automatic.
    d. coming in is to going out.
    e. cooling is to heating.

Answer: a
The architecture of the nervous system
p. 28

36. The radial nerve activates several muscles in the forearm. The radial nerve is thus a part of the:
    a. peripheral nervous system.
    b. central nervous system.
    c. autonomic nervous system.
    d. transducer system.

Answer: b
The architecture of the nervous system
p. 28

37. The sciatic nerve activates muscles that move the legs. The sciatic nerve is thus a part of the:
    a. central nervous system.
    b. peripheral nervous system.
    c. sympathetic nervous system.
    d. transducer system.

Answer: d
The architecture of the nervous system
p. 28

38. Which of the following are divisions of the peripheral nervous system?
    a. spinal cord and somatic division
    b. spinal cord and autonomic division
    c. CNS and ANS divisions
    d. ANS and somatic divisions

Answer: c
The cortex
p. 29

39. Throughout evolution, the process of increasing "braininess" is most evident by observing differences in the _____ of various species.
    a. midbrain
    b. cerebellum
    c. cortex
    d. hypothalamus

Answer: a
The cortex
p. 31

40. A general characteristic of the primary motor areas is that:
    a. the amount of tissue devoted to a specific area is related to that area's function.
    b. the primary motor area contains the sensory area that corresponds to the same area of the body.
    c. they are localized in only two lobes of the cerebral hemispheres.
    d. the location of a neuron in the primary motor area depends on the importance of the body area to which that neuron corresponds.

Answer: b
The cortex
p. 31

41. During brain surgery, a portion of the patient's primary motor projection area is stimulated and the patient's left leg moves. The site of stimulation is probably the _____ side of the _____ lobe.
    a. left, frontal
    b. right, frontal
    c. left, parietal
    d. right, parietal

Answer: d
The cortex
p. 32

42. What part of an elephant might you expect to have a particularly large amount of space in the motor homunculus?
    a. the ears
    b. the front legs
    c. the back legs
    d. the trunk

Answer: c
The cortex
p. 32

43. In a pig, you might expect a disproportionately large portion of the somatosensory area in the cortex to map the:
    a. hoofs.
    b. tail.
    c. snout.
    d. forelegs.

Answer: a
The cortex
p. 32

44. A general characteristic of the primary sensory areas is that:
    a. the amount of tissue devoted to a specific area is related to that area's function.
    b. the somatosensory area contains the primary motor area that corresponds to the same part of the body.
    c. they are localized in only two lobes of the cerebral hemispheres.
    d. the location of a neuron in the primary sensory area depends on the importance of the body area to which that neuron corresponds.

Answer: a
The cortex
p. 32

45. In a giraffe, we might expect a disproportionately large portion of the somatosensory area of the cortex to map the:
    a. lips and tongue.
    b. neck and chest.
    c. back and belly.
    d. legs and tail.

Answer: b
The cortex
p. 33

46. Following a stroke, a patient shows grossly diminished sensitivity to touch and other stimulation in the right hand and arm. The probable site of the lesion is:
    a. the motor homunculus.
    b. the left somatosensory area.
    c. the right somatosensory area.
    d. the left frontal area.

Answer: b
The cortex
p. 33

47. In which of the following would you expect neurons to be most reliably activated by stimulation of a nerve receiving sensory information from the skin of the knee?
    a. frontal lobe
    b. parietal lobe
    c. occipital lobe
    d. temporal lobe
    e. center lobe

Answer: e
The cortex
p. 33

48. Where should an electrode be placed to record the most electrical activity in response to a pinch of the left big toe?
    a. the left parietal lobe
    b. the right frontal lobe
    c. the left frontal lobe
    d. the left temporal lobe
    e. the right parietal lobe

Answer: a
The cortex
p. 33

49. What would most likely be reported if a conscious patient's brain was electrically stimulated at point X on the accompanying diagram?

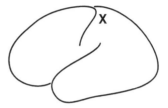

    a. a tingling on the right side of the body
    b. a memory of some past experience
    c. some kind of meaningless visual experience
    d. hearing some meaningless sounds
    e. a strong desire to move the right arm

Answer: d
The cortex
p. 33

50. In which of the following would you expect neurons to be most reliably activated by stimulation of the auditory nerve?
    a. frontal lobe
    b. parietal lobe
    c. occipital lobe
    d. temporal lobe

Answer: c
The cortex
p. 33

51. Picasso and Rembrandt are to occipital as Mozart and Beethoven are to:
    a. parietal.
    b. frontal.
    c. temporal.
    d. cerebellar.

Answer: d
The cortex
p. 33

52. Bach and Mozart are to temporal as da Vinci and Escher are to:
    a. cerebellar.
    b. frontal.
    c. detrimental.
    d. occipital.
    e. limbic.

Answer: c
The cortex
p. 33

53. During brain surgery, a portion of the patient's cortex is stimulated and she reports that she hears a loud hum. The site of stimulation is probably the _____ lobe.
    a. frontal
    b. parietal
    c. temporal
    d. occipital

Answer: d
The cortex
p. 33

54. What would most likely be reported if a conscious patient's brain was electrically stimulated at point X on the accompanying diagram?

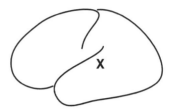

    a.   a tingling on the right side of the body
    b.   a memory of some past experience
    c.   some kind of meaningless visual experience
    d.   hearing some meaningless sounds
    e.   a strong desire to move the right arm

Answer: c
The cortex
p. 33

55. Bob is hit on the head and "sees stars." The region of the brain that was most likely affected was the:
    a.   cerebellum.
    b.   frontal cortex.
    c.   occipital lobe.
    d.   limbic system.
    e.   reticular system.

Answer: c
The cortex
p. 33

56. What would most likely be reported if a conscious patient's brain was electrically stimulated at point X on the accompanying diagram?

    a.   a tingling on the right side of the body
    b.   a memory of some past experience
    c.   some kind of meaningless visual experience
    d.   hearing some meaningless sounds
    e.   a strong desire to move the right arm

57. What's wrong with the accompanying diagram?

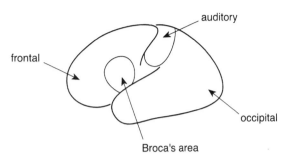

   a. It fails to show the corpus callosum.
   b. It shows Broca's area in the right hemisphere.
   c. The labels for the frontal and occipital lobes should be reversed.
   d. The auditory area is shown in the wrong lobe of the brain.

58. What's wrong with the accompanying diagram?

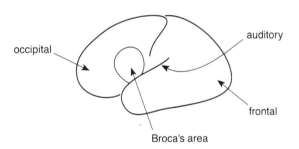

   a. It fails to show the corpus callosum.
   b. It shows Broca's area in the right hemisphere.
   c. The labels for the frontal and occipital lobes should be reversed.
   d. The auditory area is shown in the wrong lobe of the brain.

59. You observe a man brushing his teeth, and you notice that as he puts the toothpaste on the brush, he keeps squeezing and squeezing the tube until the toothpaste drips all over the sink. Then you observe that he sticks the tube of toothpaste in his mouth instead of the brush. This problem of selecting the right components and fitting them together to carry out an activity is known as:
   a. agnosia.
   b. apraxia.
   c. aphasia.
   d. split brain.

Answer: a
The cortex
p. 34

60. Apraxic patients can sometimes perform actions as part of automatic routines despite their inability to perform these acts on command. This suggests:
    a. different levels of organization for motor function.
    b. a disorganization of the sensory world.
    c. a lesion in Broca's area.
    d. a disruption of function in the brainstem.

Answer: d
The cortex
p. 34

61. Apraxia is:
    a. a sensory deficit, such as blindness, deafness, or insensitivity to touch.
    b. a disturbance in the organization of sensory input.
    c. a paralysis of some part of the body.
    d. a disturbance in the organization of voluntary action.

Answer: b
The cortex
p. 34

62. A woman slaps accurately at a mosquito biting her leg, yet she is completely unable to get a key out of her pocket and use the key to open adoor. This woman most likely suffers from damage to her:
    a. somatosensory cortex—projection area for skin of legs.
    b. frontal lobe—area just in front of motor cortex.
    c. temporal lobe—cortex surrounding Wernicke's area.
    d. corpus callosum—tissue connecting the parietal lobes.

Answer: a
The cortex
p. 34

63. Tom isn't paralyzed, but he has great trouble organizing the steps that must be taken to cook an egg. A CAT scan is most likely to reveal damage to his:
    a. frontal association area.
    b. cerebellum.
    c. motor projection cortex.
    d. temporal association areas.

Answer: c
The cortex
p. 34

64. Former Presidential press secretary James Brady has severe damage to his right frontal lobe. If he is right-handed, one expects him to have difficulty:
    a. expressing his thoughts verbally.
    b. recognizing objects in his left visual field.
    c. tying his shoes.
    d. telling when his right hand is touched if he's not looking.

65. James Brady was shot in the head in an assassination attempt on former President Reagan. Mr. Brady can now see, hear, and speak fluently, but he has a persisting paralysis on the left side of his body and serious trouble planning complex voluntary actions. Which of the following brain diagrams best shows the probable damage to Mr. Brady's brain?

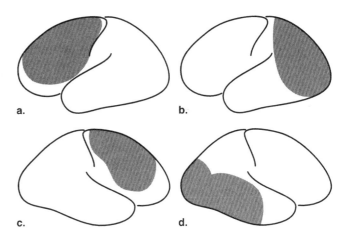

66. In theology, an *agnostic* is one who does not know if God exists. In neurology, a person with visual agnosia:
    a.   can't see his or her own body.
    b.   sees God, but can't believe it.
    c.   doesn't realize what it is he or she sees.
    d.   has difficulty dealing with abstract concepts, like that of God.
    e.   has a disconnection between Broca's area and the visual projection area.

67. Knowledge is to action as:
    a.   aphasia is to apraxia.
    b.   apraxia is to agnosia.
    c.   agnosia is to aphasia.
    d.   apraxia is to aphasia.
    e.   agnosia is to apraxia.

68. Action is to knowledge as:
    a.   apraxia is to agnosia.
    b.   aphasia is to apraxia.
    c.   aphasia is to agnosia.
    d.   agnosia is to apraxia.
    e.   apraxia is to aphasia.

69. An agnosia is:
    a.   a sensory deficit, such as blindness, deafness, or insensitivity to touch.
    b.   a disturbance in the organization of sensory input.
    c.   a paralysis of some part of the body.
    d.   a disturbance in the organization of voluntary action.

70. A patient has a cortical lesion. When shown a drawing of a camel, he painstakingly identifies several parts and then ventures a guess: "Eyes . . .mouth . . . of course, it's an animal." He probably suffers from:
    a. an agnosia.
    b. an apraxia.
    c. nonfluent aphasia.
    d. fluent aphasia.

71. A patient suffers from a visual agnosia. Her lesion is probably in:
    a. the primary visual projection area.
    b. an association area in the frontal lobe.
    c. an association area in the parietal lobe.
    d. an association area in the occipital lobe.

72. A neurological bestseller describes a man with damage to the association cortex who mistook his wife for a hat. Just by looking, he coudn't tell them apart, but he could as soon as his wife spoke. The disturbance of this patient is:
    a. fairly common after cutting the corpus callosum for relief of epilepsy.
    b. probably due to damage in Wernicke's area.
    c. an agnosia.
    d. caused by cataracts in the lens of the eye.

73. Neglect syndrome is most apt to follow damage to:
    a. the right frontal association cortex.
    b. the left temporal association cortex.
    c. the left occipital lobe.
    d. the right parietal lobe.

74. Which of the following is closest in symptoms to an apraxia?
    a. fluent aphasia
    b. agnosia
    c. nonfluent aphasia
    d. paralysis

75. The region of the brain closest to Broca's area is the:
    a. motor representation for the hand.
    b. somatosensory representation for the hand.
    c. motor representation for the tongue.
    d. somatosensory representation for the tongue.

76. From what you know about the position of the various brain areas, which of the following seems most probable?
    a. Damage to Wernicke's area is more likely to be accompanied by paralysis than is damage to Broca's area.
    b. Damage to Wernicke's area is more likely to be accompanied by deafness in the left ear than in the right ear.
    c. Damage to Broca's area is more likely to be accompanied by paralysis of the left arm than by paralysis of the right arm.
    d. Damage to Broca's area is more likely to be accompanied by paralysis than is damage to Wernicke's area.

77. After a stroke involving Broca's area, a person would have the most trouble:
    a. making hand gestures.
    b. reading silently.
    c. pronouncing words.
    d. listening to a radio talk show.
    e. listening to Roy Clark play the banjo.

78. A right-handed stroke victim has a slight paralysis of his right arm and leg, as well as a severe speech defect. He seems to be able to understand what is said to him, but all he can say is "tan." His brain damage is probably centered in the:
    a. right frontal region.
    b. right temporal region.
    c. right parietal region.
    d. left frontal region.
    e. left temporal region.

79. What's wrong with the accompanying diagram of a right-handed person's brain?

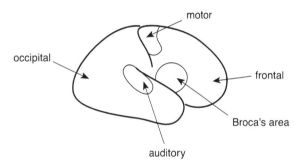

    a. It fails to show the corpus callosum.
    b. It shows Broca's area in the right hemisphere.
    c. The labels for the frontal and occipital lobes should be reversed.
    d. The auditory area is shown in the wrong lobe of the brain.

80. Carl Sagan, the astronomer, wrote a book called *Broca's Brain*. If you were an editor, which of the following pictures should you select for the dust jacket?

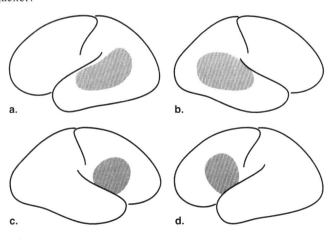

Answer: a
The cortex
p.36

81. Which region on the accompanying diagram is Broca's area?

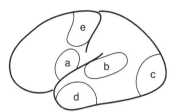

Answer: c
The cortex
p. 36

82. Non-fluent aphasia is to fluent aphasia as:
    a. Broca's area is to the adjacent regions of motor cortex.
    b. Wernicke's area is to the adjacent auditory projection area.
    c. agnosia is to apraxia.
    d. minor hemisphere is to dominant hemisphere.
    e. parietal lobe is to temporal lobe.

Answer: c
The cortex
p. 36

83. Broca's is to Wernicke's as:
    a. receptive is to expressive.
    b. left is to right.
    c. frontal is to parieto-temporal.
    d. all of the above

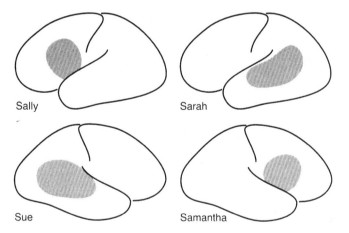

Answer: d
The cortex
p. 36

84. Shown above are imaginary CT scans of the brains of four women who have experienced strokes. Which woman is the least likely to show a language impairment?
    a. Sally, who is left-handed
    b. Sarah, who is right-handed
    c. Sue, who is left-handed
    d. Samantha, who is right-handed

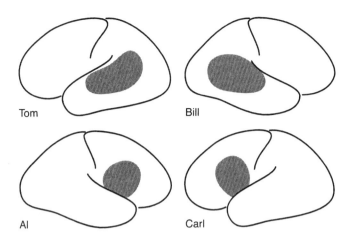

85. Shown above are imaginary CT scans of the brains of four men who haveexperienced strokes. Which man is the least likely to show a serious language impairment?
    a. Tom, who is left-handed.
    b. Bill, who is left-handed.
    c. Al, who is right-handed.
    d. Carl, who is right-handed.

86. Which region on the accompanying diagram is Wernicke's area?

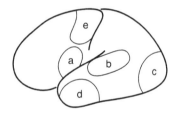

87. Betty, when shown a simple oral thermometer, described shiny glass, little red lines, a silvery bulb, and said, " . . . Of course, it's a whatchamicallit . . . a small machine." Which brain diagram is most likely to show the location of Betty's stroke?

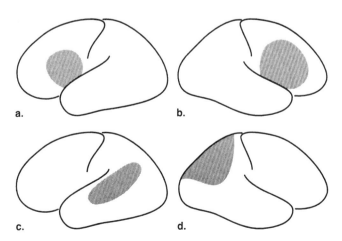

Answer: a
The cortex
p. 36

88. Broca's area is located in the _____ lobe. Wernicke's area is located in the _____ lobe.
    a. frontal; temporal
    b. parietal; occipital
    c. parietal; frontal
    d. temporal; occipital
    e. parietal; temporal

Answer: b
The cortex
p. 36

89. The region of brain closest to Wernicke's area is the:
    a. motor projection area related to the lips.
    b. auditory projection area.
    c. somatosensory representation of the earlobe.
    d. Broca's area.

Answer: c
The cortex
p. 36

90. In observing fluent and nonfluent aphasics one finds:
    a. that neither nonfluent nor fluent aphasics can produce speech.
    b. that neither nonfluent nor fluent aphasics can comprehend speech.
    c. that nonfluent aphasics can comprehend but not produce speech.
    d. that fluent aphasics can comprehend but not produce speech.

Answer: d
The cortex
p. 36

91. After a stroke involving Wernicke's area, a person would have the most trouble:
    a. making hand gestures.
    b. understanding nonverbal traffic signs.
    c. pronuncing words.
    d. listening to a radio talk show.
    e. listening to Roy Clark play the banjo.

Answer: b
The cortex
p. 36

92. Which of the following might best be called an "agnosia for language"?
    a. disconnection of the two hemispheres by cutting the corpus callosum
    b. fluent aphasia
    c. certain kinds of apraxias
    d. deafness

Answer: c
The cortex
p. 38

93. In 1848, Phineas Gage was the victim of a severe accident in which an iron rod penetrated his skull and passed through a large part of his brain. Following the accident, Gage seemed like an entirely different person. For instance, he could no longer form plans and execute them to achieve a goal. What was the site of Gage's brain damage?
    a. the brainstem
    b. the temporal lobe
    c. the prefrontal cortex
    d. the parietal lobe

Answer: d
The cortex
p. 38

94. Damage to the _____ of the human brain is associated with difficulties in planning and social cognition.
    a. corpus callosum
    b. primary motor cortex
    c. sensory projection areas
    d. prefrontal cortex

Answer: b
One brain or two?
p. 38

95. In right-handed individuals, the _____ of the human brain has been shown to be important for recognizing faces, comprehending spatial relationships, and perception of music.
    a. occipital lobe
    b. right hemisphere
    c. frontal lobe
    d. left hemisphere

Answer: b
One brain or two?
p. 39

96. What part of the brain did early twentieth-century neuropsychologists call the "minor hemisphere"?
    a. the cerebellar hemispheres
    b. the right cerebral hemisphere
    c. the left cerebral hemisphere
    d. the thalamus
    e. the association cortex

Answer: b
One brain or two?
p. 39

97. Recovery from aphasia:
    a. is more likely to occur in right-handers than left-handers.
    b. is more likely to occur in left-handers than right-handers.
    c. is equally likely in right- and left-handers and occurs to a limited extent.
    d. is equally unlikely in right- and left-handers and occurs very rarely for anyone.

Answer: a
One brain or two?
p. 39

98. The corpus callosum consists mainly of:
    a. myelinated axons or nerve fibers.
    b. neuronal cell bodies with processes that extend into each hemisphere.
    c. connective tissue of the same type that makes up skin and tendons.
    d. sensory neurons of a variety of types.

Answer: d
One brain or two?
p. 39

99. During an epileptic attack, abnormal seizure "waves" are commonly recorded in both hemispheres. One major reason for this is that:
    a. EEG recording devices are not very sensitive to the location of the abnormal waves.
    b. both hemispheres are damaged in most cases of epilepsy.
    c. the dominant hemisphere exerts control over the nondominant hemisphere.
    d. seizure activity is propagated across the corpus callosum.

Answer: c
One brain or two?
p. 39

100. Neurosurgeons sometimes cut the corpus callosum in cases of:
    a. extreme obesity.
    b. multiple sclerosis.
    c. intractable epilepsy.
    d. chronic alcoholism.
    e. mental retardation.

Answer: b
One brain or two?
p. 39

101. The rationale for cutting the corpus callosum in epilepsy is that:
    a. the corpus callosum contains axons that have low thresholds for seizures.
    b. seizures will not spread from one hemisphere to the other.
    c. the corpus callosum is a brain structure that was damaged at the time of birth, and this can be confirmed with CT-scan prior to surgery.
    d. it decreases excitation in the reticular formation, which is often responsible for the start of the seizures.

Answer: d
One brain or two?
p. 40

102. Studies on lateralization often present pictures to one or the other cerebral hemisphere. This presentation is usually very brief, say about 150 milliseconds. Why are the presentations so brief?
    a. to make sure the research participant isn't threatened by continued exposure to materials that one or the other hemisphere cannot understand
    b. because quick reactions are more reliable than long-lasting ones which the participant can think about consciously
    c. because the experimenter wants to make sure that the stimulus is no longer in view when the participant responds
    d. to make sure that the participant cannot move his eyes when the stimulus is present, because moving the eyes could allow both hemispheres to receive the information

Answer: a
One brain or two?
p. 40

103. A woman with a severed corpus callosum looks at the words "Dixie Cup" flashed on a screen in a position where her eyes arew fixated on the space between the two words. Which of the following is she most likely to touch with her left hand to indicate what she saw?
    a. a Confederate flag
    b. a coffee cup
    c. a cold drink paper cup of the "Dixie Cup" brand
    d. a tennis trophy

Answer: c
One brain or two?
p. 40

104. A woman with a split-brain operation fixates the exact center of the screen as the word *eaten* is very briefly flashed. What is she most likely to report seeing?
    a. *eaten*
    b. *eat*
    c. *ten*
    d. a hodgepodge of lines, but no meaningful word

Answer: a
One brain or two?
p. 40

105. Which of the following would be the best evidence that the right hemisphere understands some language?
    a. People with severed corpus callosums can respond to simple written commands presented in their left visual field.
    b. Most normal right-handed people can write awkwardly with their left hands.
    c. People with severed corpus callosums can answer questions heard by either ear.
    d. Strokes in the left hemisphere of right-handed people severely disrupt language understanding.

106. A man fixates on the exact center of the screen just as the word *Springtime* is flashed for a quarter of a second. With his left hand, he selects a picture of a metal spring to indicate what he saw. Which of the following is most likely to be true about this man?
    a. He is a normal right-hander.
    b. He is blind in his left eye.
    c. He is blind in his right eye.
    d. He is a normal left-hander.
    e. He has a severed corpus callosum.

107. A man with a split-brain operation looks at the exact center of the screen when this jack-o-lantern is very briefly flashed. What is he most likely to report seeing?

    a. a happy pumpkin
    b. a sad pumpkin
    c. a pumpkin that can't decide if it is happy or sad
    d. a meaningless hodgepodge of lines
    e. some kind of vegetable, without being able to specify the kind

108. A right-handed woman with a severed corpus callosum fixates on the exact center of a screen just as the word *pineapple* is flashed for a quarter of a second. She must indicate what she saw by reaching with her left hand into a grab bag filled with a variety of objects. Which object is she most likely to select?
    a. a small pineapple
    b. a bough of a pine tree
    c. an apple
    d. the letters *E* and *A* made from wire

109. A right-handed, split-brain patient is briefly shown a picture of an ashtray in the right visual field. When asked to say what he saw, he:
    a. says "an ashtray."
    b. cannot produce the correct name, but will pantomime use of the object.
    c. cannot provide an answer and only knows that it is some object.
    d. cannot provide an answer and has no idea what, if anything, was shown.

Answer: b
One brain or two?
p. 40

110. A person with a severed corpus callosum reaches blindly into a bag with his left hand and feels a comb, but does not remove it from the bag. After removing his hand he will be able to:
    a. say that it is a comb, but he will not be able to point to a picture of a comb with his right hand unless he hears himself talk.
    b. point to a comb with his left hand, but he will not be able to say what he felt unless he sees his left hand pointing.
    c. point to a comb with either hand, but he will not be able to say what he felt unless he sees his hand pointing.
    d. none of the above

Answer: a
One brain or two?
p. 40

111. Suppose a spoon is felt only by the left hand of a right-handed split-brain patient wearing a blindfold. After the blindfold is removed, he will most likely:
    a. point to a picture of a spoon with the left hand.
    b. say the word *spoon*.
    c. pantomime using a spoon with his right hand.
    d. write the word *spoon* with his right hand.

Answer: c
One brain or two?
p. 40

112. Why is the use of the adjective *minor* for the right hemisphere misleading and inappropriate?
    a. The right hemisphere is actually somewhat larger than the left hemisphere.
    b. Ten to fifteen percent of people are left-handed.
    c. The right hemisphere is more competent than the left for some activities.
    d. The right hemisphere developed over ten million years before the left hemisphere.

Answer: c
One brain or two?
p. 41

113. In studies of hemispheric lateralization in normal participants, visual stimuli are presented to either the left or right visual field. The researcher then assesses _____ as a means of determining which hemisphere was primarily involved in processing the visual information.
    a. self-report data
    b. uptake of radioactive glucose
    c. response time
    d. rate of speech

Answer: c
One brain or two?
p. 42

114. Which of the following is (are) true?
    a. Zen masters have somewhat larger right than left hemispheres.
    b. Psychological research focuses on the left hemisphere of the brain.
    c. Spatial knowledge is disrupted more by damage to the right than to the left hemisphere.
    d. all of the above

Answer: a
One brain or two?
p. 42

115. According to some theorists, the left and right hemispheres should not be referred to as the *linguist* and the *map maker*, respectively. Instead, they should be viewed as important for organizing information about:
    a. time and space.
    b. faces and music.
    c. words and numbers.
    d. sensation and movement.

Answer: d
One brain or two?
p. 42

116. Which of the following statements best describes the current scientific view regarding the functioning of our left and right hemispheres?
    a. The hemispheres constantly compete for dominance over our daily activities.
    b. The left hemisphere is our major hemisphere, while the right hemisphere plays only a minor role in daily activities.
    c. The left hemisphere tends to be analytic, while the right hemisphere tends to be artistic.
    d. Together, the left and right hemispheres contribute their specialized abilities to every task.

Answer: c
Brain functions and neural hierarchies
p. 43

117. In swallowing, over twenty pairs of muscles contract in a stereotyped sequence, with little influence by feedback. In this sense, swallowing is less like a simple reflex and more like a process controlled by a(n):
    a. central excitatory state.
    b. disinhibitor.
    c. central pattern generator.
    d. afferent ganglion.

Answer: b
Brain functions and neural hierarchies
p. 43

118. Which of the following best exemplifies the concept of disinhibition?
    a. wavering between choosing psychology or anthropology then finally choosing an anthropology course
    b. saying something while under hypnosis that you'd never say otherwise
    c. holding on to a valuable teapot even though it's excruciatingly hot
    d. shaking a parking meter when it fails to go off *Violation*, but quitting the shaking when it doesn't work.

Answer: a
Brain functions and neural hierarchies
p. 43

119. In the normal frog, a pinprick on the toe produces a small, reflexive withdrawal of the hindleg. After decapitation, the same pinprick produces a much larger reaction. This strongly suggests that:
    a. the brain has an inhibitory effect on spinal reflexes.
    b. the brain has an excitatory effect on spinal reflexes.
    c. the spinal cord has an inhibitory effect on cerebral reflexes.
    d. the spinal cord has an excitatory effect on cerebral reflexes.

Answer: d
Brain functions and neural hierarchies
p. 43

120. After the spinal cord is disconnected from the brain some spinal reflexes have lowered thresholds. This phenomenon best illustrates the concept of:
    a. temporal summation.
    b. apraxia.
    c. reciprocal inhibition.
    d. disinhibition.

Answer: b
Brain functions and neural hierarchies
p. 43

121. Which of the following best illustrates the concept of disinhibition?
    a. wavering between choosing cake or pie, then finally choosing the pie
    b. saying something while under the influence of alcohol that you'd never say otherwise
    c. holding on to a valuable tea cup even though it's excruciatingly hot
    d. shaking a parking meter when it fails to go off *Violation*, but quitting when the shaking doesn't work

Answer: d
Brain functions and neural hierarchies
p. 43

122. The praying mantis manages to survive as a species despite the fact that the female mantis often eats the male. One reason for this is that:
    a. the female usually eats the male only after she has consumed other food.
    b. the males that are caught and eaten by the females are usually those too old to be of much reproductive value.
    c. copulation reflexes are directly controlled by the male's subesophageal ganglion.
    d. the female begins to eat the male from the head down toward the reproductive organs.

Answer: d
Brain functions and neural hierarchies
p. 43

123. The male praying mantis:
    a. possesses a clump of neurons in his head, which excites copulatory movements.
    b. must approach the female from the front in order to grab her so that she doesn't eat him.
    c. can copulate only while the female is looking him in the eye.
    d. none of the above

Answer: a
Brain functions and neural hierarchies
p. 43

124. The "brain" of the male praying mantis:
    a. usually acts to inhibit sexual reflexes.
    b. usually acts to excite sexual reflexes, but on occasion can inhibit them.
    c. is a special delicacy to the female.
    d. ceases functioning at the sight of a moving female.

Answer: c
Brain functions and neural hierarchies
p. 44

125. The best analogy for the hierarchical system in the brain is:
    a. an army, with a well-specified chain of command.
    b. a balance between two opposing systems, like the American criminal justice system.
    c. a distributed system of interlocking hierarchies, like the American political system.
    d. a baseball team, with a single manager but many players of roughly equal status.

Answer: e
Building blocks of the nervous system
p. 45

126.
    ———— cell body
neuron ———— dendrite
    ————————

The blank above should be filled in by:
    a. nerve impulse
    b. myelin sheath
    c. synapse
    d. neurotransmitter
    e. axon

Answer: b
Building blocks of the nervous system
p. 45

127. Which of the following is the most appropriate metaphor for a dendrite?
    a. a ladder
    b. a branch of a bush
    c. a flower on the end of a long stem
    d. a vacuum cleaner for synaptic transmitters

Answer: b
Building blocks of the nervous system
p. 45

128.

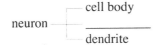

The blank above should be filled in by:
a. nerve impulse.
b. axon.
c. neurotransmitter.
d. synapse.
e. myelin sheath.

Answer: b
Building blocks of the nervous system
p. 45

129 The sending end of a neuron is the:
a. synapse.
b. axon.
c. dendrite.
d. myelin.
e. transducer.

Answer: b
Building blocks of the nervous system
p. 45

130. Nerve impulses in this neuron usually travel in the direction marked by:

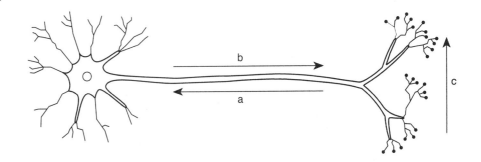

a. a.
b. b.
c. a and c simultaneously.
d. either a or b, depending upon whether the muscle end is active or the other end is active.

Answer: b
Building blocks of the nervous system
p. 46

131. Which of the following is the best example of transduction?
a. a node of Ranvier, which has many "gates" for sodium ions
b. a cell in the ear, which converts pressure into graded membrane potentials
c. a tendon, which transmits force from muscle to bone
d. an efferent nerve, which transmits information from the spinal cord to a muscle

Answer: a
Building blocks of the nervous system
p. 46

132. Dendrite is to tree as _____ is to garden hose.
a. axon
b. synapse
c. ion
d. nucleus

Answer: c
Building blocks of the nervous system
p. 46

133. Axon is to garden hose as _____ is to tree.
    a. nerve impulse
    b. synapse
    c. dendrite
    d. myelin sheath
    e. nucleus

Answer: d
Building blocks of the nervous system
p. 46

134. Transduction is the change of energy from one form to another. Which of the following are transducers?
    a. rods and cones in the eye
    b. taste buds on the tongue
    c. pressure receptors in the skin
    d. all of the above

Answer: c
Building blocks of the nervous system
p. 47

135. _____ provide supportive scaffolding for nerve cells and assist in the repair of damaged brain tissue.
    a. Interneurons
    b. Vesicles
    c. Glial cells
    d. Anastomoses

Answer: a
Building blocks of the nervous system
p. 47

136. Which of the following refers to the bare portions of a myelinated axon?
    a. nodes of Ranvier
    b. glial cells
    c. white matter
    d. soma

Answer: a
Building blocks of the nervous system
p. 47

137. Nodes of Ranvier are important in:
    a. speeding up the transmission of nerve impulses.
    b. shielding the synapse from extraneous chemicals.
    c. the synthesis of fatty tissue that makes up the myelin sheath.
    d. transducing mechanical stimuli into nerve impulses.

Answer: d
Building blocks of the nervous system
p. 47

138. Which of the following can be described as the gray matter of the human brain?
    a. cell bodies
    b. interneurons
    c. unmyelinated axons
    d. all of the above

Answer: b
Building blocks of the nervous system
p. 48

139. In the embryo, glial cells are best described as _____ for developing neurons.
    a. competitors
    b. guidewires
    c. catalysts
    d. caretakers

Answer: d
Building blocks of the nervous system
p. 48

140. In embryonic development, the possibility of neuronal "wiring errors" is minimized through:
    a. the reduction of glial cells.
    b. the destruction of glial cells.
    c. cooperation among neurons.
    d. competition among neurons.

Answer: d
Building blocks of the nervous system
p. 48

141. Which of the following would be the least useful for recording the resting potential of an axon?
    a. an oscilloscope
    b. an especially large axon
    c. a microelectrode
    d. a microscope

Answer: a
Building blocks of the nervous system
p. 48

142. Which of the following would be the most useful for recording the action potential of an axon?
    a. an oscilloscope
    b. a device for measuring polarized light
    c. an electron microscope
    d. a PET scanner

Answer: c
Building blocks of the nervous system
p. 48

143. What was the big advantage of studying nerve impulses in squid?
    a. Axons in squid are plentiful.
    b. Axons in squid have no resting potential so it is easy to detect their nerve impulses.
    c. Some axons in squid are huge.
    d. Some axons in squid have no thresholds.

Answer: c
Building blocks of the nervous system
p. 48

144.   neuronal potentials —— resting
                              _____

    The blank above should be filled in by:
    a. threshold.
    b. synaptic.
    c. action.
    d. frequency.

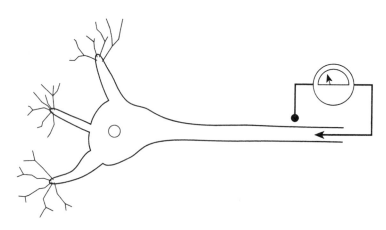

Answer: b
Building blocks of the nervous system
p. 49

145. Assume a physiologist has inserted a microelectrode at the arrow tip in the diagram above. When the neuron is at rest the voltage recorded at the arrow tip will be:
    a.   zero millivolts.
    b.   –70 mV
    c.   +50 mV
    d.   negative, neutral, or positive depending upon what kind of neuron it is.

Answer: c
Building blocks of the nervous system
p. 49

146. The resting potential of a neuron:
    a.   is an electrical phenomenon unique to the squid giant neuron.
    b.   refers to the electrical current spread associated with the action potential.
    c.   is such that the inside of the neuron is negatively charged relative to the outside.
    d.   refers to the electrical difference induced by the introduction of a microelectrode into the cell.

Answer: c
Building blocks of the nervous system
p. 49

147. Which of the following concepts applies best to action potentials?
    a.   graded potentials
    b.   synaptic transmitter substances
    c.   threshold
    d.   negative feedback

Answer: c
Building blocks of the nervous system
p. 50

148. What is wrong with the accompanying graph of an action potential?

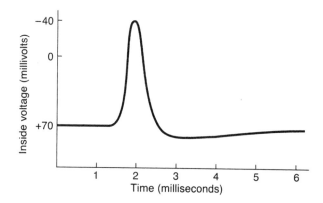

a. Its peak is about 1000 times too long.
b. Its peak is about 1000 times too brief.
c. The signs (+ and –) on the voltage axis are opposite of what they should be.
d. It should only go as high as –40mV, not beyond it.
e. It does not appear to be "all-or-none."

149. A neuron is stimulated by a stimulus that just achieves threshold. After aninterval of a few seconds, a new stimulus is applied that is half as intenseas the previous one. The resulting action potential will have what peak voltage?
    a. 2mV
    b. 5mV
    c. 10mV
    d. 20mV
    e. There will be no action potential.

150. The action potential:
    a. consists of a transition from a negative charge (inside the neuron) to a persisting positive charge (inside).
    b. consists of a transition from a positive charge (inside) to a negative (inside) and a quick return to a positive charge (inside).
    c. consists of a transition from a negative charge (inside) to a positive (inside) and a quick return to a negative charge (inside).
    d. consists of the flow of negative ions into the cell followed by the pumping out of these negative ions from the inside of the axon.

151. Which of the following cannot be used for signaling the intensity of a stimulus?
    a. the type of neuron activated (e.g., low vs. high threshold neurons)
    b. the number of neurons activated
    c. amplitude of action potentials
    d. the frequency of firing along axons

152. The greater the stimulus intensity, the greater:
    a. the negativity of the boltage changes.
    b. the rate at which action potentials are produced.
    c. the magnitude of the action potential.
    d. all of the above

153. Above-threshold depolarizing currents are repeatedly applied at a rate of 1 per second to a single neuron. If we increase the frequency of stimulation to 10 per second we can expect:
    a. an increase in the number of action potentials per second.
    b. an increase in the magnitude of the action potential(s).
    c. the number of action potentials per second will remain the same.
    d. none of the above

154. C. S. Sherrington, in his work on synapses with dogs:
    a. recorded synaptic events with microelectrodes.
    b. discovered that synapses function through the release of packets of transmitter substances.
    c. inferred the presence of synapses by doing behavioral experiments on reflexes.
    d. found that conduction along axons is substantially slower than through reflex arcs.

155. In the early 1900s, Sherrington arrived at his ideas about synapses and their mechanisms largely on the basis of inferences from:
    a. behavior.
    b. neuroanatomy.
    c. the chemistry of neurotransmitters.
    d. electrophysiological recordings from neurons.

156. Sherrington's spinal animals were ones that:
    a. had the spinal cord removed.
    b. had the spinal cord disconnected from the brain.
    c. had the spinal cord disconnected from the peripheral nerves.
    d. had most of the interneurons in the spinal cord removed.

157. A *spinal animal* is one in which:
    a. the spinal cord has been destroyed.
    b. the spinal cord has been disconnected from the brain.
    c. the spinal cord has been disconnected from the peripheral nerves.
    d. the spinal cord has been disconnected from both the brain and the peripheral nerves.

158. According to Sherrington, a central excitatory state accumulates at the synapse and is built up until it reaches a threshold value. This hypothesis about accumulation at a single synapse can account for:
    a. temporal summation.
    b. spatial summation.
    c. funneling into a final common path.
    d. one-way conduction across the synapse.

159. Which of the following behaviors illustrates the concept of reciprocal inhibition most clearly?
    a. Your arm hangs limp when you are completely relaxed.
    b. You hold your arm stiff and it takes great effort for someone else to move it in any direction.
    c. You pick up a pencil and raise it level with your shoulder.
    d. A spinal cord injury makes it so that all your arm muscles twitch uncontrollably.

160. Reciprocal inhibition, as applied to typing, would mean that:
    a. when the muscles contract pulling your index finger away from a key, the muscles that pull your middle finger away are inhibited.
    b. when a flex or motor neuron is inhibited, so is an extensor motor neuron.
    c. when you lift your index finger off a key, the flexors for your index finger are inhibited.
    d. the two hands must take turns at pressing down the keys.

161. The existence of reciprocal inhibition means that:
    a. two extensor muscles can't contract at the same time.
    b. in humans, the right arm can't be moved forward and the right leg backward at the same time.
    c. an antagonistic pair of muscles can't contract at the same time.
    d. the greater the number of muscles, the harder it is to control their timing accurately.
    e. for many of us, it's hard to read and chew gum at the same time.

162. Which of the following is the best example of reciprocal inhibition?
    a. When you want to flex your wrist, one set of muscles contract and a different set of muscles relax.
    b. When you are speaking, it is the right hand, more than the left, that makes movements for emphasis.
    c. When sitting, the right arm and the left leg cannot be moved forward at the same time.
    d. When a dog scratches, it often makes little movements with its tongue at the same time.
    e. A neuron can't secrete both inhibitory and excitatory synaptic transmitter substances at the same time.

163. Inhibition and excitation at synapses operate by:
    a. some synapses being inhibitory, others excitatory.
    b. transport of negative ions under some conditions, positive ones under others.
    c. release of one transmitter substance under some conditions and release of other transmitter substances under different contitions, all by the same neuron.
    d. taking in (inhibition) and releasing (excitation) transmitter substances.
    e. all of the above

164. Neurotransmitters originating in neuron A excite neuron B by:
    a. increasing the voltage of neuron A.
    b. decreasing the voltage of neuron A.
    c. increasing the voltage of neuron B.
    d. decreasing the voltage of neuron B.

165. Neurotransmitters:
    a. are released into synaptic gaps.
    b. change the voltage of nearby neurons.
    c. are stored in tiny sacs.
    d. all of the above

Answer: d
Interaction among nerve cells
p. 56

Answer: a
Interaction among nerve cells
p. 56

Answer: a
Interaction among nerve cells
p. 56

Answer: b
Interaction among nerve cells
p. 45

Answer: b
Interaction among nerve cells
p. 56

Answer: b
Interaction among nerve cells
p. 58

Answer: d
Interaction among nerve cells
p. 58

166. Transmission of information across the synaptic gap occurs by means of:
    a. electrical charges.
    b. movement of synaptic vesicles.
    c. fine neurotubules.
    d. chemical diffusion.
    e. contact of a synaptic knob with a receptor site.

167. Synaptic vesicles are structures:
    a. in which transmitters are stored.
    b. from which axon collaterals extend.
    c. in the shape of bulbs, which protrude into the synaptic gap.
    d. found in the postsynaptic membrane.

168. Which of the following is smallest?
    a. a synaptic vesicle
    b. an axon
    c. a dendrite
    d. a micrometer

169. Which of the following is the smallest?
    a. a dendrite
    b. a synapse
    c. an axon
    d. a cell body

170. If you want a neuron to fire, you'd better bathe it with a transmitter substance that will:
    a. stabilize its threshold.
    b. decrease its voltage.
    c. make its membrane more polarized.
    d. carry a substantial electrical charge across the synapse.
    e. none of the above

171. Transmission of messages across synapses is almost always by means of:
    a. inorganic ions, like sodium and potassium.
    b. organic molecules, like acetylcholine and dopamine.
    c. electrical impulses.
    d. intermittent physical contact of the relevant neurons.

172. In the lock-and-key model of synaptic transmission, the "key" gets to the "lock":
    a. by removal of synaptic vesicles.
    b. by rapid conduction down to the axon.
    c. by weak attractive forces of the lock.
    d. by diffusion across the cleft.

Answer: a
Interaction among nerve cells
p. 59

173. Which of the following is a very common way for drugs to act on the nervous system?
    a. altering recycling of the transmitter
    b. changing the size of action potentials
    c. slightly changing the size of the synapse
    d. blocking conduction down the axon

Answer: a
Interaction among nerve cells
p. 59

174. Drugs can act on neurons in a variety of ways. Which is a fairly uncommon way?
    a. blocking conduction down the axon
    b. stimulating release of a neurotransmitter
    c. blocking receptor sites, thus making neurotransmitters less effective
    d. interfering with the recycling of neurotransmitters

Answer: b
Interaction among nerve cells
p. 59

175. If you wanted to prevent a synapse from working, you might:
    a. supply it with Loewi's "vagus stuff."
    b. prevent it from packaging neurotransmitters in the synaptic vesicles.
    c. prevent the synaptic knobs from making direct physical contact with the receptor surface of the dendrite.
    d. all of the above

Answer: b
Interaction among nerve cells
p. 59

176. If you wanted to prevent a synapse from working you might:
    a. activate the axon leading to its synaptic knobs.
    b. prevent it from packaging neurotransmitters in the synaptic vesicles.
    c. prevent the synaptic knobs from contacting the receptor surface of the dendrite.
    d. all of the above

Answer: d
Interaction among nerve cells
p. 60

177. Amphetamine and cocaine and most other excitatory drugs work by:
    a. reducing the threshold at which the action potential is triggered.
    b. facilitating the mechanisms of reciprocal inhibition.
    c. inhibiting the autonomic nervous system.
    d. changing levels of certain neurotransmitters in the synapse.
    e. activating the endorphin system.

Answer: b
Interaction among nerve cells
p. 31

178. Most mood-altering drugs, such as cocaine and heroin, create their effects by:
    a. eliminating all-or-none nerve impulses.
    b. altering activity at synapses through specific neurotransmitters.
    c. reducing the release of endorphins.
    d. activating the autonomic nervous system.

Answer: b
Interaction among nerve cells
p. 60

179. Schizophrenia is a mental disorder that seems to involve:
    a. functional disconnection of the corpus callosum, resulting in two distinct personalities.
    b. a neurotransmitter that can be blocked by certain drugs.
    c. damage to the speech areas resulting from psychological or physical abuse.
    d. loss of normal reciprocal inhibition.
    e. all of the above

Answer: b
Interaction among nerve cells
p. 60

180. Which of the following would most likely make schizophrenia worse?
    a. chlorpromazine, which blocks dopamine synapses
    b. amphetamine, which increases the activity at dopamine synapses
    c. placebos, which work in part by increasing endorphin levels
    d. curare, which blocks certain acetylcholine receptors

Answer: b
Interaction among nerve cells
p. 60

181. Neurotransmitters and many psychoactive drugs have their effects at the:
    a. cerebrum.
    b. synapse.
    c. neuromuscular junction.
    d. axon.

Answer: a
Interaction among nerve cells
p. 60

182. Antipsychotic drugs typically make the symptoms of Parkinson's disease worse. Why?
    a. They block dopamine, which is in short supply in Parkinson's disease.
    b. They cause norepinephrine to be released, producing overarousal.
    c. They block acetylcholine, which weakens muscle control in patients with Parkinson's disease.
    d. They kill neurons that secrete dopamine.

Answer: c
Interaction among nerve cells
p. 60

183. Some drugs used to treat Parkinson's disease cause the symptoms of schizophrenia to worsen. Why might this be?
    a. They block acetylcholine agonists.
    b. They block receptors for dopamine.
    c. They increase levels of dopamine.
    d. They increase levels of acetylcholine.

Answer: a
Interaction among nerve cells
p. 60

184. Why don't drugs that are precursors to dopamine work as permanent treatments for Parkinson's disease?
    a. Because the neurons that make dopamine continue to die.
    b. Because dopamine levels eventually rise too high.
    c. Because the brain eventually builds barriers to these precursors.
    d. Because the drugs are toxic to dopaminergic neurons.

Answer: b
Interactions through the bloodstream
p. 61

185. The development of medicines to help people with brain disorders is complicated by the brain's natural defense system called:
    a. the blood-neuronal barrier.
    b. the blood-brain barrier.
    c. the glial-neuronal barrier.
    d. the glial-brain barrier.

Answer: a
Interaction through the bloodstream
p. 62

186. A fundamental difference between the endocrine and nervous systems is the:
    a. distance the chemicals must travel to have an effect.
    b. types of chemicals used as transmitters.
    c. means by which messages travel from one cell to another (chemical vs. electrical).
    d. presence vs. absence of target organs.

Answer: b
Recovery from brain injury
p. 63

187. Recovery from brain damage:
    a. is usually complete, but it takes more than a decade.
    b. is common, but is only pronounced during the first year after the trauma.
    c. is more complete in older people than in infants.
    d. is rare unless special therapies are employed.

Answer: a
Recovery from brain injury
p. 63

188. Recovery from brain damage often occurs when:
    a. causes of temporary damage to neurons are removed.
    b. processes of dead neurons are recycled to synthesize new neurons.
    c. precursors to missing neurotransmitters are incorporated into the diet.
    d. massive doses of vitamin C are taken.
    e. all of the above

Answer: d
Recovery from brain injury
p. 64

189. In young children, recovery of speech and other brain functions following injury is more likely than it is for adults. Thus, we say that a child's brain has:
    a. less specificity.
    b. more specificity.
    c. less plasticity.
    d. more plasticity.

Answer: d
Recovery from brain injury
p. 65

190. Why are ethical issues concerning abortion currently relevant to recovery from brain damage?
    a. Genetic screening has identified the causes of Alzheimer's and Parkinson's disease, therefore fetuses with high risk for these diseases might be aborted.
    b. Fetal brain damage leads to cerebral palsy, therefore fetuses with this damage might be aborted.
    c. Ultrasound has shown that certain neural defects can be corrected in fetuses, but there is a chance that such fetuses would be spontaneously" aborted.
    d. Brain cells from fetuses might be used in transplants for patients with neurological diseases.

Answer: a
Recovery from brain injury
p. 66

191. Which of the following statements best describes the current status of research concerning treatment of spinal cord injuries and degenerative brain disorders in humans?
    a. Neuronal transplantation and the design of growth-promoting chemicals provide hope that effective treatments will be developed in the future.
    b. The outlook for obtaining regeneration of function in these cases is dismal, with little or no evidence that effective treatments will be developed in the future.
    c. Transplantation of adult neuronal tissue into the sites of brain or spinal cord damage in young children has been moderately successful in the treatment of these afflictions.
    d. The use of growth-promoting chemicals to treat brain and spinal cord damage has been shown to be effective in children, but not in adults.

Answer: c
Recovery from brain injury
p. 66

192. Long-term rehabilitation following brain damage in humans or other species is likely to be improved if the afflicted individuals:
    a. ingest daily doses of chemicals known as growth factors.
    b. are provided long periods of rest and relaxation in stress-free environments.
    c. are exposed to highly stimulating environments that encourage use of lost skills.
    d. avoid situations that elicit behaviors that were directly affected by damage to the brain.

Answer: b
Some final comments
p. 67

193. "Even our most sublime thoughts and emotions are produced by chemical systems in the brain." This statement:
    a. is true, and implies that most important psychological questions will eventually be answered at a chemical level.
    b. is true, but says little about appropriate levels for answers.
    c. is false, since the higher levels of CNS functions are largely independent of chemistry.
    d. is false; "chemical" should be replaced by "subatomic particle."

CHAPTER 3 | Motivation

Answer: b
Motivation
p. 71

1. The classes of motives included in self-regulation, self-preservation, and self-restoration share the underlying similarity that:
   a. each depends upon a different specific center in the hypothalamus.
   b. they direct behavior and make some acts more likely than others.
   c. they each can be adequately explained by the drive reduction theory.
   d. they are all encompassed within opponent-process theory.

Answer: a
Motivation
p. 71

2. When we say that motives potentiate some feelings and behaviors, we mean that they:
   a. make some feelings and behaviors more likely than others.
   b. act as positive feedback systems for those feelings and behaviors.
   c. set up opponent processes for those feelings and behaviors.
   d. are essentially like the input component of Descartes' machines.

Answer: b
Motivation as directed action
pp. 71–72

3. Comparing the behavior of Descartes' reflexive machines with that of dogs reveals that
   a. only dogs can accomplish goals.
   b. dogs can approach goals much more flexibly than Descartes' machines can.
   c. the behavior of both is best described in terms of simple sensory-motor reflexes.
   d. neither can accomplish goals.

Answer: b
Motivation as direced action
p. 72

4. Which of the following best exemplifies the concept of positive feedback?
   a. panting by a dog, which lowers body temperature on a hot day
   b. the start of an argument, where one person raises his voice, causing the other person to raise his voice, which in turn makes the first person shout
   c. vasoconstriction when body temperature drops below a certain level
   d. a person who walks two hundred miles through snow to get a beer but is so cold when she gets there she takes cocoa instead

Answer: d
Motivation as directed action
p. 72

5. An example of a positive feedback system is:
   a. an electric light that automatically fades as the day breaks.
   b. a system that keeps the blood level of sodium in balance.
   c. a person digging a hole who digs faster in the morning than at the end of the day.
   d. a magnet pulling a piece of metal toward it.

Answer: b
Motivation as directed action
p. 72

6. In positive feedback systems:
   a. the feedback weakens or stops the response that produces it.
   b. the feedback strengthens the response that produces it.
   c. the feedback may either stop or strengthen the response that produces it depending upon the level of the setpoint.
   d. the feedback will stop the response that produces it if the stimulus is below the setpoint and will strengthen it if the stimulus is above the setpoint.
   e. both c and d

Answer: a
Motivation as directed action
p. 72

7. Positive feedback means that:
   a. there is an ever-increasing level of activity.
   b. there is a decrease in the level of activity.
   c. there is a steady ongoing level of activity.
   d. there is a random fluctuation in the level of activity.

Answer: c
Motivation as directed action
p. 72

8. When a neuron fires, the membrane lets in a little sodium, which alters the membrane so as to let in more sodium, which makes the membrane let in even more. Within a thousandth of a second, as much sodium comes in as is possible (all-or-none law). This process is a good example of:
   a. homeostasis.
   b. a negative feedback system.
   c. a positive feedback system.
   d. a biological motive.

Answer: b
Motivation as directed action
p. 72

9. In a nerve impulse, when a little sodium goes into the axon it changes the membrane so that a lot more can come in. This process is an example of:
   a. a situation similar to homeostasis.
   b. a positive feedback system.
   c. a servomechanism.
   d. an opponent-process system.

Answer: d
Motivation as directed action
p. 72

10. Bob has a chigger bite on his ankle, which he scratches a bit, making the bite itch even more, so he scratches it some more. This scenario best exemplifies:
    a. the opponent-process system.
    b. drive reduction.
    c. reciprocal inhibition.
    d. positive feedback.

11. Which of the following best exemplifies negative feedback?
    a. Your freezer unit, set for 0°F, is getting too cold so an alarm rings. You then come running and unplug the compressor for a little while until the freezer warms up to 0°F.
    b. Your oven is set for 350°F but a bell goes off when it reaches 300°F. You then reset the gauge so the oven will get hotter.
    c. Your oven lets 5 amps of current run through it when set on "hot," 3.5 amps when set on "medium."
    d. Your lab freezer is set on 0°F, but when it gets there the compressor keeps running. The colder it gets, the harder the compressor runs until the temperature reaches that needed to liquify air.

12. Which of the following works on the basis of negative feedback?
    a. a firecracker—a little heat gets some powder burning.
    b. cruise control on a car—if the car starts to slow down the engine runs harder; if the car speeds up the engine runs less hard.
    c. the start of a war—one country provokes an action by the opponent, which in turn elicits a full scale attack by the provoker.
    d. addiction to a drug—a little bit makes you want more.

13. In negative feedback systems:
    a. the feedback stops, or even reverses, the response that produces it.
    b. the feedback strengthens the response that produces it.
    c. the feedback may either stop or strengthen the response that produces it, depending upon the level of the setpoint.
    d. The feedback causes the response that produces it to continue at the same level.

14. An example of a negative feedback system is:
    a. a magnet pulling a piece of metal toward it.
    b. a light source that automatically fades as the day breaks.
    c. a dog that is given food when he barks.
    d. a slot machine.

15. Negative feedback _____ the original behavior.
    a. accelerates
    b. stops
    c. reverses
    d. either b or c

16. Which of the following is an example of a negative feedback system in operation?
    a. maintenance of body temperature
    b. maintenance of water intake
    c. a baby who cries until her dirty diaper is removed and then stops
    d. All of the above are examples of negative feedback.

Answer: d
Motivation as directed action
pp. 72–73

17. Which of the following is an example of a negative feedback system?
    a. a missile that increases its velocity as it gets closer to its target
    b. a machine that dispenses a candy bar whenever someone deposits a coin and pulls a lever
    c. two nations that engage in an escalating arms race that finally ends in war
    d. a device that keeps a naval gun aimed at a target despite the ship's roll

Answer: c
Motivation as directed action
p. 73

18. Homeostasis is:
    a. a dilation of the blood vessels.
    b. controlled by the pancreas.
    c. a stable internal equilibrium.
    d. a mechanism of nerve potentials.

Answer: b
Motivation as directed action
p. 73

19. Homeostasis is:
    a. a theory of need reduction.
    b. a built-in tendency to regulate bodily conditions.
    c. the psychological representation of a need.
    d. the diffusion of fluids in a cell.

Answer: b
Motivation as directed action
p. 73

20. Homeostatic behaviors:
    a. act to orient the animal in its environment.
    b. act to stabilize the conditions within the body.
    c. do not involve feedback mechanisms.
    d. are only involved in thermoregulation.

Answer: c
Motivation as directed action
p. 73

21. When blood pH shifts to acid, both respiration and kidney function change to bring the acidity back to about the normal pH of 7.4. This process best exemplifies:
    a. drive reduction.
    b. positive feedback.
    c. homeostasis.
    d. an opponent-process system.

Answer: d
Motivation as directed action
p. 73

22. The level of salt in our blood is kept constant at about the concentration of the oceans in the era of the first lungfish. Such internal consistency is termed:
    a. evolution.
    b. motivation.
    c. biochemistry.
    d. homeostasis.
    e. thirst.

Answer: c
Temperature regulation
p. 74

23. Which of the following statements is true?
    a. Endothermic animals are incapable of thermoregulation.
    b. Ectothermic animals are incapable of thermoregulation.
    c. Endothermic animals regulate temperature primarily through internal adjustments.
    d. Ectothermic animals regulate temperature primarily through internal adjustments.

Answer: d
Temperature regulation
p. 74

24. Which is not a mechanism by which the body cools itself?
    a. sweating
    b. vasodilation
    c. panting
    d. salivating

Answer: b
Temperature regulation
p. 74

25. When your body is too hot, a process called _____ occurs.
    a. vasoconstriction
    b. vasodilation
    c. piloerection
    d. lateralization
    e. none of the above

Answer: a
Temperature regulation
p. 74

26. Piloerection and vasoconstriction are part of physiological efforts to
    a. raise the body's temperature.
    b. lower the body's temperature.
    c. send blood to the body's surface.
    d. maintain appropriate fluid levels.

Answer: a
Temperature regulation
p. 74

27. When your body is too cold, a process called _____ occurs.
    a. vasoconstriction
    b. vasodilation
    c. hyperventilation (more rapid respiration)
    d. metabolic lowering

Answer: c
Temperature regulation
p. 74

28. Vasoconstriction is a _____ of the blood's capillaries that occurs when your body is too _____.
    a. widening; cold
    b. widening; hot
    c. narrowing; cold
    d. narrowing; hot

Answer: a
Temperature regulation
p. 74

29. If the body temperature in an endothermic animal is too high there will be:
    a. increased parasympathetic activity and vasodilation.
    b. increased sympathetic activity and vasodilation.
    c. increased parasympathetic activity and vasoconstriction.
    d. increased sympathetic activity and vasoconstriction.

Answer: a
Temperature regulation
p. 74

30. If the internal temperature of an endothermic animal is too high, which of the following might occur?
    a. vasodilation
    b. vasoconstriction
    c. ruffling of the fur
    d. both b and c

31. Rover, an English sheepdog, has mistakenly entered the sauna, which his owner has forgotten to turn off. What bodily reflexes would we expect from Rover as he sits in the sweltering heat?
    a. vasodilation
    b. vasoconstriction
    c. piloerection
    d. inhibited salivation

32. Which of the following is a reflexive homeostatic adjustment to a body temperature that is too low?
    a. vasodilation
    b. fur-licking
    c. ruffling of the fur
    d. moving into the sun

33. A setpoint for temperature:
    a. is the body temperature that homeostatic processes attempt to maintain.
    b. is constant throughout the year for all endothermic animals.
    c. is constant throughout each day for humans.
    d. is the minimum body temperature needed to keep an organism alive.
    e. is the maximum body temperature with which an organism can survive.

34. Anton's body temperature averages 98.2 degrees Fahrenheit. That temperature is his:
    a. trigger for positive feedback.
    b. setpoint.
    c. thermoregulatory maximum.
    d. thermoregulatory minimum.

35. Which of the following statements is true?
    a. The sympathetic and parasympathetic divisions of the autonomic nervous system usually work together.
    b. Sympathetic activation leads to increased body temperature.
    c. Parasympathetic activation leads to increased heart rate.
    d. b and c

36. The two divisions of the autonomic nervous system are:
    a. the glands and the smooth muscles.
    b. the endocrine system and the smooth muscles.
    c. the sympathetic branch and the endocrine system.
    d. the sympathetic and parasympathetic branches.

37. Which of the following is responsible for decelerating an excited heart?
    a. sympathetic nervous system
    b. parasympathetic nervous system
    c. endocrine system
    d. the pituitary

Answer: a
Temperature regulation
p. 76

Answer: b
Temperature regulation
p. 76

Answer: b
Temperature regulation
p. 76

Answer: a
Temperature regulation
p. 76

Answer: a
Temperature regulation
p. 76

Answer: b
Temperature regulation
p. 76

Answer: b
Temperature regulation
p. 76

38. Which of the following is most directly responsible for accelerating the rate at which the heart beats?
   a. sympathetic nervous system
   b. parasympathetic nervous system
   c. hypothalamus
   d. the endocrine system

39. Which brain structure is responsible for temperature regulation?
   a. pituitary
   b. hypothalamus
   c. pons
   d. medulla

40. The sensing mechanism for the homeostatic control of temperature is located in:
   a. an endocrine gland other than the pituitary.
   b. the hypothalamus.
   c. the pituitary.
   d. the cerebrum.

41. Temperature of the body is regulated by:
   a. the hypothalamus.
   b. the adrenal gland.
   c. the pituitary.
   d. the ovaries.

42. Increasing the temperature of brain cells that regulate body temperature will cause an animal:
   a. to act as if it were hot.
   b. to act as if it were cold.
   c. to attack the experimenter.
   d. to behave as if nothing had happened.

43. Decreasing the temperature of brain cells that regulate body temperature will elicit:
   a. biting.
   b. vasoconstriction.
   c. chewing.
   d. vasodilation.

44. When the hypothalamus of a comfortably warm rat is cooled directly, the rat will:
   a. experience vasodilation.
   b. press a lever it has learned to press in order to release a blast of hot air.
   c. not demonstrate any systematic response.
   d. pant and sweat.

Answer: d
Temperature regulation
p. 76

Answer: c
Temperature regulation
pp. 76–77

Answer: a
Temperature regulation
p. 77

Answer: d
Thirst
pp. 77–79

Answer: d
Thirst
p. 78

Answer: d
Thirst
p. 78

Answer: a
Thirst
p. 78

45. A big hairy dog is in a room comfortably heated to 65 degrees Fahrenheit. Its hypothalamus is warmed experimentally. Consequently:
   a. it will shiver and its body temperature will go up.
   b. it will shiver and its body temperature will go down.
   c. it will pant and its body temperature will go up.
   d. it will pant and its body temperature will go down.

46. Which of the following statements is false?
   a. A rat's thermoregulatory system makes use of voluntary as well as reflexive behaviors.
   b. Different brain areas seem to control the thermoregulatory actions of voluntary versus reflexive behavior in rats.
   c. For rats, thermoregulation relies solely on reflexive behaviors.
   d. a and b

47. The onset of a fever is marked by chills because
   a. body temperature is below the newly raised setpoint.
   b. body temperature matches the newly raised setpoint.
   c. body temperature is above the newly lowered setpoint.
   d. body temperature matches the newly lowered setpoint.

48. The body regulates water intake by monitoring
   a. blood pressure.
   b. water volume within cells.
   c. volume of bodily fluids outside of cells.
   d. all of the above

49. Vasopressin (antidiuretic hormone) is released by the:
   a. kidney.
   b. liver.
   c. hypothalamus.
   d. pituitary.
   e. medulla.

50. Vasopressin (ntidiuretic hormone) is related to:
   a. sex.
   b. hunger.
   c. temperature regulation.
   d. thirst.

51. One consequence of a decrease in fluid volume is:
   a. secretion of Vasopressin (antidiuretic hormone).
   b. sweating.
   c. a decrease in concentration of the salts in body fluids.
   d. increased electrical activity in the parietal lobe of the cerebral cortex.

Answer: a
Thirst
p. 78

Answer: b
Thirst
p. 78

Answer: a
Thirst
p. 78

Answer: c
Thirst
p. 79

Answer: c
Thirst
p. 79

Answer: a
Thirst
p. 78

Answer: e
Thirst
pp. 78–79

52. Vasopressin:
   a. causes the kidneys to retain fluid.
   b. is secreted because of an increase in blood pressure.
   c. causes vasodilation.
   d. is secreted by the hypothalamus.

53. One consequence of a decrease in fluid volume is the liberation of:
   a. large amounts of perspiration.
   b. angiotensin II.
   c. the kidney from hormonal control.
   d. the hypothalamus from negative feedback control.

54. One consequence of a decrease in blood volume is:
   a. a desire to drink.
   b. sweating.
   c. a decrease in concentration of the salts in body fluids.
   d. increased electrical activity in the parietal lobe of the cerebral cortex.
   e. all of the above

55. Why does drinking seawater lead to *de*hydration?
   a. It causes body cells to swell, which produces thirst.
   b. It causes the kidney to release angiotensin.
   c. It causes water to leak out of cells by osmosis.
   d. The premise is wrong. Drinking seawater leads to *re*hydration.

56. Osmoreceptors:
   a. detect changes in blood pressure.
   b. influence only reflexive behavior.
   c. detect changes in water volume within cells.
   d. can lead to the inhibition of vasopressin.

57. Which of the following produces drinking?
   a. decrease in total blood volume
   b. an increase in blood glucose concentration
   c. heating of the posterior hypothalamus
   d. a and c

58. The fluid volume of the body is controlled by:
   a. receptors in the veins that detect drops in blood pressure.
   b. receptors in the brain that respond to chemical messages from the kidney.
   c. cells in the body that respond to salt concentration of bodily fluids.
   d. b and c
   e. all of the above

Answer: c
Thirst
pp. 78–79

59. Which of the following would not be a signal for an organism to drink?
    a. a drop in blood pressure
    b. an increase in salt concentration in the hypothalamus
    c. a drop in blood sugar level
    d. a chemical messenger released by the kidney

Answer: b
Hunger
p. 79

60. Basal metabolic rate refers to:
    a. the standard energy value of a calorie.
    b. the rate at which calories are converted to energy in different organisms.
    c. the rate at which different organisms are able to gather food.
    d. the time it takes the brain to sense that eating has begun.

Answer: c
Hunger
p. 79

61. If animal *A* has a higher basal metabolic rate than animal *B*, then
    a. animal *A* is more likely to be an ectotherm and animal *B* is more likely to be an endotherm.
    b. animal *A* is probably larger than animal *B*.
    c. animal *A* needs to eat proportionately more calories than animal *B* to maintain body weight.
    d. animal *A* needs to eat proportionately fewer calories than animal *B* to maintain body weight.

Answer: b
Hunger
p. 80

62. A rat is fed a diet that contains 10 calories per gram. On this diet, the rat's daily intake is 30 grams. The diet is now diluted to contain only 5 calories per gram. The rat will now ingest approximately:
    a. 30 grams per day.
    b. 60 grams per day.
    c. 15 grams per day.
    d. an unknown amount per day, since its daily intake cannot be determined from the information provided.

Answer: a
Hunger
p. 80

63. A rat is fed a diet that contains 5 calories per gram. On this diet, the rat's daily intake is 60 grams. The diet is now concentrated to contain 10 calories per gram. The rat will now ingest approximately:
    a. 30 grams per day.
    b. 60 grams per day.
    c. 15 grams per day.
    d. an unknown amount per day, since its daily intake cannot be determined from the information provided.

Answer: b
Hunger
p. 80

64. Which of the following is the major source of short-term energy?
    a. glycogen
    b. glucose
    c. fats
    d. animal starch

Answer: b
Hunger
pp. 80–81

65. We are most apt to stop eating when:
    a. we have swallowed about the appropriate number of times.
    b. when liver chemistry is converting glucose to glycogen.
    c. we have about the "right" number of fat cells.
    d. our stomach has some food in it.

66. When a rat or a person is satiated and wants no more food, the liver is converting:
    a. fat to glycogen.
    b. fat to glucose.
    c. glucose to glycogen.
    d. glycogen to glucose.

67. During fasting our livers:
    a. convert glycogen to glucose.
    b. convert glucose to glycogen.
    c. convert glycogen to fat.
    d. are involved in little biochemical activity.

68. Right after we stuff ourselves at Thanksgiving dinner, our livers:
    a. convert glycogen to glucose.
    b. convert fat to glycogen.
    c. secrete insulin.
    d. convert glucose to glycogen.

69. When metabolism in the liver is going in the direction
    glucose ⟶ glycogen ⟶ fat:
    a. it signals satiety.
    b. it signals hunger.
    c. it signals either of the above, depending upon the hormonal output of the pituitary and thyroid glands.
    d. it signals hunger if the organism has a high basal metabolic rate and satiety if the organism has a low basal metabolic rate.

70. A certain metabolic reaction in the liver triggers a signal that leads to eating. What is this signal?
    a. Glucose is converted into fat.
    b. Glycogen is converted into fat
    c. Glucose is converted into glycogen
    d. Glycogen is converted into glucose

71. When an animal is hungry the liver is converting:
    a. glucose to glycogen.
    b. glucose to fat.
    c. glycogen to glucose.
    d. glycogen to fat.

72. Glucoreceptors:
    a. are located primarily in the cerebral cortex.
    b. control glucose use by influencing insulin release from the pancreas.
    c. detect the amount of glucose available for metabolism.
    d. aid in the conversion of glycogen to glucose.

73. What was the main point of the experiments in which an injected chemical made particular hypothalamic neurons unable to respond to glucose?
    a. It showed that eating increased when the brain no longer could respond to negative feedback signals from food.
    b. It showed that particular hypothalamic neurons store glucose shortly after eating and convert it to glycogen.
    c. It provided an explanation for why obesity is common in certain animals and people.
    d. It led to the correct conclusion that the brain, not the liver, is the important organ for detecting the consequences of eating.

74. The pattern of blood glucose levels that most likely signals hunger is:
    a. a slow rise, followed by a quick drop.
    b. a slow drop, followed by a quick rise.
    c. a slow steady rise until food is eaten to compensate.
    d. a slow steady drop until food is eaten to compensate.

75. Which of the following statements about the stomach's role in the cessation of eating is true?
    a. Receptors in the stomach walls measure the volume of stomach contents.
    b. When the stomach's contents reach a certain volume, the animal stops eating.
    c. Receptors in the stomach walls measure the nutrients in the stomach's contents.
    d. a and b

76. If a rat was injected with the hormone cholecystokinin, you might expect it to:
    a. drink more water than its body needed.
    b. shiver and show ruffling of the fur.
    c. eat more than it normally would.
    d. stop eating.

77. Adipose cells secrete:
    a. leptin, which may lead to decreased eating.
    b. CCK, which leads to increased eating.
    c. glucose, which leads to decreased eating.
    d. glycogen, which leads to decreased eating.

78. Leptin:
    a. is secreted by fat cells.
    b. can be detected by hypothalamic receptors.
    c. may signal sufficient fat supplies and thereby lead to decreased eating.
    d. all of the above

79. Peter became very hungry at noon when he skipped lunch to attend a meeting, but he wasn't hungry at 3 P.M., even though his schedule was so busy he still hadn't eaten. What best accounts for this?
    a. His body began to mobilize glucose from his fat cells.
    b. His body converted glucose into glycogen.
    c. Peter is working on a schedule of intermittent reinforcement.
    d. Hunger is sensitive to external factors.
    e. Peter is probably obese.

80. External cues such as the sight of food:
    a. act independently of internal cues such as feelings of satiety.
    b. are more likely to lead to eating in the context of hunger than satiety.
    c. are more likely to lead to eating in the context of satiety than hunger.
    d. have no effect on the hypothalamus.

81. Neurons in the hypothalamus that respond to the sight of food probably do so most strongly when:
    a. the liver is converting glucose to glycogen.
    b. the liver is converting glycogen to glucose.
    c. cholecystokinin levels are high.
    d. fat cells are secreting leptin.

82. According to the dual-center theory, the "off" center for feeding is the:
    a. lateral zone of the hypothalamus.
    b. ventromedial region of the hypothalamus.
    c. vein that leads into the liver.
    d. artery that comes out of the liver.

83. According to the dual-center theory, the "on" center for feeding is the:
    a. lateral zone of the hypothalamus.
    b. ventromedial region of the hypothalamus.
    c. vein that leads into the liver.
    d. artery that comes out of the liver.

84. The term *aphagia* refers to:
    a. inability to speak.
    b. inability to comprehend.
    c. not eating.
    d. excess eating.

85. Hyperphagia means:
    a. excess eating.
    b. not eating.
    c. excess sleeping.
    d. fever.

Answer: c
Hunger
p. 83

86. You meet an old high-school friend at a party and are startled to learn he went from 150 to 280 pounds in the year since his automobile accident. Damage to which of the following areas would best account for this weight gain?
    a. aphagial hypothalamus
    b. hyperphagial hypothalamus
    c. ventromedial hypothalamus
    d. lateral hypothalamus

Answer: d
Hunger
p. 84

87. Rats with lesions in the ventromedial zone of the hypothalamus will:
    a. refuse to eat until they starve to death.
    b. refuse to eat until they have lost almost 50 percent of their body weight and then slowly begin to eat again.
    c. overeat and continue to gain weight until they finally die of obesity.
    d. overeat and gain weight for about 2 months, at which time they maintain themselves at this higher weight.

Answer: a
Hunger
p. 83

88. Rats with lesions in the lateral region of the hypothalamus will
    a. refuse to eat, possibly to the point of starving to death.
    b. decrease eating until they lose about 10 percent of their body weight.
    c. overeat until they increase their body weight by about 10 percent.
    d. overeat for about 2 months and then maintain themselves at their new higher weight.

Answer: b
Hunger
p. 83

89. Your pet rodent was attacked by a cat. Although recovered, your pet has a ravenous appetite and cannot get enough to eat. You suspect:
    a. adypsia.
    b. brain damage in the ventromedial hypothalamus.
    c. lesions in the lateral hypothalamus.
    d. a change in locus of control.

Answer: a
Hunger
p. 84

90. What is the apparent effect of destroying the ventromedial area of the hypothalamus?
    a. It raises the setpoint for body weight.
    b. It lowers the setpoint for body weight.
    c. It destroys the setpoint for body weight.
    d. It has no effect on the setpoint for body weight.

Answer: a
Hunger
p. 83

91. After an accident, your friend refuses to eat or drink. You suspect he has brain damage in the:
    a. lateral hypothalamus.
    b. ventromedial hypothalamus.
    c. lateral pituitary.
    d. ventromedial pituitary.
    e. lateral medulla.

92. After an accident, your friend cannot stop eating. You suspect she has brain damage to the:
    a. lateral hypothalamus.
    b. ventromedial hypothalamus.
    c. lateral pituitary.
    d. ventromedial pituitary.
    e. lateral medulla.

93. According to the dual-center theory, destruction of the hypothalamic "off" center leads to:
    a. a decrease in sensitivity to food tastes.
    b. weight loss.
    c. aphagia.
    d. hyperphagia.

94. According to the dual-center theory, destruction of the hypothalamic "on" center leads to:
    a. unusual sensitivity to food tastes.
    b. increased glycogen levels.
    c. aphagia.
    d. hyperphagia.

95. Current research suggests that:
    a. the lateral hypothalamus is the main center for the regulation of feeding.
    b. all neurochemicals known to stimulate eating have their strongest effects in the lateral hypothalamus.
    c. the lateral hypothalamus does not control eating in a simple or direct way.
    d. a and b

96. Rats *A* and *B* are the same weight. Then the ventromedial region of the hypothalamus in rat *A* is lesioned. Which of the following statements is false?
    a. If rats *A* and *B* are given the same amount of food, they will continue to weigh the same as one another.
    b. Allowed to eat what they want, rat *A* will eat more than rat *B*.
    c. Rat *A* will convert more of its intake to fat than will rat *B*.
    d. Rat *A* will need to eat more than rat *B* for the same amount of energy.

97. Current research suggests that lesions of the ventromedial hypothalamus:
    a. destroy the "off" switch for eating.
    b. destroy the "on" switch for eating.
    c. lead to an increase in the proportion of glucose stored as fat.
    d. lead to a decrease in the proportion of glucose stored as fat.

Answer: b
Hunger
p. 85

98. That rats will ingest a solution containing noncaloric saccharin indicates that:
    a. a saccharin receptor exists in the liver.
    b. taste factors influence food intake.
    c. food preferences are culturally transmitted.
    d. saccharin levels in blood are regulated.

Answer: c
Hunger
p. 85

99. Which substance do newborn babies have a built-in preference for?
    a. a bitter substance
    b. a sour substance
    c. a sweet substance
    d. a spicy substance

Answer: d
Hunger
p. 86

100. When rats shy away from a food that they have never tasted before, they are being affected by:
    a. nutriphobia.
    b. starvation.
    c. hyperphobia.
    d. neophobia.

Answer: c
Hunger
p. 86

101. Four-year-old Sarah has just been given asparagus for the first time. She wrinkles up her mouth and nose in an expression of disgust and spits them right out. Here, Sarah is exhibiting:
    a. hyperphagia.
    b. aphagia.
    c. neophobia.
    d. a learned taste aversion.
    e. common sense.

Answer: d
Hunger
p. 86

102. One might expect food neophobias to be most common in:
    a. herbivores with specialized diets, like koalas and pandas.
    b. carnivores.
    c. insectivores like many bats.
    d. omnivores.

Answer: a
Hunger
p. 86

103. Little Joey has just been given brussel sprouts for the first time. He makes a terrible face and spits them out immediately. Joey is exhibiting:
    a. neophobia.
    b. hyperphagia.
    c. aphagia.
    d. common sense.

Answer: b
Hunger
p. 86

104. The function of neophobia seems to be:
    a. to prevent organisms from overgrazing certain plants.
    b. to prevent organisms from poisoning themselves by eating toxic substances.
    c. to prevent overeating and obesity.
    d. to transmit cultural preferences regarding food.

Answer: d
Hunger
p. 87

105. One plausible reason some people are constitutionally predisposed to become obese is that they:
    a. absorb calories less efficiently than normal and hence must eat more.
    b. have more neurons than normal in specialized areas of their hypothalamus.
    c. live in a culture that provides abundant cues for eating food high in calories.
    d. burn nutrient fuel more efficiently than normal.

Answer: d
Hunger
pp. 87–89

106. Weight is determined by:
    a. caloric intake.
    b. amount of exercise.
    c. metabolic efficiency.
    d. all of the above

Answer: b
Hunger
p. 87

107. When identical twins are equally overfed:
    a. they gain about the same amount of weight, but store the weight in different places.
    b. they gain about the same amount of weight, and store the weight in the same places.
    c. they gain different amounts of weight, and store weight gains in different places.
    d. they gain different amounts of weight, but store any weight gains in the same places.

Answer: a
Hunger
p. 88

108. According to the thrifty gene hypothesis:
    a. those predisposed to obesity would have survived better in the world of our ancestors than would those predisposed to thinness.
    b. those predisposed to thinness would have survived better in the world of our ancestors than would those predisposed to obesity.
    c. those predisposed to obesity are better suited to today's affluent cultures than are those predisposed to thinness.
    d. those predisposed to obesity and those predisposed to thinness are equally well-suited to today's affluent cultures.

Answer: c
Hunger
p. 87

109. A recent study on twins seems to indicate that metabolic patterns:
    a. are very dependent on the amount of energy a person expends daily.
    b. are not genetically linked.
    c. are probably inherited.
    d. can be controlled through biofeedback.

Answer: c
Hunger
p. 88

110. Billy is like most two-year-olds; every time he sees a potty he decides that he needs to go to the bathroom. Investigators of obesity have found that some people have an analogous response to food. This is known as the:
    a. setpoint hypothesis.
    b. restrained eating hypothesis.
    c. externality hypothesis.
    d. stimulus-dependent hypothesis.
    e. automatic hypothesis.

111. Obese and average weight people are given two brands of ice cream; one brand (*X*) tastes good, the other (*Y*) does not taste good. We measure how much each group eats of each brand (in grams). Which of the numbers below are the most likely results?
    a. obese: *X*-200, *Y*-50; average weight: *X*-100, *Y*-80
    b. obese: *X*-200, *Y*-150; average weight: *X*-100, *Y*-80
    c. obese: *X*-200, *Y*-100; average weight: *X*-100, *Y*-100
    d. obese: *X*-200, *Y*-80; average weight: *X*-100, *Y*-80

112. According to the externality hypothesis:
    a. obese people are more sensitive to internal signals for hunger than for satiety.
    b. average weight people are particularly sensitive to external cues for eating.
    c. obese people are particularly sensitive to external cues for eating.
    d. obese people have a defect in the ventromedial hypothalamus.

113. The externality hypothesis for obesity:
    a. has empirical support.
    b. is no longer in favor.
    c. probably describes the effects of restrained eating rather than the cause of obesity.
    d. all of the above

114. According to the setpoint hypothesis, when the amount of body fat is significantly above the setpoint:
    a. appetite increases.
    b. appetite diminishes.
    c. the number of body fat cells decreases.
    d. the number of body fat cells increases.

115. Dieting:
    a. is the best way to lose weight and keep it off.
    b. leads in to an increase in the basal metabolic rate.
    c. leads to a decrease in the basal metabolic rate.
    d. leads to a weight reduction which is then maintained when caloric intake is returned to normal.

116. Which of the following statements is false?
    a. Evidence indicates that health is better predicted by activity levels than by obesity.
    b. Sedentary people of average weight have been found to live longer than active overweight people.
    c. When appetite suppressing medications are stopped, weight losses are typically reversed.
    d. Exercise is a healthier way to lose weight and maintain losses than is dieting.

Answer: a
Hunger
pp. 89–90

117. Which of the following statements is true?
    a. Aesthetics regarding weight are culturally determined.
    b. Thinness is invariably healthier than moderate obesity.
    c. Thinness is an ideal in all societies that have been studied.
    d. b and c

Answer: d
Hunger
p. 89

118. Stuart is overweight. He goes on a starvation diet in the hopes of slimming down before graduating from college. He starts consuming about 1,000 calories a day. He loses some weight, but not nearly as much as he thought he would. You would tell Stuart the reason he is not losing great amounts of weight is:
    a. he has a larger number of fat cells.
    b. he is probably just losing excess water, which is easily replaced.
    c. his activity level needs to be greatly increased.
    d. his body has compensated for this caloric reduction by reducing its metabolism.

Answer: d
Hunger
pp. 83, 90

119. Anorexia nervosa is a syndrome involving a prolonged and severe refusal by people to eat enough to maintain body weight. With respect to food intake, this syndrome seems most similar to the symptoms shown by rats with:
    a. high levels of sympathetic arousal.
    b. addictions to morphine or endorphins.
    c. REM sleep deprivation.
    d. damage to the lateral part of the hypothalamus.
    e. parasympathetic overshoot.

Answer: c
Hunger
p. 90

120. A typical characteristic of anorexia nervosa is:
    a. a physical trauma that has affected the hypothalamus.
    b. lethargy and a loss of interest in exercising.
    c. an obsession with thinness.
    d. binge-and-purge cycles.

Answer: d
Hunger
p. 90

121. A problem with concluding that anorexia is caused by some kind of hypothalamic malfunction is that:
    a. there is no evidence of hormonal disturbances that are related to the hypothalamus.
    b. damage to other regions of the brain can produce anorexia, but there is no evidence that hypothalamic damage can produce it.
    c. anorexia is caused by social factors, not biological ones.
    d. it is not clear whether the hypothalamic-like symptoms in anorexia are causes of the problem or results of it.

Answer: a
Hunger
p. 90

122. According to some researchers, why might anorexia be more common in late 20th-century America than in Europe from the 17th to the 19th century?
    a. Because in modern America, "thin is in."
    b. Because more people are living to late adolescence now than in the Europe of earlier times.
    c. Because many Americans are obese, and being underweight is a way to increase longevity.
    d. Because there is now less call for hard physical labor.

Answer: a
Hunger
p. 91

123. Which of the following statements is false?
    a.   There is no evidence for a genetic predisposition to anorexia.
    b.   Anorexics often combine starvation diets with strenuous exercise.
    c.   Anorexia may be the result of an adolescent's attempt to exercise autonomy.
    d.   Female anorexics often stop menstruating.

Answer: d
Hunger
p. 91

124. Bulimia differs from anorexia in that:
    a.   people with bulimia typically maintain normal weights while anorexics become abnormally underweight.
    b.   people with bulimia often eat large amounts of food while anorexics eat very little.
    c.   bulimia is more common.
    d.   all of the above

Answer: c
Hunger
p. 91

125. Bulimia is characterized by:
    a.   starvation.
    b.   strenuous exercise.
    c.   binging and purging.
    d.   severe weight loss.
    e.   all of the above

Answer: a
Threat
pp. 92–93

126. Walking into a class that you've foolishly ignored for a month, you discover that it's exam day. As part of your panic, which of the following happens?
    a.   Your sympathetic nervous system becomes aroused.
    b.   Your parasympathetic nervous system becomes aroused.
    c.   Your hindbrain shuts down to conserve energy.
    d.   Your midbrain shuts down to conserve energy.

Answer: a
Threat
p. 93
Diff. = .72   Discrim. = .50

127. Meditation involves a slowing of respiration and heart rate. In order to effect these changes the activity of the _____ increases.
    a.   parasympathetic nervous system
    b.   sympathetic nervous system
    c.   thalamus
    d.   cerebellum

Answer: c
Threat
p. 93

128. The sympathetic nervous system is concerned with:
    a.   vegetative functions.
    b.   slowing of the heart.
    c.   activation.
    d.   digestion.

Answer: d
Threat
p. 92

129. Epinephrine is produced by the:
    a.   hypothalamus.
    b.   thalamus.
    c.   pituitary.
    d.   adrenal medulla.

130. Which statement is false?
    a. The action of the adrenal medulla facilitates the action of the sympathetic nervous system.
    b. The adrenal medulla produces adrenaline.
    c. Adrenaline is often called epinephrine.
    d. Epinephrine is responsible for all vegetative functions.

131. The _____ of the autonomic nervous system is responsible for preparing the body to spend energy for an emergency.
    a. homeostatic branch
    b. activating branch
    c. sympathetic branch
    d. parasympathetic branch

132. The adrenal medulla _____ arousal by releasing _____ into the bloodstream.
    a. decreases; norepinephrine
    b. decreases; dopamine
    c. increases; serotonin
    d. increases; epinephrine
    e. The adrenal medulla has no effect on arousal.

133. On Halloween, you were frightened by a ghost. Your heart began to pound and your face became flushed. This reaction resulted from activationof your:
    a. central nervous system.
    b. parasympathetic nervous system.
    c. sympathetic nervous system.
    d. homeostatic nervous system

134. The parasympathetic nervous system handles
    a. fight.
    b. flight.
    c. vegetative functions.
    d. a and b

135. The sympathetic branch of the ANS:
    a. arises from the brain and the lowest levels of the spinal cord (i.e., toward the tail), but not from the middle regions of the spinal cord.
    b. has a more widespread action than the parasympathetic.
    c. facilitates the storage of excess glucose as fat.
    d. all of the above

136. One sign of sexual arousal is salivation, another is penile erection, both of which are controlled by the:
    a. somatic nervous system.
    b. sympathetic nervous system.
    c. parasympathetic nervous system.
    d. thalamus.

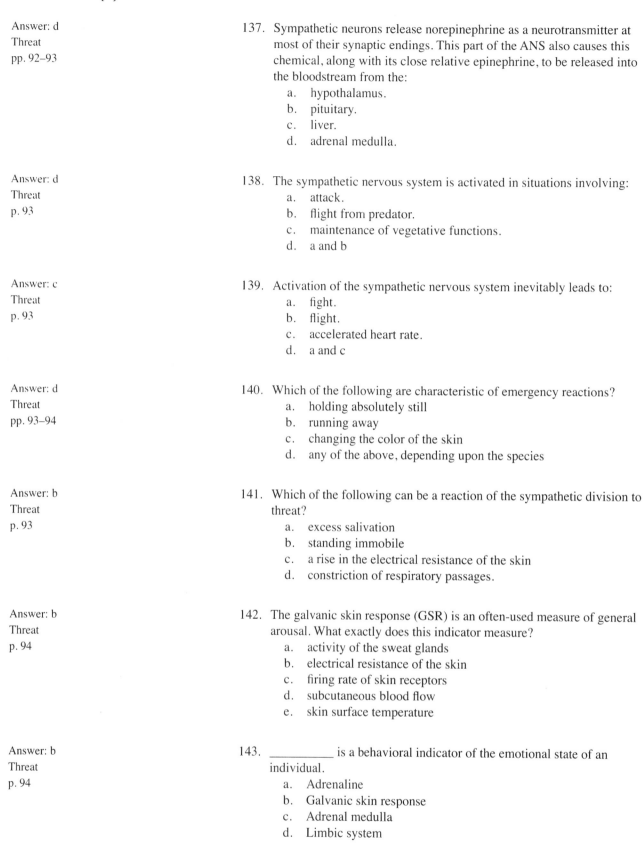

Answer: d
Threat
pp. 92–93

137. Sympathetic neurons release norepinephrine as a neurotransmitter at most of their synaptic endings. This part of the ANS also causes this chemical, along with its close relative epinephrine, to be released into the bloodstream from the:
    a. hypothalamus.
    b. pituitary.
    c. liver.
    d. adrenal medulla.

Answer: d
Threat
p. 93

138. The sympathetic nervous system is activated in situations involving:
    a. attack.
    b. flight from predator.
    c. maintenance of vegetative functions.
    d. a and b

Answer: c
Threat
p. 93

139. Activation of the sympathetic nervous system inevitably leads to:
    a. fight.
    b. flight.
    c. accelerated heart rate.
    d. a and c

Answer: d
Threat
pp. 93–94

140. Which of the following are characteristic of emergency reactions?
    a. holding absolutely still
    b. running away
    c. changing the color of the skin
    d. any of the above, depending upon the species

Answer: b
Threat
p. 93

141. Which of the following can be a reaction of the sympathetic division to threat?
    a. excess salivation
    b. standing immobile
    c. a rise in the electrical resistance of the skin
    d. constriction of respiratory passages.

Answer: b
Threat
p. 94

142. The galvanic skin response (GSR) is an often-used measure of general arousal. What exactly does this indicator measure?
    a. activity of the sweat glands
    b. electrical resistance of the skin
    c. firing rate of skin receptors
    d. subcutaneous blood flow
    e. skin surface temperature

Answer: b
Threat
p. 94

143. _____ is a behavioral indicator of the emotional state of an individual.
    a. Adrenaline
    b. Galvanic skin response
    c. Adrenal medulla
    d. Limbic system

144. Which of the following is produced in a flight-or-fight reaction?
    a. secretion of insulin by the pancreas
    b. secretion of extra saliva and other digestive juices
    c. galvanic skin response (GSR)
    d. all of the above
    e. none of the above

145. A polygraph test:
    a. often includes a measure of galvanic skin response.
    b. cannot falsely indicate that an innocent person is guilty.
    c. cannot falsely indicate that a guilty person is innocent.
    d. all of the above

146. A polygraph measures:
    a. parasympathetic activation.
    b. autonomic arousal.
    c. adrenaline levels in the bloodstream.
    d. willingness to lie.

147. The limbic system is:
    a. involved in mediating emotional behavior.
    b. part of the hypothalamus.
    c. involved in intellectual functioning.
    d. part of the cerebellum.

148. Predatory attacks and attacks in self-defense:
    a. are behaviorally indistinguishable.
    b. are controlled by different areas of the brain.
    c. both entail rage.
    d. all of the above

149. Tom is usually laid-back and a good companion, but when an electrode is activated in his _____, he first becomes anxious and, as the stimulus remains on, he smashes his guitar on the head of his therapist.
    a. limbic system
    b. motor cortex
    c. cerebellum
    d. pituitary
    e. lateral hypothalamus

150. Jane is usually calm and friendly, but when an epileptic seizure (abnormal overstimulation of neurons) begins in her _____, she becomes agitated and extremely aggressive.
    a. motor cortex
    b. Broca's area
    c. corpus callosum
    d. limbic system
    e. cerebellum

Answer: c
Threat
p. 96

151. Sexual behavior is largely controlled by:
    a. the sympathetic nervous system.
    b. the motor projection area.
    c. the parasympathetic nervous system.
    d. the sensory projection area.

Answer: d
Threat
p. 96

152. Periods of autonomic arousal may lead to:
    a. digestive problems.
    b. sexual dysfunction.
    c. hypertension.
    d. all of the above

Answer: d
Threat
p. 96

153. Which of the following are most likely to be disrupted by sympathetic nervous system arousal?
    a. water balance and ability to maintain blood pressure
    b. respiration and ability to maintain an adequate heart rate
    c. swallowing and muscle tone
    d. sexual performance and digestion

Answer: b
Threat
p. 96

154. Pain:
    a. is a learned response.
    b. is a protective warning signal.
    c. is a result of autonomic arousal.
    d. all of the above

Answer: c
Threat
p. 97

155. Analgesia means:
    a. numbness.
    b. lack of sexual function.
    c. pain relief.
    d. unwillingness to eat.

Answer: c
Threat
pp. 97–98

156. Which of the following statements is false?
    a. There are external mechanisms that produce analgesia.
    b. There are internal mechanisms that produce analgesia.
    c. Acupuncture is not an effective analgesic.
    d. Endorphins produce analgesia.

Answer: c
Threat
p. 97

157. Endorphins are:
    a. morphine and heroin.
    b. a class of neurotransmitters including nalaxone and naltrexone.
    c. opiate-like neurotransmitters.
    d. responsible for causing pain.

Answer: b
Threat
p. 97

158. Which of the following drugs or groups of drugs is the most similar in its actions to the naturally occurring endorphins?
    a. depressants, like alcohol and the barbiturates
    b. heroin and other opiates
    c. amphetamine and cocaine
    d. the combination of sugar and caffeine

Answer: c
Threat
p. 97

159. _____ are a group of neurotransmitters secreted by cells in the brain, which disrupt messages coming from pain receptors.
    a. Amphetamines
    b. Placebos
    c. Endorphins
    d. a and b

Answer: b
Threat
p. 97

160. Quarterback Joe sprained his ankle during the last quarter of the big game, yet he didn't feel any pain until after the game was over. Joe's body administered _____ to him.
    a. amphetamines
    b. endorphins
    c. a placebo
    d. morphine

Answer: d
Threat
pp. 97–98

161. Electrical stimulation at a certain place in the midbrain reduces pain substantially, but this effect is blocked by injections of naloxone. A likely mechanism involved is that the electrical stimulation causes the release of:
    a. naloxone.
    b. morphine.
    c. adrenaline.
    d. endorphins.

Answer: b
Threat
p. 97

162. In a fakir who sleeps on a bed of nails you might most expect to find:
    a. a deficiency of neurotransmitters in the pleasure centers of the brain.
    b. unusually high levels of endorphins.
    c. an absence of REM sleep.
    d. traces of amphetamine or cocaine.
    e. atrophy of the reticular formation.

Answer: d
Threat
p. 98

163. The "runner's high," which many avid joggers and marathon runners talk of, is most plausibly related to the:
    a. production of naloxone.
    b. conversion of glycogen to glucose in the liver.
    c. loss of bodily fluids resulting in hypovolemia.
    d. release of endorphins.

Answer: a
Threat
pp. 97–98

164. A(n) _____ is a chemically inert substance that a patient believes will help her or him.
    a. placebo
    b. endorphin
    c. amphetamine
    d. analgesic

Answer: d
Threat
pp. 96–98

165. Other things being equal, in which of the following people or animals would you expect to have the least production of endorphins?
    a. a person given a placebo
    b. a rat subjected to cold stress
    c. a horse given acupuncture before minor surgery
    d. a person with congenital insensitivity to pain

Answer: d
Threat
pp. 97–98

166. Which of the following has (have) analgesic effects?
    a. placebos
    b. acupuncture
    c. hypnosis
    d. all of the above

Answer: c
Threat
pp. 97–98

167. A horse is given acupuncture prior to minor surgery. The most likely effect of an injection of naloxone along with the acupuncture will be to:
    a. increase the effectiveness of the acupuncture in alleviating pain.
    b. increase the chance that the horse will become addicted to acupuncture treatments.
    c. decrease the effectiveness of the acupuncture as an analgesic.
    d. have no effect one way or the other on the effectiveness of the acupuncture.

Answer: c
Threat
p. 98

168. A serious sprain of the ankle will hurt more if it is followed by an injection of:
    a. a placebo.
    b. morphine.
    c. naloxone.
    d. endorphins.
    e. any of the above

Answer: b
Threat
p. 98

169. For what emergency condition will the drug naloxone be the most useful?
    a. blockage of the parasympathetic nerves to the heart
    b. a heroin overdose
    c. a severed limb
    d. the violent diarrhea that accompanies heroin withdrawal

Answer: d
Threat
p. 98

170. Curare blocks the effect of acetylcholine on skeletal muscle just like naloxone blocks the effects of _____ on the _____ system.
    a. amphetamine, dopamine
    b. adrenaline, sympathetic nervous
    c. parasympathetic overshoot, sympathetic
    d. endorphins, pain

Answer: d
Threat
p. 98

171. Which of the following will probably make pain feel worse?
    a. endorphins
    b. placebos
    c. acupuncture
    d. naloxone

Answer: d
Threat
p. 98

172. A study suggests that the *shiver of thrill* that for some people accompanies listening to certain music is blocked by naloxone. This finding suggests most directly that the *shiver of thrill* is mediated by:
    a. the thermoregulatory area of the hypothalamus.
    b. an opponent process.
    c. parasympathetic overshoot.
    d. endorphins.
    e. the reticular activating system.

173. A person arrives in an emergency ward in a coma from an overdose of heroin. The physician on duty will most likely give a prompt injection of:
    a. endorphin.
    b. amphetamine or cocaine.
    c. morphine.
    d. glucose.
    e. naloxone.

174. Analgesic effects of which of the following do not seem to be due in large part to the release of endorphins?
    a. placebos
    b. quelling of pain during the heat of battle
    c. hypnosis
    d. acupuncture

175. Sleep and waking are controlled by:
    a. the parasympathetic system.
    b. the sympathetic system.
    c. the limbic system.
    d. the hypothalamus.
    e. several structures in the core of the mid- and hindbrain.

176. The sympathetic branch of the ANS is to arousal processes of the body as _____ is (are) to arousal processes of the _____.
    a. the limbic system, cerebral cortex
    b. pituitary gland, limbic system
    c. structures in the core of the mid- and hindbrain, cerebral cortex
    d. the parasympathetic branch of the ANS, limbic system

177. In order for the cerebral cortex to govern its own level of arousal it seems essential to have neural connections from:
    a. one hemisphere to the other hemisphere via the corpus callosum.
    b. the cortex to the autonomic nervous system.
    c. the hypothalamus to the cortex.
    d. the cortex to subcortical systems in the mid- and hindbrain.

178. Which of the following would be likely to produce the most profound reduction of cortical arousal?
    a. damage to the connections between the cortex and subcortical systems in the mid- and hindbrain
    b. destruction of both the parasympathetic and sympathetic divisions of the autonomic nervous system
    c. prolonged deprivation of REM sleep, without deprivation of slow-wave sleep
    d. chronic addiction to amphetamines

Answer: a
Sleep and waking
p. 99

179. The fact that the sound of your own name is more likely to wake you than is the sound of someone else's name indicates that:
    a. the cortex can stimulate the subcortical arousal system.
    b. structures in the hindbrain are responsible for arousal.
    c. structures in the midbrain are responsible for arousal.
    d. b and c

Answer: a
Sleep and waking
p. 99

180. An electroencephalogram (EEG) is a record of:
    a. voltage changes over time that represent the summed activity of millions of nerve cells in the brain.
    b. different voltages in dozens of neurons at one point in time.
    c. either a or b, depending upon the precision of the electrical amplifier.
    d. either a or b, depending upon the placement of the electrodes on the patient's head.

Answer: a
Sleep and waking
p. 99

181. A participant in an EEG study is letting her thoughts drift and is in a quiet, relaxed, and peaceful state. During this time it is likely that her EEG shows:
    a. alpha rhythm
    b. beta rhythm
    c. gamma rhythm
    d. delta rhythm

Answer: d
Sleep and waking
p. 100

182. When a person performs mental arithmetic, the EEG will show:
    a. alpha rhythms.
    b. alpha rhythm blocking.
    c. low voltage and fast activity.
    d. both b and c

Answer: a
Sleep and waking
pp. 99–100

183. The alpha rhythm is characteristic of:
    a. relaxed wakefulness.
    b. deep sleep.
    c. intense arousal.
    d. normal arousal.

Answer: c
Sleep and waking
pp. 99–100

184. When the alpha rhythm is blocked by arousing a person, the frequency of the brain waves:
    a. stays the same.
    b. decreases.
    c. increases.
    d. becomes 8–10 cycles per second.

Answer: d
Sleep and waking
p. 100

185. A research participant has his eyes closed and is thinking about nothing in particular. What happens to his EEG when he begins to perform some mental arithmetic?
    a. There will be an increase in the proportion of alpha waves.
    b. The alpha rhythm will become more regular.
    c. The brain waves will decrease in both voltage and in frequency.
    d. The alpha rhythm will be blocked.

186. The frequency of alpha waves is:
    a. 408 cycles per second.
    b. 8–12 cycles per second.
    c. 16–20 cycles per second.
    d. 20–30 cycles per second.

Answer: b
Sleep and waking
p. 99

187. The alpha rhythm:
    a. is not subject to voluntary control.
    b. seems related to visual input.
    c. represents many neurons firing independently of one another.
    d. b and c

Answer: b
Sleep and waking
p. 99

188. What EEG waves are most characteristic of people who are alert and wide awake?
    a. low voltage waves that are high in frequency
    b. alpha waves
    c. delta waves
    d. gamma rho waves

Answer: a
Sleep and waking
pp. 99–100

189. The deeper stages of sleep are characterized by brain waves:
    a. of high voltage and low frequency.
    b. of high voltage and high frequency.
    c. of low voltage and low frequency.
    d. of low voltage and high frequency.

Answer: a
Sleep and waking
pp. 99–100

190. Comparing REM sleep with slow-wave sleep, REM sleep is characterized by:
    a. less relaxed body muscles; less sensitivity to external stimuli.
    b. less relaxed body muscles; more sensitivity to external stimuli.
    c. more relaxed body muscles; less sensitivity to external stimuli.
    d. more relaxed body muscles; more sensitivity to external stimuli.

Answer: c
Sleep and waking
p. 100

191. Sleep throughout a night is characterized generally by:
    a. a single cycle from Stage 1 to Stage 4 sleep.
    b. a single sequence of sleep stages from REM to slow-wave sleep.
    c. multiple transitions from slow-wave to REM sleep.
    d. a single sequence of sleep stages from slow-wave to REM sleep.

Answer: c
Sleep and waking
pp. 100–101

192. Why might REM sleep sometimes be called *paradoxical* sleep?
    a. The EEG appears like that of deep sleep, but the person is almost awake.
    b. Alpha waves intrude into an EEG record that otherwise looks very similar to that during wakefulness.
    c. The sleeper's postural muscles are tense, yet she is sound asleep.
    d. The EEG resembles that of wakefulness, yet the person is definitely relaxed and asleep.

Answer: d
Sleep and waking
pp. 100–102

Answer: b
Sleep and waking
pp. 100–101

193. How many sleep cycles do humans experience each night on the average?
    a. 0–1
    b. 4–5
    c. 8–9
    d. greater than 10

Answer: c
Sleep and waking
pp. 100–101

194. The order of sleeping states is:
    a. REM sleep, alpha sleep, slow-wave sleep.
    b. slow-wave sleep, REM sleep, alpha sleep.
    c. alpha sleep, slow-wave sleep, REM sleep.
    d. alpha sleep, REM sleep, slow-wave sleep

Answer: b
Sleep and waking
pp. 101–102

195. Prolonged sleep deprivation in people leads to:
    a. overactivation of the sympathetic nervous system.
    b. a desperate motivation to sleep.
    c. death.
    d. all of the above

Answer: a
Sleep and waking
pp. 101–102

196. Which of the following is the most accurate summary of many studies of sleep deprivation?
    a. Selective deprivation of either REM or slow-wave sleep results in more of that particular kind of sleep the next night.
    b. Selective deprivation of REM, but not of slow-wave sleep, results in more of that kind of sleep the next night.
    c. Selective deprivation of slow-wave sleep, but not of REM sleep, results in more of that kind of sleep the next night.
    d. Selective deprivation of the main phases of sleep, REM or slow-wave, results in no net change in the type of sleep the next night.

Answer: b
Sleep and waking
pp. 101–102

197. Sleep deprivation studies show that:
    a. people really don't need to sleep more than two or three hours a night.
    b. one can be deprived of particular states of sleep.
    c. everyone needs 7–9 hours' sleep in each 24 hours for optimal functioning.
    d. after all-night deprivation there is a reduced ability to dream during the next few nights.

Answer: d
Sleep and waking
p. 103

198. Which of the following possible outcomes would be most damaging to the hypothesis that REM sleep is related to the consolidation of experiences from the previous day?
    a. Rats show more REM sleep the day after they spend five hours learning mazes.
    b. Rats given a drug that reduces REM the night before a day spent learning mazes remember better than rats that have had a normal night's sleep before the big maze day.
    c. Rats that spend five hours in an exercise wheel fail to increase the amount of REM sleep the next night.
    d. Rats deprived of REM the night after a day of maze learning remember the maze better than rats deprived of slow-wave sleep.

Answer: d
Sleep and waking
p. 102

199. The surest way to increase the amount of time a person spends in REM sleep is to:
    a. get the sleeper's blood alcohol to level about .1 percent just before sleep.
    b. have the person fly across several time zones.
    c. have the person eat a heavy meal just before retiring.
    d. selectively deprive her of REM sleep for two or three nights prior to the target night.

Answer: a
Sleep and waking
p. 103

200. An investigator found that rats had more REM sleep after learning several mazes than after a day of simple running in an exercise wheel. Such data would tend to:
    a. support the theory that REM sleep is involved in memory consolidation.
    b. refute the idea that REM sleep is important in memory consolidation.
    c. support the theory that REM deprivation is motivating.
    d. refute the theory that REM deprivation is motivating.

Answer: d
Sleep and waking
p. 103

201. Circadian rhythms are about:
    a. the tempo of the heartbeat.
    b. the length of a lunar month (about 28 days).
    c. 90 minutes.
    d. 24 hours.

Answer: b
Sleep and waking
p. 103

202. Jet lag is most closely and directly related to disruption of:
    a. the autonomic nervous system.
    b. circadian rhythms.
    c. particular phases of sleep.
    d. endorphins produced by the hypothalamus and pituitary.

Answer: a
Sleep and waking
p. 103

203. One recommended treatment for jet lag is to get plenty of natural daylight in the afternoon on the day of arrival at your destination. The rationale for this treatment is that it:
    a. is likely to reset circadian rhythm control systems.
    b. increases your overall level of arousal.
    c. is likely to act as a delayed trigger for later REM sleep.
    d. suppresses the tendency to go into slow-wave sleep.

Answer: a
Sleep and waking
p. 103

204. Recovering from jet lag:
    a. implies you have reset your biological clock.
    b. involves restoring motivational regulatory systems from negative feedback to positive feedback.
    c. is basically due to one making up for lost sleep.
    d. is due to a REM-rebound phenomenon.

Answer: b
Sleep and waking
p. 103

205. Why might exposure to bright natural daylight at the point of arrival be helpful in the treatment of jet lag?
    a. When one comes in out of such light one will be sleepy.
    b. Such light could reset one's biological clock.
    c. Light on the face stimulates endorphin systems, which regulate the biological clock.
    d. Exposure to bright natural daylight can replace the loss of sleep accumulated during travel.

Answer: c
Sleep and waking
p. 104

206. An ultradian rhythm refers to a cycle that occurs:
    a. roughly every 24 hours.
    b. roughly every 12 hours.
    c. many times per day.
    d. roughly every 48 hours.

Answer: a
Sleep and waking
p. 104

207. When awakened, you can remember every detail of your dream. You were most likely awakened during which sleep cycle?
    a. REM sleep
    b. alpha wave sleep
    c. slow-wave sleep
    d. beta rhythm sleep

Answer: c
Sleep and waking
p. 104

208. If you want to maximize the chance that you will awaken your roommate during a dream you should:
    a. put his hand in a bucket of cool water.
    b. waken him after about 20 minutes of sound sleep.
    c. waken her about 10 minutes after you see jerky eye movements begin.
    d. gently poke him when you see definite nodding during a lecture.

Answer: c
Sleep and waking
p. 105

209. In a sleep laboratory, the amount of time a research participant spends in REM sleep is recorded. The total REM time is:
    a. approximately twice the amount of time spent dreaming.
    b. approximately half the amount of time spent dreaming.
    c. approximately equal to the amount of time spent dreaming.
    d. not related to the amount of time spent dreaming.

Answer: c
Sleep and waking
p. 104

210. A research participant is most likely to remember a dream if awakened during:
    a. Stage 4 sleep.
    b. Stage 3 sleep.
    c. REM sleep.
    d. Stage 1 sleep.

Answer: b
Sleep and waking
pp. 104–105

211. Which of the following statements is true?
    a. Dreaming occurs only in REM sleep.
    b. Sleepers awakened from slow-wave sleep have less vivid recall of a cartoon viewed just prior to sleep than do sleepers awakened from REM sleep.
    c. Dreaming in slow-wave sleep is more vivid than is dreaming in REM sleep.
    d. Dreaming in slow-wave sleep is less vivid than is dreaming in REM sleep.

Answer: c
Sleep and waking
pp. 104–105

212. Can we say with certainty that dreaming is less vivid in slow-wave sleep than in REM sleep?
    a. Yes, because sleepers awakened from REM sleep report more vivid dreams than do sleepers awakened from slow-wave sleep.
    b. No, because sleepers awakened from REM sleep report less vivid dreams than do sleepers awakened from slow-wave sleep.
    c. No, because sleepers awakened from REM sleep become fully conscious more quickly than do sleepers awakened from slow-wave sleep.
    d. Yes, because the physiological mechanism underlying dreaming is not in operation during slow-wave sleep.

Answer: d
Sleep and waking
p. 105

213. Dreams:
    a. take about the same time as the dream event would have taken.
    b. are frequently forgotten.
    c. are accompanied by rapidly moving eyes.
    d. all of the above

Answer: b
Sleep and waking
p. 105

214. The average amount of time an average adult spends dreaming is over an hour every night. But even so, it seems to most of us that we spend much less time dreaming than that. This discrepancy is best explained by:
    a. assuming that the figure of one hour or more per night is an over-estimate.
    b. the fact that most dreams are not remembered for long.
    c. the fact that dreams can occur without any external stimulus trigger.
    d. the hypothesis that most dreams are in highly condensed, symbolic form.

Answer: d
Sleep and waking
pp. 105–106

215. "All of the interesting things we experience during dreaming may have no psychological function whatsoever." Which of the following people would be most likely to make such a statement?
    a. an ancient prophet
    b. Sigmund Freud
    c. an advocate of memory consolidation theory
    d. an advocate of the activation-synthesis hypothesis

Answer: d
Sleep and waking
p. 106

216. According to the activation-synthesis hypothesis:
    a. the cortex is largely cut off from sensory information during REM sleep.
    b. the cortex connects disjointed images into a story line.
    c. the cerebral cortex shows fairly high activity levels.
    d. all of the above

Answer: a
Sleep and waking
p. 106

217. According to the activation synthesis hypothesis, dreams:
    a. represent the brain's attempt to connect randomly stimulated images and memories.
    b. represent unfulfilled wishes.
    c. represent the brain's attempt to make sense of the day's experiences.
    d. are often forgotten because of the very disturbing images they contain.
    e. b and d

Answer: d
What different motives have in common
p. 107

218. According to drive-reduction theory, what is intrinsically rewarding about sexual activity is:
    a. the built-in reinforcing quality of sexual stimulation and orgasm.
    b. the built-in tendency toward reproduction.
    c. the rise in tension that occurs during sexual stimulation and the subsequent fall in that tension during orgasm.
    d. the fall of tension during orgasm.

Answer: d
What different motives have in common
p. 107

219. Saccharin is rewarding. To explain this, drive-reduction theorists might suggest that:
    a. sweet tastes are intrinsically rewarding.
    b. there is a built-in preference for sweets, which has survival value because most sweet things are nutritious.
    c. sweet tastes change the glucose-glycogen balance in the body.
    d. sweet tastes have become associated with the cessation of hunger tension produced by real foods.

Answer: d
What different motives have in common
p. 107

220. Which of the following seems inconsistent with drive reduction theory?
    a. seeking erotic stimulation
    b. seeking nonnutritive saccharin solutions
    c. seeking activity for its own sake
    d. all of the above

Answer: e
What different motives have in common
pp. 107–108

221. Evidence against the drive-reduction theory is that:
    a. monkeys solve puzzles even if they are not externally rewarded for doing so.
    b. rats like drinking artificially sweetened water even though it's non-nutritive.
    c. many humans like roller coasters.
    d. some humans go skydiving for pleasure.
    e. all of the above

Answer: c
What different motives have in common
p. 107

222. According to drive-reduction theory, what is rewarding about eating a really good dinner?
    a. the anticipation of how good it will taste when you see it and smell it
    b. the eating itself
    c. the relaxed full feeling when you're finished
    d. the long-term consequences of weight gain (note: Until fairly recently thin was not fashionable.)

Answer: c
What different motives have in common
pp. 107–108

223. Which statement is false?
    a. When arousal level is unduly high we seek to reduce it.
    b. When arousal level is unduly low we seek to increase it.
    c. When arousal level is zero we experience perfect satisfaction.
    d. Optimum arousal varies from person to person.

Answer: b
What different motives have in common
p. 108

224. Alcohol is:
    a. an opiate.
    b. a depressant.
    c. an amphetamine.
    d. a stimulant.

225. If alcohol is a depressant, why are people who are drunk often loud and aggressive?
    a. Their hyperexcitability is caused by disinhibition.
    b. It affects certain neurons in the brain, which in turn make the person act this way.
    c. People expect drunks to be this way so they encourage this behavior.
    d. This phenomenonis still a mystery.

226. Amphetamines produce:
    a. rapid heart rate.
    b. behavioral quieting.
    c. decreased appetite.
    d. all of the above

227. A person begins having delusions of persecution, irrational fears, and some hallucinations. You know for sure that the person is not schizophrenic. What is the most logical explanation for her behavior?
    a. A key neurotransmitter is missing or impaired.
    b. The person is addicted to alcohol.
    c. The person is addicted to barbiturates.
    d. The person is addicted to amphetamines or cocaine.

228. Administration of X grams of amphetamine to a person who uses the drug for the first time leads to a fourfold increase in heart rate. Administration of an identical dose to an experienced user elicits only a twofold increase in heart rate. This discrepancy is an example of:
    a. a withdrawal symptom.
    b. tolerance.
    c. stimulation seeking.
    d. drive reduction.

229. A drug addict will need more of a drug than a first-time drug user to get the same effect. This phenomenon most specifically illustrates:
    a. addiction.
    b. tolerance.
    c. withdrawal symptom.
    d. learning.

230. A consequence of drug addiction is:
    a. increased tolerance to the drug.
    b. decreased tolerance to the drug.
    c. mild withdrawal symptoms.
    d. increased obesity.

Answer: a
What different motives have in common
p. 110

231. Why is it often necessary for addicts to take more and more of a drug to get the same high feeling?
    a. The drug's effects are countered by their opposites. With additional exposures to the drug, these opposite effects become stronger and more of the drug is needed to overcome them.
    b. It is psychological. If the person thinks a little of the drug gives him a high, then more of the drug will be even better.
    c. It is caused by the placebo effect.
    d. There is no known reason for this phenomenon.

Answer: a
What different motives have in common
p. 110

232. The opponent-process theory of drug addiction:
    a. relies on homeostatic mechanisms.
    b. can explain drug tolerance but not drug withdrawal.
    c. can explain drug withdrawal but not drug tolerance.
    d. argues that the opponent-process is strongest initially because the body is taken by surprise.

Answer: a
What different motives have in common
p. 110

233. The symptoms of drug withdrawal:
    a. are generally the opposite of the drug's effects.
    b. are the same for all different types of drugs.
    c. vary widely among individuals addicted to the same drug.
    d. cannot be predicted.
    e. c and d

Answer: d
What different motives have in common
p. 110

234. Each of four research participants is presented with a different stimulus. Participant *1* gets a stimulus that produces intense joy, participant *2* gets one that leads to mild joy, participant *3* gets one that produces mild fear, and participant *4* gets one that produces terror. After a period of time, the stimuli are withdrawn. According to opponent-process theory, which participant will feel best?
    a. *1*
    b. *2*
    c. *3*
    d. *4*

Answer: d
What different motives have in common
p. 110

235. According to opponent-process theory, why would people keep engaging in very arousing but dangerous activities, such as skydiving?
    a. Their parents opposed such danger seeking, and they rebelled.
    b. They have a "death instinct" which motivates them.
    c. There are a variety of secondary reinforcers associated with such activities.
    d. It feels so good when the danger is over.

Answer: c
What different motives have in common
p. 111

236. Rats taught to press a lever to administer electrical stimulation to certain regions of the hypothalamus and limbic systems:
    a. will do so only if they're not hungry.
    b. will do so only if they're hungry.
    c. will do so persistently, even passing up opportunities to eat.
    d. will do so roughly once per hour regardless of their hunger.

Answer: c
What different motives have in common
p. 111

237. The effect of electrical stimulation of the brain:
    a. is aversive as a result of the passing of current through the brain.
    b. is often seen to be a less effective reward than natural biological reinforcers, such as food to a hungry rat.
    c. resembles addiction.
    d. provides support for the opponent-process theory of motivation.

Answer: e
What different motives have in common
pp. 72, 111

238. Which statement accurately describes electrical self-stimulation of the brain?
    a. It produces a negative feedback cycle.
    b. It serves as a reward.
    c. It produces a positive feedback cycle.
    d. a and b
    e. b and c

Answer: b
What different motives have in common
pp. 111–112

239. To produce the most reliable self-stimulation in a rat, one should direct the stimulating electrodes into the:
    a. axon systems in the basal forebrain that liberate acetylcholine.
    b. systems in the midbrain and forebrain whose axons liberate dopamine.
    c. the ventromedial satiety region of the hypothalamus.
    d. the brainstem systems related to the sympathetic nervous system.

Answer: a
What different motives have in common
pp. 111–112

240. An investigator plans to let a rat inject minute amounts of cocaine into its own brain. According to what you know about electrical self-stimulation effects, where should you suggest this investigator direct the electrodes?
    a. basal forebrain dopamine system (e.g., nucleus accumbens)
    b. ventromedial satiety region of the hypothalamus
    c. brainstem systems controlling the sympathetic nervous system
    d. axons entering the brain from the spinal cord that carry messages related to pain

Answer: d
What different motives have in common
pp. 111–112

241. Which neurotransmitter seems to be most relevant to electrical self-stimulation effects in the basal forebrain of rats?
    a. acetylcholine
    b. serotonin
    c. curare
    d. dopamine

Answer: c
What different motives have in common
pp. 111–112

242. Which of the following drugs should be most effective at reducing the rate that a rat presses a lever for electrical stimulation of its medial forebrain bundle or nucleus accumbens?
    a. curare, which blocks many acetylcholine synapses
    b. naloxone, which blocks enkephalin and endorphin synapses
    c. dopamine antagonists
    d. amphetamines, which enhance levels of dopamine

Answer: d
What different motives have in common
pp. 111–112

243. Which of the following classes of drugs are most likely to increase the rate at which a rat will press a lever for electrical stimulation of its medial forebrain bundle?
    a. acetylcholine antagonists, like curare
    b. endorphin antagonists, like naloxone
    c. dopamine antagonists
    d. dopamine agonists, like amphetamines

Answer: c
What different motives have in common
pp. 111–112

244. The good feeling or "high" that comes from heroin, amphetamines, and possibly alcohol, probably arise because these drugs all seem to:
    a. depress the brainstem regions related to REM sleep.
    b. increase activity in various hypothalamic satiety regions.
    c. increase dopamine release in the nucleus accumbens.
    d. block the transmission of pain signals as they enter the brain.

Answer: b
What different motives have in common
pp. 111–112

245. If research on electrical self-stimulation in rats is relevant to our understanding of natural rewards in people, then listening to a beautiful piece of music, the thrill of a wonderful sunset, and sexual orgasm might all share the characteristic of:
    a. increasing acetylcholine transmission in the hypothalamus.
    b. increasing dopamine release in nucleus accumbens.
    c. blocking transmission of pain signals as they enter the brain.
    d. acting in a manner similar to dopamine antagonists.

Answer: b
The nature of motives
p. 112

246. Which of the following motives is the most difficult to explain in terms of principles of negative feedback?
    a. temperature regulation
    b. sex
    c. thirst
    d. hunger

Answer: d
The nature of motives
p. 112

247. Which of the following motives is the easiest to explain in terms of principles of negative feedback?
    a. sex
    b. curiosity
    c. sleep
    d. thirst

Answer: a
The nature of motives
p. 112

248. Which of the following motives is the easiest to explain in terms of principles of negative feedback?
    a. temperature regulation
    b. sex
    c. sleep
    d. curiosity

Answer: d
The nature of motives
pp. 112–113

249. Few Americans will eat snake, even though it may be as nutritious as chicken. This phenomenon is most relevant to the principle:
    a. that homeostasis is based on negative feedback.
    b. that only certain food rewards will trigger the release of dopamine in "pleasure centers" of the forebrain.
    c. of neophobia.
    d. that our motives are regulated in part by cultural learning.

Answer: d
The nature of motives
pp. 112–113

250. Why do Americans seldom consider eating insects as part of a well-balanced diet?
   a. Many insects contain poisons that would make us sick.
   b. Insects breed in dirty places and would most likely carry various germs.
   c. Eating insects would make maintenance of homeostasis difficult.
   d. Our cultural learning regulates our choices of foods.
   e. all of the above

CHAPTER 4 | Learning

Answer: c
Learning
p. 117

1. In Rene Descartes' conception, reflexes can be characterized as:
    a. changeable, but not necessarily changed, synaptic connections.
    b. rewired.
    c. hardwired.
    d. highly contingent on previous experience.

Answer: c
Learning
p. 117

2. Which of the following sayings fits best with learning theory during the first part of the twentieth century?
    a. "You can't teach an old dog new tricks."
    b. "You can lead a horse to water, but you can't make him drink."
    c. "I can do anything you can do, better."
    d. "The poor will always be with us."

Answer: c
Learning
p. 117

3. Modern learning theory:
    a. suggests that learning requires disconnecting all of the inborn prewired neural connections of the body.
    b. contends that the principles of learning can only be understood through an analysis of human behavior.
    c. suggests that complex behavior is made up of simple components.
    d. is applicable primarily to the learning of digestive responses.

Answer: d
Habituation
p. 118

4. _____ is a decline in the tendency to respond to stimuli that have become familiar due to repeated exposure.
    a. Acclimation
    b. Assimilation
    c. Discrimination
    d. Habituation

Answer: d
Habituation
p. 118

5. You set your alarm clock for medium loud at the start of the semester. At first, you hear it on the first ring but by the second week, you sleep right through it and need to reset the intensity to extra loud. This is an example of:
    a. classical conditioning.
    b. successive approximations (shaping).
    c. secondary (conditioned) reinforcement.
    d. habituation.
    e. drive reduction.

Answer: b
Habituation
p. 118

6. The loud noises from your neighbor's party distract you from your studying. After some time, you are able to concentrate on your work even though the noise has not stopped or lessened. What process has likely occurred?
    a. sensitization
    b. habituation
    c. classical conditioning
    d. instrumental conditioning
    e. none of the above

Answer: b
Habituation
p. 118

7. Professor James was hoping to get a lot of work done on the train. Unfortunately, he was seated next to a bunch of screaming children. At first it was difficult for him to concentrate, but gradually, he was able to ignore the noise completely. What type of learning does this exemplify?
    a. sensitization
    b. habituation
    c. extinction
    d. reconditioning
    e. blocking

Answer: b
Habituation
p. 118

8. The adaptive significance of habituation is that it:
    a. greatly attenuates the effects of sensitization.
    b. allows animals to ignore familiar but harmless stimuli.
    c. paves the way for associative conditioning.
    d. keeps neurons active that otherwise might degenerate.

Answer: a
Habituation
p. 118

9. When speaking of habituation, familiarity breeds:
    a. a tendency to respond with "so what."
    b. a tendency to treat the stimulus as a reinforcer.
    c. spontaneous recovery.
    d. a large number of associations to the stimulus.

Answer: b
Habituation
p. 118

10. By the end of the semester your alarm clock sounds just as loudly as ever, but it fails to awaken you on many occasions. You borrow your roommate's clock, which has a somewhat different sound, and it wakes you up on the first try, even though it is less loud than your own clock. What has happened here?
    a. short-term habituation followed by spontaneous recovery
    b. a mismatch between the new sound and the memory you have of your own clock's sound
    c. long-term habituation followed by spontaneous recovery
    d. formation of a memory trace of the sound of your own clock followed by classical conditioning to the sound of your roommate's clock

11. Which of the following types of learning is best called *nonassociative*?
    a. classical conditioning
    b. instrumental conditioning
    c. the development of a cognitive map
    d. habituation

12. Which of the following observations was most directly responsible for the redirection of Pavlov's research from the study of digestive reflexes to investigations of conditioning?
    a. the finding that salivary secretions could be collected by implantation of a fistula
    b. that in the adult dog, eating is accompanied by secretions of saliva
    c. that the secretion of saliva was elicited, via a reflex mechanism, by food in the mouth
    d. that stimuli, which were initially neutral, could come to elicit digestive reflexes

13. _____ is credited with discovering classical conditioning.
    a. John B. Watson
    b. Ivan Pavlov
    c. B. F. Skinner
    d. Edward L. Thorndike
    e. Little Albert

14. Which of the following is the best example of classical conditioning?
    a. Bob buys a lottery ticket each time he gets his car inspected because four years ago he won $100 on a ticket he bought after a car inspection.
    b. Sam underwent a painful dental procedure, and now his palms sweat when he sees the door to his dentist's office.
    c. Sally's dog brings her the newspaper and gets in return a pat on the head.
    d. Ted drops his economics course after failing the first exam.

15. A tap to the leg just below the knee leads to the knee-jerk response. This response can be elicited even in newborns. The knee jerk following a tap of the leg is an example of a(n):
    a. unconditioned response.
    b. conditioned response.
    c. unconditioned stimulus.
    d. conditioned stimulus.

16. The pupil of the eye automatically constricts when a bright light is directed at the eye. This illustrates:
    a. a conditioned stimulus.
    b. habituation.
    c. a conditioned response.
    d. an unconditioned reflex.

Answer: a
Classical conditioning
p. 120

17. A(n) _____ is elicited by a stimulus regardless of an animal's history of experiences.
    a.   unconditioned reflex
    b.   unconditioned stimulus
    c.   conditioned reflex
    d.   conditioned response

Answer: a
Classical conditioning
p. 120

18. Unconditioned reflexes, according to Pavlov, are:
    a.   inborn.
    b.   acquired.
    c.   conditioned.
    d.   nonexistent.

Answer: c
Classical conditioning
p. 120

19. An event that elicits a response without prior learning is called a(n):
    a.   unconditioned response.
    b.   conditioned response.
    c.   unconditioned stimulus.
    d.   conditioned stimulus.

Answer: b
Classical conditioning
p. 120

20. Salivation as a reaction to lemon juice in the mouth is a(n):
    a.   conditioned response.
    b.   unconditioned response.
    c.   conditioned stimulus.
    d.   unconditioned stimulus.

Answer: c
Classical conditioning
p. 120

21. The electric current producing shock from faulty wiring is an example of a potential:
    a.   conditioned stimulus.
    b.   conditioned response.
    c.   unconditioned stimulus.
    d.   unconditioned response.

Answer: b
Classical conditioning
p. 120

22. According to Pavlov, what is the basis for all learning?
    a.   the orienting reflex
    b.   the conditioned reflex
    c.   the unconditioned reflex
    d.   the conditioned stimulus

Answer: a
Classical conditioning
p. 120

23. _____ occurs when a neutral stimulus is repeatedly paired with a stimulus that already elicits a reflexive response.
    a.   Classical conditioning
    b.   Instrumental conditioning
    c.   Reflex learning
    d.   more than one of the above

Answer: d
Classical conditioning
p. 120

24. A(n) _____ is elicited by a US.
    a.   conditioned response
    b.   learned response
    c.   secondary response
    d.   unconditioned response
    e.   none of the above

25. The knee-jerk reflex, made famous in doctors' offices, is an example of a(n):
    a. operant response.
    b. instrumental response.
    c. contiguous response.
    d. conditioned response.
    e. none of the above

26. A roadside sign advertising cheeseburgers causes a driver to salivate and swallow. Here, the sign for the burgers is the:
    a. CS.
    b. US.
    c. CR.
    d. UCR.

27. Pavlov found that dogs salivated when shown food, before it actually reached the mouth. Here, he would call sight of the food the _____.
    a. conditioned reflex
    b. conditioned response
    c. conditioned stimulus
    d. unconditioned response
    e. unconditioned stimulus

28. The basic procedure that produces classical conditioning is that a _____ is followed, after a very brief interval, by a _____.
    a. desired response, reinforcement
    b. US, UCR
    c. CS, CR
    d. CS, US
    e. US, CS

29. Which is the best example of a classically conditioned response?
    a. A gun-shy dog cowers when he sees a shotgun.
    b. A child flinches when a balloon bursts a foot away from her face.
    c. A snail withdraws into its shell when the shell is tapped.
    d. A dog perks up its ears and turns toward the source of an unexpected sound.

30. Testosterone levels rise in male rats if they smell a nearby female rat that is in heat. One male rat was allowed to smell and mate only with females that wore oil of wintergreen "perfume." After several such exposures, this male's testosterone levels rose whenever he smelled oil of wintergreen. In this example the CS was the:
    a. opportunity to mate.
    b. testosterone level.
    c. natural smell of the female.
    d. oil of wintergreen.

Answer: b
Classical conditioning
p. 120

31. Benny, a family dog, has been brought up in an abusive environment. His owners routinely beat him with a broomstick so that Benny cries and whimpers anytime he sees a broom. In this example, the broom is a(n):
    a. unconditioned stimulus.
    b. conditioned stimulus.
    c. instrumental stimulus.
    d. contingent stimulus.
    e. negative reinforcer.

Answer: d
Classical conditioning
p. 120

32. The presentation of an air puff to the eye leads reflexively to closure of the eyelid. The air puff is an example of a(n):
    a. conditioned response.
    b. unconditioned response.
    c. conditioned stimulus.
    d. unconditioned stimulus.

Answer: d
Classical conditioning
p. 120

33. Injection of an animal with amphetamine leads to heart rate acceleration. With repeated injections, however, the injection procedure alone (i.e., when an inert substance is injected) can elicit heart-rate acceleration. In this situation:
    a. the injection procedure is the CS.
    b. heart rate acceleration is both the UR and the CR.
    c. amphetamine is the US.
    d. all of the above

Answer: a
Classical conditioning
p. 121

34. The tendency of the CS to elicit the CR is related to:
    a. the number of CS-US pairings.
    b. the number of times the US has elicited the CR.
    c. the intensity of the CR.
    d. none of the above

Answer: c
Classical conditioning
p. 121

35. In classical conditioning, an unreinforced trial is one in which:
    a. the CR does not occur.
    b. the CS is not presented.
    c. the US is not presented.
    d. the orienting action does not appear.

Answer: d
Classical conditioning
p. 121

36. Which of the following would be the best measure for assessing of the strength of a conditioned response?
    a. latency from the CS to the US
    b. amplitude of the UR
    c. probability that the US will follow the CS
    d. latency from the CS to the CR

Answer: a
Classical conditioning
p. 121

37. In a classical conditioning experiment, the magnitude of the response to the _____ varies with the number of CS-US pairings.
    a. CS
    b. US
    c. orienting reflex
    d. unconditioned reflex

Answer: c
Classical conditioning
p. 122

Answer: a
Classical conditioning
p. 122

Answer: c
Classical conditioning
p. 122

Answer: c
Classical conditioning
p. 122

Answer: d
Classical conditioning
p. 122

38. The most effective way to form a second-order CR would be to:
   a. reverse the order of the CS and US presentation sequence.
   b. extinguish the CR to the original CS; then condition a new CS to the original US.
   c. pair a new CS with the original CS, which now functions as a US.
   d. habituate responses to both the first and the second CS; then pair the two as a compound CS with an effective US.

39. A person is given an insulin injection each day with the same syringe. After a few injections, the mere sight of the syringe results in a rise in blood sugar. Which of the following is the best example of second-order conditioning that might follow this conditioning?
   a. The syringe no longer contains insulin, but now music paired with the presentation of the syringe results in a rise in blood sugar.
   b. The syringe contains twice the dose of insulin, but it takes several such presentations before there is an appropriate increase in the amount of rise in blood sugar to presentation of the syringe.
   c. The syringe no longer contains insulin and after repeated presentations of it there is no longer a rise in blood sugar.
   d. A loud gong sounded just after the presentation of the syringe results in a pronounced startle response to simply seeing the syringe.

40. Once a CS-US relationship is established, the CS can serve to condition other stimuli. This is called:
   a. stimulus generalization.
   b. experimental extinction.
   c. second-order conditioning.
   d. reconditioning.

41. Biff had always thought of himself as a great student until Professor Merlin began failing him on every paper. Gradually, the sight of Prof. Merlin caused Biff anxiety. Soon, even when Biff saw the professor's car, he got anxious. This anxious response to the car is an example of:
   a. backward pairing.
   b. stimulus generalization.
   c. second-order conditioning.
   d. discriminative learning.
   e. shaping.

42. A metronome that served as the CS in first-order conditioning serves as the US for a second-order conditioned response. The CS for this second-order response was a light. The results show that the second-order conditioning is much weaker than the first-order conditioning. Why?
   a. There is generalized inhibition from the light to the metronome.
   b. There is generalized inhibition from the metronome to the light.
   c. The CR to the light extinguishes during second-order conditioning trials.
   d. The CR to the metronome extinguishes during second-order conditioning trials.

Answer: d
Classical conditioning
p. 122

43. When the CR becomes weaker because the US has been omitted, it is called:
    a. conditioning.
    b. spontaneous recovery.
    c. generalization.
    d. extinction.

Answer: a
Classical conditioning
p. 122

44. Experimental extinction:
    a. results from repeated presentations of the CS without the US.
    b. results from repeated presentations of the US without the CS.
    c. both a and b
    d. neither a nor b

Answer: b
Classical conditioning
p. 122

45. After 40 CS-US pairings, presentation of the CS elicits 20 drops of saliva. The response is then extinguished so that the CS elicits no salivation. On the following day, the CS is presented again. One may expect about _____ drops of saliva to presentation of the CS.
    a. 0
    b. 10
    c. 20
    d. 30

Answer: a
Classical conditioning
p. 122

46. You have not paid your Visa bill, and as a result you receive frequent phone calls from a bill collector. You come to associate the sound of a ringing telephone with a feeling of dread. After you pay your Visa bill, the threatening phone calls stop, and you no longer react with dread to the sound of a ringing telephone. This is an example of:
    a. extinction.
    b. second-order conditioning.
    c. reconditioning.
    d. discrimination.

Answer: b
Classical conditioning
p. 122

47. Which of the following is an example of extinction?
    a. After repeated presentations of the sound of a bell, a dog ceases to turn his head toward it.
    b. A rat stops pressing a bar when food is no longer presented after a lever press.
    c. Over a period of time, a man requires larger doses of drug Z to obtain the same effect.
    d. As a result of brain damage, a woman enters a coma.
    e. all of the above

Answer: e
Classical conditioning
p. 122

48. Imagine that you are a student who suffers from "test anxiety." You ask your instructor not to criticize you after an exam. In Pavlovian terms, you are trying to set up a situation where the CS will be presented with out theUCS. This should lead to the _____ of the anxiety response.
    a. suppression
    b. substitution
    c. contiguity
    d. contingency
    e. extinction

Answer: b
Classical conditioning
p. 122

49. To an evolutionary biologist the term *extinction* means the vanishing of a species; to Pavlov it meant the vanishing of the:
   a. CS.
   b. CR.
   c. dog.
   d. UCR.

Answer: a
Classical conditioning
p. 122

50. When a conditioned stimulus loses its relationship to a given unconditioned stimulus, the conditioned response diminishes. This is known as:
   a. extinction.
   b. generalization.
   c. reconditioning.
   d. counterconditioning.
   e. blocking.

Answer: c
Classical conditioning
p. 122

51. Which of the following phenomena demonstrate conclusively that extinguished CRs are not forgotten?
   a. sharp generalization gradients
   b. the partial reinforcement effect
   c. reconditioning with fewer trials
   d. the presence of higher-order conditioning

Answer: e
Classical conditioning
p. 122

52. Presenting further reinforced trials after a conditioned response has been extinguished is called:
   a. stimulus generalization.
   b. second-order conditioning.
   c. extinction.
   d. discrimination.
   e. reconditioning.

Answer: a
Classical conditioning
p. 122

53. An extinguished CR will reappear if the CS is accompanied by a novel stimulus (i.e., disinhibition). The fact that extinction does not completely abolish the CR is also shown by:
   a. reconditioning with savings.
   b. stimulus generalization.
   c. the partial reinforcement effect.
   d. orienting reflexes.
   e. all of the above

Answer: b
Classical conditioning
p. 122

54. After a conditioned response is extinguished, an animal is given twenty-four hours of rest. The next day, if the animal is presented with the CS, it will:
   a. not respond.
   b. respond at a lower rate than during conditioning.
   c. respond at a higher rate than during conditioning.
   d. respond to the same degree as during conditioning.

55. A conditioned response that has been extinguished is resurrected in a process called:
    a. backward conditioning.
    b. reconditioning.
    c. operant conditioning.
    d. spontaneous recovery.

56. During _____, a former CS becomes a signal that the US is not going to be presented.
    a. stimulus generalization
    b. extinction
    c. forward pairing
    d. secondary reinforcement

57. A human research participant is touched on the shoulder whenever he receives electric shock. Subsequent tests show that he will give a more vigorous galvanic skin response when touched on the shoulder, less vigorous when touched on the lower back, still less vigorous when touched on the thigh, and least when touched on the calf. The results are plotted with the galvanic skin response on the y-axis and the parts of the body on the x-axis. The resulting curve is called:
    a. an acquisition curve.
    b. an excitation gradient.
    c. a spread of inhibition curve.
    d. a generalization gradient.

58. Stimulus generalization is said to have occurred when:
    a. a number of stimuli produce the same response.
    b. one stimulus produces several responses.
    c. the US produces the CR.
    d. the CS produces the UR.

59. Little Jimmy has met his grandmother only once, but that experience was a very positive one. It was so great that every time he sees an older-looking woman, he runs over to her with a big smile and his arms outstretched. Jimmy demonstrates which conditioning phenomenon?
    a. shaping
    b. stimulus generalization
    c. second-order conditioning
    d. reconditioning
    e. counterconditioning

60. Stimulus generalization refers to the fact that:
    a. the conditioned response can be elicited by a conditioned stimulus that resembles the CS used during acquisition.
    b. in general, any stimulus can be used as a CS in a classical conditioning situation.
    c. after extinction of a conditioned response, presentation of the CS on the next day will still lead to some conditioned responding.
    d. the reason classical conditioning works is because the UR generalizes to the CS.

61. A dog is conditioned with a 1000Hz tone as a CS and it secretes 10 drops of saliva when presented with this CS. How many drops of saliva should we expect if we then present the dog with a tone of 750 and 500 cycles respectively?
    a. about 7 drops, about 7 drops
    b. about 3 drops, about 7 drops
    c. about 7 drops, about 3 drops
    d. about 2 drops, about 3 drops

62. An animal is conditioned with a 500 Hz tone as a CS and it responds with 5 drops of saliva. How many drops of saliva would be expected if it hears a 700 Hz tone?
    a. 0 drops
    b. about 3 drops
    c. about 5 drops
    d. about 7 drops

63. Concerning the generalization gradient, which of the following statements is true?
    a. The weaker the stimulus, the weaker the response.
    b. The more similar the stimulus is to the original CS, the stronger the response.
    c. The more similar the stimulus is to the original CS, the weaker the response.
    d. The stronger the stimulus, the stronger the response.

64. A dog is classically conditioned to salivate when it sees a blue light. When tested for generalization, it responds more to a green light than to a red light. In later tests, it is given two kinds of discrimination training. In procedure I, the blue light serves as CS+ and the green light serves as CS–. In procedure II, the blue light serves as CS+ and the red light as CS–. Which of the two procedures will lead to faster discrimination?
    a. procedure I
    b. procedure II
    c. There will be no difference.
    d. It is hard to predict because there is no control procedure in which the green light is CS+ and the red light is CS–.

65. Discrimination learning can be viewed as the opposite of:
    a. spontaneous conditioning.
    b. backward conditioning.
    c. stimulus generalization.
    d. second-order conditioning.

66. A male rat was repeatedly exposed to female rats in heat sprayed with the scent of wintergreen. He was also exposed repeatedly to oil of cloves "perfume" on female rats that were not in heat. When tested later, testosterone levels rose whenever he smelled oil of wintergreen but not when he smelled oil of cloves. Thus, this male rat has exhibited:
    a. extinction.
    b. generalization.
    c. discrimination.
    d. all of the above

Answer: d
Classical conditioning
p. 123

67. Learning to respond to one special CS and not respond to other similar stimuli constitutes:
    a. assimilation.
    b. generalization.
    c. extinction.
    d. discrimination.
    e. biofeedback.

Answer: d
Classical conditioning
p. 123

68. Which of the following statements is false?
    a. Initially, discrimination training results in generalization.
    b. Discrimination learning is difficult when stimuli are similar.
    c. Fewer discrimination trials are needed when stimuli are very different.
    d. While the CS+ predicts the occurrence of the US, the CS– conveys little or no information.

Answer: c
Classical conditioning
p. 123

69. In discrimination learning, the CS– is:
    a. a stimulus that precedes an aversive US.
    b. a stimulus that precedes appetitive CS.
    c. a stimulus that precedes a time internal without the US.
    d. none of the above.

Answer: b
Classical conditioning
p. 124

70. Fear conditioning can be accomplished by:
    a. pairing a painful CS with a neutral US.
    b. pairing a neutral CS with a painful US.
    c. pairing a painful CS with a neutral CR.
    d. pairing a neutral CS with a painful CR.

Answer: a
Classical conditioning
p. 124

71. Tom has a strong phobia of motorcycles after nearly being killed by riding his Harly Davison too fast. When Tom hears or sees a motorcycle he starts to sweat, his heart races, and he trembles. Tom's phobia best fits the phenomenon of:
    a. classical conditioning.
    b. sensitization.
    c. belongingness or preparedness.
    d. instrumental conditioning.
    e. latent learning.

Answer: b
Classical conditioning
p. 124

72. A Conditioned Emotional Response (CER), such as fear can be acquired by:
    a. cognitive learning.
    b. classical conditioning.
    c. instrumental conditioning.
    d. latent learning.

Answer: b
Classical conditioning
p. 124

73. The view that classical conditioning is a kind of expectancy involves the idea that:
    a. the CS takes the place of the US.
    b. the CS signals the arrival of the US.
    c. the CR becomes associated to the US.
    d. the CS becomes unassociated with the UR.

74. Although the CR is typically similar to the UR, the two responses are not identical. Evidence for this is clear in fear conditioning experiments in which the CR, but not the UR, involves:
    a. cessation of movement.
    b. fearful anticipation.
    c. reduction of heart rate.
    d. all of the above.

75. Conditioned drug effects, such as those to injections of insulin or heroin, offer the strongest support for the idea that:
    a. the CR is a weak duplicate of the UR.
    b. extinction is more a suppression of the CR than a forgetting of the conditioning process.
    c. the CS acts as an anticipatory signal for the US.
    d. conditioned response suppression is a good index of CERs.

76. When heroin addiction is viewed as an opponent-process reaction, the sight of the hypodermic needle acts as a:
    a. CS.
    b. CR.
    c. US.
    d. UR.

77. When heroin addiction is viewed as an opponent-process reaction, the compensatory response is the _____, while the drug's euphoric effect is the _____.
    a. UR; CR
    b. US; CS
    c. CR; UR
    d. CS; US

78. The danger of a lethal overdose of morphine or heroin is greatest for an experienced user if:
    a. he sees the familiar syringe several minutes prior to injecting the drug.
    b. he injects the usual dose in an unfamiliar environment.
    c. he injects the drug's antagonist, naloxone, prior to injecting the drug itself.
    d. he follows injection of the drug with an injection of its antagonist, naloxone.

79. A recovering heroin addict has been free of the drug for a month, yet when she sees a picture of a syringe she feels restless, has an increased sensitivity to pain, and a strong craving for heroin. What has happened here?
    a. The picture is a CS for the state usually induced by heroin.
    b. Extinction of the drug habit has resulted in an increase in the body's own natural opiates, the endorphins.
    c. Seeing the syringe is a CS for a compensatory mechanism for the arrival of heroin.
    d. Seeing the picture of the syringe has resulted in second-order conditioning.

Answer: a
Classical conditioning
p. 127

80. What do conditioned compensatory reactions to drugs like insulin and heroin tell us about conditioning?
    a. The CS serves as a warning that the US will arrive.
    b. The CR is a weak replica of the UR.
    c. The US must follow CS by less than one second if conditioning is to occur.
    d. all of the above

Answer: a
Instrumental conditioning
p. 128

81. Instrumental conditioning differs from classical conditioning in which of the following ways?
    a. Reinforcement is contingent upon a response in instrumental conditioning, but not in classical conditioning.
    b. Instrumental conditioning requires "insight," but classical conditioning does not.
    c. Classical, but not instrumental, conditioning is impossible with autonomic responses.
    d. Instrumental conditioning involves S-S associations, while conditioning involves S-R associations.

Answer: d
Instrumental conditioning
p. 128

82. In classical conditioning, the animal must learn about the relation between _____; in instrumental conditioning, it must learn about the relation between _____.
    a. CR and US; stimulus and response
    b. CS and UR; stimulus and response
    c. CR and UR; response and reward
    d. CS and US; response and reward

Answer: d
Instrumental conditioning
p. 128

83. Instrumental conditioning involves:
    a. extinguishing incorrect responses.
    b. associating a stimulus with a response.
    c. strengthening correct responses with rewards.
    d. all of the above

Answer: d
Instrumental conditioning
p. 129

84. Which of the following was Edward L. Thorndike's major contribution to the field of psychology?
    a. the discovery that reflexive responses can be affected by environmental contingencies
    b. the demonstration that rats and other species can behave adaptively using cognitive maps
    c. the development of evidence that species such as chimpanzees use *insight* to solve complex problems
    d. the design of systematic, objective, well-documented research on animal learning and behavior

Answer: b
Instrumental conditioning
p. 129

85. Which of the following would probably result in a learning curve that looks like those produced by Thorndike's cats in the puzzle boxes?
    a. groping around for a solution to a physics problem and suddenly understanding the way to do it
    b. learning to ride a bicycle
    c. learning to dislike Dobermans after being bitten by one
    d. performance on a variable ratio schedule plotted on a cumulative recorder

86. The cats in Thorndike's puzzle boxes typically:
    a. at first, struggled to get out, but once they got out successfully they caught on and got out very quickly on the next try.
    b. were let out of the box after they produced the required amount of saliva.
    c. learned in a smooth way, with each trial taking slightly less time than the preceding trial.
    d. learned gradually, but with an irregular series of slower and faster trials.

87. Which of the following is most like the learning curves for individual cats in one of Thorndike's puzzle box experiments?

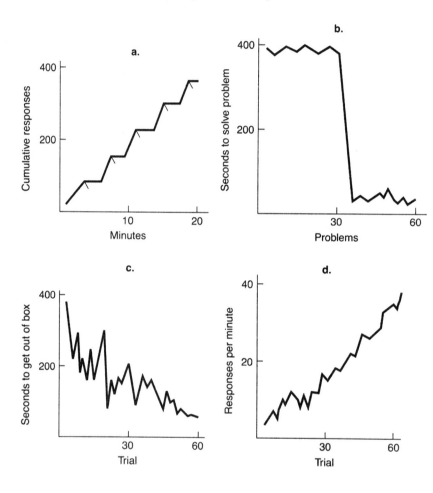

88. According to Thorndike, instrumental learning involves the formation of an association between:
    a. two stimuli.
    b. two responses.
    c. a stimulus and a response.
    d. a motor act and a response.

Answer: a
Instrumental conditioning
p. 130

89. Thorndike proposed that what the animal learned in a puzzle box was an association between:
    a. a stimulus situation and a motor response.
    b. a conditioned stimulus and a conditioned response.
    c. a stimulus situation and a reward.
    d. all of the above

Answer: c
Instrumental conditioning
p. 130

90. In Thorndike's law of effect, what determines whether the response will be strengthened or weakened?
    a. latency of the response
    b. goal of the animal
    c. consequences of the response
    d. animal's noticing the connection between act and consequence

Answer: b
Instrumental conditioning
p. 130

91. Thorndike proposed that learning occurs because certain responses become reinforced and therefore become more likely to occur. This is known as the:
    a. law of instrumentality.
    b. law of effect.
    c. law of purpose.
    d. law of determinacy.
    e. law of contingency.

Answer: d
Instrumental conditioning
p. 130

92. John cleans his room every day because then his parents allow him to watch television. John's room-cleaning illustrates:
    a. classical conditioning.
    b. learning sets.
    c. cognitive learning.
    d. the law of effect.

Answer: d
Instrumental conditioning
p. 130

93. Thorndike's law of effect is relevant to the effects of:
    a. different CS-US time intervals.
    b. effects of motivational levels on performance.
    c. rewards and punishments.
    d. S-R bonds on memory.

Answer: c
Instrumental conditioning
p. 130

94. Superstitious behavior in people shares many characteristics with the behavior of cats in puzzle boxes and pigeons in Skinner boxes. This would lead a behaviorist to conclude that superstitious behavior in people is largely a result of:
    a. rational planning.
    b. certain CS-US pairings.
    c. the law of effect.
    d. instinctive patterns of behavior.
    e. some kind of opponent process.

95. According to the principle of natural selection, some individuals within a species have adaptations that convey a reproductive advantage, thus making it more likely that their genes will be transmittted to future generations. Instrumental conditioning is analogous to natural selection in that:
    a. reinforcement acts to select only some responses.
    b. genes are ultimately responsible for what animals find reinforcing.
    c. Thorndike and other early behaviorists provided support for Darwin's theory.
    d. reinforcement is always subjectively pleasant.

96. Thorndike likened his law of effect to evolution's law of the survival of the fittest. What actually survives according to the law of effect?
    a. the "fittest" species
    b. the "fittest" individuals
    c. the "fittest" stimuli
    d. the "fittest" responses

97. Thorndike's studies of the law of effect provide an analogue of Darwinian principles in that in Thorndike's studies:
    a. the cats were chosen through natural selection.
    b. the fittest responses survived.
    c. the fittest stimuli survived.
    d. the learned responses could be transmitted to the next generation.

98. In Thorndike's "law of effect," something analogous to natural selection operates upon:
    a. the cats.
    b. the stimuli.
    c. the responses.
    d. none of the above

99. According to B.F. Skinner, operants are:
    a. voluntary responses.
    b. discriminative stimuli.
    c. elicited behaviors.
    d. environmental events.

100. The most important distinction between classical conditioning and operant conditioning is that in operant conditioning:
    a. reinforcement is contingent upon responding.
    b. the experimenter controls the response by presenting the stimuli.
    c. the ANS rather than the CNS is primarily involved.
    d. reinforcement is pleasant rather than aversive.
    e. reinforcement reduces some biological need.

101. In an operant chamber (or Skinner box), behavior is typically studied:
    a. by the method of discrete trials.
    b. by measuring the error rate.
    c. by recording the response rate.
    d. by observing how long it takes the animal to get out of the box.

Answer: c
Instrumental conditioning
p. 131

102. In which of the following is the rate of responding the most meaningful dependent variable?
    a.   a Pavlovian conditioning situation
    b.   instrumental maze learning
    c.   operant conditioning
    d.   learning to learn discrimination problems

Answer: d
Instrumental conditioning
p. 131

103. In a _____ situation, there are usually no discrete training trials.
    a.   classical conditioning
    b.   puzzle box
    c.   maze learning
    d.   operant

Answer: c
Instrumental conditioning
p. 132

104. In instrumental conditioning, which of the following will serve as a reinforcer if it is contingent on behavior?
    a.   presentation of an appetitive stimulus
    b.   termination of an aversive stimulus
    c.   both a and b above
    d.   neither a nor b above

Answer: c
Instrumental conditioning
p. 132

105. Elicited is to emitted as:
    a.   generalization is to discrimination.
    b.   extinction is to acquisition.
    c.   classical is to operant.
    d.   positive reinforcer is to negative reinforcer.

Answer: d
Instrumental conditioning
p. 132

106. According to Skinner, operants are:
    a.   best described in molecular terms.
    b.   best studied in discrete trials.
    c.   elicited.
    d.   emitted.

Answer: c
Instrumental conditioning
p. 132

107. A major difference between classical and operant conditioning is that in classical conditioning, the US is presented:
    a.   during every test trial.
    b.   immediately after the response.
    c.   no matter what the research participant does.
    d.   more often in the early training than later.

Answer: c
Instrumental conditioning
p. 133

108. Based on what you've learned about classical and operant conditioning, which of the following pairings is incorrect?
    a.   S⁻—"there's no point responding now"
    b.   S⁺—"If you respond now, you will get a reward"
    c.   CS⁻—"If you respond now, you'll be punished"
    d.   CS⁺—"The US is coming"

Answer: b
Instrumental conditioning
p. 133

109. Another name for the method of reinforcing successive approximations is:
    a.   extinction.
    b.   shaping.
    c.   biofeedback.
    d.   selective reinforcement.

Answer: d
Instrumental conditioning
p. 133

Answer: b
Instrumental conditioning
p. 133

Answer: d
Instrumental conditioning
p. 133

Answer: a
Instrumental conditioning
p. 134

Answer: d
Instrumental conditioning
p. 134

Answer: b
Instrumental conditioning
p. 134

110. Shaping:
   a. involves rewarding the organism after the desired response has been performed.
   b. involves presentation of a reinforcement intermittently regardless of the organism's behavior.
   c. refers to that part of the reinforcement schedule that marks the transition from continuous reinforcement to extinction.
   d. involves reinforcing responses that are more and more similar to the desired response.

111. If the presentation of a reinforcer is delayed after a response occurs, the reinforcer will:
   a. serve as the discriminative stimulus for the next response.
   b. have less effect on behavior than if there were no delay.
   c. act as a punisher, reducing the likelihood of the desired response.
   d. none of the above

112. In order to shape performance of a difficult response, all but one of the following procedures should be followed. Which procedure is not appropriate?
   a. Provide a clear signal for the arrival of reinforcement.
   b. Present the reinforcement immediately after the response is performed.
   c. Initially reinforce approximations to the desired response.
   d. Begin by reinforcing the most difficult component in the response sequence.

113. An "A" in an Introductory Psychology course is to most students a(n):
   a. conditioned reinforcer.
   b. unconditioned stimulus.
   c. primary reinforcer.
   d. extinguished conditioned reward.
   e. instance of self-actualization.

114. Food, water, or the termination of an electric shock are examples of:
   a. conditioned reinforcers.
   b. conditioned stimuli.
   c. aversive stimuli.
   d. primary reinforcers.

115. Conditioned reinforcement:
   a. is typically given after primary reinforcement.
   b. acquires its properties by being paired with primary reinforcement.
   c. is more effective than primary reinforcement.
   d. is usually food or water.

Answer: c
Instrumental conditioning
p. 134

116. Some laboratory rats are always fed in a black box, never in a white box. They are then placed in a T-maze, one side of which contains a black box, the other a white box. Neither box contains food, but even so, the rats will learn to run to the black box. According to B. F. Skinner, it can be assumed that:
    a. the black box acted as a primary reinforcer.
    b. the white box is not a conditioned reinforcer.
    c. the black box is a conditioned reinforcer.
    d. the rats expected to be fed in the black box.

Answer: c
Instrumental conditioning
p. 134

117. In training your dog to retrieve, it is not always possible to deliver the reinforcer (e.g., food or a pat on the head) immediately. Therefore, you might use another stimulus, like "Good dog," when your dog picks up the object it is to retrieve. Soon, the phrase "Good dog" will serve as:
    a. a primary reinforcer.
    b. a partial reinforcer.
    c. a conditioned reinforcer.
    d. a gradient of reinforcer.

Answer: d
Instrumental conditioning
p. 134

118. Learning theorists would argue that conditioned reinforcement is established by a process that is similar to:
    a. expectancy learning.
    b. free operant conditioning.
    c. instrumental conditioning.
    d. classical conditioning.

Answer: a
Instrumental conditioning
p. 134

119. To establish a conditioned reinforcer:
    a. the conditioned reinforcer must be paired with the primary reinforcement.
    b. the conditioned reinforcer must have similar properties to the primary reinforcer.
    c. the conditioned reinforcer must be presented repeatedly without the primary reinforcer.
    d. none of the above

Answer: b
Instrumental conditioning
p. 135

120. Reinforcement is probably BEST defined as a(n):
    a. stimulus that satisfies a biological requirement.
    b. opportunity to engage in a preferred activity.
    c. event that maintains homeostasis.
    d. experience that results in a CER.

Answer: d
Instrumental conditioning
p. 135

121. A rat that only receives 5 food pellets per lever press, after being used to receiving 15 food pellets per lever press, is most likely to exhibit:
    a. stimulus generalization.
    b. intrinsic motivation.
    c. insight learning.
    d. behavioral contrast.

122. Nursery school children typically enjoy drawing pictures. Which of the following is likely to reduce their intrinsic motivation for engaging in this activity?
     a. reward the children with "Good Player" certificates for drawing pictures
     b. only allow the children to draw pictures once per week
     c. encourage the children to draw by praising the drawings of their friends
     d. tell the children that they can draw pictures of anything they wish

123. In instrumental learning, the schedule of reinforcement used:
     a. can affect the rate of learning.
     b. has very little effect on behavior.
     c. can make the animal nauseous.
     d. should always be a fixed ratio.

124. In ratio schedules of reinforcement, the organism is reinforced after:
     a. emitting a certain number of responses.
     b. emitting a certain ratio of responses.
     c. a specific length of time.
     d. a variable length of time.

125. A rat in a Skinner box has a characteristic pattern of behavior. Immediately after reinforcement, it pauses before it starts to respond again. Once it starts, however, it picks up its usual rate. On what schedule was this rat most probably trained?
     a. fixed ratio
     b. variable ratio
     c. fixed interval
     d. variable interval

126. If you are reinforced for selling greeting cards according to a VR 20 schedule, then you should expect:
     a. to earn $20 for every major sale.
     b. to receive payment after every 20th sale.
     c. to be paid after every 20 days.
     d. none of the above.

127. The highest response rates are obtained with:
     a. fixed-ratio schedules.
     b. variable-ratio schedules.
     c. fixed-interval schedules.
     d. variable-interval schedules.

128. To ensure a very high rate of responding without pauses after reinforcement, one should use a:
     a. fixed-ratio schedule.
     b. fixed-interval schedule.
     c. variable-ratio schedule.
     d. variable-interval schedule.

129. After which schedule of reinforcement would you predict a child would show the most resistance to extinction?
    a. continuous reinforcement
    b. fixed ratio
    c. fixed interval
    d. variable ratio

Answer: d
Instrumental conditioning
p. 136

130. Working as a car mechanic for a taxi company, you receive a paycheck every two weeks. You are being reinforced according to a _____ schedule of reinforcement.
    a. VR
    b. VI
    c. FR
    d. FI

Answer: d
Instrumental conditioning
p. 137

131. A rat in an operant chamber is reinforced according to a VI 30 schedule of reinforcement. This means that it will receive food pellets for responding:
    a. on average, every 30 seconds.
    b. on average, after every 30th response.
    c. after every 30-second interval.
    d. after every 30th response.

Answer: a
Instrumental conditioning
p. 137

132. "The fisherman does not hook a fish with every cast of the line" best describes:
    a. stimulus generalization.
    b. shaping.
    c. primary reinforcement.
    d. partial reinforcement.

Answer: d
Instrumental conditioning
p. 137

133. If a response was acquired during partial reinforcement through it will be _____ through than if it had been acquired during continuous reinforcement.
    a. more resistent to extinction
    b. more easily shaped
    c. less resistent to extinction
    d. less easily shaped

Answer: a
Instrumental conditioning
p. 137

134. The partial-reinforcement effect refers to:
    a. increased resistance to extinction.
    b. decreased response rates during training.
    c. emergence of superstitious behavior.
    d. all of the above

Answer: a
Instrumental conditioning
p. 137

135. Which rat would show the most rapid extinction of lever pressing? The one trained with:
    a. a VR 10 schedule of reinforcement.
    b. a VR 5 schedule of reinforcement.
    c. a FR 12 schedule of reinforcement.
    d. continuous reinforcement.

Answer: d
Instrumental conditioning
p. 137

136. Gamblers often persist at gambling even when they very rarely receive a payoff. This persistence is predicted by:
    a. the gradual increase in performance with successive approximations.
    b. resistance to extinction when performance has been maintained with variable schedules of reinforcement.
    c. the fact that there is typically a pause in performance after each reinforcement.
    d. research on learned helplessness.

137. Pigeon *A* is trained on a VR 10 schedule of reinforcement, pigeon *B* on a FR 5 schedule, and pigeon *C* on a continuous reinforcement schedule. The correct ranking of birds in terms of the number of responses each will emit during extinction is (ranked from fewest responses to greatest number of responses):
    a. *A, B, C.*
    b. *B, C, A.*
    c. *C, B, A.*
    d. *A, B,* and *C* will emit an approximately equal number of responses.

138. According to your textbook authors, instrumental conditioning techniques have applications in:
    a. psychotherapy.
    b. prison settings.
    c. parenting.
    d. all of the above

139. Aversive stimuli:
    a. are reinforcing upon their removal.
    b. are events that organisms avoid.
    c. are necessary for escape learning.
    d. all of the above

140. There is a type of instrumental learning in which a response is followed by an aversive stimulus, reducing the likelihood of the response on subsequent occasions. This type of learning is called:
    a. avoidance learning.
    b. escape learning.
    c. punishment.
    d. none of the above

141. Jenny is a chubby six-year-old who has a penchant for cookies. Her affection for cookies is so strong that she is constantly trying to steal them when her parents are otherwise occupied. Her parents decide that they will have to spank Jenny each time she steals one. The spanking acts as a(n):
    a. avoidance stimulus.
    b. aversive stimulus.
    c. blocking stimulus.
    d. effect stimulus.
    e. reconditioning stimulus.

Answer: a
Instrumental conditioning
p. 138

142. If you want punishment to work as you housebreak your dog, you must make the punishment:
    a. both contingent and contiguous.
    b. severe.
    c. preceded by a clear warning signal.
    d. occur according to a partial-reinforcement schedule.
    e. all of the above

Answer: a
Instrumental conditioning
p. 138

143. In _____, a response stops an aversive event that has already begun.
    a. escape learning
    b. avoidance learning
    c. punishment training
    d. latency learning

Answer: d
Instrumental conditioning
p. 139

144. Treatment of phobias is most closely related to:
    a. spontaneous recovery of CRs after extinction.
    b. opponent-processes related to drug addictions.
    c. the difficulty of training complex responses using shaping.
    d. the difficulty extinguishing avoidance responses.

Answer: b
Cognitive learning
p. 140

145. E. C. Tolman is an adherent of which general approach to animal learning?
    a. operant theory
    b. cognitive theory
    c. behavior theory
    d. two-factor theory

Answer: b
Cognitive learning
p. 140

146. In a backward conditioning situation:
    a. the US is presented after the CS.
    b. the US is presented before the CS.
    c. the US is presented with the CS.
    d. the US is presented without the CS.

Answer: b
Cognitive learning
p. 140

147. The most effective conditioning occurs when:
    a. the CS follows the US by about 0.5 seconds.
    b. the CS precedes the US by about 0.5 seconds.
    c. the CS and US the occur simultaneously.
    d. the CS and US the occur on alternate trials.
    e. responses to the US are well habituated before training begins.

Answer: a
Cognitive learning
p. 141

148. In backward conditioning:
    a. the CS is uninformative about the onset of the US.
    b. the CR is presented shortly after the UR.
    c. there is a fairly high ratio of unreinforced trials.
    d. all of the above

Answer: a
Cognitive learning
p. 141

149. The fact that conditioning is most effective when the US immediately follows the CS suggests that:
    a. classical conditioning involves learning that the CS is a predictive signal for the occurrence of the US.
    b. classical conditioning does not produce an association between the CS and US.
    c. classical conditioning depends on the close temporal contiguity of CS and US.
    d. extinction is a major factor that weakens conditioned responses.

Answer: a
Cognitive learning
p. 141

150. What will happen in a classical conditioning experiment if the likelihood of the US following the CS is 30 percent and the likelihood of the US being presented alone is also 30 percent?
    a. There will be no conditioning no matter how contiguous the CS and US.
    b. There will be strong conditioning if the US arrives about half a second after the CS.
    c. There will be no obvious effect at first, but after a rest period the CR will appear when the CS is presented.
    d. The animal will show surprise reactions when the CS is presented.

Answer: d
Cognitive learning
p. 142

151. Which word or phrase best captures the meaning of the term "contingency"?
    a. comes after
    b. supports
    c. precedes
    d. depends upon

Answer: c
Cognitive learning
p. 142

152. In the typical classical conditioning experiment performed by Pavlov, the relationship between the CS and the US was:
    a. contiguous.
    b. contingent.
    c. both contiguous and contingent.
    d. neither contiguous nor contingent.

Answer: c
Cognitive learning
p. 142

153. Pavlov's dogs learned that it was the metronome and not other events in the laboratory that were associated with meat powder. According to a contingency view of classical conditioning, this is not only because the CS preceded the US but also because:
    a. the experiments were well-controlled and there were no other stimuli near the dog.
    b. the dog was unable to make responses other than salivation because it was held in a harness.
    c. the absence of the metronome predicted the absence of meat.
    d. all of the above

154. The table below shows the results of forty trials in a classical conditioning experiment. The CS was presented on some trials and not others, and the same is true for the US.

	US	no US
CS	17	3
No CS	3	17

Experiments like this illustrate:
   a. the steady performance levels one sees with variable interval schedules of reinforcement.
   b. that even nonhuman animals can show insight under particular conditions.
   c. extinction and spontaneous recovery.
   d. the importance of contingencies.

155. What is the contingency learned in classical conditioning?
   a. If CS, then US and if not CS, then not US.
   b. If CS, then CR and if not CS, then not CR.
   c. If US, then UR and if not US, then not UR.
   d. If US, then CS and if not US, then not CS.

156. Based on what you know about contingencies, what does the CS predict in classical conditioning?
   a. the CR
   b. the US
   c. the UR
   d. extinction

157. In determining whether two events are contingent, one must consider:
   a. the number of times the two events have co-occurred.
   b. the number of times the two events have not co-occurred.
   c. both a and b above
   d. neither a nor b above

158. The most important thing that animals learn in classical conditioning is:
   a. the contingency between the CS and the US.
   b. the motivational significance of the US.
   c. the degree of contiguity between stimuli and particular responses.
   d. the predictive power of the US.

159. In an experiment, a dog undergoes 20 trials on which he hears a tone and gets meat powder in various combinations. On nine of the trials, he gets tone and meat powder; on 1 trial, he gets tone and no meat powder; on 1 trial, he gets meat powder and no tone; on 9 trials, he gets no tone and no meat powder. In this situation, there is:
   a. a contingency between the sound of tone and meat powder.
   b. a contingency between the sound of the tone and absence of meat powder.
   c. a negative contingency.
   d. a zero contingency.

Answer: d
Cognitive learning
p. 142

160. An animal hears 100 tones and experiences 100 shocks. Shock only follows the tone closely in time on 2 trials. According to a contingency view, the animal would learn:
    a. nothing, since tone is both paired and not paired with shock.
    b. a weak tone-shock relationship.
    c. a contrast effect, because shock was expected but not delivered on many trials.
    d. that tone is a safety signal predicting that shock is unlikely.

Answer: c
Cognitive learning
p. 142

161. "If . . . then . . . and if not . . . then not . . ." comes closest to what the learning theorist means by:
    a. contiguity.
    b. reinforcement.
    c. contingency.
    d. consequences.

Answer: c
Cognitive learning
p. 143

162. Under which condition is a rat most likely to experience anxiety rather than fear?
    a. When a CS precedes shock 100 percent of the time.
    b. When a CS is followed by shock on 50 percent of the trials but when there is no CS there is no shock.
    c. When the probability of shock following a CS is 40 percent and the probability of shock happening when there is no CS is also 40 percent.
    d. When the probability of shock following a CS is 90 percent and the probability of shock occurring when there is no CS is 5 percent.

Answer: d
Cognitive learning
p. 143

163. Signaled is to unsignaled shock as:
    a. US is to UR.
    b. UR is to US.
    c. anxiety is to fear.
    d. fear is to anxiety.

Answer: b
Cognitive learning
p. 143

164. Which of the following is a cognitive interpretation of classical conditioning?
    a. CSs are associated with USs and their elicited URs.
    b. CSs produce expectancies of USs.
    c. Pavlov's demonstrations were really of latent learning.
    d. S-R bonds are formed because the US acts as a reinforcer.

Answer: a
Cognitive learning
p. 143

165. Surprise appears to play an important role in classical conditioning. For which of the following events is surprise most important if effective conditioning is to occur?
    a. US follows CS
    b. CS occurs alone
    c. CS provides redundant information
    d. CR follows CS

Answer: c
Cognitive learning
p. 143

166. Research on which of the following best shows the importance of surprise in forming strong classical conditioning?
    a. spontaneous recovery
    b. intermittent reinforcement
    c. blocking
    d. latent learning

Answer: c
Cognitive learning
p. 144

167. When one stimulus overshadows another because of an animal's prior experience, this is known as:
    a. contingency.
    b. contiguity.
    c. blocking.
    d. fear conditioning.

Answer: b
Cognitive learning
p. 144

168. A rat is placed in a maze for an hour per day during 10 consecutive days so that it can explore the corridors of the maze. On the 11th day, food is placed in the goal box. The animal learns immediately, and without errors, to run to the goal box for food. What type of learning is illustrated here?
    a. generalization
    b. latent learning
    c. intrinsic learning
    d. insightful behavior

Answer: a
Cognitive learning
p. 145

169. Your textbook authors described an elegant study (Colwill and Rescorla, 1985) that demonstrated that rats can learn act-outcome associations. Specifically, rats were trained to press a level for food and pull a chain for sugar water. What was the next step in this research that provided evidence that rats can learn the relationships between their own actions and the associated reward?
    a. Sugar water was paired with the injection of a mild toxin.
    b. Food pellets were paired with a mild electric shock.
    c. Lever pressing was paired with a novel food.
    d. Chain pulling was paired with a loud noise.

Answer: a
Instrumental conditioning
p. 145

170. In instrumental conditioning, reinforcement is _____ upon the response.
    a. contingent
    b. contiguous
    c. both a and b
    d. neither a nor b

171. Imagine that your infant, Betty, has a colorful mobile suspended over her crib. There is a sensing device under her pillow so that when Betty moves her head, the mobile turns and its colorful shapes move enticingly. Betty enjoys making the mobile move and she smiles whenever the mobile is in motion. Now, imagine that Betty's twin brother, Frank, has an identical mobile suspended over his crib. However, Frank's mobile only moves when Betty sets hers in motion. What is the likely outcome in this situation?
    a. Betty will pay less attention to the mobile than Frank because the movements of hers are predictable.
    b. Betty will have intelligence scores that are significantly higher than Frank's when the twins are two years old.
    c. Frank will lose interest in the movements of his mobile while Betty will continue to enjoy hers.
    d. Frank will attempt to reach out and grasp the colorful shapes in motion above his crib, while Betty will just move her head to set her mobile in motion.

172. Which of the following is critical for the development of learned helplessness?
    a. the organism's lack of control over events
    b. the delivery of a substantial amount of punishment
    c. a contingent relationship between some response and punishment
    d. the presence of a "yoked" control

173. An investigator plans to use Seligman's (1975) procedures to study the effects of learned helplessness on immune functioning in rats. What control condition or control group is most important for an unambiguous interpretation of the results?
    a. a group of rats given a pleasant event instead of an aversive event in the presence of the CS
    b. a group of rats given the same amount of an aversive event, but the event is under the rats' control
    c. a group of rats exposed to the CS but given neither pleasant nor aversive stimuli
    d. a group of rats given some kind of virus that impairs the immune system by a nonbehavioral means

174. Rats *A* and *B* receive shock in a Skinner box. Rat *A* can terminate the shock by pressing a bar. For rat *B*, there is no response that leads to shock termination. The experimenter then tries to teach both rats another similar shock-avoidance task. One expects that:
    a. rat *A* will learn faster than rat *B*.
    b. rat *B* will learn faster than rat *A*.
    c. the rats will learn at equal rates.
    d. neither rat *A* nor rat *B* will learn the new task.

175. Person *X* lost both his wife and his job in the last two years. Person *Y* had no significant personal or professional losses in the past two years. Which person is more vulnerable to depression?
    a. person *X*
    b. person *Y*
    c. neither person *X* nor person *Y*
    d. There is no relevant data on this issue.

176. In the past, psychologists have focused on identifying general laws of learning. Today, many researchers are more interested in investigating species differences in learning. These modern researchers typically study animal behavior using a(n) _____ perspective.
    a. radical behaviorist
    b. evolutionary
    c. information processing
    d. none of the above

177. If one wishes to teach rats an aversion to a stimulus using shock as the US, what would be an effective CS?
    a. a taste
    b. a tone
    c. either a or b above
    d. neither a nor b above

178. What general principle of learning was most seriously challenged by the results of learned taste aversion studies?
    a. the contingency principle
    b. the principle of preparedness
    c. the principle of biological constraints
    d. the equipotentiality principle

179. The equipotentiality principle involves the assumption(s) that:
    a. all mammals are capable of the same levels of cognition and performance.
    b. mammals are capable of associating any response with any reinforcer.
    c. certain CSs just seem to "go naturally" with particular USs.
    d. all of the above

180. The equipotentiality principle makes the assumption(s) that:
    a. mammals are capable of associating almost any CS to almost any US.
    b. all mammals are capable of the same levels of cognition and performance.
    c. some responses seem to "go naturally" with particular reinforcers.
    d. all of the above

181. A demonstration that salivation can be conditioned to any conceivable CS would be strong evidence for:
    a. belongingness.
    b. equipotentiality.
    c. contingency.
    d. contiguity.

182. Suppose that you could teach a cat to press a lever in order to either get any conceivable incentive or to avoid any conceivable punishment. If you could do this, it would be strong evidence for:
    a. belongingness.
    b. contiguity.
    c. contingency
    d. equipotentiality.

183. Suppose that a dog is able to associate food with practically any conditioned stimulus. This illustrates the principle of:
    a. belongingness.
    b. biological constraint.
    c. equipotentiality.
    d. none of the above

184. Which of the following provides evidence for learned taste aversion?
    a. An organism, on its first response to a bitter taste, avoids eating that food again.
    b. An organism avoids a food that it ate just prior to getting sick.
    c. An organism that avoids lemon-flavored food also avoids any food that tastes sour.
    d. all of the above

185. Rats easily associate illness with:
    a. a touch on the whiskers.
    b. sounds.
    c. sights.
    d. tastes.

186. When an animal learns to avoid certain foods, this is called:
    a. learned taste aversion.
    b. unnatural belongingness.
    c. response-suppressed arbitrariness.
    d. reduced extinction.

187. What is the significance of the fact that the stimuli most easily associated with nausea are quite different in quail than in rats?
    a. The equipotentiality principle holds for some species but not for others.
    b. Belongingness is species-specific.
    c. Contingencies are less important in some species than in others.
    d. Some species develop learned helplessness more easily than others.

188. Coyotes often stop killing sheep if they become ill after eating sheep. This phenomenon seems to violate the principle of:
    a. temporal contiguity.
    b. contingency.
    c. cause and effect.
    d. relatedness.
    e. specific nerve energies.

Answer: b
Varieties of learning
p. 150

189. When a rat or a coyote acquires a taste aversion to poisoned meat, what principle of learning does this seem to violate?
    a.   the law of effect
    b.   the principle that immediate reinforcement is necessary for conditioning to occur
    c.   the principle that there must be a discriminative stimulus for having to occur
    d.   the principle that there are prepackaged correlations between certain kinds of stimuli and certain reinforcements

Answer: d
Varieties of learning
p. 149

190. A strong argument that contiguity is not absolutely essential for classical conditioning comes from studies of:
    a.   spontaneous recovery.
    b.   generalization gradients.
    c.   extinction of conditioned avoidance.
    d.   learned taste aversions.

Answer: b
Varieties of learning
p. 150

191. Taste aversion studies have important medical implications in treatment of:
    a.   depression.
    b.   cancer.
    c.   cardiovascular disease.
    d.   hypertension.

Answer: a
Varieties of learning
p. 151

192. Which of the following would be the most difficult to do?
    a.   train a pigeon to peck a key to avoid shock
    b.   train a cat to rub your legs to get you to open the can of cat food
    c.   train a rat to avoid a certain flavor of ice cream with a mild poison as punishment
    d.   train a rat to jump over a hurdle to avoid shock

Answer: b
Varieties of learning
p. 151

193. Which of the following would be the hardest task to train?
    a.   train a pigeon to flap its wings to avoid shock
    b.   train a rat to associate a flashing light with nausea
    c.   train a pigeon to peck a piano key to get a food reward
    d.   train a cat to rub your legs to get you to open a can of cat food

Answer: b
Varieties of learning
p. 151

194. The normal defense reaction of a certain species involves freezing in the face of danger. For these animals, which of the following responses wouldbe easy to learn in order to avoid shock?
    a.   pressing a bar in order to avoid shock
    b.   staying immobile in order to avoid shock
    c.   turning a wheel in order to avoid shock
    d.   all of the above

195. You are training a chicken to peck a key for a food reward and you want it to hold its feet absolutely still. You try and try, but your chicken keeps moving its feet while pecking. Why can't you extinguish this response?
    a. Although pecking naturally occurs while eating, so does scratching.
    b. You have set up a contingency between scratching and getting rewarded.
    c. You are not feeding your chicken enough. As it gets full, it will give up the scratching.
    d. The response that you are reinforcing is too equipotential.

196. What is the significance of the fact that pigeons use a different position of the beak when pecking a key for water than for food?
    a. It suggests that the operant is not an arbitrary response.
    b. It suggests that the principle of preparedness is invalid.
    c. It suggests that contingencies are less important than contiguity.
    d. It suggests that instrumental conditioning is the opposite of classical conditioning.

197. Which of the following would provide the clearest evidence that key pecking by pigeons may be a classically conditioned response, not an arbitrary operant?
    a. Key pecking still occurs when the absence of this response is reinforced with food.
    b. Pecks occur in rapid succession if water is the reinforcer.
    c. Key pecking is reduced if it is punished by a loud sound.
    d. Key pecking is difficult to establish if the reinforcement is shock avoidance.

198. Breland and Breland (1961) attempted to train a raccoon to drop a coin in a toy piggy bank to receive food as reinforcement. They reported that the raccoon began to "misbehave," spending longer and longer periods of time rubbing the coin between its forepaws and refusing to drop the coin in the slot of the piggy bank. What psychological principle does this raccoon's "misbehavior" illustrate?
    a. conditioned emotional responding
    b. latent learning
    c. the law of effect
    d. biological constraints on learning

199. Clark's nutcracker hides pine nuts in trees and later retrieves them. How does it do this?
    a. It carefully places small marks on the trees where the nuts are hidden.
    b. It randomly moves through the trees, finding the nuts accidentally.
    c. It hides most of the pine nuts in the same few trees over and over again.
    d. It actually remembers where it put them.

Answer: d
Varieties of learning
p. 153

200. The hippocampus appears to be larger in species of birds that:
    a. learn to speak
    b. can solve problems by insight.
    c. are good at forming learning sets.
    d. make heavy use of spatial memory.

Answer: d
Varieties of learning
p. 154

201. How do evolutionary psychologists explain the existence of general laws of learning, common to many species of animals?
    a. Different species of animals have the same neural circuitry, causing them to form stimulus-response relationships in exactly the same way.
    b. Brain processes are similar across a wide range of species, resulting in similarities of learning styles.
    c. Evolutionary forces have acted on different species to produce a single, effective form of learning that increases the likelihood of survival.
    d. Different species of animals all live in environments that share the same physical laws of nature, thus constraining mental processes and behavioral outcomes.

Answer: d
The neural basis for learning
p. 154

202. Which of the following is an aspect of neural plasticity that allows learning to occur?
    a. the formation of synapses
    b. changes in neuronal sensitivity to stimulation
    c. inactivation of existing synapses
    d. all of the above

Answer: c
The neural basis for learning
p. 155

203. The marine mollusk *Aplysia* is extremely useful for investigating the basic neural mechanisms of learning because:
    a. *Aplysia* have very simple nervous systems.
    b. *Aplysia* exhibit only a few simple behaviors.
    c. both a and b
    d. neither a nor b

Answer: c
The neural basis for learning
p. 155

204. Classical conditioning studies with *Aplysia* have involved training these animals to retract their gills in response to light touches on their tubular siphons. Which of the following pairings is incorrect?
    a. CS—light touch on the tubular siphon
    b. US—electric shock on the tail
    c. CR—extension of the tubular siphon
    d. UR—retraction of the gill

Answer: a
The neural basis for learning
p. 156

205. Which of the following is the apparent neural basis for conditioned gill retractions in *Aplysia*?
    a. Sensory neurons that carry information about light touches to the siphon increase their release of neurotransmitters across trials.
    b. Motor neurons that activate gill retractions become less sensitive to neurotransmitter substances across trials.
    c. New sensory neurons are formed that are specifically sensitive to light touches on the siphon.
    d. Old motor neurons are eliminated that interfere with the tail retraction response.

206. Which of the following is true regarding long-term potentiation (LTP)?
    a. LTP involves presynaptic facilitation of excitatory neuronal potentials.
    b. LTP serves as a correlation detector when two functionally significant events are related.
    c. LTP has only been demonstrated to occur in the primary sensory areas of the human cerebral cortex.
    d. LTP has been demonstrated to occur in only a few species of mammals.

207. Learning in the form of _____ involves postsynaptic mechanisms in which receiving neurons become increasingly sensitive with repeated stimulation.
    a. instrumental conditioning
    b. negative reinforcement
    c. stimulus generalization
    d. long-term potentiation

208. Imagine that neuron C receives input from two other neurons, A and B. Neuron C will act as a correlation detector if:
    a. long-term potentiation is prevented.
    b. the spread of potentiation is activity dependent.
    c. neurons A and B fire in alternation.
    d. all of the above

209. Which of the following is false regarding long-term potentiation?
    a. It is long term because the neuronal effect can last several days, or even weeks.
    b. It involves presynaptic facilitation, resulting in detection of uncorrelated neuronal events.
    c. It is an activity-dependent event, so that potentiation spreads when nearby neuronal events occur simultaneously.
    d. It occurs when the responsiveness of a postsynaptic neuron is increased as a function of environmental events.

210. Studies designed to test an animal's ability to create a mental representation of spatial layout show that rats trained to find food in an 8-arm radial maze are likely to:
    a. lack the ability to remember multiple locations of food.
    b. enter the center platform rarely, if ever.
    c. search for food in a systematic fashion.
    d. fail tests for the formation of spatial maps.

211. Insight refers to:
    a. arriving at a solution to a problem after encountering that same problem on a number of repeated trials.
    b. a highly stereotyped, species-specific response to a problem.
    c. the long period of cognition required before solving a complex problem.
    d. none of the above

Answer: a
Complex cognition in animals
p. 159

212. Kohler's chimpanzee, Sultan, was said to show evidence of insight learning when he:
    a. connected two sticks to obtain a banana.
    b. used a least-distance path to locate hidden food.
    c. showed an empathetic response to an injured kitten.
    d. none of the above.

Answer: d
Complex cognition in animals
p. 160

213. Which of the following is the most convincing evidence that an animal has learned by through "insight" rather than by trial and error?
    a. a smooth, continuous performance
    b. an absence of errors
    c. a sudden drop in the learning curve
    d. a transfer of training

Answer: c
Complex cognition in animals
p. 160

214. Archimedes had the "aha," experience when he discovered that when the king's crown was submerged, it displaced its own volume of water. Kekule had a similar experience when he discovered that benzene had a ring structure. Which of the following came the closest to exhibiting this kind of "insightful" learning?
    a. Skinner's pigeons
    b. Pavlov's dogs
    c. Kohler's chimps
    d. Thorndike's cats

Answer: a
Complex cognition in animals
p. 160

215. Insight in the context of learning refers to:
    a. comprehending the principles underlying the solution to a problem.
    b. understanding the mechanisms underlying the bar-pressing behavior of the rat.
    c. understanding one's own emotional state.
    d. none of the above

Answer: b
Complex cognition in animals
p. 160

216. To show that an animal understands the principle of *sameness* a match-to-sample task, one must show that the animal:
    a. performs the response consistently, even when reward is delayed.
    b. transfers the response to a new and different stimulus.
    c. is able to discriminate between physically similar stimuli.
    d. all of the above

Answer: c
Complex cognition in animals
p. 161

217. In studies of concept formation in pigeons, discriminative stimuli included photographs of each of the following except:
    a. trees.
    b. a particular human.
    c. three apples.
    d. water.

Answer: b
Complex cognition in animals
p. 161

218. Correct performance on a match-to-sample task requires:
    a. acquisition of a concept of "sameness."
    b. discrimination between stimuli.
    c. selection of a stimulus that is unrelated to the sample.
    d. demonstration of a third-order concept.

219. In order to demonstrate that an organism is responding on the basis of a learned concept rather than on the basis of a specific stimulus, one must demonstrate that:
    a. learning transfers to a situation with perceptually different stimuli.
    b. learning persists over many trials on many consecutive days.
    c. the animal can use symbols to correctly select its response.
    d. all of the above

220. Pigeons in operant chambers would be said to have successfully learned the concept of *sameness* if they learned to peck green keylights when shown green lights, red keylights when shown red lights, and then could demonstrate transfer of training by:
    a. selecting yellow keylights when shown yellow lights.
    b. selecting keylights with triangles when shown triangles.
    c. generalizing to other green and red stimuli.
    d. avoiding pecking keylights with unfamiliar colors.

221. Premack's chimpanzee, Sarah, learned to place a token between two objects to indicate if the objects shown were:
    a. toys or tools.
    b. edible or nonedible.
    c. manmade or natural.
    d. same or different.

222. Your textbooks authors suggest that recent historical changes in psychological investigations of animal learning included a shift from studying what animals _____ to what they _____.
    a. do; know
    b. want; have
    c. ignore; learn
    d. think; perceive

223. Pigeons are remarkable navigators and can find their way home over huge distances, an ability that is comparable to what humans can do using special equipment. But despite this, we don't regard the pigeon as particularly intelligent. Why not?
    a. The pigeon cannot use special man-made equipment to navigate.
    b. The pigeon lacks language and speech comprehension.
    c. The pigeon's navigational achievements are species-specific abilities.
    d. The pigeon has no access to its own intellectual operations as it navigates.

224. Unlike pigeons, chimpanzees are able to:
    a. solve match-to-sample problems.
    b. access their own intellectual operations.
    c. solve problems by using language.
    d. discriminate moving from stationary stimuli.

CHAPTER 5 | Sensory Processes

Answer: a
The origins of knowledge
p. 170

1. A fundamental tenet of British empiricism is that:
   a. all knowledge is acquired through the senses.
   b. some individuals enter life with a tabula rasa; others don't.
   c. some basic categories of human knowledge, such as time, space, and causality, are presented at birth.
   d. the doctrine of specific nerve energies explains why we hear sound rather than see it.

Answer: a
The origins of knowledge
p. 170

2. John Locke was once asked how a person would see who had been born blind, but suddenly had vision restored. Locke's answer, consistent with his philosophy, was that the person would:
   a. need to learn about the visual world in order to see clearly.
   b. be unable to see light because the retina would have atrophied.
   c. be able to see size, color, distance, and depth because perception of these is innate.
   d. see normally, just as if vision had been functioning all along.

Answer: a
The origins of knowledge
p. 170

3. A distal stimulus is:
   a. an object or event in the world.
   b. a pattern of activity in a sensory organ.
   c. a sensation.
   d. a Weber fraction.

Answer: a
The origins of knowledge
p. 170

4. A man sees a tree. What is the distal stimulus?
   a. the tree
   b. the light waves reflected by the tree
   c. the image on the man's retina cast by the tree
   d. the pattern of nerve impulses triggered by the retinal image and conducted by the optic nerve to the brain

Answer: c
The origins of knowledge
p. 170

5. A man sees a tree. What is the proximal stimulus?
   a. the tree
   b. the light waves reflected by the tree
   c. the image cast by the tree on the man's retina
   d. the pattern of nerve impulses triggered by the retinal image and conducted by the optic nerve to the brain

Answer: a
The origins of knowledge
p. 170

6. Sounds in the environment enter the ear and cause a membrane in the inner ear to vibrate. In the case of audition, vibration of this inner ear membrane represents the:
   a. proximal stimulus.
   b. distal stimulus.
   c. sensation.
   d. neural basis of the tabula rasa.

Answer: b
The origins of knowledge
p. 171

7. Which of the following is an example of a sensation?
   a. our perception of a tree
   b. the experience of *bitter*
   c. the absolute threshold for hearing
   d. Weber's law

Answer: c
The origins of knowledge
p. 172

8. To an empiricist, one sensation is linked to another through:
   a. transduction.
   b. sensitization.
   c. association.
   d. distal stimuli.

Answer: b
The origins of knowledge
p. 173

9. The nativist philosopher Immanuel Kant argued that human knowledge derives from sensory experience, as well as preexisting categories for interpreting sensations. Which of the following is not one of these perceptual categorizations mentioned by your textbook authors?
   a. causality
   b. identity
   c. space
   d. time

Answer: c
The origins of knowledge
p. 173

10. A fundamental tenet of nativists such as Immanuel Kant is that:
    a. all knowledge is acquired through the senses.
    b. some individuals enter life with a tabula rasa; others don't.
    c. some basic categories of human knowledge, such as time, space, and causality are present at birth.
    d. the doctrine of specific nerve energies explains why we hear sound.

Answer: d
The origins of knowledge
p. 173

11. _____ refers to the scientific study of the relationships between sensory experiences and the physical characteristics of the environmental stimuli that give rise to these experiences.
    a. Psychology
    b. Biology
    c. Ethnophysics
    d. Psychophysics
    e. Psychobiology

12. The technical term for describing the conversion of energy into a neural impulse is:
    a. transformation.
    b. transduction.
    c. transposition.
    d. conversion.

13. Transduction refers to:
    a. the point at which a proximal sensory stimulus impinges upon the organism.
    b. the conversion of a proximal stimulus into a receptor process, giving rise to a neural impulse.
    c. the psychological sensation associated with a stimulus.
    d. the electrical activity in the cerebral cortex associated with by the perception of a stimulus.

14. Which of the following is an example of transduction?
    a. sound waves in the air are translated into neural impulses
    b. a light touch on the arm translated into neural impulses by sensory receptors in the skin
    c. light energy is converted into neural impulses in the retina of the eye
    d. all of the above

15. Psychophysics is a branch of psychology that studies the relationship between:
    a. physical stimuli and sensory experiences.
    b. physical stimuli and neural events.
    c. distal stimuli and perceptual interpretation.
    d. the proximal stimuli and distal stimuli.

16. The major goal of psychophysics is to:
    a. relate physical intensity of stimuli to neuronal functioning.
    b. understand the processes of transduction.
    c. understand how psychological processes can result in physical actions.
    d. relate the properties of physical stimuli to attributes of sensation.

17. Research in psychophysics addresses which of the following types of questions?
    a. What types of stimuli can be detected?
    b. What types of stimuli can be discriminated?
    c. What types of stimuli can be recognized?
    d. all of the above

18. The difference threshold refers to:
    a. the concept of individual differences.
    b. the maximum amount of energy needed to perceive a change in the original stimulus.
    c. the minimum amount of energy needed to perceive a change in the original stimulus.
    d. the minimum amount of energy required for detection of a stimulus.

Answer: d
The origins of knowledge
p. 174

19. A certain species of rodent can just tell the difference between plain water and water that contains one gram of salt per liter of water (a 1 percent solution). This best illustrates:
    a. Fechner's law.
    b. the constancy of the Weber fraction.
    c. signal-detection theory.
    d. a special case of difference thresholds.
    e. a signal-detection experiment.

Answer: a
The origins of knowledge
p. 174

20. If there is a jnd between two stimuli, then:
    a. they are detectably different.
    b. they cannot be identified as different.
    c. Fechner's law is supported.
    d. an empiricist approach to psychophysics is appropriate.

Answer: b
The origins of knowledge
p. 174

21. A 1,000 Hz tone is played to a subject. The frequency of the tone is then slowly increased, and the subject is instructed to inform the experimenter when the pitch of the tone changes. At 1,050 Hz, the subject says that the pitch of the tone is not the same as it was before. This experiment has just determined that for a 1,000 Hz tone, a change of 50 Hz represents:
    a. the absolute threshold.
    b. the difference threshold.
    c. the magnitude of the sensation.
    d. the magnitude of the stimulus.

Answer: b
The origins of knowledge
p. 174

22. Typically, what are the units for describing a jnd, according to Gustav Fechner?
    a. hypothetical units of psychological sensation
    b. the same as for the physical stimulus that produces it
    c. frequency of neural impulses per second
    d. a description of a jnd should not include units

Answer: a
The origins of knowledge
p. 174

23. $\dfrac{\Delta I}{I} = c$ is:

    a. Weber's law.
    b. Fechner's law.
    c. the equation for measuring the strength of a sensation.
    d. the equation for measuring psychological intensity.

Answer: c
The origins of knowledge
p. 175

24. The Weber fraction for discrimination of lifted weights is about 1/40. How many grams heavier than a 240 gram standard weight would a second weight need to be before it would be judged heavier than the standard?
    a. 2 grams heavier
    b. 3 grams heavier
    c. 6 grams heavier
    d. 40 grams heavier

25. Suppose we can just tell the difference between 50 and 51 candles burning in an otherwise unilluminated room. According to Weber's law, we should then be able to just distinguish 300 candles from:
    a. 301 candles.
    b. 303 candles.
    c. 306 candles.
    d. 310 candles.

26. The Weber fraction for lifted weights is about 1/50. This means that a person would be barely able to detect the difference between a 300 gram weight and one of:
    a. 300.02 grams
    b. 300.5 grams
    c. 306 grams
    d. 330 grams
    e. 350 grams

27. Suppose you can just tell the difference between lifting 100 grams and 102 grams. According to Weber's law, you would need to add _____ grams to tell the new weight from a standard weight of 1000 grams.
    a. 1
    b. 2
    c. 10
    d. 20
    e. 100

28. Most people can just detect the difference between 6 spoonfuls of sugar in a gallon of water and 5 spoonfuls of sugar in a gallon of water. If Weber's law holds, these same people should be just able to tell 30 spoonfuls from _____ per gallon.
    a. 6
    b. 25
    c. 31
    d. 50
    e. 100

29. The Weber fraction is:
    a. the absolute threshold divided by the comparison stimulus.
    b. the standard stimulus divided by the jnd.
    c. the difference threshold divided by the standard stimulus.
    d. the jnd divided by the absolute threshold.

30. If Weber's fraction is smaller for vision than for hearing, this means:
    a. vision is more sensitive than hearing.
    b. hearing is more sensitive than vision.
    c. vision is more functionally important than hearing.
    d. hearing is more functionally important than vision.

31. A psychologist asserts that a certain animal's sense of vision is more sensitive than its sense of hearing. What does she mean?
    a. The animal's absolute threshold for vision is lower than its absolute threshold for hearing.
    b. The animal's difference threshold for vision is smaller than its difference threshold for hearing.
    c. The animal's Weber fraction for vision is smaller than its Weber fraction for hearing.
    d. all of the above

32. Assume that an experiment has determined that, for monkeys, the Weber fraction for vision is 1/25 while that for audition is 1/5. This tells us that:
    a. the monkey can make finer visual discriminations than auditory ones.
    b. the monkey can make finer auditory discriminations than visual ones.
    c. over the range of perceptible stimuli, the monkey's visual sense is as keen as its auditory sense.
    d. an auditory stimulus is perceived as being five times as intense as a visual stimulus.

33. According to Weber's Law:
    a. only three types of color receptors are required to see the full color spectrum.
    b. a constant and low stimulus intensity produces a stronger sensation.
    c. different sound frequencies trigger activity in different neurons.
    d. the difference threshold is a constant proportion of stimulus intensity.

34. The equation $S = k \log I$ is Fechner's law. This law states that:
    a. increases in sensation are associated with logarithmic increases in the stimulus intensity.
    b. increases in the magnitude of a stimulus causes logarithmic increases in sensation.
    c. increases in sensation are associated with logarithmic decreases in the magnitude of a stimulus.
    d. increases in the magnitude of a stimulus causes logarithmic decreases in sensation.

35. Fechner's law specifically states that:
    a. the greater the intensity of a stimulus, the more that stimulus must be increased in order to produce a jnd.
    b. the ratio of stimulus change to a standard stimulus is a constant.
    c. the intensity of a sensation increases as a constant ratio of the physical intensity of the stimulus.
    d. the intensity of a sensation increases as the logarithm of stimulus intensity.

Answer: b
The origins of knowledge
p. 175

36. According to Fechner's law:
    a. the strength of stimulus intensity grows as the intensity of a sensation.
    b. the strength of a sensation grows as the logarithm of stimulus intensity.
    c. the logarithm of the strength of a sensation is a linear function of the logarithm of stimulus intensity.
    d. the strength of a sensation is a linear function of stimulus intensity.

Answer: a
The origins of knowledge
p. 175

37. Fechner's law is most closely related to the fact that:
    a. most senses operate over a huge range of stimulus intensities.
    b. transducers are present in all sensory systems.
    c. different sensory qualities are carried to the brain over different neural pathways.
    d. a given neuron fires completely or not at all.

Answer: a
The origins of knowledge
p. 176

38. Which of the following psychophysical techniques or concepts has been applied to studies of decision making in fields outside of traditional psychology, including criminal justice and medicine?
    a. signal detection
    b. Fechner's law
    c. the Weber fraction
    d. the difference threshold

Answer: a
The origins of knowledge
p. 176

39. Which of the following assumptions of classical psychophysics is seriously questioned by signal-detection theorists?
    a. the concepts of zero stimulus and absolute threshold
    b. the concept of sensory adaptation
    c. the logarithmic relation between stimulus intensity and perceived magnitude of sensation
    d. that there are individual differences in sensory acuity

Answer: d
The origins of knowledge
p. 176

40. According to signal-detection theory, a subject's criterion for decision making in an auditory psychophysical task is:
    a. relative to the proportion of stimulation resulting from external signal.
    b. the condition of silence referred to as zero stimulus.
    c. the Weber fraction for monaural stimulation.
    d. the amount of background noise in the absence of a stimulus.

Answer: c
The origins of knowledge
p. 178

41. On a particular trial in a detection experiment, no stimulus is presented but the participant reports having perceived one. This is called a:
    a. hit.
    b. miss.
    c. false alarm.
    d. correct negative.

Answer: c
The origins of knowledge
p. 178

42. In a detection experiment, the payoff matrix is changed so as to increase the bias toward saying yes. This change will lead to an increase in the number of:
    a. hits.
    b. false alarms.
    c. both a and b
    d. none of the above

Answer: c
The origins of knowledge
p. 177

42. A candidate for the state police passes the qualifying exam with a high score, yet flunks out of the police academy. In signal-detection terms, a passing grade on a qualifying exam is a:
    a. miss.
    b. correct negative.
    c. false alarm.
    d. hit.

Answer: b
The origins of knowledge

p. 177

43. In a signal-detection experiment, a miss has occurred when:
    a. the participant reports seeing a stimulus when none was presented.
    b. the participant fails to report seeing a stimulus when one was presented.
    c. the participant reports seeing a stimulus when one was presented.
    d. the participant fails to report seeing a stimulus when none was presented.

Answer: a
The origins of knowledge
p. 177

44. A candidate for the state police fails the exam and does not qualify for training at the police academy, yet in fact this person would have made a very good police officer. In signal-detection terms, this person's test results represent a:
    a. miss.
    b. correct negative.
    c. false alarm.
    d. hit.

Answer: b
The origins of knowledge
p. 178

45. The major advantage of signal-detection theory over classical psychophysical theory is that signal-detection theory includes in its formulation the concepts of both:
    a. absolute and difference thresholds.
    b. sensitivity and response bias.
    c. Weber's and Fechner's laws.
    d. transduction and detection.

Answer: a
The origins of knowledge
p. 178

46. In a particular experiment, the payoff matrix is established as follows: + 5 for a hit; +5 for a correct negative; –5 for a false alarm; and –15 for a miss. In order to maximize his "winnings," the participant should establish a criterion:
    a. biased toward answering yes.
    b. biased toward answering no.
    c. equally biased toward yes and no.
    d. biased toward saying maybe.

47. In a detection experiment, the payoff matrix is changed so as to increase the bias toward saying no. This change will increase the number of:
    a. hits
    b. false alarms
    c. both a and b
    d. none of the above

48. In a detection experiment, there are two payoff matrices. In I, it is: +5 for a hit, −15 for a false alarm, +5 for correct negative, and −5 for a miss. In II it is: +5 for a hit, −5 for a false alarm, +5 for a correct negative, and −15 for a miss. We would expect the subject to establish a response criterion:
    a. biased toward *yes* judgments for both I and II.
    b. biased toward *no* judgments for both I and II.
    c. biased toward *yes* judgments for I; biased toward *no* judgments for II.
    d. biased toward *no* judgments for I; biased toward *yes* judgments for II.

49. In a particular experiment, the payoff matrix is established as follows: +5 for a hit; +5 for a correct negative; −5 for a false alarm; and −15 for a miss. In order to maximize his "winnings," the participant should establish a criterion:
    a. biased toward answering yes.
    b. biased toward answering no.
    c. equally biased toward yes and no.
    d. There is no way to know, given the above information.

50. A meteorologist examines computer data and must decide "will it rain?" She answers yes and takes an umbrella home from work. It turns out not to rain. What can we conclude probably was true for this meteorologist?
    a. The reward for a hit was quite low.
    b. The penalty for a miss was quite low.
    c. The penalty for a false alarm was quite low.
    d. all of the above

51. A major advantage of signal-detection methods over traditional ways of measuring thresholds is that signal-detection methods allow the investigator to:
    a. distinguish between sensitivity effects and tendencies to respond too conservatively or too liberally.
    b. separate hits and misses from correct negatives and false alarms.
    c. introduce occasional "catch" trials to eliminate response biases.
    d. multiply the effects of sensitivity by the magnitude of the response bias to produce an ROC curve.

52. Signal-detection theory:
    a. allows one to separate actual perceptual ability from response tendencies.
    b. suggests that, for each participant, there exists a constant stimulus intensity corresponding to a zero stimulus.
    c. suggests that perceived sensation occurs only in the presence of an external stimulus.
    d. suggests that confusion about whether a stimulus has been presented or not is most likely to occur when the signal is much greater than the noise.

53. The fact that a blow to the ear can result in an auditory stimulus ("ringing of the ear") is consistent with:
    a. the concept of an absolute threshold for sensation.
    b. Muller's doctrine of specific nerve energies.
    c. Fechner's rules for measuring sensation intensity.
    d. the concept embodied in Weber's law.

54. The experiences of *blue-green, A-sharp,* and *sour* clearly have different qualities. According to the doctrine of specific nerve energies, this difference is caused by differences:
    a. in the physical energies that serve as the stimuli for vision, hearing, and taste.
    b. in the neural structures excited by stimuli associated with these experiences.
    c. in the absolute thresholds for vision, hearing, and taste.
    d. in the jnd's for vision, hearing, and taste.

55. Differences in our experiences of iced tea, birds singing, and the sight of a fireworks display are due to:
    a. our past experiences with these stimuli.
    b. differences in the sense organs that respond to the stimuli.
    c. physiological differences in the conduction velocities of the neurons attached to the associated sense organs.
    d. all of the above

56. In a simple computer system, pressing 1 = A, pressing 2 = B, 3 = C, 1 + 2 = D, 1 + 3 = E, and 2 + 3 = F. This scheme is most similar to the sensory quality principle of:
    a. specificity theory.
    b. signal-detection theory.
    c. pattern theory of sensory encoding.
    d. sensory coding of stimulus intensity.

57. Which of the following theories involves the idea that responses across different sets of sensory neurons give rise to qualitatively different sensory experiences?
    a. specificity theory
    b. pattern theory
    c. place theory
    d. cross-excitation theory

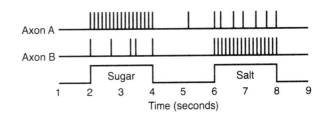

58. Suppose a physiologist simultaneously recorded nerve impulses from two different axons, *A* and *B,* in the gustatory system. She exposed the taste receptors to a weak sugar solution, then to a weak salt solution, obtaining the results shown above. Each vertical bar stands for one nerve impulse. These findings would be most consistent with:
    a. Fechner's law.
    b. signal-detection theory.
    c. pattern theory.
    d. specificity theory.

59. Which of the following is currently accepted as an explanation of how the human nervous system encodes qualitative differences in sensations?
    a. Different sensory qualities are signaled by different neurons.
    b. Different sensory qualities are signaled by different patterns of activity across a set of neurons.
    c. both a and b
    d. none of the above

60. Kinesthetic receptors provide information about:
    a. skeletal muscle activity.
    b. the position of the body in space.
    c. passive rotation of the body.
    d. all of the above

61. The receptors that signal rotation of the head are found in the:
    a. auditory nerves.
    b. joints of the neck.
    c. semicircular canals.
    d. cerebellum.

62. A collective term for information that comes from receptors in the skeletal muscles, tendons, and joints is:
    a. somesthesis.
    b. kinesthesis.
    c. the vestibular sense.
    d. the gravitational sense.

63. A major function of the semicircular canal system is to:
    a. prevent nausea when the head moves too quickly.
    b. allow comparison of head movement with simultaneous movement of the eyes.
    c. signal the body's position relative to gravity.
    d. help to control the skeletal musculature of the body.

64. The semicircular canals signal:
    a. the position of the head when a person is at rest.
    b. the position of the head relative to the rest of the body.
    c. the motion of the head when it rotates.
    d. the position of the eyes as the head rotates.

65. The semicircular canals provide information about the rotation of the head via a mechanism that involves:
    a. receptor hair cells that fire when bent by the movement of a viscous liquid.
    b. the integration of information from three semicircular canals oriented differently from one another in space.
    c. both a and b.
    d. neither a nor b.

66. The best two-point discrimination, with the lowest thresholds, would be obtained if the skin is tested on the:
    a. underside of the forearm.
    b. thigh.
    c. lips.
    d. middle of the back.

67. Most psychologists believe that there are at least _____ different skin sensations. They are _____.
    a. 3; pressure, temperature, pain
    b. 3; pressure, warmth, cold
    c. 4; pressure, itch, temperature, pain
    d. 4; pressure, warmth, cold, pain

68. Most taste buds are located:
    a. in the cheeks.
    b. on the roof of the mouth.
    c. in the throat.
    d. on the tongue.

69. According to most investigators, how many primary taste qualities can we experience?
    a. 3
    b. 4
    c. 5
    d. 6

Answer: c
A survey of the senses
p. 183

70. The basic taste qualities are:
    a. cool, cold, warm, hot.
    b. sour, spicy, bland, sweet.
    c. sweet, salty, bitter, sour.
    d. none of the above

Answer: a
A survey of the senses
p. 183

71. Why does sugar taste sweet and vinegar taste sour? According to specificity theory:
    a. they activate different fibers that carry the information to the brain.
    b. the threshold for sour is lower than the threshold for sweet tastes.
    c. the size of the jnds for sugar are smaller than those for vinegar.
    d. they trigger different patterns of nerve impulses, generating a type of taste code, analogous to the bar codes on consumer products.

Answer: b
A survey of the senses
p. 183

72. Why does NutraSweet taste a lot like sugar? According to specificity theory:
    a. they have the same chemical structure.
    b. they both stimulate "sugar-best fibers."
    c. they both stimulate a variety of different taste receptors.
    d. for both substances, the intensity of taste sensation increases in proportion to the logarithm of the solution's concentration.

Answer: b
A survey of the senses
p. 183

73. Tonic water tastes bitter because the quinine in it activates:
    a. "sweet-best" and "sour-best" fibers in roughly equal amounts.
    b. "bitter-best" fibers more than any other fiber type.
    c. all four types of taste fibers in roughly equal amounts.
    d. the salivary glands.

Answer: c
A survey of the senses
p. 183

74. According to specificity theory, why might the fairly high concentration of the artificial sweetner saccharine taste somewhat bitter as well as sweet?
    a. because at high concentrations all sweet substances taste bitter
    b. because Fechner's law fails to apply at high concentrations
    c. because saccharine stimulates more than one kind of taste fiber
    d. because sweet fibers respond only to purely sweet substances, not to mixtures

Answer: b
A survey of the senses
p. 184

75. A 2 percent solution of sugar is given repeatedly to a subject. The subject reports that over time the sugar tastes less and less sweet. This is an example of:
    a. sensory interaction.
    b. sensory adaptation.
    c. Weber's law.
    d. Fechner's law.

76. The sensory experience that will be elicited by a specific taste stimulus depends on:
    a. which other sensory modalities are also excited by that stimulus.
    b. the interaction of that stimulus with other co-occurring taste stimuli.
    c. how often that stimulus has been applied over the recent past.
    d. all of the above

77. Which of the following human senses involves distal stimuli in the form of chemicals suspended in the air around us?
    a. vision
    b. olfaction
    c. audition
    d. all of the above

78. The pepperoni on pizza tastes like it does because:
    a. it activates sweet and salt receptors in about equal ratio.
    b. we smell it even though it is in our mouth.
    c. we have olfactory images of how it smells in our unconscious memory.
    d. we are insensitive to the bitter chemicals it contains.

79. Although humans are less competent at assessing odors than many other land-dwelling animals, we are capable of using our olfactory sense effectively in many situations. Which of the following is not within the range of human olfactory abilities?
    a. as young adults, identifying the gender of the person wearing clothing over 24 hours without deodorants or other masking odors
    b. as babies, identifying the breast odor of one's own mother compared to the breast odors of other women
    c. as young adults, distinguishing between different types of strong emotional responses in the people around us
    d. as babies, detecting the underarm odors of one's own mother in clothing worn 24 hours without deodorants or other masking odors

80. A pheromone is:
    a. any olfactory stimulus that has a specific meaning for a given organism, such as carrion for a hyena.
    b. a special chemical substance secreted by a given organism that produces a particular reaction in another member of the same species.
    c. any chemical substance, such as sweat, that provides a distinct olfactory stimulus for another member of the same species.
    d. a built-in, species-specific signal that advertizes sexual receptivity.

81. Rats working in a Skinner box are exposed to air taken from the vicinity of a group of rats that suffered electric shock. What will be the probable result?
    a. the rats will exhibit aggressive behaviors
    b. there will be no effect
    c. the rats will exhibit fear
    d. none of the above

82. The vomeronasal organ is also known as:
    a. the emotional eye.
    b. the sexual nose.
    c. the sexual eye.
    d. the emotional nose.

83. Which of the following types of people are most sensitive to musky compounds similar to those secreted by boars (i.e., male pigs)?
    a. young boys
    b. young girls
    c. mature men
    d. mature women

84. Which of the following lines of research is most relevant to advertising a new aftershave?
    a. gender differences in sensitivity to boar's musk
    b. body odor effects on menstrual synchrony
    c. the effects of pheromones on sexual maturation
    d. territorial marking with urine by dogs

85. A perfume chemist should be most interested in which of the following lines of research?
    a. the close relationship between taste and smell
    b. menstrual synchrony arising from body odors
    c. gender differences in sensitivity to boar's musk
    d. accident victims who are anosmic

86. In hearing, the distal stimulus is:
    a. the change in sound pressure level at the eardrum.
    b. the event that causes sound waves to be transmitted through air.
    c. the vibrations in the fluid inside of the cochlea.
    d. the wavelike movements of the basilar membrane.

87. Wavelength refers to:
    a. the maximum height of a wave crest in a sound wave.
    b. the distance between successive wave crests in a sound wave.
    c. the number of sound waves per second.
    d. the pitch of a sound wave.

Answer: c
A survey of the senses
p. 187

88. Two sound waves are equal in amplitude but differ in frequency. The two sounds produced by these waves:
    a. will differ in loudness.
    b. will differ in decibel level.
    c. will differ in pitch.
    d. will differ in complexity.

Answer: a
A survey of the senses
p. 187

89. Two sound waves are generated. The second has a larger amplitude but a lower frequency than the first. The second sound will be perceived as:
    a. louder and lower pitched than the first.
    b. louder and higher pitched than the first.
    c. softer and lower pitched than the first.
    d. softer and higher pitched than the first.

Answer: b
A survey of the senses
p. 187

90. The amplitude of a sound wave:
    a. is inversely proportional to the sound wave's wavelength.
    b. corresponds to the psychological dimension of loudness.
    c. represents the distance between successive crests of the sound wave.
    d. is measured in units termed hertz.

Answer: b
A survey of the senses
p. 188

91. The average range of hearing in normal young adults is roughly:
    a. 4 to 40,000 hertz.
    b. 20 to 20,000 hertz.
    c. 100 to 100,000 hertz.
    d. 30 to 6,000 hertz.

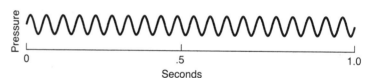

Answer: a
A survey of the senses
p. 188

92. The accompanying graph represents well a:
    a. simple sound at about the lowest frequency people can hear.
    b. simple sound at about the highest frequency people can hear.
    c. complex sound at about the lowest frequency people can hear.
    d. complex sound at about the highest frequency people can hear.
    e. There is no way to answer this question, given the above data.

Answer: c
A survey of the senses
p. 188

93. Below are frequency ranges for several individuals. Which is most likely to be the hearing range of an elderly person?
    a. 4 to 40,000 hertz
    b. 20 to 20,000 hertz
    c. 30 to 10,000 hertz
    d. 1,000 to 20,000 hertz

Answer: b
A survey of the senses
p. 190

94. Movements of the eardrum are changed into patterns of neural activity in the:
    a. pinna.
    b. cochlea.
    c. stirrup.
    d. middle ear.

95. Which of the following is not a transducer?
    a.   the eardrum
    b.   the rods and cones
    c.   the olfactory receptors
    d.   the taste buds

96. From the outside of the body inward, a sound wave travels from:
    a.   the external ear, to the cochlea, then to the ossicles.
    b.   the eardrum, to the ossicles, then to the cochlea.
    c.   the ossicles, to the eardrum, then to the oval window.
    d.   the ossicles, to the oval window, then to the eardrum.

97. The eardrum is _____ the oval window, which causes vibrations in the fluid of the cochlea. This is biologically adaptive because it _____.
    a.   20 times smaller than; protects the eardrum from excess pressure
    b.   20 times larger than; amplifyies the physical stimulus
    c.   roughly the same size as; transmits the appropriate proximal stimulus to the receptors
    d.   similar in shape to; transmits high amplitude wave forms to the cochlea

98. The auditory receptors are located in the:
    a.   eardrum.
    b.   ossicles.
    c.   middle ear.
    d.   cochlea.

99. According to place theory, what structure in the human ear moves in response to sound, causing different hair cells to bend and allowing our perceptions of different sound frequencies?
    a.   the ossicles
    b.   the eardrum
    c.   the oval window
    d.   the basilar membrane

100. The idea that different sound frequencies trigger different neurons is called:
    a.   frequency theory.
    b.   volley theory.
    c.   Young-Helmholtz theory.
    d.   place theory.

101. Different frequencies of sound waves maximally deform different parts of the basilar membrane, a phenomenon that supports:
    a.   opponent-process theory.
    b.   impulse frequency theory.
    c.   Fechner's law.
    d.   place theory.
    e.   the all-or-none law.

Answer: b
A survey of the senses
p. 191

102. The place theory is particularly useful in explaining the phenomena of:
    a. loudness.
    b. pitch.
    c. saturation.
    d. brightness.
    e. afterimages.

Answer: b
A survey of the senses
p. 191

103. When a sound stimulus is transmitted to the cochlea:
    a. for low-frequency sound, only one place on the basilar membrane vibrates.
    b. for high-frequency sound, the whole basilar membrane moves, but one place moves maximally.
    c. the frequency of vibration of the basilar membrane always equals the frequency of the sound wave.
    d. the frequency of vibration of the basilar membrane never equals the frequency of the sound wave

Answer: a
A survey of the senses
p. 191

104. Compare two tones of 1,000 hertz and 500 hertz. What can we say about the movement of the basilar membrane in response to these tones?
    a. The peak of the vibratory wave will be closer to the oval window for the 1,000-hertz tone than for the 500-hertz tone.
    b. The peak of the vibratory wave will be closer to the oval window for the 500-hertz tone than for the 1,000-hertz tone.
    c. There will be a peak in the vibratory wave for the 500-hertz tone; but there will be no such peak for the 1,000-hertz tone, which affects the entire membrane equally.
    d. There will be a peak in the vibratory wave for the 1,000-hertz tone; but there will be no such peak for the 500-hertz tone, which affects the entire membrane equally.

Answer: a
A survey of the senses
p. 191

105. According to the place theory of pitch, high frequency tones cause the basilar membrane to vibrate maximally:
    a. in the portion closest to the oval window.
    b. in the portion farthest from the oval window.
    c. in the middle of the membrane.
    d. in the portion without hair cells.

Answer: d
A survey of the senses
p. 192

106. The place theory of pitch is inconsistent with the finding that:
    a. high-frequency tones cause peak deformations close to the oval window, while tones of lower frequencies have their peaks farther away from this structure.
    b. for high frequency tones, the site of peak deformation along the basilar membrane does not correspond to stimulus characteristics.
    c. normal adults can discriminate the frequencies of tones considerably higher than 500 hertz.
    d. for low frequency sounds, the basilar membrane is deformed almost equally along its entire length.

107. Frequency coding in sensory systems refers to:
    a. decoding of messages by the parietal, temporal, and occipital lobes.
    b. encoding of stimulus by the frequency of neuronal firing.
    c. special tuning of sensory receptors to specific sound frequencies.
    d. none of the above

108. At low frequencies (e. g., below 50 hertz), the entire basilar membrane deforms almost equally, posing a problem for the place theory of pitch. To account for our ability to sense low frequency sounds, another mechanism involves:
    a. the frequency of neural impulse firing.
    b. the dilation of the inner ear.
    c. the activation of the semicircular canals.
    d. all of the above

109. The perceived pitch of an auditory stimulus depends upon:
    a. for high frequency sounds, the place on the basilar membrane that is maximally deflected by the auditory stimulus.
    b. for low frequency sounds, the frequency of impulses in the auditory nerve generated by the auditory stimulus.
    c. both a and b
    d. none of the above

110. A 200-hertz tone is sounded continuously. Under these circumstances, one would expect:
    a. a frequency of impulse firing in the auditory nerve of approximately 200 hertz.
    b. the entire basilar membrane to vibrate at an average of 200 hertz, with one area vibrating at a substantially faster rate.
    c. one place in the basilar membrane to undergo large deflection, whereas adjacent places will not be deflected.
    d. a vibratory wave to travel along the basilar membrane at a frequency of approximately 200 hertz.

111. Which of the following statements is false?
    a. Pitch perception involves two separate mechanisms.
    b. High frequency sounds above 20,000 Hz are typically out of the range of human hearing.
    c. Below 400 hertz neural, frequency coding is unlikely to occur.
    d. Humans easily discriminate between 1,000 and 2,000 hertz sounds.

112. The amplitude of a sound wave, which corresponds to its intensity, is measured in:
    a. Hertz.
    b. wavelengths.
    c. decibels.
    d. cycles per second.

113. Which of the following characteristics of light is the most important determinant of our sense of color?
    a. intensity
    b. accommodation
    c. saturation
    d. wavelength

114. An individual sees 2 equal-sized trees. One tree is 100 feet away from the person, and the other is only 40 feet away. The retinal image of the closer tree will be _____ that of the farther tree.
    a. larger than
    b. smaller than
    c. equal to
    d. reversed in relation to

115. The lens in the human eye:
    a. transduces light energy into neural impulses.
    b. controls the amount of light entering the eye.
    c. is the device responsible for accommodation.
    d. represents the proximal stimulus for vision.

116. The lens in the human eye flattens for objects at a distance, and thickens for objects nearby. This process is called:
    a. refraction.
    b. accommodation.
    c. pupillary contraction.
    d. convergence.

117. Which of the following is a receptor for visual sensations?
    a. a cone cell
    b. a bipolar cell
    c. a ganglion cell
    d. all of the above

118. In what order does visual information travel to the brain?
    a. photoreceptor, bipolar cell, ganglion cell
    b. photoreceptor, ganglion cell, bipolar cell
    c. bipolar cell, ganglion cell, photoreceptor
    d. bipolar cell, photoreceptor, ganglion cell
    e. bipolar cell, rod, cone

119. As they travel toward the receptors in the retina of the human eye, light rays first pass through a layer of:
    a. ganglion cells.
    b. bipolar cells.
    c. foveal cells.
    d. rods and cones.

Answer: d
Vision
p. 195

120. Which of the following is not a receptor organ or cell?
    a. hair cells of the semicircular canal
    b. taste buds
    c. cochlea
    d. optic nerve

Answer: a
Vision
p. 195

121. The neural links that relay the messages of the receptors are the:
    a. bipolar and the ganglion cells.
    b. rods and the cones.
    c. retina and the lens.
    d. cornea and the optic nerve.

Answer: d
Vision
p. 195

122. The optic nerve consists of the axons of:
    a. rod cells.
    b. cone cells.
    c. bipolar cells.
    d. ganglion cells.

Answer: b
Vision
p. 195

123. The optic nerve is composed of:
    a. the dendrites of ganglion cells.
    b. the axons of ganglion cells.
    c. the dendrites of cone cells.
    d. the axons of rod cells.

Answer: d
Vision
p. 195

124. Which of the following is true regarding the distribution of rods and cones in the retina?
    a. Both rods and cones increase in density as one progresses from the fovea to the periphery.
    b. Rods are most plentiful at the fovea, while cones are most plentiful at the periphery.
    c. Both rods and cones are absent at the site where the optic nerve leaves the retina.
    d. all of the above

Answer: a
Vision
p. 195

125. The blind spot on the retina is where:
    a. there are no receptors at all.
    b. there are only cones.
    c. there are only rods.
    d. there are both rods and cones.

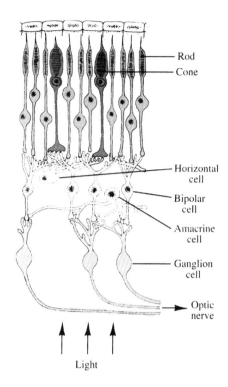

Rod
Cone
Horizontal cell
Bipolar cell
Amacrine cell
Ganglion cell
Optic nerve

Light

Answer: d
Vision
p. 195

126. What is wrong with the accompanying diagram of the human retina?
    a. There should be more cones than there are rods.
    b. The axons of the bipolar cells should exit the eye as the optic nerve.
    c. There should be a layer of horizontal cells on each side of the receptors.
    d. The light is shown coming in from the wrong direction.

Answer: b
Vision
p. 195

127. The duplex theory of vision involves the idea that we have:
    a. two eyes, each with a slightly different view of the world.
    b. both rods and conesin the retinas of our eyes.
    c. ganglion cells that are activated when lights go on and others that are activated when lights go off.
    d. better vision when our eyes have saccadic movement than when our eyes are absolutely motionless.

Answer: a
Vision
p. 195

128. We cannot see colors in very dim light because:
    a. receptors for color are not sensitive to dim light.
    b. lateral inhibition is activated.
    c. opponent processes cannot operate at low levels of light.
    d. all of the above

Answer: c
Vision
p. 196

129. An optometrist asks you to read the letters on an eye chart in order to determine whether or not you have the ability to distinguish between separate points that are projected onto your retina. Your ability to make such distinctions is known as:
    a. retinal disparity.
    b. perceptual constancy.
    c. visual acuity.
    d. the duplicity theory of vision.
    e. none of the above

130. Animals that live in caves and thus are exposed to only low-intensity light would be expected to have:
    a. a large number of rod-type visual receptors.
    b. very good color vision.
    c. both a and b.
    d. neither a nor b.

131. We can discriminate between two touches close together on our fingertips more easily than on the middle of our back. This difference in two-point discrimination threshold is most like:
    a. hearing high frequency sounds via vibrations at one end of the basilar membrane and low frequency sounds via vibrations at the other end.
    b. visual acuity being far better at the fovea than in the peripheral retina.
    c. some small spots on the skin being more sensitive to pressure, others to cold.
    d. having color vision only with high levels of illumination, achromatic vision with much lower levels.

132. Assume that scientists have collected the following data regarding the density of visual receptors for two areas, *A* and *B*, in the retina of an organism. Area *A* contains 100 receptors per square millimeter and Area *B* contains 1,000 receptors per square millimeter. Which of the following is true?
    a. This organism would show greater visual acuity for stimuli activating Area *A*.
    b. This organism would show greater visual acuity for stimuli activating Area *B*.
    c. This is impossible to determine since visual acuity is unrelated to the density of receptors.
    d. The organism would show equal acuity in both areas since the maximal visual acuity has been determined to exist for receptive areas containing as few as 50 receptors per square millimeter.

133. In order to maximize visual acuity in a normally illuminated classroom, you should:
    a. stare slightly away from the thing that you are trying to see.
    b. use only one eye at a time to reduce interocular rivalry.
    c. reduce the luminance of the room in order to activate the more sensitive rod system.
    d. look directly at the objects in the room.

134. In order to maximize visual acuity at noon, you should:
    a. stare slightly away from the object that you are trying to see.
    b. use only one eye at a time to reduce interocular rivalry.
    c. reduce luminance in order to activate the more sensitive rod system.
    d. look directly at the objects around you.
    e. dilate your pupils.

135. An object seen only out of the corner of the eye, in the peripheral vision:
     a. is best seen in infrared light.
     b. can only be seen at night.
     c. activates the opponent-color system.
     d. primarily stimulates rods.

136. If one wants to best see an object in dim light conditions, one should orient one's eyes so that the object projects an image on:
     a. the fovea of the retina.
     b. the periphery of the retina.
     c. the area where the optic nerve exits the retina.
     d. cone-shaped receptors.

137. In determining the spectral sensitivity curve for rods, a light is projected on the periphery of the retinal surface:
     a. because more direct light would disrupt the orderly relationship between amplitude and wavelength.
     b. to ensure that only rod receptors are activated by the light stimulus.
     c. since this involves testing an area with relatively poor visual acuity, and this is the case at the periphery of the retina.
     d. because light elsewhere would elicit color sensations, confounding the results in spectral sensitivity testing.

138. We ask a research participant to tell us when he can see a dim light, varying the intensity until he reports that he just barely sees it. We then record the luminance level. Now, we change the wavelength and repeat the experiment. Finally, we draw a figure, plotting sensitivity wavelength. This figure is a function know as:
     a. dark adaptation curve.
     b. spectral sensitivity curve.
     c. ROC curve.
     d. sensory adaptation curve.

139. A spectral sensitivity curve shows:
     a. the sensitivity to various wavelengths of light.
     b. which color will be perceived as the wavelength of a light is systematically altered.
     c. the visual acuity of the rods relative to the cones of the human eye.
     d. the distribution of rods and cones on the surface of the retina.

140. Spectral sensitivity curves for rods and cones:
     a. are the same, but the cone curve has three components.
     b. overlap, but cones are more sensitive to longer wavelength light.
     c. are in nonoverlapping parts of the visible spectrum.
     d. none of the above

141. In the rods and cones of the human eye, transduction of light energy into neural signals is best described as a _____ process.
    a. mechanical
    b. electrical
    c. chemical
    d. none of the above

142. The energy that we perceive as light can be described as a waveform with intensity corresponding to our perception of _____ and wavelength corresponding to our perception of _____.
    a. color; saturation
    b. brightness; color
    c. saturation; color
    d. color; brightness

143. When light strikes the rods, it begins a chemical breakdown of a visual pigment called:
    a. the bromide molecule.
    b. rhodopsin.
    c. achromaton.
    d. photodopsin.

144. Looking directly at the sun or at a welding arc is likely to:
    a. activate receptors in the fovea.
    b. cause sensory adaptation.
    c. reduce visual acuity.
    d. all of the above

145. Which of the following neurophysiological recordings from a single neuron best illustrates the phenomenon of adaptation? Note: Each vertical line represents one nerve impulse.

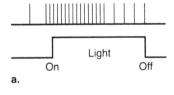
a.

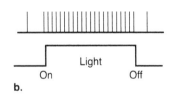
b.

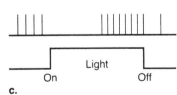
c.

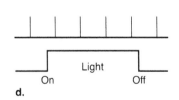
d.

146. In your textbook the term "stabilized image" refers to:
    a. the effects of normal fixation.
    b. the compensatory effect produced by stabilizing visual input through adjustments of the vestibular system.
    c. the visual effect of manipulating size, angle of regard, and illumination.
    d. the adaptation effect produced by moving the entire visual stimulus along with the moving eye.

147. What major experimental use can be made of a tiny slide projector that attaches to a contact lens?

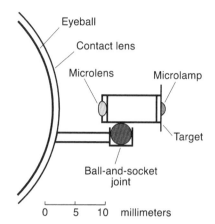

a. measurement of the bleaching of rhodopsin in the light
b. measurement of tiny eye movements
c. stabilization of an image on the retina
d. determination of the position of the optic nerve as it leaves the retina

148. As a result of nervous system damage, a patient has lost the ability to move his eyes. The head of the patient is fixed in space and the patient stares at a visual pattern. After a time:
    a. the color of the stimulus will shift to the violet portion of the visual spectrum.
    b. the pattern will no longer be perceived.
    c. the stimulus will appear to be brighter than it was orginally.
    d. the pattern will seem to move erratically.

149. The first time you see a friend's new light blue car, it is parked against a black wall. Later, you see the same car parked against a white backdrop at the same time of day. You comment that the car seemed to be much brighter the last time you saw it. This is an example of:
    a. brightness contrast.
    b. adaptation.
    c. temporal interaction.
    d. lightness constancy.

150. A gray piece of cardboard is placed next to the following stimuli: 1 cm away from a black patch, 10 cm away from a black patch, and then immediately adjacent to a white patch. The gray patch will:
    a. look brightest when placed 1 cm away from the black patch.
    b. look brightest when placed 10 cm away from the black patch.
    c. look brightest when placed immediately adjacent to the white patch.
    d. will look equally bright when placed next to the black patch, regardless of the distance.

151. The visual system sharpens fuzzy boundaries by creating sharp boundaries where physically, none are present. This effect is exemplified by:
  a. brightness contrast.
      b. the stabilized image.
      c. Mach bands.
      d. the Purkinje effect.

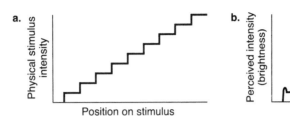

152. The accompanying graphs best illustrate the phenomenon of:
      a. contrast effects.
      b. adaptation effects.
      c. duplex theory.
      d. opponent-process theory.

153. The physiological basis of brightness contrast is:
      a. Mach bands.
      b. lateral inhibition.
      c. receptive field excitation.
      d. inhibition of ganglion cells by bipolar cells.

154. The physiological basis of brightness contrast is:
      a. inhibition of rods by cones.
      b. lateral inhibition.
      c. receptive field excitation.
      d. inhibition of ganglion cells by bipolar cells.

155. The physiological mechanism that underlies brightness contrast is possible because:
      a. adjacent cells in the visual system are mutually excitatory.
      b. bright lights inhibit the firing of retinal cells.
      c. the absence of light inhibits cell firing in the visual system.
      d. adjacent cells in the visual system are mutually inhibitory.

156. The accompanying diagram of a receptive field for a retinal ganglion cell is most relevant to:
    a. contrast efffects and lateral inhibition.
    b. adaptation effects and opponent-process theory.
    c. duplex theory and different types of retinal receptors.
    d. Fechner's law and psychophysical scaling.

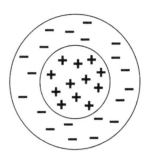

157. Assume that cell *A* of the visual system laterally inhibits the output of an adjacent cell *B*. This is the basis of brightness contrast because:
    a. the more cell *A* is excited, the more its excitation will spread to cell *B*.
    b. the more cell *A* is excited, the greater the lateral inhibition effect.
    c. the more cell *A* is excited, the more it will reduce the receptive field of cell *B*.
    d. none of the above

158. Hue:
    a. varies with the wavelength of light.
    b. is the appropriate term for both chromatic and achromatic colors.
    c. describes a physical property of a light stimulus.
    d. all of the above

159. The greater the saturation, the greater:
    a. the extent to which a color has one of the four unique hues.
    b. the extent to which a color is mixed with gray.
    c. the extent to which a color can be described by a point in the color solid.
    d. the extent to which a color is chromatic rather than achromatic.

160. The greater the saturation, the greater the extent to which a color:
    a. has one of the four unique hues.
    b. is mixed with gray.
    c. can be described as a point in the color solid.
    d. is chromatic rather than achromatic.

161. The colors that represent the extremes for the brightness dimension in a "color solid" are:
    a. gray and blue.
    b. white and black.
    c. yellow and green.
    d. red and blue.

Answer: a
Vision
p. 203

162. When one set of wavelengths is taken away from another set, the resulting mixture is called a(n):
    a. subtractive mixture.
    b. additive mixture.
    c. complementary mixture.
    d. none of the above

Answer: a
Vision
p. 202

163. To have maximal saturation:
    a. a color's brightness has to be at a medium value.
    b. a color's brightness has to be at its maximum value.
    c. a color's hue has to be at its maximum value.
    d. a color's hue should be as unique as possible.

Answer: c
Vision
p. 203

164. A white light is passed through a filter. The white light now appears blue. This occurs because:
    a. the filter imparts a color to previously white light.
    b. the filter has added certain wavelengths to the previously white light.
    c. the filter has removed certain wavelengths from the white light.
    d. in essence, we have performed an additive mixture experiment.

Answer: d
Vision
p. 204

165. All of the following are examples of additive color mixtures except:
    a. color printing.
    b. color television.
    c. human color vision.
    d. mixing of crayons.

Answer: b
Vision
p. 205

166. Any wavelength will stimulate:
    a. all four color receptors, but will do so unequally.
    b. all three color receptors, but will do so unequally.
    c. only one or two of the four color receptors.
    d. only one or two of the three color receptors.

Answer: c
Vision
p. 202

167. Persons with normal color vision can typically distinguish over __________ different shades of colors.
    a. one hundred
    b. three thousand
    c. seven million
    d. five trillion

Answer: c
Vision
p. 206

168. An additive color mix is made between two complementary colors. The resultant mixed color:
    a. will look white.
    b. will look black.
    c. will look gray.
    d. The color of the mixture will depend on the hues of the two components.

Answer: a
Vision
p. 206

169. Complementary colors:
    a. result in desaturation when additively mixed.
    b. represent the saturation point for another color.
    c. result from passing a single color through a filter.
    d. result in a gray stimulus in a subtractive mixture.

Answer: b
Vision
p. 206

170. Unique green is additively mixed with an orange exactly midway between unique red and unique yellow. The resulting mixture will be:
    a. a desaturated orange.
    b. a desaturated yellow.
    c. a desaturated blue.
    d. gray.

Answer: a
Vision
p. 207

171. According to opponent-process theory, what color is perceived when there is excitation of both blue and red systems, with concomitant inhibition of their antagonists?
    a. violet
    b. black
    c. achromatic
    d. white

Answer: c
Vision
p. 207

172. The negative afterimage of a violet color is:
    a. purplish blue.
    b. black.
    c. greenish yellow.
    d. orange.

Answer: b
Vision
p. 207

173. A _____ has the complementary hue and the opposite brightness of the original stimulus.
    a. simultaneous color contrast
    b. negative afterimage
    c. unique color
    d. subtractive mixture

Answer: a
Vision
p. 207

174. The negative afterimage of a greenish-yellow square is:
    a. a violet-colored square.
    b. a yellow-orange square.
    c. a black circle.
    d. a fog of red which occupies the entire visual field.

Answer: a
Vision
p. 205

175. Televisions are designed in a way that is consistent with the Young-Helmholtz theory of color vision. Specifically, a television image is composed of small dots of colors that seem to blend together to form visual images in a variety of colors. What colors are these dots?
    a. red, green, and blue
    b. red, yellow, and blue
    c. red, green, yellow, and blue
    d. red, yellow, black, and blue

<table>
<tr><td>

Answer: d
Vision
p. 207

</td><td>

176. According to Ewald Hering and others, red is to green as blue is to:
    a. violet.
    b. white.
    c. black.
    d. yellow.

</td></tr>
</table>

Answer: d
Vision
p. 207

177. According to opponent-process theory, a visual stimulus that results in a perfect balance of both red-green and yellow-blue systems would be perceived as:
    a. mixed colors.
    b. blankness.
    c. vividly colorful.
    d. achromatic.

Answer: d
Vision
p. 207

178. In the theory developed by Hurvich and Jameson there are _____ primary color qualities, which are organized in three opponent-process pairs.
    a. 3
    b. 10
    c. 9
    d. 6

Answer: d
Vision
p. 209

179. If you have the most common kind of color blindness, you are:
    a. one of about every million people.
    b. likely to see everything as shades of yellow.
    c. unable to distinguish blue from red.
    d. more likely to be male than female.
    e. all of the above

Answer: d
Vision
p. 209

180. According to your textbook authors, the discovery of neural cells that act as feature detectors has been one of the most exciting achievements in visual physiology in recent history. What technique(s) was(were) used in this research?
    a. signal detection
    b. PET scans and MRIs
    c. controlled drug testing
    d. electrophysiological recording

Answer: b
Vision
p. 210

181. The so-called "bug detectors" in the visual systems of frogs occur at the level of the:
    a. receptors.
    b. ganglion cells.
    c. superior colliculus.
    d. optic tectum.

Answer: c
Vision
p. 210

182. The receptive field of a cell includes:
    a. the total area of a receptor's surface, the stimulation of which leads to an increase of that cell's firing.
    b. the total area of a receptor's surface, the stimulation of which leads to a decrease of that cell's firing.
    c. the total area of a receptor's surface, the stimulation of which leads to either a decrease or increase of that cell's firing.
    d. the total area on a receptor's surface, which represents the transition zone from stimulation to excitation effects.

Answer: d
Vision
p. 210

183. Regardless of the intensity of light projected onto a particular spot of the retina, no electrical responses are elicited in a specific cell. That retinal spot is outside of that cell's:
    a. field potential.
    b. brightness-contrast zone.
    c. zone of lateral inhibition.
    d. receptive field.

Answer: d
Vision
p. 210

184. In cats, monkeys, and humans, most visual analysis occurs at the level of the:
    a. receptors.
    b. optic nerve.
    c. lateral geniculate nucleus.
    d. visual cortex.

Answer: d
Vision
p. 211

185. In the cats studied by Hubel and Wiesel, feature detectors in the visual cortex responded optimally to:
    a. small, dark objects that moved like bugs.
    b. chromatic changes in visual stimuli.
    c. visual images at specific brightness levels.
    d. lines at specific orientations.

Answer: d
Vision
p. 211

186. The neurons in the visual cortex of normal cats will probably respond best to:
    a. diffuse lighting of the entire visual field.
    b. small circular spots of light on specific areas of the retina.
    c. complex learned shapes like the outline of another cat.
    d. borders and lines at specific orientations.

Answer: d
Vision
p. 211

187. Adaptations of feature detectors in the human visual system are most likely to result in perception of:
    a. erratically moving bugs after staring at a blank wall.
    b. small moving dots after staring at a large moving circle.
    c. moving lines of various orientations after staring at stationary lines.
    d. an upward moving afterimage after staring at a brightly lit waterfall.

Answer: d
Vision
p. 212

188. Imagine that you are using an electrophysiological recording procedure to investigate the functioning of the monkey visual system. You are least likely to locate cortical cells that respond optimally to:
    a. lines of specific orientation.
    b. objects that move in specific directions.
    c. pictures of monkey hands.
    d. images of tree branches.

CHAPTER 6 | Perception

Answer: c
The problem of perception
p. 217

1. The fundamental issue in the study of perception is how a particular stimulus is:
   a. judged as a particular kind of object.
   b. composed of smaller parts.
   c. seen or otherwise judged as an object.
   d. associated with other, similar, stimuli.

Answer: b
The problem of perception
p. 217

2. The field of perception addresses:
   a. how we learn what name goes with what object.
   b. how we determine which aspects of what we're looking at go together to form an object.
   c. how we detect brightness.
   d. how we register colors.

Answer: c
The perception of depth
p. 218

3. _____ are the features of a stimulus situation that allow the observer to judge the physical distance of the object from the observer or from other objects.
   a. Transposition cues
   b. Subjective contours
   c. Depth cues
   d. a and b

Answer: c
The perception of depth
pp. 218–219

4. Suppose the distance between the eyes was substantially decreased, so that the two eyes touched in the middle of the forehead. This change would have the effect of:
   a. increasing binocular disparity.
   b. enhancing the effect of motion parallax.
   c. decreasing the binocular disparity.
   d. decreasing the effect of motion parallax.

Answer: a
The perception of depth
pp. 218–219

Answer: b
The perception of depth
pp. 218–219

Answer: c
The perception of depth
pp. 218–219

Answer: d
The perception of depth
pp. 219–219

Answer: a
The perception of depth
pp. 218–219

Answer: c
The perception of depth
pp. 218–219

Answer: a
The perception of depth
pp. 218–219

Answer: e
The perception of depth
pp. 219–221

5. Suppose the distance between the eyes was significantly increased. This would have the effect of:
   a. increasing binocular disparity.
   b. decreasing binocular disparity.
   c. enhancing the effect of motion parallax.
   d. decreasing the effect of motion parallax.

6. Binocular disparity:
   a. is a depth cue used even by those blind in one eye.
   b. occurs because the retina of each eye receives a different image.
   c. is responsible for good continuation.
   d. both b and c

7. Binocular disparity means that:
   a. there is feedback from the strain on the eye muscles.
   b. gradients of texture cannot be depth perception cues.
   c. the images falling on the retinas of each eye differ slightly.
   d. some depth perception cues conflict.
   e. figure-ground relations don't always fit our expectancies.

8. Which of the following requires the use of two eyes?
   a. motion parallax
   b. relative size
   c. optic flow
   d. binocular disparity

9. Binocular disparity exists because:
   a. our eyes are about two inches apart.
   b. most people tend to see somewhat better in their right eye.
   c. many people are somewhat nearsighted.
   d. the cornea is not a perfect hemisphere.
   e. the retina is not perfectly flat.

10. Which of the following is a binocular cue of depth?
   a. texture gradients
   b. motion parallax
   c. disparity
   d. interposition

11. Devices that make photographs appear three-dimensional do so by:
   a. presenting slightly different images to each eye.
   b. presenting slightly different images, one right after the other.
   c. slowly moving the photograph toward the viewer.
   d. quickly moving the photograph toward the viewer.

12. A person with only a single eye could perceive depth by using the cue of:
   a. linear perspective.
   b. motion parallax.
   c. texture gradients.
   d. interposition.
   e. all of the above

Answer: d
The perception of depth
p. 219

13. A person who is blind in one eye is likely to have the most trouble in which of the following situations?
    a. seeing depth in a realistic painting of a basket of fruit
    b. seeing apparent movement
    c. seeing details in a fine coin
    d. judging how far away a stationary white cat is in an otherwise dark hallway

Answer: b
The perception of depth
p. 219

14. Pictorial cues include:
    a. motion parallax.
    b. interposition.
    c. binocular disparity.
    d. all of the above

Answer: b
The perception of depth
p. 219

15. Which depth cue is most helpful in determining which of the Mona Lisa's hands is meant to be closest to the viewer?
    a. linear perspective
    b. interposition
    c. texture gradients
    d. disparity
    e. motion parallax

Answer: a
The perception of depth
p. 219

16. If you want to use interposition to indicate that the apples are closer to the viewer than the oranges in your still life, you should:
    a. paint half-moon contours of oranges right next to full, round, apple contours.
    b. make the apples smaller than the oranges.
    c. make the apples larger than the oranges.
    d. paint the apples in brighter colors than the oranges.

Answer: a
The perception of depth
p. 219

17. As you look down a long street, the buildings on the right side of the street seem to be getting closer to the buildings on the left side of the street. This apparent convergence is an example of:
    a. linear perspective.
    b. motion parallax.
    c. binocular disparity.
    d. interposition.

Answer: a
The perception of depth
p. 219

18. As an art class exercise, you have painted identical twins on opposite sides of a canvas. One twin is larger than the other, and the rest of the canvas is just white. Which of the following statements is true?
    a. The viewer will perceive the larger twin as closer because of relative size.
    b. The viewer will perceive the smaller twin as closer because of relative size.
    c. The viewer will perceive the larger twin as closer because of interposition.
    d. The viewer will perceive the smaller twin as closer because of interposition.
    e. The viewer will perceive the larger twin as closer because of texture gradient.

Answer: a
The perception of depth
pp. 219–220

19. When looking down a rocky beach you see individual stones nearby, but farther away you can see only a rough-looking terrain. This example best shows us judging distance from:
    a. texture gradients.
    b. interposition.
    c. shape constancy.
    d. linear perspective.
    e. motion parallax.

Answer: c
The perception of depth
pp. 219–220

20. Suppose you look out over a football stadium. You can see the people nearby as individuals, but in the distance you see only a solid "sea" of blue and white. This example shows how we use _____ to judge distance.
    a. shape constancy
    b. linear perspective
    c. texture gradients
    d. interposition

Answer: a
The perception of depth
pp. 220–221

21. Motion parallax:
    a. makes use of relative movement.
    b. needs sources of information from both eyes.
    c. occurs mostly when we look at two-dimensional stimuli.
    d. is very difficult to demonstrate.

Answer: c
The perception of depth
pp. 220–221

22. Which of the following is a cue for depth?
    a. apparent movement
    b. induced movement
    c. motion parallax
    d. all of the above

Answer: d
The perception of depth
pp. 220–221

23. One of the most effective monocular depth cues is _____, which is absent in pictorial representation but present in real life.
    a. linear perspective
    b. relative size
    c. interposition
    d. motion parallax

Answer: b
The perception of depth
pp. 220–221

24. *A* is farther away from an observer than is *B*. As the observer moves his head from right to left:
    a. *A* will seem to move more quickly than *B* in a direction opposite to that of the observer.
    b. *B* will seem to move more quickly than *A* in a direction opposite to that of the observer.
    c. *A* will seem to move more quickly than *B* in the same direction as that of the observer.
    d. *B* will seem to move more quickly than *A* in the same direction as that of the observer.

Answer: d
The perception of depth
pp. 218–221

25. In basketball it is easier to see how far away the basket is if you: 1) use both eyes and 2) move your head and body with respect to the basket. These two cues to depth are called:
    a. binocular disparity and texture gradients.
    b. interposition and binocular disparity.
    c. texture gradients and apparent (stroboscopic) movement.
    d. binocular disparity and motion parallax.

Answer: d
The perception of depth
p. 221

26. As a passenger, you look out the windshield as the car is backed out of the garage. The texture of the wooden walls seems to move from the periphery of your vision toward the center, a phenomenon called:
    a. linear perspective.
    b. motion parallax.
    c. induced motion.
    d. optic flow.

Answer: c
The perception of depth
p. 221

27. As you drive a car into a garage the texture of the wooden walls seems to move from near the center of your visual field toward your periphery, a phenomenon called:
    a. motion parallax.
    b. induced motion.
    c. optic flow.
    d. linear perspective.

Answer: b
The perception of depth
pp. 220–221

28. As you're sitting in a moving train, looking out the window, it appears that:
    a. things far from the train are moving very quickly in the opposite direction.
    b. things near to the train are moving very quickly in the opposite direction.
    c. things far from the train are moving very quickly in the same direction.
    d. things near to the train are moving very quickly in the same direction.

Answer: b
The perception of depth
p. 222

29. The most likely reason why multiple depth cues are available to us is that:
    a. none of the cues alone is very informative.
    b. different cues are effective under different circumstances.
    c. some of the cues often give misleading information.
    d. There is no good explanation for redundancy in depth perception.

Answer: a
The perception of depth
p. 222

30. Which of the following statements is true?
    a. Some depth cues only work if objects are moving.
    b. Binocular disparity is most informative regarding distant objects.
    c. Texture gradient is informative regarding depth in any context.
    d. all of the above

Answer: c
The perception of movement
pp. 222–223

31. Which of the following statements is false?
    a. There are cells in the visual cortex that fire when a stimulus moves from left to right across the visual field.
    b. There are cells in the visual cortex that fire when a stimulus moves from right to left across the visual field.
    c. We perceive motion only when an image moves across the retina.
    d. Apparent movement can be indistinguishable from real movement.

Answer: d
The perception of movement
p. 223

32. Apparent movement results when:
    a. the head is stationary but an object is moved in the visual field.
    b. an object is held stationary in the visual field but the head is moved.
    c. the head and an object in the visual field are moved at somewhat different speeds.
    d. two points of the visual field are stimulated sequentially at certain intervals.

Answer: b
The perception of movement
p. 223

33. Animated neon signs seem to move even though there is no actual (that is, physical) movement. This illusion is a case of:
    a. induced movement.
    b. apparent movement.
    c. motion parallax.
    d. all of the above

Answer: c
The perception of movement
p. 223

34. A neon sign for a bowling alley has flashing lights that make it seem like a ball has gone down the alley and knocked over some pins. This illusion of motion is called:
    a. induced movement.
    b. motion parallax.
    c. apparent movement.
    d. optic flow.

Answer: b
The perception of movement
p. 223

35. A series of projections of stills can seem to move, as in movies. This is most clearly an example of:
    a. optic flow.
    b. apparent movement.
    c. induced movement.
    d. motion parallax.

Answer: a
The perception of movement
pp. 223–224

36. What would happen if you suddenly had an involuntary twitch of one of your eye muscles, a twitch analogous to the jerks one sometimes has prior to going to sleep?
    a. The world would seem to move.
    b. The world would remain stationary.
    c. There would be a momentary "blank" time in your perceptual experience.
    d. You would experience both motion parallax and optic flow.

Answer: b
The perception of movement
pp. 223–224

37. Why does the world seem to move when you push your eyeball through the side of your eyelid?
    a. Because the retinal receptors have been stimulated both by what you are looking at and the gentle mechanical force of the finger pressing against your lid.
    b. Because your eye has moved without a corresponding signal that a message has been sent out from the brain to the eye muscles.
    c. Because your eye has moved without any corresponding signals that some part of your body is causing your eye to move.
    d. Because you have moved some part of your body voluntarily rather than involuntarily.

Answer: c
The perception of movement
pp. 223–224

38. Under what conditions will the world seem to jump to the right?
    a. You move your eyes to the left.
    b. You move your eyes to the right.
    c. Your eye muscles are paralyzed and you try to move your eyes to the left.
    d. Your eye muscles are paralyzed and you try to move your eyes to the right.

Answer: b
The perception of movement
pp. 223–224

39. As we look from left to right, objects in front of us do not seem to move from right to left because:
    a. there is no relative displacement on the retina.
    b. information regarding voluntary eye movement compensates for information regarding retinal displacement.
    c. there is relative displacement on the retina.
    d. there is no absolute displacement on the retina.

Answer: b
The perception of movement
p. 224

40. Which of the following provides the most convincing evidence that there must be a brain process that serves as a marker that the eyes are scheduled to move a particular amount?
    a. We can perceive the difference between an object that is stationary and one that is moving.
    b. The world seems to jump to the left if, when your eye muscles are paralyzed, you try to move your eyes to the right.
    c. When everything in your visual field is moving in one direction you feel that you are moving in the opposite direction, even though you are really stationary.
    d. When you are moving, objects in the foreground seem to zoom by whereas those farther away seem to move at a more leisurely pace.

Answer: b
The perception of movement
pp. 224–225

41. Two-dimensional spinning spirals appear to be moving toward or away from us because:
    a. of motion parallax.
    b. we have trouble determining which component of what we're currently seeing goes with which component of our previous view.
    c. of optic flow.
    d. of induced motion of the self.

Answer: d
The perception of depth
pp. 218–221, 225

42. Which of the following is not a cue for depth?
    a. binocular disparity
    b. interposition
    c. motion parallax
    d. induced movement

Answer: b
The perception of movement
p. 225

43. A subject stands on a bridge that she perceives as moving in a direction opposite to that of the river below. This is an example of:
    a. apparent movement.
    b. induced movement.
    c. motion parallax.
    d. the Barber pole illusion.

Answer: a
The perception of movement
p. 225

44. Which of the following best illustrates induced movement?
    a. The moon seems to race across the sky on a windy night with a few clouds.
    b. The wagon wheels look like they turn backwards in an old episode of *Death Valley Days*.
    c. It's easy to tell how far away the green is when you walk a few steps back and forth across the fairway.
    d. When you bowl a strike, it always seems like one pin takes a long time to fall.

Answer: a
The perception of movement
p. 225

45. A ball is moving on a table. The table is:
    a. a frame of reference.
    b. the enclosed figure.
    c. a depth cue.
    d. a reversible figure.

Answer: b
The perception of movement
p. 225

46. The moon appears to drift through the clouds. This is an example of:
    a. apparent movement.
    b. induced movement.
    c. motion parallax.
    d. all of the above

Answer: a
The perception of movement
p. 225

47. Seated on a stationary train, you can see out the window another stationary train on the next track. One of the trains begins to move and you aren't sure whether it's yours or the other train. This confusion arises because of:
    a. induced movement.
    b. apparent movement.
    c. motion parallax.
    d. the correspondence problem.

Answer: d
The perception of movement
p. 225

48. In a dark room, all that's visible is a luminous triangle surrounding a luminous dot. As the triangle is moved upwards, it will appear that:
    a. the triangle is moving up.
    b. the triangle is moving down.
    c. the dot is moving up.
    d. the dot is moving down.

49. A problem for form perception is explaining how we recognize:
    a. an elephant as an elephant from any of a variety of angles.
    b. an elephant when its body is partially occluded by a tree.
    c. elephants of all different sizes and shades as elephants despite their differences.
    d. all of the above

Answer: d
Form perception
pp. 225–226

50. In some cases of brain damage the patient fails to recognize faces, yet can point out the individual components like eyes and nose. Such patients seem to have the most trouble with:
    a. segregating figure from ground.
    b. compensating for their own eye movements.
    c. seeing the Gestalt.
    d. binocular disparity.

Answer: c
Form perception
p. 226

51. The Gestalt group of psychologists are most well known for their work on:
    a. adjustment to stressful perceptual situations.
    b. the development of thought processes as they influence perception.
    c. issues of free will and personal responsibility.
    d. organizational processes in perception.
    e. the physiology of the eye.

Answer: d
Form perception
p. 226

52. Gestalt psychologists argue that:
    a. forms are defined by their component parts.
    b. forms are recognized by the firing of relevant feature detectors.
    c. the whole form is not simply the sum of its parts.
    d. a and b

Answer: c
Form perception
p. 226

53. A close English translation of the German word *Gestalt* is:
    a. figure.
    b. whole form.
    c. background.
    d. illusion.
    e. quality.

Answer: b
Form perception
p. 226

54. The information-processing approach to studying perception got its main impetus from:
    a. Gestalt principles.
    b. behaviorism.
    c. computer science.
    d. the study of brain-damaged patients.

Answer: c
Form perception
p. 227

55. Flowcharts intended to show the sequence of events in the processing of signals by the nervous system grew mainly out of work:
    a. in Gestalt psychology.
    b. with computers.
    c. in animal training.
    d. with brain-damaged patients.

Answer: b
Form perception
p. 227

56. The information-processing approach relies on an analogy between the mind and:
    a. computer.
    b. mechanical statue.
    c. combustion engine.
    d. telephone switchboard.

57. Earlier metaphors of how the nervous systems work emphasized transformations of _____, whereas the computer metaphor emphasizes transformations of _____.
    a. mechanical energy; electrical energy
    b. nonspecific information; specific information
    c. energy; information
    d. input; output
    e. output; input

58. How could one best tell if curvature is truly a primitive perceptual feature?
    a. Determine whether the threshold for curvature is lower than for other attributes, such as color.
    b. Determine whether the observer can describe a curved line in detail.
    c. See whether a stimulus having one curvature is immediately noticed in an array of other stimuli having a different curvature.
    d. Have the observer stare at a curved line and then see whether that observer has an afterimage of curvature upon looking at something else.

59. What inference is most reasonable from studies of visual searches where some stimuli "pop out" almost immediately when an observer looks at an array of many stimuli that are exactly the same and one that differs in only one way?
    a. that the attribute that makes the one stimulus differ from the others may be a perceptual primitive
    b. that looking at such an array requires a series of steps of information processing
    c. that figure-ground separation requires sharp boundaries
    d. that perception requires top-down processing as well as bottom-up processing
    e. that illusory conjunctions occur because various perceptual primitives are free-floating early in the information-processing sequence

60. A subject is asked to locate a horizontal line in an array of vertical lines. Which of the following statements is true?
    a. The more vertical lines there are in the array, the longer it will take the subject to locate the one horizontal line.
    b. The time it takes to locate the horizontal line will not vary as a function of the number of vertical lines in the array.
    c. The more similar the vertical and horizontal lines are in color, the longer it will take the subject to locate the one horizontal line.
    d. The darker in color the vertical lines are, the longer it will take the subject to locate the one horizontal line.

61. What type of experiments could best be used to study just which attributes of stimuli are perceptually primitive for people?
    a. determining which aspects of stimuli are also seen by lower vertebrates and by insects
    b. determining the relative sensitivity to different sense modalities
    c. search tasks involving displays containing one "oddball" stimulus
    d. studying the time it takes observers to see figure-ground reversals in ambiguous figures

62. You show observers the display below for 200 msec. Many report seeing a few short slanted lines and a few long horizontal ones, along with the lines that were actually shown. What do such illusory conjunctions imply?

    a. that the threshold for length is lower than the threshold for orientation
    b. that early in processing there are perceptual primitives that are isolated from each other, here length and orientation
    c. that the primitive of horizontal pops out from among the array of less primitive slanting lines
    d. that an opponent system operates at the level of the visual cortex, with slanting lines being opponents of horizontals and short lines being opponents of long ones

63. A subject is shown a display containing blue Bs and yellow Ts for 200 milliseconds. Which of the following is the subject most likely to mistakenly claim she has seen?
    a. yellow Bs
    b. green Bs
    c. green Ts
    d. b and c

64. An example of an illusory conjunction would be reporting having seen:
    a. purple Rs in a display when there were only purple Gs and orange Rs.
    b. As and Bs in a display when there were As and Cs.
    c. only As in a display when there were As and Bs.
    d. As and Bs in a display when there were only As.

65. Perceptual parsing means:
    a. sensing (looking at, listening to, etc.) the stimulus.
    b. determining which aspects of the stimulus go together.
    c. breaking the stimulus into component parts.
    d. detecting the primitive features of the stimulus.

66. A major issue in perception of a visual scene that goes well beyond the detection of primitive features is determining:
    a. which of the areas of the scene have which colors and brightness.
    b. which of the stimuli in the scene are large and which are small.
    c. which parts of the scene go together.
    d. whether the scene is viewed in central or peripheral vision.

67. Visual parsing:
    a. results in a segregation process on the object to be recognized.
    b. is performed by the perceptual system and is not a part of the stimulus pattern.
    c. is completed during a single stage of the perceptual process.
    d. a and b

68. Visual parsing implies performing a(n):
    a. conjunction.
    b. segregation.
    c. threshold determination.
    d. association with auditory stimuli.

69. Perceptual parsing of speech that we listen to is necessary because:
    a. people, when speaking, don't put in pauses between words.
    b. we need to associate what the speaker says with how we plan to respond.
    c. speech many times contains words with which we are unfamiliar.
    d. the speech stream is broken up into small bits of sound, which need to be synthesized by the listener.

70. The separation of figure from ground is:
    a. inherent in the figure.
    b. an illusion.
    c. a perceptual process, accomplished by the brain.
    d. a sensory process, accomplished by the receptors.

71. In a scene of a tree against a blue sky, the sky would be called the:
    a. reversible pattern.
    b. picture.
    c. figure.
    d. ground.

72. Reversible figures are those in which:
    a. the figure is darker than the ground.
    b. the figure is lighter than the ground.
    c. the same section of the display can be seen as figure or as ground.
    d. the figure and ground appear to move in opposite directions.

73. Reversible figures demonstrate that:
    a. perceptual parsing is not inherent in the stimulus.
    b. perceptual parsing is inherent in the stimulus.
    c. figure-ground relationships are inherent in the stimulus.
    d. figure-ground relationships are stable.
    e. c and d

74. Some artists create paintings where the figure and the background relations are deliberately reversible and ambiguous. Such ambiguity illustrates the important general point about human perception that:
    a. adaptation to steady or repeated stimulation happens in almost all of the senses.
    b. different proximal stimuli can be parsed in the same way.
    c. only a few basic perceptual abilities are inborn.
    d. the same proximal stimuli can be parsed in more than one way.
    e. sensation and perception are on a continuum.

75. When you first look at a certain painting by Salvador Dali you see an archway filled with people fighting. But when you look a bit longer the archway seems to become a horse and many of the people become textures in the landscape. As you continue to look your perception keeps flip-flopping. This exemplifies the general principle about human perception that:
    a. the same stimulus can be parsed in more than one way.
    b. the next likely event is for the image to gradually fade away.
    c. we pay attention to stimuli that are the most meaningful at the time.
    d. only a few basic perceptual abilities are inborn.
    e. different distal stimuli can give rise to the same proximal stimuli.

76. Patients with certain kinds of brain damage have difficulty in establishing and maintaining figure-ground relationships. In which of the following tasks would you expect them to do worse than normal subjects?
    a. tracing the shortest route from New York to Chicago on an ordinary road map
    b. locating the Big Dipper in the sky
    c. reading a letter that has been scribbled over in the same color ink
    d. all of the above

77. A black spot on the side of an otherwise white dog is perceived as:
    a. a figure on a ground.
    b. a reversible figure.
    c. an afterimage.
    d. a subjective contour.

78. An example of a figure-ground perception is:
    a. an inkblot on a sheet of white paper.
    b. a cloud in an otherwise cloudless sky.
    c. a single tea leaf at the bottom of an empty tea cup.
    d. all of the above

79. A horse standing in a meadow is perceived as a distinct entity that stands out against its surroundings. This phenomenon illustrates:
    a. constancy.
    b. the principle of similarity.
    c. the use of binocular cues.
    d. figure-ground relationships.

80. In reversible figure-ground patterns:
    a. the figure is seen as being more formless and less cohesive than the ground.
    b. the contour or border is perceived to belong to both figure and ground simultaneously.
    c. discrimination of detail is best in the part seen as figure.
    d. border is subjective and is brought about by a closure-like process.

81. A subject is asked how he perceives the following stimulus: -* -* -*. He says he perceives it as three pairs, each containing a dash and an asterisk. He has grouped the stimulus on the basis of:
    a. similarity.
    b. proximity.
    c. good continuation.
    d. closure.

82. Look at the figure below. It is usually perceived as a diamond inside of a rectangle. The Gestalt principle that applies to this percept is called:

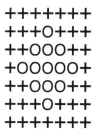

    a. proximity.
    b. good continuation.
    c. similarity.
    d. closure.
    e. transposition of form.

83. When we see a pattern of dots and we group certain dots together based on their color, we are grouping according to the principle of:
    a. figure.
    b. similarity.
    c. proximity.
    d. subjective contours.

84. Proximity is the law of perceptual grouping which says that:
    a. stimuli are perceived as a perceptual whole due to the emphasis placed upon relationships between component parts.
    b. figures close together in space or sounds made in rapid succession are perceived as belonging together.
    c. we tend to separate figure from ground.
    d. we tend to complete figures that have gaps in them.

85. An example of grouping by proximity in time is:
    a.   induced motion.
    b.   adaptation of directional movement.
    c.   the waterfall illusion.
    d.   auditory rhythm.

86. Most of us see the figure below as rows instead of columns. This is an example of the Gestalt principle of:

    O   O   O   O   O

    S   S   S   S   S

    O   O   O   O   O

    S   S   S   S   S

    a.   closure.
    b.   transposition of form.
    c.   similarity.
    d.   construction.

87. Camouflage is frequently possible because of the perceptual organizing principle of:
    a.   good continuation.
    b.   proximity.
    c.   closure.
    d.   similarity.

88. Some insects have body markings that help to conceal them from predators who tend to see various parts of the insect's body as continuations of the twig on which it stands. This fact suggests that:
    a.   good continuation cannot be attributed to prior experience in looking at line drawings.
    b.   subject contour is a special case of good continuation.
    c.   good continuation is based on feature detectors that signal the direction of contour.
    d.   good continuation cannot be affected by learning.

89. The principle of good continuation suggests that someone who has never seen an X is most likely to describe it as consisting of:
    a.   a "v" over an upside down "v".
    b.   two sideways "v"s next to each other.
    c.   two crossed diagonal lines.
    d.   four diagonal lines meeting at a central point.

Answer: d
Form perception
p. 232

90. According to some authors, subjective contours are created by a process similar to that which underlies:
    a. reversible figure-ground patterns.
    b. proximity.
    c. similarity.
    d. good continuation.

Answer: a
Form perception
pp. 231–232

91. One of the following isn't a Gestalt principle. Which is it?
    a. size constancy
    b. good continuation
    c. proximity
    d. similarity

Answer: d
Form perception
pp. 232–233

92. The principle of maximum likelihood suggests that:
    a. we use proximal stimuli to make a good guess about distal stimuli.
    b. stimuli that are close together probably go with the same object.
    c. regions that are the same in texture usually go with the same object.
    d. all of the above

Answer: d
Form perception
pp. 232–233

93. A principle that seems to tie together many of the Gestalt laws of perceptual organization is:
    a. primitive features.
    b. constancy.
    c. opponent-processing.
    d. maximum likelihood.

Answer: d
Form perception
pp. 230–232

94. Proximity, similarity, closure, and good continuation are all _____ laws of perceptual organization that theorists attempt to subsume under the _____ principle.
    a. primitive; maximum likelihood
    b. primitive; opponent-processing
    c. primitive; constancy
    d. Gestalt; maximum likelihood
    e. Gestalt; opponent-processing

Answer: d
Form perception
pp. 230–232

95. According to several theorists, the _____ laws of perceptual organization, like similarity and closure, are explained by the _____ principle.
    a. primitive; constancy
    b. Gestalt; constancy
    c. primitive; maximum likelihood
    d. Gestalt; maximum likelihood
    e. primitive; opponent-processing

96. People are apt to see the figure below as an outline square covered in its lower right corner by a white line than as a rearrangement of the two separate figures on the right.

What principle can explain this?
   a. constancy
   b. opponent-processing
   c. maximum likelihood
   d. geon

97. Pattern perception is most concerned with the question:
   a. "Where is the object?"
   b. "What is the object?"
   c. "When did the object appear?"
   d. "Why is that object present?"

98. If pattern recognition is accomplished with feature nets:
   a. each distinct shape (e.g., circle, triangle) directly triggers the firing of a detector for that shape.
   b. many of the cells firing do so in response to the firing of other cells rather than directly in response to the stimulus.
   c. many of the cells firing do so as a result of the perceiver's expectations.
   d. complex shapes will prompt firing in about the same number of cells as will simple shapes.

99. A professor constructs a device for sorting handwritten zip codes that determines whether a line segment is straight or curved, its angle, and whether and where that line segment intersects with other line segments. This device seems to be based on:
   a. bottom-up processing.
   b. context effects.
   c. the maximum likelihood principle.
   d. top-down processing.

100. Bottom-up processing means:
   a. using context to determine what is being seen.
   b. using expectations to determine what is being seen.
   c. using induced motion and optic flow to determine what is being seen.
   d. using features of the stimulus to determine what is being seen.

101. When pattern recognition starts with features and gradually builds up to letters, words, phrases, etc., it is referred to as a:
    a. component process.
    b. differentiated process.
    c. bottom-up process.
    d. top-down process.

102. A computer device is capable of recognizing handwritten zip code by examining particular features of lines and their various combinations, exciting processing units that match the combinations and inhibiting those that do not. This pattern recognition device, as described above:
    a. probably operates in one step.
    b. makes important use of context effects.
    c. depends on bottom-up processing.
    d. operates similarly to the way that Renaissance painters showed depth.

103. In comparison to bottom-up processing, top-down processing:
    a. matches particular features of a given stimulus to objects in visual memory.
    b. activates higher-order units of perception, which in turn influence items of lower order.
    c. is only applicable in cases of ambiguous stimuli.
    d. employs more innate mechanisms of perception.

104. Students working on an experiment with rats tended to see the figure below as a rat, physicians working on a geriatric ward tended to see the same drawing as an old man with glasses.

This example demonstrates the power of:
    a. Gestalt principles of organization.
    b. bottom-up processing.
    c. perceptual constancies.
    d. top-down processing.

105. Expectancies and context effects are especially important in:
    a. Gestalt principles of organization.
    b. feature detection.
    c. bottom-up processing.
    d. top-down processing.

106. The 13s in the top and bottom rows are identical but the one on top is perceived as a number, the one on the bottom as a letter. This example best illustrates:

A I3 C
I2 I3 I4

    a.   top-down processing.
    b.   Gestalt principles of organization.
    c.   feature detection in a data-drive process.
    d.   perceptual constancies.

107. Subjects told they are about to see an instrument will recognize the word *guitar* _____ subjects told they are about to see a form of transportation. This finding is called the _____.
    a.   more quickly than; priming effect
    b.   more quickly than; feature net model
    c.   as quickly as; priming effect
    d.   as quickly as; feature net model

108. During bidirectional processing, a subject shown only part of a word may employ the following methods to guess its correct meaning:
    a.   Allow recent experience with similar words to influence the choice.
    b.   Rule out certain letters that would not combine with the word fragment to spell any recognizable word.
    c.   Create a new category in visual memory for that word fragment.
    d.   a and b

109. The idea of bidirectional activation implies that we tend:
    a.   both to see what we believe and to believe what we see.
    b.   to process information from central and peripheral vision simultaneously and in parallel.
    c.   to have lower thresholds for motion in a particular direction if we have just been adapted to motion in the opposite direction.
    d.   to see stationary objects in central vision as moving if all of the background is moving in the opposite direction.

110. To study bidirectional processing, a subject is primed with the instructions *nonword,* then shown the letters R__T, and finally needs to identify as quickly as possible the letter shown below.

Almost all quickly respond "H". To make a good case for bidirectional processing the investigator should also study:
   a. how fast subjects respond "A" when primed with *word.*
   b. how fast subjects respond "H" and respond "A" without priming.
   c. the proportion of subjects who respond "A" and respond "H" without priming.
   d. how fast subjects do all of the above.

111. With only top-down processing we would:
   a. believe what we sense.
   b. perceive only the individual features of objects.
   c. perceive only what we expect.
   d. believe one can see almost any object in a huge number of different ways.

112. Professor Stone believes that perceptions are constructions made by top-down processing. If so, she probably stresses the importance of:
   a. nativism and genetics as explanations.
   b. Weber's and Fechner's laws.
   c. expectations and hypotheses.
   d. the grouping of primitive features.

113. Geons are:
   a. ways of representing objects in three dimensions, which were established by early Egyptian artists.
   b. ways of capturing light and shadow with dots, as done by various Impressionist painters.
   c. components of objects above the level of primitive features.
   d. memory groups of entire objects that we have seen before, as in recognizing a "shotgun" formation in a football offense.

114. Which of the following is an example of a geon?
   a. cube
   b. red
   c. vertical line
   d. all of the above

Answer: d
Form perception
p. 237

115. Which of the following is proposed as an intermediate perceptual component in models of object recognition?
    a. meaning
    b. icon
    c. primitive feature
    d. geon
    e. context

Answer: c
Form perception
p. 238

116. Assembly of geons into an object:
    a. guarantees form perception.
    b. requires that meaning be extracted first.
    c. is an intermediate step in bottom-up processing.
    d. guarantees that meaning will be extracted.

Answer: b
Form perception
p. 238

117. In visual agnosia, patients have the most trouble:
    a. remembering what particular words mean.
    b. recognizing what it is that they see.
    c. perceiving motion in particular directions.
    d. perceiving and copying lines at particular orientations.

Answer: b
Form perception
p. 238

118. A patient with visual agnosia is looking at his house key. He is most likely to have difficulty:
    a. describing the key.
    b. identifying the object as a key.
    c. seeing the key.
    d. using the depth cues needed to insert the key into the lock.

Answer: d
Form perception
p. 238

119. A problem with the view that processing for object recognition occurs in the order, figure/ground segregation, geons, meaning, is that:
    a. these events may occur simultaneously.
    b. top-down as well as bottom-up processing occurs.
    c. parallel processing is likely.
    d. all of the above

Answer: d
Perceptual problem solving
pp. 238–240

120. According to the perceptual problem-solving hypothesis, a viewer:
    a. waits to form a hypothesis until the primitive features have been adequately analyzed.
    b. examines features for fit, or failure to fit, an expectation.
    c. uses both bottom-up and top-down processing.
    d. b and c
    e. all of the above

Answer: d
Perceptual problem solving
pp. 238–240

121. Being able to identify black and white horses painted on a background of snow-covered rocks illustrates a major point about perception. What is it?
    a. Perceptual systems are not a blank slate but they are hightly vulnerable to certain early experiences.
    b. Perceptual systems adapt and hence are most responsive to changing stimuli.
    c. Color is not the only perceptual process set up in an opponent-process way.
    d. Perception is a joint product of what you sense and what you already know.

122. Subjects see a backwards R and an R in the regular orientation repeatedly flashed in a sequence. They perceive an R rotating in three dimensions around its vertical line. This illusion of rotation probably occursas a result of:
    a. the familiarity of English letters.
    b. perceptual problem solving.
    c. opponent processes.
    d. adaptation to repeated presentations of stimuli.

123. In impossible figures:
    a. primitive features do not connect with each other in logical ways.
    b. bottom-up processing cannot occur.
    c. individual parts of the figure make sense.
    d. we process the entire array simultaneously, and in parallel, which results in a top-down overload.

124. In which of the accompanying figures does the perceptual hypothesis fail?

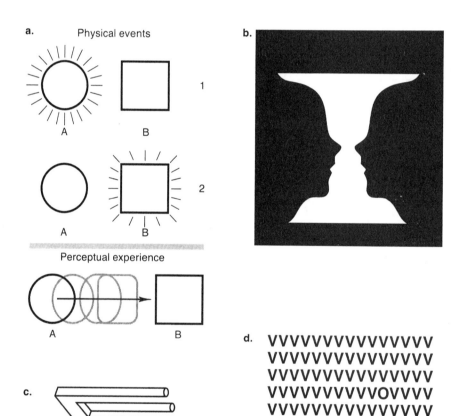

125. Which of the the following illustrates or assumes that perception involves both top-down and bottom-up processing?
    a. bidirectional models
    b. impossible figures
    c. the perceptual hypothesis
    d. all of the above

Answer: e
Form perception and the nervous system
pp. 241–242

126. Parvo cells:
    a. are smaller than magno cells.
    b. are spread throughout the retina.
    c. are sensitive to differences in hue.
    d. seem to play a key role in the perception of pattern and form.
    e. all of the above

Answer: b
Form perception and the nervous system
pp. 241–242

127. Magno cells:
    a. continue to fire in response to an unchanging stimulus.
    b. seem to play a key role in motion detection.
    c. are sensitive to differences in hue.
    d. are smaller than parvo cells.
    e. all of the above

Answer: d
Form perception and the nervous system
pp. 242–243

128. Cerebral processing of visual information:
    a. begins in the occipital cortex.
    b. involves the temporal cortex.
    c. involves the parietal cortex.
    d. all of the above

Answer: a
Form perception and the nervous system
p. 243

129. A monkey is trained to press a button once if a picture of a banana appears on his right and to press the same button twice if any other picture appears on his right or if any picture appears on his left. The pathway from his occipital to his temporal cortex is then damaged. He is now most likely to give the wrong response when:
    a. a picture of an apple appears on his right.
    b. a picture of an apple appears on his left.
    c. a picture of a banana appears on his left.
    d. all of the above

Answer: c
Form perception and the nervous system
p. 243

130. A monkey is trained to press a button once if a picture of a banana appears on his right and to press the same button twice if any other picture appears on his right or if any picture appears on his left. The pathway from his occipital to his parietal cortex is then damaged. He is now most likely to give the wrong response when:
    a. a picture of an apple appears on his right.
    b. a picture of an apple appears on his left.
    c. a picture of a banana appears on his left.
    d. all of the above

Answer: e
Form perception and the nervous system
p. 243

131. T. C. has visual agnosia. She often can't recognize objects, even very common ones. She most likely has damage to her:
    a. right frontal lobe.
    b. left frontal lobe.
    c. parietal cortex.
    d. occipital-parietal pathway.
    e. occipital-temporal pathway.

Answer: b
Form perception and the nervous system
pp. 243–244

132. The *binding problem* focuses on:
    a. how movement is perceived.
    b. how all the elements of a stimulus detected by separate systems are integrated.
    c. how depth is perceived.
    d. how an object is identified.

Answer: c
Perceptual selection
p. 244

133. The fact that we attend to only certain aspects of the total stimulus array impinging on our sensory receptor surfaces describes the concept of:
    a. mental set.
    b. motor set.
    c. selective attention.
    d. perceptual constancy.

Answer: d
Perceptual selection
p. 244

134. Head turning, quick eye movements, and finger movements are all manifestations of:
    a. figure/ground segregation.
    b. top-down processing.
    c. perceptual constancy.
    d. orienting.

Answer: a
Perceptual selection
p. 244

135. Orienting in humans is accomplished:
    a. by adjusting so that the stimulus falls on the fovea.
    b. by relying on peripheral acuity.
    c. primarily through audition.
    d. primarily through touch.

Answer: c
Perceptual selection
pp. 245–246

136. The visual search procedure:
    a. requires subjects to attend to all parts of the presented stimuli.
    b. employs the use of top-down processing more than bottom-up methods.
    c. is used to study the mechanisms of visual attention.
    d. becomes easier as the stimuli become more similar.

Answer: b
Perceptual selection
p. 246

137. When one is examining an array for a conjunction of features the search is:
    a. parallel.
    b. serial.
    c. done equally fast with from 5 to 75 items in the array.
    d. conducted independently of expectations.

Answer: a
Perceptual selection
p. 246

138. When a visual search target differs from other array items by only one feature:
    a. the search is parallel.
    b. the time taken for the search depends on the number of items in the array.
    c. the search is serial.
    d. b and c

Answer: c
Perceptual selection
p. 246

Answer: d
Perceptual selection
p. 246

Answer: b
Perceptual selection
p. 246

Answer: d
Perceptual selection
p. 247

Answer: d
Perceptual selection
p. 247

Answer: a
Perceptual selection
p. 247

Answer: b
Perceptual selection
p. 247

139. Mental searchlight models of attention are most useful when attempting to explain performance in tasks that involve:
    a. moving the eyes when a sudden stimulus comes into peripheral vision.
    b. parallel processing of primitive features in an array.
    c. serial processing for a conjunction of features.
    d. size and shape constancy.

140. Priming
    a. facilitates perception of the expected stimulus.
    b. hinders perception of the unexpected stimulus.
    c. facilitates perception of any stimulus.
    d. a and b

141. In spatial or directional priming,
    a. the prime only has its effect if subjects have time to move their eyes before the stimulus is presented.
    b. priming may lead to slower responding than in conditions without primes.
    c. the arrow remains visible while the stimulus is presented.
    d. the prime indicates what the stimulus is going to be.

142. One of perception's major characteristics, _____, is illustrated by the cocktail-party effect.
    a. ambiguity
    b. constancy
    c. adaptation
    d. selectivity

143. Which of the following is most closely associated with the concept of central selection in attention?
    a. the fact that a door looks rectangular even if the proximal stimulus for it is a trapezoid
    b. the aftereffects of looking for many seconds at a bright red square
    c. texture gradients are potent monocular cues to depth
    d. the cocktail-party effect

144. In a dichotic listening task:
    a. information is presented to both ears simultaneously.
    b. information is presented alternately, first to one ear and then to the other.
    c. information is presented to only one ear at random intervals.
    d. identical information is presented to both ears simultaneously.

145. In a dichotic listening experiment, the subject is often asked to shadow:
    a. the message that comes through both ears.
    b. the message that comes through the to-be-attended-to ear.
    c. the message that comes through the not-to-be-attended-to ear.
    d. text shown to the subject.

146. Apparently, in a dichotic listening task:
    a. the auditory stimulus is received by the receptors in the unattended-to ear, but that information is only partly processed.
    b. the auditory stimulus is filtered before it has an opportunity to impinge on the receptor surface in the unattended-to ear.
    c. auditory stimuli to the attended-to ear are filtered for special relevance.
    d. a sensory filter is produced first in one ear and, after some very brief time interval, is produced in the second ear.

147. Research suggests that in a task in which separate messages are simultaneously played in each ear of the subject:
    a. the auditory stimulus is received by the receptors in the unattended-to ear, but the information is only partly processed.
    b. the auditory stimulus is filtered before it has an opportunity to get beyond the receptor level in the unattended-to ear.
    c. the information from auditory stimuli from the unattended-to ear reach the cortex, but even one's own name is filtered out.
    d. a sensory filter is produced first in one ear and, after some very brief time interval, is switched to the second ear.

148. In a dichotic listening task, which of the following is most likely to be noticed in the unattended ear?
    a. a shift in the speaker's language
    b. a change in the speaker's gender
    c. discussion of a controversial topic
    d. All of the above are equally likely or unlikely to be noticed.

149. Which of the following statements about dichotic listening tasks is true?
    a. Changes in some characteristics of the unattended message are noticed.
    b. No aspect of the unattended message reaches consciousness.
    c. Subjects almost always hear their name in the unattended message.
    d. Subjects typically find the shadowing task very difficult.

150. Perceptual constancy refers to the ability to:
    a. see figures standing out against a ground.
    b. resolve ambiguities in patterns of stimuli.
    c. perceive depth in paintings.
    d. perceive objects as invariant despite changes in sensory activity.

151. Perceptual constancy describes the phenomenon that our perception of:
    a. a stimulus remains the same in spite of changes in the distal stimuli it provides.
    b. a stimulus remains the same in spite of changes in the proximal stimuli it provides.
    c. an object changes when the distal stimuli it provides change.
    d. an object changes when the proximal stimuli it provides change.

Answer: c
Perceiving constancy
p. 248

152. Size constancy refers to the phenomenon of seeing objects:
    a. as the same size even if they are really different sizes.
    b. as different in size even though they are really the same size.
    c. as the same size even if they move to a different distance.
    d. as the same size even when they get smaller, as when a balloon loses air.

Answer: c
Perceiving constancy
p. 248

153. A train car 500 meters away looks substantially larger than a Honda at 25 meters despite the fact that the retinal image of the Honda is greater than that of the train car. This phenomenon is analogous to:
    a. a single tea leaf standing out as a figure in the bottom of an otherwise empty cup.
    b. the vase and the face reversing when drawn just right.
    c. a book that looks rectangular even when seen at a 45-degree angle.
    d. interposition of people's bodies in a group photograph.

Answer: d
Perceiving constancy
pp. 248–249

154. An example of a perceptual invariant in a size constancy experiment is the:
    a. size of an object's retinal image.
    b. actual size of the image out in the world.
    c. apparent size of the object as the subject perceives it.
    d. ratio between the retinal size of the object and the retinal size of its background.

Answer: d
Perceiving constancy
p. 231

155. An invariant size relationship is one that:
    a. changes frequently.
    b. changes depending upon the size of the objects.
    c. changes depending upon the distance of the objects from the observer.
    d. does not change.

Answer: e
Perceiving constancy
pp. 249–250

156. The size of the distal stimulus can be determined by a simple calculation of:
    a. the shape of the proximal stimulus.
    b. the distance of the proximal stimulus.
    c. the size of the proximal stimulus.
    d. the distance of the distal stimulus.
    e. c and d.

Answer: d
Perceiving constancy
pp. 249–250

157. The unconscious inference proposed by Helmholtz:
    a. takes distance into account when judging size.
    b. can explain size constancy.
    c. is similar to aspects of modern perception theories.
    d. all of the above

Answer: b
Perceiving constancy
pp. 249–250

158. Objects *A* and *B* both cast the same size image on your retina, yet distance cues indicate that *A* is closer to you. You therefore perceive:
    a. *A* and *B* to be objects of the same size at different distances.
    b. *A* to be smaller than *B*.
    c. *A* to be larger than *B*.
    d. *A* and *B* to be objects of the same size, equally far from you.

Answer: a
Perceiving constancy
p. 251

159. Lightness constancy occurs because:
    a. a figure maintains the same proportion of luminance with the background.
    b. light has no effect on how bright something is.
    c. feature detectors maintain the same level of brightness.
    d. both a and c

Answer: b
Perceiving constancy
p. 251

160. The fact that a swan will not suddenly seem to turn gray when a cloud hides the sun, but appears just as white, but in shadow, is an example of:
    a. color constancy.
    b. lightness constancy.
    c. reflectance.
    d. retinal disparity.

Answer: a
Perceiving constancy
p. 251

161. For lightness constancy to occur:
    a. the background must receive the same light as the figure.
    b. the background must proportionately receive less light than the figure.
    c. there must be a sharp brightness contrast between background and figure.
    d. the subject must be informed about the reflectance of the figure.

Answer: b
Perceiving constancy
p. 251

162. The crucial invariant relationship in lightness constancy is that between:
    a. illumination and reflectance.
    b. luminance of object and its background.
    c. reflectance and luminance of the object.
    d. level of illumination and luminance.

Answer: c
Perceiving constancy
p. 251

163. Two objects of the same reflectance are placed in different light; one in shadow, the other in sunlight. The one in the shadow will be perceived as:
    a. lighter than the one in sunlight.
    b. darker than the one in sunlight.
    c. about the same lightness as the one in sunlight.
    d. cannot be determined from information given

Answer: a
Perceiving constancy
p. 251

164. The reason that changes of illumination have relatively little effect on the perceived lightness of objects is that:
    a. the same illumination falls on the object as on the background.
    b. we have learned that increasing illumination increases luminance, and we have unconsciously compensated for this.
    c. we know that swans are white and crows are black, for example, regardless of illumination.
    d. we have built-in visual search mechanisms.

165. Assume two papers, *A* and *B*, are of equal reflectance. The light shining onto paper *A* and its background has twice the illumination of that shining onto *B* and its background. An observer would perceive paper *B* as being:
    a. approximately half as light as paper *A*.
    b. approximately equal in lightness to paper *A*.
    c. approximately twice as light as paper *A*.
    d. No judgment could be made under this set of experimental conditions.

166. Dr. Pepper believes that perceptual capabilities are inborn and little affected by learning. From this you should guess that Dr. Pepper is a(n):
    a. interactionist.
    b. dualist.
    c. empiricist.
    d. nativist.
    e. fool who will never catch up with Drs. Pepsi and Coke.

167. Perceptual processes are probably best described by
    a. an interaction between innate structures and learning.
    b. nativists.
    c. empiricists.
    d. dualists.

168. The visual representations of Egyptian artists concentrated on:
    a. what the artists saw.
    b. conveying a momentary impression.
    c. rendering the best possible copy of the retinal image.
    d. representing enduring and characteristic attributes of their models.

169. The Renaissance masters tried to paint pictures that would:
    a. correspond to the image the model cast on the eye.
    b. represent enduring and characteristic attributes of the model.
    c. convey the momentary impression the scene produced in the artist's mind.
    d. indicate what the model looks like, not just from one orientation but from several different ones.

170. According to some authors, the special vitality found in the works of some Impressionist masters derives from:
    a. their deliberate violations of linear perspective.
    b. their use of warm colors.
    c. the alternation between the sight of separate dots and mixed colors as the observer moves his eyes over a painting.
    d. the fact that they painted what they knew rather than what they saw.

| Memory

1. The name of your first grade teacher is probably stored in your _____ memory. As you try to recall the name, you are engaging in an _____ memory task.
   a. working; explicit
   b. working; implicit
   c. long-term; explicit
   d. long-term; implicit

2. As you work on a complex multiplication problem in your head, the numbers you're manipulating are in your _____ memory, and the multiplication tables you're drawing on are in your _____ memory.
   a. working; generic
   b. working; episodic
   c. long-term; generic
   d. long-term; episodic

3. Generic memory:
   a. refers to what you're thinking about now.
   b. includes your knowledge that George Washington was the first President of the United States.
   c. includes your memory of your tenth birthday.
   d. is where you store a phone number for the brief period between when you look it up and when you dial it.

4. You're presented with some anagrams you solved last month. Though you don't remember working on the problems previously, you now solve them faster than you did initially. This difference demonstrates:
   a. working memory.
   b. implicit memory.
   c. explicit memory.
   d. episodic memory.

Answer: c
Studying memory
p. 262

5. With respect to memory, conscious is to unconscious as:
   a. generic is to episodic.
   b. long term is to working.
   c. explicit is to implicit.
   d. cortex is to hippocampus.

Answer: c
Studying memory
p. 262

6. The best reason that we have trouble remembering a car's license number that we just passed ten minutes ago while going south on US 322 to Harrisburg is that:
   a. working memory lasts only a minute or so.
   b. seven digit numbers are too difficult to remember easily.
   c. we probably never encoded the number in the first place.
   d. the memory, though present, is too difficult to retrieve except under special circumstances, such as hypnosis or substantial amounts of stress.

Answer: c
Studying memory
pp. 262–263

7. If you "can't think of it now" but do remember it later, there was an initial failure of:
   a. acquisition.
   b. retention.
   c. retrieval.
   d. recognition.

Answer: a
Studying memory
p. 263

8. Recognition and recall tasks both ask subjects to:
   a. retrieve information.
   b. encode information.
   c. store information.
   d. acquire information.

Answer: a
Studying memory
p. 263

9. A test where you fill in the blanks is an example of a:
   a. recall test.
   b. recognition test.
   c. savings test.
   d. mnemonic.
   e. rehearsal.

Answer: a
Studying memory
p. 263

10. Essay exams measure retention by what method?
    a. recall
    b. recognition
    c. savings
    d. latent learning

Answer: c
Studying memory
p. 263

11. Though you can't name all fifty states, you insist that you know them. Which type of test will most likely allow you to demonstrate that knowledge?
    a. rehearsal
    b. recall
    c. recognition
    d. reminiscence

12. You moved from West Virginia to Pennsylvania 10 years ago. A researcher now wants to know how many of the West Virginia counties you remember from when you memorized them in fifth grade. The researcher gives you a list of 30 counties with 15 from West Virginia mixed in with 15 from other states. Your job is to pick out those from West Virginia. This is a test that uses the method of:

    a. rehearsal.
    b. recall.
    c. recognition.
    d. reminiscence.

13. A researcher wants to know how many of the West Virginia county seats you remember from when you memorized them as a fifth grader in Morgantown. The researcher says "Tell me all of the county seats that you remember, and the county that each one goes with." This is a test that uses the method of:

    a. rehearsal.
    b. recall.
    c. recognition.
    d. reminiscence.

14. Which of the following methods is most likely to demonstrate that you do, in fact, remember the list of Nebraska counties that you learned in the third grade in Omaha?

    a. Think of your third grade teacher's name. Then try to recall the county names.
    b. Be hypnotized and then try to recall the county names under hypnosis.
    c. First think of the counties you know in Pennsylvania. Then recall them in Nebraska.
    d. Have a friend prepare a list of all the counties in both Nebraska and Illinois, with those from Nebraska and Illinois thoroughly mixed. Then select those that are Nebraska counties.
    e. Have someone at a good neurological clinic stimulate the appropriate area of your temporal lobe while you are under local anesthesia.

15. Memory span tasks are used to assess

    a. recognition memory.
    b. working memory capacity.
    c. long-term memory capacity.
    d. speed of processing in working memory.

16. In a memory span task, subjects are asked to:

    a. identify items they've just learned from among a list of learned and novel items.
    b. remember as many items as they can from lists they studied at least an hour earlier.
    c. listen once to a series of items and then repeat the list back, in order.
    d. study some items just once and others more than once and then immediately try to remember as many items as they can from each list.

Answer: b
Encoding
p. 264

17. The capacity of working memory seems to be about:
    a. 3 items.
    b. 7 items.
    c. 10 items.
    d. 15 items.

Answer: a
Encoding
p. 264

18. The "magic number 7" refers to:
    a. the capacity of working memory.
    b. the capacity of long-term memory.
    c. the number of seconds it takes to transfer an item from working to long-term memory.
    d. the number of seconds it takes to process an item in working memory.

Answer: d
Encoding
p. 264

19. The capacity of a normal person's working memory:
    a. depends substantially on what particular type of items are in store.
    b. is practically unlimited.
    c. is limited primarily by the capacities of the long-term storage system.
    d. is roughly seven items.

Answer: a
Encoding
pp. 264–265

20. The best explanation for our difficulty in remembering new phone numbers is that:
    a. items quickly decay or are displaced form working memory.
    b. information received visually is difficult to process.
    c. long-term memory is unrelated to short-term memory.
    d. seven digit numbers are too difficult to remember easily.

Answer: a
Encoding
pp. 264–265

21. When an item fades from working memory our best guess is that:
    a. it is usually gone forever.
    b. it can be recalled when we need it.
    c. we are left with only a sensory impression.
    d. we store only its emotional impressions.

Answer: b
Encoding
pp. 264–265

22. According to the stage theory:
    a. items enter memory in pieces rather than as wholes.
    b. items must pass through working memory to get into long-term memory.
    c. all items that get into working memory are eventually transferred to long-term memory.
    d. b and c

Answer: d
Encoding
pp. 264–265

23. A memory theorist likens the relationship between one kind of memory and another kind to the relationship between a loading dock and a large warehouse. This theorist is most likely:
    a. one who takes a depth-of-processing approach.
    b. one who makes a distinction between procedural and declarative knowledge.
    c. an interference theorist.
    d. a stage theorist.

24. Experimenter: "The words are: *cat, rat, crumb, cow, scrap, fantastic, dog, excitement*. Please tell me what you recall."
Subject: "Cat, rat, cow, dog, fantastic, excitement, scraps, crumb."
Here, the method used to study recall was most likely:
    a. serial anticipation.
    b. paired association.
    c. recognition.
    d. free recall.
    e. serial reproduction.

25. If you tried to learn the serial list: BOZ, ZIR, JEV, VID, LEQ, SAR, RAK, NUD, FUH, you would probably have the most trouble recalling:
    a. BOZ.
    b. JEV.
    c. LEQ.
    d. RAK.
    e. FUH.

26. A subject is required to report as much of a poem as he can remember after having read the poem once immediately prior to recall. In reciting the poem from memory, one expects the greatest number of errors in lines:
    a. at the beginning of the poem.
    b. in the middle of the poem.
    c. at the end of the poem.
    d. Errors will be independent of the position of the line in the poem.

27. The primacy effect refers to the fact that:
    a. the most important items in a list are more likely to be remembered than less important items.
    b. the first-presented items in a list are more likely to be remembered than items in the middle of the list.
    c. the items presented most recently in a list are more likely to be remembered than items presented earlier.
    d. those items in a list which have the greatest emotional impact are those with the greatest likelihood of recall.

28. The recency effect refers to the fact that:
    a. the last several items on a list are more likely to be remembered than the middle items.
    b. the first several items on a list are more likely to be remembered than the middle items.
    c. rehearsed items are more likely to be remembered than unrehearsed items.
    d. the most personally relevant items on a list are most likely to be remembered.

29. Items in which of the following parts of the serial position are most likely being drawn directly from working memory?

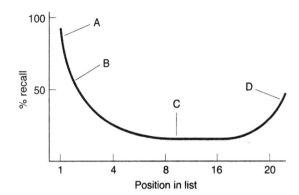

   a. A
   b. B
   c. C
   d. D

30. The primacy effect probably results from the retrieval of items:
   a. from generic memory.
   b. from working memory.
   c. from long-term memory.
   d. from retentive memory.

31. Which of the following points of the serial position curve can be explained best by rehearsal?

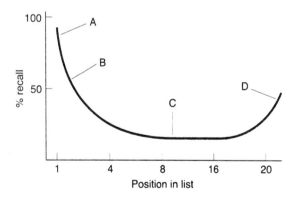

   a. A
   b. B
   c. C
   d. D

Answer: a
Encoding
p. 266

32. Two groups hear a list of 20 unrelated items at the same 1-item-per-second rate and are then tested for free recall. For group I, the test comes 1 second after hearing the last item in the list. For group II, the test comes 30 seconds after hearing the last item, with the 30 seconds filled with backward counting. We would expect:
   a. the same primacy effect for both groups; a greater recency effect for group I.
   b. the same primacy effect for both groups; a greater recency effect for group II.
   c. the same recency effect for both groups; a greater primacy effect for group I.
   d. the same recency effect for both groups; a greater primacy effect for group II.

Answer: a
Encoding
p. 266

33. A group of subjects hears a list of 15 words after which there is a delay of 30 seconds before they are asked to recall the words. During this delay period, rehearsal is prevented. When asked for free recall of the words, the _____ will be affected the most.
   a. recency effect
   b. primacy effect
   c. memory span
   d. long-term memory

Answer: d
Encoding
p. 266

34. Subjects in memory experiments are sometimes asked to count backward by threes during a retention interval between presentation of the material and test. What is most likely the point of the backward-counting task?
   a. It helps subjects to concentrate.
   b. It keeps the subjects interested.
   c. It prevents interference by other materials.
   d. It displaces the contents of working memory.

Answer: d
Encoding
p. 266

35. Two groups hear a list of 20 unrelated items and are tested for immediate recall a few seconds after they hear the last word. In group I, the items are presented at the rate of 1 second per item; in group II, they are presented at 2 seconds per item. We would expect:
   a. the same primacy effect for both groups; a greater recency effect for group I.
   b. the same primacy effect for both groups; a greater recency effect for group II.
   c. the same recency effect in both groups; a greater primacy effect for group I.
   d. the same recency effect for both groups; a greater primacy effect for group II.

Answer: a
Encoding
p. 266

36. A drug that prevents processing of information into long-term memory is administered to a subject prior to a memory task. Under these conditions one expects to see the elimination of:
   a. the primacy effect.
   b. the recency effect.
   c. any recall of items.
   d. a and b.

37. The formation of "chunks" involves:
    a. recoding of the stimulus input.
    b. restricting the capacity of working memory.
    c. restricting the capacity of long-term memory.
    d. increasing working memory capacity from about 7 chunks to about 12 chunks.

38. The capacity of working memory, in chunks, is about the same as the number of:
    a. wheels on a tricycle.
    b. days in a week.
    c. months in a year.
    d. days in a month.

39. Which of the following lists exceeds the capacity of the average person's working memory?
    a. BOATLOADDOCKROPELAND
    b. MNOPQRSTUVWXYZABCDEF
    c. MQTLNRAZPCDBLQNVUDSD
    d. all of the above

40. Subject *A* has learned a list of letters by organizing it into four chunks, each chunk containing two letters. Subject *B* has learned another list of letters by organizing it into four chunks, each chunk containing four letters. Which of the following statements is true?
    a. Only subject *A* will be able to transfer the list to long-term memory.
    b. Subject *B* is placing a far larger load on his working memory than subject *A*.
    c. In a recall test one hour later, subject *B* will be able to recall more letters than subject *A*.
    d. In a recall test one hour later, subjects *A* and *B* will be able to recall approximately the same number of letters.

41. Subjects were given several lists of words, some of which began with the letter *G*. At the end of each list, which were of varying length, the subjects were asked to recall the last word that started with *G*. At the end of the entire session they were asked to recall all of the words that began with *G*. What is the major conclusion one can reach from that experiment?
    a. Transfer from working memory to long-term memory takes time, a process the investigators called trace consolidation.
    b. Retrieval can be partial in that one can have a feeling of knowing and be able to recognize, yet not be able to recall.
    c. Maintenance rehearsal provides little or no benefit in helping recall.
    d. Proactive interference limits recall. The more previous words beginning with the letter *G* one has seen the harder it is to recall additional words starting with that letter.

Answer: c
Encoding
pp. 268–269

42. Subjects are told they will hear a list of words and will be asked to remember the last word on the list beginning with *T*. The list is:
    "carrot, paper, football, table, toaster, record, camel, jacket, picture, thunder". Afterwards, subjects are unexpectedly asked to recall all the words they can remember. The results are,
    a. consistent with the claim that maintenance rehearsal increases the likelihood of transfer to long-term memory; "toaster" and "table" are equally likely to be remembered.
    b. consistent with the claim that maintenance rehearsal increases the likelihood of transfer to long-term memory; "toaster" is more likely to be remembered than "table".
    c. contradicting the claim that maintenance rehearsal increases the likelihood of transfer to long-term memory; "toaster" and "table" are equally likely to be remembered.
    d. contradicting the claim that maintenance rehearsal increases the likelihood of transfer to long-term memory; "toaster" is more likely to be remembered than "table".

Answer: a
Encoding
pp. 268–269

43. If you are serious about learning the names and positions of China's fifteen most populous cities you will not use:
    a. maintenance rehearsal.
    b. mnemonics.
    c. chunking.
    d. declarative knowledge.

Answer: b
Encoding
pp. 268–269

44. Which of the following tends most strongly to refute the original stage theory of memory?
    a. The capacity of working memory is severely limited.
    b. Maintenance rehearsal does little to aid recall.
    c. Damage of the hippocampus produces more severe anterograde amnesia than it does retrograde amnesia.
    d. Electroconvulsive shock disrupts the memory of material learned just before the shock more than it does more distant memories.

Answer: b
Encoding
pp. 268–269

45. Which of the following facts about memory undoubtedly has the most relevance for a student who is currently in the process of studying for an exam?
    a. The capacty of working memory is severely limited.
    b. Maintenance rehearsal confers little or no benefit in aiding recall.
    c. Items are easily displaced from working memory.
    d. The video-recorder theory of memory is almost certainly false.

Answer: d
Encoding
p. 267

46. Which of the following is true of the capacity of the average adult's working memory (i.e., memory span)?
    a. It never varies.
    b. It has not been determined.
    c. It differs by about 80 percent for different types of items.
    d. It contains approximately seven items.

47. Working memory is to short-term memory as:
    a. loading dock is to warehouse.
    b. active is to passive.
    c. procedural is to declarative.
    d. passive is to depth-of-processing.

48. Using the metaphor of long-term memory as a warehouse, working memory (as opposed to "short-term memory") is best thought of as:
    a. the high shelves in the warehouse where boxes are safely out of reach.
    b. the packer who organizes the contents of each box.
    c. the truck that brings boxes to the warehouse.
    d. the loading dock where boxes sit before they're taken into the warehouse.

49. Working memory differs from long-term memory in terms of:
    a. the length of time information can be stored before it is lost or forgotten.
    b. the degree to which information has been processed before being stored.
    c. the capacity of the memory store.
    d. all of the above

50. The "depth-of-processing" approach:
    a. assumes that the longer material is in working memory the more deep will be its memory traces.
    b. is primarily concerned with a type of memory called "procedural."
    c. suggests that thinking about material leads to better memory than does maintenance rehearsal.
    d. says that meaningless material produces greater depth of processing than does material that can easily be fitted into meaningful contexts.
    e. all of the above

51. An investigator asks some participants to count the number of letters in each of the names on a long list of Russian rivers. She asks other participants to pronounce each river's name and asks, for instance, "Does it rhyme with Vienna?" (for Lenna). She asks still other participants to place the river on a map and to observe into which body of water it flows. This investigator is probably interested in the approach to memory and forgetting called:
    a. interference theory.
    b. stage theory.
    c. script theory.
    d. the depth-of-processing approach.

Answer: b
Encoding
p. 270

52. Subjects are presented with a list of words. They are asked to count the letters in the words in group 1, come up with rhymes for the words in group 2, and come up with synonyms for the words in group 3. Later, their memory for all of the words is tested. Going from best to worst, which pattern correctly indicates how well words in each group will be remembered?
    a. 1, 2, 3
    b. 3, 2, 1
    c. 3, 1, 2
    d. There's no basis for predicting differences among the groups.

Answer: d
Encoding
p. 271

53. The absolute amount of information that can pass from working to long-term memory can be increased by:
    a. fragmenting the information input into the largest number of chunks.
    b. increasing the number of chunks so that each chunk contains the least possible amount of information.
    c. processing the input data exactly as it is presented by the experimenter.
    d. organizing individual pieces of information into larger groups.

Answer: d
Encoding
p. 271

54. Study guides often suggest beginning a chapter by looking through it to notice the headings of the main subdivisions within it. This advice is based on the general principle that:
    a. rote memory can be used for learning longer lengths of material than can memory for meaningful material.
    b. recognition is a more sensitive measure of learning than is recall.
    c. unfamiliar material causes proactive interference.
    d. it is easier to remember materials if relationships are perceived among them than if no relationship is perceived.

Answer: c
Encoding
p. 271

55. Topic sentences in writing are most relevant to what important principle of human memory?
    a. retroactive and proactive interference effects
    b. consolidation effects
    c. organizational effects
    d. recency effects
    e. savings effects

Answer: b
Encoding
p. 271

56. You are preparing for a test. Which of the following suggestions is least likely to result in a better score, keeping total amount of study time constant at 6 hours?
    a. spending a substantial amount of the time thinking about what the material means
    b. reading and underlining each chapter 3 times
    c. outlining the chapter to help you organize the important points
    d. using mental imagery to help you to encode and relate the various facts

Answer: b
Encoding
p. 271

57. From what you know about memory, what is the best organizational advice for a high school student writing her first term paper?
    a. Save the most important information until the end of the paragraph. That is the part that the reader will recall best. (recency effect)
    b. Write a good topic sentence for each paragraph and subordinate the rest of the information in the paragraph to it. (organizational effect)
    c. Space the important information out enough to let the reader have time to consolidate the information. (consolidation effect)
    d. Add a little color to the paper (at least metaphorically) to break up the automatization that the reader is likely to fall into.
    e. Try not to make any explicit conclusions at the end of the paper, to avoid that material interfering with what was read at the start of the paper. (retroactive interference effect)

Answer: d
Encoding
p. 272

58. Techniques used to improve one's memory are collectively called:
    a. image productions.
    b. verbal organizations.
    c. peg methods.
    d. mnemonics.

Answer: a
Encoding
p. 272

59. A mental device for improving memory is called:
    a. a mnemonic.
    b. incidental learning.
    c. latent learning.
    d. anterograde amnesia.

Answer: a
Encoding
p. 272

60. For most people, eighty consecutive syllables of a Shakespeare soliloquy are far easier to learn than a string of ten nonsense syllables, illustrating the effect of:
    a. organization.
    b. serial positioning.
    c. order.
    d. all of the above

Answer: d
Encoding
p. 272

61. If you remember linguist Noam Chomsky's name by visualizing a small elf (a gnome) chomping on a ski you would be using a:
    a. strategy for transferring information from working memory to long-term memory.
    b. mnemonic device.
    c. way of uniting the separate names.
    d. all of the above

Answer: a
Encoding
p. 272

62. "Thirty days hath September, April, June and November . . ." is an example of:
    a. a mnemonic device.
    b. serial reproduction.
    c. retroactive interference.
    d. an attentional process.

Answer: a
Encoding
p. 272

63. "On old Olympus towering top a Finn and German . . . " (first letter of each word is first letter of each cranial nerve, in correct order) is an example of:
    a. a mnemonic.
    b. proactive interference.
    c. serial reproduction.
    d. incidental learning.

Answer: c
Encoding
pp. 272–273

64. "Somewhere between,
    her blue eyes and jeans,
    there's a heart that's been broken
    along with her dreams."

    These lines from a Conway Twitty song are far easier to remember than a string of 8 of Ebbinghaus's 3-letter syllables. This is primarily because:
    a. there are 24 letters in the Ebbinghaus string but only 17 words in this part of the song.
    b. the song is written down as 4 lines rather than as a complete sentence, with all words in a row.
    c. the song is meaningful, it rhymes, and it has a meter to it.
    d. many Americans are quite familiar with Conway Twitty's songs.

Answer: c
Encoding
p. 272

65. Memorizing material using the method of loci:
    a. involves using some image to peg the position of a particular piece of information in a long list.
    b. generally results in a greater difficulty of retrieval.
    c. involves mentally locating each piece of information in a different spatial location.
    d. involves repeating the item over and over in working memory.

Answer: d
Encoding
pp. 272–273

66. Why does imagery help in remembering?
    a. It helps to unify different parts of the material.
    b. It is another way of chunking.
    c. It allows one to create interactive relationships.
    d. all of the above

Answer: d
Encoding
pp. 272–273

67. If you remember Ebbinghaus's name by visualizing a large house ebbing and flowing in a sea of nonsense syllables you would be using a:
    a. scheme for moving information from working to long-term memory.
    b. mnemonic device.
    c. more useful technique than maintenance rehearsal.
    d. all of the above

Answer: c
Encoding
pp. 272–273

68. Mental imagery results in the best facilitation of recall:
    a. when the subject can mentally place each of the items in a different spatial location.
    b. in paired associate learning.
    c. when the image acts to unify the individual component items.
    d. when the image degrades a chunk into its component parts.

Answer: c
Encoding
pp. 272–273

69. Suppose you learn to associate pairs of words by using visual chunking. You would then have the easiest time recalling:
   a. creation-consolidation.
   b. impeach-imagine.
   c. alligator-apple.
   d. loci-lacquer.

Answer: d
Encoding
pp. 272–273

70. The superiority of mnemonic systems over rote learning can be shown for:
   a. material to be recalled immediately.
   b. material to be recalled after a few hours.
   c. material to be recalled the next day.
   d. all of the above

Answer: a
Encoding
p. 273

71. What is the main reason that various mnemonic schemes, like the method of loci, are of limited usefulness in remembering information for most college courses?
   a. The material to be learned usually has an intrinsic organization.
   b. Mnemonic schemes can only be used with meaningless material.
   c. Abstract, rather than concrete, examples are most helpful in learning most course material.
   d. The delay between study and examinations is usually too long for mnemonic schemes to work.

Answer: d
Retrieval
p. 274

72. When a piece of information is said to be inaccessible, it:
   a. was never placed into long-term memory.
   b. cannot be retrieved from working memory.
   c. is lost forever in working memory.
   d. is presently unretrievable from long-term memory.

Answer: c
Retrieval
p. 274

73. You haven't remembered much about your Caribbean voyage of several years ago, but as soon as you feel the ship roll and smell the salty air you recall several details about the voyage. The rolls and smells acted as:
   a. mnemonic devices.
   b. autonomic nervous system stimulants.
   c. retrieval cues.
   d. episodic memories.

Answer: e
Retrieval
p. 274

74. Why are tests of recognition typically easier than tests of recall?
   a. Only working memory is needed to store the material for recognition tests.
   b. Recall is usually limited to about 5 to 7 items.
   c. Recall, but not recognition, requires consolidation.
   d. Recall requires verbal encoding but recognition requires only visual imagery.
   e. Recognition tests usually provide better retrieval cues.

75. When a memory is presently inaccessible it may sometimes be recalled by using an appropriate:
    a. chunk.
    b. nonsense syllable.
    c. retrieval cue.
    d. mnemonic device.

76. An effective way to get access to a forgotten memory is via a:
    a. chunk.
    b. retrieval cue.
    c. rehearsal.
    d. both a and b.

77. You haven't remembered much about your camping trip to Vermont for several years, but as soon as you smell bacon and pine smoke you recall lots of details about the trip. The smells acted as:
    a. loci.
    b. mnemonics.
    c. primacy effects.
    d. recency effects.
    e. retrieval cues.

78. You want to use what you've learned about encoding specificity as you study for your next psychology test. To take advantage of this principle, you should:
    a. always study in the same place.
    b. always study in the same place and then imagine that location while you're taking the test.
    c. always study in the room where the test will be given.
    d. b or c

79. Your introductory psychology class is held in room *A*. For the tests, students are divided among rooms *A*, *B*, and *C*. Given what you've learned about memory, your memory for the material is likely to be best if you take the test in:
    a. room *A*.
    b. the largest of the three rooms.
    c. the smallest of the three rooms.
    d. Where you take the test isn't relevant to your ability to remember the material.

80. Suppose that you always study psychology in a particular part of the library. According to the encoding-specificity principle, you will do best on the tests if you:
    a. imagine that you are in the library as you take the test.
    b. associate the various concepts in the text with the places in the library you would be likely to find relevant books.
    c. pay attention to the details in the materials as you read it.
    d. put yourself into a hypnotic trance prior to each study session.

Answer: d
Retrieval
pp. 274–275

81. A student is presented with a list of word pairs including the pair "stone-chair." According to the encoding-specificity principle, which word would be the best cue for the recall of "chair" on a subsequent task?
    a. table
    b. furniture
    c. charity
    d. stone

Answer: d
Retrieval
pp. 274–275

82. On a test of recall, subjects who learn a list of words in one room do better if tested in that same room than if tested in a different room. This finding is best explained by:
    a. habituation.
    b. method of loci.
    c. positive transfer.
    d. encoding specificity.

Answer: d
Retrieval
p. 275

83. The _____ the processing (encoding) of information, the _____ the likelihood of later remembering it.
    a. simpler; less
    b. simpler; greater
    c. more elaborate; less
    d. more elaborate; greater

Answer: c
Retrieval
p. 275

84. The more elaborate the rehearsal:
    a. the more confused a person is likely to be at the time of retrieval.
    b. the greater the chance for proactive interference.
    c. the greater the likelihood of retrieval.
    d. the less is the need for chunking.

Answer: b
Retrieval
p. 275

85. Elaborative rehearsal seems to be effective because:
    a. like maintenance rehearsal, it increases the amount of time material is in working memory.
    b. it increases the number of retrieval cues linked to the item.
    c. it leads to shallower processing which improves memory.
    d. it makes use of mnemonic devices which improve memory.

Answer: b
Retrieval
p. 275

86. Subjects in group I were asked to judge whether or not a particular word, for instance "breath," would fit into a particular sentence, for instance "He drew his . . . ." Those in group II were asked whether or not the particular word would fit into a sentence like "Mimi was dying of T.B., yet she sang until the end of the opera, when she gasped, looked in the direction of her lover, and took her last . . . ." After a long series of such judgments, all subjects were unexpectedly asked to recall all the words they had judged. Those in group II recalled substantially more, supporting the importance of:
    a. maintenance rehearsal.
    b. elaborative rehearsal.
    c. priming.
    d. trace consolidation.

Answer: c
Retrieval
p. 276

87. When people report how they recall the names of high school classmates after 20 years or so they report that:
    a. the names simply pop up without any special cues.
    b. they must have photos to look at to recall more than a few class-mates.
    c. they hunt through memory by thinking of familiar high school situations.
    d. the number of names remembered immediately varies widely, but names that are not retrieved within the first hour turn out to be almost impossible to retrieve.

Answer: c
Retrieval
p. 276

88. Which of the following would be the least helpful thing to do in trying to remember who played the leads in your sixth grade production of *The Sound of Music*?
    a. Think of each of the songs in the show and try to remember who sang them.
    b. Revisit your old school, especially the room where the rehearsals and performances were held.
    c. Think about unrelated things like the courtroom thriller you're reading, and wait for the names to pop into your head.
    d. Try to picture your sixth grade music class, whom you sang near, whom you could see in the other sections, etc.

Answer: d
Retrieval
pp. 276–277

89. You are about to take your psychology final, for which you've studied very hard. Just before the exam, the person sitting next to you asks you the name of the physiologist who worked on classical conditioning. You suddenly realize that you can't quite remember the name, but it starts with a *p* and is two syllables long. You are experiencing:
    a. repression (motivated forgetting).
    b. fatigue from information overload.
    c. proactive interference.
    d. the tip-of-the-tongue phenomenon.

Answer: b
Retrieval
pp. 276–277

90. The tip-of-the-tongue phenomenon is evidence for the role of _____ in recall.
    a. recognition
    b. memory search
    c. reconstruction
    d. intentional learning

Answer: d
Retrieval
pp. 276–277

91. Subjects who have a tip-of-the-tongue experience are compared with others who have no such experience but who are also unable to come up with the desired target word. The tip-of-the-tongue subjects will probably be better:
    a. at picking out the correct word if it is presented in a list of false alternatives.
    b. able to guess the first letter.
    c. able to guess how many syllables the word is composed of.
    d. all of the above

Answer: c
Retrieval
pp. 276–277

92. When a piece of information is "on the tip of our tongue":
    a. we are unable to recall anything about that piece of information.
    b. that piece of information is irretrievably lost in long-term memory.
    c. some of the aspects of that information are accessible.
    d. a and b

Answer: c
Retrieval
pp. 276–277

93. Almost everybody has had the feeling of knowing the answer to a question, but not being quite able to say it. This is known as the "tip-of-the-tongue" phenomenon, and is a failure of:
    a. retention.
    b. storage.
    c. retrieval.
    d. trace consolidation.
    e. all of the above

Answer: a
Retrieval
p. 277

94. Suppose that you are driving the same route to work you always take. As you listen to the radio you make several correct turns, yet you are not conscious of the cues you used to make the turns. Here, retrieval of your memories:
    a. is implicit.
    b. demonstrates the importance of context specificity for declarative memory.
    c. demonstrates repetition priming.
    d. was similar to that which occurs in flashbulb memory.

Answer: b
Retrieval
p. 278

95. Which of the following methods would be most likely to show the effects of implicit retrieval?
    a. serial reproduction
    b. repetition priming
    c. elaborative rehearsal
    d. trace consolidation

Answer: d
Retrieval
p. 278

96. In studies using repetition priming:
    a. words that were seen recently are recognized more quickly than words that were not seen recently.
    b. priming effects demonstrate implicit memory.
    c. performance on an implicit memory measure seems unrelated to performance on a measure of explicit memory.
    d. all of the above

Answer: b
Retrieval
p. 278

97. Which can be used to demonstrate of implicit memory?
    a. recall
    b. word identification
    c. recognition
    d. all of the above

Answer: a
Retrieval
p. 279

98. Implicit is to explicit as:
    a. word fragment completion is to recall.
    b. recognition is to recall.
    c. recall is to recognition.
    d. word identification is to word fragment completion.

99. Traditional tests of recall and recognition, such as those used in college courses:
    a. assess procedural learning.
    b. depend upon elaborative rehearsal done at the time of studying.
    c. assess explicit learning.
    d. employ repetition priming.

100. Subjects are asked to identify the parts of speech of each word in the sentence, "Orangutans like chocolate yogurt". Later, they're shown the same sentence and asked to rate its truth. Which of the following is true?
    a. Subjects who have seen the sentence previously are more likely to rate it as true than are those who have not.
    b. Only those subjects who remember having seen the sentence previously are more likely to rate it as true than are those who have not.
    c. Subjects who have seen the sentence previously are less likely to rate it as true than are those who have not.
    d. Only those subjects who remember having seen the sentence previously are less likely to rate it as true than are those who have not.

101. In the study about becoming famous overnight:
    a. subjects mistakenly recognized random names seen a day or a few minutes earlier, as belonging to famous people.
    b. subjects mistakenly recognized random names seen a day but not a few minutes earlier, as belonging to famous people.
    c. subjects mistakenly recognized random names seen a few minutes but not a day earlier, as belonging to famous people.
    d. subjects seem to make mistakes because of their explicit memory of having seen the names earlier.

102. Implicit memory differs from explicit memory in that:
    a. the extent to which a subject thinks about the meaning of words to be remembered is more relevant for explicit than implicit memory.
    b. superficial characteristics of words to be remembered, like the way they're written, are more relevant to explicit than implicit memory.
    c. explicit memory effects are stimulus-specific.
    d. all of the above
    e. b and c

Answer: a
When memory fails
p. 280

103. Which of the graphs shown below is the most typical curve for the forgetting of unrelated verbal material?

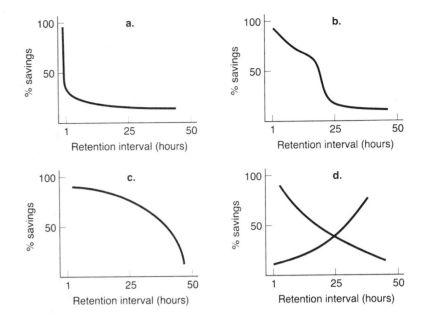

Answer: d
When memory fails
p. 280

104. The forgetting curve indicates that:
    a. the longer the retention interval, the greater the chance of forgetting.
    b. things are forgotten most quickly shortly after they're learned.
    c. at long retention intervals the rate of forgetting tends to flatten out.
    d. all of the above

Answer: b
When memory fails
p. 280

105. A psychologist who believes that memories are traces left in the brain that, if not routinely reactivated, will gradually fade away, would subscribe to which of the following theories of forgetting?
    a. interference
    b. decay
    c. motivated forgetting
    d. amnesia-induced forgetting

Answer: d
When memory fails
p. 280

106. A loss of stored information as a function of time is called:
    a. deterioration.
    b. erosion.
    c. disintegration.
    d. decay.

Answer: d
When memory fails
p. 280

107. The assumption that time plays an important role in forgetting is part of the:
    a. interference theory of forgetting.
    b. repression theory of forgetting.
    c. retrograde amnesia theory of forgetting.
    d. decay theory of forgetting.

Answer: d
When memory fails
p. 280

108. Subjects have been tested for forgetting after long intervals spent awake or asleep. The results of such experiments pose a problem to the:
    a. interference theory of forgetting.
    b. retrieval theory of forgetting.
    c. reconstruction theory of forgetting.
    d. decay theory of forgetting.

Answer: a
When memory fails
p. 280

109. Forgetting is studied in four groups. Groups I and II are fish who are taught a discrimination and tested two months later. Group I spends the interval in a very cold tank; group II spends the same interval in a tank that is much warmer than average. Groups III and IV are rats who are also taught the discrimination and then tested after two months, having spent the two months in either a cold (group III) or a warm (group IV) cage. What differences in forgetting should we expect?
    a. Group I will forget less than group II; groups III and IV should forget the same amount.
    b. Group III will forget less than group IV; groups I and II will forget the same amount.
    c. Group I will forget more than group II; group III will forget more than group IV.
    d. Group II will forget more than group I; group IV will forget more than group III.

Answer: a
When memory fails
p. 280

110. Two groups of subjects learn a task and are tested after a six-hour retention interval. For group I, this interval is spent awake. For the subjects in group II, the interval is passed in sleep, mostly of the slow-wave type. Which group will forget more?
    a. I
    b. II
    c. There will be no difference.
    d. Group I will forget more if the room in which the group II subjects sleep is kept at a cooler than average temperature; II will forget more if the room is kept at warmer than average temperature.

Answer: c
When memory fails
p. 281

111. You listen to a talk radio program with great interest. You then listen to a second similar program. You later find it difficult to remember details of the first. What has probably occurred?
    a. decay of the memory trace
    b. consolidation of the memory trace
    c. retroactive interference
    d. negative transfer

Answer: a
When memory fails
p. 281

112. You watch a new TV program with enthusiasm. You then watch a second similar program. You later find it difficult to remember the details of the second program in that things about the first one keep intruding. What has probably occurred?
    a. proactive interference
    b. trace consolidation
    c. mnemonic transfer
    d. decay of the memory trace

Answer: c
When memory fails
p. 281

113. In a certain verbal learning study, proactive interference was the main cause of forgetting. The study showed, then, that the more lists of material a subject had previously learned the:
     a. better his retention of the newly learned list.
     b. better his retention of the original lists.
     c. poorer his retention of the newly learned list.
     d. poorer his retention of the original lists.

Answer: b
When memory fails
p. 281

114. After losing the combination lock for your bicycle, you buy a new combination lock and use it for a couple of weeks. Then you find your old lock and decide to use it again. When you try to remember the combination, you keep bringing in numbers from the new combination. This difficulty indicates:
     a. proactive interference.
     b. retroactive interference.
     c. motivated forgetting.
     d. decay.

Answer: d
When memory fails
p. 281

115. John is painting numbers on the wall mural for an elementary school. John's friend then calls him over to help paint her mural of the alphabet. When he returns, John begins to paint letters all over his number mural. What is the best explanation for John's mistake?
     a. proactive interference
     b. retrograde amnesia
     c. recall clustering
     d. retroactive interference
     e. decay

Answer: b
When memory fails
p. 281

116. Which of the following is the best example of proactive interference?
     a. You forget your old friend's original family name after she's been married and has had her husband's name for five years.
     b. You forget your old friend's current, married, last name and can only recall the last name she had when you knew her in high school.
     c. You forget exactly where you were when you learned John Lennon was shot, but you remember where you were when you learned the U.S. had invaded Grenada.
     d. You forget all details leading up to the accident in which you hit your head on the car windshield.

Answer: a
When memory fails
p. 281

117. In retroactive interference:
     a. new learning interferes with old learning.
     b. old learning interferes with new learning.
     c. amnesia occurs for recently learned material.
     d. both a and c

Answer: c
When memory fails
p. 281

118. _____ is a theory of forgetting in which a memory is said to be forgotten, not because it was lost or damaged, but rather because it was misplaced among other memories learned before or after it.
     a. Decay
     b. The peg method
     c. Interference
     d. The method of loci

119. In _____ newly learned material hampers the recall of old material.
    a. retroactive interference
    b. proactive interference
    c. decay
    d. extra-experimental interference

120. In proactive inhibition:
    a. old learning interferes with new learning.
    b. new learning interferes with old learning.
    c. amnesia occurs for long-term memory.
    d. both b and c

121. Which of the following is not a likely cause of forgetting?
    a. decay
    b. interference
    c. retroactive interference
    d. mnemonics
    e. proactive interference

122. Bill finds that with each vocabulary list he learns, it becomes harder for him to remember the first list. According to the interference theory of forgetting, this is due to:
    a. retroactive interference.
    b. proactive interference.
    c. disinhibition.
    d. reciprocal inhibition.

123. When you try to give your friends your new phone number you always seem to give them the old number. You are experiencing:
    a. proactive interference.
    b. retroactive interference.
    c. negative feedback.
    d. unconscious inhibition.

124. Which of the following statements is false? Interference:
    a. is more likely to occur when the competing stimulus materials are similar.
    b. can explain the finding that subjects who are asleep retain more over the same retention interval than do subjects who are awake.
    c. always occurs when related material is learned at different times.
    d. suggests that forgotten material has been misplaced rather than erased.

125. Runway performance of rats declines after a retention interval of two months in which all physical conditions were kept constant. This result has been regarded as an argument against one major theory of forgetting. Which?
    a. decay
    b. interference by proactive interference
    c. interference by retroactive interference
    d. change of retrieval cues

126. Returning home after many years causes memories to resurface. In this case, *home* serves as:
    a. an icon.
    b. a retrieval cue.
    c. a mnemonic device.
    d. a memory chunk.

127. That retrieval cues play an important role in memory might be illustrated by the fact that:
    a. we have difficulty recalling events of our childhood.
    b. recognition is easier than recall.
    c. a smell can trigger an image of grandmother's kitchen.
    d. all of the above

128. Which is a potentially plausible account of childhood amnesia?
    a. retroactive interference
    b. change of retrieval cues
    c. poor quality of initial encoding
    d. all of the above

129. Childhood amnesia seems to be related to:
    a. encoding difficulty for implicit memories.
    b. late maturation of brain structures involved in procedural knowledge.
    c. changes in retrieval cues.
    d. proactive inhibition effects.

130. Which of the following is a plausible partial explanation for childhood amnesia?
    a. changed retrieval cues
    b. immaturity of some neural structures
    c. poorly developed schemas for encoding information
    d. Each of the above is plausible.

131. Theories have been proposed that suggest that forgetting occurs because:
    a. the person has lost access to the memory (the index card is incorrect) but the memory is still there.
    b. the memory has decayed (similar to the atrophy of unused muscles).
    c. other memories have interfered with the forgotten memory.
    d. all of the above

132. Which of the following is not a cause of forgetting?
    a. change in retrieval cues
    b. proactive interference
    c. decay
    d. All of the above are causes of forgetting.

Answer: d
When memory fails
p. 283

133. Suppose that you studied Russian during your first 3 years in college, between the ages 18 and 20. When are you likely to forget the most Russian?
     a. between the time that you are 50 and 60
     b. between the ages 40 and 50
     c. between the ages 25 and 35
     d. during your senior year and the first year after college

Answer: d
When memory fails
p. 283

134. What is the major conclusion from studies on the retention of material from college courses across very long periods of time?
     a. Retention is excellent for the first few years, but it then gradually declines.
     b. Retention declines in an almost linear way across the lifespan.
     c. Retention is excellent for the first few years, but by middle age there is a precipitous drop off.
     d. Retention declines rapidly for the first two or three years after which there is not much additional loss.

Answer: b
When memory fails
p. 283

135. Items which are retained over decades are:
     a. in working memory.
     b. said to be in permastore.
     c. equally likely to have been well or poorly learned initially.
     d. b and c

Answer: d
When memory fails
p. 283

136. Bob got grades of A and Bill grades of C during their 3 years of Russian in the late 1940s. What will have happened to their competence at Russian if they haven't used it since 1950?
     a. Bob will have remained competent at almost his original level until the 1960s but Bill will have lost most of what he learned by that time.
     b. Bob will have remained more competent than Bill for about 10 years, but after that the two will be about the same.
     c. Bob's competence will hardly decline until he reaches advanced old age but Bill will show virtually no competence even in the 1960s.
     d. The competence of both will decrease rapidly for a few years, but when they level off Bob will remain substantially more competent than Bill.

Answer: a
When memory fails
p. 283

137. The curve of long-term forgetting for such things as memory for a foreign language:
     a. falls off quickly, then levels off.
     b. falls off gradually during its entire course.
     c. falls off slowly at first, then quickly thereafter.
     d. shows that all learners achieve the same baseline after many years have passed.

Answer: b
When memory fails
p. 284

138. The concept of a flashbulb memory comes from:
     a. the detailed memories that people have of facts that they learned early in life.
     b. the detailed memories that people have of certain important events.
     c. the fact that our memories for some events contain detail only about the central features of the event, and not peripheral details.
     d. the fact that memory for visual stimuli varies as a function of how well lit the stimuli were in their initial presentation.

Answer: a
When memory fails
p. 284

139. Flashbulb memories:
     a. typically concern major, unexpected, public, or personal events.
     b. are remarkably accurate even years after the initial event.
     c. must be due to special encoding mechanisms for emotionally charged events.
     d. all of the above

Answer: d
When memory fails
p. 284

140. Which of the following is a major reason that many researchers doubt that there is anything really special about "flashbulb memory"?
     a. Very few people say that they have experienced such memories.
     b. Although people seem to have them, they are not very confident in their recall.
     c. It seems impossible in terms of what we know about encoding in the brain.
     d. It is usually very hard to validate the details people recall.

Answer: c
When memory fails
p. 284

141. Which of the following is a major reason that many researchers doubt that there is anything really special about "flashbulb memory"?
     a. Very few people say that they have experienced such memories.
     b. Although people seem to have them, they are not very confident in their recall.
     c. Much of what is recalled has been subsequently rehearsed.
     d. It seems impossible in terms of what we know about encoding in the brain.

Answer: a
When memory fails
p. 285

142. If subjects are asked to recall meaningful verbal material, as in Bartlett's stories taken from the folklore of other cultures, there is a tendency to:
     a. recall things as similar to familiar events.
     b. report images rather than meanings.
     c. make errors in terms of acoustic confusions.
     d. show an inability to chunk information.

Answer: b
When memory fails
p. 285

143. Immediately after spending a brief period of time in a professor's office, subjects:
     a. forgot some of the things they had seen in the office but did not claim to have seen things that were not there.
     b. reported having seen books in the office even though there were no books.
     c. reported having seen a microwave oven in the office even though there was no microwave oven.
     d. correctly remembered that there were no books in the office, but a day later, they mistakenly claimed that there were books.

Answer: b
When memory fails
p. 285

144. After reading a story about two people going to a movie, the reader is most likely to make which of the following errors in recalling the story?
    a. forgetting the fact that the fire alarm went off during the movie
    b. claiming that the protagonists bought tickets even though the story didn't mention that
    c. claiming that the movie was a comedy even though it was a drama
    d. claiming that the people behind the protagonists were men when, in fact, they were women

Answer: b
When memory fails
pp. 285–286

145. How does use of a schema improve memory?
    a. It improves memory for details.
    b. It provides a framework to use in interpreting a situation.
    c. It helps avoid making errors in remembering the details of a situation.
    d. all of the above

Answer: a
When memory fails
p. 286

146. A schema is:
    a. a conceptual framework for interpreting a situation.
    b. a form of proactive interference.
    c. a form of retroactive interference.
    d. an item that has been forgotten.

Answer: d
When memory fails
pp. 285–286

147. A big disadvantage to schema-based memory is that:
    a. the main concepts are often forgotten.
    b. it requires substantially more processing capacity than does more data-driven memory.
    c. it is more subject to interference than is more data-driven memory.
    d. memory for details is often faulty.

Answer: b
When memory fails
p. 286

148. _____ are the special schemas we have for recurring everyday events, like checking out at a supermarket.
    a. Cues
    b. Scripts
    c. Mnemonics
    d. Accommodative distortions

Answer: a
When memory fails
pp. 286–287

149. A major problem in eyewitness testimony is the influence of:
    a. reconstructive memory.
    b. long-term memory.
    c. retroactive inhibition.
    d. retrograde amnesia.
    e. mnemonic devices.

Answer: a
When memory fails
p. 287

150. What is a major concern about the way questions are worded during an interrogation in terms of their potential influence on what is recalled at a subsequent trial?
    a. They can implant false memories.
    b. They can produce retrograde amnesia.
    c. They can produce proactive interference.
    d. They can reactivate repressed memories.

Answer: d
When memory fails
pp. 287–288

151. Errors in memory for events are often due to:
    a. general knowledge intruding into the specific recollection.
    b. aspects of more than one event being confused.
    c. source confusion.
    d. all of the above

Answer: a
When memory fails
pp. 287–288

152. Source confusion:
    a. can explain errors in memory.
    b. refers to forgetting the source of things learned in childhood.
    c. is another term for a lack of retrieval cues.
    d. only occurs as a result of hypnosis.

Answer: b
When memory fails
pp. 287–288

153. Which of the following statements is false?
    a. Memory retrieval may involve some memory reconstruction.
    b. Memory errors are due to problems at retrieval, not encoding.
    c. Memory errors may be due to source confusion.
    d. It's unclear whether storied memories can be erased or altered.

Answer: c
When memory fails
pp. 287–288

154. Included in an eyewitness' report is the accurate claim that the thief wore a red jacket. The eyewitness then sees a lineup in which the thief is wearing a blue jacket. She later reports that the thief wore a blue jacket during the theft. This error is most likely due to
    a. retrieval confusion.
    b. an error in initial encoding.
    c. source confusion.
    d. proactive interference.

Answer: c
When memory fails
pp. 288–289

155. Hypnosis allows people to:
    a. relive their past.
    b. perform feats of agility of which they would otherwise be incapable.
    c. be unusually cooperative and believe in another person.
    d. all of the above

Answer: d
When memory fails
pp. 288–289

156. Hypnosis:
    a. convinces a person that his or her reconstructions are the real thing.
    b. allows people to relive their childhoods.
    c. can yield inaccurate and untrue memories.
    d. all of the above

Answer: d
When memory fails
pp. 288–289

157. You are a trial lawyer defending your client against a murder charge. The district attorney introduces testimony obtained from an eyewitness through hypnosis. You immediately object because:
    a. the testimony is damaging.
    b. 90 percent of hypnotized subjects recall lost memories.
    c. the witness is near-sighted.
    d. the witness is likely to be very confident of a memory that could be completely inaccurate.

Answer: b
When memory fails
pp. 288–289

158. Which of the following statements is false?
     a. Apparent reliving of childhood experiences through hypnosis is actually pretense.
     b. If memory obtained through hypnosis is recalled with great confidence, it must be accurate.
     c. Drawings produced by adults hypnotized and told to relive their sixth birthday are more sophisticated than drawings they actually produced at six.
     d. a and c

Answer: c
When memory fails
pp. 288–289

159. Dan is hypnotized and told he's back in his kindergarten class. Which of the following statements is true?
     a. His drawings will be indistinguishable from those he made in kindergarten.
     b. His answers to questions about how things work will be indistinguishable from the answers of actual kindergartners.
     c. His behavior will represent the adult Dan's expectations of how a kindergartner would behave.
     d. a and b

Answer: b
When memory fails
pp. 288–289

160. A witness sees a car leaving the scene of a crime. She says she doesn't remember the car's license plate number. Under hypnosis she is told she can see the car and read its plate. She produces a number which:
     a. is probably accurate.
     b. is probably stated confidently.
     c. demonstrates that she must have seen the plate initially.
     d. all of the above

Answer: e
When memory fails
pp. 289–290

161. How would you reply to a friend who says "Memory is like a videotape recording; you may misplace the tape but if you can locate it everything isstill there"?
     a. The only good evidence for this comes from studies of recall under hypnosis.
     b. The only good evidence for this comes from studies in which people have had their temporal lobes electrically stimulated while undergoing surgery for relief of epilepsy.
     c. The only good evidence for this comes from studies of making free associations while in a very relaxed and trusting state.
     d. Yes. There is good evidence from all three of the above sources.
     e. There is no good evidence for this view; it's very unlikely memory works this way.

Answer: c
When memory fails
p. 290

162. Under hypnosis Sam recalls painfully and vividly being sexually abused from ages 3–4 by his aunt and uncle. Passport and visa records, however, show that his aunt and uncle had been out of the country continuously during that entire period of Sam's life. Research on repressed memories indicates that Sam's therapist should:
     a. infer that the documents of the relatives have been altered.
     b. infer that Sam had probably been out of the country with his aunt and uncle during that time.
     c. be aware that his or her own talk with Sam may have created false memories.
     d. be aware that there could be minor distortions but should infer that Sam was almost certainly sexually abused by someone while he was very young.

Answer: a
When memory fails
pp. 290–292

163. Memories that are said to be "recovered" after years of being repressed:
    a. are quite possibly false.
    b. are typically minor distortions of real childhood experiences.
    c. generally emerge full-blown without any prodding.
    d. may or may not be accurate, though the phenomenon of repression clearly does exist.

Answer: d
When memory fails
pp. 290–291

164. Therapists:
    a. may, through their use of hypnosis, lead subjects to fabricate memories.
    b. may, through their use of "memory-promoting drugs," lead subjects to fabricate memories.
    c. may, through their use of suggestive questions, lead subjects to fabricate memories.
    d. all of the above

Answer: c
When memory fails
pp. 291–292

165. Memory without bottom-up processing would result in:
    a. hallucinations.
    b. highly accurate recall.
    c. perpetual delusions and reconstructions.
    d. overloading of the storage capacity with irrelevant detail.

Answer: c
When memory fails
pp. 291–292

166. A major cost to top-down processing in memory is that it:
    a. requires more storage capacity than does bottom-up.
    b. makes it difficult to take context into account.
    c. can lead to distortions.
    d. restricts the use of schemas.

Answer: a
When memory fails
pp. 291–292

167. A major cost to purely bottom-up processing in memory is that it would:
    a. be very demanding of our limited cognitive machinery.
    b. overemphasize the central features to be recalled and omit the details.
    c. distort memory by reorganizing on the basis of subsequent information.
    d. lead to memory much like that of a patient with Korsakoff's syndrome.

Answer: b
When memory fails
pp. 292–293

168. A patient with anterograde amnesia will:
    a. have a shorter memory span than normal persons.
    b. have serious difficulties in learning any new information and retaining it.
    c. suffer a loss of memories for at least 5 years prior to the cerebral trauma that caused his condition.
    d. have difficulties remembering the names for common objects.

Answer: b
When memory fails
p. 292

169. Korsakoff's syndrome is most often found in:
    a. infants with fetal alcohol syndrome.
    b. chronic alcoholics.
    c. adults with protein-calorie malnutrition.
    d. epileptics.
    e. schizophrenics.

170. In Korsakoff's syndrome a part of the thalamus degenerates. What part of the cerebrum is this part of the thalamus most likely to be connected with?
    a. limbic areas, like the hippocampus
    b. motor regions, like the primary motor cortex
    c. motor association regions, like Broca's area
    d. visual areas, like those in the occipital lobe
    e. interhemispheric connections, like the corpus callosum

171. A patient with Korsakoff's syndrome will:
    a. have a shorter memory span than normal persons.
    b. have serious difficulties in learning any new information and retaining it.
    c. suffer a loss of memories for at least 5 years prior to the cerebral trauma that caused his condition.
    d. have difficulties remembering the names for common objects.

172. Patients with anterograde amnesia:
    a. cannot remember events before their injuries.
    b. cannot remember their names.
    c. cannot hold anything in working memory.
    d. cannot learn new facts after their injuries.

173. Sarah has a mild anterograde amnesia. At which of the following will she probably do most poorly?
    a. remembering where she parked her car this morning
    b. recalling the multiplication tables from 1×1 to 11×11
    c. recognizing her husband when he phones but doesn't say his name
    d. recalling how to swim
    e. remembering that all English words need at least one vowel

174. Damage to which of the following regions of the human brain is most likely to produce anterograde amnesia?
    a. left frontal cortex, especially near Broca's area
    b. left parietal-temporal cortex, especially near Wernicke's area
    c. hippocampus and related temporal areas
    d. corpus callosum

175. A person who, following brain surgery, is unable to transfer new information from working memory to long-term memory would most likely:
    a. fail to recognize members of his family.
    b. fail to recognize someone he met a few minutes ago.
    c. forget his name.
    d. be unable to carry out mental arithmetic.
    e. be diagnosed with retrograde amnesia.

176. H.M. is a neurological patient who has severe _____ amnesia as a result of damage to his _____.
   a.   retrograde; corpus callosum
   b.   retrograde; hippocampus
   c.   retrograde; cerebral cortex
   d.   anterograde; hippocampus
   e.   anterograde; cerebral cortex

177. The parts of the nervous system concerned with memory that were damaged in the famous neurological patient H.M. were in the:
   a.   frontal lobe.
   b.   occipital lobe.
   c.   parietal lobe.
   d.   temporal lobe.

178. The famous neurological patient H.M. lost much of his ability to consolidate memories when regions of his temporal lobe were removed in an attempt to:
   a.   alleviate his schizophrenia.
   b.   control his epilepsy.
   c.   reduce the symptoms of Korsakoff's disease.
   d.   reduce his severe mental retardation.
   e.   alleviate the apraxia caused by a tumor in the frontal lobe.

179. Lesions of the hippocampus and related temporal lobe structures lead to an impairment in the ability to:
   a.   transfer information from perception to working memory.
   b.   retrieve information from working memory.
   c.   retrieve information from long-term memory.
   d.   learn new information.

180. In cases of anterograde amnesia patients have trouble:
   a.   remembering what they learned prior to the brain trauma.
   b.   remembering what they learned during the periods immediately prior to and immediately following the brain trauma, but memory capacities eventually recover.
   c.   retrieving information initially encountered after the brain trauma.
   d.   remembering those past events, the representation of which is stored in the hippocampus.

181. Who of the following is likely to have the most difficult time remembering a person she first met half an hour ago?
   a.   a mnemonist with Ebbinghaus's syndrome
   b.   a chronic alcoholic with Korsakoff's syndrome
   c.   an eleven-year-old girl with anorexia nervosa
   d.   a depressed patient who received electroconvulsive therapy three months ago

182. Mr. Jones hits his head on the windshield in an auto accident and can now recall none of the events that led up to the accident. This memory problem is called:
    a. traumatic amnesia.
    b. repression.
    c. anterograde amnesia.
    d. retrograde amnesia.

183. Paula received a severe blow to the head in a car accident. What is the most reasonable explanation for her amnesia of what led up to the accident?
    a. The information wasn't yet consolidated in long-term memory.
    b. Working memory interfered with the long-term memory storage.
    c. Semantic memory has been disrupted.
    d. She has lost the use of her hippocampus. That is, she is like H.M., but not as severely impaired.

184. Rambo was hit across the head with a rifle. What is the most plausible explanation for his amnesia of what led up to his getting hit?
    a. His semantic memory was disrupted.
    b. There was a disruption of trace consolidation.
    c. Neither his right nor his left hippocampus now function properly, so that he is similar to the neurological patient H.M.
    d. There has been massive proactive interference.

185. A sudden blow to the head often causes forgetting of the events in the few seconds or minutes that preceded the blow. This finding is most consistent with which of the following ideas about memory?
    a. New memory traces require consolidation.
    b. Temporal contiguity is impressed upon the mind.
    c. Memory often depends upon organizational factors.
    d. There is a limit of about seven items that can be held in working memory at one time.

186. The principle distinction between retrograde and anterograde amnesia is that:
    a. retrograde is inherited; anterograde is learned.
    b. anterograde is temporary; retrograde is permanent.
    c. anterograde involves forgetting things after a certain time; retrograde involves forgetting things prior to a certain time.
    d. anterograde affects long-term memory; retrograde affects working memory.

187. Retrograde amnesia:
    a. is the condition representing the inability to learn new information following some neural trauma.
    b. results from interference with retrieval from working memory.
    c. is not constant in the sense that some of the memories preceding the accident that are "lost" do reappear with time.
    d. all of the above

188. A cartoon staple is a character who is hit on the head and can no longer remember who he is or what's going on. This condition most closely resembles:
    a. anterograde amnesia.
    b. retrograde amnesia.
    c. proactive interference.
    d. retroactive interference.

189. You might expect an anterograde amnesiac to be unable to do which of the following tasks?
    a. learn to solve a complicated maze
    b. tell you about an event that occurred in his childhood
    c. recall having met his newborn grandchild yesterday
    d. utter a complete sentence
    e. read the newspaper aloud

190. A recent news report tells that a patient with serious and permanent anterograde amnesia has, through special training, been able to remember some things well enough to use them at a job. From what you know about memory you should guess that the kinds of things this patient has acquired entail:
    a. verbal memory.
    b. procedural memory.
    c. nonverbal declarative memory.
    d. episodic memory.
    e. explicit memory.

191. H.M., the famous neurological patient who has serious and permanent amnesia, can remember some things. For the most part, these things are:
    a. aspects of declarative memory acquired prior to his surgery and procedural memory of things learned both before and since his surgery.
    b. procedural memory for most things acquired prior to his surgery and episodic memory of things learned both before and since his surgery.
    c. procedural memory for most things acquired prior to his surgery and semantic memory for events that have happened since his surgery.
    d. verbal memories prior to his surgery and episodic ones since then.

192. For several years researchers thought that damage to the hippocampus in nonhuman animals produced no defects in memory. This is now known not to be true. The inference that the hippocampus is not involved in memory except in people would, at first, seem sensible. Most tests of memory in animals involve memory for tasks learned by instrumental or classical conditioning, kinds of memory closest to those classed as:
    a. semantic.
    b. declarative.
    c. explicit.
    d. procedural.

193. Special tests are needed to reveal any defects in memory by nonhuman animals that have had their hippocampus removed. Such animals show no abnormal forgetting of classically or instrumentally conditioned responses. These findings make sense in light of what we know about the hippocampus and human memory, because even H.M. shows good acquisition of knowledge classed as:
    a. semantic.
    b. declarative.
    c. episodic.
    d. procedural.

194. Encephalitis left a musician without his hippocampus and much of the cerebral cortex that feeds into it. He still carries on a good conversation with everyday chit-chat, but can recall virtually nothing from his past nor can he learn what just happened in his life. Which of the following kinds of memory does it seem most likely still functions for him?
    a. episodic
    b. semantic
    c. procedural
    d. mnemonic
    e. declarative

195. Anterograde amnesiacs:
    a. can learn lists of words for a later recognition test.
    b. can learn to identify people and recognize them later.
    c. get better at some motor skills with practice.
    d. all of the above

196. In 1975, a cardiac arrest resulted in Peter, who was fifty at the time, losing a crucial part of his hippocampus in both cerebral hemispheres. He now has severe anterograde amnesia. With what will he have the most trouble?
    a. throwing a bowling ball well, a skill he acquired in 1985
    b. identifying pictures of John F. Kennedy and Lyndon Johnson
    c. remembering the names of his parents, who were killed in a car crash in the late 1960s
    d. remembering his social security number
    e. identifying a picture of Madonna

197. Procedural is to declarative as:
    a. explicit is to implicit.
    b. top-down is to bottom-up.
    c. implicit is to explicit.
    d. working memory is to long-term memory.

198. Declarative memory, is:
    a. conscious and explicit.
    b. conscious and implicit.
    c. unconscious and explicit.
    d. unconscious and implicit.

Answer: b
When memory fails
p. 295

199. The priming procedures with word fragments used to reveal memory in amnesiacs:
    a. work only when the patient consciously tries to recall.
    b. take advantage of their spared implicit memory.
    c. are a way of testing procedural memory.
    d. all of the above

Answer: b
When memory fails
p. 295

200. An anterograde amnesiac, Dawn, is shown a list of words including "toothpaste". Shortly thereafter, she's shown "_ O _ T _ P _ S _ E" and asked to fill in the blanks. Another anterograde amnesiac, Rodney, is given the fill-in-the-blank task without the initial word list. Results on the fill-in-the-blank task are most likely to indicate that:
    a. Dawn does as poorly as Rodney because she's forgotten the words on the list.
    b. Dawn does better than Rodney because her implicit memory was spared.
    c. Dawn does better than Rodney because her procedural memory was spared.
    d. Dawn does as poorly as Rodney because they've both suffered losses to their problem solving skills.

Answer: a
When memory fails
pp. 296–297

201. Which of the following statements is false?
    a. Associative retrieval involves actively searching for a memory.
    b. Associative retrieval and strategic retrieval seem to rely on different areas of the brain.
    c. Certain kinds of brain damage lead not only to memory loss, but also to false recollections.
    d. Certain kinds of brain damage may disrupt episodic memory while leaving memory for generic information intact.

Answer: b

When memory fails
pp. 296–297

202. Evidence from people with different types of brain damage indicates that:
    a. the neurological control center for all types of memory is the hippocampus.
    b. some types of memory can be disrupted while other types remain intact.
    c. episodic memory is a specific type of generic memory.
    d. strategic retrieval is a specific type of associative retrieval.

Answer: b
When memory fails
pp. 296–297

203. Strategic retrieval:
    a. is primarily controlled by the hippocampus.
    b. involves actively searching for a memory.
    c. is a specific type of associative retrieval.
    d. all of the above

Answer: d
When memory fails
pp. 296–297

204. Some brain-damaged patients:
    a. seem to be incapable of fear conditioning.
    b. can't remember details of specific events they experienced, but can remember general information.
    c. lose memory for a lot of general knowledge like the names of U.S. Presidents, but retain memory for events they have experienced.
    d. all of the above

Answer: c
When memory fails
pp. 296–297

205. The amygdala plays an important role in:
    a. generic memory.
    b. procedural memory.
    c. memory for emotional events.
    d. visual memory.

| # Thought and Knowledge

Answer: c
Thought and knowledge

p. 301

1. Which of the following is not an example of directed thinking?
   a. trying to identify a partially completed word in a crossword puzzle
   b. trying to figure out how to make your paper airplane more aero-dynamic
   c. remembering and laughing over the previous night's escapades
   d. planning how to break off a relationship without having anything thrown at you

Answer: b
Thought and knowledge
p. 301

2. The way or ways that psychologists use the term *think* is or are:
   a. interchangeable with the way *believe* is used in ordinary speech.
   b. substantially narrower than the way or ways it is used in ordinary speech.
   c. considerably broader than the way or ways it is used in ordinary speech.
   d. defined in terms of the underlying neural processes.

Answer: b
Thought and knowledge
p. 301

3. Figuring out "who done it" in a mystery is an example of what psychologists would include under the term:
   a. thinking, as it is used as a close synonym for a system of beliefs.
   b. directed thinking.
   c. chunking.
   d. mental set.

Answer: a
Thought and knowledge
p. 301

4. Psychological research on thinking is mainly directed at the meaning of the term closest to:
   a. reasoning.
   b. attending.
   c. believing.
   d. remembering.

Answer: d
Thought and knowledge
p. 301

5. Which of the following best exemplifies the use of the word *think* as it is typically studied by psychologists?
   a. "I think that the U.S. policy toward Central America in the 1980s was immoral."
   b. "I think she really is in love with me."
   c. "I couldn't think of who John Locke was."
   d. "I can think through the answer to the physics problem even though I've not seen that kind before."

Answer: d
Thought and knowledge
p. 301

6. Thinking that is aimed at the solution of a well-defined problem is called:
   a. concentration.
   b. reflection.
   c. reasoning.
   d. directed thinking.

Answer: d
Analogical representations
p. 301

7. Our thoughts are composed of:
   a. images of analogical representations.
   b. mental representations.
   c. both analogical and symbolic representations.
   d. all of the above

Answer: c
Analogical representations
pp. 301–302

8. The information contained in a satellite weather map that is shown on TV, a map which shows cloud cover and the outlines of rivers, lakes, and the sea, is in the form of:
   a. a mental representation.
   b. a hypothetical representation.
   c. an analogical representation.
   d. a symbolic representation.

Answer: b
Analogical representations
pp. 301–302

9. A road sign showing the silhouette of a jumping deer is an example of a(n) _____ representation.
   a. symbolic
   b. analogical
   c. hypothetical
   d. mental

Answer: a
Analogical representations
pp. 301–302

10. The Roman numeral *X* is an example of a(n) _____ representation.
    a. symbolic
    b. analogical
    c. hypothetical
    d. mental

Answer: d
Analogical representations
pp. 301–302

11. The Arabic number *3* is an example of a(n) _____ representation.
    a. mental
    b. hypothetical
    c. analogical
    d. symbolic

12. A cartoon of President Clinton with a big chin and a burger in his hand is an example of a(n) _____ representation.
    a. mental
    b. hypothetical
    c. analogical
    d. symbolic

13. Your exam comes back with the marking at the top "89%". In this example, the:
    a. 89 is a symbolic representation, the % an analogical one.
    b. 89 is an analogical representation, the % a symbolic one.
    c. 89 and the % are both symbolic representations.
    d. 89 and the % are both analogical representations.

14. On the door to the women's room is a silhouette of a person in a skirt. This exemplifies:
    a. an analogical representation.
    b. a symbolic representation.
    c. a hypothetical representation.
    d. a mental representation.

15. Which of the following cases is most on the borderline between a symbolic and an analogical representation?
    a. the Roman numeral III
    b. the green light on a traffic signal
    c. the words "Her Royal Highness," meaning Queen Elizabeth II
    d. an aerial photograph of Manhattan, Brooklyn, and Queens

16. Unlike images, words are typically:
    a. analogical.
    b. not arbitrary.
    c. non-representational.
    d. symbolic.

17. Compared to the word *train*, the word *choo-choo* is:
    a. more symbolic.
    b. more analogical.
    c. more mental.
    d. more arbitrary.

18. A line drawing that can be seen as either a mouse or an old man is an example of:
    a. a symbolic representation.
    b. an analogical representation.
    c. a hypothetical representation.
    d. a mental representation.

Answer: b
Analogical representations
pp. 301–302

19. A painter fills a shotgun shell with black paint, shoots it at a canvas and titles the result "Holocaust." This painting is a:
    a. mental representation.
    b. symbolic representation.
    c. analogical representation.
    d. hypothetical representation.

Answer: b
Analogical representations
p. 303

20. Mental images are:
    a. not found in blind persons.
    b. not necessarily visual.
    c. dependent upon vision.
    d. not analogical.

Answer: a
Analogical representations
p. 303

21. A group of ninety people take a test composed of items like telling which of two gloves seen in an unusual position is a right and which is a left, or telling which of two pictures of knots shows a knot that will come untied by simply pulling on the rope's ends. What will be the relationship between performance on this test and the self-reports of visual imagery?
    a. On average, there will be little relationship.
    b. There will be a strong and positive relationship. People who report the strongest visual imagery will do the best on the test.
    c. There will be a strong, but negative, relationship. People who report the strongest visual imagery will do the worst on the test.
    d. Those who report strong or poor visual imagery will do worst on the test. Those who self-report moderate imagery will do best.

Answer: c
Analogical representations
p. 303

22. Suppose we ask people whether they have vivid imagery or do not, and then measure their memory for spatial designs. We are most likely to find:
    a. that people who say they have vivid imagery are better at remembering spatial designs.
    b. that people who say that they have vivid imagery are worse at remembering spatial designs.
    c. that there is no relation between self-rating of imagery vividness and memory for spatial designs.
    d. that there is a positive relation between self-rating and spatial memory, but only for those persons who have eidetic imagery.

Answer: c
Analogical representations
p. 303

23. Self-reports of visual imagery:
    a. are positively correlated with spatial skills.
    b. are negatively correlated with spatial skills.
    c. may over- or underestimate the quality of visual images.
    d. provide a reasonably accurate way of ranking subjects for visual imagery skills.

Answer: d
Analogical representations
pp. 303–304

24. Eidetic imagery is more frequent in:
    a. adults than in children; in children it occurs in about one child in three.
    b. adults than in children; in children it occurs in about one child in twenty.
    c. children than in adults; in children it occurs in about one child in three.
    d. children than in adults; in children it occurs in about one child in twenty.

Answer: a
Analogical representations
pp. 303–304

25. Lila can recall every detail of a picture she glances at. This *photographic* memory is known as:
    a. eidetic imagery.
    b. episodic memory.
    c. generic memory.
    d. Korsakoff's syndrome.

Answer: a
Analogical representations
pp. 303–304

26. Among which group of people would you be most likely to find a person with eidetic imagery?
    a. schoolchildren
    b. memory experts
    c. women over fifty
    d. people who have had the corpus callosum severed

Answer: d
Analogical representations
pp. 303–304

27. A person looks at a picture of a lion. After the picture is removed the person is unexpectedly asked some questions about the picture and is able to count the number of whiskers on the animal's face by examining her mental image. Most likely, this person:
    a. is over age thirty.
    b. has excellent episodic memory.
    c. has had the corpus callosum cut.
    d. has eidetic imagery.

Answer: d
Analogical representations
pp. 303–304

28. Sam tells you that he has eidetic imagery. You have him look at the first five lines of this very test question for thirty seconds, after which he knows that you will ask him to recall something. At the end of thirty seconds you remove the printed item. Which would now be the best test, if he really has what he says he has?
    a. Have him count the number of words in the first five lines.
    b. Have him repeat the entire five lines, verbatim.
    c. Have him describe in detail just what his visual image is like.
    d. Have him read off the last letter of the last word in each line.

Answer: d
Analogical representations
pp. 303–304

29. The term *eidetic imagery* is what is commonly known as:
    a. mental imagery.
    b. visual imagery.
    c. the type of imagery used by most memory experts.
    d. photographic memory.

Answer: c
Analogical representations
pp. 303–304

30. When we say someone has a "photographic memory," we are saying that the person is capable of:
    a. iconic memory.
    b. short-term memory.
    c. eidetic imagery.
    d. mental rotation.

Answer: a
Analogical representations
p. 304

31. Subjects were shown Rs rotated by various degrees. Sometimes they were genuine Rs that were rotated; sometimes they were mirror image Rs. The subjects' task was to decide whether the rotated Rs were normal or mirror reversed. The results showed that the time needed to make this decision was:
    a. directly proportional to the angle of rotation from the upright.
    b. increased with the angle of rotation, but not proportionally; the first ten degrees took more time than the next ten degrees, and so on.
    c. increased with the angle of rotation, but not proportionally; the first ten degrees took less time than the next ten degrees, and so on.
    d. unaffected by the angle of rotation from the upright.

Answer: a
Analogical representations
p. 304

32. You look at two arrangements of blocks and mentally rotate one to see whether it is exactly like the other. What is the most reasonable inference you can make from such studies?
    a. In doing this your mental processes are analogical and in some ways similar to those used in actually rotating the blocks by hand.
    b. In doing this the time that you take to determine whether they are the same or different will be influenced by top-down processes but not by the relative orientation of the two sets of blocks.
    c. You must rely on top-down processing that involves your knowledge of verbal concepts like *up*, *down*, *right*, and *left*.
    d. The rapidity with which you respond is unrelated to how many degrees one construction is rotated from the other.

33. Which of the following graphs best shows the relationship between the tilt of a letter *E* and the reaction time to respond as to whether it is a normal or a mirror-reversed example of the letter?

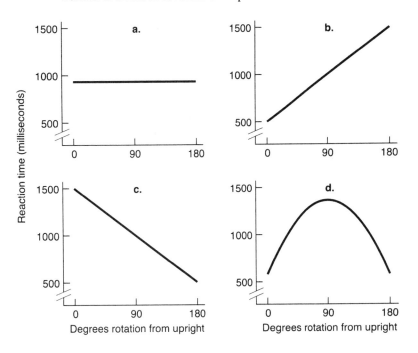

34. Which of the following graphs best shows the relationship between the tilt of a letter *G* and the reaction time to determine if the letter is a normal *G* or one that is a mirror reversal of the letter?

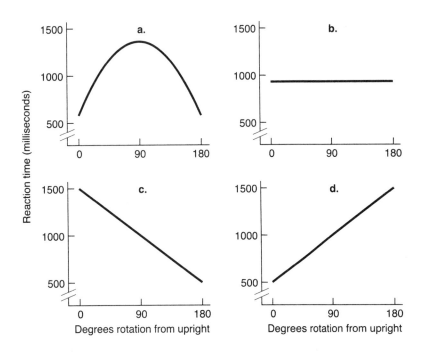

Answer: b
Analogical representations
pp. 304–305

35. Subjects are given an unfamiliar map with several points highlighted and are asked to study it. Later, without looking at the map, they are asked to picture an object moving from one of the highlighted points to another. Results will most likely:
    a.   be that response time is unrelated to how far apart the points are.
    b.   be that response times vary such that points that are further apart take longer than points that are closer together.
    c.   indicate that this task does not involve analogical processes.
    d.   contradict the findings from mental rotation studies.

Answer: d
Analogical representations
pp. 301–305

36. Studies of both image scanning and mental rotation indicate that in important ways, visual imagery is:
    a.   symbolic.
    b.   present mainly in children of grade-school age.
    c.   generic.
    d.   analogical.

Answer: e
Analogical representations
pp. 301–305

37. Research on mental rotation and image scanning suggests that mental images:
    a.   cannot be studied experimentally.
    b.   are identical to the perception that produced them.
    c.   are generally eidetic.
    d.   are primarily symbolic representations.
    e.   are primarily analogical representations.

Answer: d
Analogical representations
pp. 305–306

38. Research indicates that:
    a.   the same brain areas are involved in visual perception and visual imagery.
    b.   people who lose the ability to perceive colors often also lose the ability to imagine colors.
    c.   people who lose the ability to perceive fine detail often also lose the ability to see fine detail in visual imagery.
    d.   all of the above

Answer: c
Analogical representations
p. 306

39. Images are picture-like, but they are not mental pictures. This is indicated by the fact that:
    a.   they can be rotated.
    b.   they can be scanned.
    c.   they are already somewhat encoded.
    d.   all of the above

Answer: a
Analogical representations
p. 306

40. A drawing that can look like either a man or a rat is viewed for a few seconds. After the drawing is removed the subject is asked to describe the visual image that can still be "seen." What will the subject most likely describe?
    a.   either the man or the rat, whichever was perceived originally
    b.   a reversal of the perception, from man to rat and vice versa
    c.   a figure that looks in part like a man, in part like a rat
    d.   The subject is about equally likely to describe any of the above.

41. Many Pennsylvanians are surprised to learn that Sao Paolo, Brazil, is substantially east of Philadelphia, yet they have no hesitation about saying Anchorage, Alaska, is a lot to the west. Chances are that they make the Brazil mistake because:
    a. they know that if one goes by land one must go west to get to Mexico, through which one must go on the way to South America.
    b. they don't know that Brazil is in South America.
    c. one must do a mental rotation of the map of the Americas to figure out about time zones.
    d. mental scanning is primarily analogical.

42. Research participants are asked to estimate the distance between 1) a city on the East Coast of the U.S. and one on the West Coast and 2) between a city on the East Coast of the U.S. and one in the Midwest. Results will:
    a. demonstrate the use of symbolic representations.
    b. be that participants take about the same amount of time to make each judgment, and are more accurate for #2.
    c. be that participants take about the same amount of time to make each judgment, and are about equally accurate.
    d. be that participants take slightly longer for judgment #1 than #2.

43. Two research participants are given pairs of cities in North America and asked to judge which member of the pair is further east, west, north, or south. Both participants have frequently seen maps of North America, but only one is allowed to use a map during this task. Their responses are most likely to differ for a comparison that requires them to:
    a. judge that a city on the East Coast is east of a city on the West Coast.
    b. judge that a city on the East Coast is east of a city in the Midwest.
    c. judge that a city in Canada is south of a city in the U.S.
    d. judge that a city in the U.S. is south of a city in Canada.
    e. all of the above

44. A subject is asked to picture a map of the U.S. and judge relations between pairs of cities. He wrongly indicates that San Diego, California is west of Reno, Nevada. This mistake indicates his use of:
    a. eidetic imagery.
    b. symbolic representations.
    c. analogical representations.
    d. image scanning.

45. Assume a subject is asked to estimate four distances from a given location. Which estimation would take the most time?
    a. 1 mile
    b. 5 miles
    c. 1/2 mile
    d. 3 miles

46. Mental constructs that allow one to group or categorize similar events or objects are called:
    a. algorithms.
    b. concepts.
    c. heuristics.
    d. propositions.
    e. thoughts.

47. One comes to realize that *dog, cow, hen, rat, etc.*, all belong to that class we call *animal*. In this sense, *animal* is a:
    a. relational concept.
    b. concept.
    c. proposition.
    d. mental image.

48. A(n) _____ makes a statement about a relationship between a noun phrase (the subject) and a verb phrase (the predicate).
    a. attitude.
    b. category.
    c. concept.
    d. proposition.

49. *Propositions* are:
    a. relationships between subjects and predicates.
    b. another word for *concepts*.
    c. categories.
    d. invariably true.

50. In the sentence "The zebra is suspicious of the zookeeper," the phrase "is suspicious of the zookeeper" is:
    a. the proposition.
    b. the subject.
    c. the predicate.
    d. a relational concept.

51. In the sentence "The zebra came over to the zookeeper," the phrase "The zebra" is:
    a. a proposition.
    b. the subject.
    c. the predicate.
    d. a relational concept.

52. A distinction between the memory for particular events in one's life and memory for the meaning of concepts and knowledge about the world is known as the:
    a. procedural-declarative distinction.
    b. autobiographical-declarative distinction.
    c. parallel-hierarchical distinction.
    d. episodic-generic distinction.

Answer: c
Symbolic representations
p. 308

53. When you remember what you were doing when you heard about the death of Princess Diana, you're drawing on:
    a. semantic memory.
    b. hierarchical memory.
    c. episodic memory.
    d. generic memory.

Answer: a
Symbolic representations
p. 309

54. Semantic memory is a form of:
    a. generic memory.
    b. episodic memory.
    c. hierarchical memory.
    d. visual memory.

Answer: c
Symbolic representations
p. 309

55. A subject is presented with a word. The task for the subject is to come up with an antonym for the word in the shortest possible interval. The experimenter records the reaction time of the subject. This experiment taps:
    a. episodic memory.
    b. short-term memory.
    c. semantic memory.
    d. visual memory.

Answer: b
Symbolic representations
pp. 308–309

56. One's knowledge of the multiplication tables resides in:
    a. episodic memory.
    b. generic memory.
    c. semantic memory.
    d. short-term memory.

Answer: d
Symbolic representations
p. 309

57. In a hierarchical model, examination of the concept *furniture* would reveal
    a. the property *inanimate* at the level of *furniture*.
    b. the property *has legs* at the level of *tables* rather than *coffee tables*.
    c. *chairs* at a higher level than *recliners*.
    d. all of the above

Answer: a
Symbolic representations
p. 309

58. According to the hierarchical model of semantic memory:
    a. *chair* would be a subcategory of *furniture*.
    b. *instrument* would be a subcategory of *violin*.
    c. *bird* and *fish* would be in close proximity in the hierarchy.
    d. all of the above

Answer: a
Symbolic representations
p. 309

59. When things are organized into broad categories and, in turn, each of these is organized into narrower categories, this type of organization is called:
    a. hierarchical.
    b. chunking.
    c. differentiation.
    d. restructuring.

Answer: d
The process of thinking: solving problems
p. 309

60. *Superhighway, highway,* and *byway* as a classification system for roads is an example of:
    a. a parallel distributed processing network.
    b. restructuring.
    c. a set of nodes.
    d. hierarchical organization.

Answer: d
Symbolic representations
p. 309

61. An investigator asks you to respond *true* or *false* as fast as you can to the question "Is a _____ a car?" filling in the blank on different occasions with examples like Ford, Packard, BMW, Dodge, and Yugo. This research is probably studying:
    a. semantic priming and implicit knowledge.
    b. the Stroop effect in automatization.
    c. the feeling of knowing in unconscious processing.
    d. the influence of typicality in a hierarchical network.

Answer: d
Symbolic representations
p. 309

62. To which of the following questions will you probably respond most slowly?
    a. Is a cat an animal?
    b. Is aluminum a metal?
    c. Is a pine a tree?
    d. Is a penguin a bird?

Answer: c
Symbolic representations
p. 309

63. From what you know about hierarchical networks in human thinking, to which of the following questions should it take people the longest to respond *yes* or *no*?
    a. Is a rabbit an animal?
    b. Is iron a metal?
    c. Is a gingko a tree?
    d. Is a robin a bird?

Answer: d
Symbolic representations
p. 309

64. Verification time for the sentence "Robins are birds" is shorter than verification time for the sentence "Penguins are birds." This difference probably reflects differences in:
    a. hierarchical structure of these concepts in semantic memory.
    b. relative difficulty in access to episodic memory.
    c. memory activation.
    d. typicality.

Answer: c
Symbolic representations
p. 309

65. From what you know about hierarchical networks in human thinking, to which of the following questions should it take people the longest to respond *yes* or *no*?
    a. Is a trout a fish?
    b. Is a grasshopper an insect?
    c. Is a porpoise a mammal?
    d. Is a robin a bird?

66. Based on what you know about hierarchical networks in human thoughts, to which of the following statements would a subject take longest to respond *true* or *false*?
    a. Is a maple a tree?
    b. Is a table furniture?
    c. Is a tomato a fruit?
    d. Is a rose a flower?

67. From what you know about hierarchical networks in human thought, to which of the following should it take Americans the longest to answer?
    a. Are the Yankees a baseball team?
    b. Is a Maserati a car?
    c. Is the Mississippi a river?
    d. Is Chicago a city?

68. When we think of an animal we're likely to think of a cat or a dog; of a fruit, an apple; and of a bird, a robin. This tendency has been taken as evidence that we encode concepts like *animal, fruit,* and *birds* according to:
    a. lists of features that define the category.
    b. typical representatives of instances of the category.
    c. a hierarchical model.
    d. a strategy in which we store each instance of the category independently.

69. The spreading activation model of conceptual organization:
    a. includes links based on hierarchical knowledge.
    b. includes links based on nonhierarchical knowledge.
    c. is inconsistent with priming data.
    d. a and b

70. Research participants are asked to think of an animal beginning with *d* and their responses are timed. Just prior to this task, some participants (group 1) were asked to think of an animal beginning with *p* and others (group 2) were asked to think of a vegetable beginning with *p*. Results on the *d* question will show that:
    a. consistent with the spreading activation model, people in group 1 respond more quickly than those in group 2.
    b. consistent with the spreading activation model, people in groups 1 and 2 respond equally quickly.
    c. contrary to the spreading activation model, people in group 1 respond more quickly than those in group 2.
    d. contrary to the spreading activation model, people in groups 1 and 2 respond equally quickly.

Answer: a
Symbolic representations
p. 310

71. In a lexical decision task in which subjects must judge whether a string of letters forms a word in English, subjects are given the string "BANANA." They will be fastest to next judge which of the following strings?
    a. APPLE
    b. TOWER
    c. MAVEN
    d. POWER

Answer: b
Symbolic representations
p. 310

72. Research participants are asked to judge whether a string of letters forms a word in English. They are first given the string "CABBAGE." They will be fastest to next judge which of the following strings?
    a. CRIBBAGE
    b. CARROT
    c. TOILET
    d. CABOOSE

Answer: d
Symbolic representations
p. 310

73. Subjects are asked to judge whether a string of letters forms a word in. English They are first given the string "VIOLIN." They then are substantially faster at answering "yes" to "PIANO" than to "TOILET" or "BASKET." This result exemplifies:
    a. episodic memory.
    b. mental set.
    c. automatization.
    d. semantic priming.

Answer: b
Symbolic representations
p. 310

74. Research on semantic priming:
    a. contradicts the spreading activation model.
    b. indicates that *saddle* will be recognized more quickly if it is preceded by *horse* than by *house*.
    c. indicates that *guitar* will be recognized equally quickly whether it is preceded by *drum* or by *sofa*.
    d. a and c

Answer: a
Symbolic representations
p. 310

75. According to the spreading activation model, when the word *girl* is applied to a twenty-year-old woman, the mental nodes that are activated in the hearer probably:
    a. include *child*.
    b. include only those which are appropriate in this case (e.g., *female*).
    c. include only those with a hierarchical relationship (e.g., *person*).
    d. do not include any antonyms for *girl*.

Answer: c
Symbolic representations
p. 311

76. In a parallel distributed processing network, a symbolic representation of something like "banana" is:
    a. a particular node in the network.
    b. located in a particular part of the cerebral cortex.
    c. a particular activation pattern in the network as a whole.
    d. represented in a spatial configuration like that of a real banana.

Answer: b
Symbolic representations
p. 311

77. The key assumption in parallel distributed processing networks is that symbolic representations are:
    a. represented in essentially analogical form within the network.
    b. properties of the network as a whole.
    c. located at particular nodes in the network.
    d. determined by where a particular node is located in the cerebral cortex.

Answer: c
Symbolic representations
p. 311

78. Models of parallel distributed processing networks assume:
    a. separate sets of connections for semantic and episodic memory.
    b. that symbolic representations are essentially analogical.
    c. that symbolic representations are properties of the network as a whole.
    d. that each symbolic representation has its own node in the network.

Answer: c
Symbolic representations
p. 311

79. In a parallel distributed processing network, knowledge of a particular visual pattern is stored:
    a. at a particular node in the network.
    b. in a way that requires a particular set of a few neurons to access it.
    c. as a set of connections in the network as a whole.
    d. in parallel in two places in the network, once in a generic store and another in an episodic store.

Answer: a
Symbolic representations
p. 311

80. In the parallel distributed processing model, the term *parallel* refers to the fact that:
    a. relevant units are activated simultaneously.
    b. relevant neurons are located in parallel lines.
    c. associative links are generally depicted in parallel lines.
    d. relevant areas of the temporal cortex are located parallel to relevant areas of the parietal cortex.

Answer: d
Symbolic representations
pp. 311–312

81. The textbook's story of the master spy is analogous to parallel distributed processing models in that:
    a. elements of the plan or representation are divided up.
    b. the plan or representation can be assembled even in the absence of an overview residing in a single location.
    c. holders of elements of the plan or representation need not know what the final product will be.
    d. all of the above

Answer: b
Symbolic representations
pp. 311–312

82. A jigsaw puzzle is analogous to a parallel distributed processing model in that:
    a. the person who assembles the puzzle is often guided by a picture of how it will look when assembled.
    b. the picture is divided into a number of pieces.
    c. the pieces can only be assembled in one way.
    d. all of the above

Answer: c
Symbolic representations
p. 312

83. Parallel distributed processing models:
    a.   use local representations.
    b.   have only been applied to conceptual organization.
    c.   seem to do a better job of modelling brain functioning than do spreading activation models.
    d.   are simple extensions of hierarchical network models.

Answer: d
The process of thinking: solving problems
pp. 312–313

84. In a problem-solving situation, the things that are considered in an attempt to solve the problem are:
    a.   random associations.
    b.   determined only by the eventual goal one seeks.
    c.   determined only by the immediately preceding thought.
    d.   determined by both the preceding thought and the eventual goal.

Answer: c
The process of thinking: solving problems
p. 313

85. In much of human problem solving, like driving to an airport or making a medical diagnosis, each mental step toward the solution is usually:
    a.   the next logical one.
    b.   triggered or determined by the step that just preceded it.
    c.   relevant to the original problem and determined by both it and the preceding step.
    d.   tried out in action before the next mental step is taken.

Answer: d
The process of thinking: solving problems
p. 313

86. In solving both anagram problems and problems involving spatial mazes, the person is guided by:
    a.   the eventual goal.
    b.   the step of the solution that came just before.
    c.   the same set of brain processes
    d.   a and b

Answer: a
The process of thinking: solving problems
p. 313

87. Going home involves going to bus depot, then buying a ticket, then getting on the bus, . . . Buying a ticket involves getting in line, then waiting, then asking for a ticket, then . . . .This simple scheme is an example of:
    a.   hierarchical organization.
    b.   restructuring.
    c.   a set of nodes.
    d.   a parallel distributed processing network.

Answer: d
The process of thinking: solving problems
p. 313

88. Going to class involves walking to the classroom building, finding the correct room, and finding a seat. Finding a seat involves looking around the classroom, seeing which chairs are empty, selecting an empty one that is in the desired part of the room, and so on. This simple scheme is an example of:
    a.   restructuring.
    b.   a set of nodes.
    c.   a parallel distributed processing network.
    d.   hierarchical organization.

Answer: a
The process of thinking: solving problems
p. 314

89. Learning a skill involves:
    a. increases and plateaus in performance.
    b. steady increases in performance.
    c. a constant plateau in performance.
    d. a Stroop effect.

Answer: b
The process of thinking: solving problems
p. 314

90. Bryan and Harter's study of the way apprentice telegraph operators learned to send and receive Morse code messages found that the learning curve for this task is characterized by:
    a. repeated dips in the curve in which the operator gets worse than he had been previously, followed by spurts above the previous high.
    b. long plateaus followed by ascents to a new plateau and so on.
    c. slow and steady improvement, which decelerates with increasing sessions.
    d. slow and steady improvement, which accelerates with increasing sessions.

Answer: a
The process of thinking: solving problems
p. 314

91. Bob is learning a difficult Chopin waltz, which must be played at a fast tempo. At first he steadily increases the tempo, but then for a time he is unable to increase it. Eventually, he is able to increase it again. The period of time during which he was unable to increase the tempo was a:
    a. plateau.
    b. circular reaction.
    c. consolidation period.
    d. proactive period.

Answer: c
The process of thinking: solving problems
p. 314

92. A violinist and guitarist worked for several months to perfect their playing of a complex Paganini sonata. Weekly audiotapes of their playing throughout their practice period were rated by music critics. The resulting curve of the critics' judgments is shown below. These findings are most similar to those obtained by:

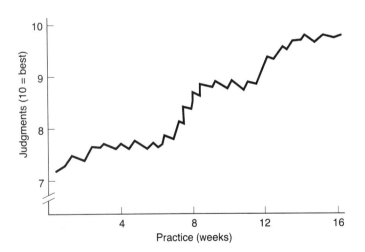

    a. Skinner in studying instrumental conditioning by pigeons.
    b. Kohler in his work with chimps getting bananas.
    c. Bryan and Harter's work with learning Morse code.
    d. Ebbinghaus in his study of his own forgetting of nonsense syllables.

93. A diver works on a complicated dive for four years. Videotapes of her dives throughout the training period were rated by judges. The resulting curve of the judgments is shown below.

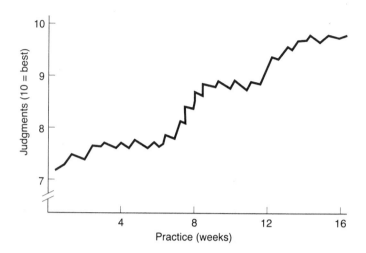

These findings are most similar to those obtained by:
a. Ebbinghaus in studying his own forgetting of nonsense syllables.
b. Tolman in studying the acquisition of maze learning by rats where reinforcement was not available in the early trials.
c. Pavlov in studying the acquisition of salivary CSs.
d. Bryan and Harter studying the acquisition of Morse code by telegraphers.

94. One of the hallmarks of learning a skill such as typing, receiving Morse code, tying one's shoes, etc., is:
a. a smooth increase in the level of skill.
b. a jumpy change in skill, alternating periods of rapid improvement with periods of little apparent change.
c. periods of learning alternating with periods of apparent forgetting.
d. a sudden increase in learning after long periods of little apparent change in activity.

95. The book suggests that skill acquisition is marked by alternating periods of improvement and plateaus because:
a. the learners periodically tire of trying to improve.
b. measurement techniques aren't sensitive enough to detect the slow but steady improvement that's actually present.
c. low level skills (subroutines) are honed during the plateau and then combined into bigger chunks during the periods of improvement.
d. learners expect that pattern, so they modify their behavior to create it.

Answer: a
The process of thinking: solving problems
p. 315

96. Compared to chess players who are competent but are below the master level, chess masters:
    a. can remember positions of a chess game better.
    b. have better visual memory.
    c. have better working memory.
    d. a and b

Answer: a
The process of thinking: solving problems
p. 315

97. Chess masters are distinguished from novices by all of the following except:
    a. master analysts encode complex patterns of players into a small number of chunks.
    b. most people have interfering heuristics that hinder recall; master analysts have learned to inhibit these.
    c. master analysts have a generally larger capacity for independent items of all kinds in their working memories.
    d. master analysts have learned to use their eidetic imagery.

Answer: a
The process of thinking: solving problems
p. 315

98. Chess masters are not distinguished from novices by:
    a. better memory in general.
    b. better chunking of chess information on a board.
    c. better evaluation of chess positions.
    d. better skill at looking ahead to future moves.

Answer: c
The process of thinking: solving problems
p. 315

99. The difference between chess masters and average chess players is that masters:
    a. are superior in restructuring.
    b. have better short-term memory.
    c. chunk chess in larger units.
    d. have better visual imagery.

Answer: b
The process of thinking: solving problems
p. 315

100. When chess masters and average chess players are briefly shown a chess board with pieces randomly arranged on it:
    a. both groups remember as much of the arrangement as when the pieces are in the middle of a game.
    b. the masters remember less of the arrangement than when the pieces are in the middle of a game.
    c. the masters remember more of the arrangement than the average players.
    d. b and c

Answer: c
The process of thinking: solving problems
p. 315

101. The essence of mastership in typing, athletics, chess, and a variety of other skills is the ability to:
    a. memorize.
    b. use mnemonics.
    c. organize material from the area of expertise into larger chunks.
    d. attend to the relevant stimuli for sustained periods of time.

Answer: c
The process of thinking: solving problems
p. 316

102. In the Stroop task, subjects are asked to identify the color of the ink in which random words are printed, and the color of the ink in which color names are printed (with the words and the ink mismatching). The results are that:
    a. subjects with good visual imagery do the tasks equally quickly.
    b. subjects do the task more quickly when the words are color names.
    c. subjects do the task more quickly when the words are random.
    d. semantic priming improves performance with the color names, but not with the random words.

Answer: a
The process of thinking: solving problems
p. 316

103. A major point demonstrated by the Stroop color naming task is:
    a. once certain procedures are learned really well they can be very hard not to use.
    b. sharpness of perception is important in how people associate what they view and how they think.
    c. that what is easy to learn when young can be hard to learn when adult.
    d. the importance of the ability to associate color with objects and patterns common in society.

Answer: d
The process of thinking: solving problems
p. 316

104. The Stroop color-naming task demonstrates a major point about thinking. What is it?
    a. Most people tend to see almost everything as color, which can make reading difficult.
    b. Some concepts are difficult to name.
    c. It helps to determine color preferences and color dominance of observers.
    d. Highly learned skills can be difficult to turn off.

Answer: b
The process of thinking: solving problems
p. 316

105. The Stroop effect demonstrates a phenomenon called:
    a. chunking.
    b. automatization.
    c. chaining.
    d. task transformation.

Answer: a
The process of thinking: solving problems
p. 316

106. The Stroop effect is concerned with:
    a. automatization.
    b. chunking.
    c. the feeling of knowing.
    d. selective forgetting.

Answer: b
The process of thinking: solving problems
p. 316

107. The Stroop effect, in which individuals find it difficult to name the colors in which words such as *red* are printed, illustrates:
    a. framing effects.
    b. the automaticity of some mental processes.
    c. that typicality is important for the speed with which activation spreads in mental networks.
    d. that we can ignore virtually any information that we don't want to attend to.

Answer: a
The process of thinking: solving problems
pp. 316–317

108. A person is asked to think of all the words she can beginning with the letters "squ" (e.g., "squeak"). She is then given a fill-in-the-blank task on which one of the items is "s _ _ o n g". She keeps tying to make "squong" a word, and has great difficulty coming up with the common word, "strong". Her ability to solve this problem has been hampered by:
    a. mental set.
    b. a lack of analogy.
    c. hierarchical thinking.
    d. automatization.

Answer: c
The process of thinking: solving problems
pp. 316–317

109. A plumber can't repair a pump because he can only see the conventional use for his tools. Which of the following does this best exemplify?
    a. a well-defined problem
    b. heuristic problem solving
    c. a form of mental set
    d. representational thinking

Answer: a
The process of thinking: solving problems
pp. 316–317

110. Which of the following would be most likely to decrease mental set, for example, to facilitate using a hammer to prop open a door?
    a. having just used a hammer as a weight to pull a hollow toy under water
    b. seeing the hammer lying with a saw, a chisel, and a screwdriver
    c. having just used a hammer to pull out a nail
    d. being in a race with three others to solve the most problems the fastest

Answer: d
The process of thinking: solving problems
pp. 316–317

111. A jeweler isn't able to fix a particular mounting in a ring because she can see only the conventional uses for her tools. This best demonstrates which of the following?
    a. a hierarchical organization of thought
    b. algorithmic thinking
    c. representational thinking
    d. a special kind of mental set

Answer: b
The process of thinking: solving problems
pp. 316–317

112. Failing to see that a fifty-cent piece can be used as an emergency plug for a wash basin is an example of:
    a. a heuristic approach.
    b. a mental set.
    c. restructuring.
    d. representational thinking.

Answer: a
The process of thinking: solving problems
pp. 316–317

113. A person would not be as likely to blow out a burning candle to use as a weight for a pendulum as to use a candle just lying on its side for such a weight when he was trying to solve a problem that necessitated a pendulum for its solution. This difference best illustrates:
    a. mental set.
    b. lack of goal-directed thinking.
    c. parallel distributed processing.
    d. lack of an appropriate incubation period.

114. Suppose that someone is stuck on a very difficult problem. One problem-solving technique that is often successful is:
    a. providing a large reward, to intensify motivation.
    b. working backwards.
    c. mental set.
    d. all of the above

115. Suppose that someone is stuck on a very difficult problem. One problem-solving technique that is often successful is:
    a. mental set.
    b. finding an analogy.
    c. providing a large reward, to intensify motivation.
    d. all of the above

116. It has been shown that the use of analogy:
    a. is automatic: people use analogies in problem solving when they are present.
    b. is not readily apparent to subjects unless they are aware that there is an analogy between a present problem and a previous one.
    c. works much better for novices than for experts in a problem domain.
    d. works better if there is only one potential analog in memory than if there are two or more.

117. The key to using analogy in problem solving is to:
    a. notice the surface similarity between a problem and its potential analog.
    b. be a novice in a field so that the analogy becomes readily apparent.
    c. be able to hone in on a single potential analog and not be distracted by other previous problems that also might be similar to the present one.
    d. notice the underlying structural similarity between a present problem and a potential analog.

118. Reorganization of a problem to produce a shift in the way it is viewed is called:
    a. a heuristic.
    b. restructuring.
    c. functional fixedness.
    d. forming a mental set.

119. The term *incubation:*
    a. refers to creative problem solutions that occur after long and intense effort that for a long time seemed to go nowhere.
    b. is a hypothetical process of problem solution that operates unconsciously, occurring after a thinker turns away from the conscious pursuit of a problem.
    c. refers to insights that come at unexpected times and places.
    d. refers to sudden restructurings in the way in which a problem is viewed.

Answer: c
The process of thinking: solving problems

pp. 320–321

120. After a subject stops thinking about a problem and turns to another activity, the problem may be solved by an unconscious process known as:
 a. directed thinking.
 b. mental set.
 c. incubation.
 d. reconstruction.

Answer: c
The process of thinking: solving problems
pp. 320–321

121. Research on incubation:
 a. demonstrates that time away from a problem leads to solving the problem.
 b. demonstrates that incubation works because it breaks false mental sets.
 c. has produced mixed findings and multiple interpretations.
 d. demonstrates that incubation works because it allows fatigue and frustration to dissipate.

Answer: d
The process of thinking: solving problems
pp. 320–321

122. Which of the following characteristics of creative thinking is most likely to be emphasized by a person who believes that creativity expresses the contents of the unconscious?
 a. its tendency to occur infrequently
 b. the intense study of the problem that often precedes insight
 c. the importance of context for coming up with a good solution
 d. the suddenness of creative solutions at what seem like strange times

Answer: c
The process of thinking: solving problems
pp. 320–321

123. Which of the following characteristics of creativity is most likely to be cited by those who believe that creativity is an expression of the unconscious?
 a. its tendency to occur repeatedly in the same people
 b. the role of settings in developing creativity
 c. an incubation period followed by sudden solution
 d. the intense study that often precedes solutions

Answer: a
The process of thinking: solving problems
pp. 320–321

124. The effect of *incubation:*
 a. may seem more prevalent than it is because examples of it are more likely to be reported than are examples of other types of problem solving.
 b. is well-established.
 c. could only be due to unconscious processing.
 d. b and c

Answer: d
The process of thinking: solving problems
pp. 321–322

125. What is the essential similarity between insight and humor?
 a. Both depend upon the processing of cognitive information.
 b. Both are usually sudden.
 c. In both, an initial expectation is unfulfilled.
 d. Both involve a sharp shift from one cognitive organization to another.

Answer: a
The process of thinking: solving problems
pp. 321–322

126. Restructuring in problem solving and humor share which of the following features?
   a. They both require a change in cognitive organization.
   b. They both require an incongruous ending.
   c. They both require a person to be ignorant of the subject matter at hand.
   d. all of the above

Answer: b
The process of thinking: solving problems
pp. 321–322

127. In a good joke, the punch line often requires the listener to:
   a. be naive to the subject matter at hand.
   b. restructure what was just heard.
   c. selectively forget some of the earlier material to fully process the end of the joke.
   d. suspend the tendency to think in terms of cause-effect relations.

Answer: a
The process of thinking: solving problems
pp. 321–322

128. The book argues that jokes often involve trios because:
   a. the first two items create a pattern which is then sensibly but unexpectedly broken by the third.
   b. *three* represents male genitalia according to Freud and jokes often have an underlying sexual content.
   c. presentation of the second item allows time for the first item to incubate before presentation of the third item.
   d. jokes typically turn on an ambiguity that can be resolved in one of three ways.

Answer: d
The process of thinking: solving problems
p. 323

129. Humans and computers are examples of:
   a. visual memory systems.
   b. memory machines.
   c. algorithms.
   d. information-processing systems.

Answer: a
The process of thinking: solving problems
pp. 323–324

130. If the problem is soluble, an appropriate algorithm:
   a. always leads to a solution to a problem.
   b. represents the quickest way of solving a problem.
   c. involves forming some hypothesis about a likely solution to the problem and using this hypothesis to direct the problem solving.
   d. guarantees subgoals that need to be satisfied in order to reach a solution to the problem.

Answer: c
The process of thinking: solving problems
p. 323

131. The term *artificial intelligence:*
   a. refers to pretending to be intelligent.
   b. is a field of study of memory and reasoning in nonhuman animals.
   c. refers to constructing computer programs that simulate how people think.
   d. is a field of drug research that attempts to restore some intellectual functions to people who are demented.

Answer: c
The process of thinking: solving problems
p. 323

132. Sarah is a computer science major interested in human problem solving. These interests correspond best to the field of:
    a. learning and memory.
    b. unconscious processing.
    c. artificial intelligence.
    d. heuristics.

Answer: b
The process of thinking: solving problems
p. 323

133. Despite enormous differences in their underlying machinery, humans and computers both exemplify:
    a. algorithms.
    b. information-processing systems.
    c. visual memory systems.
    d. memory machines.

Answer: c
The process of thinking: solving problems
pp. 323–324

134. Investigators concerned with artificial intelligence use the term *algorithm*. This is:
    a. a procedure by which computers render ill-defined problems into well-defined ones.
    b. a description of the physical machinery that makes up the computer.
    c. a procedure by which all of the operations required to reach problem solutions are specified step by step.
    d. a set of tricks and rules of thumb that have worked in the past and may work again in the future.

Answer: b
The process of thinking: solving problems
pp. 323–324

135. To find the area of a rectangle, one multiplies the length by the width. This is an example of:
    a. a heuristic.
    b. an algorithm.
    c. a mental set.
    d. artificial intelligence.

Answer: a
The process of thinking: solving problems
pp. 323–324

136. To find the circumference of a circle one multiplies the diameter by pi. This exemplifies:
    a. an algorithm.
    b. an expert system.
    c. a mental set.
    d. a heuristic.

Answer: a
The process of thinking: solving problems
p. 324

137. An industrial recipe for the manufacture of toothpaste specifies how much of each ingredient is to be added, under what conditions, and at which time in the processing. Such a recipe is a(n):
    a. algorithm.
    b. heuristic.
    c. hierarchy.
    d. reversible operation.

Answer: b
The process of thinking: solving problems
p. 324

138. A big advantage of using algorithms to solve problems is that algorithms:
    a. take less time than other methods.
    b. guarantee a solution.
    c. take a hierarchical approach.
    d. most closely duplicate the way that human experts solve problems in their area of expertise.

Answer: a
The process of thinking: solving problems
p. 324

139. A big advantage of using algorithms for solving problems is that they:
    a. will eventually result in a correct solution.
    b. work more efficiently than do heuristics.
    c. are the methods used by experts when solving difficult problems in their own area of expertise.
    d. all of the above

Answer: d
The process of thinking: solving problems
p. 324

140. Young Karl Gauss quickly discovered that the sum of a continuous even-numbered series is always equal to half the number of elements in the series times the quantity (first element of the series plus last element of the series). What Gauss came up with here is a good example of:
    a. an analogy.
    b. a heuristic.
    c. an ill-defined problem.
    d. an algorithm.
    e. a hierarchy.

Answer: d
The process of thinking: solving problems
p. 324

141. Tom gives you precise, step-by-step directions about how to get to his house. These directions are:
    a. a heuristic.
    b. an example of syllogistic reasoning.
    c. an example of inductive reasoning.
    d. an algorithm.

Answer: d
The process of thinking: solving problems
p. 324

142. A solution algorithm:
    a. guarantees a solution if one exists.
    b. is the most efficient way to solve crossword puzzles.
    c. would consider all possible combinations in a chess position.
    d. both a and c

Answer: a
The process of thinking: solving problems
p. 324

143. If one wished always to arrive at the correct solution to a problem and one did not care about the amount of time it took to solve the problem, one would be best advised to develop a(n) _____ for that type of problem.
    a. algorithm.
    b. heuristic.
    c. mental set.
    d. either a or b

Answer: c
The process of thinking: solving problems
p. 324

144. Solving crossword puzzles requires certain rules of thumb called:
    a. algorithms.
    b. reconstructions.
    c. heuristics.
    d. mental sets.

Answer: d
The process of thinking: solving problems
p. 324

145. An issue of *Science* magazine contains a two-page article by James Watson of DNA fame on "How to Succeed in Science." From its title you should guess that this article contains:
    a.   advice on chunking.
    b.   an expert system.
    c.   algorithms.
    d.   heuristics.

Answer: b
The process of thinking: solving problems
p. 324

146. A $29.95 video with the title "How to Get Rich Selling Antiques" is most likely to contain:
    a.   expert systems.
    b.   heuristics.
    c.   hierarchies.
    d.   algorithms.

Answer: c
The process of thinking: solving problems
p. 324

147. You pick up a pamphlet at the counseling center entitled "How to Succeed at College Course Work." This pamphlet is most likely to contain:
    a.   algorithms.
    b.   mental sets.
    c.   heuristics.
    d.   syllogisms.

Answer: b
The process of thinking: solving problems
p. 324

148. What's the term for problem-solving strategies that use "rules of thumb"?
    a.   syllogisms
    b.   heuristics
    c.   mnemonics
    d.   insights

Answer: c
The process of thinking: solving problems
p. 324

149. Heuristics are most likely to be contained in:
    a.   a chemical equation for the synthesis of sulfuric acid.
    b.   a recipe for making cookies on the back of a box of corn flakes.
    c.   an article by a Nobel Prize winner on "How to Succeed in Science."
    d.   a computer program for keeping track of inventory at a K-Mart store.

Answer: c
The process of thinking: solving problems
p. 324

150. "When you have trouble in a class, try outlining the book in your own words." This general rule for solving some academic problems is called a(n):
    a.   syllogism.
    b.   hierarchy.
    c.   heuristic.
    d.   insight.
    e.   mnemonic.

Answer: b
The process of thinking: solving problems
p. 324

151. A big advantage of using a heuristic rather than an algorithm is that the heuristic:
    a. allows for more creativity in responses.
    b. is often a lot faster.
    c. is more certain to result in a correct response.
    d. ends up with only one possible solution.

Answer: d
The process of thinking: solving problems
pp. 324–325

152. Investigators concerned with artificial intelligence use the term *heuristics*. These are:
    a. procedures by which computers render ill-defined problems into well-defined ones.
    b. descriptions of the physical machinery that makes up a computer.
    c. procedures by which all of the operations required to reach a problem solution are specified step by step.
    d. a set of tricks and rules of thumb that have worked in the past and may work again in the future.

Answer: c
The process of thinking: solving problems
pp. 324–325

153. Heuristics:
    a. always lead to correct solutions of a problem.
    b. are slower ways to solve problems than are algorithms.
    c. represent approaches to the solution of a problem.
    d. are used by computers but not by humans as problem-solving tools.

Answer: d
The process of thinking: solving problems
p. 324

154. Mechanic Sally believes that the best way to correct a faulty distributor is to think about the things most likely to be wrong and to check those. Her problem-solving strategy is clearly:
    a. algorithmic.
    b. analogous.
    c. hierarchical.
    d. heuristic.

Answer: b
The process of thinking: solving problems
p. 325

155. Which of the following is an ill-defined problem?
    a. navigating to a museum in a nearby city.
    b. composing a good concerto.
    c. finding out where several well-known authors were born.
    d. playing Scrabble.

Answer: c
The process of thinking: solving problems
p. 325

156. Which of the following statements is false?
    a. Computers are better at solving well-defined than ill-defined problems.
    b. Humans are better than computers at solving ill-defined problems.
    c. Solutions to well-defined problems are generally difficult to evaluate.
    d. Ill-defined problems can be redefined through the use of subgoals.

Answer: a
The process of thinking: solving problems
p. 325

157. Which of the following statements about solving a 15-letter anagram is false?
   a. This problem is ill-defined.
   b. There is an algorithm available for solving this problem.
   c. Using a heuristic would involve considering common letter combinations in English.
   d. This problem is well-suited to an appropriately programmed computer.

Answer: b
The process of thinking: solving problems
pp. 325–326

158. Computers can be programmed to do all of the following things except:
   a. play chess.
   b. make moral decisions.
   c. prove theorems in logic.
   d. decipher cryptograms.

Answer: c
The process of thinking: solving problems
pp. 325–326

159. Artificial intelligence programs seem to lack common sense, which is to say they lack:
   a. well-defined solutions.
   b. heuristics.
   c. a broad understanding of the questions posed to them.
   d. algorithms.

Answer: b
The process of thinking: solving problems
pp. 325–326

160. Consider a well-trained reference librarian and a computer programmed to serve the functions of a reference librarian. Both are instructed to alert a supervisor to problems. Both are asked by a library user how much arsenic it would take to kill an adult male of average build. Which of the following outcomes is most likely?
   a. Because the problem is ill-defined, the computer will not be able to answer it and will have to alert the supervisor. The human will have no trouble.
   b. The human will alert the supervisor to the possibility that a murder is being planned; lacking common sense, the computer will not do so.
   c. The computer will alert the supervisor to the possibility that a murder is being planned, but the human will not.
   d. The computer will be able to find the answer, but the human will not.

Answer: e
The process of thinking: solving problems
pp. 325–326

161. Computer problem solvers differ from human problem solvers in that the former:
   a. lack common sense.
   b. do very poorly with ill-defined problems.
   c. don't understand the intentions underlying questions.
   d. can't make value-based judgments.
   e. all of the above

Answer: b
The process of thinking: solving problems
p. 326

162. Computer systems, such as those used for medical diagnosis:
   a. store less of the detailed information than physicians.
   b. lack the breadth of relevant knowledge of physicians.
   c. take substantially longer to process the relevant information than do physicians.
   d. contain few interlocking networks of commands.
   e. all of the above

Answer: b
The process of thinking: solving problems
p. 326

163. An expert system is:
    a. a chunking process.
    b. a problem-solving computer program with a narrow scope of knowledge.
    c. a plan with a hierarchical organization.
    d. a system developed to explain the Stroop effect.

Answer: d
The process of thinking: solving problems
p. 326

164. An expert system:
    a. attempts to enhance creativity in small groups of experts.
    b. is a type of computer program that simulates the methods of problem solving done by experts.
    c. is a group of specialists in human cognition that communicate via the internet.
    d. is a computer program that gives expert-level advice in a restricted domain.

Answer: c
The process of thinking: solving problems
p. 326

165. MYCIN is an example of a(n):
    a. algorithm.
    b. heuristic.
    c. expert system.
    d. ill-defined solution.

Answer: d
The process of thinking: solving problems
p. 326

166. MYCIN and other artificial intelligence programs are not like humans in that:
    a. they have knowledge about a wide range of situations.
    b. they fail to solve the problems with which they are faced.
    c. they do not reason like humans about the problems in their domain.
    d. their knowledge is limited in its scope to a narrow domain.

Answer: d
The process of thinking: reasoning and decision making
p. 327

167. All *A* are *B*. All *B* are *C*. Therefore all *A* are *C* is an example of a(n):
    a. algorithm.
    b. heuristic.
    c. invalid statement.
    d. syllogism.

Answer: c
The process of thinking: reasoning and decision making
p. 327

168. In deductive reasoning, the task is to:
    a. consider a number of instances and try to determine a rule that covers them.
    b. remove extraneous information until only key information remains.
    c. determine whether conclusions can logically be drawn from premises.
    d. remove implausible premises until only plausible premises remain.

Answer: b
The process of thinking: reasoning and decision making
p. 327

169. Each syllogism contains two _____ and a(n) _____.
    a. statements; answer
    b. premises; conclusion
    c. premises; judgment
    d. transformations; conclusion

Answer: a

The process of thinking: reasoning
  and decision making

p. 327

170. In deductive reasoning, the validity of a syllogism is determined by:
  a. the logical relationship between the premises and the conclusion.
  b. the plausibility of the conclusion.
  c. hypothesis testing.
  d. b and c

Answer: a

The process of thinking: reasoning
  and decision making

p. 327

171. Which statement regarding the following syllogisms is true?
  1) All men are mortal. All mortals are women. Therefore, all men are women.
  2) All men are mortal. Some mortals are human. Therefore, all men are human.
  a. number 1 is valid and number 2 is invalid.
  b. number 1 is invalid and number 2 is valid.
  c. Both are valid.
  d. Both are invalid.

Answer: b

The process of thinking: reasoning
  and decision making

p. 327

172. Research on deductive reasoning indicates that:
  a. research participants are generally quite good at judging the validity of syllogisms.
  b. research participants frequently assess a syllogism's conclusion based on its plausibility.
  c. research participants usually evaluate a syllogism by determining whether the conclusion logically follows from the premises.
  d. a and c

Answer: b

The process of thinking: reasoning and
  decision making

p. 328

173. When we consider a number of different instances and try to determine a general rule that covers them all we are using:
  a. hypothetical reasoning.
  b. inductive reasoning.
  c. deductive reasoning.
  d. confirmational reasoning.

Answer: d

The process of thinking: reasoning
  and decision making

pp. 328–329

174. Frequency estimates are:
  a. judgments of how often we've encountered something.
  b. often inaccurate.
  c. often made with the availability heuristic.
  d. all of the above

Answer: a

The process of thinking: reasoning and
  decision making

p. 329

175. Motorcycle accidents account for more deaths than airplane crashes, but airplane crashes get more publicity. If Mike hears about an airplane crash on the news, and decides to ride his motorcycle instead of flying from Washington to Atlanta, he is making a reasoning error due to:
  a. the availability heuristic.
  b. mental set.
  c. a syllogistic error.
  d. a problem of framing.

Answer: b
The process of thinking: reasoning and
    decision making
p. 329

176. A lawyer represents a client who is accused of robbery. The client has previously been proven guilty of assault and has served three years in jail. When asked to estimate the man's chances of acquittal for the second crime the lawyer's judgment is likely to be affected by:
    a. inductive reasoning.
    b. the availability heuristic.
    c. irrationality.
    d. deductive reasoning.

Answer: b
The process of thinking: reasoning and
    decision making
p. 330

177. When you use the representativeness heuristic, you:
    a. make frequency estimates based on the ease with which things come to mind.
    b. assume that something is typical of its class.
    c. mistake visual images and other forms of mental representations for reality.
    d. consistently convert analogical representations into symbolic representations.

Answer: a
The process of thinking: reasoning and
    decision making
p. 330

178. The one person Craig has ever met from New Zealand strikes him as quite friendly and funny. When asked what he would expect to find if he went to New Zealand, Craig says that he would expect the people to be quite friendly and funny. His judgment seems to have been made using:
    a. the representativeness heuristic.
    b. confirmation bias.
    c. framing effects.
    d. the availability heuristic.

Answer: c
The process of thinking: reasoning and
    decision making
p. 330

179. Research participants are shown a videotape of a police officer from City X talking with relish about harassing people he doesn't like and beating confessions out of suspects. Half the participants (group 1) are told that this officer is a typical member of the department, and half (group 2) are told he is quite extreme and atypical in his views. They are then asked to judge the brutality of City X's police force. Research on the representativeness heuristic suggests that
    a. group 1 will judge the force to be much more brutal than will group 2.
    b. group 2 will judge the force to be much more brutal than will group 1.
    c. both groups will judge the force to be quite brutal.
    d. neither group will judge the force to be very brutal.

Answer: d
The process of thinking: reasoning and
    decision making
pp. 331–332

180. In hypothesis testing, a frequent error is "confirmation bias," which means:
    a. testing more examples than are necessary to confirm the hypothesis.
    b. looking for evidence against the hypothesis, rather than considering all evidence equally.
    c. assuming that any hypothesis that sounds reasonable with respect to prior knowledge is true.
    d. paying more attention to evidence that is consistent with the hypothesis than to contradictory evidence.

Answer: c
The process of thinking: reasoning and
   decision making
pp. 331–332

181. A person who believes in astrology reads in his horoscope that today will
be his lucky day. He gets so excited that he spills coffee all over himself,
has to go change his clothes and, because of the extra time, gets to work
too late for a big meeting and gets in serious trouble with his boss. Later,
in the hospital parking lot, on his way to the emergency room where his
mother has just been taken, he finds a dime on the ground. Research on
confirmation bias suggests that:
   a. he will renounce astrology as completely wrong because of all
      the horrible things that happened on his "lucky day".
   b. he will begin to question his belief in astrology because of all the
      horrible things that happened on his "lucky day".
   c. he will seize on the dime he found as evidence of astrology's
      accuracy.
   d. Confirmation bias has no relevance to how this person will think
      about astrology in the future.

Answer: d
The process of thinking: reasoning and
   decision making
pp. 331–332

182. "Lucky" Lou considers himself quite lucky while his friend "Loser"
Larry considers himself quite unlucky. They each take $100 to a casino
and play blackjack for 3 hours. When they leave, they have each lost
$20. Research on confirmation bias suggests that:
   a. Because of their losses, "Loser" will maintain his view of himself
      and "Lucky" will begin to change his view of himself.
   b. Both men will reason that they were willing to lose $100 but only
      lost $20, so it's like they won $80. So "Lucky" will maintain his
      view of himself and "Loser" will begin to change his.
   c. "Loser" will begin to change his view of himself, reasoning that
      he was willing to lose $100 but he only lost $20, so it's like he
      won $80. Because of his loss, "Lucky" will also begin to change
      his view of himself.
   d. "Loser" will maintain his view of himself because of his loss.
      "Lucky" will also maintain his view of himself, reasoning that he
      was willing to lose $100 but he only lost $20, so it's like he won
      $80.

Answer: d
The process of thinking: reasoning and
   decision making
pp. 331–332

183. Research on confirmation bias suggests that a person who believes that
students at Learning-'R-Us University are stupid will:
   a. look for examples of stupid students at LRU U.
   b. look for examples of smart students at LRU U.
   c. when confronted with examples of smart students at LRU U, play
      them down as very atypical.
   d. a and c
   e. all of the above

Answer: c
The process of thinking: reasoning and
   decision making
pp. 332–333

184. Statistical training:
   a. encourages people to test hypotheses by seeking confirming
      evidence.
   b. increases the likelihood that people will use the representative-
      ness and availability heuristics.
   c. makes people less prone to making errors in inductive reasoning.
   d. is unrelated to everyday reasoning.

Answer: c

The process of thinking: reasoning and
   decision making

pp. 333–334

185. Faced with a new disease that will kill 1000 people, research participants in group A are asked to choose between plan 1, with a 60 percent chance of saving no one and a 40 percent chance of saving everyone, or plan 2, guaranteed to save 400 people. Research participants in group B are offered plan 1, with a 60 percent chance of all 1000 people dying and a 40 percent chance of no one dying, or plan 2, in which 600 people will die. Research on framing indicates that:
    a. majorities of both sets of participants will choose plan 1.
    b. majorities of both sets of participants will choose plan 2.
    c. most participants in group A will choose plan 2 and most participants in group B will choose plan 1.
    d. most participants in group A will choose plan 1 and most participants in group B will choose plan 2.

Answer: a

The process of thinking: reasoning and
   decision making

pp. 333–334

186. Research on framing indicates that people are most willing to:
    a. take risks to avoid losses.
    b. take risks to increase gains.
    c. choose options that emphasize the low possibility for loss rather than those that emphasize the high possibility for gain.
    d. all of the above

Answer: b

The process of thinking: reasoning and
   decision making

pp. 333–334

187. Saying that people are "risk averse":
    a. is the same as saying that they're loss averse.
    b. means that they're unwilling to risk losing a sure gain for the possibility of greater gains.
    c. means that they're unwilling to risk increasing losses for the possibility of decreasing a sure loss.
    d. b and c

Answer: d

The process of thinking: reasoning and
   decision making

pp. 333–334

188. If someone is loss averse and risk averse:
    a. her behavior will be consistent across a large range of decisions.
    b. she is unlikely to risk increasing a sure loss in an attempt to decrease it.
    c. she is likely to risk losing a sure gain to try to increase the gain.
    d. she is likely to respond to the same choice differently depending on whether it is framed in terms of gains or losses.

Answer: c

The process of thinking: reasoning and
   decision making

pp. 333–334

189. Gambler 1 has won $100 and Gambler 2 has lost $100. They're both offered a double-or-nothing coin flip. In other words, rather than winning $100, Gambler 1 will end up winning either $200 or $0, and rather than losing $100, Gambler 2 will end up losing either $200 or $0. Research suggests that which of the following outcomes is most likely?
    a. Both will take the bet.
    b. Neither will take the bet.
    c. Gambler 2 will take the bet and Gambler 1 will not.
    d. Gambler 1 will take the bet and Gambler 2 will not.

Answer: a
The process of thinking: reasoning and
    decision making
pp. 333–334

190. Suppose that people think the country's economic problems aren't so bad if the government reports the employment rate at 80 percent instead of reporting a 20 percent *un*employment rate. If so, the public's relatively positive judgments have been manipulated most by the:
    a. government's framing of the announcement.
    b. statement ignoring base rates.
    c. representativeness.
    d. government betting that people will use confirmation biases.

Answer: b
The process of thinking: reasoning and
    decision making
pp. 333–334

191. The public may think the economic situation is not so bad if the government reports employment as 82 percent instead of saying that there is an 18 percent unemployment rate. If so, the increase in relatively positive judgments has been influenced by:
    a. confirmation biases.
    b. framing.
    c. ignoring the base rates.
    d. the availability heuristic.

Answer: c
The process of thinking: reasoning and
    decision making
pp. 333–334

192. If the government decides to report unemployment statistics in terms of the number of people working instead of the number of people out of work, and the basic information is the same, the public may react more positively due to the effect of _____ on judgments.
    a. mental set
    b. availability and representativeness
    c. framing
    d. confirmation biases

Answer: d
The process of thinking: reasoning and
    decision making
p. 335

193. An occasional lack of rationality:
    a. probably doesn't do major damage to scientific research because it can be corrected by the communal nature of the scientific enterprise.
    b. may be the price paid for the ability to make timely judgments and decisions.
    c. is less likely following statistical training.
    d. all of the above

Answer: a
The thinking brain
p. 336

194. Patients with damage to the prefrontal cortex:
    a. often perseverate.
    b. have difficulty in speaking.
    c. often lose the ability to form visual images.
    d. are better at working on a series of different tasks rather than repeating the same task several times.

Answer: a
The thinking brain
p. 336

195. The prefrontal cortex seems to:
    a. play an important role in working memory.
    b. be the primary center for linguistic processing.
    c. be the primary center for visual processing.
    d. be the primary center for auditory processing.

Answer: c
The thinking brain
p. 336

196. _____ seems to play a direct and central role in may aspects of thought and memory.
   a. The hindbrain
   b. Broca's area
   c. The prefrontal cortex
   d. The occipital lobe

Answer: b
The thinking brain
p. 337

197. Psychologists in the 19th century were keenly interested in consciousness. Why did this interest wane during most of the 20th century?
   a. Most of the fundamental issues were solved when psychologists began to examine behavior with rigorous experimental methods.
   b. Conscious experience was too subjective for investigators to repeat each other's observations.
   c. There were no methods available until neurophysiology discovered how synapses work and how neurons conduct nerve impulses.
   d. Computers had not yet been invented, and the data from research on consciousness were simply too voluminous and complex to work with by hand.

Answer: d
The thinking brain
p. 337

198. How did 19th-century investigators attempt to gather data on conscious experience?
   a. Following Darwin's lead, they worked with intelligent nonhuman animals.
   b. They primarily studied patients who suffered various neurological defects.
   c. Most of the research was based on dreaming and other altered states of consciousness.
   d. They tried to describe the contents and processes of their own conscious experience.

Answer: c
The thinking brain
pp. 338–339

199. The term *blindsight* seems like a contradiction in terms. Which of the following is true?
   a. It is seen in patients with multiple personalities, one of which has sight, the other being blind.
   b. It refers to the development of acute sensitivity to touch in many blind people, such that they are actually conscious of seeing things when they touch them.
   c. It describes a dissociation between perception and the conscious experience of perception.
   d. It describes people who think that they can see, but when tested they fail badly at most visual tasks.

Answer: a
The thinking brain
pp. 338–339

200. The *blind* in the term *blindsight* refers to:
   a. the absence of awareness of stimuli in some parts of the visual field.
   b. a type of hysterical blindness brought on by extreme anxiety, as in post-traumatic stress disorders.
   c. an objective blindness, as shown by the inability to orient to objects that appear suddenly in the visual field.
   d. the inability to use vision by partially blind people who have become highly skilled in using touch and hearing.

Answer: b
The thinking brain
pp. 338–339

201. Suppose a person reports being totally deaf. Yet the person gives vigorous startle responses to loud sounds. Of such occasions the person reports "I just felt I had to crouch quickly." Such findings would be most similar to those from studies of:
 a. selective attention to one ear when conflicting messages arrive at the other ear.
 b. people with blindsight.
 c. the effects of mental set on the perception of ambiguous figures.
 d. people who have reasonably good generic memory but virtually no procedural memory.

Answer: d
The thinking brain
p. 339

202. "Bill got a Big Mac at MacDonald's and ate it" is taken by almost everybody to mean Bill ate the burger, not the restaurant. The process at work here seems to be:
 a. an explicit search of semantic memory.
 b. an unconscious grammatical algorithm that divides the proposition into unambiguous parts, a noun phrase and a verb phrase.
 c. our mindful choice of alternatives.
 d. implicit retrieval.

Answer: b
The thinking brain
p. 339

203. Which of the following statements is false?
 a. Memory retrieval often takes place without conscious awareness.
 b. Cognitive scientists use the term *unconscious* in the same way the Freud did.
 c. Studying behaviors that are done automatically can improve our understanding of consciousness.
 d. Some people are unaware that they can see.

Answer: c
The thinking brain
pp. 338–340

204. Studies of blindsight and automatization study consciousness:
 a. by asking the participants in the research to look within and to describe the processes involved.
 b. by comparing the processes involved with those of complex computers.
 c. by examining what happens in the absence of conscious awareness.
 d. in ways that have little or no relevance to issues about the way or ways that consciousness might be related to behavior.

Answer: c
Cognition and consciousness
pp. 338–340

205. Processes like blindsight and automatization:
 a. confirm Freud's basic ideas about the role of anxiety in repression.
 b. are independent ways of substantiating what Freud meant by the term *unconscious*.
 c. demonstrate that complex processes can be inaccessible to consciousness.
 d. all of the above

Answer: d
The thinking brain
p. 340

206. Which of the following statements is true?
 a. Several explanations have been offered for the purpose of consciousness.
 b. Consciousness may serve more than one function.
 c. We don't know exactly what the purpose of consciousness is.
 d. all of the above

Answer: d
Taking stock
p. 341

207. A subject is asked to write down three landmarks he passes on his way to work each morning. In order to do this, he makes use of:
    a. perception.
    b. thinking.
    c. memory.
    d. all of the above

CHAPTER 9 | Language

Answer: a
Language
p. 345

1. To Descartes, languages:
   a. are the only certain evidence of thinking.
   b. are based on a system of complex reflexes.
   c. both of the above
   d. none of the above

Answer: b
Language
p. 345

2. To Descartes, languages:
   a. are based on a system of complex reflexes.
   b. make humans qualitatively different from any other animal.
   c. both of the above
   d. none of the above

Answer: d
Language
p. 345

3. A serious objection to the view that the foundations for language are built into the biology of humans is that:
   a. all normal humans have language.
   b. humans born without forebrains do not develop language.
   c. chimpanzees can acquire some of the rudiments of language.
   d. there are many different human languages.

Answer: d
Major properties of human language
p. 345

4. All of the following are major properties of human language except one. Which is it?
   a. Human language is creative.
   b. Human language is structured.
   c. Human language is referential.
   d. Human language is not rule-governed.

Answer: a
Major properties of human language
p. 346

5. The response to "How are you?" is almost invariably "Fine." This is:
   a. one of the few examples of speech behavior that easily fits into a behavioral account of language learning.
   b. an illustration of a frozen metaphor that provides evidence against an associative basis for language learning.
   c. a demonstration of the difference between semantics and syntax.
   d. a manifestation of a conversational rule that is both descriptive and prescriptive.

257

Answer: c
Major properties of human language
p. 346

Answer: d
Major properties of human language
p. 347

Answer: d
Major properties of human language
p. 349

Answer: a
Major properties of human language
p. 347

Answer: a
Major properties of human language
p. 347

Answer: d
Major properties of human language
p. 347

Answer: d
Major properties of human language
p. 347

6. A serious objection to the argument that language is a complicated habit is:
    a.   that vocabulary can be acquired by imitation.
    b.   children can memorize complex sentences.
    c.   there are an infinite number of understandable sentences.
    d.   that we can apply rules like "I before E, except after C."

7. A prescriptive rule is:
    a.   a rule formed by us about how we never speak.
    b.   a rule formed by us about how we speak.
    c.   a rule formed by authorities about how we speak.
    d.   a rule formed by authorities about how we should speak.

8. In the United States, the prescriptive rules for language are usually set by:
    a.   users of new technology who must coin new phrases to describe new concepts.
    b.   a formalization of the descriptive rules of the language.
    c.   the way in which Wernicke's and Broca's areas are interconnected.
    d.   the educational system and other authorities.

9. Which of the following is a prescriptive rule for English speakers?
    a.   A sentence must not end in a preposition.
    b.   No word can start with the letter combination *xl*.
    c.   A sentence contains both a noun and a verb.
    d.   Sentences are made up of words.

10. Which of the following is a prescriptive rule for speaking English?
    a.   A sentence must not end in a preposition.
    b.   No word can start with the letter combination *tl*.
    c.   A sentence contains a noun phrase and a verb phrase.
    d.   all of the above

11. The language that most of us use in daily life:
    a.   is less governed by structural principles than the standard dialect.
    b.   is acquired more easily by children than the standard dialect.
    c.   is less likely to be disrupted by brain damage than standard dialects.
    d.   often violates prescriptive rules of the language.

12. Descriptive rules are to prescriptive rules as:
    a.   reflexes are to thought.
    b.   meaning is to referents.
    c.   sentences are to morphemes.
    d.   implicit is to explicit.

Answer: a
Major properties of human language
p. 347

13. Each word in a language has its own:
    a. meaning.
    b. phrase.
    c. tense.
    d. none of the above

Answer: c
Major properties of human language
p. 348

14. Which of the following sentences will be the easiest for most people to understand?
    a. one that is meaningless and ungrammatical
    b. one that is meaningless and grammatical
    c. one that is meaningful and grammatical
    d. one that is meaningful and ungrammatical

Answer: b
Major properties of human language
p. 348

15. If a child says, "That's a shoe." when she sees a truck, the parent could reasonably assume that the child is:
    a. experiencing retrograde amnesia.
    b. exhibiting a problem of reference.
    c. fond of shoes.
    d. too young to verbalize "truck."

Answer: d
Major properties of human language
p. 349

16. A person who simply answers "Yes!" when you say "Could you pass me the salt?" has failed to obey:
    a. principles of phonetic use.
    b. principles of morphetic use.
    c. principles of description.
    d. principles of conversation.

Answer: d
Major properties of human language
p. 349

17. Most people interpret the sentence "Can you pass me the butter?" to mean "Please pass me the butter." This is an illustration of:
    a. the fact that meaning and reference are not the same thing.
    b. the inability of an associationist theory to explain language.
    c. prescriptive rules that govern language.
    d. conversational principles that affect communication.

Answer: d
Major properties of human language
p. 349

18. Most people interpret the sentence "Can you pass me the butter?" to mean "Please pass me the butter." This is an illustration of:
    a. the fact that meaning and reference are not the same thing.
    b. the inability of an associationist theory to explain our speaking behavior.
    c. our daily violation of descriptive rules of language.
    d. our tendency to make complicated inferences about meaning and intent.

Answer: c
The basic units of language
p. 350

19. For any specific language, speech sounds are called different phonemes if substituting one for another changes the:
    a. sound of the word.
    b. loudness of the speech.
    c. meaning of the word.
    d. movements of the tongue and lips in speech.

Answer: b
The basic units of language
p. 350

20. In order to correctly interpret phonemes, one needs a(n):
    a. built-in interpreter.
    b. context of other phonemes.
    c. comparative signal generator.
    d. mental word processor.

Answer: c
The basic units of language
p. 350

21. Phonemes are:
    a. the smallest language units that carry bits of meaning.
    b. the smallest word structures in speech that are universally understood by all language speakers.
    c. the smallest distinctions in speech sounds that signal a difference in meaning between words.
    d. all of the above

Answer: c
The basic units of language
p. 351

22. Why is it fairly easy, out of context, to mistake the spoken sentence "The sky is falling" for the sentence "This guy is falling"?
    a. They contain the same morphemes, but in different orders.
    b. They contain ambiguous or vague referents.
    c. The speech stream rarely contains silences between words.
    d. There are only about 40 phonemes used in English, not enough to distinguish between sentences that sound the same.

Answer: b
The basic units of language
p. 351

23. English contains about _____ phonemes.
    a. 13
    b. 40
    c. 5,000
    d. 50,000

Answer: b
The basic units of language
p. 351

24. Which of the following is a structural principle of English speech?
    a. A sentence must not end in a preposition.
    b. No word can start with the letter combination *tl*.
    c. The typical meaning of "Can you pass the salt?" is "Please pass me the salt."
    d. all of the above

Answer: a
The basic units of language
p. 351

25. Morphemes are to phonemes as meanings are to:
    a. sounds.
    b. words.
    c. structural principles.
    d. syntax.

Answer: b
The basic units of language
p. 352

26. Examine the sentence "The strangers left." The *s* at the end of the word *strangers* is a:
    a. functional phoneme.
    b. functional morpheme.
    c. content phoneme.
    d. content morpheme.

Answer: b
The basic units of language
p. 352

27. Examine the phrase "Isn't it?" The *it* at the end is a:
    a. phoneme.
    b. morpheme.
    c. both a and b above
    d. neither a nor b above

Answer: d
The basic units of language
p. 352

28. Take the phrase "Aren't I?" The *I* at the end is a:
    a. functional morpheme.
    b. content phoneme.
    c. functional phoneme.
    d. content morpheme.

Answer: c
The basic units of language
p. 352

29. Which of the following statements regarding morphemes is true?
    a. Rearrangement of the morphemes within an utterance does not alter the meaning of the utterance.
    b. The total number of morphemes is approximately equal to the total number of phonemes.
    c. There may be more than one morpheme within a word, although there are one-word morphemes.
    d. none of the above

Answer: d
The basic units of language
p. 352

30. Japanese linguist: "What does 'k' mean in English?" Reply by American linguist: "It doesn't mean anything. It's a _____, not a _____."
    a. consonant, vowel
    b. referent, structural principle
    c. prescriptive structure, word
    d. phoneme, morpheme

Answer: c
The basic units of language
p. 352

31. In English, *ing* is a:
    a. word.
    b. syntax.
    c. morpheme.
    d. phoneme.

Answer: c
The basic units of language
p. 352

32. A local meteorologist calls the big hunks of frozen slush left by road crews *slument*. This word shows:
    a. the importance of imitation in the acquisition of vocabulary.
    b. that descriptive rules of English can be violated, yet have little effect on meaning.
    c. morphemes carry meaning even when used in unusual ways.
    d. phonemes in English are less restrictive than many linguists would suggest.

Answer: b
The basic units of language
p. 352

33. The word *studying* contains _____ morphemes.
    a. 1
    b. 2
    c. 3
    d. 8

34. The word *breadwinner* contains _____ morphemes.
    a. 1
    b. 2
    c. 3
    d. 5
    e. 11

35. The number of morphemes in the sentence "He kicked the ball," is:
    a. 2.
    b. 3.
    c. 4.
    d. 5.

36. The word *cowboys* contains _____ morphemes.
    a. 1
    b. 2
    c. 3
    d. 7

37. The fact that two expressions can have different meanings yet refer to the same thing is evidence against a _____ theory of meaning.
    a. definitional
    b. prototype
    c. referential
    d. family resemblance

38. The definitional theory of meaning suggests that we understand the meaning of words because:
    a. we form mental images of their meanings.
    b. we know the particular objects to which words refer.
    c. we associate words with specific actions.
    d. we understand the semantic elements that constitute words.

39. According to the definitional theory of word meaning, we tend to see a group of words as having similar meaning when:
    a. the words sound the same.
    b. the words share features of meaning.
    c. the words refer to the same object.
    d. the words elicit similar mental images.

40. Definitional theories of meaning pose a serious problem in that:
    a. relationships can be explained in terms of groups of semantic features.
    b. we have relatively few words that describe elementary concepts.
    c. the words *wife, sister,* and *daughter* all contain the concept of female.
    d. some members of a meaning category fit the category far better than do other members.

Answer: d
The basic units of language
p. 354

41. According to prototype theory, a prototype is:
    a. a list of all the features that characterize a category.
    b. a list of all the defining features that characterize a category.
    c. a family resemblance among examples of a category.
    d. a mental average of all the various examples of a category.

Answer: b
The basic units of language
p. 354

42. Which of the following concepts is most consistent with the basic ideas of prototype theory?
    a. dictionary definitions
    b. family resemblance structures
    c. bundles of semantic features
    d. prescriptive rules

Answer: c
The basic units of language
p. 355

43. A concept has a family resemblance structure if:
    a. its meaning is very different from its reference.
    b. it is described by a set of defining features.
    c. it is described by a set of defining features, no one of which is individually either necessary or sufficient.
    d. it cannot be represented by a mental image, but it shares features with other words.

Answer: b
The basic units of language
p. 355

44. According to prototype theory, a prototype for a concept:
    a. embodies the feature element that necessarily defines one as a member of that class.
    b. embodies many, but not necessarily all, of the features that characterize a class.
    c. embodies all of the features that characterize a class.
    d. is an internal representation of all of the features that characterize a class.

Answer: a
The basic units of language
p. 356

45. It seems most plausible that the limits on categories like *grandmother* are set by:
    a. memory storage of definitional features.
    b. a collection of features that fit grandmothers especially well.
    c. descriptive rules of language that require features like noun phrases and verb phrases to produce meaningful thought.
    d. the time required to analyze family resemblance structures.

Answer: d
The basic units of language
p. 357

46. The word *predicate* comes closest to the meaning of the word or phrase:
    a. concept.
    b. prototype.
    c. phrase structure.
    d. propose.

Answer: c
The basic units of language
p. 358

47. Instead of producing sentences, we might invent a new word for each idea we want to convey. The problem with this is that:
    a. all the words have already been used.
    b. some letter combinations cannot occur.
    c. the number of words would be too huge to remember.
    d. none of the above

Answer: c
The basic units of language
p. 358

48. Syntax refers to:
    a. the meanings of words.
    b. the sounds of words.
    c. the rules by which words are combined.
    d. the symbols used to designate words.

Answer: c
The basic units of language
p. 358

49. Syntax is the general name for the system that arranges:
    a. sounds together to form meaningful speech units.
    b. morphemes together to form words.
    c. words together to form sentences.
    d. all of the above

Answer: d
The basic units of language
p. 359

50. In the sentence "The ball was hit by the boy," what is the verb phrase?
    a. "The ball was hit"
    b. "was hit"
    c. "hit"
    d. "was hit by the boy"

Answer: c
The basic units of language
p. 359

51. In the sentence "The cook squeezed the lemon," what is the verb phrase?
    a. "The cook squeezed"
    b. "squeezed"
    c. "squeezed the lemon"
    d. There is no verb phrase.

Answer: d
The basic units of language
p. 359

52. When one divides a sentence into a noun phrase and a verb phrase, and then subdivides each of these, with appropriate connecting lines, into their components, one has:
    a. constructed a phrase structure description.
    b. produced a hierarchical structure.
    c. used a tree diagram notation.
    d. all of the above

Answer: b
The basic units of language
p. 359

53. A linguist constructs a phrase structure description of a sentence, using the appropriately placed lines to connect the various parts. This will most likely reveal a(n):
    a. diagram of the semantics of the sentence.
    b. hierarchical structure.
    c. family resemblance structure.
    d. underlying structure diagram.

Answer: a
The basic units of language
p. 359

54. You would be helped most in memorizing a list of seven nonsense syllables if you could:
    a. add function morphemes to the syllables in the list.
    b. add the suffix *-ly* to each of the syllables in the list.
    c. change the syllables so that each one starts with the same letter.
    d. remove the vowel from the middle of each syllable to reduce the list size.

55. Memorizing Lewis Carroll's famous poem "Jabberwocky" ("Twas brillig, and the slithy tove . . .") is made tolerably easy because:
    a. morphemes enable us to chunk nonsense words into phrases.
    b. the underlying phrase structure becomes clear after we have recited the poem a few times.
    c. there is little meter or rhyme in the poem.
    d. all of the above

56. If the phrase structure descriptions of two seven-word sentences look dramatically different, these sentences must differ in:
    a. over half of their words.
    b. surface structures.
    c. underlying structures.
    d. all of the above

57. If the tree diagrams of the structure of two seven-word sentences look dramatically different, these sentences must differ in their:
    a. meanings.
    b. clarity.
    c. surface structures.
    d. family resemblance structure.

58. What does examining a structural diagram of a sentence enable one to determine?
    a. who did what to whom
    b. the meaning of the various words
    c. the truth or falsity of the sentence
    d. whether or not the sentence is ambiguous

59. Assertions, negatives, passives, and questions of the same basic proposition differ in their:
    a. referents for the proposition.
    b. presence or absence of hierarchical structure.
    c. ambiguity.
    d. attitude.

60. People often make errors in recalling sentences they have heard very recently. When this happens, they are most apt to accurately remember:
    a. the underlying structure of the sentence.
    b. the attitude that the speaker took toward the proposition.
    c. the specific phonemes used by the speaker.
    d. the surface structure of the sentence.

61. What people are most apt to remember about a sentence is its:
    a. attitude.
    b. surface structure.
    c. family resemblence structure.
    d. underlying structure.

Answer: c
The basic units of language
p. 362

Answer: d
The basic units of language
p. 362

Answer: c
The basic units of language
p. 362

Answer: d
The basic units of language
p. 362

Answer: d
The basic units of language
p. 362

Answer: d
Comprehension
p. 363

Answer: c
Comprehension
p. 363

62. Paraphrases are to language as _____ are to perception.
  a. meanings
  b. constancies
  c. sensations
  d. associations

63. When two sentences have the identical surface structure but differ in their underlying structure there is:
  a. paraphrasing.
  b. semantic isomorphism.
  c. a family resemblence hierarchy.
  d. ambiguity.

64. When the same string of words can indicate two propositions, there is:
  a. paraphrasing.
  b. a difference in attitude.
  c. ambiguity.
  d. the same underlying structure.

65. Mom failed to segregate her phonemes well and little Billy heard her prayer " . . . lead us not into temptation . . . " as " . . . lead us not into Penn Station . . . ." This illustrates:
  a. a form of linguistic constancy.
  b. a violation of phonemic rules of English.
  c. that young children are able to hear phonemes that are not used in the language of their parents.
  d. a type of ambiguity.

66. Ambiguity occurs at the level of:
  a. underlying structure.
  b. segmenting words.
  c. word meaning.
  d. all of the above

67. In German it's *klein*, in French it's *petite*, and in English it's *small*. This example from three languages is most similar to the psychological phenomenon involving:
  a. monocular depth cues.
  b. sensory integration.
  c. visual ambiguities.
  d. perceptual constancies.

68. In German it's *schwartz*, in English it's *black*, and in French it's *noir*. This example from languages is most similar to the psychological phenomenon of:
  a. ambiguities.
  b. opponent processes.
  c. perceptual constancies.
  d. differentiation.

69. Understanding that the sentence "Bob hit the ball" means the same thing as "The ball was hit by Bob" is most similar to which of the following perceptual phenomenon?
    a. the ambiguity of reversible figures
    b. the bottom-up approach of feature detectors for lines
    c. perpetual constancy of size and shape
    d. the dot techniques used by the Impressionist painters

Answer: c
Comprehension
p. 363

70. The default or "factory setting" for the Sentence Analyzing Machinery discussed by psycholinguists seems to:
    a. expect sentences in which the object of the action comes before the doer of the action.
    b. identify function words that let the reader know if there are any propositions embedded within other propositions.
    c. assume a "doer first" form of the proposition.
    d. know that there will be distinct pauses between the various phrases of a sentence.

Answer: c
Comprehension
p. 364

71. A commonly used method for determining the relative ease with which the Sentence Analyzing Machinery works on different kinds of sentences is to:
    a. ask native speakers of the language if they can repeat the sentence.
    b. measure reaction times for responding to one or another possible meaning of a sentence.
    c. determine the accuracy with which the listener can indicate the gist of the sentence after a 24-hour retention interval.
    d. count the number of function words used in the sentences.

Answer: b
Comprehension
p. 365

72. If the psycholinguists are correct about the way in which the Sentence Analyzing Machinery works, which of the following sentences should result in the fastest reaction times?
    a. The apple which the beautiful princess ate was poisoned by the wicked witch.
    b. The apple which the wicked witch poisoned was eaten by the beautiful princess.
    c. The beautiful princess was poisoned by the apple the wicked witch poisoned.
    d. The wicked witch poisoned the apple and the beautiful princess ate that apple.

Answer: d
Comprehension
p. 365

73. Which of the following propositions should be processed almost as quickly when presented in the passive form as in the active form?
    a. The cow licked the calf.
    b. The farmer plowed the field.
    c. The frog jumped over the rabbit.
    d. The ball hit the boy.

Answer: b
Comprehension
p. 365

74. Which of the following propositions would be processed substantially more slowly in the passive form than in the active form?
    a. The boy weeded the carrots.
    b. Big Bird greeted Grover.
    c. The car drove through the puddle.
    d. The manager drank her coffee.

75. Which of the following propositions would be processed substantially more slowly in the passive form than in the active form?
    a. The car hit the rock.
    b. The girl mowed the grass.
    c. The car drove through the puddle.
    d. The bird flew into the tree.

76. What makes it difficult to understand the sentence "The truck towed slowly past the car crashed"?
    a. The second proposition "the truck was towed slowly past the car" is inserted into the middle of the first proposition.
    b. The sentence omits some helpful function words like "which was" that could precede the word "towed."
    c. The proposition regarding the truck being towed is in the passive form.
    d. all of the above

77. What makes it difficult to understand the sentence "The truck towed slowly by the car crashed"?
    a. The sentence omits some helpful function words like "which was" that could precede the word "towed."
    b. Use of the word "by" is ambiguous. The car could have towed the truck or the truck could have been towed "past" the car.
    c. The proposition regarding the truck being towed is in the passive form.
    d. all of the above

78. Spoken utterances of garden-path sentences such as, "The cabin struck by the tree fell" are less likely to result in confusion than written statements. Why is this?
    a. Spoken utterances are accompanied by extralinguistic factors.
    b. Spoken utterances are processed more rapidly than written statements.
    c. Written statements are accompanied by extralinguistic factors.
    d. Written statements are processed more rapidly than written statements.

79. Which of the following would not clarify the spoken utterance, "Put the orange on the table in the dining room"?
    a. the addition of function words
    b. the physical presence of the objects
    c. the use of timing as an extralinguistic cue
    d. the omission of repetitive morphemes

80. Consider the following conversation about a family's cat:
    Marty: "I opened the kitchen door."
    Mustafa: "Was she limping?"
    Marty: "She wasn't happy."
    Which of the following statements is probably false about this conversation?
    a.   Mustafa violated the maxim of relevancy.
    b.   Marty probably used extralinguistic factors to convey meaning.
    c.   The circumstances allowed Mustafa to understand Marty's initial statement.
    d.   Bystander comprehension errors are likely to occur.

81. Which of the following is least likely to affect language comprehension as two people have a conversation over the telephone?
    a.   timing and intonation
    b.   syntax
    c.   extralinguistic factors
    d.   inference

82. The idea that imitation is the method by which children acquire language is contradicted by the observation that:
    a.   children are not capable of imitation at the age they acquire language.
    b.   reinforcement, and not imitation, appears to be the mechanism by which children acquire language.
    c.   children utter sentences that they have never heard spoken by the people around them.
    d.   children who frequently imitate others tend to acquire language faster than children who do not imitate.

83. If language were acquired strictly by imitation, then one would predict that:
    a.   children would not become proficient in a second language.
    b.   adults would learn no more than 100–200 words.
    c.   adults would speak their languages no better than children.
    d.   children would not generate a novel utterance.

84. Imitation is least likely to explain how children produce sentences like:
    a.   "Bye, Bye Mommy."
    b.   "Grandma and Grandpa live in Davenport, Iowa."
    c.   "I goed to the store today."
    d.   "We're going to go to Aunt Betty's house for Thanksgiving."

85. Reinforcement theory is particularly poor in explaining how:
    a.   children say one word rather than another when referring to a particular object.
    b.   children learn to take turns in conversation.
    c.   children learn grammar even though they are seldom corrected for mistakes.
    d.   children talk for no reason except to get attention.

Answer: b
The growth of language in the child
p. 372

86. Parents of two- and three-year-olds are most likely to correct their children's:
    a. grammatical errors.
    b. factual errors.
    c. errors of both grammar and fact.
    d. sentences that show ambiguity in the use of words.

Answer: d
The growth of language in the child
p. 372

87. Analyses of the linguistic abilities of children in the first year of life indicate that:
    a. children begin to babble in order to initiate communication with their parents.
    b. deaf children do not babble and they never develop speech.
    c. infants have no means, other than babbling, to communicate with parents.
    d. none of the above

Answer: c
The growth of language in the child
p. 373

88. Which of the following statements is false?
    a. Initially, Japanese babies can distinguish between the sounds *l* and *r*.
    b. Japanese adults cannot perceive the difference between the sound *l* and *r*.
    c. American-born children and adults can respond to all sound distinctions in any language.
    d. Children learn the phonemes of their languages by ignoring the sound distinctions that are not used in their language.

Answer: c
The growth of language in the child
p. 373

89. How could you best determine if infants prefer Motherese to normal adult speech?
    a. Determine if infants who hear one type of speech are happier and more well-adjusted than infants who hear adult-to-adult speech.
    b. Record EEGs from the left hemisphere as the infants listen to the two different types of speech.
    c. See if infants orient to a speaker emitting one kind of speech more than they do to a speaker emitting the other kind.
    d. all of the above

Answer: b
The growth of language in the child
p. 373

90. How does Motherese help infants to learn where one sentence stops and another begins?
    a. It has normal conversational pauses to demarcate sentences.
    b. It has exaggerated intonations, like drops in pitch.
    c. It has a special low and attractive tone of voice.
    d. It has a somewhat more rapid delivery than characterizes adult speech.

Answer: a
The growth of language in the child
p. 373

91. Motherese is characterized by:
    a. exaggerated intonations.
    b. a monotone delivery.
    c. rapid rates of speech.
    d. all of the above

92. The first words of infants:
    a. are typically function words.
    b. generally describe the child's emotional state.
    c. commonly refer to familiar objects.
    d. generally occurs at about age five to six months.

93. Which of the following words is the "one-word speaker" least likely to utter?
    a. ball
    b. Mama
    c. be
    d. no

94. When a young child thinks that the word *grandmother* refers to any older woman with white hair, he is:
    a. undergeneralizing.
    b. overgeneralizing.
    c. categorizing.
    d. prototyping.

95. If a child overgeneralizes based on perceptual properties, he might say "ball" to refer to:
    a. a beach ball.
    b. the moon.
    c. a face.
    d. all of the above

96. Which of the following methods would be the fastest and easiest means of determining whether an infant understands the sentence "Maria pats Grover"?
    a. Ask the infant, "who pats whom?"
    b. Reinforce looking at Maria when this sentence is presented and reinforce looking at Grover when the sentence "Grover pats Maria" is presented.
    c. Use a selective looking experiment to determine whether infants prefer to look at a video screen that shows events matching this verbal statement.
    d. all of the above

97. A selective looking experiment would be most appropriate for determining:
    a. if two-year-olds can imitate three-word sentences.
    b. the rate at which infants will suck a pacifier to hear various phonemes.
    c. if infants understand that "Maria pats Grover" means something different from "Grover pats Maria."
    d. whether infants prefer to hear Motherese over ordinary speech.

Answer: b
The growth of language in the child
p. 377

98. Two-word sentences, such as "Mommy throw," are characteristic of most children at what age?
    a. 1 year
    b. 2 years
    c. 3 years
    d. 4 years

Answer: a
The growth of language in the child
p. 378

99. Four-year-old Jimmy tells you he "runned fast but falled down." You note that he:
    a. exhibits overregularization errors.
    b. is omitting functional morphemes.
    c. is communicating using Motherese.
    d. all of the above

Answer: a
The growth of language in the child
p. 379

100. Which of the following clues is a youngster most likely to use to discover the meaning of the question "Can you see fiffining?"
    a. syntax
    b. the sounds of unusual phonemes
    c. configuration
    d. word length

Answer: b
The growth of language in the child
p. 379

101. If an experimenter points to an object and says "That's foff," children will almost always guess that *foff* refers to:
    a. some part of the object.
    b. the whole object.
    c. the material of which the object is made.
    d. the color of the object.

Answer: a
The growth of language in the child
p. 380

102. If an experimenter points to two objects with the same shape but with different colors, a child is likely to:
    a. think they have the same linguistic label.
    b. assume no relation between the two.
    c. ignore the shapes and focus on the colors.
    d. none of the above

Answer: d
The growth of language in the child
p. 381

103. Based on current evidence, language learning in humans seems to be facilitated by:
    a. sensitivity to sound patterns.
    b. preparedness for acquiring a universal language structure.
    c. the presence of brain structures specialized for language.
    d. all of the above

104. An eight-month-old infant listens to audiotape recordings of nonsense sounds. Which of the following is likely to be true in this situation?
    a. After hearing "bobusismetapogbobusispogmetabobusis . . ." for two minutes, the infant will perceive "bobusis" as a word and will show surprise if "bobumet" is presented.
    b. After hearing "bobusismetapogbobusispogmetabobusis . . ." for two minutes, the infant will perceive "metapog" as a word and will show surprise if "pogmeta" is presented.
    c. After hearing "bobusismetapogbobusispogmetabobusis . . ." for two minutes, the infant will perceive "bobumet" as a word and will show surprise if "bobupog" is presented.
    d. none of the above

105. According to Noam Chomsky and many other psychologists, if there is a genetic basis for human language learning, then:
    a. non-human animals will be unable to learn rudimentary components of language.
    b. the parameters of language will be identical across cultures.
    c. there must be an innate universal structure for all languages.
    d. all of the above

106. In deaf individuals, Broca's and Wernicke's areas of the brain are:
    a. smaller and less active than in persons with hearing.
    b. crucial for learning sign language.
    c. located in the right hemisphere, even in right-handed individuals.
    d. none of the above

107. The human mouth and larynx appear to have evolved to facilitate speech production. Which of the following is true in this context?
    a. The arrangement of human teeth is less adaptive for biting and chewing than that of most other animals, but it allows easy control of air flow in and out of the mouth.
    b. The shape of the adult human larynx prevents simultaneous breathing and eating, but it allows control of air through the vocal tract.
    c. The shape of the adult human larynx increases the likelihood of choking on food compared to other animals, but it is well designed for speech production.
    d. all of the above

108. The evidence regarding language learning in isolated children:
    a. suggests that there is a critical period for language acquisition.
    b. shows that after about fifteen years of isolation, language basics can be acquired but language elaborations cannot.
    c. indicates that after six years or so of isolation, language can be acquired normally.
    d. all of the above

Answer: c
Language learning in changed environments
p. 386

109. Research on language acquisition in deaf individuals indicates that:
    a. no system of functional communication can be developed in the absence of auditory stimuli.
    b. sign language is unlike spoken language because it has few morphemes and it lacks syntactical structure.
    c. similar developmental stages exist for the acquisition of sign language in deaf children and spoken language in hearing children.
    d. sign language only permits very primitive and basic communication between individuals.

Answer: d
Language learning in changed environments
p. 386

110. American Sign Language:
    a. is a system of easy-to-comprehend gestures, somewhat similar to what hearing persons use when they play charades.
    b. manual version of English, based on finger spelling and supplemented with a few charade-like gestures.
    c. is not a true language because it lacks the functional morphemes and grammatical principles that characterize spoken communication.
    d. is a language with morphemes, ways of building up complex words out of simple ones, and grammatical rules for combining words into sentences.

Answer: b
Language learning in changed environments
p. 387

111. Studies of deaf children with hearing parents who are not taught ASL are important because they demonstrate that:
    a. both language basics and language elaborations like complex syntax are invented without the need of models.
    b. using words and syntax to organize thoughts is a basic property of human minds.
    c. without models, children will not exhibit even the basics of language.
    d. such children are quite similar to birds that do not hear their species' songs until they are adults.

Answer: c

Language learning in changed environments
p. 388

112. Children who are blind from birth tend to respond to commands like "look up":
    a. in an almost random way, indicating that they really do not understand the visually related concept.
    b. by pointing their heads upward, much like sighted children do.
    c. by raising their arms and hands to feel the space above them.
    d. with confusion because of their problems understanding terms of spatial relations.

Answer: a
Language learning in changed environments
p. 388

113. Children who are blind from birth initially show confusion about:
    a. referents to pronouns.
    b. prepositions in speech.
    c. words involving spatial relationships.
    d. all of the above

Answer: b
Language learning in changed environments
p. 389

114. If isolated from all forms of language, an infant such as Helen Keller would be likely to:
   a. lack communication skills.
   b. invent her own language forms.
   c. develop severe mental retardation.
   d. remain socially isolated.

Answer: b
Language learning in changed environments
p. 389

115. Helen Keller is not an ideal case for understanding how someone can acquire language in the absence of early exposure to it because:
   a. she began learning ASL when she was about three.
   b. she became blind and deaf after exposure to spoken English.
   c. besides being blind and deaf, she was born with brain damage.
   d. she did not learn finger-spelling or Braille until she was a teenager.

Answer: b
Language learning with changed endowments
p. 390

116. When a patient uses few, if any, function words but can use many content words properly, he is probably afflicted with:
   a. Wernicke's aphasia.
   b. Broca's aphasia.
   c. congenital deafness.
   d. cortical aphasia.

Answer: a
Language learning with changed endowments
p. 390

117. Language in persons with damage to Broca's area:
   a. has some similarities to the language used by children in the early stages of language acquisition.
   b. is impaired primarily in the patient's ability to understand language.
   c. is characterized by the overuse of function words like *the* and *on*.
   d. is impaired as a result of brain damage that interferes with the motor control of the vocal cords and mouth.

Answer: c
Language learning with changed endowments
p. 390

118. When a patient has no trouble with function words but has an extremely deficient use of content morphemes, he is probably afflicted with:
   a. expressive aphasia.
   b. morphemic aphasia.
   c. Wernicke's aphasia.
   d. Broca's aphasia.

Answer: b
Language learning with changed endowments
p. 390

119. A person utters the following sequence of words: "Tree . . . squirrel . . . bird." This person most likely:
   a. suffers from Wernicke's aphasia.
   b. suffers from Broca's aphasia.
   c. has receptive aphasia.
   d. learned English as a second language.

Answer: a
Language learning with changed endowments
p. 390

120. A person utters the following sentence: "And then they went and did it and got the what-do-you-call-it and that all over there." This person most likely:
    a. suffers from Wernicke's aphasia.
    b. suffers from Broca's aphasia.
    c. has an expressive aphasia.
    d. was exposed to spoken language after the critical period.
    e. learned English as a second language after the critical period.

Answer: b
Language learning with changed endowments
p. 390

121. What isolated children, very young children, and many aphasics have in common with respect to language is:
    a. a defective capacity for forming mental images from words.
    b. difficulty with functional morphemes and other language elaborations.
    c. trouble with the gestural and emotional components of normal speech.
    d. a lack of good role models for language.

Answer: d
Language learning with changed endowments
p. 390

122. After damage to Broca's area, someone would have the greatest difficulty with:
    a. reading written words.
    b. understanding spoken language.
    c. making lip and tongue movements.
    d. using words like *for* and *the*.

Answer: b
Language learning with changed endowments
p. 390

123. After damage to Wernicke's area, someone would have the greatest difficulty with:
    a. making the hand movements needed to converse in ASL.
    b. understanding the content words of spoken language.
    c. making lip and tongue movements.
    d. using words like *for* and *the*.

Answer: b
Language learning with changed endowments
p. 391

124. A critical period for language acquisition refers to:
    a. the period of transition between one-word and two-word utterances.
    b. the time in one's childhood in which language must develop if it is to be fully learned.
    c. the period that isolated children spend by themselves before someone begins to teach them language.
    d. the period from 6–10 years of age during which certain complex aspects of syntax are learned.

Answer: a
Language learning with changed endowments
p. 391

125. Assume that a critical period exists for learning to write and that this critical period is from age two to fifteen years. If someone has not yet learned to write by the time he is twenty, one would predict that:
    a. he will have great difficulty ever learning to write.
    b. he can still learn to write as easily as he would have during the critical period for writing.
    c. he can learn to write faster now than during the critical period.
    d. he will have great difficulty reading two- and three-letter words.

126. Seven-year-olds have a better chance of recovering from aphasia than fifty-year-olds with similar brain damage. This fact:
    a. is consistent with the critical period hypothesis if there are no sex differences in recovery from such brain damage.
    b. is consistent with the critical period hypothesis if one assumes there is a biological basis for language acquisition.
    c. is consistent with the critical period hypothesis if young brains utilize the remaining parts of the brain better than older brains.
    d. refutes the critical hypothesis.

127. In order for a young male white- crowned sparrow to sing its species-specific song, it must hear an adult's song sometime between its 7th and 60th days of life. If not, it will never learn the song. Therefore, the time from the 7th to the 60th day of the sparrow's life is called:
    a. the fledgling stage.
    b. pre-puberty.
    c. the critical period.
    d. the early social learning stage.

128. Which of the following persons would find it easiest to learn to be fluent in a second language?
    a. a fifty-year-old woman
    b. a sixty-five-year old man
    c. a fourteen-year-old boy
    d. a five-year-old girl

129. Which of the following is most plausible, according to recent research on human speech?
    a. Humans do not show species-specific behavior relevant to speech.
    b. Deaf children cannot benefit from language training after they are four years old.
    c. There is a critical period for language acquisition in humans.
    d. People can only learn to speak one language fluently.

130. The most convincing evidence that first languages are easiest to learn in childhood comes from studies of:
    a chimpanzees learning ASL.
    b. deaf middle-aged adults learning ASL.
    c. language acquisition in children who are blind from birth.
    d. so-called "wild children" and children raised in social isolation.

131. When deaf people learn ASL as a first language in adolescence, they:
    a. have difficulty in communicating in ASL even after over 30 years of practice.
    b. have an easier time learning to read English compared to congenitally deaf people who learned ASL earlier.
    c. fail to use function items consistently even after 30 years of using ASL.
    d. all of the above

Answer: e
Language learning with changed endowments
p. 392

132. Which aspects of language are the most defective in people who are not exposed to their first language until late childhood or early adolescence?
   a. use of function words
   b. use of phonemes
   c. use of noun phrases
   d. use of verb phrases

Answer: b
Language learning with changed endowments
p. 393

133. There is general agreement among psychologists that chimpanzees can:
   a. learn to utter most human speech sounds, even though they do not understand what it is that they utter.
   b. learn a substantial number of manual signals for "words."
   c. learn rules to put words together in different sequences so as to express different meanings.
   d. all of the above

Answer: a
Language learning with changed endowments
p. 394

134. According to your textbook authors, there is evidence that chimpanzees are capable of:
   a. some propositional thought.
   b. a fair amount of human phonology.
   c. learning complex syntactical rules.
   d. all of the above

Answer: c
Language learning with changed endowments
p. 394

135. Which of the following statements is false?
   a. Chimpanzees can learn manual signals as "words."
   b. Chimpanzees are capable of some propositional thought.
   c. Chimpanzees can learn complex syntactical rules.
   d. Chimpanzee vocal tracts cannot produce human speech.

Answer: d
Language learning with changed endowments
p. 394

136. Human language can be differentiated from most or all animal behavior because:
   a. only humans can communicate with others.
   b. the ability to solve problems is unique to humans.
   c. animals are unable to emit communcatory sounds.
   d. human language has rules for arranging sounds into meaningful combinations.

Answer: d
Language learning with changed endowments
p. 394

137. There is little satisfactory evidence to show that chimpanzees:
   a. can show relational thought.
   b. can be taught to communicate.
   c. can learn sign language.
   d. can acquire syntax.

Answer: c
Language learning with changed endowments
p. 394

138. Which of the following is a fair summary of language learning?
   a. Human children are born with a "blank slate" for learning language.
   b. Spoken language is not unique to humans.
   c. Human children are biologically predisposed to acquire language.
   d. Language learning must be a fairly simple process if virtually all human babies do it.

139. Antropologist Benjamin Whorf argued that human thought is shaped, in part, by:
    a. vocabulary.
    b. food availability.
    c. sociality.
    d. dominance relationships.

140. Which of the following research findings is inconsistent with Whorf's hypothesis about the relationship between language and thought?
    a. The Dani people of New Guinea have only two color names and they tend to agree with American observers about which colors are particularly good examples of their categories.
    b. The Mayan people who speak Tzeltal have no language labels for "left of" or "right of," nor do they distinguish between mirror-images.
    c. The Australian people who speak Guugu Yimithrr only speak of objects as positioned north, south, east, or west of other objects and they regard layouts of objects as similar only if they are aligned in these ways.
    d. all of the above

141. Verbalizations can seriously disrupt our memories of events, unless:
    a. our verbalizations immediately follow the related experiences.
    b. our vocabulary allows adequate descriptions of our experiences.
    c. our experiences are accompanied by strong emotions.
    d. our language allows dramatic descriptions of related experiences.

142. Which of the following is true regarding language and gender?
    a. Males show better recall of material written with female pronouns than with male pronouns.
    b. Females tend to interpret male pronouns as referring to both females and males.
    c. Females remember material better when it is written with male and female pronouns, rather than male pronouns alone.
    d. none of the above

CHAPTER 10 | The Biological Basis of Social Behavior

Answer: b
The social nature of humans and animals
p. 405

1. Thomas Hobbes, a seventeenth-century philosopher, argued that human beings are naturally:
   a. inclined to social interaction and cooperation.
   b. solitary, selfish, and competitive.
   c. good, until spoiled by society.
   d. heroic and self-sacrificing.

Answer: b
The social nature of humans and animals
pp. 405–406

2. Thomas Hobbes made several strong statements about basic human nature. Which of his assertions are we now most confident is false?
   a. People are basically nasty and selfish.
   b. People are basically solitary.
   c. People are prone to enter into social contracts.
   d. People are constrained by their societies.
   e. People are basically loving and loyal.

Answer: c
The social nature of humans and animals
pp. 405–406

3. According to Thomas Hobbes:
   a. people are by nature gregarious and social beings.
   b. society and civilization act to distort the basic goodness of human nature.
   c. people are, by nature, asocial brutes with no regard for others.
   d. both a and b

Answer: e
The social nature of humans and animals
p. 406

4. Thomas Malthus:
   a. argued that populations grow faster than their food supplies, so that there is always scarcity.
   b. provided Darwin with the explanatory principle for evolution.
   c. argued for the evolution of acquired (rather than inherited) characteristics.
   d. all of the above
   e. a and b only

Answer: a
The social nature of humans and animals
p. 406

Answer: a
The social nature of humans and animals
p. 406

Answer: d
The social nature of humans and animals
p. 406

Answer: c
The social nature of humans and animals
pp. 406–408

Answer: c
The social nature of humans and animals
p. 407

Answer: c
The social nature of humans and animals
p. 407

Answer: d
The social nature of humans and animals
p. 407

5. Which of the following authors was most influential in giving Darwin a possible explanatory principle for biological evolution?
   a. Thomas Malthus
   b. Thomas Hobbes
   c. Adam Smith
   d. Karl Marx

6. The man who developed the theory of natural selection was:
   a. Darwin.
   b. Malthus.
   c. Hobbes.
   d. Lorenz.

7. *Natural selection* refers to the process or principle:
   a. whereby organisms can identify mates of their own species.
   b. whereby animals avoid potentially harmful foods.
   c. that explains how environmental factors limit natural resources.
   d. that explains why organisms with certain hereditary attributes will eventually outnumber organisms who lack these attributes.

8. Which is the best answer to the question "What is evolution?"
   a. survival of the fittest and most selfish
   b. gradual improvement of the health and strength of a species
   c. gradual change in the hereditary makeup of members of a species
   d. gradual inheritance of characteristics acquired by the parents during their lifetime

9. When we talk about the evolutionary "fitness" of an organism we are referring to characteristics that:
   a. contribute to the organism's health and survival.
   b. enhance the organism's longevity, regardless of its health.
   c. contribute to the organism's reproductive success.
   d. make the organism larger and stronger than other members of its species.
   e. all of the above are equally good ways to describe "fitness."

10. The biological survival value of a particular behavior is measured best by seeing whether the behavior:
    a. leads to a relatively long adult life for the animal.
    b. allows the animal to mate more often.
    c. increases the average number of descendants.
    d. makes the animal more aggressive.
    e. all of the above are roughly equally good ways to assess survival value.

11. Which of the following is the best measure of the biological "fitness" of an animal?
    a. its longevity
    b. the number of times it succeeds in mating
    c. the number of offspring it produces
    d. the number of its grandchildren

Answer: d
The social nature of humans and animals
pp. 407–408

12. According to Darwin, which of the following could be (or are) the result of evolution?
   a. the size and strength of a bear which allow it to overpower many animals as prey
   b. the shape of a bird's beak which is well-suited to the tight places it ordinarily finds food
   c. the grooming behavior which may play a role in cooperative relationships in primates
   d. all of the above
   e. a and b only

Answer: d
The social nature of humans and animals
p. 407

13. "Survival of the fittest" means survival of the _____ organism.
   a. physically strongest
   b. least cooperative
   c. most aggressive
   d. most reproductively successful

Answer: c
The social nature of humans and animals
p. 407

14. According to evolutionary theory, what is the most basic unit of heredity?
   a. species
   b. individual organisms
   c. genes
   d. adaptive physical structures

Answer: a
The social nature of humans and animals
p. 407

15. What Darwin referred to as "survival of the fittest" is the animal that is:
   a. most likely to survive and reproduce.
   b. most concerned with self-protection.
   c. most aggressive.
   d. healthiest.

Answer: a
The social nature of humans and animals
p. 408

16. The branch of biology that studies animal behavior under natural conditions is:
   a. ethology.
   b. zoology.
   c. psychology.
   d. histology.

Answer: a
The social nature of humans and animals
p. 408

17. The two people usually credited with founding ethology as a branch of biology are:
   a. Lorenz and Tinbergen.
   b. Hobbes and Malthus.
   c. Darwin and Richardson.
   d. Wilson and Hailman.
   e. Sears and Roebuck.

Answer: a
The social nature of humans and animals
p. 408

18. An ethologist, as opposed to a behavioral psychologist, would be most apt to study which of the following?
   a. nest building in robins
   b. dolphins doing tricks at Disneyworld
   c. dogs salivating when particular tones sounded
   d. a rat learning a complex maze

Answer: d
The social nature of humans and animals
p. 408

19. Ethologists primarily study:
    a. learning and motivation.
    b. sensory and cognitive processes of nonhuman animals in the laboratory.
    c. laboratory rats and pigeons.
    d. many different species in their natural habitats.
    e. non-Western cultures.

Answer: c
The social nature of humans and animals
pp. 409–410

20. Fixed-action patterns are:
    a. behavioral tendencies that are shared by a number of different species.
    b. behaviors acquired as a result of experiences in a particular environment.
    c. genetically pre-programmed behavior sequences.
    d. agonistic displays that occur at the beginning of mating rituals.

Answer: c
The social nature of humans and animals
pp. 409–410

21. Fixed-action patterns are normally elicited by genetically pre-programmed:
    a. pair-bonding.
    b. sexually arousing photographs.
    c. releasing stimuli.
    d. aggressive behavior.

Answer: d

The social nature of humans and animals
pp. 409–410

22. Fixed-action patterns are _____ behaviors or behavioral sequences.
    a. stereotyped
    b. species-specific
    c. genetically pre-programmed
    d. all of the above

Answer: b
The social nature of humans and animals
pp. 409–410

23. A releasing stimulus is one that:
    a. is learned.
    b. is the key to unlock a fixed-action pattern.
    c. guides the way in a cognitive map.
    d. acquires its meaning during an early critical period.

Answer: c
The social nature of humans and animals
pp. 409–410

24. According to Tinbergen, the releasing stimulus for the food-begging response of the young herring gull is:
    a. the internal cues provided by its empty stomach.
    b. the presence of other chicks in the nest.
    c. the sight of its parent's red-tipped beak.
    d. the sound of its parent's distinctive "food here" call.

Answer: b
The social nature of humans and animals
pp. 409–410

25. In studying the development of the food-begging response of young herring gulls we find that the newly-hatched gull chick:
    a. will peck only at a herring gull beak.
    b. will peck at a range of beak-like stimuli, indicating that experience is required to restrict its response to a herring gull beak.
    c. will peck at the first moving object it sees, which is usually (but not always) a herring gull beak.
    d. learns to associate its parent's beak with food through classical conditioning.

Answer: b
The social nature of humans and animals
pp. 409–410

26. Which of the following is the best example of a releasing stimulus?
    a. an alarm call
    b. the shape and marking of an adult gull's beak
    c. the sound of a bell that signals food in a salivary condition
    d. the tap on the knee that elicits the knee jerk

Answer: b
The social nature of humans and animals
pp. 409–410

27. A gull chick pecks the parent's beak when begging for food. Here the beak serves as:
    a. a display.
    b. a releasing stimulus.
    c. a visual cue.
    d. a fixed-action pattern.

Answer: b
The social nature of humans and animals
p. 410

28. Which of the following is not an example of a built-in display?
    a. the male peacock's opening up its colorful tailfeathers
    b. the beaver's dam-building
    c. the human baby's smile
    d. a male robin's song

Answer: d
The social nature of humans and animals
p. 410

29. A display is:
    a. a behavior.
    b. a releasing stimulus.
    c. part of a built-in communication system.
    d. all of the above

Answer: c
Aggression
pp. 410–411

30. Psychobiologists generally use the term *aggression* to refer to conflicts between:
    a. predator and prey.
    b. different species claiming the same territory.
    c. members of the same species.
    d. different species claiming the same food.

Answer: b
Aggression
pp. 410–411

31. Neurological evidence concerning the relationship between predation and aggression indicates that, in cats:
    a. both behaviors are elicited by stimulation of the same hypothalamic area.
    b. each behavior is elicited by stimulation of a different area of the hypothalamus.
    c. both behaviors are elicited by stimulating an area of the hypothalamus that controls eating.
    d. both a and c

Answer: b
Agression
pp. 410–411

32. Studies of the relationship between predation and aggression in cats indicates that:
    a. both behaviors are elicited by stimulating an area of the hypothalamus that controls eating.
    b. predation, but not aggression, is elicited by stimulating an area of the hypothalamus that controls eating.
    c. aggression, but not predation, is elicited by stimulating an area of the hypothalamus that controls sexual behavior.
    d. both b and c

Answer: c
Agression
pp. 410–411

33. Which of the following behaviors seems to have the same motivational basis as predatory attack?
    a. self-defense
    b. threat displays
    c. feeding
    d. escape

Answer: a
Agression
pp. 410–411

34. Sometimes it is difficult to tell whether a particular behavior pattern represents aggression. One such borderline case is:
    a. the mobbing of a cat by bluejays.
    b. the stalking of a gazelle by a lion.
    c. a male redwing blackbird attacking another male redwing that has invaded the territory of the first.
    d. a person eating a steak and a baked potato.

Answer: c
Agression
pp. 410–411

35. According to your text, the mobbing of an intruding cat or hawk by a flock of birds:
    a. clearly does not fit the psychobiologists' definition of aggression.
    b. is more closely related to feeding than to aggression.
    c. is a defensive reaction that is probably close to true aggression.
    d. is an example of a social behavior that is clearly neither aggressive nor predatory.

Answer: a
Agression
pp. 410–411

36. Which of the following best illustrates aggression between members of different species?
    a. A cornered rabbit kicks and bites a cat.
    b. A cat stalks a mouse.
    c. A pack of wild dogs chases and kills a deer.
    d. Each of the above illustrates interspecies aggression.

Answer: a
Agression
p. 411

37. Most truly aggressive encounters take place between:
    a. males of the same species.
    b. predator and prey.
    c. males and females of the same species.
    d. members of different species competing for food.

Answer: a
Agression
p. 411

38. Which of the following hormones leads to an increase in aggressiveness in males?
    a. testosterone
    b. estrogen
    c. progesterone
    d. adrenaline

Answer: a
Agression
p. 411

39. According to your text, if we examine the relationship between testosterone and aggression we find that:
    a. high testosterone levels are associated with increased aggressiveness in a wide range of species.
    b. only in mammals are high testosterone levels associated with increased aggressiveness.
    c. only in humans are high testosterone levels associated with increased aggressiveness.
    d. a relationship between testosterone levels and aggression is found only when animals (including humans) are defending a mate.

Answer: c
Agression
p. 411

40. Which of the following best describes the relationship between sex hormones and aggressive behavior?
    a. The two are not related to each other.
    b. People with higher estrogen levels are more likely to be aggressive.
    c. People with higher testosterone levels are more likely to be aggressive.
    d. Drugs that reduce testosterone levels produce increased aggressive behavior as a side effect.
    e. both c and d

Answer: d
Agression
p. 411

41. Injection of testosterone into a male cat will make the animal:
    a. more alert.
    b. a better hunter.
    c. more territorial.
    d. more aggressive.

Answer: e
Aggression
p. 411

42. Testosterone:
    a. is found only in males.
    b. levels increase following successful aggressive encounters.
    c. increases lead to increased aggression.
    d. all of the above
    e. b and c only

Answer: c
Aggression
p. 411

43. In females:
    a. testosterone is not present.
    b. hormones are unrelated to aggression.
    c. elevated testosterone levels are associated with aggression.
    d. tomboy behaviors lead to lower levels of testosterone.

Answer: b
Aggression
p. 411

44. Which of the following statements is false?
    a. Low serotonin levels are associated with increased aggression in monkeys.
    b. Drug-induced serotonin increases in monkeys have no effect on the monkeys' positions in their dominance hierarchies.
    c. Serotonin seems to inhibit impulsive aggression.
    d. Low serotonin levels in humans are associated with increased aggression toward the self and others.

Answer: a
Aggression
p. 411

45. Compared to a monkey with high serotonin levels, a monkey with low serotonin levels is likely:
    a. to show more impulsive aggression and be lower in the dominance hierarchy.
    b. to show more impulsive aggression and be higher in the dominance hierarchy.
    c. to show less impulsive aggression and be lower in the dominance hierarchy.
    d. to show less impulsive aggression and be higher in the dominance hierarchy.

Answer: d
Aggression
p. 411

46. In examining animal aggression we find that:
    a. males are generally more aggressive than females in most vertebrate species.
    b. male aggressiveness is associated with high levels of testosterone in the blood.
    c. most animal aggressiveness is linked to struggles over scarce resources.
    d. all of the above

Answer: b
Aggression
p. 412

47. An ultimate purpose of territorial behavior is to:
    a. reduce the numbers within a species by increasing the death rate.
    b. secure a supply of resources for the next generation.
    c. give the holders of territories a feeling of possession.
    d. prevent massive migrations of groups of animals.

Answer: d
Aggression
p. 412

48. Territoriality seems to have adaptive value mainly in that it:
    a. promotes tests of strength between rival males.
    b. distributes the species so that all will not be destroyed in an attack, disaster, etc.
    c. guarantees each "family" a certain spot on which to live, thereby enabling the construction of stable, durable shelters.
    d. helps ensure adequate resources for each "family."

Answer: d
Aggression
p. 412

49. The male bird's song serves to advertise:
    a. the location of his territory.
    b. his readiness to mate.
    c. his readiness to fight intruding males.
    d. any of the above

Answer: d
Aggression
p. 412

50. Which of the following is not a resource that animals might fight about?
    a. food
    b. mate
    c. water
    d. offspring

Answer: a
Aggression
p. 412

51. A territory-holder is usually most aggressive:
    a. on his home ground.
    b. after he crosses his border and enters another animal's territory.
    c. away from his immediate neighborhood.
    d. when accompanied by his mate.

Answer: a
Aggression
p. 412

52. Aggressive behavior in many species of vertebrates often serves the function of:
    a. defense of the territory.
    b. releasing excessive testosterone.
    c. preparing the animals to defend themselves against predators.
    d. killing potential competitors for mates and thus improving the gene pool.

Answer: a
Aggression
p. 412

53. Territoriality limits combat, because:
    a. animals are courageous on their own territory, and more timid outside it.
    b. animals generally do not fight on unfamiliar territory.
    c. animals spend so much time on their own territory, that there is little time left for combat.
    d. all of the above

Answer: b
Aggression
p. 412

54. Although natural selection seems to favor aggressive songbirds, aggression in any species does not go on increasing indefinitely. This fact is best explained in terms of:
    a. limitations on hormonal levels.
    b. the relative cost and benefits of the behavior.
    c. the slow rate of evolutionary change.
    d. the existence of a territorial advantage.

Answer: d
Aggression
p. 412

55. Aggression may be either adaptive or detrimental, in that:
    a. more aggressive songbirds will conquer a larger or more desirable territory.
    b. aggression may distract animals from important pursuits like mating.
    c. aggression is inherently dangerous, and may lead to injury or death.
    d. all of the above

Answer: c
Aggression
p. 413

56. When two males roar at each other prior to fighting,
    a. they are more aggressive when they begin the fight.
    b. they are engaging in a type of appeasement display.
    c. they may be able to determine which is likely to win the fight.
    d. the one with softer roar will initiate the fight.

Answer: d
Agression
pp. 412–414

57. Evolved strategies like _____ serve to limit the costs of aggression.
    a. threat displays and ritualized combat
    b. territoriality and dominance hierarchies
    c. appeasement displays
    d. all of the above

Answer: d
Agression
pp. 413–414

58. John and Phil have been fist fighting for a few minutes. Gradually, it becomes clear that Phil is going to hurt John if the fight lasts much longer. John stops punching and huddles up, putting his hands over his head. A number of animals have postures such as that displayed by John that signify admission of defeat. These are known as:
    a. resignation patterns.
    b. yielding displays.
    c. submissive intention movements.
    d. appeasement displays.
    e. deference responses.

Answer: b
Agression
pp. 413–414

59. Physical battles between animals usually end when one of the combatants:
    a. is dead, or too badly injured to continue.
    b. communicates submission with an appeasement display.
    c. intimidates the other with a threat signal.
    d. finds himself in his own territory.

Answer: d
Agression
pp. 412–414

60. Several mechanisms or factors limit aggression, including:
    a. territoriality.
    b. threat displays.
    c. appeasement displays.
    d. all of the above

Answer: d
Agression
pp. 412–414

61. There are several ways in which animal aggression and fighting within a species is minimized. For example:
    a. territoriality limits combat, since animals are timid away from their own territory, and less likely to fight.
    b. most quarrels begin with threat displays, and may be settled by bluff rather than fighting.
    c. fighting is often done in a ritualized manner that limits the amount of harm inflicted.
    d. all of the above

Answer: c
Agression
pp. 412–414

62. Territoriality, dominance hierarchies, and appeasement signals all help to reduce:
    a. bonding.
    b. personal space.
    c. aggression.
    d. resources.

Answer: b
Aggression
pp. 413–414

63. An ethologist would most likely describe the practice of "crying uncle" to end a losing battle as a(n):
    a. passive-aggressive display.
    b. appeasement display.
    c. threat display.
    d. territoriality display.
    e. dominance hierarchy.

Answer: a
Agression
p. 414

64. The social order that many animal species establish is a distinction of rank called:
    a. a dominance hierarchy.
    b. a hierarchical organization.
    c. a descriptive rule.
    d. natural selection.

Answer: a
Agression
p. 414

65. In baboon dominance hierarchies, the male that outranks all of the other males is known as the _____ male.
    a. alpha
    b. center
    c. identified
    d. prescriptive

Answer: e
Agression
pp. 414–415

66. In discussing the role of dominance hierarchies in lessening aggression your text points out that:
    a. there is still considerable aggression within groups, even when a dominance hierarchy has been established.
    b. the alpha male in a baboon dominance hierarchy spends considerable effort defending and consolidating his position.
    c. there is actually more aggression in baboon troops that have strong dominance hierarchies than there is in troops with no dominance hierarchy.
    d. all of the above
    e. a and b only

Answer: a
Agression
pp. 414–415

67. The alpha male in a baboon dominance hierarchy:
    a. enjoys a number of privileges, including greater access to females.
    b. is altruistic, since the time he devotes to the defense of the troop might otherwise have been used to mate.
    c. enjoys greater access to food and sleeping sites, but otherwise has no reproductive advantages over other males in the troop.
    d. is typically an older male who is past his reproductive prime.
    e. both c and d

Answer: b
Aggression
pp. 414–415

68. Among primates with dominance hierarchies, subordinate males:
    a. do not sire offspring.
    b. may form coalitions to depose the alpha male.
    c. ignore females because they have no mating privileges.
    d. a and c

Answer: b
Agression
pp. 414–415

69. Studies of primate dominance hierarchies indicate that:
    a. only males develop dominance hierarchies.
    b. females may also develop dominance hierarchies that are often more stable than those of males.
    c. only males develop dominance hierarchies, but they can pass on their status to their primary female mate.
    d. females often establish the primary dominance hierarchy, with the mate of the leading female becoming the alpha male in the troop.
    e. both b and d

Answer: b
Agression
pp. 414–415

70. Dominance hierarchies among primate females have long-term importance because:
    a. the breeding preferences of the dominant female determines which male will lead the troop.
    b. mothers may pass their social ranking in the troop to their offspring, especially daughters.
    c. the struggle of females for dominance is often more disruptive to the troop than is the fighting of males.
    d. all of the above
    e. b and c only

Answer: c
Aggression
p. 415

Answer: c
Agression
pp. 415–416

Answer: e
Agression
pp. 415–416

Answer: e
Agression
pp. 415–416

Answer: a
Mating
p. 416

Answer: b
Mating
p. 417

Answer: a
Mating
p. 417

71. Research suggests that if you sit down next to the only other person in an empty subway car,
    a. he will be perfectly comfortable.
    b. you will elicit an innate territorial response from him.
    c. he will fidget and possibly try to move away.
    d. he will lean closer to you.

72. Human attempts to maintain a minimum personal space are most likely prompted by:
    a. misinterpretations of foreigners' actions.
    b. a built-in "territorial imperative."
    c. cultural factors.
    d. an innately based fear of strangers.

73. According to your text, studies of personal space suggest that:
    a. the necessity for personal space is largely culturally determined.
    b. the amount of personal space an individual seeks is influenced by his culture.
    c. personal space and animal territoriality clearly stem from the same evolutionary roots.
    d. all of the above
    e. a and b only

74. If we examine research on personal space we find that:
    a. the physical dimensions of personal space seem to be the same for all cultures.
    b. the older we are, the more personal space we seem to want.
    c. people of high socioeconomic status maintain a larger personal space than do people of low socioeconomic status.
    d. all of the above
    e. b and c only

75. Asexual reproduction:
    a. creates genetically identical replicas of the original organism.
    b. is not possible.
    c. produces individuals which vary widely in reproductive fitness.
    d. uses a process called fusion.

76. In sexual reproduction, a new individual is created by joining two specialized cells called the _____ and _____.
    a. zygote; sperm
    b. sperm; ovum
    c. zygote; ovum
    d. gene; sperm

77. A zygote is:
    a. a fertilized egg, produced by the joining of sperm and ovum.
    b. a cell (sperm or ovum) with only half the number of normal chromosomes.
    c. any cell that contains the normal complement of chromosomes.
    d. a fertilized egg that has only half the normal number of chromosomes.

Answer: d
Mating
p. 417

78. The biological advantage of sexual, as compared with asexual, reproduction is that it:
    a. is more enjoyable.
    b. leads to a greater number of offspring.
    c. guarantees the genetic similarity between parents and offspring and thus the transmission of adaptive attributes.
    d. leads to more differences among the offspring so that natural selection can come into play.

Answer: d
Mating
p. 417

79. In sexual reproduction, chance partially determines:
    a. which sperm will join with which ovum.
    b. which genes are contained in each sperm and ovum.
    c. the genetic makeup of the zygote.
    d. all of the above

Answer: b
Mating
p. 417

80. From an evolutionary perspective, sexual, as opposed to asexual, reproduction may be desirable because:
    a. offspring are certain to be fitter on average than their parents.
    b. pathogens typically have more difficulty attacking genetically novel than genetically familiar organisms.
    c. egg cells and sperm cells are formed from the fittest genes within each individual.
    d. asexual reproduction leads to too much genetic variation in offspring.

Answer: c
Mating
p. 417

81. In a study of widow birds, the length of males' tail feathers was artificially altered. The result was that:
    a. alterations had no effect on the number of nests within each male's territory.
    b. unaltered males had the most nests in their territories, followed by shortened and then extended males.
    c. extended males had the most nests in their territories, followed by unaltered and then shortened males.
    d. shortened males had the most nests in their territories, followed by unaltered and then extended males.

Answer: c
Mating
pp. 418–419

82. Courtship rituals:
    a. are typically forms of appeasement displays.
    b. are very rare in nonprimates.
    c. are highly species-specific.
    d. encourage cross-species breeding for increased genetic variation.

Answer: c
Mating
p. 419

83. Interbreeding between species:
    a. benefits both species by increasing genetic variation in the next generation.
    b. is more likely in species with elaborate courtship rituals than in species without such rituals.
    c. often produces infertile offspring.
    d. is impossible in mammals.

Answer: b
Mating
pp. 418–419

84. Imagine the fictitious male discomoronicus whose courtship display consists of an odd and energetic dance in front of the female. Most likely:
    a. males use the same dance as a threat display.
    b. only discomoronicus females are driven to mate after seeing this dance.
    c. males learn this courtship ritual by imitating older males in the group.
    d. all of the above

Answer: d
Mating
pp. 418–419

85. Courtship rituals serve to:
    a. ensure that mates are members of the same species.
    b. communicate that one's intentions are not aggressive.
    c. advertise one's own sex.
    d. all of the above

Answer: b
Mating
pp. 418–419

86. Which of these purposes is not served by courtship rituals?
    a. the exhibition of structural sex differences
    b. the lowering of sexual drive levels
    c. the maintenance of within-species mating
    d. the communication of nonhostile intentions

Answer: c
Mating
p. 419

87. In the dancing fly, the male presents the female with a ball of silk which she plays with while he mounts her and copulates. Which of the following statements is false?
    a. In related species, the female sometimes eats the male which is attempting to mount her.
    b. In related species, the male sometimes gives the female a small insect prior to mounting her.
    c. There is no reasonable basis for drawing inferences about how the dancing fly's courtship ritual evolved.
    d. Distracting the female with the silk ball may save the male's life during copulation.

Answer: b
Mating
pp. 419–420

88. In most animal species the final choice of a mate is made by:
    a. the male, who usually initiates courtship.
    b. the female, who bears the major costs of reproduction.
    c. both male and female equally, during courtship.
    d. the arbitrary mechanisms of chance.

Answer: c
Mating
pp. 419–420

89. In most species:
    a. males choose their mates rather than being chosen.
    b. males and females share roughly equally in the care of the off-spring.
    c. females invest more in reproduction than do males.
    d. final mate choice is equally likely to be made by the male or the female.

Answer: d
Mating
pp. 419–420

90. In which of the following situations should the male be choosier than the female he mates with?
   a. when the male must show colorful plumage and a complex courtship display
   b. when several males in succession mate with one female
   c. when the reproductive group is a dominant male and several females
   d. when the male cares for the infants

Answer: d
Mating
pp. 419–420

91. The sea horse is a small fish, the male of which has a brood pouch in which he carries the young. Research suggests that:
   a. male sea horses will have rigid dominance hierarchies.
   b. male sea horses will show an unusual degree of territorial aggressiveness.
   c. the sexual behavior of male sea horses will be partially under the control of female hormones.
   d. the male sea horse will be more discriminating in its choice of a sexual mate than are the males of most other fish.

Answer: a
Mating
p. 420

92. When a female mammal is in estrus, it is unlikely that:
   a. she will fight off all male advances.
   b. her ova are ripe for fertilization.
   c. she will become pregnant if mated.
   d. her overt behavior is affected.

Answer: d
Mating
pp. 420–421

93. _____ are mechanisms that help to ensure the appropriate timing of fertilization.
   a. Hormonal cycles
   b. Courtship rituals
   c. Female estrus periods
   d. a and c

Answer: c
Mating
pp. 420–421

94. The biological value of the estrus period is that it:
   a. reduces the level of aggressiveness among the males, who would otherwise fight among themselves, not just when the female is in estrus, but at all times.
   b. conserves the female's energy for other activities such as food-gathering, care of the young, and so forth.
   c. synchronizes the time when the animals mate with the time that the female's ova are ready for fertilization.
   d. makes it unnecessary to learn how to mate and copulate since the entire sequence is pre-programmed.

Answer: b
Mating
p. 420

95. The follicles in the ovary produce the female sex hormone called:
   a. testosterone.
   b. estrogen.
   c. androgen.
   d. serotonin.

Answer: b
Mating
pp. 420–421

96. Today you noticed your pet rat Juliet kicking and biting her cagemate Romeo as he tried to nuzzle her. Chances are that:
    a. Juliet is in estrus.
    b. if Juliet had intercourse today she would not become pregnant.
    c. Juliet has higher than usual levels of estrogen in her bloodstream.
    d. Juliet was engaging in a courtship ritual.

Answer: b
Mating
p. 420

97. The female rat enters estrus immediately after:
    a. an ovarian follicle begins to mature under the influence of pituitary secretions.
    b. the ovarian follicle ruptures and releases the mature ovum.
    c. the hypothalamus directs the pituitary to begin producing estrogen.
    d. the ovarian follicle begins to produce progesterone.

Answer: d
Mating
p. 420

98. The hormone progesterone is produced by:
    a. the developing testes.
    b. the female pituitary in response to signals from the hypothalamus.
    c. the ovarian follicle before it ruptures.
    d. the ovarian follicle after it ruptures.

Answer: d
Mating
p. 420

99. The hormone that is responsible for thickening the wall of the uterus (to prepare for the potential embryo) is called:
    a. testosterone.
    b. estrogen.
    c. androgen.
    d. progesterone.

Answer: c
Mating
p. 420

100. The hormone progesterone:
    a. causes the ovarian follicle to develop.
    b. causes the developed ovarian follicle to rupture, releasing the mature ovum.
    c. causes the lining of the uterus to thicken in preparation for receiving the embryo.
    d. causes the thickened lining of the uterus to be reabsorbed or sloughed off.

Answer: c
Mating
p. 421

101. The behavioral effects of sex hormones have been shown to be triggered by hormone receptors in the:
    a. pituitary.
    b. ovaries.
    c. hypothalamus.
    d. bloodstream.

Answer: c
Mating
p. 421

102. When estrogen is implanted into the hypothalamus of a spayed (neutered) female cat:
    a. she becomes sexually unreceptive.
    b. she shows sexual behaviors typical of male cats, including mounting.
    c. she enters estrus and becomes sexually receptive.
    d. she shows no change in her sexual receptivity.

Answer: c
Mating
pp. 420–421

103. Which of the following statements is false?
    a. Small amounts of hormones injected into the hypothalamus can cause the animal to behave as though large amounts of the hormones were in its bloodstream.
    b. Sexual behavior can increase hormone production.
    c. Removing the ovaries of a female rat leaves the rat incapable of sexual receptivity.
    d. Hormone levels affect sexual behavior.

Answer: b
Mating
p. 421

104. If we look at the effect of sexual behavior and hormone secretion in female rats we find that copulation:
    a. decreases the secretion of estrogen and progesterone.
    b. increases the secretion of progesterone.
    c. increases the secretion of estrogen but decreases the secretion of progesterone.
    d. has no effect on the levels of either estrogen or progesterone.

Answer: a
Mating
p. 421

105. The male rat's contribution to the reproductive effort:
    a. includes stimulating the release of more progesterone in the female.
    b. consists solely of delivering sperm.
    c. includes stimulating follicle rupture and the release of the mature ovum.
    d. includes stimulating the release of more estrogen in the female.

Answer: a
Mating
pp. 421–422

106. Which of the following is found only in humans?
    a. female sexual receptivity independent of hormonal state
    b. elaborate courtship rituals and displays
    c. existence of mechanisms for limiting aggressive behavior
    d. greater mate selectivity in the female

Answer: a
Mating
pp. 421–422

107. Human sexuality, when compared with that of other species, seems to reflect a general evolutionary trend toward:
    a. greater flexibility in behavior.
    b. less reliance on previous learning.
    c. greater dependence upon hormonal regulation.
    d. weaker bonds between partners.

Answer: b
Mating
p. 422

108. When male homosexuals with an abnormally low testosterone level are injected with testerone:
    a. they become more sexually active and direct this activity toward females.
    b. they become more sexually active and direct this activity toward males.
    c. they become less sexually active.
    d. their sexual activity and interest are unaffected.

Answer: d
Mating
p. 422

Answer: d
Mating
p. 422

Answer: a
Mating
p. 422

Answer: c
Mating
p. 422

Answer: d
Mating
p. 422

Answer: b
Mating
p. 422

Answer: c
Mating
pp. 422–423

109. Injections of testosterone into humans with abnormally low testosterone levels:
    a. cause increased sex drive in heterosexual men.
    b. cause increased sex drive in homosexual men.
    c. cause increased sex drive in women.
    d. all of the above

110. Sexual desire in the woman tends to be the highest:
    a. during ovulation.
    b. during the part of the menstrual cycle when other animals would be in estrus.
    c. during menstruation.
    d. both a and b

111. In examining the role of hormones in controlling human sexuality, we note that:
    a. the sexual desires of human females are somewhat higher at the time of ovulation than at other points during their menstrual cycle.
    b. testosterone injections do not increase the sexual drives of men with low hormone levels.
    c. homosexual males injected with testosterone show increased interest in female partners, and reduced interest in male partners.
    d. all of the above

112. Mate guarding:
    a. is when the male prevents other females from attacking his mate.
    b. increases the female's chances of reproductive success.
    c. increases the male's chances of reproductive success.
    d. is when the male protects his mate from predators.

113. _____ refers to the mating system in which a family consists of one male, several females, and their various offspring.
    a. Monogamy
    b. Polyandry
    c. Heterogamy
    d. Polygyny

114. _____ refers to the mating system in which a family consists of one female and several males.
    a. Monogamy
    b. Polyandry
    c. Heterogamy
    d. Polygyny

115. The most common mating system among birds is _____, and the most common mating system among mammals is _____.
    a. monogamy; monogamy
    b. polygyny; monogamy
    c. monogamy; polygyny
    d. polyandry; polygyny
    e. polygyny; polygyny

Answer: a
Mating
p. 423

116. Evolutionary biologists suggest that birds are generally monogamous because:
    a. the cooperative efforts of both parents are required to incubate the young.
    b. the high metabolic rate of birds makes it difficult for a single male to meet the reproductive needs of several mates.
    c. the short breeding season makes it impossible for males to court and mate with more than one mate.
    d. all of the above

Answer: a
Mating
p. 423

117. Evolutionary biologists argue that mammals are generally polygynous because:
    a. the male is not required to invest time and energy in the raising of the young.
    b. male mammals are able to control large territories, making the support of multiple mates possible.
    c. male mammals are generally unable to remember which female is their mate, so they accidentally mate with many others.
    d. female mammals want diversity in their mates.

Answer: c
Mating
p. 423

118. Sexual dimorphism refers to:
    a. the existence of two different sexes in a plant or animal species.
    b. differences in the sexual behavior of the two sexes.
    c. differences in the size or body structures of the two sexes.
    d. the existence of two different phases of sexual receptivity (receptive or nonreceptive) in the females of an animal species.

Answer: a
Mating
p. 423

119. Sexual dimorphism is:
    a. more pronounced in polygynous than monogamous species.
    b. more pronounced in monogamous than polygynous species.
    c. more pronounced in monogamous than either polygynous or polyandrous species.
    d. more pronounced in polygynous and monogamous species than in polyandrous species.
    e. none of the above

Answer: b
Mating
p. 423

120. A new species of primate is discovered, and we note that the males and females of this species are almost indistinguishable in size and coloration. This observation indicates that:
    a. the species is more likely to be polygynous than monogamous.
    b. the species is more likely to be monogamous than polygynous or polyandrous.
    c. the species is more likely to be polyandrous than polygynous or monogamous.
    d. the species is likely to be polygynous, and to show high levels of sexual dimorphism.

121. A new species of animal is discovered in which the females are much larger and more brightly colored than the males. Chances are that this species:
    a. is monogamous.
    b. is polygynous.
    c. is polyandrous.
    d. is polygynous and has high levels of sexual dimorphism.

122. In sexually dimorphic species, fancy attributes like extravagant tails:
    a. serve no purpose.
    b. are important in determining whether an individual will be chosen for a mate, but are otherwise unrelated to the individual's fitness.
    c. are important in determining whether an individual will be chosen for a mate, probably because they give some indication of the individual's health and strength.
    d. are most likely to be found in females in polygynous species.

123. Studies of human mate selection indicate that:
    a. men are more influenced by a partner's physical attractiveness than are women.
    b. men are interested in younger mates, while women are more attracted to older men.
    c. a partner's social and financial status is more important to women than it is to men.
    d. all of the above

124. Studies of human mate selection indicate that the criteria for mate selection:
    a. are the same for men and women, and are the same in a variety of cultures.
    b. are the same for men and women within a single culture, but the criteria vary between cultures.
    c. differ for men and women, and male-female differences in mate-selection criteria vary from culture to culture.
    d. differ for men and women, but male-female differences in mate-selection criteria are the same across a range of cultures.

125. Which of the following statements is false?
    a. Across a variety of cultures, physical attractiveness in a mate is more important for men than for women.
    b. Across a variety of cultures, women are more concerned about a potential mate's financial status than are men.
    c. Human mate choice is as strongly biologically determined as is mate choice in other primates.
    d. Across a variety of cultures, men generally prefer younger women as mates and women prefer older men.
    e. all of the above

Answer: d
Mating
p. 424

126. According to David Buss, male-female differences in the criteria for mate selection:
    a.   are shaped by our culture's views of "ideal" males and females.
    b.   are based (for males) on the fact that younger, more attractive females are likely to be healthier and more fertile.
    c.   are based (for females) on the fact that males of higher social and economic status have more resources to support children.
    d.   both b and c

Answer: d
Mating
p. 424

127. Critics of David Buss's sociobiological views on mate-selection criteria argue that:
    a.   females prefer higher status males simply because a male's economic position determines the economic future of his mate and offspring.
    b.   gender differences in mate selection criteria should be smaller in societies where women are approaching economic equality with men.
    c.   although males and females report different mate-selection criteria, the criteria they actually use are the same.
    d.   both a and b

Answer: b
Mating
pp. 424–425

128. An examination of human mating patterns across 185 cultures indicates that the majority of human cultures endorse _____, with _____ being the second most common marriage arrangement.
    a.   monogamy; polygyny
    b.   polygyny; monogamy
    c.   monogamy; polyandry
    d.   polygyny; polyandry
    e.   polyandry; monogamy

Answer: b
Mating
pp. 424–425

129. An evolutionary theorist would expect _____ to be more common than _____ in humans because of our _____ .
    a.   monogamy; polygyny; sexual dimorphism
    b.   polygyny; monogamy; sexual dimorphism
    c.   monogamy; polygyny; tendency to jealousy
    d.   monogamy; polyandry; tendency to jealousy
    e.   c and d

Answer: e
Mating
pp. 424–425

130. Studies of mating patterns in our own culture indicate that:
    a.   women express more interest in having a variety of sexual partners than do men.
    b.   men express more interest in having a variety of sexual partners than do women.
    c.   men and women differ with regard to interest in having a variety of sexual partners in a way that is consistent with evolutionary theory.
    d.   men and women differ with regard to interest in having a variety of sexual partners in a way that is inconsistent with evolutionary theory.
    e.   b and c

Answer: d
Mating
pp. 424–425

131. Evolutionary theorists argue that women are more cautious than men in evaluating sexual partners because:
    a. our cultural norms dictate that women should be more reticent in sexual matters than men.
    b. there is more variability in the reproductive potential of men than in the reproductive potential of women.
    c. women have learned that men cannot always be trusted to fulfill their parental responsibilities.
    d. a woman's biological investment in children is greater than a man's.

Answer: d
Mating
p. 425

132. Critics of the evolutionary explanation for human mating patterns argue that:
    a. cultural norms are more important than evolutionary history in determining mating patterns.
    b. polygyny is likely to occur where men are dominant and women are perceived as property.
    c. men prefer more variety in sexual partners than do women because boys learn that sexual conquests are proof of "manliness."
    d. all of the above

Answer: e
Mating
p. 425

133. When the sexual practices of homosexual and heterosexual men and women were compared prior to AIDS:
    a. homosexual men were more interested in a variety of sexual partners than were homosexual women.
    b. heterosexual men were more interested in a variety of sexual partners than were heterosexual women.
    c. homosexual men (like heterosexual women) were less interested than heterosexual men in a variety of sexual partners.
    d. homosexual men and women were more interested in a variety of sexual partners than were heterosexual men and women.
    e. both a and b

Answer: b
Mating
pp. 425–426

134. Your text suggests that:
    a. human sexual behavior is as biologically determined as is that of other primates.
    b. research on human sexual behavior reveals patterns that are consistent with evolutionary theory.
    c. behavior that is found across cultures and is consistent with evolutionary theory must be genetically programmed.
    d. b and c

Answer: b
Parenting
p. 426

135. The young of many bird and mammal species become "attached" to their mothers. Certain ethologists believe that this phenomenon is the product of a basic biological fact, namely:
    a. that the mother-infant relationship helps the infant to learn how to acquire later social ties.
    b. that animals who are alone are most vulnerable to starvation and predators.
    c. that all infants must be fed.
    d. that imprinting can only occur during a "critical period."

Answer: b
Parenting
p. 427

136. For the mother, the biological function of the mother-infant bond is:
     a. personal survival.
     b. genetic survival.
     c. to help a member of the species that is helpless.
     d. to feel good about herself.

Answer: a
Parenting
p. 427

137. Birds feed their young because:
     a. they are genetically programmed to do so.
     b. they know that's the only way their genes will survive.
     c. they are imitating the behavior they saw their own parents engage in.
     d. the baby birds will return the favor when the parents are too old to gather their own food.

Answer: d
Parenting
pp. 427–428

138. Motherese:
     a. is the name for the distinctive way that humans talk to infants.
     b. occurs across a variety of cultures.
     c. helps the child learn language.
     d. all of the above

Answer: d
Parenting
pp. 427–428

139. Which of the following of the baby's behavior serves to solidify the mother-child relationship?
     a. suckling
     b. distress calls
     c. smiling
     d. all of the above

Answer: c
Parenting
p. 428

140. All of the following except one are characteristics of "babyness." Which one is not?
     a. chubby cheeks
     b. the smile
     c. long thin face
     d. upturned nose

Answer: a
Parenting
p. 428

141. According to ethologists, one reason that human mothers care for their infants is that:
     a. They are responding to "babyness" cues.
     b. The biological costs are not great.
     c. Society stresses the value of mothering.
     d. Early doll-play has given them practice.

Answer: a
Parenting
p. 428

142. To ethologists, the facial characteristics of human infants, like short upturned noses, big eyes, and smiles, are:
     a. built-in releasers of nurturing behavior by parents.
     b. the ways in which people learn to recognize the ages of different individuals.
     c. the features that make contact comfort possible.
     d. displays analogous to intention movements in nonhuman animals.

143. Human infants provide stimuli in the form of _____ that release parental behaviors.
   a. facio-cranial features such as large eyes, an upturned nose, and a large protruding forehead
   b. hand gestures such as pointing
   c. special pheromones that endow the baby (to the age of 14–18 months) with a unique scent
   d. all of the above

144. The infant's smile:
   a. is probably learned through imitation.
   b. first appears around six months.
   c. seems to be innate.
   d. appears only in sighted children.
   e. a and d

145. In order to determine the meaning of a particular display, ethologists study the correlation between the display and:
   a. the behavior preceding the display.
   b. the behavior following the display.
   c. the contents of the animal's most recent meal.
   d. a and b

146. Displays sometimes convey:
   a. intentions.
   b. sexual receptivity.
   c. age.
   d. all of the above

147. Someone says "Display systems—in both humans and animals—are just like a human language that has a very small vocabulary." Why is this statement false?
   a. because some animals have a large number of displays, and some human languages have a rather small vocabulary
   b. because display systems lack rules for putting individual displays together to form new messages
   c. because displays are completely unaffected by the context in which the display is made
   d. all of the above

148. Which statement is false?
   a. The animal display system is rigid and conveys limited information.
   b. Human language is based on a creative principle and is very flexible.
   c. Most mammals display about 500 distinguishable signals.
   d. The average human vocabulary is about 50,000 words.

Answer: d
Communication
p. 430

149. In comparing animal displays and human language we find that:
    a. most mammals have a repertoire of displays and signals that is nearly half as large as the word vocabulary of the average human adult.
    b. the animal display "language" is a flexible creative system.
    c. animal displays are often chained together or organized to form longer and more complex messages.
    d. each human language can produce an infinite number of utterances.

Answer: c
Communication
p. 431

150. Research on food calls in roosters indicates that:
    a. food calls are automatically elicited by the presence of food.
    b. the extent to which a rooster emits food calls depends solely on the amount of food present.
    c. roosters seem to manipulate their food calling to attract hens.
    d. displays are elicited by certain stimuli and are unaffected by context beyond those stimuli.

Answer: b
Communication
p. 431

151. When Cheney and Seyfarth played the distress call of a vervet monkey infant to its mother and two nearby females, they noted that:
    a. all three females looked toward the sound.
    b. the mother looked toward the sound, but the other females looked toward the mother.
    c. the mother looked toward the sound, but the other females looked toward each other.
    d. the mother looked toward the sound, but the other females made no response at all.

Answer: a
Communication
p. 431

152. Cheney and Seyfarth played the distress call of a vervet monkey infant to its mother and two nearby females. The responses of these monkeys suggested that the monkeys:
    a. had a considerable knowledge of the kinship relation in their group.
    b. were able to distinguish the vocal expression of negative from positive emotions.
    c. were able to identify the meaning of the distress call even though there was no visual sign of a predator.
    d. were willing to make altruistic sacrifices for offspring that were not their own.
    e. shared a collective responsibility for the well-being of the young in the troop.

Answer: b
Communication
p. 431

153. To say that chimpanzees have a "theory of mind" is to say that they:
    a. have an elaborate display system.
    b. attribute states of mind to others.
    c. are altruistic because they empathize with others.
    d. have mental states.

Answer: e
Communication
pp. 431–432

154. Evidence that monkeys may have a "theory of mind" comes from the observation that:
    a. monkeys recognize kinship relations in their groups
    b. chimpanzees may deliberately deceive human caretakers.
    c. monkeys recognize their own reflections in a mirror.
    d. all of the above
    e. a and b only

Answer: b
Communication
p. 432

155. When chimpanzees were shown a piece of fruit hidden out of reach and introduced to a selfish attendant and an altruistic attendant, they would:
    a. point either attendant to the hidden fruit.
    b. point the altruistic, but not the selfish attendant, to the hidden fruit.
    c. withhold information from the selfish attendant, but would never actually mislead him.
    d. not point either attendant to the hidden fruit.

Answer: a
Communication
pp. 432–433

156. Many people assume that the theory of evolution means that all animals, including people, by nature must be selfish and competitive. Yet there is strong evidence that individuals of many species engage in seemingly unselfish acts toward others who are not even their offspring. This phenomenon is called:
    a. altruism.
    b. fitness.
    c. reciprocity.
    d. selection.

Answer: a
Communication
pp. 432–433

157. When a bird feigns injury to draw a predator away from her nest:
    a. she is increasing her chances of genetic survival.
    b. she is increasing her chances of personal survival.
    c. her behavior makes no sense.
    d. the genes responsible for this behavior are likely to be less common in the next generation than the genes of a bird who, in similar circumstances, abandoned the nest.

Answer: a
Communication
p. 433

158. On the face of it, altruism seems to go against evolutionary principles. Why?
    a. because there is little or no apparent personal gain for the altruist
    b. because altruistic animals are usually less "fit"
    c. because altruism is unrelated to genetic inheritance
    d. because it is rare and most animals engage in it to about the same degree

Answer: c
Communication
p. 433

159. Genes for altruism (e.g., the alarm call in birds) manage to survive because altruistic individuals:
    a. sacrifice one group of young but live to breed again.
    b. put the welfare of the young ahead of the welfare of the old.
    c. contribute to the survival of relatives with some of the same genes.
    d. put their own welfare before that of the group.

Answer: d
Communication
pp. 433–434

160. Altruistic behavior in animals:
   a. may actually increase the altruist's chances of personal survival.
   b. may help to ensure the survival of the altruist's genes in its offspring.
   c. may be supported by a built-in predisposition toward reciprocal altruism.
   d. all of the above

Answer: a
Communication
pp. 433–434

161. According to one hypothesis, altruistic behavior should be more likely among relatives than among unrelated individuals. This is known as the _____ hypothesis.
   a. kin selection
   b. self-preserving
   c. genetic
   d. social cognition

Answer: b
Communication
pp. 433–434

162. According to the kin-selection hypothesis:
   a. animals are more likely to choose related rather than unrelated animals as mates.
   b. altruistic behavior should be more likely among relatives than among unrelated individuals.
   c. reciprocal altruism is observed only between closely related individuals.
   d. an animal's relatives punish those who fail to reciprocate the animal's altruism.

Answer: b
Communication
p. 434

163. Reciprocal altruism:
   a. explains altruism among kin.
   b. is more likely to be found in stable social groups than in impromptu interactions.
   c. is not susceptible to cheating.
   d. all of the above

Answer: c
Communication
p. 434

164. Grooming:
   a. is irrelevant to other aspects of social relationships.
   b. is equally common among kin and non-kin.
   c. may be a form of reciprocal altruism.
   d. serves a purely hygienic function.

Answer: d
Communication
p. 434

165. In the primate troop you've been observing, two members spend an inordinate amount of time grooming each other. Chances are:
   a. they're related to each other.
   b. they forage for food together.
   c. they would help each other fight a common enemy.
   d. all of the above

Answer: a
Communication
p. 434

166. One possible biological foundation for altruism is a built-in tendency:
   a. toward reciprocity.
   b. to be more active, vigorous, and aggressive in the presence of members of one's own species.
   c. to imitate the behaviors of other members of one's species.
   d. to feel more comfortable and secure in the presence of familiar (and presumably related others).

167. Research indicates that:
     a. consistent with evolutionary theory, people are more likely to be helped by close than distant relatives.
     b. consistent with evolutionary theory, people are equally likely to be helped by close as by distant relatives.
     c. contrary to the predictions of evolutionary theory, people are more likely to be helped by non-kin than by relatives.
     d. contrary to the predictions of evolutionary theory, people are more likely to be helped by close than by distant relatives.

168. According to some evolutionary theorists, tendencies toward tribalism:
     a. may be based on kinship selection.
     b. must be purely cultural, since they are inconsistent with the biological good of the species.
     c. arise from a complex interaction between the biological instincts of selfishness and altruism.
     d. are based primarily on reciprocal altruism.

169. According to Edward Wilson's evolutionary perspective, human heroism has a genetic basis. Critics of this view contend that:
     a. human heroism cannot be explained without reference to cultural factors.
     b. humans do not inherit social behaviors.
     c. human heroism is too rare to be an inherited trait.
     d. all of the above

170. Evolutionary theorists argue for the biological basis of altruism in humans. Critics of this view point out that:
     a. the most altruistic cultures we know of are also the smallest and most primitive.
     b. selective pressures on our human ancestors would have eliminated any genetic tendency toward altruism.
     c. human altruism, as a social behavior, depends much more on social and cultural variables than on biology.
     d. people help each other based more on perceived closeness than on genetic relatedness.
     e. both c and d

171. According to the textbook, if human men are biologically predisposed to seek sexual variety:
     a. then male promiscuity is natural and, therefore, good.
     b. then there are no implications for the moral appropriateness of male promiscuity.
     c. then men cannot control their tendency to promiscuity.
     d. then evolutionary theorists are wrong.

172. According to the text, the most definite conclusion we can draw about human nature is that we are basically:
     a. altruistic.
     b. selfish.
     c. social.
     d. aggressive.
     e. monogamous.

CHAPTER 11 | Social Cognition and Emotion

Answer: e
Social cognition and emotion
p. 441

1. Which of the following factors affects our social behavior?
   a. our evolutionary past
   b. our personal past
   c. our socialization into particular cultural patterns
   d. the present situation
   e. all of the above

Answer: a
Social cognition and social reality
p. 442

2. Social cognition:
   a. has to do with the way we interpret and comprehend social events.
   b. is quite different from other forms of cognition.
   c. does not involve memory.
   d. does not involve interpretive activity.
   e. all of the above

Answer: a
Social cognition and social reality
pp. 442–443

3. In Asch's line-judgment task:
   a. most research participants gave an obviously wrong answer at least once.
   b. research participants gave the correct response over 90 percent of the time, regardless of how others in the group responded.
   c. most research participants were unable to distinguish between a 6.25-inch line and an 8-inch line.
   d. only about 25 percent of the research participants gave an obviously wrong answer at least once.

Answer: a
Social cognition and social reality
pp. 442–443

4. In Asch's line-judging experiment on social cognition:
   a. fewer than one in three research participants never went along with a wrong answer given by the rest of the group.
   b. nearly three in four participants never went along with a wrong answer given by the rest of the group.
   c. about half of all participants never went along with a wrong answer given by the rest of the group.
   d. at least 90 percent of the participants never went along with a wrong answer given by the rest of the group.

Answer: c
Social cognition and social reality
p. 443

5. In Asch's social pressure experiments, when the confederates said that a 6-inch line is equal to an 8-inch line, most real participants:
   a. did not yield.
   b. yielded, but were sure that the group was wrong even though they pretended to agree.
   c. yielded, and were not sure who was right even though they still saw the 8-inch line as bigger than the 6-inch line.
   d. yielded, because the group pressure changed their perception so that they saw the 8-inch line as equal to the 6-inch line.

Answer: a
Social cognition and social reality
pp. 443–444

6. The reactions of Asch's research participants to their experience in his study suggest that:
   a. we believe that physical reality is socially shared.
   b. public opinion has little impact on privately held views.
   c. our belief in physical reality is immune to social pressure.
   d. human cognitive and social processes are separate and distinct.

Answer: d
Social cognition and social reality
pp. 443–444

7. Which of the following is a criterion for determining physical reality?
   a. consistent sensory information over time
   b. consistent confirmation from the behavior of others
   c. consistent information from the different senses
   d. all of the above

Answer: b
Social cognition and social reality
pp. 444–445

8. In an Asch-style social pressure experiment, what is the effect of making the judgments difficult (for example, 6.5 vs. 6.25 inches) compared to the effect when the judgments are easy (for example, 6 inches vs. 8 inches)? The real research participants will:
   a. yield more, and be more emotionally disturbed.
   b. yield more, and be less emotionally disturbed.
   c. yield less, and be more emotionally disturbed.
   d. yield less, and be less emotionally disturbed.

Answer: b
Social cognition and social reality
pp. 444–445

9. The results of a standard Asch line-judgment task compared to one in which the lines are difficult to distinguish indicate that:
   a. a dissenting minority cannot withstand the opinion of the majority.
   b. social comparison is especially important in ambiguous situations.
   c. uncertainty increases emotional disturbance.
   d. ambiguity produces more rigid responses.

Answer: b
Social cognition and social reality
p. 445

10. People are most likely to seek social comparison when:
    a. decisions are easy and obvious in order to confirm their choices.
    b. decisions are difficult and a situation is not fully understood.
    c. a situation is well understood and social consensus is needed.
    d. they have sufficient time to gather information.

Answer: d
Social cognition and social reality
pp. 445–446

11. Asch's experiments deal with consistency across individuals. What happens when there is inconsistency within a person's own beliefs?
   a. She will faithfully maintain the inconsistent information and deal with it as best she can.
   b. She will accentuate the inconsistencies in the information.
   c. She will invariably seek outside assistance to deal with the inconsistency.
   d. She will try to restore cognitive consistency by reinterpreting the situation.

Answer: b
Social cognition and social reality
pp. 445–446

12. Cognitive dissonance is an internal state that is the result of:
   a. disorientation due to strong emotion.
   b. perceived inconsistencies among one's own behavior, beliefs, and feelings.
   c. lack of unanimity in group judgments.
   d. conflict between conscious and unconscious motives.

Answer: b
Social cognition and social reality
pp. 445–446

13. Judy idolizes a famous person, then finds out that he is actively supporting a terrorist group Judy despises. The unpleasant internal state that results in Judy is called:
   a. reaction formation.
   b. cognitive dissonance.
   c. repression.
   d. reciprocal inhibition.

Answer: c
Social cognition and social reality
pp. 445–446

14. Fred supports the cause of the *As* in their war against the *Bs*. He then sees on television that the *As* are killing innocent children. He decides that the *As* must be being forced to do this by the *Bs*, and that the *As* have no choice. This type of thinking in Fred is an example of:
   a. social comparison.
   b. stimulus-response association.
   c. resolution of cognitive dissonance.
   d. reference to comparison groups to change attitudes.

Answer: d
Social cognition and social reality
pp. 445–446

15. Mitzi has paid a great deal to a dating service because she believes it will find her perfect match. However, her first date from the service is a disaster. Based on cognitive dissonance theory, which of the following outcomes is most likely?
   a. Mitzi will decide that the service is a scam and she will report them to the Better Business Bureau.
   b. Mitzi will be so horrified that she won't be able to date again for at least one year.
   c. Mitzi will decide that she has thrown her money away, but she won't do anything about it.
   d. Mitzi will convince herself that the date wasn't really that bad after all.

Answer: d
Attitudes
pp. 446–447

16. Which of the following beliefs would not be classified by social
psychologists as an attitude?
   a. The courts deal more harshly with the poor.
   b. My closest friend can be trusted with my money.
   c. Shakespeare was an immensely gifted playwright.
   d. The earth rests on the back of a large tortoise.

Answer: c
Attitudes
pp. 446–447

17. An attitude differs from a belief in that:
   a. a belief is more strongly held.
   b. an attitude is more strongly held.
   c. an attitude is a belief with emotional investment as well.
   d. an attitude and a belief are the same.

Answer: b
Attitudes
p. 447

18. In the 1930s, Richard LaPiere stopped at hotels and restaurants with a
Chinese couple. Later, he asked each establishment by letter whether
they would house or serve Chinese persons. LaPiere found that:
   a. most establishments actually discriminated against the Chinese
couple, but later wrote that they did not discriminate against Chinese persons.
   b. most establishments did not discriminate against the Chinese
couple, but later wrote that they did not serve or house Chinese
persons.
   c. most establishments served the Chinese couple, and later wrote
that they did so.
   d. most establishments refused to serve the Chinese couple, and
later wrote that they did not serve or house Chinese persons.

Answer: e
Attitudes
pp. 447–448

19. One of the factors that influences whether there is a relationship between
attitudes and behavior is:
   a. whether the attitude is specific or general.
   b. whether the behavior is specific or general.
   c. whether the attitude is about a personal issue or an issue that affects others.
   d. whether the attitude is strongly held or weakly held.
   e. a and d

Answer: e
Attitudes
pp. 447–448

20. As your text notes, one reason that attitudes do not always predict
behavior is that:
   a. situational pressures may cause people to behave in ways that are
inconsistent with their attitudes.
   b. general attitudes may not predict specific behaviors.
   c. people often lie about attitudes.
   d. all of the above
   e. a and b only

Answer: d
Attitudes
p. 448

21. Messages that are openly persuasive in attempting to change an attitude
are called:
   a. subliminal communications.
   b. cognitive consistencies.
   c. forced compliances.
   d. persuasive communications.

22. Imagine that research participants read an essay arguing that most people could do fine with just four hours of sleep per night. Though they read the same essay, half the participants are told that it was written by a sleep researcher at a prestigious university, and half are told that it was written by a college undergraduate. Most likely:
    a. participants in the group told it was written by a sleep researcher will be more persuaded than the other subjects.
    b. participants in the group told it was written by an undergraduate will be more persuaded than the other subjects.
    c. both groups of participants will be equally persuaded.
    d. neither group of participants will be persuaded at all.

23. Which of the following will make a persuasive communication more effective?
    a. a very credible source
    b. advocating a position in line with the speaker's self-interest
    c. speaking loudly
    d. both a and b

24. There is a good deal of controversy about the best way to control cholesterol level. Which of the following is likely to influence the behavior of a person suffering from a high cholesterol level?
    a. an article in a popular magazine, because it will be written for the layperson.
    b. an article in the *Journal of the American Medical Association* because it is an authoritative source
    c. an article in the local newspaper, because it feels "close to home"
    d. the recommendation of a friend who is a lawyer

25. Which of the following will be better believed?
    a. an argument to lower malpractice insurance premiums by the American Medical Association
    b. an argument to increase the use of litigation in injury cases by the Bar Association
    c. an argument to lower the incidence of dental decay by fluoridation by the Dental Association
    d. an argument to increase the number of police officers in a city by the Police Benevolent Association

26. Tony's back injury could be treated by surgery or by chiropracty, and neither option is clearly better than the other. Which of the following is most likely to persuade him to have surgery?
    a. a surgeon arguing that he should have surgery
    b. an article in a popular news magazine suggesting that surgery is often a better option than chiropracty
    c. a chiropractor arguing that he should have surgery
    d. All of the above would be equally persuasive.

Answer: a
Attitudes
p. 449

27. According to Petty and Cacioppo, the central route to persuasion involves:
   a. careful attention to the message and its arguments.
   b. subtle attempts to change our attitudes.
   c. appealing to our emotions.
   d. changing our attitudes by changing our behaviors.

Answer: a
Attitudes
p. 449

28. The central route to persuasion involves:
   a. reasoned thought.
   b. emotional responses.
   c. behavioral change.
   d. all of the above

Answer: e
Attitudes
p. 449

29. The central route to persuasion:
   a. is more likely to be used if the issue involved is important to us.
   b. is more likely to be used if we are not distracted by other concerns.
   c. relies primarily on the source and context of the message rather than on its content.
   d. all of the above
   e. a and b only

Answer: a
Social cognition and social reality
p. 449

30. If you are listening to an argument on an issue that is very important to you, the aspect of the communication most likely to persuade you is:
   a. the logic of the arguments.
   b. the speaker's credibility.
   c. the speaker's likability.
   d. the number of arguments offered.
   e. all of the above

Answer: d
Attitudes
p. 449

31. The peripheral route to persuasion:
   a. is more likely to be used if the issue involved is not important to us.
   b. is more likely to be used if we are distracted by other concerns.
   c. relies primarily on the source and context of the message rather than on its content.
   d. all of the above
   e. a and b only

Answer: b
Attitudes
p. 449

32. The peripheral route to persuasion:
   a. is only effective if we have an emotional response to the message.
   b. involves the use of heuristics to decide whether to accept the message.
   c. is most effective when the speaker is disliked, but the speaker's arguments are strong.
   d. all of the above

Answer: d
Attitudes
p. 449

33. The peripheral route to persuasion involves the use of mental shortcuts, or heuristics, to decide whether to accept the message. These heuristics might include:
    a. the number of arguments that are presented.
    b. the length of the arguments.
    c. how expert or likable the speaker is.
    d. all of the above

Answer: b
Attitudes
p. 449

34. The peripheral route to persuasion involves the use of mental shortcuts, or heuristics, to decide whether to accept the message. Which of the following is not likely to be one of these heuristics?
    a. the number of arguments that are presented
    b. the logic or reasonableness of the arguments presented
    c. the length of the arguments
    d. the expertise of the speaker
    e. the likability of the speaker

Answer: a
Social cognition and social reality
p. 449

35. While trying to watch a debate on TV because he knows the moderator, Charles is distracted by constantly having to chase his toddler around the room. Which aspects of the debate are least likely to affect his attitude toward the debate topic?
    a. the logic of the arguments offered
    b. the length of the arguments offered
    c. the expertise of the debaters
    d. the appearance of the debaters

Answer: b
Social cognition and social reality
p. 449

36. In preparing your candidate for a debate, you realize that the arguments on your side are very weak. Instead of giving your candidate strong arguments, you load her up with a bunch of tangentially relevant statistics. With this strategy, your candidate is most likely to persuade
    a. someone for whom the debate topic is very important.
    b. someone accessible through the peripheral route to persuasion.
    c. someone who is able to pay close attention to the debate.
    d. a and c

Answer: b
Attitudes
p. 449

37. What is it about peripheral arguments that leads to persuasion?
    a. They are forceful because they present the critical facts that are persuasive.
    b. They lead one to use rules of thumb, such as reliance on experts, to evaluate them regardless of the message.
    c. They are more resistant to the effects of distracting events.
    d. all of the above

Answer: a
Attitudes
p. 450

38. According to cognitive dissonance theory, we value a goal more highly if it was difficult to reach because:
    a. we need to justify the effort we exerted to reach the goal.
    b. we need to reduce our feeling of forced compliance.
    c. we need to make our emotions consistent with our cognitions.
    d. we are more aware of high effort behaviors than of low effort behaviors.

39. Suppose you are a struggling athlete with little natural talent, yet you work years and years to develop your tennis skills, finally honing them sufficiently to make the professional tour. You struggle on the tour, with others beating you regularly. Your opponents can't understand your attitude: You are always exuberant and happy, even in the face of repeated defeat. Which of the following explains your positive outlook?
    a. You have been forced to comply with the rigors of the tour.
    b. You have increased your dissonance between the work you do and the results you get.
    c. You have decreased your dissonance, valuing the result because of the work you put in getting there.
    d. You have no more cares; having put in all that work to get there, you are now just coasting.

Answer: c
Attitudes
p. 450

40. According to cognitive dissonance theory, justification of effort is responsible for the fact that:
    a. we tend to downplay the amount of effort we exerted to reach a goal.
    b. we have fewer negative emotions while engaging in an effortful task.
    c. we value a goal more highly if it was difficult to reach.
    d. both a and b

Answer: c
Attitudes
p. 450

41. A defense attorney must defend a client in whose innocence she doesn't believe. According to dissonance theory, under what conditions might she be more likely to come to believe in her client's innocence?
    a. She gets a higher fee than usual.
    b. She gets a lower fee than usual.
    c. The client is quite friendly to her.
    d. The client is in fact guilty.

Answer: b
Attitudes
pp. 450–451

42. The members of a club you run tend to take the club for granted. According to cognitive dissonance theory, if you want members to value their membership more, you should:
    a. let more people join.
    b. lower membership fees.
    c. increase membership fees.
    d. improve the facilities.

Answer: c
Social cognition and social reality
pp. 450–451

43. Two actors are paid to make commercials that explain the need for a new gasoline tax—something which both men privately oppose. Actor *A* is well known, and actor *B* is just starting his career. The ad agency hires each man for the same fee. After the commercials are aired, the attitudes of each actor toward the tax are assessed. What do you expect will be found?
    a. Actor *A*'s attitude is more positive than before.
    b. Actor *B*'s attitude is more positive than before.
    c. *A* and *B* have both become more positive.
    d. Neither actor's attitude has changed.

Answer: a
Attitudes
pp. 450–451

44. In a classic study, research participants did an extremely boring task and were then paid either $1 or $20 to tell someone else that it was interesting. When their actual attitudes toward the task were later measured:
    a. consistent with cognitive dissonance theory, participants paid $20 thought the task was more interesting than did participants paid $1.
    b. consistent with cognitive dissonance theory, participants paid $1 thought the task was more interesting than did participants paid $20.
    c. contrary to cognitive dissonance theory, participants paid $20 thought the task was more interesting than did participants paid $1.
    d. contrary to cognitive dissonance theory, participants paid $1 thought the task was more interesting than did participants paid $20.

45. Three students are paid different amounts of money to give a speech in support of more difficult final exams, a position that is contrary to the attitudes of each of them. Sarah is paid $1, Lynn is paid $5, and Kelly is paid $20. According to dissonance theory, which student will be most likely to support difficult exams after giving the speech?
    a. Kelly
    b. Lynn
    c. Sarah
    d. Each student will support difficult exams equally.

46. More recent dissonance research suggests that:
    a. we strive to reduce dissonance because of a need for logical consistency.
    b. participants in dissonance studies don't really change their attitudes.
    c. unresolved dissonance often threatens a person's self-image and the need to protect that self-image leads to a reduction in dissonance.
    d. dissonance effects can be explained purely in terms of cognitive inconsistency.

47. Forced compliance may result in changing one's strongly held attitude because:
    a. a large reward awaits later.
    b. the resulting cognitive dissonance is emotionally unpleasant.
    c. one finally sees the light.
    d. reversing one's opinion is rewarding.

48. We often try to reduce dissonance in order:
    a. to reduce negative emotions such as guilt or shame.
    b. to maintain a favorable self-picture or self-image.
    c. to increase our status in the eyes of others.
    d. all of the above
    e. a and b only

49. According to the textbook, attitudes are generally:
    a. stable, because we actively resist efforts to change them.
    b. in flux, because we frequently experience dissonance and need to reduce it by changing our attitudes.
    c. in flux, because we are bombarded by persuasive communications.
    d. stable, because our social contexts are fairly constant.

Answer: b
Perceiving others
p. 453

50. Person perception is similar to object perception in that:
    a. the percept resembles the proximal stimulus more than the distal stimulus.
    b. situational variation is often disregarded so that stable characteristics can be extracted.
    c. both largely rely on the visual medium.
    d. both involve the same kinds of hierarchical information processing.

Answer: a
Perceiving others
p. 453

51. A trait in person perception is most analogous to _____ in visual perception.
    a. shape
    b. distance
    c. illumination
    d. angle of regard

Answer: c
Perceiving others
p. 454

52. In an experiment performed by Asch, substitution of the term _____ for _____ in a seven-trait list was sufficient to change subjects' total impression of the person described.
    a. intelligent; stupid
    b. obedient; disobedient
    c. cold; warm
    d. determined; cautious

Answer: d
Perceiving others
p. 454

53. Asch's concept of a central trait is one which:
    a. appears in the middle of a list of traits.
    b. has a moderate, rather than an extreme connotation.
    c. has an extreme, rather than a moderate connotation.
    d. plays a disproportionate role in shaping the impression conveyed by a group of traits.

Answer: b
Perceiving others
p. 454

54. Asch suggested that people form total impressions of others by organizing their attitudes around a single attribute known as the _____ trait.
    a. schematic
    b. central
    c. primary
    d. dispositional

Answer: c
Perceiving others
p. 454

55. Solomon Asch argued that our impression of others is often shaped by primacy effects. In other words:
    a. the most recent information we receive about a person affects our impression of that person more than does previous information.
    b. there are certain characteristics (traits) of a person that are especially likely to determine our impression of that person.
    c. we tend to be more influenced by the first information we get about a person than by later information.
    d. some things we learn about a person are better remembered than other things.

56. In evaluating information about a person in order to form an impression of his personality we tend to:
    a. form an impression on the basis of the most recent information we have about him.
    b. integrate initial and later information in order to form a well-rounded impression of a person's personality.
    c. rely most heavily on the information which we first received about a person in forming our impressions about that person's personality.
    d. rely most heavily on recent information in forming an impression of a person, especially if our initial impression was unfavorable.

57. In impression formation the primacy effect refers to the observation that:
    a. our initial impression of an individual tends to be positive, regardless of the information we are given about him or her.
    b. our initial impression of a person tends to be unfavorable, and it is only with repeated exposure to the individual that we form more favorable impressions.
    c. our first impression of an individual tends to color our judgment of that individual more than does later information.
    d. our most recent interaction with an individual tends to color our judgment of that individual more than do earlier impressions.

58. Studies of general impression formation by Asch suggest that:
    a. there is a primacy effect, in that our first impressions of an individual are weighted more heavily than later information.
    b. a single trait or characteristic can act as a central focus around which our impression of another is organized.
    c. we generally change our impressions of others rapidly as we receive new information about them.
    d. both a and b

59. When Asch presented research participants with lists of traits ordered from positive to negative or vice versa, he found that the impression which was formed depended most heavily on:
    a. the first traits in the list.
    b. the trait in the center of the list.
    c. the last traits in the list.
    d. all listed traits equally.

60. Professor Hall is asked to add one adjective to a list of traits made up for a graduate school applicant. The professor wishes to add a positive trait to the list of negative traits. Based on Asch's experiments, where is the best place to place this adjective if the professor wants to create a favorable tone for the application reader?
    a. Each position would have the same impact.
    b. at the end of the list
    c. in the middle of the list
    d. at the beginning of the list

Answer: b
Perceiving others
p. 455

61. Recent authors have cast Asch's analogy between impression formation and perception in terms of:
    a. cognitive consistency.
    b. schemas.
    c. episodic memory.
    d. cognitive dissonance.

Answer: a
Perceiving others
p. 455

62. Research participants are asked to read a group of traits that all describe the same friendly person. Research indicates that when memory for the list is tested, participants are most likely to mistake _____ as having been on the list even though it wasn't.
    a. *outgoing*
    b. *nasty*
    c. *industrious*
    d. all of the above

Answer: d
Perceiving others
p. 455

63. Recent authors argue that our impressions of others are based on schemas. These schemas:
    a. are organized expectations about how different kinds of behaviors or characteristics are related.
    b. are equivalent to implicit theories of personality.
    c. can lead to stereotypes if they are simplified and applied to groups rather than individuals.
    d. all of the above

Answer: c
Perceiving others
p. 455

64. Social schemas are useful to us because:
    a. they permit us to view the world accurately.
    b. they allow us to keep cognitive dissonance to a minimum.
    c. they allow us to overcome our limited cognitive capacities when interpreting events.
    d. they are algorithms for solving social problems.

Answer: b
Perceiving others
pp. 455–456

65. As a general impression of others, the statement "blondes have more fun" is an example of:
    a. cognitive dissonance.
    b. a stereotype.
    c. the fundamental attribution error.
    d. a situational attribution.

Answer: b
Perceiving others
pp. 455–456

66. Your text argues that the relationship between schemas and stereotypes is that:
    a. schemas arise when group stereotypes are applied to individuals.
    b. stereotypes arise when schemas are simplified and applied to groups.
    c. stereotypes arise when several schemas are combined into a more complex perceptual Gestalt.
    d. schemas consist of a combination of stereotypes.
    e. none of the above

Answer: a
Perceiving others
pp. 455–456

67. Illusory correlation refers to:
    a. relationships that are seen because they are expected, even when they're not present.
    b. a tendency to see positive correlations even when there's a negative correlation.
    c. a tendency to see negative correlations even when there's no correlation.
    d. a tendency to see negative correlations even when there's a positive correlation.

Answer: c
Perceiving others
pp. 455–456

68. One factor that perpetuates social stereotypes is illusory correlations, which are due to:
    a. inattention to co-occurrences in the world.
    b. paying attention to too many co-occurrences in the world.
    c. noting and remembering just some co-occurrences in the world.
    d. paying particular attention to those co-occurences which are unexpected.

Answer: c
Perceiving others
pp. 455–456

69. Imagine that participants are asked to determine what symptoms predict a fictitious new disease by reviewing a list of people, each of whom is described as having the disease or not, and as having either a fever, a rash, or a craving for popcorn. If the list is set up such that 60 percent of the people with each symptom have the disease, participants most likely will conclude that:
    a. none of the symptoms predicts the disease.
    b. each of the symptoms is good at predicting the disease.
    c. fever and rash are better predictors of the disease than is popcorn craving.
    d. popcorn craving is a better predictor of the disease than is fever or rash.

Answer: a
Perceiving others
pp. 456–457

70. An in-group is defined as:
    a. a group that a target person belongs to.
    b. a group that is highly valued in the society.
    c. a collection of people who are currently physically closest to a target person (though they may be strangers to the target).
    d. a group with power.
    e. b and d.

Answer: d
Perceiving others
pp. 456–457

71. When participants were asked to rate the pleasantness of nonsense words that had previously been paired with *we, us,* or *ours* or with *they, them,* or *theirs,* they:
    a. were unable to comply.
    b. rated all the words as equally pleasant.
    c. rated the words with two syllables as more pleasant than the words with one syllable.
    d. rated the words that had been association with first person pronouns as more pleasant than the words that had been associated with second person pronouns.

Answer: a
Perceiving others
p. 457

72. Studies of the perception of in-groups (*us*) versus out-groups (*them*) indicate that we tend:
    a. to see out-group members as being more similar to each other than are in-group members.
    b. to see in-group members as being more similar to each other than are out-group members.
    c. to notice the presence of out-group members more rapidly than we notice the presence of in-group members.
    d. to see most other people as members of an out-group.

Answer: b
Perceiving others
p. 457

73. The out-group homogeneity effect refers to the observation that we tend to:
    a. see all out-groups as having the same set of (generally negative) characteristics.
    b. see out-group members as being more similar to each other than are in-group members.
    c. perceive most other people as members of an out-group.
    d. see out-group members as having the same characteristics and beliefs as members of our smallest in-group.

Answer: d
Perceiving others
p. 457

74. In a laboratory study, subjects from Rutgers saw a student (call him *A*) make a choice. Some research participants were told that *A* was also from Rutgers, while other participants were told that *A* was from Princeton. The study found that participants:
    a. who thought *A* was from Rutgers believed that most Rutgers students would make the same choice *A* had made.
    b. who thought *A* was from Princeton believed that most Princeton students would make the same choice *A* had.
    c. who thought *A* was from Rutgers drew no inferences about the behavior of other Rutgers students from *A*'s choice.
    d. both b and c

Answer: c
Perceiving others
p. 458

75. Erving Goffman has likened social interactions to:
    a. medical skills.
    b. object perceptions.
    c. theatrical performances.
    d. cocktail parties.

Answer: a
Perceiving others
p. 457

76. Person perception differs crucially from visual perception in that in person perception:
    a. the stimulus is aware of being perceived.
    b. schema-based expectations are important.
    c. invariant characteristics must be extracted.
    d. initial information is unimportant.

Answer: c
Perceiving others
p. 458

77. Impression management refers to:
    a. remembering which impression goes with which person.
    b. using schemas to organize impressions.
    c. trying to create particular impressions of yourself.
    d. trying to extract invariant characteristics from impressions.

78. Which of the following statements is true of impression management as described by Erving Goffman?
    a. An actor may gradually come to believe in his own performance.
    b. An audience will often help an actor to preserve his self-presentation.
    c. Many roles require a team effort for successful presentation.
    d. all of the above

79. Self-handicapping means:
    a. picking race horses without professional help.
    b. performing poorly on a task to deceive people about your true abilities.
    c. performing worse than you could to make someone else look better.
    d. providing yourself with an excuse for an anticipated failure.

80. Sheila is worried that she won't do well on an upcoming exam. Then she spends the night before the exam partying rather than studying. She seems to be engaging in:
    a. self-handicapping.
    b. cognitive dissonance.
    c. the fundamental attribution error.
    d. a self-serving bias.

81. Which of the following would lead you to feel empathetic embarrassment?
    a. watching your brother score a basket for the other team
    b. watching your friend forget his lines during a play
    c. seeing your roommate come out of the shower and lose his towel in front of a group of women
    d. watching your dad split his pants while bending over within sight of some of his friends
    e. all of the above

82. According to a recent account, empathetic embarrassment is (at least partly) due to:
    a. the disruption of a social interaction that cannot be repaired.
    b. the deviation of a social actor from the prescribed script for the current interaction.
    c. a social actor misreading the key that indicates the nature of the current social interaction.
    d. the substitution, by one social actor, of a new interaction script that is not agreed upon by others in the social relationship.

83. The term *attribution* refers to our tendency to:
    a. resolve inconsistencies in our attitudes.
    b. resolve inconsistencies between attitudes and behavior.
    c. form impressions of people based on their credibility.
    d. assign causes to events in the world.

Answer: d
Attribution
p. 460

84. Attribution theory is concerned with:
    a. how people resolve internal inconsistencies.
    b. how social norms affect the perception of physical reality.
    c. the distinction between attitudes and beliefs.
    d. how people infer the causes of behavior.

Answer: b
Attribution
p. 460

85. Attribution theory focuses on the assignment of either _____ or _____ causes for behavior:
    a. dispositional; attributional
    b. situational; dispositional
    c. attributional; situational
    d. rational; emotional

Answer: b
Attribution
p. 460

86. A dispositional cause for behavior is one which:
    a. is beyond the control of the individual.
    b. refers to an underlying characteristic of the individual.
    c. is due to the pressures of the situation in which the individual finds him or herself.
    d. is due to the presence of others.

Answer: a
Attribution
p. 460

87. After failing a recent exam you exclaim that the questions were too difficult and the professor is terrible. You are making a(n) _____ attribution for your failure.
    a. situational
    b. dispositional
    c. emotional
    d. physical

Answer: c
Attribution
p. 460

88. We tend to attribute an individual's behavior to dispositional qualities if we believe that:
    a. the behavior was heavily influenced by the demands placed on the individual by the situation.
    b. the individual is not aware of the reasons for his or her actions.
    c. the behavior was based on some underlying characteristic or quality of the individual.
    d. the individual's behavior was more influenced by emotional than by rational factors.

Answer: d
Attribution
p. 460

89. A child's favorite prank is to push a friend so that he bumps into a stranger. The idea is to have the stranger think that the bump was intentional. That is, the child is trying to have the stranger attribute the bump to:
    a. the fundamental attribution error.
    b. situational factors.
    c. the actor-observer difference.
    d. a dispositional quality.

Answer: b
Attribution
p. 461

90. The fundamental attribution error is that in making attributions for the behavior of others, we tend to:
    a. overemphasize situational factors.
    b. overemphasize dispositional factors.
    c. assume that their behavior has the same causes as our own behavior.
    d. overemphasize the role of chance.

91. When making attributions for the behavior of others, people tend to:
    a. overestimate both situational and dispositional factors.
    b. underestimate situational and overestimate dispositional factors.
    c. overestimate dispositional and underestimate situational factors.
    d. underestimate both situational and dispositional factors.

92. When people attempt to determine why an individual behaved as he or she did, they tend to:
    a. be equally likely to infer situational or dispositional causes.
    b. infer dispositional causes more readily than situational causes.
    c. infer situational causes more readily than dispositional causes.
    d. overlook both situational and dispositional causes in assigning reasons for behavior.

93. The fact that we tend to overestimate the importance of dispositional factors in the behavior of others is referred to as:
    a. the fundamental attribution error.
    b. cognitive dissonance.
    c. the above-average effect.
    d. the undersituational attribution effect.

94. The fundamental attribution error is:
    a. taking a behavior as a sign of internal dispositions and downplaying obvious or potential situational determinants.
    b. placing too much weight on situational determinants in making attributions for behavior.
    c. the tendency to see conformity in behavior across situations based on an inferred internal disposition.
    d. overemphasizing chance factors in determining behavior.

95. In the quiz master study:
    a. consistent with the fundamental attribution error, research participants who were randomly chosen to ask tough questions were viewed as as knowledgeable as those who were randomly chosen to answer the questions.
    b. consistent with the fundamental attribution error, research participants who were randomly chosen to ask tough questions were viewed as more knowledgeable than those who were randomly chosen to answer the questions.
    c. contrary to the predictions of the fundamental attribution error, research participants who were randomly chosen to ask tough questions were viewed as as knowledgeable as those who were randomly chosen to answer the questions.
    d. contrary to the predictions of the fundamental attribution error, research participants who were randomly chosen to ask tough questions were viewed as more knowledgeable than those who were randomly chosen to answer the questions.

Answer: b
Attribution
p. 461

96. You are defending a client wrongly accused of theft, and are deciding whether the jury should see a tape showing your client confessing under extreme duress. Your knowledge of the fundamental attribution error leads you to the conclusion that the jury would probably:
    a. disregard your client's confession, and concentrate on the circumstances under which it was extracted.
    b. deplore the police brutality involved, but still tend to believe that the confession was sincere.
    c. weigh the confession against the circumstances under which it was made, and be more convinced of your client's innocence.
    d. not be influenced by either your client's confession or the circumstances under which it occurred.

Answer: b
Attribution
p. 462

97. There are differences between the attribution processes applied to the behavior of others, and those applied to our own behavior. For example, it seems that:
    a. the fundamental attribution error is much more prominent when we are attributing causes to our own behavior.
    b. we tend to see our own behavior as much more determined by the situation than do observers.
    c. we are more likely to attribute our own behavior to dispositional factors than we are to attribute the behavior of others to such factors.
    d. both a and c

Answer: c
Attribution
pp. 462–463

98. When we make attributions for our own behavior (as opposed to the behavior of others), we tend to:
    a. overestimate the importance of dispositional factors.
    b. ignore the importance of salient situational factors.
    c. see our behavior as more governed by situational factors than observers do.
    d. both a and b

Answer: d
Attribution
pp. 462–463

99. Which of the following contributes to the actor-observer difference?
    a. better knowledge of oneself than of others
    b. different perception of the situation by the actor and observer
    c. different perception of actions by the actor and observer
    d. all of the above

Answer: c
Attribution
pp. 462–463

100. According to the cognitive interpretation of the actor-observer bias:
    a. we pay more attention to our own behavior than we do to the behavior of others.
    b. we need to preserve cognitive consistency between our behaviors and our dispositions.
    c. we have more information about our own dispositions and behaviors than we have about the dispositions and behaviors of others.
    d. we tend to see others as members of out-groups, and apply biased schemas to their behavior.

Answer: a
Attribution
pp. 462–463

101. Research on the actor-observer bias indicates that:
    a. consistent with the cognitive interpretation, people are less likely to make dispositional attributions for close friends than for mere acquaintances.
    b. consistent with the cognitive interpretation, people are more likely to make dispositional attributions for close friends than for mere acquaintances.
    c. in contrast to the predictions of the cognitive interpretation, people are less likely to make dispositional attributions for close friends than for mere acquaintances.
    d. in contrast to the predictions of the cognitive interpretation, people are more likely to make dispositional attributions for close friends than for mere acquaintances.

Answer: c
Attribution
pp. 462–463

102. Jorge's best friend is Sarah and he has a passing acquaintance with Lucia. The cognitive interpretation of the actor-observer difference suggests that of himself and the two others, Jorge will offer the most dispositional attributions for _____ and the most situational attributions for _____.
    a. himself; Lucia
    b. Lucia; Sarah
    c. Lucia; himself
    d. himself; Sarah
    e. Lucia or Sarah (equally likely); himself

Answer: b
Attribution
pp. 462–463

103. According to the perceptual interpretation of the actor-observer bias:
    a. we are more aware of ourselves when we are behaving, and more aware of the situation when see another person behaving.
    b. we tend to attribute behavior to what is perceptually salient, which differs depending on whether we are the actor or only an observer.
    c. we perceive our own thoughts and emotions.
    d. our sense of self conveys a sense of stability, whereas we see others as constantly in flux and situationally driven.

Answer: d
Attribution
pp. 462–463

104. In an experiment by Storms, research participants saw a tape of a conversation they had had with a stranger. The tape showed the interaction either from the participant's own perspective, or from the perspective of the stranger. Storms found that participants tended to describe their own behavior:
    a. in dispositional terms when shown the conversation from the stranger's perspective.
    b. in situational terms, regardless of the perspective from which the conversation was shown.
    c. in situational terms when shown the conversation from their own perspective.
    d. both a and c

Answer: a
Attribution
pp. 463–464

105. The self-serving attribution bias refers to the observation that we tend to:
  a. attribute our successes to dispositional factors and our failures to situational factors.
  b. attribute both our successes and failures to situational rather than dispositional factors.
  c. attribute our successes to situational factors and our failures to dispositional factors.
  d. attribute both our successes and failures to dispositional rather than situational factors.

Answer: b
Attribution
pp. 463–464

106. Game show contestants who lose often attribute their loss to poor choice or bad luck in the particular questions that were asked. This is an example of:
  a. immunity to the fundamental attribution error.
  b. self-serving attribution bias.
  c. attention to dispositional factors.
  d. all of the above

Answer: c
Attribution
pp. 463–464

107. The comments made by college and professional sports figures indicate that they tend to:
  a. attribute their successes to external factors (e.g., luck), and their failures to internal factors (e.g., skill).
  b. attribute both their successes and failures to external factors (e.g., luck).
  c. attribute their successes to internal factors, and their failures to external factors.
  d. attribute both their successes and failures to internal factors.(e.g., skill).

Answer: c
Attribution
pp. 464–465

108. The above-average effect is one example of:
  a. the actor-observer bias.
  b. inconsistency in self-perception.
  c. the self-serving bias.
  d. the fundamental attribution error.

Answer: c
Attribution
pp. 464–465

109. The above-average effect refers to the observation that we tend to:
  a. attribute dispositional causes to our own behavior if we think our performance is above average.
  b. judge ourselves as above average in both favorable and unfavorable characteristics.
  c. judge ourselves as above average in various favorable characteristics.
  d. judge others primarily in terms of characteristics or skills on which we are (or think we are) above average.

Answer: b
Attribution
pp. 464–465

110. One explanation for the above-average effect is that:
  a. we reinterpret the centerpoint of the scale on which we are rating ourselves so that it falls below our skill level.
  b. we redefine the trait on which we are rating ourselves to make it more consistent with our actual characteristics or abilities.
  c. we judge what is "average" by considering the characteristics or abilities of individuals that we know or believe are inferior to us.
  d. it is a case of impression management, and occurs only for traits or characteristics on which others could easily evaluate us.

Answer: c
Attribution
pp. 464–465

111. The above-average effect is most likely to be occur:
    a. for traits or characteristics that are easily measured or quantified.
    b. when most of the people we know exceed us in the characteristic or ability being rated.
    c. for characteristics or abilities that are ambiguously or imprecisely defined.
    d. all of the above
    e. b and c only

Answer: d
Attribution
pp. 464–465

112. We would expect the above-average effect to be least noticeable if we rated ourselves in terms of which of following traits or abilities?
    a. sophisticated
    b. intelligent
    c. skilled driver
    d. well read

Answer: a
Attribution
p. 465

113. Which of the following statements is false?
    a. Self-serving biases only appear when the failure to be explained is public.
    b. Impression management cannot account fully for self-serving bias effects.
    c. People who demonstrate a self-serving bias are probably deluding themselves.
    d. b and c

Answer: a
Perceiving oneself
p. 466

114. One factor leading to the development of a self-concept is:
    a. the perception that others have of us.
    b. the perception that we have of others.
    c. the perception that others have of themselves.
    d. b and c

Answer: d
Perceiving oneself
pp. 466–467

115. According to self-perception theory, our sense of self is derived from:
    a. direct access to our cognitions.
    b. the opinions of others.
    c. direct access to our emotions.
    d. inferences from observations of our own behavior.

Answer: b
Perceiving oneself
pp. 466–467

116. According to self-perception theory, we come to know ourselves:
    a. through processes which are fundamentally different from those we use to learn about others.
    b. by applying to our own behavior the same rules of inference we use in interpreting and understanding the behavior of others.
    c. intuitively, and by watching the reactions of others to us.
    d. all of the above

Answer: b
Perceiving oneself
pp. 466–467

117. _____ states that we really don't know ourselves directly, but that self-knowledge is achieved indirectly through the same methods that we use to understand others.
    a. Attribution theory
    b. Self-perception theory
    c. The James-Lange theory of emotions
    d. Cognitive dissonance theory

Answer: c
Perceiving oneself
pp. 466–467

118. The effectiveness of the foot-in-the-door technique of persuasion suggests that:
    a. actions always reflect prior beliefs about the self.
    b. we are more prone to do favors for people we like.
    c. our beliefs can change as a result of our own actions.
    d. we tend to like those who do favors for us.

Answer: c
Perceiving oneself
pp. 466–467

119. The foot-in-the-door method of persuasion is successful because people:
    a. are susceptible to dogma.
    b. like assertive behavior.
    c. attribute their actions to their attitudes.
    d. can't bring themselves to insult other people.

Answer: c
Perceiving oneself
pp. 466–467

120. Who would be most likely to use the foot-in-the-door technique?
    a. a lawyer
    b. an accountant
    c. a political campaigner
    d. a nurse

Answer: a
Perceiving oneself
pp. 466–467

121. In an experiment described in your text, homeowners were asked to put a small sign concerning auto safety in their window. Several weeks later they were asked to place a large billboard on their front lawn. The study showed that:
    a. compliance with the second request was higher among those who had agreed to the first request.
    b. compliance with the second request was lower among those who had agreed to the first request.
    c. those who had agreed to the first request tended to refuse the second, while those who had refused the first tended to agree to the second.
    d. responses to the first and second requests were completely unrelated.

Answer: a
Perceiving oneself
pp. 466–467

122. A father wants his adolescent son to be more responsible in his use of the family car. Based on self-perception research, which of the following actions would you recommend as most likely to promote this goal?
    a. Put the son in complete charge of maintenance of the car.
    b. Take care to consistently punish each irresponsible act.
    c. Have the boy's mother talk to him about the virtue of responsible behavior.
    d. Make himself (father) more likable so his son will want to please him.

Answer: b
Perceiving oneself
pp. 466–467

123. Self-perception theory implies that role-playing would:
    a. help a person understand a particular position, but not affect her attitude toward the position.
    b. lead to increased sympathy for the role played.
    c. make a person more aware of the difference between her own position and the one she's playing.
    d. a and c

124. Compared to individualist cultures, collectivist cultures emphasize:
    a. interdependence.
    b. self-reliance.
    c. a person's needs, desires and emotions.
    d. all of the above

125. Compared to collectivist cultures, individualist cultures:
    a. include the dominant culture in the United States.
    b. emphasize independence.
    c. emphasize family and community relationships in defining goals.
    d. all of the above
    e. a and b

126. Glen and Steve are research participants in an Asch-type study. Although both conform, Glen is much more uncomfortable doing so than Steve is. Most likely:
    a. Glen is from an individualist culture and Steve is from a collectivist culture.
    b. Steve is from an individualist culture and Glen is from a collectivist culture.
    c. Steve is experiencing cognitive dissonance.
    d. Both men are from collectivist cultures.

127. Research on attributions indicates that:
    a. people from collectivist cultures tend to make more dispositional attributions than do people from individualist cultures.
    b. people from collectivist cultures are unwilling to make attributions.
    c. people from individualist and collectivist cultures don't differ in their tendency to make dispositional or situational attributions.
    d. people from collectivist cultures tend to make more situational attributions than do people from individualist cultures.

128. Two research participants read a story about a waiter who maintains his cool in the face of a very rude customer. Asked to explain the waiter's behavior, person *A* says that a crucial part of the waiter's job is to accept mistreatment from customers. Person *B* says that the waiter is a very secure, unflappable person. Most likely:
    a. both participants are from individualist cultures.
    b. person *A* is falling prey to the fundamental attribution error.
    c. person *A* is from a collectivist culture and person *B* is from an individualist culture.
    d. person *A* is from an individualist culture and person *B* is from a collectivist culture.

Answer: a
Culture and social cognition
p. 469

129. Wei is from China and Peter is from the U.S. Regarding their decisions about where to go to college, which of the following is true?
    a. Wei is likely to give more weight to his parents' advice than is Peter.
    b. Peter is likely to give more weight to his parents' advice than is Wei.
    c. Wei and Peter will both give the most weight to what they want to major in and the quality of that major at each of the schools they're considering.
    d. Peter is more likely to choose a school close to his family and friends than is Wei.

Answer: d
Culture and social cognition
p. 469

130. Which of the following statements about members of collectivist and individualist cultures is false?
    a. Collectivists are less likely to conform with members of an out-group than are individualists.
    b. Collectivists' friendships tend to be deeper and more lasting than those of individualists.
    c. Collectivists are more likely to conform with members of an in-group than are individualists.
    d. Collectivists tend to make friends more easily than do individualists.

Answer: d
Culture and social cognition
p. 470

131. Research on the above-average effect indicates that:
    a. the effect is found to the same extent in both individualist and collectivist cultures.
    b. the effect is found in both individualist and collectivist cultures, but it's much stronger in individualist cultures.
    c. the effect is found in both individualist and collectivist cultures, but it's much stronger in collectivist cultures.
    d. the effect is found individualist cultures but not in collectivist cultures.

Answer: c
Emotion
p. 471

132. One similarity in the treatment of emotion and sensation by psychologists in the 1800s was that:
    a. both were largely ignored.
    b. both were treated theoretically but not empirically.
    c. both were the subject of cataloging efforts.
    d. both were rejected in principle as topics for study.

Answer: d
Emotion
pp. 471–472

133. The James-Lange theory of emotions asserts that:
    a. emotional experience is by definition private and inaccessible.
    b. overt behavior is largely the result of emotional experience.
    c. different people classify the same emotions differently.
    d. emotion is the awareness of the bodily changes that result from arousing stimuli.

Answer: b
Emotion
pp. 471–472

134. According to the James-Lange theory of emotion:
   a. our emotional response to a situation leads to a set of physiological responses associated with that emotion.
   b. our behavioral and physiological response to a situation precedes and determines the emotion we feel in that situation.
   c. the behavioral, physiological, and cognitive components of emotion occur simultaneously.
   d. our cognitive evaluation of a situation leads to emotional and behavioral responses.

Answer: c
Emotion
pp. 471–472

135. The James-Lange theory of emotion and the self-perception theory both assert that:
   a. our actions rarely reflect our true feelings or beliefs.
   b. our actions are usually determined by our self-perceptions.
   c. our feelings or beliefs are often the result of our action.
   d. our emotions and beliefs interfere with accurate self-perception.

Answer: a
Emotion
pp. 471–472

136. The James-Lange theory of emotion asserts that feelings:
   a. are the awareness of bodily changes.
   b. precede bodily changes.
   c. precede behavior.
   d. both b and c

Answer: a
Emotion
pp. 472–473

137. One of Cannon's major objections to the James-Lange theory of emotion was that:
   a. fear, anger, and even joy produce the same bodily changes; how does a person know what she feels?
   b. the sympathetic nervous system was not given a more prominent role.
   c. emotions have different intensities.
   d. emotions are subjective experiences; therefore, no theory can be adequate in explaining them.

Answer: c
Emotion
pp. 472–473

138. Which of the following has been raised as an argument against the James-Lange theory of emotions?
   a. Different cultures recognize the same basic emotions.
   b. Emotions have standard, measurable physiological consequences.
   c. There are more subjective emotions than different autonomic reaction patterns.
   d. The precise meanings of emotional terms vary from person to person.

Answer: b
Emotion
pp. 472–473

139. Among the criticisms of the James-Lange theory of emotion is (are) which of the following?
   a. Our subjective experience of an emotion generally does not occur until we have cognitively interpreted the situation as emotion-arousing.
   b. Although emotional experiences vary widely, sympathetic reactions to arousing stimuli are very similar.
   c. Artificial autonomic arousal is generally accompanied by the experience of an emotional state.
   d. all of the above

Answer: c
Emotion
pp. 472–473

140. When research participants are simply injected with epinephrine, they report:
    a. no awareness of the physiological results.
    b. a relatively mild, euphoric response.
    c. an "as if" or "cold emotion" response.
    d. a feeling of intense fear or rage.

Answer: d
Emotion
pp. 473–474

141. The cognitive arousal theory attributes emotion to:
    a. arousal by bodily processes in response to stimuli.
    b. cognitive appraisal of a situation.
    c. a kind of attribution process.
    d. all of the above

Answer: c
Emotion
pp. 473–474
32

142. According to Schachter and Singer, our emotions are based upon:
    a. physical behavior.
    b. attribution and social perception.
    c. a physiological response and cognitive evaluation.
    d. reasoning and decision making.

Answer: a
Emotion
pp. 473–474

143. Schachter and Singer's position on the nature of emotions is often referred to as:
    a. attribution-of-arousal theory.
    b. emotional dissonance theory.
    c. emotional self-perception theory.
    d. cold emotions theory.

Answer: a
Emotion
pp. 473–474

144. According to Schachter and Singer's view of emotion:
    a. autonomic arousal is interpreted as different emotions (or as no emotion) depending on the individual's interpretation of the situation.
    b. each emotion is preceded and determined by the particular pattern of autonomic arousal produced by the situation.
    c. the autonomic components of emotion follow and are caused by our cognitive experience of an emotional state.
    d. our behavior in a situation determines the pattern of emotional responses and cognitions which will follow that behavior.

Answer: b
Emotion
pp. 473–474

145. In an experiment by Schachter and Singer, research participants were injected with a drug that produced autonomic arousal. The study found that the emotion experienced by these participants:
    a. was always anxiety, regardless of the situation in which arousal occurred.
    b. depended on the situation at the time of arousal, and could be positive, negative, or absent.
    c. was nonexistent; participants reported no experience of emotion solely as a result of autonomic arousal.
    d. tended to be positive or euphoric in the absence of specific cues suggesting any other emotional state.

146. Although the groups in Schachter and Singer's study were exposed to the same angry confederate, one group reported more subsequent feelings of anger than the other. Why?
    a. The angrier group had been injected with adrenaline.
    b. The angrier group had to wait longer in the confederate's company.
    c. The angrier group had been led to expect that they would become angry.
    d. The angrier group were not informed about the physical effects of the drug they were given.

147. Schachter and Singer investigated physiological concomitants of emotion. In general their results suggest that:
    a. different amounts of epinephrine produce different emotions.
    b. the same state of arousal is interpreted as the same emotional experience across different situations.
    c. different attributions yield different emotional experiences from the same state of arousal.
    d. different arousal patterns underlie different emotional experiences.

148. The results of the Schachter-Singer experiment indicate that:
    a. emotional experience and visceral reaction are the same thing.
    b. emotions are actually the result of parasympathetic rebound.
    c. emotional experience is the cognitive interpretation of arousal.
    d. people can never experience "true" emotions.

149. The results of the Schachter-Singer experiment with epinephrine-treated research participants indicate that:
    a. emotions are the result of cognitive dissonance.
    b. environment has little to do with the nature of the emotion.
    c. self-perception theorists are incorrect.
    d. visceral reactions by themselves do not produce genuine emotions.

150. In Schachter and Singer's experiment on emotion:
    a. participants informed of drug effects showed more emotion than other participants.
    b. participants misinformed of drug effects showed less emotion than other participants.
    c. informed and misinformed participants showed the same amount of emotion.
    d. participants informed of drug effects showed less emotion than other participants.

151. The Schachter and Singer experiment in which participants were injected with epinephrine showed that:
    a. physiological state produces emotional state.
    b. reactions to external stimuli produce emotional state.
    c. anger and euphoria are the result of quite different physiological states.
    d. anger and euphoria can result from the same physiological state.

Answer: b
Emotion
pp. 474–475

152. Excitation transfer effects occur when:
   a. our expectations about the emotions appropriate to a situation lead us to misinterpret our actual experiences in that situation.
   b. physiological arousal from a previous situation enhances emotions produced by events in our current situation.
   c. emotions from a previous situation cause us to misinterpret physiological arousal occurring in the current situation.
   d. emotions directed toward one aspect of the current situation are redirected to a different aspect.

Answer: c
Emotion
pp. 474–475

153. Shortly after finishing several vigorous squash games, Carrie found herself attracted to a man she passed near the locker room. To say that her attraction was due to excitation transfer would mean that:
   a. Carrie was attracted to the man because he looked a bit like her former boyfriend.
   b. Carrie found herself flirting with the man and assumed she must be attracted to him.
   c. Carrie was still somewhat aroused from the exercise and misinterpreted the arousal as indicative of a feeling of attraction.
   d. Carrie was in a good mood from having won and so decided to view everything and everyone in a more positive light than usual.

Answer: b
Emotion
p. 475

154. The _____ seems to be largely responsible for marking the emotional meaning of stimuli.
   a. hippocampus
   b. hindbrain
   c. autonomic nervous system
   d. amygdala

Answer: d
Emotion
p. 475

155. Karl has a tumor that has destroyed much of his amygdala. In a classical conditioning study, he is given an electric shock whenever a blue light flashes and no shock when a yellow light flashes. Most likely:
   a. he will be unable to distinguish between the two lights and will not fear either.
   b. he will be unable to distinguish between the two lights and will fear both.
   c. he will be afraid of the blue light but not the yellow light.
   d. he will be able to state that the blue light is accompanied by shock, but he will not fear the blue light.

Answer: d
Emotion
p. 475

156. Complex partial seizure disorder:
   a. makes neurons in the amygdala hyperactive.
   b. leads people to tag stimuli with inappropriate emotional meanings.
   c. might make someone feel very comfortable and at-home in a completely unfamiliar place.
   d. all of the above

Answer: b
Emotion
p. 476

157. Facial expressions seem to mimic:
    a. the expressions they follow.
    b. the action that is implied by the emotion.
    c. the culture of the person.
    d. nothing; they are arbitrary.

Answer: a
Emotion
p. 476

158. Darwin argued that human facial expressions:
    a. would be the same across cultures.
    b. differed dramatically from those of other primates.
    c. had to be learned.
    d. were arbitrary.

Answer: c
Emotion
pp. 476–478

159. Which of the following statements about cross-cultural studies of facial expressions is false?
    a. People in a variety of cultures recognize smiles more reliably than they recognize other facial expressions.
    b. No studies have tested people who have had no contact with Western cultures.
    c. Studies of spontaneous facial expressions across a wide range of cultures are consistent with the universality thesis.
    d. The status of the universality thesis is still under debate.

Answer: a
Emotion
pp. 478–479

160. A study of the emotional expressiveness of American and Japanese research participants while observing an unpleasant film found that:
    a. both groups showed the same emotions when viewing the film alone, but the Japanese were more polite and reserved when viewing the film with another.
    b. Japanese participants showed less emotion while observing the film, whether alone or with another, than did Americans.
    c. American participants expressed less emotion than Japanese participants, whether viewing the film alone or with another.
    d. American participants expressed more unpleasant emotions than Japanese participants, whether viewing the film alone or with another.
    e. both groups showed the same emotions when viewing the film with another, but the Japanese were more expressive than the Americans when viewing the film alone.

Answer: b
Emotion
pp. 478–479

161. Cultural display rules:
    a. are innate.
    b. indicate when different expressions are appropriate.
    c. rely on facial feedback.
    d. a and b

Answer: b
Emotion
p. 479

162. The facial feedback hypothesis:
    a. contradicts the James-Lange theory.
    b. argues that emotions are partially determined by facial expressions.
    c. has no experimental support.
    d. b and c

Answer: a
Emotion
p. 479

163. When research participants were asked to view cartoons while holding a pen in their mouths in a way that would either produce a smile or puckered lips:
    a. consistent with the facial feedback hypothesis, the smiling participants rated the cartoons as more amusing than did the other participants.
    b. contrary to the facial feedback hypothesis, the smiling participants rated the cartoons as more amusing than did the other participants.
    c. contrary to the facial feedback hypothesis, the smiling participants rated the cartoons as as amusing as did the other participants.
    d. contrary to the facial feedback hypothesis, the smiling participants rated the cartoons as less amusing than did the other participants.

Answer: c
Emotion
pp. 479–480

164. The communicative view of facial expressions suggests that facial expressions:
    a. automatically communicate our emotional states.
    b. are automatic responses indicating that we have understood communications from others.
    c. are designed to convey our intentions to others.
    d. a and b

Answer: a
Emotion
pp. 479–480

165. The communication hypothesis of facial expressions of emotions is supported by the observation that:
    a. facial expressions occur mostly when we are in the presence of others and make eye contact with them.
    b. there are many more distinct facial expressions than there are distinct emotional states.
    c. we tend to interpret the facial expressions of others as calls for action rather than as read-outs of their internal emotional states.
    d. all of the above

Answer: d
Emotion
pp. 479–480

166. A bowler who makes a strike is most likely to smile:
    a. the moment the ball leaves her hand.
    b. the moment the first pin goes down.
    c. the moment she realizes she's made a strike.
    d. when she turns to face others.

Answer: b
Emotion
pp. 479–480

167. Imagine that subjects are asked to watch a film under various circumstances. Under which of the following pairs of circumstances are a research participant's facial expressions likely to differ the most?
    a. watching unobserved versus watching while being observed but thinking you're unobserved
    b. watching unobserved versus watching with another person
    c. watching with another person versus watching unobserved but thinking you're being observed
    d. b and c

Answer: a
Emotion
pp. 480–481

168. Which of the following statements is false?
    a. Most researchers agree on which emotions should be called "basic".
    b. Not all emotions have distinct neural circuitry.
    c. The same emotions can be combined to produce different effects.
    d. all of the above

169. The emotions of pity, anger, and guilt are similar in that:
    a. they appear in the facial expressions of all primates, but in no animals below the primates.
    b. they are all emotions that seem to involve a blend of positive and negative emotions.
    c. they are all aroused by the experience of misfortune.
    d. all of the above

170. The dimension of controllability seems to be an important one in determining which emotion we experience. It can determine which of the following emotions?
    a. anger
    b. guilt
    c. pity
    d. all of the above

171. Your text distinguishes between the related emotions of pity, anger, and guilt by noting that:
    a. we feel guilt if we caused some misfortune to others and we could have avoided it.
    b. we feel anger if someone else caused us misfortune that he or she could have avoided.
    c. we feel pity if someone else experienced misfortune that he or she could not avoid.
    d. all of the above
    e. a and c only

172. Your text distinguishes between the related emotions of pity, anger, and guilt by noting that we feel:
    a. either guilt or pity if a misfortune was unavoidable.
    b. either anger or guilt depending on whether misfortune was caused by another person or by ourselves.
    c. either pity or anger depending on whether a misfortune was caused by ourselves or by another person.
    d. all of the above

173. Anger seems to be determined at least in part by which of the following factors?
    a. physiological state
    b. interpretive processes
    c. moral considerations
    d. all of the above

174. Your text notes that some emotions involve an appreciation of a moral order. These emotions include:
    a. pity and sadness.
    b. anger and guilt.
    c. regret and anger.
    d. sadness and regret.

Answer: a
Emotion
pp. 482–483

175. Regret involves an assessment of:
    a. what is and what might have been.
    b. what is and what could be.
    c. what is and what should be.
    d. all of the above

Answer: d
Emotion
pp. 483–484

176. Inga and Tarika both get on line early one morning for concert tickets. Both are too far back to get tickets. Tarika is the first person in line not to get tickets and Inga is the thirtieth. Research indicates that most people would expect:
    a. both women to be equally upset.
    b. both women to feel angry at the people who managed to get tickets.
    c. both women to feel more self-pity than guilt.
    d. Tarika to be more upset than Inga.

Answer: d
Emotion
pp. 484–485

177. Cross-cultural research on emotions indicates that:
    a. in some cultures there are no words for some emotions that are common in Western cultures.
    b. in Western culture there are no words for some emotions that are common in other cultures.
    c. it is unclear whether people in different cultures can experience all of the same feelings.
    d. all of the above

Answer: b
Emotion
pp. 485–486

178. Your text suggests that the emotions we experience when watching a play or movie:
    a. are fundamentally identical to those we experience in "real life."
    b. result from a different cognitive interpretation of the same physiological arousal we experience in "real life" emotions.
    c. do not involve either the same cognitive interpretation nor the same physiological arousal as real emotions.
    d. include only a small subset of the full range of human emotions.

Answer: b
Emotion
pp. 486–487

179. In a theatrical performance, an adult audience is most likely to obtain the appropriate esthetic experience:
    a. if the performance is perceived coolly and dispassionately.
    b. if the performance gives the viewer an "as if" emotion.
    c. if the performance gives the viewer a true emotion without any sense of "as if."
    d. if the performance has a minimum of psychical distance.

CHAPTER 12 | Social Interaction

Answer: c
Relating to others: one-on-one interactions
p. 491

1. The concept of a social exchange implies:
   a. that one partner in a relationship will give something to the other.
   b. that an opponent in a relationship will exchange his animosity for a favor.
   c. that each partner in a relationship gives and expects something in return.
   d. that relationships are primarily asymmetrical.

Answer: e
Relating to others: one-on-one interactions
p. 491

2. The commodity that is exchanged in a social exchange is:
   a. affection.
   b. goods.
   c. money.
   d. loyalty.
   e. any of the above

Answer: b
Relating to others: one-on-one interactions
p. 491

3. According to social exchange theory:
   a. human relationships have nothing to do with economics.
   b. relationships in which one person takes without giving will not last.
   c. all relationships require some financial interchange.
   d. all relationships require the exchange of something tangible like money, food, or gifts.

Answer: c
Relating to others: one-on-one interactions
p. 492

4. The reciprocity principle refers to:
   a. the fact that our impression of ourselves is very much influenced by the impression that others have of us.
   b. the observation that we tend to like someone who also likes us.
   c. the social rule that we are obligated to repay whatever favor we have been given by another person.
   d. an argument against social exchange theory.

Answer: c
Relating to others: one-on-one interactions
p. 492

5. Some charities send out fundraising letters with a small gift (like return address labels for the recipient) enclosed. Their strategy seems to rely on:
   a. the foot-in-the-door technique.
   b. the door-in-the-face technique
   c. the reciprocity principle.
   d. the reciprocal-concession effect.

Answer: a
Relating to others: one-on-one interactions
pp. 492–493

6. The reciprocity principle can be turned to one's favor by using it in bargaining. In order to do this one must:
   a. give a small concession to create a feeling of obligation in the other member of the transaction.
   b. give a large concession to get a deal consummated.
   c. give a large concession to force the other bargainer's hand.
   d. give a small concession to make the other bargainer feel small.

Answer: d
Relating to others: one-on-one interactions
pp. 492–493

7. In bargaining for a car with you, the dealer has just dropped $1,000 off the asking price. You now feel obliged to increase your offer. The dealer has made use of:
   a. the door-in-the-face technique.
   b. the self-disclosure principle.
   c. the foot-in-the-door technique.
   d. the reciprocal-concession effect.

Answer: a
Relating to others: one-on-one interactions
pp. 492–493

8. The door-in-the-face technique involves:
   a. making a large request in the expectation that if it is rejected, the individual will feel obligated to agree to a subsequent smaller request.
   b. bestowing a small gift or favor in the expectation that the individual will feel obligated to grant a larger one in return.
   c. making a small request so that once it is accepted, the individual will be inclined to agree to a subsequent larger request.
   d. making a small request so that once it is rejected, the individual will be inclined to agree to a subsequent larger request.

Answer: a
Relating to others: one-on-one interactions
pp. 492–493

9. The door-in-the-face technique is based on:
   a. the reciprocal-concession effect.
   b. the self-disclosure principle.
   c. social impact theory.
   d. the bystander effect.

Answer: b
Relating to others: one-on-one interactions
pp. 492–493

10. Suppose you are asked for a loan of $100, which you refuse. Then you are asked for a loan of $25 by the same person.
    a. You are more likely to refuse the second request than if you had not been asked for the first.
    b. You are more likely to grant the second request than if you had not been asked for the first.
    c. There will be no effect of the first request on the probability of your granting the second.
    d. The first and second requests will yield the same probability of acceptance or refusal.

11. The reciprocity principle may also apply to self-disclosure. Studies of self-disclosure indicate that:
    a. individuals feel obliged to reciprocate when others disclose information about themselves.
    b. patterns of self-disclosure seem to be independent of culture, and are the same in societies as different as the U.S. and China.
    c. men are more willing to reveal themselves to women, while women are equally likely to reveal themselves to either men or women.
    d. all of the above
    e. a and b only

12. Which of the following statements is false?
    a. Self-disclosure always enhances a relationship.
    b. The reciprocity principle applies to self-disclosure.
    c. In Western culture women tend to be more self-disclosive than men.
    d. Gender differences in self-disclosure patterns seem to be culturally determined.

13. The reciprocity principle:
    a. is valuable because the things that are exchanged are often quite important.
    b. is valuable because the social system it creates is quite important.
    c. only applies to the exchange of desirable things.
    d. all of the above
    e. a and b

14. Cosmides and Tooby argue that exchange rules and the reciprocity principle are:
    a. an elaboration of our biological tendency toward reciprocal altruism.
    b. universal not because of any biological basis, but simply because they are a rational way for people to live together.
    c. tied to economics: In cultures where families are self-sufficient, social interactions are not governed by the reciprocity principle.
    d. ultimately based on the phenomenon of self-attribution: We interpret our giving behavior as evidence of a giving nature.

15. Latané and Darley suggest that none of the bystanders helped Kitty Genovese because:
    a. they didn't care.
    b. they weren't sure whether she really needed help.
    c. they wanted to see her hurt.
    d. they were afraid to get involved.

16. Pluralistic ignorance refers to the fact that:
    a. if nobody knows what to do in an emergency, no action will be taken.
    b. when there are a large number of people present, there is a tendency for bystanders to pretend that nothing is happening.
    c. when other bystanders do not take action, those present are likely to define the situation as a nonemergency.
    d. in an emergency, large groups of people are easily swayed by a single dominant individual.

17. Which of the following clearly illustrate(s) or involve(s) pluralistic ignorance?
    a. A bystander decides not to help a car accident victim because there are others present who will undoubtedly do so.
    b. A passerby decides the man lying on the sidewalk is not in trouble because nobody else in the vicinity is stopping to assist him.
    c. Nobody in a group of bystanders helps a heart attack victim because they are not sure what to do.
    d. all of the above

18. Diffusion of responsibility refers to the fact that:
    a. people are more likely to intervene in an emergency if they alone will not be responsible for the results of that intervention.
    b. people are less likely to act in an emergency if there are others present, because they feel less responsible for taking action.
    c. when others do not act in an emergency, the bystander is less likely to define the situation as an emergency requiring action.
    d. people are likely to follow the lead of a single dominant individual in the group.

19. Studies of bystander intervention in emergencies indicate that, in order to help, the bystander must:
    a. recognize that the situation is an emergency.
    b. accept responsibility for providing assistance.
    c. be a member of an emergency squad.
    d. possess an M.D.
    e. both a and b

20. What are some of the factors involved in people's inaction in emergency situations?
    a. Situations are often ambiguous.
    b. People look to other observers and see that they are calm.
    c. Responsibility for action is diffused among all observers.
    d. all of the above

21. Diffusion of responsibility leads to a(n) _____ probability of bystander intervention.
    a. decreased
    b. increased
    c. neutral
    d. It depends on the situation.

Answer: d
Relating to others: one-on-one interactions
p. 497

22. The bystander effect obeys which of the following effects?
    a. The larger the crowd, the faster the response.
    b. The larger the crowd, the higher the probability of response.
    c. The smaller the crowd, the slower the response.
    d. The larger the crowd, the lower the probability of response.
    e. a and c

Answer: d
Relating to others: one-on-one interactions
p. 497

23. The bystander effect:
    a. has been well-supported by research.
    b. is consistent with the diffusion of responsibility hypothesis.
    c. refers to the fact that bystanders are more likely to help someone in trouble the fewer other bystanders there are.
    d. all of the above

Answer: c
Relating to others: one-on-one interactions
pp. 496–497

24. Research on bystander intervention suggests that if you are attacked on the street:
    a. you are more likely to get help if there are several people nearby than just one (besides your attacker).
    b. you should yell "Fire!", rather than "Help!", to attract attention and increase the odds that someone will help you.
    c. and there are several bystanders, your chances of getting help are better if you look directly at one while you yell for help, rather than looking all around.
    d. in a city, the only way you'll be helped is if there happens to be a police officer nearby.

Answer: b
Relating to others: one-on-one interactions
p. 498

25. We know that in a group, various factors will influence the probability that an observer will react to an emergency. But we also know that regardless of these factors:
    a. people will generally respond in spite of any cost to themselves.
    b. people will respond less when there is any cost to themselves.
    c. people will respond less when there is cost to themselves if the cost is potential bodily harm only.
    d. only women are less likely to respond because of potential bodily harm.

Answer: d
Relating to others: one-on-one interactions
p. 498

26. In a study by Darley and Batson, seminary students rushing to give a talk passed by a man groaning in a doorway. The results of this study indicated that:
    a. a majority of all seminary students stopped to help.
    b. seminary students stopped to help only if the topic of the talk they were about to give was the parable of the Good Samaritan.
    c. seminary students were more likely to stop and offer help if the man was neatly dressed than if he was shabbily dressed.
    d. only about 10 percent of seminary students stopped to help.
    e. both b and c

Answer: c
Relating to others: one-on-one interactions
p. 498

27. In one study, stranded motorists tried to flag down a passing car. The results were that:
    a. male and female motorists were equally likely to stop and help.
    b. people were equally likely to stop and help whether they were traveling alone or with others.
    c. female stranded motorists received more help than male stranded motorists.
    d. b and c

Answer: c
Relating to others: one-on-one interactions
pp. 498–499

28. Altruistic behavior:
    a. is typically not influenced by personal gain.
    b. is not a function of the cost to the actor.
    c. is sensitive to the personal gain of the actor.
    d. is influenced by the time of day.

Answer: b
Relating to others: one-on-one interactions
p. 499

29. With regard to genuine altruism, the textbook argues that:
    a. there's no such thing; all altruistic acts benefit the actor.
    b. acts which should be viewed as genuinely altruistic are those which provide nothing to the actor except the satisfaction of knowing that he or she has helped another.
    c. there's no such thing; people only help another when the cost of helping is less than the benefits gained from helping.
    d. a and c

Answer: a
Relating to others: one-on-one interactions
pp. 499–500

30. Proximity:
    a. enhances liking.
    b. decreases familiarity.
    c. is unrelated to liking.
    d. is unrelated to familiarity.

Answer: d
Relating to others: one-on-one interactions
pp. 499–500

31. Familiarity may be one factor involved in the relationship between proximity and attraction. We know that:
    a. the closer two people live, the more likely that they will be familiar to one another.
    b. familiarity breeds liking.
    c. the more often a person encounters most anything, the more he will like it.
    d. all of the above

Answer: b
Relating to others: one-on-one interactions
pp. 499–500

32. Research on attraction suggests that if you want to make a lot of friends in your new dorm you should try to get a room:
    a. as far from the stairs as possible.
    b. next to the lounge where all the students hang out.
    c. with a good view.
    d. with a roommate.

Answer: d
Relating to others: one-on-one interactions
p. 500

33. Consistent with the familiarity hypothesis, we prefer to look at:
    a. pictures of both ourselves and our friends rather than mirror images of both.
    b. mirror images of both ourselves and our friends rather than pictures of both.
    c. pictures of ourselves and mirror images of our friends.
    d. mirror images of ourselves and pictures of our friends.

Answer: c
Relating to others: one-on-one interactions
pp. 500–501

34. It is generally true that:
    a. people who live far apart tend to find one another more attractive.
    b. opposites attract.
    c. people with similar characteristics and interests are attracted to one another.
    d. people who differ on some critical dimension, such as skill in sports, are attracted to one another.

Answer: a
Relating to others: one-on-one interactions
pp. 500–501

35. The idea that opposites attract seems to be:
    a. generally untrue.
    b. true with respect to beliefs, but not for personality characteristics.
    c. true with respect to personality characteristics, but not for beliefs or opinions.
    d. true with respect to personality characteristics, but not for social status or religion.

Answer: b
Relating to others: one-on-one interactions
p. 501

36. Homogamy refers to our tendency to:
    a. like members of the same sex.
    b. marry individuals who are similar to ourselves.
    c. bring our attitudes and behaviors into agreement with those of others.
    d. meet and like individuals who live nearby.

Answer: b
Relating to others: one-on-one interactions
pp. 499–501

37. All of the following are factors that make people like one another except:
    a. similarity.
    b. homogamy.
    c. physical attractiveness.
    d. proximity.

Answer: d
Relating to others: one-on-one interactions
pp. 499–501

38. Evidence suggests that people tend to like those who:
    a. are similar to them.
    b. live close by.
    c. are opposite to them.
    d. both a and b

Answer: e
Relating to others: one-on-one interactions
pp. 499–501

39. Bob is attracted to a particular woman in his class. Research suggests that if he wants this woman to be attracted to him, he should:
    a. move his desk closer to hers.
    b. express similar interests to hers.
    c. exclaim his love for her in class.
    d. be coy and ignore her.
    e. a and b

Answer: a
Relating to others: one-on-one interactions
p. 501

40. Given several dimensions on which one might choose a date, the most influential seems to be:
    a. physical attractiveness.
    b. intelligence.
    c. mutual interests.
    d. All of the above are equivalent.

Answer: d
Relating to others: one-on-one interactions
pp. 501–502

41. Physically attractive people are assumed to be:
    a. smarter than others.
    b. more socially skilled than others.
    c. happier than others.
    d. all of the above

Answer: b
Relating to others: one-on-one interactions
p. 502

42. A person is likely to be paired with a mate:
    a. more attractive than she is.
    b. equally attractive as she is.
    c. less attractive than she is.
    d. There is no basis for predicting the attractiveness of a person's mate.

Answer: a
Relating to others: one-on-one interactions
p. 502

43. The matching hypothesis suggests that we tend to mate with someone:
    a. whose physical attractiveness is similar to our own.
    b. whose personality characteristics are similar to our own.
    c. whose personality characteristics are opposite to, or complement, our own.
    d. whose social background and religion are similar to our own.

Answer: a
Relating to others: one-on-one interactions
pp. 502–503

44. When American college men judged the physical attractiveness of photographs of white, black, and Asian women:
    a. they preferred facial features (like small chins) that are found in children.
    b. they seemed to use different criteria for judging in-group as opposed to out-group women.
    c. there was considerable individual variation in what was judged to be attractive.
    d. all of the above
    e. a and c only

Answer: b
Relating to others: one-on-one interactions
pp. 502–503

45. Research indicates that physical attractiveness:
    a. is in the eye of the beholder.
    b. may be a cue to health and, therefore, genetic fitness.
    c. is rated higher in the context of asymmetry than symmetry.
    d. is rarely agreed upon within any culture at any point in time.
    e. a and d

Answer: c
Relating to others: one-on-one interactions
p. 503

46. Cross-culturally:
    a. thinness is considered attractive.
    b. signs of aging are considered attractive.
    c. signs of ill health are considered unattractive.
    d. all of the above

Answer: a
Relating to others: one-on-one interactions
p. 504

47. Although love is difficult to define, there seem to be at least _____ basic kinds of love.
    a. two
    b. three
    c. four
    d. five

48. Most psychologists agree that there are at least two crude categories of love, which are:
    a. emotional and instrumental
    b. passionate and compassionate
    c. romantic and companionate
    d. amative and erotic
    e. Platonic and Erotic

49. Romantic love:
    a. is primarily passionate.
    b. is centered on trust and care.
    c. allow partners to see each other very objectively.
    d. is experienced more often by women than by men.

50. Which of the following theories could readily account for why pain or anxiety might lead to sexual arousal?
    a. attribution of arousal theory
    b. the James-Lange theory of emotion
    c. cognitive dissonance theory
    d. the matching hypothesis

51. Attribution-of-arousal theory:
    a. doesn't seem to hold for romantic love.
    b. predicts that fear could be misinterpreted as romantic love.
    c. predicts that romantic love will wilt under adversity.
    d. predicts that romantic love will eventually fade.

52. In one study, young men were approached by an attractive young woman either while they were crossing a frightening bridge (group *A*), or shortly after they had safely crossed (group *B*). A later measure of how much the men had been attracted to the woman indicated that
    a. consistent with attribution-of-arousal theory, men in group *A* seem to have been more attracted than men in group *B*.
    b. consistent with attribution-of-arousal theory, men in group *B* seem to have been more attracted than men in group *A*.
    c. contrary to attribution-of-arousal theory, men in group *A* seem to have been more attracted than men in group *B*.
    d. contrary to attribution-of-arousal theory, men in group *B* seem to have been more attracted than men in group *A*.

53. At the local multiplex, you run into someone you're interested in dating. You suggest going to a movie together. According to attribution of arousal theory, your best chance of getting this person interested in you is to go with him or her to a:
    a. romantic film.
    b. comedy.
    c. fairly boring documentary.
    d. very suspenseful thriller.

Answer: a
Relating to others: one-on-one interactions
pp. 505–506

54. Love tends to heighten under conditions:
    a. that hinder it.
    b. that ignore it.
    c. that foster it.
    d. What matters are the two people in love, not the surrounding circumstances.

Answer: c
Relating to others: one-on-one interactions
p. 506

55. The Romeo-and-Juliet effect refers to the finding that:
    a. romantic love leads to suicide pacts more often than does companionate love.
    b. grief over a lost romantic love is the most long-standing and deepest of all types of grief.
    c. parental opposition tends to enhance a couple's romantic love.
    d. young lovers experience romantic love more intensely than do older lovers.

Answer: b
Relating to others: one-on-one interactions
p. 506

56. Companionate love typically:
    a. precedes romantic love.
    b. follows romantic love.
    c. is independent of romantic love.
    d. is opposite to romantic love.

Answer: b
Relating to others: one-on-one interactions
p. 506

57. Companionate love:
    a. emphasizes passion.
    b. emphasizes mutual trust, concern, and similarity of outlook.
    c. is typically briefer than romantic love.
    d. includes an obsession with the loved one.

Answer: d
Social influence: many-on-one interactions
pp. 507–508

58. Social facilitation:
    a. occurs for highly stereotyped and dominant responses.
    b. is ineffective for complex and non-dominant behaviors.
    c. is more likely for more skilled performers.
    d. all of the above

Answer: a
Social influence: many-on-one interactions
p. 507

59. Social facilitation
    a. refers to enhanced performance when an audience is present.
    b. is equally likely for dominant or nondominant responses.
    c. is more likely for nondominant than for dominant responses.
    d. refers to poorer performance when an audience is present.

Answer: a
Social influence: many-on-one interactions
p. 507

60. According to Zajonc's theory, the presence of others has its effects by:
    a. increasing the drive or arousal level of the performer.
    b. increasing the performer's ability to focus on the essential aspects of the task being performed.
    c. reducing the number of alternative responses which the performer will make in a given situation.
    d. altering the performer's ability to recall essential elements of the task being performed.

Answer: b
Social influence: many-on-one interactions
p. 507

Answer: a
Social influence: many-on-one interactions
p. 507

Answer: a

Social influence: many-on-one interactions
p. 507

Answer: e
Social influence: many-on-one interactions
pp. 507–508

Answer: c
Social influence: many-on-one interactions
pp. 507–508

Answer: e
Social influence: many-on-one interactions
pp. 508–509

61. Zajonc's theory of social facilitation effects assumes that the presence of others:
    a. increases the variability of the performer's responses.
    b. enhances highly dominant responses.
    c. increases the strength of relatively weak (nondominant) responses.
    d. increases the performer's concentration.

62. According to Zajonc, the presence of others:
    a. strengthens the dominant response whether the task being performed is simple or complex.
    b. weakens the dominant response when the task being performed is simple, but strengthens it when the task is complex.
    c. changes the dominant response from an error to a correct response when the task being performed is simple.
    d. has no effect on the nature or strength of the dominant response.

63. According to Zajonc, the effect of others on performance will depend on:
    a. whether the dominant response is correct or incorrect with respect to the task being performed.
    b. the difference in probability between the dominant response and other nondominant responses.
    c. the number of nondominant responses available in that situation.
    d. the total number of responses involved in the task to be performed.

64. Which of the following statements is true?
    a. Good pool players do worse in the presence of an audience.
    b. Good pool players do better in the presence of an audience.
    c. Poor pool players do worse in the presence of an audience.
    d. Poor pool players do better in the presence of an audience.
    e. b and c

65. Social facilitation effects:
    a. have only been found in humans.
    b. are due to concerns about being evaluated.
    c. seem to be due to the arousal caused by the presence of others.
    d. occur whenever others are present.

66. What are the causes of conformity?
    a. People want to be liked.
    b. People want to be correct, but they don't trust others to show them what is correct.
    c. People want to be correct, and they trust others to indicate what is correct.
    d. a and b
    e. a and c

Answer: b
Social influence: many-on-one interactions
pp. 508–509

67. Consider two people, one a quality-control supervisor in a pickle factory and the other a person off the street. Which one of the two will be more influenced by group opinion about the level of brine to use in pickling?
   a. the quality-control supervisor
   b. the person off the street
   c. They will be equally influenced.
   d. Expertise has no effect on susceptibility to group influence.

Answer: a
Social influence: many-on-one interactions
p. 509

68. When research participants in an Asch line-judgment study wrote their answers down instead of saying them aloud:
   a. consistent with a motivational account, they showed less conformity than in the aloud condition.
   b. consistent with an informational account, they showed less conformity than in the aloud condition.
   c. consistent with a motivational account, they showed as much conformity as in the aloud condition.
   d. consistent with an informational account, they showed as much conformity as in the aloud condition.

Answer: d
Social influence: many-on-one interactions
pp. 509–510

69. In an Asch experiment, the target line is 5 inches long but the confederates say the 6-inch line is the one that matches it. The real research participant will be more likely to give the correct answer if:
   a. the confederates unanimously give the wrong answer.
   b. one confederate gives the right answer (5-inch line) while the rest all say it's the 6-inch line.
   c. one confederate wrongly states that the 7-inch line matches while the rest all say it's the 6-inch line.
   d. b or c

Answer: d
Social influence: many-on-one interactions
pp. 509–510

70. A consistent minority in a group is most likely to influence the _____ of members of the majority. A consistent majority is most likely to influence the _____ of members of the minority.
   a. behavior alone; thinking
   b. behavior alone; behavior alone
   c. thinking; thinking
   d. thinking; behavior alone

Answer: c
Social influence: many-on-one interactions
p. 510

71. Consistent minorities:
   a. have very little influence over other group members.
   b. have faster effects than do consistent majorities.
   c. often bring about social innovations.
   d. have the same effects as consistent majorities do.

Answer: d
Social influence: many-on-one interactions
pp. 511–512

72. According to the original investigators who studied the so-called authoritarian personality, such individuals:
   a. believe in the importance of power and authority, and tend to be prejudiced against various minority groups.
   b. develop as a result of specific childhood experiences.
   c. employ reaction formation in dealing with repressed hostility toward harsh and punitive fathers.
   d. all of the above

Answer: c
Social influence: many-on-one interactions
pp. 511–512

73. According to the original investigators who studied the so-called authoritarian personality, such individuals:
    a. have trouble taking orders from those in authority.
    b. are no more likely to be prejudiced against minority groups than anyone else.
    c. are likely to endorse slogans such as "my country right or wrong."
    d. had upbringings that were permissive to the point of being neglectful.

Answer: c
Social influence: many-on-one interactions
pp. 511–512

74. Persons who believe in the importance of power and dominance and respect for authority are called:
    a. dictators.
    b. obedient personalities.
    c. authoritarian personalities.
    d. war criminals.

Answer: b
Social influence: many-on-one interactions
pp. 511–512

75. Authoritarian personalities would agree with all of the following statements except one. Which one?
    a. Obedience and respect for authority are the most important virtues children should learn.
    b. Although superiors have the authority to order subordinates to do things, subordinates have the right to refuse orders from a superior.
    c. Most of our social problems would be solved if we could get rid of immoral people.
    d. People can be divided into two classes: the weak and the strong.

Answer: b
Social influence: many-on-one interactions
pp. 511–512

76. Authoritarianism:
    a. is more prevalent among the better educated.
    b. is more prevalent among the poorly educated.
    c. is more prevalent among those of higher intelligence.
    d. is uninfluenced by education and intelligence.

Answer: d
Social influence: many-on-one interactions
pp. 511–512

77. People with authoritarian personalities tend to:
    a. vote for conservative candidates.
    b. believe in disciplining children harshly.
    c. be less educated than others.
    d. all of the above

Answer: a
Social influence: many-on-one interactions
p. 512

78. One valid criticism of original studies on the authoritarian personality is:
    a. accounts of childhood experience came from the research participants themselves.
    b. prejudice is not usually accompanied by authoritarian sentiments.
    c. authoritarian people have no hostility toward their parents.
    d. authoritarian personalities are found in all social classes.

Answer: b
Social influence: many-on-one interactions
p. 513

79. Stanley Milgram's experiment where the research participant acted as a "teacher" and thought he administered shock to a "learner" was designed to investigate:
    a. the effects of punishment on speed of learning.
    b. the effects of situational factors upon obedience.
    c. learned responses to uncontrollable shock.
    d. emotional reactions to increasing punishment.

Answer: a
Social influence: many-on-one interactions
p. 513

80. In Milgram's experiment, research participants who were fully obedient
    a. thought they were delivering potentially lethal electric shocks to an innocent man.
    b. had no reason to think that the *learner* was suffering.
    c. typically had no qualms about their behavior.
    d. had to be threatened in order to continue.

Answer: b
Social influence: many-on-one interactions
p. 514

81. In Milgram's experiment on obedience:
    a. only pathological research participants used the maximum shock intensity.
    b. about 65 percent of the research participants used the maximum shock intensity.
    c. about 90 percent of the research participants used the maximum shock intensity.
    d. about 25 percent of the research participants used the maximum shock intensity.

Answer: d
Social influence: many-on-one interactions
p. 514

82. Approximately what proportion of the research participants in Milgram's original experiment administered shocks of maximum intensity?
    a. 2 percent
    b. 18 percent
    c. 35 percent
    d. 65 percent

Answer: d
Social influence: many-on-one interactions
p. 514

83. Milgram's obedience study demonstrated that most research participants would:
    a. refuse to administer shocks to humans.
    b. deliver shocks to humans under vigorous protest.
    c. deliver mild but not strong shocks to humans.
    d. give lethal shocks to humans.

Answer: b
Social influence: many-on-one interactions
pp. 514–515

84. Increasing the psychological distance of a research participant from the administration of shocks in Milgram's experiments results in:
    a. less obedience.
    b. more obedience.
    c. no obedience.
    d. no effect on obedience.

Answer: a
Social influence: many-on-one interactions
pp. 514–515

85. In a variation of Milgram's experiment, research participants played an essential part in "teaching," but a confederate administered the shocks. Under these conditions about _____ of the research participants continued to the end of the experiment.
    a. 90 percent
    b. 65 percent
    c. 30 percent
    d. 2 percent

Answer: c
Social influence: many-on-one interactions
pp. 514–515

86. When Milgram's research participants were seated next to the "learner" and had to hold his hand down on a shock plate to administer shocks:
    a. about the same percentage were fully obedient as in the standard condition.
    b. none of the participants was fully obedient.
    c. 30 percent of the participants were fully obedient.
    d. 70 percent of the participants were fully obedient.

Answer: d
Social influence: many-on-one interactions
p. 515

87. An obedient person sees himself as a(n) _____ of an authority, and he sees the victim as a(n) _____.
    a. scapegoat; subject
    b. subject; survivor
    c. friend; prisoner
    d. instrument; object

Answer: d
Social influence: many-on-one interactions
p. 515

88. Those who comply with immoral orders often employ cognitive strategies like _____ to cope with their dilemma.
    a. attribution of fault to the victim
    b. dehumanization of the victim
    c. seeing themselves as merely instruments
    d. all of the above

Answer: b
Social influence: many-on-one interactions
p. 515

89. Victim dehumanization:
    a. is a purely experimental phenomenon with no obvious real world parallels.
    b. was a common strategy of Milgram's research participants.
    c. makes obedience in Milgram's study more difficult.
    d. is more difficult when the victim is out of sight.

Answer: c
Social influence: many-on-one interactions
p. 515

90. Suppose Milgram had asked his research participants to begin punishment at the highest shock intensity. Given the nature of cognitive reorientation processes, it is likely that:
    a. more people would have complied.
    b. people would have reinterpreted the situation as the experiment progressed.
    c. more people would have disobeyed.
    d. the results would have been the same.

Answer: b
Social influence: many-on-one interactions
p. 515

91. In regard to the Milgram study, *slippery slope* refers to:
    a. the way the experimenter became progressively nastier to the research participants.
    b. the gradual increase in shock intensities.
    c. the fact that the initial act of obedience was so harsh, it was like falling off a mountain.
    d. the fact that the learner's pain increased each time he screamed.

Answer: c
Social influence: many-on-one interactions
p. 516

92. When experts heard a description of Milgram's study and were asked to predict the results:
    a. consistent with the fundamental attribution error, their predictions were fairly accurate.
    b. contrary to the fundamental attribution error, their predictions were fairly accurate.
    c. consistent with the fundamental attribution error, they vastly underestimated the percentage of research participants who would be fully obedient.
    d. contrary to the fundamental attribution error, they vastly underestimated the percentage of research participants who would be fully obedient.

Answer: c
Social influence: many-on-one interactions
pp. 516–517

93. Social impact theory predicts that:
    a. a performer will be more intimidated by a lower-status audience than by a higher-status audience.
    b. expectation of being watched on video is more intimidating than performance before a live audience.
    c. a larger audience will be more intimidating than a smaller one.
    d. women are more intimidated by audience reaction than men.

Answer: d
Social influence: many-on-one interactions
pp. 516–517

94. Bibb Latané's social impact theory argues that:
    a. the individual is exposed to a field of converging social forces.
    b. the impact of others on an individual is greater if the others are of high status or power.
    c. the total social impact on an individual increases with the number of others who affect the individual.
    d. all of the above

Answer: d
Social influence: many-on-one interactions
p. 517

95. Which of the following observations is (or would be) inconsistent with social impact theory?
    a. Performers are more anxious in front of a large audience than in front of a small audience.
    b. Performers are more anxious when playing in front of a high status audience than when playing in front of a low status audience.
    c. Performing in front of a live audience produces more stage fright than performing for a remote audience watching on a television monitor.
    d. Performing with a group produces as much stage fright as does performing alone.

Answer: a
Social influence: many-on-one interactions
pp. 517–518

96. Stage fright and the bystander effect are similar in that both the actor and the bystanders are affected by:
    a. the number of other principals.
    b. the intelligence of the other principals.
    c. the social status of the other principals.
    d. the educational level of the other principals.

Answer: c
Social influence: many-on-one interactions
p. 518

97. Social loafing refers to the finding that:
    a. people are unwilling to look like shirkers in front of others.
    b. people work less when they can be seen by others than when they can't.
    c. people generally put less effort into a group task than they would doing the same task individually.
    d. people generally prefer spending leisure time with others than alone.

Answer: d
Social influence: many-on-one interactions
p. 518

98. When students were asked to clap and cheer as loudly as they could, either alone or in groups of various sizes:
    a. individuals cheered more vigorously alone than in groups, but the size of the group did not matter.
    b. vigorousness of clapping and cheering was unrelated to the number of people involved.
    c. each individual clapped and cheered more vigorously the more people were involved.
    d. each individual clapped and cheered less vigorously the more people were involved.

Answer: a
Leadership: one-on-many interactions
pp. 519–520

99. Questions about whether historical events were primarily determined by a confluence of circumstances or by the leadership of particular individuals are most analogous to questions about _____ in social psychology.
    a. attribution
    b. social impact theory
    c. diffusion of responsibility
    d. social facilitation

Answer: e
Leadership: one-on-many interactions
pp. 520–521

100. Laboratory studies of leadership indicate that:
    a. people perceived as leaders tend to be more intelligent and more outgoing than those not regarded as leaders.
    b. leaders are most effective when the task to be performed is unclear or open-ended.
    c. leaders are most effective when they have considerable authority, and group members get along well with each other.
    d. all of the above
    e. a and c only

Answer: c
Leadership: one-on-many interactions
pp. 520–521

101. Laboratory studies indicate that leaders are least likely to be effective:
    a. if they are more intelligent and dominant than others in the group.
    b. if the task to be performed is clear-cut rather than ambiguous.
    c. if they have relatively little authority within the group.
    d. if the members of the group get along well with each other.
    e. a and c only

Answer: b
Leadership: one-on-many interactions
pp. 520–521

102. Studies of leadership indicate that effective leadership:
    a. is determined by the potential leader's personal characteristics.
    b. is more likely in some situations than in others.
    c. in one group means that the leader will be an effective leader for another group.
    d. a and c

Answer: b
Crowd behavior: many-on-many interactions
p. 522

103. Gustav Le Bon held that the individual in a crowd:
    a. is still subject to the law of individual functioning.
    b. descends to the level of primitive, barbarous instincts.
    c. acts in accordance with his own best interests.
    d. still feels very much alone.

Answer: c
Crowd behavior: many-on-many interactions
p. 522

104. Deindividuation:
    a. leads to an increased sense of responsibility.
    b. tightens inhibitions on impulses.
    c. is most likely under conditions of anonymity.
    d. seems to be a laboratory phenomenon that does not exist in the real world.

Answer: a
Crowd behavior: many-on-many interactions
p. 522

105. A key characteristic of crowd behavior is deindividuation in which:
    a. each individual loses his own identity and becomes an anonymous member.
    b. each individual contributes equally to a group identity for the crowd.
    c. a panicky response by an individual spreads to other individuals in the crowd.
    d. each individual tries to serve her own best interests rather than the best interests of the crowd.

Answer: e
Crowd behavior: many-on-many interactions
pp. 522–523

106. In one study, trick-or-treaters were more likely to steal Halloween candy if they:
    a. were wearing dark costumes.
    b. had come alone.
    c. were anonymous.
    d. had come with other children.
    e. c and d

Answer: c
Crowd behavior: many-on-many interactions
p. 523

107. In some situations (e.g., fire in a crowded theater), crowds may panic and rush for the exits, resulting in injury and loss of life. According to the cognitive interpretation of crowd behavior, panic occurs when:
    a. members of the crowd experience intense fear.
    b. members of the crowd believe that all escape routes are blocked.
    c. members of the crowd believe that escape routes are limited or are closing.
    d. all of the above
    e. b and c only

Answer: d
Crowd behavior: many-on-many interactions
pp. 523–524

108. In the prisoner's dilemma:
   a. achieving the best outcome requires a great deal of trust.
   b. each individual can act rationally and yet produce a nonoptimal outcome.
   c. the prisoners' behavior is irrational.
   d. a and b

Answer: d
Crowd behavior: many-on-many interactions
pp. 523–524

109. In the prisoner's dilemma, two prisoners (*X* and *Y*) have to decide whether to betray each other or remain silent. In the payoff matrix for this situation, the outcome:
   a. is best for both *X* and *Y* if they both remain silent.
   b. is worst for *X* if *Y* confesses and *X* does not.
   c. is best for both *X* and *Y* if they both confess.
   d. both a and b

Answer: c
Crowd behavior: many-on-many interactions
pp. 524–525

110. When the logic of the prisoner's dilemma is applied to panic situations, it seems clear that panic behavior would not occur if each individual:
   a. maximized his own payoff.
   b. disapproved of others who pushed ahead.
   c. could trust the others to calmly take their turns.
   d. acted rationally regardless of others' behavior.

Answer: d
Crowd behavior: many-on-many interactions
pp. 524–525

111. Which of the following statements is false? Panic in a crowd:
   a. generally leads to much worse outcomes than calmness would have.
   b. seems to be governed by the same principles as the prisoner's dilemma.
   c. may result from each individual acting rationally.
   d. has purely an emotional, rather than a cognitive, basis.

Answer: c
Crowd behavior: many-on-many interactions
pp. 525–526

112. Imagine that several clothing manufacturers have to choose between producing inexpensive products by exploiting unprotected workers (including children) in other countries, or paying more to produce the same products in this country. Which of the following statements about this situation is false?
   a. It fits the structure of the prisoner's dilemma.
   b. Considering only the information included above, the rational thing for each company to do is to move production facilities overseas.
   c. Short of barring them from having products made elsewhere, there would be no way to get companies to choose to make their products in this country.
   d. Based only on the information described above, a company that chooses to make their goods in this country is likely to suffer financially.

Answer: c
Some final comments
pp. 526–527

113. Which of the following is not a dichotomy that seems to be prevalent in social psychological theories?
    a. reason versus passion
    b. situation versus disposition
    c. continuity versus discontinuity
    d. cognitive versus motivational

Answer: d
Some final comments
pp. 527–528

114. In considering the generality of social psychology, your text notes that:
    a. critics of social psychology argue that many of its findings are relevant only to our own culture.
    b. a genuine science of social behavior will integrate information from social sciences, such as anthropology and sociology, as well as from psychology.
    c. there are invariant properties of social behavior that cut across time and cultural differences.
    d. all of the above
    e. a and b only

CHAPTER 13 | Physical and Cognitive Development

Answer: b
What is development?
p. 534

1. A progressive change from the more general to the more specific is called:
   a. developmental progression.
   b. differentiation.
   c. embryonic development.
   d. specific progression.

Answer: c
What is development?
p. 534

2. A very young human embryo looks much like a very young rabbit embryo. The fact that they're initially so similar and yet they develop so differently is due to:
   a. cell specificity.
   b. distinctiveness.
   c. differentiation.
   d. specific progression.

Answer: a
What is development?
p. 534

3. A child might initially say "bow-wow" to describe any sort of animal. Later she might say "bow-wow" for anything that walks and "birdie" for anything that flies. Eventually she will learn distinct names for each type of animal she encounters. This progression is an example of:
   a. differentiation.
   b. maturation.
   c. concrete operations.
   d. habituation.
   e. object distinction.

Answer: a
Cognitive development
p. 535

4. Two weeks after conception, the developing fertilized egg is called _____ .
   a. an embryo
   b. a fetus
   c. a pupa
   d. any of the above

5. At two months after conception, we refer to the developing fertilized egg as _____, rather than as _____.
    a. an embryo; a fetus
    b. a fetus; an embryo
    c. a child; a fetus
    e. an embryo; a child

6. A 3-month-old fetus:
    a. has fully developed reflex patterns, and can cry, breathe, and swallow.
    b. looks like a little worm, and is only about a fifth of an inch long.
    c. is 3 inches long, and has some early reflexes and some functioning organ systems.
    d. has mature neurons with complex interconnections of axons and dendrites with other nerve cells.

7. Early in its development, an embryo:
    a. has fully developed reflex patterns, and can cry, breathe, and swallow.
    b. looks like a little worm, and is only about a fifth of an inch long.
    c. is three inches long, and has some early reflexes and some functioning organ systems.
    d. has mature neurons with complex interconnections of axons and dendrites with other nerve cells.

8. From among the following, identify the youngest that would have a good chance of surviving outside the womb.
    a. 3-month-old fetus
    b. embryo
    c. 9-month-old fetus
    d. 7-month-old fetus

9. What percent of the adult cranial capacity has a human newborn achieved at birth?
    a. 60 percent
    b. 10 percent
    c. 75 percent
    d. 23 percent

10. Which of the following statements is false?
    a. Humans are born more immature than most animals.
    b. Differentiation begins during embryonic development.
    c. The brains of full-term newborns are fully developed.
    d. Adults have fewer synapses that they had at age two.

11. The number of neural interconnections:
    a. increases dramatically after birth.
    b. decreases after age two.
    c. is constant through infancy and childhood.
    d. a and b

12. Which of the following is probably experiencing the fastest physical growth?
    a. a 4-year-old girl
    b. a 14-year-old boy
    c. an 8-year-old boy
    d. a 17-year-old girl

13. Physical growth happens _____ in childhood; brain size and complexity increase _____ in childhood.
    a. in spurts; in spurts
    b. in spurts; continuously
    c. continuously; in spurts
    d. continuously; continuously

14. The long period of dependency in human development:
    a. is about as long as periods of dependency in most other mammals.
    b. seems well-suited to learning and cultural transmission of knowledge.
    c. seems primarily to serve the purpose of allowing sensory abilities to develop fully.
    d. means that the child's behavior is either random or reflexive for the first several years.

15. Which of the following is an infantile reflex?
    a. grasp reflex
    b. sucking reflex
    c. rooting reflex
    d. all of the above

16. The rooting reflex is concerned with:
    a. crying.
    b. feeding.
    c. waste elimination.
    d. grasping.

17. A 6-month-old infant makes a move to grasp a toy that he wants. His action is:
    a. a voluntary action.
    b. a reflexive action.
    c. an involuntary action.
    d. a rooting reflex.

18. Infant reflexes:
    a. take several months to develop.
    b. often disappear early in development.
    c. include movement of the head toward the source of light stroking of the cheek.
    d. b and c

Answer: d
What is development?
p. 537

19. Your text notes that newborns:
    a. can discriminate between tones of different pitch and loudness.
    b. show a preference for their mother's voice over that of a stranger.
    c. can discriminate brightness and color.
    d. all of the above

Answer: b
What is development?
p. 537

20. Which of the following statements about the sensory capabilities of newborns is not true?
    a. They can discriminate between tones of different pitch and loudness.
    b. They can focus on objects as far away as 30–40 feet.
    c. They prefer their mother's voice to that of a stranger.
    d. They can discriminate brightness and color.

Answer: d
What is development?
pp. 538–539

21. Which child will have the greatest linguistic competence later on in life?
    a. the child who begins speaking at ten months
    b. the child who begins speaking at fifteen months
    c. the child who begins speaking at twenty months
    d. Age of language onset is not a predictor of later linguistic competence.

Answer: b
What is development?
pp. 537–539

22. Which of the following statements is true?
    a. Linguistic development follows a different progression for each child.
    b. Physical and mental development proceed by an orderly sequence of steps.
    c. The sequence of language acquisition is: babbling, cooing, one-word speech, two-word speech, multi-word sentences.
    d. The optimal time for initial language onset is 10 months of age.

Answer: d
What is development?
pp. 537–539

23. Development as orderly progression refers to the fact that:
    a. all infants reach motor milestones (e.g., walking) at the same age.
    b. all infants reach linguistic milestones (e.g., babbling) at the same age.
    c. all infants reach physical growth milestones (e.g., increase in brain weight) at the same age.
    d. many aspects of development involve invariantly ordered sequences.

Answer: c
What is development?
pp. 537–539

24. Two women are good friends who happen to give birth to full-term babies on the same day. Which of the following statements about the babies' motor development is most likely to be true?
    a. The babies will begin walking within a week of each other.
    b. The babies will begin sitting within two days of each other.
    c. Both babies will develop the ability to sit before they develop the ability to walk.
    d. all of the above

Answer: a
The physical basis of development
p. 539

25. All genes are contained in the:
    a. chromosomes.
    b. sperm cells.
    c. egg cells.
    d. phenotype.

Answer: b
The physical basis of development
pp. 539–540

26. Which of the following statements is true?
    a. Y chromosomes are inherited from the mother.
    b. An X chromosome can be inherited from either parent.
    c. X and Y chromosomes are the same size.
    d. Each sperm cell contains two sex chromosomes.

Answer: d
The physical basis of development
pp. 540–541

27. What is the genotype of a brown-eyed individual?
    a. brown-brown
    b. brown-blue
    c. blue-brown
    d. Any of the above could be the genotype of a brown-eyed person.

Answer: c
The physical basis of development
p. 540

28. Which of the following characteristics is recessive?
    a. dark hair
    b. brown eyes
    c. hemophilia
    d. all of the above

Answer: c
The physical basis of development
p. 540

29. If a characteristic is recessive:
    a. it is harmful.
    b. it is determined by the sex chromosomes.
    c. it must be inherited from both parents in order to be manifested.
    d. only parents in whom the characteristic is manifested can have children in whom the characteristic is manifested.

Answer: d
The physical basis of development
p. 540

30. Sandy does not have hemophilia but her father did and her husband does. When Sandy and her husband have children, the children
    a. will definitely have hemophilia.
    b. will definitely not have hemophilia.
    c. may have hemophilia, but if they do not, it means they do not have a hemophilia gene to pass on to their own children.
    d. may have hemophilia, but even if they do not, they may still have a hemophilia gene to pass on to their own children.

Answer: a
The physical basis of development
p. 541

31. The phenotype of an individual:
    a. is his or her overt behavior or visible appearance.
    b. is the individual's genetic blueprint.
    c. is completely determined by the individual's genotype.
    d. both a and c

Answer: a
The physical basis of development
p. 541

32. An individual's genotype:
    a. is his or her genetic blueprint.
    b. completely determines his or her phenotype.
    c. changes over the course of development.
    d. all of the above
    e. a and b only

Answer: a
The physical basis of development
p. 541

33. In one study, cells in a very early-stage salamander embryo that would have developed into skin were transplanted to the embryo's mouth region. The results were that the transplanted cells:
    a. became teeth as was appropriate for their new location.
    b. developed into skin as was appropriate for their original location but not their new location.
    c. remained undifferentiated.
    d. died, leaving the salamander to develop without a section of skin and teeth.

Answer: d
The physical basis of development
p. 541

34. Which of the following factors plays an important role in the development of an embryo?
    a. cell environment
    b. heredity
    c. hormonal environment
    d. all of the above

Answer: b
The physical basis of development
p. 542

35. If we consider the internal events that determine whether an individual is male or female we find that:
    a. genetic sex (XX or XY) is the crucial factor: An XY fetus invariably develops as a male.
    b. male hormones (androgens) are critical: In the absence of male hormones an XY fetus will develop as a female.
    c. female hormones (estrogens) are critical: In the absence of female hormones an XX fetus will develop as a male.
    d. sex hormones (androgens or estrogens) are critical: Without male hormones an XY fetus develops as a female; without estrogens, an XX fetus develops as a male.

Answer: b
The physical basis of development
p. 542

36. Which of the following is false?
    a. A fetus which is exposed to sufficient levels of androgens develops male genitalia.
    b. All fetuses with a Y chromosome develop male genitalia.
    c. A fetus which is not exposed to androgens develops female genitalia.
    d. Female genitalia are the default in human development.

Answer: a
The physical basis of development
p. 542

37. The child's environment consists of:
    a. all aspects of her experience.
    b. only the people she interacts with regularly (e.g., family members, friends, etc.).
    c. only the adults she interacts with regularly (e.g., parents, teachers, etc.).
    d. only the physical world surrounding her.

Answer: d
The physical basis of development
p. 543

38. The concept of critical periods in human development:
    a. implies that certain events are more important at one particular time that they would be either earlier or later.
    b. was derived from phenomena of embryological development.
    c. is considered too rigid to explain the phenomena of human development after birth.
    d. all of the above

Answer: c
The physical basis of development
p. 543

39. Assume that in order for a rooster to crow, he must be exposed to crowing before the age of two. The two-year span of time for learning to crow is called the:
    a. learning period.
    b. initiation period.
    c. critical period.
    d. imitation period.

Answer: c
The physical basis of development
p. 543

40. Imagine that a strict critical period exists for learning to read and that the critical period is from age 2 to 15. If someone has not yet been exposed to written materials by the time he is 20:
    a. he can still learn to read as easily as he would have at age 10.
    b. he will have great difficulty ever learning to read because no one will correct him when he makes mistakes.
    c. he will have great difficulty ever learning to read because reading materials can no longer have the impact they would have had earlier.
    d. he can learn to read faster now than he would have at age 10, because he is older.
    e. From the above information one can make no prediction about his ability to learn to read.

Answer: c
The physical basis of development
pp. 543–544

41. The maturation process:
    a. is considered to result from a complex mixture of genetic and environmental factors.
    b. is responsible for the fact that the sequence of steps in motor and perceptual development is different from infant to infant.
    c. is a genetically programmed unfolding of behavior patterns that is independent of specific environmental conditions.
    d. both a and b

Answer: c
The physical basis of development
pp. 544–545

42. A pre-programmed growth process that is relatively unaffected by specific environmental conditions is called:
    a. accommodation.
    b. assimilation.
    c. maturation.
    d. conservation.

Answer: c
The physical basis of development
pp. 544–545

43. Studies of infant-rearing practices in several cultures reveal that:
    a. restricting an infant's early movements has no effect on later motor development.
    b. systematic practice of various motor activities in infancy has no effect on the rate at which later motor development takes place.
    c. although early experience may retard or accelerate the pace of basic motor development, the final level of performance is the same in either case.
    d. both a and b

Answer: a
The physical basis of development
pp. 544–545

44. Twins Jake and Evan are in an experiment. Prior to either child learning to climb stairs, Jake is given a great deal of practice in the movements used in climbing stairs, while Evan is given no special practice. Most likely:
   a. Jake will begin climbing stairs slightly earlier than Evan.
   b. Jake and Evan will begin climbing stairs at the same time.
   c. Two years later, Jake's motor skills will be better developed than Evan's.
   d. a and c

Answer: e
The physical basis of development
pp. 544–545

45. According to your text, studies of the effects of restricted or enriched environments on development indicate that:
   a. when animals are reared in total darkness, their visual systems do not develop normally.
   b. rat pups raised in an enriched sensory environment have brains with more interconnections than do rat pups raised in impoverished environments.
   c. infants who spend most of their first year strapped to a board never learn to walk properly.
   d. all of the above
   e. a and b only

Answer: b
The physical basis of development
pp. 544–545

46. Aspects of development that are best explained by maturation typically require _____ for proper development.
   a. some sort of specific experience, but not general experience
   b. general experience, but no specific experience
   c. both general experience and some sort of specific experience
   d. neither general nor specific experience

Answer: c
Piaget's theory of cognitive development
p. 546

47. Piaget's approach to cognitive development differs from that of the nativists and empiricists in that:
   a. Piaget views the cognitive abilities of the child as fundamentally similar to those of the adult.
   b. Piaget regards the child as an adult-like thinker but without the range of associations available to the adult.
   c. Piaget sees development as a progression through a series of qualitatively different states of cognitive ability.
   d. Piaget thought basic categories of adult cognition like numbers were inborn.

Answer: a
Piaget's theory of cognitive development.
p. 546

48. Piaget's stages of cognitive development are, in order of increasing age:
   a. sensory-motor, preoperational, concrete operations, formal operations
   b. preoperational, sensory-motor, concrete operations, formal operations
   c. preoperational, sensory-motor, formal operations, concrete operations
   d. sensory-motor, preoperational, formal operations, concrete operations

49. According to Piaget, a four-year-old child is probably in the:
    a. sensory-motor stage.
    b. preoperational stage.
    c. concrete operations stage.
    d. formal operations stage.

50. The age span from 2 to 7 years represents Piaget's _____ stage.
    a. preoperational
    b. sensory-motor
    c. concrete operational
    d. formal operational

51. According to Piaget, newborns must be in the _____ stage of cognitive development.
    a. preoperational
    b. concrete operations
    c. sensory-motor
    d. formal operations

52. According to Piaget, the infant gradually develops the notion that things exist independently of his own senses. This understanding is known as:
    a. reversibility.
    b. conservation.
    c. transposition.
    d. object permanence.

53. Object permanence refers to the child's awareness that:
    a. a variety of actions can be coordinated into one organized schema.
    b. the mass of an object does not change despite transformations in the shape of the object.
    c. objects exist independent of one's direct perception of them or action upon them.
    d. certain motor patterns can become permanently associated with specific environmental objects.
    e. rough handling can cause objects to break.

54. Evidence that infants lack a mature concept of object permanence comes from:
    a. the A-not-B effect.
    b. the fact that young infants don't seem concerned when a toy they were looking at with delight disappears from view.
    c. the fact that young infants who watch a cloth being placed over a toy don't attempt to uncover the toy.
    d. all of the above.

Answer: c
Piaget's theory of cognitive development
p. 547

55. The A-not-B effect:
   a. is evidence that infants have a mature concept of object permanence.
   b. refers to the fact that infants don't seem concerned when a toy they've been looking at disappears.
   c. refers to the fact that at a certain age, infants who have watched a toy hidden several times in the same location will continue to search in that location even after they watch the toy hidden in a different location.
   d. occurs during the preoperational stage.

Answer: a
Piaget's theory of cognitive development
pp. 547–548

56. For Piaget, schemas are
   a. organized patterns of behavior.
   b. reflexes that disappear after several months.
   c. isolated units of behavior that are gradually replaced by assimilations.
   d. isolated units of behavior that are gradually replaced by accommodations.

Answer: a
Piaget's theory of cognitive development
p. 548

57. The development of a schema involves modifications and alterations in response to the environment. Piaget believed the infant _____ her schema to the environment.
   a. accommodates
   b. assimilates
   c. integrates
   d. incorporates

Answer: a
Piaget's theory of cognitive development
p. 548

58. Which of the following would be an example of assimilation?
   a. A child deforms a ball somewhat in order to grasp it the same way he grasps a block.
   b. The child changes his grip so that he can grasp a ball in the same way that he grasps a block.
   c. A child develops a new schema of bouncing, and now deals with a ball differently than with a block.
   d. A child reorganizes his thinking in order to integrate his experiences with blocks, ball, and other solid objects.
   e. all of the above

Answer: a
Piaget's theory of cognitive development
p. 548

59. When a child interprets a novel event or object in terms of the information he already possesses, the child is exhibiting:
   a. assimilation.
   b. accommodation.
   c. maturation.
   d. egocentrism.

Answer: a
Piaget's theory of cognitive development
p. 548

60. According to Piaget, accommodation:
   a. takes place when current schemas are modified to deal with new objects or events.
   b. occurs when new objects or events are modified so that they can be handled by current schemas.
   c. refers to the development of new schemas when the child's internal logic is reorganized.
   d. refers to experiences with the environment that are inconsistent with the child's current logic system.

Answer: e
Piaget's theory of cognitive development
pp. 548–549

61. According to Piaget, the ability to form mental representations is evidenced in the infant by:
    a. the development of object permanence.
    b. deferred imitation.
    c. the development of sensorimotor schemas.
    d. all of the above
    e. a and b only

Answer: d
Piaget's theory of cognitive development
pp. 547–549

62. During the sensory-motor period, infants develop:
    a. the knowledge that objects exist independent of immediate perception or action upon them.
    b. the ability to imitate an action that occurred in the past.
    c. the rudiments of representational thought.
    d. all of the above

Answer: d
Piaget's theory of cognitive development
p. 549

63. As Piaget uses the term, *deferred imitation* is:
    a. genuine imitation that comes rather belatedly in the course of the child's cognitive development.
    b. illustrated by a child imitating an adult sticking out his tongue.
    c. a result of the comparative absence of representations during the sensory-motor stage.
    d. illustrated when a child imitates an action that took place in the past.

Answer: a
Piaget's theory of cognitive development
pp. 548–549

64. According to your text, both object permanence and deferred imitation:
    a. demonstrate the existence of internal representations.
    b. occur within the first month after birth.
    c. require the development of psychomotor coordination.
    d. first appear in the preoperational stage.

Answer: d
Piaget's theory of cognitive development
p. 549

65. A child in the preoperational stage of cognitive development:
    a. has yet to develop object permanence.
    b. is probably anywhere from 7 to 11 years of age.
    c. performs cognitively in a way qualitatively similar to adults.
    d. is beginning to organize menal representations.

Answer: a
Piaget's theory of cognitive development
pp. 549–550

66. Conservation refers to:
    a. the appreciation that certain properties of an object remain constant despite some perceptual changes in the object.
    b. the belief that the height of a column of liquid is the sole determinant of the liquid's total volume.
    c. the fact that the preoperational child is incapable of performing certain perceptual transformations in his head.
    d. the fact that preoperational children cannot preserve thoughts about other people.

Answer: c
Piaget's theory of cognitive development
pp. 549–550

67. A child complains to his mother that he wants more soda. The mother takes the amount of soda the child has in his glass and pours it into a taller but narrower glass. The child is now content that he has more soda. This child has failed to develop:
    a. object permanence.
    b. visual perspective taking.
    c. conservation of quantity.
    d. class inclusion.

Answer: a
Piaget's theory of cognitive development
pp. 549–550

68. A child is shown two equal amounts of water in separate glasses. One is a tall, thin glass and the other a short, wide glass. When the child is asked "which glass has more water," the person asking the question is measuring the child's ability to:
    a. conserve quantity.
    b. classify.
    c. conserve number.
    d. perceive.

Answer: a
Piaget's theory of cognitive development
p. 550

69. In a conservation problem a child grasps the principle that liquid may change form as it is poured from one container to another, but its volume does not change since it can be poured back into its original container. The child comprehends the concept of:
    a. reversibility.
    b. egocentrism.
    c. object permanence.
    d. conservation of number.

Answer: a
Piaget's theory of cognitive development
p. 550

70. A 4-year-old child is shown a row of 7 red checkers. He is asked to place a black checker immediately adjacent to each red one. Upon doing so, the child agrees that there are as many red as black checkers. The experimenter then spreads out the black checkers so that they lie in a line larger than the red checkers. The child is asked if there are more red or black checkers. The child will answer:
    a. black checkers.
    b. red checkers.
    c. that there are the same number of each.
    d. The child will be too confused to answer.

Answer: a
Piaget's theory of cognitive development
p. 550

71. A child who doesn't conserve quantity does not have an appreciation of the concept of:
    a. reversibility.
    b. accuracy.
    c. object permanence.
    d. weight.

Answer: d
Piaget's theory of cognitive development
pp. 550–551

72. Piaget would explain the preoperational child's inability to conserve by saying that:
    a. they focus on one dimension of an object to the exclusion of others.
    b. they do not yet fully comprehend that certain transformations are reversible.
    c. in social situations, they act in an egocentric fashion.
    d. a or b

73. Preoperational children are unable to understand that points of view besides their own exist. Piaget calls such thinking:
    a. egotistical.
    b. egocentric.
    c. self-reference.
    d. conservation.

74. A characteristic of preoperational thought in which a child doesn't recognize other points of view is called:
    a. conservation.
    b. assimilation.
    c. egocentrism.
    d. object permanence.

75. As Piaget uses the term, "egocentrism" is:
    a. another word for *selfishness*.
    b. a manifestation of the child's inability to form representations.
    c. the child's inability to reverse transformations mentally.
    d. the child's difficulty in recognizing that there are different points of view.

76. Piaget describes an experiment in which a 5-year-old child sees a 3-dimensional model of a mountain scene. A doll is placed at various locations around the model and the child must describe what the doll sees. The results show that the child describes _____, which Piaget interprets as indicating _____.
    a. what the child can see; failure at conservation of direction
    b. what the child can see; egocentrism
    c. what the doll can see; failure at conservation of direction
    d. what the doll can see; egocentrism

77. A child views a small table on which is arranged a number of objects. When asked to describe how the model would look to someone standing on the opposite side of the table, the child describes the table as it appears from where he is standing. This result is most clearly an example of:
    a. irreversibility.
    b. concrete operations.
    c. egocentrism.
    d. conservation failure.

78. Which of the following is characteristic of the period of concrete operations as described by Piaget? A child:
    a. demonstrates an inability to conserve number.
    b. compares a heavy weight suspended from a long string and a light weight suspended from a short string and concludes that the speed of a pendulum's swing depends solely upon its weight.
    c. understands that adding 1 to any even number must always produce a number that is odd
    d. b and c

Answer: c
Piaget's theory of cognitive development
p. 552

79. When a child is able to understand that adding 1 to 6 makes an odd number but cannot grasp that 1 added to any even number makes it odd, the child according to Piaget is in the:
    a.   sensory-motor period.
    b.   preoperational period.
    c.   concrete operations period.
    d.   formal operations period.

Answer: c
Piaget's theory of cognitive development
p. 552

80. Which of the following indicates the presence of formal operations as Piaget uses the term?
    a.   the recognition that 4, 6, and 8 are even numbers and that (4 + 1), (6 + 1), and (8 + 1) are odd numbers
    b.   conservation of number and liquid quantity
    c.   ability to entertain hypothetical questions
    d.   egocentrism

Answer: d
Piaget's theory of cognitive development
p. 552

81. According to Piaget, the child reaches the _____ stage when he can understand symbols and abstractions of thought.
    a.   preoperational
    b.   sensory-motor
    c.   concrete operational
    d.   formal operational

Answer: b
Piaget's theory of cognitive development
p. 552

82. A child is given 2 bottles of chemicals, 2 measuring cups, and many mixing bowls, and is asked to determine in what proportions the chemicals must be mixed to cause a small (harmless) explosion. The child takes 1/2 cup of one chemical and adds 1/8 cup of the other, then another 1/8 cup, and so on, until the mixture explodes. This child is most likely in the:
    a.   concrete operational period.
    b.   formal operational period.
    c.   sensory-motor period.
    d.   preoperational period.

Answer: a
Piaget's theory of cognitive development
p. 552

83. A child is given 2 bottles of chemicals, 2 measuring cups, and many mixing bowls, and is asked to determine in what proportions the chemicals must be mixed to cause a small (harmless) explosion. The child takes 1/2 cup of one chemical and adds 1/8 cup of the other. When that doesn't work, he tries 1/4 cup of the first chemical and adds one cup of the second. He keeps trying random combinations until the mixture explodes. This child is most likely in the:
    a.   concrete operational period.
    b.   formal operational period.
    c.   sensory-motor period.
    d.   preoperational period.

Answer: c
What is the cognitive starting point?
p. 553

84. Research with the visual cliff apparatus demonstrates that six-month-old infants:
    a.   lack a sense of object permanence.
    b.   have a sense of object permanence.
    c.   are able to use depth cues.
    d.   have an understanding of occlusion.

374 | *Physical and Cognitive Development [13]*

Answer: b
What is the cognitive starting point?
p. 553

85. When a six-month-old infant is placed on the center board of a visual cliff apparatus:
    a. she will be more willing to crawl over the deep side than the shallow side to get to her mother.
    b. she will be more willing to crawl over the shallow side than the deep side to get to her mother.
    c. she will be equally willing to crawl over either side to get to her mother.
    d. she will be unwilling to leave the center board.

Answer: b
What is the cognitive starting point?
pp. 553–555

86. Studies of infants' reactions to partly occluded objects:
    a. support Piaget's view that infants have no understanding of object permanence during the sensory-motor stage.
    b. indicate that infants as young as four months understand that a partly occluded object (such as a rod) is whole, even though they cannot see all of it.
    c. indicate that infants younger than 8 months do not understand that a partly occluded object (such as a rod) is a single whole rather than two separate objects.
    d. both a and c

Answer: a
What is the cognitive starting point?
pp. 553–555

87. Studies of infants' understanding of occlusion of one object by another suggest that:
    a. the infant understands that the parts of objects are connected, even when hidden.
    b. the infant must have extensive experience with overlapping objects before understanding that the parts of objects remain connected even when hidden.
    c. infants at four months of age are not surprised when a rod hidden behind a block is shown to be made up of two separate parts.
    d. 4-month-old infants lack a sense of object permanence.

Answer: b
What is the cognitive starting point?
pp. 554–555

88. Recent research using the habituation technique with infants suggests that:
    a. Piaget's observations of infant behavior were incorrect; infants do search for hidden objects.
    b. the inferences Piaget drew from his observations of infant behavior were wrong; infants have some concept of objects as independent, unitary entities.
    c. infants develop object permanence later than Piaget thought.
    d. the development of object permanence is very much as Piaget described it.

89. Studies of infants' reactions to physically possible and physically impossible events indicated that infants:
    a. were equally surprised by both sorts of events, indicating that they had no idea that two objects cannot occupy the same space at the same time.
    b. were more surprised by impossible events, indicating that they understood that two objects cannot occupy the same space at the same time.
    c. were equally uninterested in both possible and impossible events, indicating that they saw the world as a place in which the basic relationships between objects could change from moment to moment.
    d. showed more of an interest in the possible event, presumably because it was familiar.

90. Which of the following is false?
    a. Infants have a concept that two objects cannot occupy the same space at the same time.
    b. Infants know that, even when temporarily occluded, objects keep their size and shape.
    c. Infants have no concept of object permanence.
    d. Although infants may know that objects exist, they do not always search for them.

91. Recent explanations of the A-not-B effect observed by Piaget suggest that:
    a. infants may understand that objects exist, but lack the skills necessary to search for them.
    b. infants may be unable to inhibit a dominant (previously reinforced) reaching pattern, even when it is wrong.
    c. infants may look at the correct location of a hidden object even while they are reaching for an incorrect location.
    d. all of the above
    e. a and c only

92. The A-not-B effect:
    a. may be due to the immaturity of a particular region of the prefrontal cortex.
    b. has been found only in human infants.
    c. is probably due to the fact that infants don't know where the object is currently located.
    d. all of the above

93. Recent studies on children's understanding of number ("threeness or "fiveness") indicate that:
    a. Piaget was correct in arguing that this concept is not acquired until late in the preoperational stage.
    b. this understanding appears at about the age of 4, several years earlier than Piaget expected.
    c. this understanding has been observed in infants less than 7 months of age.
    d. this concept seems to be acquired nearly a year later than Piaget predicted.
    e. none of the above

Answer: b
What is the cognitive starting point?
pp. 556–557

94. In a recent habituation study, infants under 6 months of age were shown a series of slides, each showing 3 objects. After habituation had taken place, the infants were shown additional slides, some containing 3 objects, others containing only 2 objects. The results indicated that:
    a. the infants showed renewed interest in the slides containing three objects after they were intermixed with slides showing two objects.
    b. the infants looked longer at the slides of two objects, indicating that they saw them as novel.
    c. the infants showed no interest in either of the slides, indicating that the just-noticeable difference for number at this age is greater than 1 object.
    d. the infants' looking time was determined by what the objects in the slides were rather than by how many there were.

Answer: d
What is the cognitive starting point?
pp. 556–557

95. Recent studies of the infant's understanding of number indicate that:
    a. infants around the age of six months seem to have an understanding of "threeness" versus "twoness."
    b. infants apparently have a rudimentary understanding of addition.
    c. infants apparently have a rudimentary understanding of subtraction.
    d. all of the above

Answer: a
What is the cognitive starting point?
pp. 556–557

96. Which of the following statements is false?
    a. Infants need to be able to count out loud before they can understand anything about addition.
    b. Six-month-old infants seem to have some understanding of "threeness" as distinct from "twoness".
    c. It is possible to test preverbal infants for a basic understanding of subtraction.
    d. b and c

Answer: d
What is the cognitive starting point?
pp. 557–558

97. A number of studies have examined the infant's awareness of the existence of other human minds. These studies indicate that:
    a. within minutes of birth, infants seem to have a preference for human faces over other sorts of patterns.
    b. nine-month-old infants tend to look in the direction of their mother's gaze.
    c. eighteen-month-old infants who are prevented from following their mothers' gaze will look where she had been looking as soon as they are allowed to do so.
    d. all of the above

Answer: e
Cognitive development in preschoolers
pp. 558–559

98. As Piaget used the term, a developmental stage:
    a. generally involves discrete developmental plateaus rather than slow and continuous change.
    b. involves qualitative rather than quantitative differences in the individual's ability.
    c. always occurs at the same age in every child.
    d. all of the above
    e. a and b only

Answer: a
Cognitive development in preschoolers
p. 559

99. Recent analyses of Piaget's theory of cognitive development have emphasized that:
    a. the child's transition from one stage to the next may not be as abrupt as originally proposed by Piaget.
    b. conservation tasks are the only way of evaluating understanding of number in very young children.
    c. there are no stages of cognitive development beyond the age of four; once children are about four years of age, their cognitive abilities are qualitatively similar to that of adults.
    d. the ability to count is one of the best indicators of the level of cognitive development.

Answer: b
Cognitive development in preschoolers
p. 559

100. Studies of how young children count and use counting words indicate that:
    a. children who use idiosyncratic counting sequences (e.g., "one", "two", "fourteen") tend to use them inconsistently, indicating that they do not yet understand counting.
    b. children who use idiosyncratic counting sequences tend to use them consistently, indicating that they understand the basics of counting.
    c. whether they use idiosyncratic counting sequences or not, children under the age of five do not understand the one-to-one relationship between objects and numbers that is the basis of counting.
    d. both a and c

Answer: a
Cognitive development in preschoolers
p. 560

101. According to your text, recent studies suggest that Piaget's methods may have led him to underestimate the understanding of number conservation in young children. In particular:
    a. children tend to change their answers when asked the same question twice ("Does this row have more or less than this row?").
    b. children easily confuse "more" and "less" to mean "longer" and "shorter".
    c. children may forget the question in the time it takes the experimenter to rearrange the items in one row.
    d. all of the above

Answer: d
Cognitive development in preschoolers
pp. 560–561

102. The adult "theory of mind" includes the idea that:
    a. all people have beliefs and desires.
    b. the beliefs and desires of others are not necessarily the same as our own.
    c. that beliefs can be true or false.
    d. all of the above

Answer: c
Cognitive development in preschoolers
p. 561

103. In a recent study, three-year-olds were asked to show a photograph to their mother, who was seated opposite them. They turned the picture so that it faced the mother. This finding is an argument against Piaget's theory of:
    a. conservation.
    b. animism.
    c. egocentrism.
    d. higher-order schemas.

Answer: d
Cognitive development in preschoolers
pp. 561–562

104. Evidence for a developing theory of mind in children comes from the observation that:
    a. 2- and 3-year-olds hide things, indicating an understanding of how others perceive objects.
    b. 2- to 3-year-olds can predict the behavior of another child if they know what that child wants.
    c. 3-year-olds understand that others may see something different from what they themselves see.
    d. all of the above

Answer: c
Cognitive development in preschoolers
p. 562

105. A 3-year-old is told 2 stories. In both she is told that Bart wants a pretzel and that Bart believes pretzels are in the cabinet. In the first story she is told that pretzels are actually in the cabinet, but in the second she is told that Bart's mother moved the pretzels to a drawer without Bart's knowledge. When asked to predict Bart's behavior in both stories, the child will most likely:
    a. predict that Bart will go to the drawer in both stories.
    b. predict that Bart will go to the cabinet in both stories.
    c. predict that Bart will go to the cabinet in the first story and the drawer in the second.
    d. be unable to say what Bart will do next.

Answer: c
Cognitive development in preschoolers
p. 562

106. A 3-year-old and a 5-year-old watch Megan and Danika hide a cookie in a yellow box. They then watch Megan leave and Danika move the cookie to a blue box. When asked where Megan will look for the cookie, most likely:
    a. both children will say, "the yellow box".
    b. both children will say, "the blue box".
    c. the older child will say, "the yellow box"; the younger child will say, "the blue box".
    d. the younger child will say, "the yellow box"; the older child will say, "the blue box".

Answer: b
Cognitive development in preschoolers
pp. 561–562

107. Research on the child's theory of mind indicates that:
    a. 3-year-olds have an adult theory of mind.
    b. Piaget greatly overestimated egocentrism in young children.
    c. 3-year-olds have not begun to develop a theory of mind.
    d. a and b

Answer: e
Cognitive development in preschoolers
p. 562

108. A theory:
    a. serves as a basis for predictions.
    b. accounts for data.
    c. has interrelated claims.
    d. has a specific domain of application.
    e. all of the above

Answer: b
Cognitive development in preschoolers
p. 562

109. According to your textbook:
   a. it makes no sense to speak of preschoolers having theories.
   b. preschoolers have some ability to understand and predict the behavior of others.
   c. preschoolers may have a rudimentary theory of mind, but they do not seem to have theories in any other domain.
   d. the "theory" in "theory of mind" has no relation to the theories that scientists hold.

Answer: e
Cognitive development in preschoolers
p. 563

110. In evaluating the evidence concerning Piaget's stages of intellectual development your text notes that:
   a. there is no clear evidence of a sequence of cognitive milestones.
   b. although young children may understand the basics of concrete operations, an older child can apply these insights to a wider range of problems.
   c. although 3-year-olds can tell the difference between 2 and 3 objects regardless of how they are spaced, they do not understand the general principle that number is always independent of arrangement.
   d. all of the above
   e. b and c only

Answer: d
Cognitive development in preschoolers
p. 563

111. What is the difference between a 4-year-old who has some understanding of conservation of number and an 8-year-old who has an understanding of it?
   a. The older child can apply his knowledge to a wider range of problems.
   b. The younger child's conservation abilities are only isolated pockets of knowledge.
   c. The younger child needs simplification of the task to perform well; for the older child, no simplification is necessary.
   d. all of the above

Answer: c
The causes of cognitive growth
p. 564

112. According to the maturational account of cognitive development:
   a. the environment is irrelevant to cognitive development.
   b. all developmental milestones should be reached at the same age across diverse cultures.
   c. developmental milestones are genetically programmed to occur in the same order across diverse cultures.
   d. all of the above

Answer: b
The causes of cognitive growth
p. 564

113. Evidence consistent with the nativist approach to cognitive development comes from the observation that:
   a. there are wide differences across cultures in the order in which children reach various milestones of cognitive development.
   b. there is consistency across cultures in the order in which children reach various milestones of cognitive development.
   c. there is no correlation between the rate of cognitive development and the rate of physical development.
   d. both b and c

Answer: c
The causes of cognitive growth
p. 565

114. Empiricists argue that:
    a. all developmental milestones should be reached at the same age across diverse cultures.
    b. the environment is irrelevant to cognitive development.
    c. the principles of learning theory explain cognitive development.
    d. developmental milestones are genetically programmed to occur in the same order across diverse cultures.

Answer: c
The causes of cognitive growth
p. 566

115. Piaget argued that progression through his stages:
    a. is completely due to specific experiences.
    b. normally occurs at particular ages, but could happen years earlier.
    c. is dependent on intellectual readiness.
    d. varies dramatically across cultures.

Answer: d
The causes of cognitive growth
p. 566

116. Piaget's notions of assimilation and accommodation:
    a. emphasize the importance of genetic programming for cognitive development.
    b. are part of his nativist approach to cognitive development.
    c. emphasize the role of conditioning and reinforcement in cognitive development.
    d. emphasize the interaction between the organism and the environment.
    e. a and b

Answer: b
The causes of cognitive growth
pp. 565–566

117. Research examining whether training can influence intellectual development has found that:
    a. attempts to teach conservation to nonconservers have produced permanent improvements in performance on such tasks.
    b. Mexican children who had worked extensively with clay performed better on mass conservation tasks than North American children of the same age.
    c. children given practice pouring fluids between jars of various shapes and sizes achieve both fluid and mass conservation significantly earlier than children without such experience.
    d. all of the above

Answer: d
The causes of cognitive growth
pp. 566–567

118. _____ approach to cognitive development emphasizes the cognitive resources (e.g., attentional and memory skills) that children bring to tasks.
    a. Piaget's
    b. The maturational
    c. The empiricist
    d. The information-processing

Answer: e
The causes of cognitive growth
p. 567

119. In discussing memory in young children, your text points out that:
    a. infants remember in the sense that they can retain and perform an instrumental response several weeks after having learned it.
    b. a child's memory span is roughly equal to the child's age until about the age of 5.
    c. children do not have explicit memory until the age of 6 or 7 years.
    d. all of the above
    e. a and b only

Answer: b
The causes of cognitive growth
p. 567

120. In infancy:
    a. memory cannot be assessed.
    b. implicit memories can be retained for at least several weeks.
    c. memory capacity is the same as in preschool years.
    d. the only clear evidence of memory comes from the infant's apparent recognition of familiar faces.

Answer: d
The causes of cognitive growth
p. 567

121. Research suggests that a 6-year-old who is an avid baseball fan:
    a. will remember details of a baseball game she has watched better than will an accompanying adult who does not follow baseball.
    b. will remember details of a baseball game she has watched as well as will an accompanying 6-year-old who does not follow baseball.
    c. will show better memory for things related to baseball than for things in other domains.
    d. a and c

Answer: a
The causes of cognitive growth
pp. 567–568

122. The "child-as-novice" argument suggests that:
    a. children's memory appears worse than it really is because they have so little context for their experiences.
    b. improvements in children's memory are due solely to motivation.
    c. a child's memory performance will be the same in each domain.
    d. b and c

Answer: d
The causes of cognitive growth
pp. 567–568

123. Children are generally thought to have poorer memory skills than adults. Your text points out that:
    a. memory span in children increases steadily between the ages of about 1 and 5 years.
    b. children before the age of 2 are using relatively sophisticated rehearsal strategies to keep information in memory.
    c. genuine rehearsal does not appear until about the age of 5 or 6 years.
    d. both a and c

Answer: b
The causes of cognitive growth
p. 568

124. Some three-year-old children watch while an experimenter hides a toy dog under one of two containers. The children are told to remember where the dog is until the experimenter returns. Which of the following is not one of the memory strategies we would expect these children to use?
    a. Looking at the hiding place and nodding yes.
    b. Explicitly rehearsing the location of the toy.
    c. Looking at the wrong container and nodding no.
    d. Keeping their hand on the correct container.

Answer: a
The causes of cognitive growth
pp. 568–569

125. Genuine rehearsal first occurs spontaneously at age _____.
    a. 5 or 6
    b. 2 or 3
    c. 10 or 11
    d. 8 or 9

Answer: c
The causes of cognitive growth
pp. 568–569

126. In a study of memory in 5-, 7-, and 10-year-olds, research participants were required to remember three objects after an interval during which a "space helmet" prevented them from seeing the objects. The results showed that:
   a. older children recalled no better when they could not see the items than did the younger children.
   b. although older children used no obvious rehearsal strategies, the fact that they recalled better indicates the importance of brain maturation in memory capacity.
   c. older children were rehearsing the items by silently mouthing their names to themselves over and over.
   d. all of the children were equally likely to use rehearsal.

Answer: b
The causes of cognitive growth
pp. 568–569

127. Studies that have attempted to train young children to use rehearsal in a memory task have found that:
   a. the children were not able to learn to rehearse.
   b. the children successfully rehearsed on the task for which they were trained, but did not spontaneously apply the newly learned strategy to other tasks.
   c. the children rehearsed on the task for which they were trained, but their efforts weren't successful, so they gave up on rehearsal.
   d. the children successfully rehearsed on the task for which they were trained and spontaneously applied the newly learned strategy to other tasks.

Answer: c
The causes of cognitive growth
p. 569

128. *Metacognition* means:
   a. complex mental functioning.
   b. adult mental functioning.
   c. thinking about mental functioning.
   d. poorly developed mental functioning.

Answer: d
The causes of cognitive growth
p. 569

129. People with good metacognition skills will:
   a. have strategies for remembering.
   b. be able to assess when they have learned something and when they still need to study.
   c. be able to predict their memory performance.
   d. all of the above

Answer: b
The causes of cognitive growth
p. 569

130. Children:
   a. generally have metacognitive skills equal to those of adults.
   b. have smaller memory spans than adults.
   c. can predict their memory performance as accurately as adults can.
   d. all of the above

Answer: e
Cognitive development from a
   cross-cultural perspective
pp. 570–571

131. In assessing evidence of cross-cultural differences in cognitive development, your text notes that:
   a. the lives of people in most cultures do not require abstract thought or reasoning.
   b. people who do poorly on Piagetian cognitive tasks often show remarkable intellectual abilities in the context of their own lives.
   c. Piagetian tasks, like object classification, may be interpreted differently by people from other cultures.
   d. all of the above
   e. b and c only

Answer: c
Cognitive development from a
   cross-cultural perspective
p. 571

132. When unschooled Russian peasants from central Asia were asked to pick from four pictures the three that belonged together:
   a. their performance showed that they did not understand the concept of grouping.
   b. they chose according to an abstract semantic category.
   c. they chose concretely and functionally, picking three objects that would be used or found together.
   d. they based their choice on what they thought the experimenter wanted, rather than on their own natural or abstract categories.

Answer: d
Cognitive development from a
   cross-cultural perspective
pp. 570–571

133. In assessing cross-cultural differences in cognitive development, your text notes that:
   a. many such differences are related to the amount of schooling that individuals have.
   b. some such differences are artifacts of the procedures we employ to test cognitive development.
   c. some such differences come from interpreting nonwestern behavior using our Western ideas.
   d. all of the above
   e. a and c only

Answer: b
Cognitive development from a
   cross-cultural perspective
pp. 570–571

134. How would unschooled Kpelle participants in Liberia group the following objects: scissors, wood, knife, paper, axe, pear, razor, beard?
   a. scissors, knife; razor, axe; wood, paper; pear, beard
   b. scissors, paper; razor, beard; axe, wood; knife, pear
   c. They wouldn't be able to group the objects.
   d. scissors, knife, axe, razor; wood, paper; pear, beard

Answer: e
Cognitive development from a
   cross-cultural perspective
p. 571

135. Many cross-cultural differences in cognitive performance are related to schooling. Your text suggests that:
   a. schooled people are more likely to understand what the experimenter wants.
   b. Western schools teach that concepts and rules can be applied to a variety of situations and problems.
   c. it is the structure of schooling (obedience, order, and discipline) rather than its specific content, that is most important in producing formal operational thought.
   d. all of the above
   e. a and b only

Answer: a
Cognitive development from a
   cross-cultural perspective
pp. 570–571

136. Which of the following inferences is best-supported by cross-cultural research?
   a. Standard measures of concrete and formal operations may not provide the best way of assessing complex and abstract thinking.
   b. Many nonwestern adults cannot think with any greater complexity or abstractness than can western children.
   c. Formal schooling does nothing to encourage abstract thinking.
   d. Non-Westerners often respond to classification tasks in ways that make no sense.

CHAPTER 14

Social Development

1. Attachment:
   a. lasts only until the infant is able to move away from the mother.
   b. is found in many species.
   c. only occurs between infant and mother.
   d. all of the above

2. Sigmund Freud suggested that the infant becomes attached to the mother because:
   a. the mother provides the child with emotional satisfaction.
   b. the mother is a source of familiarity.
   c. the mother satisfies the child's basic needs, such as hunger.
   d. the mother is the first sexual object.
   e. the child innately responds to certain stimulus attributes.

3. The _____ theory of mother love suggests that the infant's attachment to its mother is associated with the satisfaction of basic needs such as hunger and thirst.
   a. externality
   b. attachment
   c. conditioned
   d. cupboard

4. John Bowlby argues that fear of _____ is a major cause of attachment.
   a. of adults
   b. of the unfamiliar
   c. of the dark
   d. of starvation
   e. being alone

Answer: a
Attachment
p. 576

5. Bowlby argues that attachment is due to:
   a. the infant's built-in tendency to seek contact with an adult and to fear the unfamiliar.
   b. the fact that the mother attends to the infant's basic needs like food and warmth.
   c. the fact that the mother carries the infant everywhere and the infant gets used to that closeness.
   d. the emotional satisfaction that the mother provides.

Answer: c
Attachment
p. 576

6. According to Bowlby, fear of the unfamiliar:
   a. must be learned.
   b. makes attachments more difficult to form.
   c. may keep a young organism alive.
   d. makes a young organism more susceptible to predation.

Answer: b
Attachment
p. 577

7. When a child clings to an adult:
   a. that adult must be a kind and sensitive caregiver.
   b. that adult may have hit the child numerous times.
   c. that adult is equally likely to be a stranger or a caregiver to the child.
   d. the child probably has some physical need (e.g., hunger or a dirty diaper) to be dealt with.

Answer: b
Attachment
p. 577

8. Harlow's experiments with baby monkeys showed that:
   a. when frightened, infants flock to a food-producing "mother."
   b. when frightened, infant monkeys prefer "contact comfort" above food.
   c. rhesus monkeys don't show attachment behaviors.
   d. mother ducks could successfully rear baby monkeys once the monkeys had imprinted.

Answer: d
Attachment
p. 577

9. Harlow reared monkeys with two artificial "mothers," one terry cloth and one wire. When only the wire mother provided food, the baby monkeys:
   a. seemed fearful and confused the two mothers.
   b. developed abnormalities in social relations which were not present if it was the terry-cloth mother that provided the milk.
   c. preferred the wire mother most of the time, especially when frightened.
   d. showed a strong preference for the terry-cloth mother.

Answer: c
Attachment
p. 577

10. Harlow's experiments with baby monkeys show:
    a. that, as Freud believed, a mother's main function for a baby is to satisfy the bodily needs.
    b. imprinting, as examined by Lorenz in ducklings, occurs in primates, too.
    c. baby monkeys value contact comfort over food.
    d. baby monkeys will cling to wire mothers only in fearful situations.

11. Harlow's studies of infant monkeys raised with surrogate mothers indicated that infants became attached to the surrogate mother:
    a. from which food was most often delivered.
    b. that provided the most contact comfort.
    c. that was present when danger threatened.
    d. that was present for the greatest amount of time.

12. Harlow studied the role of surrogate mothers in comforting the infant monkey during times of danger or stress. He found that:
    a. neither the wire mother nor the cloth mother were effective in comforting the infant during times of stress.
    b. the cloth mother, but not the wire mother, was effective in comforting the infant during times of stress.
    c. both the wire mother and the cloth mother comforted the infant during times of stress, but the cloth mother was more effective.
    d. only the mother (wire or cloth) that had furnished nourishment to the infant was effective in comforting the infant during times of stress.

13. Which of the following is the strongest evidence against Freud's theory that an infant's attachment to his mother is caused merely by a fear that the infant's bodily needs won't get met?
    a. A human infant is more likely to approach a stranger while his or her mother is present.
    b. Ducklings can be imprinted early in life to follow any object that moves in a manner similar to a duck.
    c. In the laboratory, an infant monkey who is frightened will more readily cling to a terry cloth figure that provides contact comfort than to a wire one that provides food.
    d. Both monkey and human infants that are raised in a motherless environment are withdrawn and tend to sit alone and rock back and forth.

14. Based on Harlow's research with monkeys, what is the most helpful thing you can do for a frightened infant or child?
    a. Leave him alone.
    b. Offer him something good to eat.
    c. Talk to him.
    d. Touch or hold him.

15. Harlow's work with terry cloth and wire mothers is closely associated with which of the following concepts?
    a. modeling
    b. accommodation
    c. stranger anxiety
    d. attachment

16. Studies of imprinting in ducks conducted by Konrad Lorenz indicated that:
    a. the duckling's maximum sensitivity to imprinting occurs about 15 hours after hatching.
    b. ducklings can be imprinted on inanimate objects.
    c. a duckling imprinted on an inanimate object will still recognize and return to its mother if it sees her within 3 or 4 days after imprinting has occurred.
    d. all of the above
    e. a and b only

Answer: e
Attachment
p. 578

17. The relatively brief sensitive period for imprinting in ducks has been attributed to:
    a. a decline in the plasticity of the duckling's brain that is somehow tied to a physiological clock.
    b. the fact that by the end of this time the duckling has learned to fear new objects.
    c. the fact that by 24–36 hours after hatching, the duckling can feed independently.
    d. all of the above
    e. a and b only

Answer: e
Attachment
pp. 578–579

18. Professor Bird finds that a recently hatched chick follows her around the lab all of the time. This following is most likely due to:
    a. the effects of prenatal sex hormones.
    b. incentive behavior.
    c. the contact comfort that Professor Bird supplies.
    d. imprinting.

Answer: d
Attachment
p. 578

19. Which of the following statements is false?
    a. Ducklings will imprint on the first thing they see for more than a few minutes.
    b. Ducklings imprinted on a triangle will show distress if they are separated from the triangle.
    c. Within several days of imprinting, ducklings demonstrate fear for all new objects.
    d. There is a *sensitive* (rather than *critical*) period for ducking imprinting.

Answer: a
Attachment
pp. 578–579

20. Research on imprinting in humans:
    a. indicates a sensitive period for forming mother-child attachments.
    b. demonstrates that it's very important for mothers and newborns to interact right after birth.
    c. indicates that normal attachments can form at various points in infancy.
    d. a and b

Answer: c
Attachment
p. 579

21. At what age will an infant first display separation anxiety?
    a. 6–8 months
    b. 2–3 months
    c. 3–5 months
    d. 10–12 months

Answer: a
Patterns of attachment
p. 579

Answer: d
Patterns of attachment
pp. 579–580

22. The most common way of assessing attachment in human infants is to:
    a. have the child track a picture of the mother with her eyes.
    b. see if the child smiles at the picture of her mother.
    c. determine the predominant child-rearing style of the parents.
    d. see how distressed the child is when separated from her mother.

Answer: b
Patterns of attachment
pp. 579–580

23. The *Strange Situation* is a procedure designed by Ainsworth to assess children's:
    a. novelty seeking.
    b. attachment.
    c. social skills.
    d. moral reasoning.
    e. information-processing abilities.

Answer: c
Patterns of attachment
pp. 579–580

24. In Mary Ainsworth's *Strange Situation*, we are primarily interested in measuring or assessing:
    a. an infant's response to the presence of a stranger.
    b. a mother's behavior in response to an infant's distress.
    c. an infant's response to separation from and reunion with mother.
    d. the infant's response to several people, including his mother, the experimenter, and a stranger.

Answer: d
Patterns of attachment
pp. 579–580

25. In Ainsworth's studies with the so-called *Strange Situation,* children are classified as securely attached if they:
    a. stay close to the mother instead of exploring the toys.
    b. continue to play with toys and ignore the mother when she returns.
    c. do not show distress when the mother leaves.
    d. seem comfortable in the mother's presence, show some distress at her absence, and greet her return enthusiastically.

Answer: a
Patterns of attachment
pp. 579–580

26. According to Ainsworth, the reaction of securely attached infants to the departure and return of their mother in the *Strange Situation* is to show:
    a. some distress when she leaves, and enthusiasm when she returns.
    b. little distress when she leaves, and mild pleasure when she returns.
    c. little distress when she leaves, and little interest when she returns.
    d. considerable distress when she leaves, and enthusiasm when she returns.

Answer: c
Patterns of attachment
pp. 579–580

27. According to Ainsworth, the reaction of insecurely attached (anxious/resistant) infants in the *Strange Situation* is to show:
    a. little distress when mother leaves, but no pleasure or relief when she returns.
    b. considerable distress and panic when mother leaves, and great enthusiasm when she returns.
    c. considerable distress and panic when mother leaves, but emotional ambivalence when she returns.
    d. no concern when mother leaves, and no response when she returns.

28. According to Ainsworth, the reaction of insecurely attached (anxious/avoidant) infants in the *Strange Situation* is to show:
    a. some distress when mother leaves, and mild pleasure or relief when she returns.
    b. considerable distress and panic when mother leaves, and great enthusiasm when she returns.
    c. considerable distress and panic when mother leaves, but emotional ambivalence when she returns.
    d. little concern when mother leaves, and ignore her when she returns.

29. What effect does the presence of a mother to whom there is a secure attachment bond have on human infants in the *Strange Situation*?
    a. It promotes impulsiveness.
    b. It inspires exploration.
    c. It promotes clinging.
    d. It increases the fear of strangers.

30. In Ainsworth's *Strange Situation*, an infant who was mildly disturbed at the departure of his mother, but approached and was easily soothed by her upon her return would most likely be described as:
    a. securely attached.
    b. insecurely attached (anxious/avoidant).
    c. insecurely attached (anxious/resistant).
    d. insecurely attached (anxious/disorganized).

31. At 12 months of age, James is classified as securely attached. Which of the following behaviors in the *Strange Situation* would be most consistent with this classification?
    a. James is moderately distressed when mother leaves him alone, and pleased when she returns.
    b. James is unconcerned when his mother leaves, and uninterested when she returns.
    c. James is very upset when his mother leaves, and seems both relieved and angry when she returns.
    d. James is very upset when his mother leaves and ignores her when she returns.

32. According to Ainsworth, 3-and-a-half-year-old youngsters who were rated as securely attached at 15 months are least likely to be described as:
    a. outgoing.
    b. unfriendly.
    c. popular.
    d. well-adjusted.

33. Ainsworth explains the correlation between a child's attachment classification at one year and his adjustment in nursery school by arguing that:
    a. both sets of behaviors reflect a constancy in the way the mother treats the child.
    b. the early relationship with the mother shapes the child's later social relationships.
    c. both sets of behaviors reflect a consistency in the child's inborn temperament.
    d. a and c

34. Attachment theorists believe that the early relationship between mother and child causes later differences in social and emotional adjustment. However, your text points out that the relationship between early attachment and later development may be due to:
    a. the child's temperament, which may also remain consistent across the childhood years.
    b. the fact that the child's social environment is also very consistent across childhood.
    c. the quality of the Strange Situation experience itself.
    d. all of the above
    e. a and b only.

35. In comparing an infant's attachment to mother and father, we find that children tend to:
    a. prefer mother over father, since father is more likely than mother to discipline the child.
    b. prefer mother over father when they need care and comfort.
    c. prefer father over mother when they are looking for a playmate.
    d. both b and c

36. In comparing the difference between mothers' and fathers' interactions with young children your text notes that:
    a. fathers are more likely to discipline children than are mothers.
    b. fathers are more likely to play with infants than mothers are.
    c. fathers handle infants more vigorously than mothers do.
    d. all of the above
    e. b and c only

37. Fathers who are primary caregivers:
    a. show the same style of interaction with their children that mothers who are primary caregivers do.
    b. show the same style of interaction with their children that fathers who are secondary caregivers do.
    c. are more likely to interact with their children through physical play than are fathers who are secondary caregivers.
    d. have children who are less strongly attached to them than do mothers who are primary caregivers.

38. Bowlby argued that disruption of a child's initial attachment:
    a. will increase the child's ability to cope with problems throughout life.
    b. will have long-term negative consequences.
    c. will have no long-term effects.
    d. will increase the child's independence and self-reliance.

39. There has been much concern over the effects of early separation from mother, and of nonmaternal care. Your text notes that:
    a. children with more than 20 hours per week of nonmaternal care are more likely to show insecure patterns of attachment.
    b. children in day-care may be more independent and self-reliant than their non-day-care peers.
    c. children in day-care have been found to be higher in measures of sociability, persistence, and achievement than non-day-care peers.
    d. all of the above

40. Which of the following statements is false?
    a. High quality daycare is probably not detrimental to young children.
    b. Children who have been in poor quality daycare are less attentive and sociable than children who have been in high quality daycare.
    c. Most daycare centers in this country are considered "high quality".
    d. Children who have been in poor quality daycare have worse social and emotional development than children who have been in high quality daycare.

41. According to the textbook:
    a. parental divorce is detrimental to children.
    b. parental divorce may lead to later emotional difficulties.
    c. family life prior to parental divorce may lead to later emotional difficulties.
    d. b and c

42. Harlow found that monkeys who spend their first three months without human or animal contact and are then exposed to social contact:
    a. show minimal long-term effects of the early isolation.
    b. spend most of their time as adults rocking and biting themselves.
    c. are sexually incompetent as adults.
    d. demonstrate very disturbed parental behavior.
    e. b, c, and d

43. Rhesus monkeys raised in isolation for a year are _____ as adults.
    a. unusually aggressive toward their peers
    b. socially withdrawn and sexually incompetent
    c. extremely dependent and clinging
    d. especially affectionate parents

Answer: c
Patterns of attachment
pp. 585–586

44. Harlow found that when his isolated 1-year-old monkeys were exposed for the first time to age-mates, a year old, the isolated monkeys:
    a. showed an abnormally high level of active chasing and romping.
    b. were hypersexual.
    c. withdrew from contact, rocked, and bit themselves.
    d. clung to the normal monkeys and refused to let go.

Answer: e
Patterns of attachment
pp. 585–586

45. Harlow found that his isolated monkeys were deficient as adults, in:
    a. attaining full adult size.
    b. learning visual discrimination problems.
    c. developing parental behaviors.
    d. engaging in appropriate sexual behavior.
    e. c and d

Answer: d
Patterns of attachment
pp. 585–586

46. Harlow's work with socially deprived monkeys suggests that early social relationships directly affect:
    a. the quality of later peer relationships.
    b. later social and mating skills.
    c. the mature offspring's own maternal behavior.
    d. all of the above

Answer: d
Patterns of attachment
pp. 585–586

47. Harlow raised some monkeys with no contact with either monkeys or humans. The main effect on adult reproductive behavior was that these deprived monkeys:
    a. were hypersexual.
    b. were extra attentive to their own infants as a compensation for their deprivation.
    c. were only attentive to the infants of other monkeys, not to other adult monkeys.
    d. had trouble in both breeding and caring for their own infants.

Answer: b
Patterns of attachment
pp. 586–587

48. Human infants raised in orphanages under conditions of comparative social isolation:
    a. showed dramatic reductions in motor skills and social responsiveness that began as early as a few days after birth.
    b. tended to become apathetic towards others, and rarely approached adults.
    c. sometimes showed deficits in language and abstract thinking, but these disappeared by 4-6 years of age.
    d. all of the above

Answer: a
Patterns of attachment
pp. 586–587

49. Infants reared in institutions with very little social stimulation will probably be similar to normally reared children in:
    a. their social responsiveness during the first 3 or 4 months of life.
    b. their social adjustment between 3 and 6 years of age.
    c. their language development at 2 years of age.
    d. their adult intellectual attainments.

50. Research on children raised in institutions indicates that:
    a. spending early childhood in an orphanage is detrimental to intellectual and social development.
    b. the detrimental effects of orphanages initially appear after 2–3 weeks.
    c. children who spend their first few years in good quality orphanages suffer no apparent ill effects.
    d. human social development is quite different from that of other primates.

51. Harlow's experiments with monkeys suggest that the effects of early prolonged social isolation are:
    a. fixed and irreversible.
    b. mostly reversible through appropriate later experience.
    c. naturally outgrown.
    d. negligible.

52. The best therapy for the effects of social isolation in 6-month-old monkeys is to:
    a. allow them to attach to a warm terry-cloth mother.
    b. allow them to be with an adult female monkey who has lost her own infant.
    c. allow them ample contact with normal young monkeys about three months older than they are.
    d. put them in a cage with normal young monkeys about three months younger than they are.
    e. give them tranquilizers before introducing them to a normal group of young and adult monkeys.

53. In discussing the possibility of "rehabilitating" monkeys who experienced social isolation in infancy, your text notes that:
    a. no procedure or program has been found that will undo or reverse the detrimental effects of early social deprivation.
    b. monkey mothers who were isolated as infants were no less abusive to their second-born offspring than to their first-born offspring.
    c. the effects of early social deprivation seem to disappear without special treatment as animals mature into adulthood.
    d. monkeys raised in social isolation were much improved in their social behavior after being paired with younger monkeys whose clinging and persistence provided "therapy" for the isolates.

54. Female monkeys who were raised for a year in isolation would, if artificially inseminated:
    a. show normal maternal behaviors once they gave birth.
    b. show normal maternal behaviors toward their second offspring, but not their first.
    c. never show normal maternal behaviors.
    d. only show normal maternal behaviors if they had been forced to spend time with normal monkeys three months younger than themselves.

Answer: d
Patterns of attachment
p. 588

55. In one study, children from an overcrowded orphanage were "adopted" by residents of an institution for mentally retarded women. When these "adopted" children were later compared with children who had remained in the orphanage, it was found that the "adopted" children:
   a. had lower intelligence test scores.
   b. had higher intelligence test scores.
   c. had reached higher levels of education by their thirties.
   d. b and c

Answer: b
Patterns of attachment
p. 588

56. Research on institutionalized children indicates that:
   a. infants who have not had the opportunity to form an attachment within their first year and a half will not be able to overcome the effects of early social isolation.
   b. later opportunities for an attachment relationship can overcome the ill effects of early social isolation.
   c. emotional and intellectual development are probably independent of one another.
   d. b and c

Answer: c
Patterns of attachment
p. 588

57. The textbook summarizes the research on early isolation by suggesting that:
   a. there is a critical period for the development of social skills.
   b. the quality of social relationships in the first years of life determines the quality of later social relationships.
   c. early social relationships lay a foundation upon which later social relationships build, but there may be ways of compensating for a missing or weak foundation.
   d. a and b

Answer: d
Childhood socialization
p. 589

58. Socialization:
   a. means teaching the child what constitutes appropriate behavior in her society.
   b. includes some goals that are common across diverse cultures.
   c. includes some goals that are specific to different cultures.
   d. all of the above

Answer: b
Childhood socialization
p. 589

59. Anthropological studies suggest that societies whose dominant means of livelihood is through agriculture as opposed to hunting stress which of thefollowing values as they raise their children?
   a. self-reliance and initiative
   b. conformity and responsibility
   c. religiousness and respect for tradition
   d. generosity and tolerance

Answer: a
Childhood socialization
p. 589

60. Anthropological studies suggest that societies whose dominant means of livelihood is through hunting or fishing as opposed to agriculture stress which of the following values as they raise their children?
   a. self-reliance and initiative
   b. conformity and responsibility
   c. religiousness and respect for tradition
   d. generosity and tolerance

Answer: c
Childhood socialization
pp. 589–590

61. Which of the following people is most likely to stress the importance of self-control in the rearing of his child?
    a. an assembly line worker
    b. a machine operator
    c. an office supervisor
    d. a dishwasher

Answer: b
Childhood socialization
pp. 589–590

62. Which of the following is most likely to stress the importance of obedience to authority in the rearing of his child?
    a. a professor
    b. an assembly line worker
    c. an office supervisor
    d. a restaurant owner

Answer: a
Childhood socialization
pp. 589–590

63. In our society, differences in child-rearing practices:
    a. often reflect the parents' work experiences.
    b. seem to be a function of geographical location.
    c. are nonexistent.
    d. seem to be arbitrary; there is no basis for predicting how parents will treat their children.

Answer: b
Childhood socialization
p. 589

64. The social learning theory of socialization stresses that a child:
    a. must be rewarded or punished in order to learn.
    b. learns by imitation and reward and punishment.
    c. must actively want to learn.
    d. learns by imitation and understanding.

Answer: c
Childhood socialization
p. 590

65. You want your child to be kind and charitable. Which of the following ways of achieving this goal does not use principles of social learning theory?
    a. Praise your child when she does something nice for someone else.
    b. Punish your child when she is mean to someone.
    c. Explain to your child why she should treat others well.
    d. Give money or food to a homeless person while your child is with you.

Answer: a
Childhood socialization
p. 590

66. In order for observational learning to occur, the learner must:
    a. observe a model performing the relevant acts.
    b. imitate a model's performance.
    c. be reinforced for imitating a model.
    d. all of the above

Answer: d
Childhood socialization
p. 590

67. Wendy sees her big sister smoking a cigarette. A few hours later she sneaks over to a pack of cigarettes, takes one out, holds it with two fingers, and puts it in her mouth while looking as debonair as possible. These actions would seem to require (in Wendy):
    a. observational learning without performance.
    b. a conception of the sister as an organism like herself.
    c. learning in the absence of a clear-cut reinforcement.
    d. all of the above

Answer: c
Childhood socialization
p. 591

68. Unlike social theories, cognitive theories assert that a child imitates an adult's action because:
    a. she knows that she will be rewarded.
    b. she has seen the action rewarded and is, therefore, vicariously re-inforced.
    c. she assumes that adults know more than she does.
    d. she is afraid of punishment.

Answer: a
Childhood socialization
p. 591

69. Cognitive theories, unlike social learning accounts, stress the notion that _____ is an important factor in socialization.
    a. a child's understanding
    b. reinforcement the child obtains
    c. performance of learned behavior
    d. behavior of a model

Answer: e
Childhood socialization
p. 591

70. Little Lisa used to always tease and poke her baby brother. Now she treats him much more gently. Which of the following possible explanations offers a cognitive developmental account of the change?
    a. Lisa's parents yelled at her whenever she bothered the baby.
    b. Lisa's parents encouraged her whenever she played nicely with the baby.
    c. As she got used to the baby, Lisa outgrew her jealousy of him.
    d. Lisa saw her parents playing fun games with the baby and she began to imitate them.
    e. Lisa began to understand her parents' explanations that the baby was a little person who probably didn't like to be poked and teased.

Answer: d
Childhood socialization
p. 592

71. Studies of the effects of breast-feeding, weaning, and toilet training on child development indicate that:
    a. breast-feeding and weaning are related to attachment behavior, but toilet training seems to have no clear connection with later development.
    b. toilet training seems to be modestly related to moral development, but neither breast-feeding nor weaning seem to play any clear role in later development.
    c. all three seem to play at least some role in the socialization of the young child.
    d. contrary to Freud's claims, none of these three aspects of child rearing seem to play any role in the socialization of the young child.

Answer: c
Childhood socialization
pp. 592–593

72. Which of the following is not a pattern of child rearing observed in parents?
    a. autocratic
    b. permissive
    c. assertive-reciprocal
    d. authoritative-reciprocal

73. "Because I'm the mother" in response to a child's "why do I have to?" is most likely to be uttered by a woman using:
    a. social learning theory.
    b. the autocratic pattern of child rearing.
    c. the permissive pattern of child rearing.
    d. the authoritative-reciprocal pattern of child rearing.

74. What is the main characteristic of authoritative-reciprocal parents?
    a. They exercise their power to the full extent.
    b. They exercise power but also respond to the child's viewpoint.
    c. They respond to the child's opinion but act on their own beliefs to set arbitrary rules.
    d. They allow the child to do what he/she wants, thus allowing for creative and intellectual growth.
    e. They wait for the child to respond and then give reward or punishment (feedback).

75. Walter's parents strongly believe that Walter should make his own decisions, and so they set very few rules about homework, bedtime, and household chores. Since they believe that freedom and responsibility are important, they patiently tolerate all of Walter's behavior, whether childish or mature. The parenting style adopted by Walter's parents is called:
    a. autocratic
    b. permissive
    c. authoritative-reciprocal
    d. indifferent

76. Joan's parents believe that parents know best. They expect Joan to obey all parental rules without question, and are quick to impose stern punishments if she does not. Joan's parents are using the child-rearing style called:
    a. autocratic
    b. permissive
    c. authoritative-reciprocal
    d. arbitrary

77. Children from permissive homes are likely to:
    a. be angry, immature, and lack social responsibility.
    b. be self-reliant, but anxious and aggressive.
    c. be self-reliant, competent, and warm.
    d. show high leadership skills, but to be manipulative and emotionally distant from others.

78. Children from authoritative-reciprocal homes are likely to be:
    a. independent and socially responsible.
    b. assertive, and low in self-control.
    c. withdrawn, angry, and defiant.
    d. good leaders, but aggressive and manipulative.

Answer: c
Childhood socialization
pp. 592–593

79. Parents who are inflexible in their thinking and control their children's behavior largely through punishment are likely to produce children who are:
    a. independent and self-reliant.
    b. immature but cheerful.
    c. withdrawn and hostile.
    d. impulsive but otherwise socially responsible.

Answer: d
Childhood socialization
pp. 592–593

80. What pattern of child rearing was used by parents whose children lacked independence and were more angry?
    a. permissive pattern
    b. autocratic pattern
    c. authoritative-reciprocal pattern
    d. a and b

Answer: a
Childhood socialization
pp. 592–593

81. Which of the following are characteristics of both autocratically and permissively raised children?
    a. more prone to anger and lacking independence
    b. withdrawn, clumsy in social situations
    c. socially responsible and generally more happy
    d. dutiful and respectful of authority
    e. all of the above

Answer: a
Childhood socialization
pp. 592–593

82. The most independent, competent, and socially responsible children are those who:
    a. are raised by the authoritative-reciprocal pattern of parenting in which the child's point of view is taken into account.
    b. are raised by the permissive pattern of parenting in which few demands are placed on the child, allowing her or him to become more independent.
    c. are raised by autocratic parents who assure responsibility in their children by using strict control of behavior.
    d. are least affected by anxiety, and therefore are less affected by internalization.

Answer: d
Childhood socialization
pp. 592–593

83. Sue thinks that children should grow up in a totally free environment, with no parentally set limits or rules. What is the best guess about what her children will be like?
    a. They will be moody and defiant but will show a striking amount of independence.
    b. They will be socially mature for their age but generally pessimistic.
    c. They will be independent and show social responsibility.
    d. They will seem immature and will not show much independence.

84. When we examine the socialization process we note that:
    a. parents may socialize children differently depending on the child's temperament.
    b. differences in parenting styles cause differences in the way children develop.
    c. recent studies suggest that parenting styles have little real effect on later social and emotional development.
    d. the classification of parenting styles formulated in the United States fits all other cultures that have been studied.

85. Differences in temperament:
    a. are present at birth.
    b. may lead children to be treated differently.
    c. may lead children to respond differently to similar treatment.
    d. all of the above

86. The way parents treat their children:
    a. is determined by the way the parents were treated as children.
    b. is determined by the parents' socialization goals.
    c. is shaped, to some extent, by the children themselves.
    d. determines how the children will develop.

87. When we say that, to some extent, an infant shapes her own environment, we are talking about:
    a. the conscious choices she makes about where to go and what to do.
    b. the way her temperament influences how others interact with her.
    c. the way her abilities influence how others interact with her.
    d. b and c

88. According to the textbook, the ultimate goal of moral development is for children to:
    a. internalize moral values.
    b. behave as they have been taught to in certain circumstances.
    c. know what's right and wrong.
    d. obey the law.

89. In moral development, the principle of minimal sufficiency states that a child:
    a. will exhibit only as much moral responsibility in a given situation as is necessary to satisfy his or her internal standards of conduct.
    b. will internalize moral principles if he or she is given little explanation of why moral behavior is appropriate.
    c. will internalize moral behavior if there is just enough pressure on him to induce the moral behavior, but not so much that the behavior seems forced.
    d. who is given very few rules will learn that better than will a child given many rules.

90. Which principle states that a child will internalize a certain way of acting if there is some pressure put on him to act this way, but not enough to feel that he was forced?
    a. principle of minimal sufficiency
    b. principle of forced compliance
    c. principle of internalization
    d. principle of socialization

91. The parenting style of _____ parents is most consistent with the principle of minimal sufficiency in moral development.
    a. autocratic
    b. permissive
    c. authoritative-reciprocal
    d. authoritarian

92. Which of the following statements is false?
    a. The permissive pattern of parenting allows children a great deal of latitude in their behavior.
    b. Autocratic parents tend to enforce rules quite sternly.
    c. The principle of minimal sufficiency is most likely to be used by autocratic parents.
    d. Authoritative-reciprocal parenting is a bit of a compromise between autocratic and permissive styles.
    e. The authoritative-reciprocal pattern of parenting is correlated with the best outcomes in children.

93. Imagine that Zack and Casey are each left in a room alone and are told not to turn on the TV in the room. Zack is told that if he turns on the TV, his mother will be disappointed and annoyed with him. Casey is told that if he turns on the TV, his mother will be furious and he won't be able to play with any friends for a week. Neither boy turns on the TV. The next time they are in the same room, with no threats:
    a. neither boy is likely to turn on the TV.
    b. both boys are likely to turn on the TV.
    c. Casey is more likely to turn on the TV than Zack.
    d. Zack is more likely to turn on the TV than Casey.

94. When a child is forced through harsh threats and punishment to behave in a certain manner, she will probably:
    a. not internalize the behavior as valuable.
    b. not comply with the pressure she's under.
    c. understand the behavior better than a child who is asked to do it rather than being forced.
    d. both comply with the pressure and internalize the behavior as valuable.

95. According to the Hobbesian position, altruistic behavior:
    a. is actually more egoistic and selfish than it appears.
    b. is an innate quality of all human beings.
    c. must be carefully nurtured by social and cultural forces if the human race is to survive.
    d. both b and c

Answer: e
The development of morality
p. 597

96. Newborns will cry in response to another newborn's cry because:
    a. sounds of that volume upset them.
    b. they may have a built-in empathic response.
    c. from their own cries, they may have come to associate the sound of crying with discomfort.
    d. all of the above
    e. b or c

Answer: b
The development of morality
p. 597

97. When a two-year-old child experiences empathic distress at another person's pain, she is most likely to:
    a. leave the situation so as to remove the cause of her own emotional distress.
    b. try to help by offering the other individual whatever she herself would find comforting if she were in pain.
    c. offer the other person some form of emotional support, such as hugs or kisses.
    d. recall the fear or anxiety that she herself has experienced at other times.

Answer: c
The development of morality
p. 597

98. A two-year-old child sees his mother burn herself on the stove. What might he give her?
    a. first aid cream
    b. a band-aid
    c. his favorite blanket
    d. ice

Answer: d
The development of morality
p. 597

99. Empathic distress:
    a. may lead to helping behavior.
    b. may interfere with helping behavior.
    c. is irrelevant to helping behavior.
    d. a and b

Answer: c
The development of morality
p. 597

100. A study of nurses dealing with very sick patients found that those who felt the greatest empathy for their patients:
    a. spent the most time with their patients.
    b. were liked the most by the patients.
    c. were the least effective in their jobs.
    d. a and b

Answer: a
The development of morality
p. 598

101. According to Kohlberg's view of moral development:
    a. the earliest form of moral reasoning tends to be based on fears of punishment or the desire for personal gain.
    b. moral reasoning based on personal principles is followed by moral reasoning based on social or cultural standards of acceptable behavior.
    c. morality based on personal fears or desires develops later than moral reasoning based on social conventions.
    d. all of the above
    e. a and b only

Answer: e
The development of morality
p. 598

102. In Kohlberg's stage of preconventional morality, our moral behavior is governed by:
    a. avoiding punishment.
    b. gaining rewards.
    c. codes of law and order.
    d. ethical principles.
    e. a and b

Answer: b
The development of morality
p. 598

103. According to Lawrence Kohlberg, moral reasoning at the highest level relies upon:
    a. the ability to anticipate the opinions of others.
    b. personal moral principles.
    c. a concern with punishment and reward.
    d. adherence to a code of "law and order."

Answer: d
The development of morality
p. 598

104. Susie tells Sally that she doesn't eat cookies before dinner because her parents will send her to her room for the rest of the night. What stage of Kohlberg's moral reasoning is Susie in?
    a. rationalization
    b. postconventional
    c. conventional
    d. preconventional

Answer: d
The development of morality
p. 598

105. There's a severe drought and a ban on outdoor watering. The Dodges decide they won't wash their car because they realize that if everyone washed a car, the town might not have drinking water. Their reasoning places them in Kohlberg's _____ stage.
    a. preconventional
    b. conventional
    c. unconventional
    d. postconventional

Answer: b
The development of morality
p. 598

106. There's a severe drought and there is a ban on outdoor watering. The Robinsons decide they won't water their new shrubs because the neighbors would disapprove. Their reasoning places them in Kohlberg's _____ stage.
    a. preconventional
    b. conventional
    c. unconventional
    d. postconventional

Answer: d
The development of morality
p. 598

107. Kohlberg's studies of moral reasoning seem to show that:
    a. most people don't attain the highest level of moral development.
    b. moral development proceeds through qualitatively different stages.
    c. moral development extends through adolescence.
    d. all of the above

Answer: e
The development of morality
p. 599

108. Carol Gilligan has suggested that men and women have different moral orientations. Which of the following statements forms the basis of her argument?
    a. Women see morality in abstract, rational terms.
    b. Men see morality in abstract, rational terms.
    c. Women see morality in concrete, social terms.
    d. Men see morality in concrete, social terms.
    e. b and c

Answer: c
The development of morality
p. 599

109. Studies comparing the moral reasoning of males and females have shown that:
    a. men tend to reason predominantly at stages 4 and 5, while women reason predominantly at stages 3 and 4.
    b. the difference in moral reasoning between males and females is greater for people over 35 than for people between the ages of 18 and 35.
    c. the literature reveals no reliable difference in moral reasoning between males and females.
    d. both b and c

Answer: c
The development of morality
pp. 599–600

110. Cross-cultural studies of moral reasoning indicate that:
    a. westerners are, on average, more moral than are members of technologically less advanced cultures.
    b. moral reasoning develops independently of one's social context.
    c. it may not be appropriate to interpret higher ratings on Kohlberg's scales as indicative of "better" moral reasoning.
    d. people in technologically less advanced cultures tend to provide more abstract justifications for moral decisions than westerners.

Answer: b
The development of morality
p. 600

111. Kohlberg's moral reasoning classification:
    a. is almost perfectly predictive of moral conduct.
    b. is somewhat predictive of moral conduct.
    c. is negatively correlated with moral conduct.
    d. is unrelated to moral conduct.

Answer: a
The development of morality
p. 600

112. A strong criticism of Kohlberg's theory of moral development is that it:
    a. assesses a person's ability to describe her moral principles rather than the principles themselves.
    b. is age based and excludes people over about the age of fourteen.
    c. is based on generalizations from behavior theory with nonhuman animals.
    d. undervalues abstract reasoning.

Answer: c
The development of sex and gender
p. 601

113. Which of the following terms refers to the "clear inner sense of being male or female"?
    a. gender role
    b. sexual orientation
    c. gender identity
    d. sex-typing

Answer: b
The development of sex and gender
p. 601

114. Gender identity is:
    a. a host of external behavior patterns that are appropriate for each sex.
    b. our inner sense of whether we are male or female.
    c. the identification of a sexual partner.
    d. a description of men or women using adjectives that generally describe each.

Answer: b
The development of sex and gender
p. 601

115. The group of behavior patterns that a culture defines as appropriate for each sex is known as:
    a. gender identity.
    b. gender role.
    c. sexual orientation.
    d. sex type.
    e. gender type.

Answer: a
The development of sex and gender
p. 601

116. A person's inclination toward a sexual partner of the same or opposite sex is called:
    a. sexual orientation.
    b. gender identity.
    c. gender typing.
    d. sexual preference.

Answer: d
The development of sex and gender
p. 601

117. Which of the following is not a societal expectation for females?
    a. greater submissiveness
    b. greater emotional expressiveness
    c. less competitiveness
    d. an interest in things rather than people

Answer: b
The development of sex and gender
p. 602

118. In one study, mothers were introduced to a 6-month-old baby ("Joey" or "Janie") and asked to play with the child. The results indicated that:
    a. unlike fathers given the same task, mothers played the same way with the infant whether they thought it was male or female.
    b. mothers treated the baby more gently if they thought it was a girl than if they thought it was a boy.
    c. mothers, unlike fathers, were just as likely to give the infant a doll when they thought it was male as when they thought it was female.
    d. both b and c

Answer: c
The development of sex and gender
pp. 601–602

119. Which of the following statements is false?
    a. People typically play more roughly with baby boys than with baby girls.
    b. By age eleven, children are well aware of gender-role stereotypes in our society.
    c. Boys and girls are equally pressured to maintain gender-role stereotypes.
    d. Fathers reinforce gender-role stereotypes somewhat more than mothers do.

Answer: c
The development of sex and gender
pp. 602–603

120. Which of the following statements is false?
    a. Girls mature faster than boys.
    b. Girls speak at an earlier age than boys.
    c. Any normally developing girl in early childhood has better language skills than any normally developing boy of the same age.
    d. The brains of men and women differ in the vicinity of the hypothalamus.

Answer: c
The development of sex and gender
p. 603

121. If a trait is strongly shaped by biology:
    a. its development will not be influenced by the environment.
    b. it is fixed.
    c. it can be changed.
    d. a and b

Answer: d
The development of sex and gender
pp. 603–604

122. If we look at sex differences in aggression we find that:
    a. male infants are more irritable and active than females.
    b. at age two, boys engage in more and rougher play-fighting, across a variety of cultures.
    c. aggressiveness is enhanced by the administration of male sex hormone.
    d. all of the above
    e. b and c only

Answer: c
The development of sex and gender
pp. 603–604

123. Which of the following provides the least support for the argument that sex differences in aggression are primarily biologically determined?
    a. Male infants are more irritable and active than females.
    b. At age two, boys engage in more and rougher play-fighting, across a variety of cultures.
    c. Men are more likely to resort to physical assault than are women.
    d. Aggressiveness is enhanced by the administration of male sex hormone.

Answer: a
The development of sex and gender
pp. 603–604

124. In our society:
    a. inborn sex differences in aggression are probably enhanced by environmental factors.
    b. boys who are physically aggressive are generally treated the same as girls who are physically aggressive.
    c. girls are less likely than boys to engage in any sort of aggression.
    d. all of the above

Answer: b
The development of sex and gender
pp. 604–605

125. On tests of verbal and mathematical/spatial aptitudes:
    a. women on average have higher scores for both types of ability.
    b. women on average have lower mathematical/spatial scores than men.
    c. men on average have lower mathematical/spatial scores than women.
    d. there are no consistent sex differences in average scores on either type of test.

Answer: a
The development of sex and gender
pp. 604–605

126. A comparison of SAT scores for males and females with the same math backgrounds and the same levels of interest in math revealed that
   a. as is usually found, the males averaged higher scores than the females.
   b. in contrast to what is usually found, the males averaged higher scores than the females.
   c. in contrast to what is usually found, the males averaged the same scores as the females.
   d. in contrast to what is usually found, the males averaged lower scores than the females.

Answer: d
The development of sex and gender
p. 605

127. In PET scans and MRIs, male and female brains:
   a. are indistinguishable.
   b. differ in regions involved in verbal tasks.
   c. differ in regions involved in visuospatial tasks.
   d. b and c

Answer: c
The development of sex and gender
p. 605

128. Which of the following statements is false?
   a. Males with abnormally low levels of testosterone have impaired visuospatial abilities.
   b. Females with abnormally high levels of testosterone have enhanced visuospatial abilities.
   c. From an evolutionary perspective, females would have more need of navigational skills than males would.
   d. Testosterone might affect visuospatial skills through its effects on the hippocampus.

Answer: d
The development of sex and gender
pp. 605–606

129. Several years ago a talking Barbie doll was produced which said, "Math is hard." Our culture, as exemplified by this doll:
   a. fully accounts for sex differences in spatial and mathematical abilities.
   b. may encourage girls with a great deal of potential in math to concentrate instead on more "acceptable" topics.
   c. probably enhances biologically based sex differences in spatial and mathematical abilities.
   d. b and c

Answer: b
The development of sex and gender
p. 606

130. Before the age of five a child usually cannot:
   a. indicate which of the people she knows are male and which are female.
   b. understand the permanence of gender.
   c. answer whether she is a girl or a boy.
   d. a and b

Answer: a
The development of sex and gender
p. 606

131. Before the age of five or six, children typically fail to recognize:
   a. the permanent nature of gender.
   b. the different genders of their parents.
   c. the different social roles of the two sexes.
   d. both a and b

Answer: a
The development of sex and gender
p. 606

Answer: b
The development of sex and gender
p. 606

Answer: c
The development of sex and gender
p. 607

Answer: a
The development of sex and gender
pp. 607–608

Answer: d
The development of sex and gender
p. 608

Answer: c
The development of sex and gender
pp. 608–609

132. The term *gender constancy* refers to:
    a. the concept that gender is a permanent attribute.
    b. behaviors that are appropriate to only one sex role.
    c. the exclusive choice of same-sex playmates.
    d. a match between chromosomes and external genitals.

133. A preschooler identifies a person in a picture as a boy. He then explains that the boy would become a girl if he grew his hair longer and put it in pigtails. This child hasn't achieved
    a. object permanence.
    b. gender constancy.
    c. gender role.
    d. pseudohermaphroditism.
    e. gender identity.

134. Pseudohermaphrodites:
    a. have XX chromosomes and male genitalia.
    b. have XY chromosomes and female genitalia.
    c. have ambiguous genitalia.
    d. have functioning reproductive tissue from both sexes.

135. The book describes the case of a boy, John, who, in infancy, lost his penis and was surgically altered and reassigned as "Joan". The most recent follow-up studies of this child (now adult) show that:
    a. the reassignment failed; Joan's gender identity was always male.
    b. gender identity is determined primarily by socialization.
    c. Joan's gender identity was uncertain until she began receiving estrogen injections at puberty; then she felt more fully female.
    d. Joan is happily married to a man and has adopted his children from a previous marriage.
    e. b and d

136. Chromosomal females who are prenatally exposed to high levels of androgens:
    a. generally have normal female genitalia.
    b. are more likely than other girls to be tomboys.
    c. have higher rates of lesbianism than other women.
    d. b and c

137. Researchers have recently found a rare genetic disorder among males in three villages in the Dominican Republic. These males look like girls at birth, and are raised as girls until normal male puberty occurs, when they find they must adopt a male gender identity. Studies of these males indicate that:
    a. they never become fully comfortable with their new role as males, and often seek sex reassignment.
    b. although they adopt a normal male identity with relatively little trouble, they are much more likely to have a homosexual orientation.
    c. they have little trouble adopting a male identity, suggesting that sex reassignment may be possible at much later ages than once thought.
    d. gender identity is completely flexible.

Answer: e
The development of sex and gender
pp. 608–609

138. There are limits on the inferences that can be drawn from guevedoces syndrome to other cases of sex reassignment, because boys with this syndrome:
    a. are relatively common in their community.
    b. have appropriately masculinized brains.
    c. were never really treated as girls.
    d. all of the above
    e. a and b only

Answer: a
The development of sex and gender
p. 609

139. Almost all homosexual men and women:
    a. have a gender identity consistent with their physical sex.
    b. have a gender identity inappropriate to their physical sex.
    c. are transsexual.
    d. would like to change their sexual orientation.

Answer: c
The development of sex and gender
p. 609

140. Over the years, a number of surveys have estimated the proportion of the population that is predominantly homosexual. Your text suggests that this number is roughly:
    a. 1 percent.
    b. 5 percent.
    c. 10 percent.
    d. 15 percent.

Answer: d
The development of sex and gender

p. 610

141. Cultures that consider homosexuality among young males to be normal:
    a. are unusual. Most cultures have strict rules against homosexuality.
    b. are those in which men have nothing to do with child rearing.
    c. are likely to have been under substantial cultural stress, which produces endocrine abnormalities during fetal development.
    d. are probably quite common.

Answer: d
The development of sex and gender
p. 610

142. One New Guinea group expects all of its young males to establish homosexual relationships prior to their eventual marriage to a woman. Such homosexuality at some point in development is:
    a. quite rare and occurs mainly in cultures with considerable in-breeding.
    b. related to the particular puberty rites of that culture.
    c. related to unusual hormone levels during fetal development.
    d. common across many cultures.

Answer: a
The development of sex and gender
p. 610

143. Compared to typical heterosexual relationships, typical homosexual relationships are:
    a. the same except for the sexes of those involved.
    b. briefer.
    c. less likely to include romantic love.
    d. less likely to include companionate love (a sense of trust and commitment).
    e. b, c, and d

Answer: d
The development of sex and gender
p. 610

144. Bisexuals:
   a. sometimes live in a long-term monogamous relationship with a member of the same sex.
   b. sometimes live in a long-term monogamous relationship with a member of the opposite sex.
   c. sometimes consider themselves heterosexual, but seek out occasional homosexual encounters.
   d. all of the above

Answer: a
The development of sex and gender
p. 611

145. According to Freud's theory, male homosexuality:
   a. is a response to fears aroused during the Oedipal conflict.
   b. is a reaction formation to phallic sexuality that occurs when the child is punished for masturbation.
   c. results from a fixation at the anal (or oral) stage that prevents sexual libido from being directed toward phallic sexuality.
   d. results from a confusion during the genital stage.
   e. none of the above

Answer: b
The development of sex and gender
p. 611

146. A survey of one thousand gays and lesbians indicated that:
   a. homosexuals were no more likely than heterosexuals to report troubled relationships with their parents.
   b. homosexual fantasies generally preceded actual homosexual experiences.
   c. homosexual desires and fantasies generally began around puberty.
   d. all of the above

Answer: e
The development of sex and gender
p. 612

147. Attempts to identify biological factors in homosexuality have found:
   a. if a twin is homosexual, the probability that his or her co-twin will be also is more than twice as high if they are identical than if they are fraternal.
   b. male homosexuality might involve the action of one or more genes in a specific area of the X-chromosome.
   c. high testosterone levels in gay males are associated with weaker homosexual urges.
   d. all of the above
   e. a and b only

Answer: d
The development of sex and gender
pp. 612–613

148. Studies of hormone levels in male homosexuals indicate that male homosexuality:
   a. is the result of low levels of testosterone.
   b. is the result of high levels of testosterone.
   c. is the result of high levels of estrogen.
   d. cannot be said to be consistently related to hormone levels.

Answer: d
The development of sex and gender
p. 613

149. Part of the hypothalamus:
   a. becomes sexually differentiated by hormones in prenatal development.
   b. affects sexual behavior in animals.
   c. has been found to be larger in heterosexual men than in heterosexual women or homosexual men.
   d. all of the above

Answer: b
The development of sex and gender
pp. 611–613

150. Which of the following statements is most consistent with the bulk of scientific evidence?
    a. Certain types of family structures and early childhood experiences lead some people to become homosexuals.
    b. Areas of the hypothalamus that affect sexual behavior in animals tend to be different sizes in homosexual than in heterosexual men.
    c. Administering male sex hormones to gay men decreases their homosexual tendencies.
    d. All cultures that have been studied regard homosexual feelings and behaviors as deviant and inappropriate.

Answer: a
The development of sex and gender
p. 613

151. Simon Le Vay's study comparing the brains of homosexual and heterosexual males revealed that:
    a. an area in the hypothalamus was significantly larger in heterosexual males than in homosexual males.
    b. the right hemispheres of homosexual males were slightly but significantly larger than the left hemispheres, a pattern opposite to that found in heterosexual males.
    c. the pituitary gland, just beneath the hypothalamus, was larger in homosexual than in heterosexual males, just as it is larger in women than in men.
    d. there were no gross or fine anatomical differences between the brains of heterosexual and homosexual males.

Answer: c
Development after childhood
pp. 614–615

152. Erik Erikson believes that all humans go through a series of major _____ during which they confront themselves and the new demands put on them by their personal and social settings.
    a. transformations
    b. regressions
    c. crises
    d. relationships

Answer: a
Development after childhood
p. 614

153. The most basic (first) of psychosocial crises to be solved according to Erikson is:
    a. trust versus mistrust.
    b. intimacy versus isolation.
    c. integrity versus stagnation.
    d. identity versus intimacy.
    e. none of the above

Answer: a
Development after childhood
p. 615

154. The age at which adolescence ends and adulthood begins:
    a. varies widely across cultures and time periods.
    b. has gotten progressively older in this country.
    c. is determined by physical growth.
    d. a and b

Answer: c
Development after childhood
p. 616

155. Initiation rites or rites of passage:
    a. occur only in preliterate cultures.
    b. occur only once during adolescence.
    c. may be particularly severe in cultures which emphasize distinctions between children and adults and between men and women.
    d. generally take place at age twenty.

156. Which of the following is not a characteristic of adolescence?
    a. a growth spurt occurs
    b. an inevitable emotional turbulence
    c. a separation between the adolescent and his parents
    d. experimentation with different social roles

157. Adolescent emotional turbulence:
    a. is a popular theme in literature.
    b. is not inevitable.
    c. probably depends on the individual's social and psychological context.
    d. all of the above

158. Body piercing in adolescents:
    a. seems to be a way for adolescents to distinguish themselves from their parents.
    b. is likely to be popular among adolescents for decades.
    c. is inconsistent with Erikson's understanding of adolescence.
    d. all of the above

159. According to Erikson, the major goal of adolescent development is:
    a. learning to deal with new sexuality.
    b. learning to think abstractly.
    c. distinguishing yourself from your younger siblings.
    d. development of a sense of identity.

160. Erikson's "identity crisis" refers to:
    a. a rare, temporary type of amnesia brought about the the hormonal changes of puberty.
    b. attempts to determine what kind of person one really is and wants to be.
    c. attempts to determine one's gender identity.
    d. a confusion brought about by the heavy drinking and drug use sometimes seen among adolescents.

161. On Monday, Jacques announces to his parents that he wants to be called "Jack". On Wednesday, he says he wants to drop out of school. On Friday, he says he wants to get a tattoo and become an architect. Erikson would say that Jacques is experiencing:
    a. a crisis of trust versus mistrust.
    b. a crisis of competence versus inferiority.
    c. an identity crisis.
    d. a crisis of productivity versus stagnation.

162. Erikson's final stage revolves around the issues of:
    a. intimacy versus isolation.
    b. competence versus inferiority.
    c. integrity versus despair.
    d. productivity versus stagnation.

Answer: a
Development after childhood
pp. 618–619

163. Erikson and other authors devoted considerable attention to the "midlife transition." This transition involves:
    a. a reappraisal of one's life and career.
    b. a redefinition of life purpose from personal to more social and altruistic goals.
    c. a turning away from more material interests to more philosophical and spiritual ones.
    d. a renewed interest in the ideas and pursuits of one's adolescence and young adulthood.

Answer: d
Development after childhood
pp. 618–620

164. The stages of adult development:
    a. are partially built around biological milestones.
    b. have not been well-studied cross-culturally.
    c. may be influenced by cultural differences in the treatment and perception of people of different ages.
    d. all of the above

CHAPTER 15 | Intelligence: Its Nature and Measurement

Answer: a
Mental tests
p. 624

1. A test that measures what a person can do now is called a(n):
   a. achievement test.
   b. aptitude test.
   c. criterion test.
   d. IQ test.

Answer: c
Mental tests
p. 624

2. Aptitude tests are designed to:
   a. measure what a person knows in a given area.
   b. identify a person's characteristic disposition.
   c. predict a person's likely performance in a given area later on, given proper training and motivation.
   d. evaluate a person's motivational state.

Answer: c
Mental tests
p. 626

3. A test that is designed to measure a very general cognitive aptitude, including the ability to benefit from schooling, is called a(n):
   a. aptitude test.
   b. achievement test.
   c. intelligence test.
   d. personality test.

Answer: d
Mental tests
p. 626

4. A test that is designed to assess someone's characteristic behavioral dispositions is called a(n):
   a. aptitude test.
   b. achievement test.
   c. intelligence test.
   d. personality test.

Answer: c
Mental tests
p. 627

5. A frequency distribution reflects:
   a. how often a particular mental test is accurate in predicting performance.
   b. the average differences between two groups on a number of different measures.
   c. the number of individual cases falling within each interval on a particular scale of measurement.
   d. the number of times a particular distribution of test items is used.

Answer: d
Mental tests
p. 627

6. The frequency distributions of many human physical characteristics closely resemble a "normal" or _____ curve.
   a. flattened
   b. bi-modal
   c. rising
   d. bell-shaped

Answer: d
Mental tests
p. 627

7. The value that is obtained by summing values and dividing by the number of cases is called the:
   a. standard deviation.
   b. median.
   c. variance.
   d. mean.

Answer: d
Mental tests
p. 628

8. Imagine that you are holding 5 pennies. You drop them onto a table and note that 3 of the pennies landed tails up. You do this again and there are only 2 pennies that are tails up. If you repeat this many times, what should you expect?
   a. The frequency distribution representing the number of times that 1, 2, 3, 4, or 5 pennies landed tails up would take the form of a bell-shaped curve.
   b. The number of times that 1 penny landed tails up would be approximately the same as the number of times that 5 pennies landed tails up.
   c. Three pennies would land tails up more often than any other number of pennies would land tails up.
   d. all of the above

Answer: a
Mental tests
p. 628

9. The Belgian scientist, Adolphe Quetelet, explained variability for characteristics such as height in terms of:
   a. chance operations.
   b. evolutionary processes.
   c. related differences.
   d. general social preferences.

Answer: b
Mental tests
p. 628

10. The Belgian scientist Adolphe Quetelet proposed that nature aims at ideal characteristics during individual development. According to Quetelet, what causes us to overshoot or fall short of this ideal?
    a. socioeconomic variables
    b. chance
    c. nutrition
    d. none of the above

Answer: b
Mental tests
p. 628

11. Variability within a species is _____ evolutionary change.
    a. an unwanted byproduct of
    b. an essential condition for
    c. a barrier to
    d. a sign of imminent

Answer: c
Mental tests
p. 629

12. Darwin's half-cousin Francis Galton spent much of his life studying:
    a. the physical characteristics of Scottish soldiers.
    b. the odds involved in games of chance.
    c. the extent to which relatives resemble one another.
    d. the results of interbreeding plants.

Answer: c
Mental tests
p. 629

13. Which of the following pairs of variables would probably result in a steeply accelerating line of best fit, if plotted as a scatter diagram?
    a. college grades and hours of television watching
    b. shoe size and intelligence scores
    c. height and weight
    d. all of the above

Answer: b
Mental tests
p. 629

14. If two variables are perfectly correlated, then the points in a scatter diagram would take the form of:
    a. a bell-shaped curve.
    b. a diagonal line.
    c. a circle.
    d. a U-shaped curve.

Answer: d
Mental tests
p. 629

15. In a scatter diagram, a diagonal line:
    a. joins all of the points in the diagram.
    b. allows error-free prediction of scores for a given individual.
    c. joins the points representing one set of scores to the points representing scores on a second measure.
    d. provides the best prediction of one score, given knowledge of the other.

Answer: a
Mental tests
p. 629

16. The information directly attainable from a scatter diagram is:
    a. whether two variables are related.
    b. the correlational coefficient.
    c. the standard deviation.
    d. all of the above

Answer: d
Mental tests
p. 629

17. In a scatter diagram, the line that would provide the best description of the relationship between two variables is:
    a. the line of intersection.
    b. the normal curve.
    c. the variance.
    d. typically a diagonal line.

18. A psychologist has given two tests to a group of college students and calculated the degree of correlation for the two sets of scores. Which of the values listed below could not possibly be the correlation here?
    a. $r = 0.50$
    b. $r = +0.60$
    c. $r = +1.50$
    d. $r = -0.95$.

19. Which of the following pairs of measures is most likely to yield a correlation coefficient close to 0.00?
    a. maternal age and number of children
    b. hair color and IQ
    c. height and weight
    d. level of education and yearly earnings

20. The more it rains, fewer people have picnics. The correlation between picnics and rain is:
    a. positive.
    b. negative.
    c. zero.
    d. There is no correlation.

21. A negative correlation indicates that:
    a. as the value of one variable increases, so does that of the other variable.
    b. as the value of one variable increases, the value of the other remains constant.
    c. as the value of one variable increases, that of the other variable decreases.
    d. all of the above

22. Which of the following correlation coefficients describes the strongest relationship between two variables?
    a. $r = -0.75$
    b. $r = 0.00$
    c. $r = +0.25$
    d. $r = +0.50$

23. Which of the following correlation coefficients describes the weakest relationship between two variables?
    a. $r = -0.75$
    b. $r = 0.00$
    c. $r = +0.25$
    d. $r = +0.50$

24. Which of the following is most likely to represent the correlation between shoe size and age?
    a. $r = -0.80$
    b. $r = -0.02$
    c. $r = +0.40$
    d. $r = +1.00$

Answer: d
Mental tests
p. 630

25. The finding that two variables are highly correlated allows a scientist to conclude:
    a. that the first causes the second.
    b. that the second causes the first.
    c. that a third factor causes both.
    d. nothing about causal relationships.

Answer: a
Mental tests
p. 629

26. Two variables have a correlation coefficient of +1.00. This indicates that:
    a. knowing the value of one variable allows prediction of the second variable.
    b. the two variables are causally related.
    c. the best fitting line in a scatter diagram will be a decelerating curve.
    d. all of the above

Answer: b
Mental tests
p. 630

27. A mental test is considered reliable if:
    a. it actually measures the characteristic that it was designed to measure.
    b. it consistently measures whatever it is designed to measure.
    c. scores obtained on the test are accurate measures of the characteristics in question.
    d. an individual's score on the test remains the same no matter what happens.

Answer: a
Mental tests
p. 631

28. The test-retest method is a method to determine:
    a. the reliability of a test.
    b. the validity of a test.
    c. the norms of a test.
    d. whether a test has appropriate standardization.

Answer: c
Mental tests
p. 631

29. If people receive similar scores when taking the same test on different occasions, the test can be described as:
    a. objective.
    b. valid.
    c. reliable.
    d. standardized.

Answer: d
Mental tests
p. 631

30. The test-retest method is sometimes used to assess the _____ of a mental test.
    a. integrity
    b. construct validity
    c. predictive validity
    d. reliability

Answer: b
Mental tests
p. 631

31. An alternative forms technique of measuring reliability is preferable to the test-retest method because:
    a. research participants are likely to get the same scores when tested on two different.
    b. what research participants learn while taking a test may improve their future scores when taking the same test twice.
    c. the split-half method requires only one form of the test.
    d. the test-retest method typically yields lower correlations.

32. Today, most psychological tests have reliability coefficients of about:
    a. $r = -0.89$.
    b. $r = +0.90$.
    c. $r = -0.01$.
    d. $r = +0.00$.

33. A test is considered valid if:
    a. it measures the characteristics that it was designed to measure.
    b. it consistently measures whatever it is designed to measure.
    c. scores obtained on the test are precise and accurate.
    d. an individual's score on the test remains the same over long periods of time.

34. The extent to which a test measures what it is designed to measure is known as the test's:
    a. criterion measure.
    b. norms.
    c. reliability.
    d. validity.

35. Dr. Williams has developed a paper-and-pencil test to assess fear of heights. He gives the test to 50 research participants, whose scores range from 0 (no fear) to 100 (intense fear). He finds that scores on the test have a correlation of only –0.25 with the physiological measures of fear. Two months later, participants take the papers-and-pencil test again. The correlation between scores on this second paper-and-pencil test and scores on the first paper-and-pencil test is 0.95. This information suggests that Dr. Williams test is:
    a. reliable, and probably valid.
    b. probably invalid, but reliable.
    c. unreliable and invalid.
    d. valid, and therefore reliable.
    e. none of the above

36. The predictive validity of most scholastic aptitude tests is in the neighborhood of +0.55. This suggests that:
    a. these tests do not really measure scholastic aptitude.
    b. factors other than scholastic aptitude influence academic performance.
    c. such tests have little or no predictive validity.
    d. such tests provide a near-perfect index of academic ability.

37. Tests can be used to facilitate some hiring decisions, but errors will always occur. This is because:
    a. a standardized sample can never be found.
    b. norms vary from person to person.
    c. predictive validity is never +1.00.
    d. these tests are subjective.

38. A mental test is said to have *construct validity* when the test results:
    a. are consistent with a larger theoretical scheme.
    b. correlate well with some criterion measure.
    c. accurately predict performance at a later time.
    d. show that the test is both reliable and valid.

39. Dr. Jamal is constructing a test of competitiveness. At the moment, she is correlating scores on this test with performance on tests of achievement, assertiveness, dominance, and other traits that she thinks are involved in competitiveness. By doing this, Dr. Jamal is trying to establish the _____ of her test.
    a. standardized reliability
    b. alternative forms reliability
    c. construct validity
    d. predictive validity
    e. standard error

40. A valid test that is consistent with contemporary theories is said to have:
    a. predictive validity.
    b. construct validity.
    c. criterion validity.
    d. a reliability coefficient.

41. If a test has a high reliability coefficient we can assume that it has:
    a. high predictive validity.
    b. high construct validity.
    c. both a and b above
    d. neither a nor b above

42. The Air Force needs a test to select people for training as pilots. There is no adequate theory regarding the acquisition of flying skills, but Air Force investigations reveal that the speed with which one can tap with the forefinger has a correlation of +0.80 with ultimate success as a flyer. On the basis of this observation, one could say that this test item has:
    a. high predictive validity and high construct validity.
    b. high predictive validity.
    c. high construct validity.
    d. good standardization.

43. In order to understand the meaning of an individual test score, it is necessary to know:
    a. an individual's score on a criterion measure.
    b. the norms of the standardization sample.
    c. the degree of construct validity.
    d. none of the above

44. A person's test score is meaningless unless it is compared with test scores of other people. In this instance, what we need are called:
    a. validity criteria.
    b. norms.
    c. reliability criteria.
    d. forms.

45. A single test score provides little information without some knowledge of the test's:
    a. cutoff scores.
    b. split-half coefficient.
    c. norms.
    d. face validity.

46. Administering a test to a large group of people so that others can be compared to this group allows:
    a. reliability.
    b. validity.
    c. standardization.
    d. correlation testing.

47. To obtain norms for a test, the test first must be administered to a group referred to as the:
    a. transfer training group.
    b. normal group.
    c. standardization sample.
    d. population.

48. The practical problem that Alfred Binet was trying to solve when he developed his intelligence test was:
    a. identifying slow learners for remedial programs.
    b. devising an uncontaminated measure of intelligence.
    c. identifying gifted children for accelerated programs.
    d. devising a culturally fair measure of intelligence.

49. The intelligence test developed by Binet and Simon was originally composed of items that:
    a. varied in both content and difficulty.
    b. required no prior knowledge.
    c. directly tapped pure intelligence.
    d. posed unfamiliar problems to be solved.

50. Binet's approach to intelligence testing was based upon which of the following assumptions?
    a. Intelligence is a general attribute, expressed in many different spheres of cognitive functioning.
    b. Intelligence, not just the store of knowledge, continues to grow until physical maturity.
    c. both a and b above
    d. neither a nor b

51. Joe has a CA of 10 and an MA of 5. His IQ would be:
    a. 50 points.
    b. 100 points.
    c. 150 points.
    d. 200 points.

52. Claire is a six-year-old who passes all the items on a Binet intelligence test that are passed by the average nine-year-old and she fails all the itemspassed by the average ten-year-old. Claire's IQ is:
    a. 50 points.
    b. 100 points.
    c. 150 points.
    d. impossible to determine with the information given.

53. The original equation for determining IQ was:
    a. $IQ = CA/MA \times 10$
    b. $IQ = MA/CA \times 10$
    c. $IQ = MA/CA \times 100$
    d. $IQ = CA/MA \times 100$

54. Within the age range of Binet's standardization group, the average IQ:
    a. increased with age.
    b. decreased with age.
    c. was 100 regardless of age.
    d. could not be determined.

55. Jim is seventeen and has a deviation IQ of 100 points. Meng is eleven and has the same deviation IQ as Jim. Which of the following statements is true?
    a. Meng has a higher IQ than an average 11-year-old.
    b. Meng has a higher mental age than Jim.
    c. Both Jim and Meng have the same mental age.
    d. Jim has the same mental age as the average seventeen-year-old.

56. Leroy is eighteen and has a deviation IQ of 110 points. Carol is ten years old and has the same deviation IQ as Leroy. In comparison, we can say that:
    a. both have the same percentile ranking in their age groups.
    b. both have the same mental age.
    c. both have the same CA
    d. none of the above

57. David Wechsler's adult intelligence scale differed from the Binet scales because it:
    a. included a large proportion of items requiring verbal skills.
    b. divided the obtained MA by a maximum CA of 16 points.
    c. included both verbal and performance subtests.
    d. designed the scale for group testing rather than individual administration.

58. The Kaufman Assessment Battery for Children (K-ABC) differs from the Stanford-Binet in that:
    a. it uses group testing.
    b. it is more culturally neutral.
    c. both a and b above
    d. neither a nor b above

59. Responding to a particular item on an intelligence test may require speech comprehension, adequate working memory, and mathematical reasoning. If a psychologist is more interested in the individual's functioning in these areas components than in a correct response to a single item, then she is conducting a test of:
    a. information processing.
    b. pre-intellectual functioning.
    c. neuropsychological assessment.
    d. none of the above

60. Neuropsychological tests are designed to:
    a. assess intelligence in individuals with neurological damage.
    b. uncover cognitive deficits by determining why individuals give incorrect answers to questions.
    c. determine the extent of normal functioning in the spinal cord and lower brain.
    d. none of the above

61. The usual definition of mental retardation is an IQ of:
    a. 100 points or below.
    b. 85 points or below.
    c. 70 points or below.
    d. 55 points or below.

62. About what percentage of the U.S. population is classified as mentally retarded?
    a. 0.1 percent
    b. 0.6 percent
    c. 2.5 percent
    d. 12 percent

63. It is irresponsible to use IQ scores alone to assess mental retardation. A diagnostician should also consider:
    a. emotional adjustment.
    b. adjustment to the demands of everyday living.
    c. performance on the K-ABC.
    d. sociocultural background.
    e. all of the above

64. Most people who are considered mentally retarded are classified as _____ in their degree of mental retardation.
    a. mild
    b. moderate
    c. severe
    d. profound
    e. There are approximately equal numbers in each category.

Answer: d
Intelligence testing
p. 638

65. What proportion of the mentally retarded are able to learn sixth-grade academic skills by their late teens?
    a. 0 percent
    b. 10 percent
    c. 50 percent
    d. 90 percent

Answer: d
Intelligence testing
p. 639

66. A cause of retardation is:
    a. brain damage occurring in the womb, during delivery, or after birth.
    b. impoverished environmental conditions.
    c. genetic disorders.
    d. all of the above

Answer: d
Intelligence testing
p. 639

67. Which of the following statements is false?
    a. About 90 percent of the mentally retarded can be categorized as "mildly" retarded.
    b. Retardation does not have a single cause.
    c. Retardation may be the result of genetic disorders.
    d. Retardation is fully assessed by intelligence testing.

Answer: d
What is intelligence?
  the psychometric approach
p. 640

68. Your textbook authors point out that when interpreting the results of intelligence tests, it is essential to recall that there may be an intermediate factor between high levels of intelligence and job performance, including:
    a. encouragement.
    b. more school.
    c. more skills.
    d. all of the above

Answer: b
What is intelligence? the psychometric
  approach
p. 640

69. When one assesses data acquired from psychological measuring instruments one is using a _____ to the study of intelligence.
    a. psychogenic approach
    b. psychometric approach
    c. psychoanalytic approach
    d. somatic approach

Answer: c
What is intelligence? the psychometric
  approach
p. 641

70. In your textbook, imaginary observations of the movements of a sea serpent were used as an analogy to illustrate:
    a. variance.
    b. validity.
    c. correlation.
    d. reliability.

Answer: b
What is intelligence? the psychometric
  approach
p. 641

71. According to your textbook, which of the following is analogous to the inference that a series of mental tests assess a single ability?
    a. the tail of one imaginary sea serpent is attached to the mouth of a second imaginary sea serpent
    b. all of the visible parts of an imaginary sea serpent tend to rise from and submerge under water together
    c. several imaginary sea serpents move together through an imaginary lake
    d. several imaginary sea serpents become entwined into a single ball

Answer: d
What is intelligence? the psychometric
    approach
p. 642

72. Which of the following techniques would be useful if you wanted to
    determine if several variables all have some commonality that affects
    their values?
    a.   variance assessment
    b.   standardization
    c.   the test-retest method
    d.   factor analysis

Answer: a
What is intelligence? the psychometric

    approach
p. 642

73. Spearman developed a statistical method to extract a common factor that
    all the various psychological tests assess. This technique is referred to
    as:
    a.   factor analysis.
    b.   general intelligence.
    c.   common feature analysis.
    d.   group analysis.

Answer: a
What is intelligence? the psychometric
    approach
p. 642

74. In Spearman's theory of intelligence, *g* stands for:
    a.   general intelligence.
    b.   group factor.
    c.   generalization gradient.
    d.   genetic influence.

Answer: a
What is intelligence? the psychometric
    approach
p. 642

75. The existence of a general intelligence *g* factor was inferred by Charles
    Spearman from:
    a.   the positive intercorrelations for tests of different intellectual
         skills.
    b.   the fact that different tests tap different specific abilities.
    c.   the tendency for people to score well on either verbal or mathe-
         matical tests, but not both.
    d.   high reliability coefficients for the results of individual tests.

Answer: c
What is intelligence? the psychometric
    approach
p. 642

76. According to CharlesSpearman, the intercorrelations among mental tests
    are not perfect due to:
    a.   variability in age.
    b.   variability in group factors.
    c.   variability in specific factors.
    d.   all of the above

Answer: c

What is intelligence? the psychometric
    approach
p. 643

77. The view that intelligence is a composite of separate abilities is called
    the:
    a.   crystallized intelligence theory.
    b.   general intelligence theory.
    c.   group factor theory.
    d.   cognitive consonance theory.

Answer: b
What is intelligence? the psychometric
    approach
p. 643

78. L. L. Thurstone's primary mental abilities are:
    a.   similar for Spearman's *g*.
    b.   several group factors, such as spatial and reasoning abilities.
    c.   fluid and crystallized intelligence.
    d.   the same as Spearman's specific factors.

Answer: b
What is intelligence? the psychometric
   approach
p. 643

79. L. L. Thurstone's primary mental abilities are:
   a. equivalent to Spearman's *g*.
   b. underlying factors inferred from clusters of positive correlations.
   c. the elements of a monarchic theory of intelligence.
   d. digit-span and paired-associate learning.

Answer: d
What is intelligence? the psychometric
   approach
p. 643

80. The ability to deal with essentially new problems is called:
   a. verbal intelligence.
   b. general intelligence.
   c. crystallized intelligence.
   d. fluid intelligence.

Answer: b
What is intelligence? the psychometric
   approach
p. 643

81. Fluid intelligence refers to:
   a. previously acquired skills and information.
   b. the ability to deal with new problems.
   c. verbal ability.
   d. performance measures.

Answer: c
What is intelligence? the psychometric
   approach
p. 643

82. Which of the following activities is likely to involve more fluid than crystallized intelligence?
   a. driving a car
   b. completing a crossword puzzle with a familiar theme
   c. repairing a toilet with a bobby pin
   d. balancing a checkbook

Answer: b
What is intelligence? the psychometric
   approach
p. 643

83. Gordon is really rather creative and he has a way of coming up with new ways of doing things. He could be described as:
   a. high in *g*.
   b. high in fluid intelligence.
   c. high in crystallized intelligence.
   d. low in *g*.

Answer: b
What is intelligence? the psychometric
   approach
p. 643

84. Janet has a knack of figuring things out. When faced with puzzles and problems she has never seen before, Janet always manages to find a solution. Janet is high in:
   a. general intelligence.
   b. fluid intelligence.
   c. primary mental ability.
   d. crystallized intelligence.
   e. analogical reasoning.

Answer: b
What is intelligence? the psychometric
   approach
p. 643

85. Crystallized intelligence refers to:
   a. aspects of intelligence that are genetically determined and resistant to environmental influence.
   b. an individual's repertoire of information, strategies, and cognitive skills.
   c. the reduction in intellectual fluidity that occurs with aging.
   d. the static nature of intellectual ability after puberty.
   e. none of the above

Answer: b
What is intelligence? the psychometric
   approach
p. 643

86. Studies of changes in intelligence as a function of aging suggest that:
   a. both fluid and crystallized intelligence tend to decline with age in adults.
   b. fluid intelligence tends to decline with age in adults, but crystallized intelligence does not.
   c. crystallized intelligence tends to decline with age in adults, but fluid intelligence does not.
   d. neither fluid nor crystallized intelligence decline with age in adults.

Answer: d
What is intelligence? the psychometric
   approach
p. 643

87. Which of the following is true regarding current interpretations of research demonstrating that certain mental abilities cluster together giving rise to *g* or a general intelligence measure?
   a. Scientists agree that *g* reflects a complex and diverse set of capacities that should not be lumped together.
   b. This general intelligence measure has been determined to be a measure of neural efficiency in the brain.
   c. Psychologists agree that *g* has neither practical nor theoretical value.
   d. none of the above

Answer: c
What is intelligence?
   the information processing approach
p. 644

88. Which of the following theoretical approaches to understanding intelligence emphasizes the fine-grained differences in the ways individuals perceive, attend, learn, remember, and think?
   a. the psychometric approach
   b. the behaviorist approach
   c. the information-processing approach
   d. the psychoanalytic approach

Answer: b
What is intelligence? the information-
   processing approach
p. 645

89. The results of studies relating intelligence to reaction time show that:
   a. simple reaction time is more strongly related to intelligence than is choice reaction time.
   b. choice reaction time is more strongly related to intelligence than is simple reaction time.
   c. the correlation between choice reaction time and intelligence decreases with the number of choices.
   d. the correlation between choice reaction time and intelligence is unrelated to the number of choices.

Answer: d
What is intelligence? the information
   processing approach
p. 645

90. According to your textbook authors, simple and choice reaction time measures may:
   a. allow study of "rock-bottom" differences in neurological functioning.
   b. be the underpinning of Spearman's *g*.
   c. be affected by many variables, including attention and comprehension.
   d. all of the above

Answer: d
What is intelligence? the information-
    processing approach
p. 646

91. There is a positive correlation between time to complete a lexical
    decision task and performances on:
    a. spatial tasks.
    b. tests of verbal intelligence.
    c. the WAIS.
    d. none of the above

Answer: b
What is intelligence? the information-
    processing approach
p. 646

92. There is a positive correlation between test scores for verbal intelligence
    and performances on:
    a. spatial tasks.
    b. lexical decision tasks.
    c. the WAIS.
    d. none of the above

Answer: b
What is intelligence? the information-
    processing approach
p. 646

93. There is a negative correlation between time to complete lexical
    identification tasks and performances on:
    a. spatial tasks.
    b. tests of verbal intelligence.
    c. the WAIS.
    d. none of the above

Answer: d
What is intelligence? the information-
    processing approach
p. 646

94. Robert Sternberg analyzed the cognitive components of _____
    tasks in standard intelligence tests?
    a. block design
    b. object assembly
    c. picture completion
    d. analogical reasoning

Answer: b
What is intelligence? the information
    processing approach
p. 646

95. According to Robert Sternberg, how many steps are required to solve an
    analogical reasoning problem such as, "Washington is to 1 as Lincoln is
    to (5, 10, 20)?"
    a. 1
    b. 3
    c. 10
    d. 15

Answer: a
What is intelligence? the information-
    processing approach
p. 646

96. Robert Sternberg's studies of analogic reasoning tasks showed that:
    a. the task involves several stages or components.
    b. the correlation between abstract reasoning ability and decision
        time on these tasks is about +0.65.
    c. performance on such analogic reasoning tasks is a good predictor
        of nonverbal intelligence, but not of verbal intelligence.
    d. all of the above

Answer: b
What is intelligence? the information
    processing approach
p. 647

97. What type of psychological test was specifically designed to assess the
    ability to store and manipulate different pieces of information
    simultaneously?
    a. matching-to-sample tasks
    b. active span tasks
    c. the WISC
    d. the Stanford-Binet test

Answer: a
What is intelligence? the information
   processing approach
p. 647

98. Suppose you are asked to perform a psychological task that takes this form:

   Part I.   4 + 5 = 9 (True or False?),
              dog;
              1 + 2 = 3 (True or False?),
              gas;
              6 + 2 = 8 (True or False?),
              nose.

   Part II.   Recall test for the words presented.

   What type of test is this?
    a.   an active span task
    b.   a spatial-analogy task
    c.   an analogical reasoning task
    d.   a form-memory task

Answer: d
What is intelligence? the information
   processing approach
p. 647

99. According to psychological research, scores on active span tasks tend to be correlated with:
    a.   verbal SAT scores.
    b.   measures of reading comprehension.
    c.   scores on some intelligence tests.
    d.   all of the above

Answer: a
What is intelligence? the information
   processing approach
p. 648

100. A(n) _____ individual is likely to use an organizational device to remember a list of words in a recall task.
    a.   adult
    b.   retarded
    c.   six-year-old
    d.   all of the above

Answer: d
What is intelligence? the information
   processing approach
p. 648

101. Six-year-old children differ from most adults in their performance on word recall tasks because:
    a.   six-year-olds tend to remember fewer words than adults.
    b.   six-year-olds are less likely to use organizational strategies than adults.
    c.   six-year-olds are less likely to use rythmic groups than adults.
    d.   all of the above

Answer: d
What is intelligence? the information

   processing approach
p. 648

102. When attempting to memorize a list of words, severely retarded individuals are likely to use _____ to enhance their performance.
    a.   rehearsal
    b.   semantic categorization
    c.   groupings of words
    d.   none of the above

Answer: c
What is intelligence? the information-
   processing approach
p. 648

103. Attempts to teach memory strategies to mentally retarded individuals have had limited success because:
    a.   these individuals could not learn the usual strategies.
    b.   memory strategies did not affect recall performance.
    c.   the learned strategies were not generalized to new task situations.
    d.   these individuals preferred to use their own strategies.

Answer: a

What is intelligence? the information-
   processing approach

p. 649

Answer: b

What is intelligence? the information-
   processing approach

p. 649

Answer: b

What is intelligence? beyond IQ

p. 650

Answer: a

What is intelligence? beyond IQ

p. 650

Answer: c

What is intelligence? beyond IQ

p. 650

Answer: a

What is intelligence? beyond IQ

p. 650

Answer: b

What is intelligence? beyond IQ

p. 650

104. Problem solving strategies learned by mentally retarded individuals will transfer to new situations if:
   a. the individuals are taught that they can be used in other situations.
   b. the strategies are based on verbal reasoning.
   c. the strategies involve repetitive rehearsal.
   d. all of the above

105. The lack of transfer of mental strategies for mentally retarded persons and children is because these individuals do not:
   a. have sufficiently developed verbal skills.
   b. develop plans for when to use their strategies.
   c. reason analogically.
   d. form complex cognitive components.

106. According to Robert Sternberg, which of the following is a form of intelligence that is typically assessed by intelligence tests?
   a. practical intelligence
   b. analytic intelligence
   c. creative intelligence
   d. all of the above

107. Which of the following forms of intelligence is probably most closely related to business success and an ability to perform well as a racetrack handicapper?
   a. practical intelligence
   b. analytic intelligence
   c. creative intelligence
   d. social intelligence

108. According to recent research findings, which of the following forms of intelligence is most likely to be the best predictor of business success?
   a. creative intelligence
   b. analytic intelligence
   c. practical intelligence
   d. none of the above

109. Practical intelligence seems to differ from analytic intelligence because:
   a. tasks demanding practical intelligence typically require some amount of information gathering.
   b. tasks demanding analytic intelligence typically require a great deal of tacit knowledge.
   c. tasks demanding analytic intelligence are typically situation-specific.
   d. all of the above

110. According to Robert Sternberg and his colleagues, tacit knowledge is most closely related to:
   a. analytic intelligence.
   b. practical intelligence.
   c. creative intelligence.
   d. social intelligence.

Answer: e
What is intelligence? beyond IQ
p. 650

111. Howard Gardner's concept of multiple intelligence includes which of the following?
    a. logical-mathematical ability
    b. bodily-kinesthetic ability
    c. linguistic ability
    d. personal intelligence
    e. all of the above

Answer: c
What is intelligence? beyond IQ
p. 650

112. One piece of evidence supporting Howard Gardner's notion of multiple intelligences is based on the fact that:
    a. there are some people who have multiple personalities.
    b. people seem to lose one type of intelligence earlier than others.
    c. brain lesions may impair some abilities while leaving others unaffected.
    d. at different times in our lives, we may excel at one type of intelligence at the expense of others.
    e. all of the above

Answer: b
What is intelligence? beyond IQ
p. 651

113. The existence of retarded savants seems to support Gardner's theory of multiple intelligences, yet the data from these individuals does not make the strongest possible case for his position because autistic savants:
    a. show skills characteristic of several intelligences, not just one.
    b. are fewer in number than one would expect if intelligences were truly independent of one another.
    c. don't live very long and they do not develop their other intelligences.
    d. none of the above

Answer: c
What is intelligence? beyond IQ
p. 651

114. The existence of retarded savants seems to support Gardner's theory of multiple intelligences, yet the data from these individuals does not make the strongest possible case for his position because:
    a. they are fewer in number than one would expect if intelligences were truly independent of one another.
    b. their abilities are often not as extraordinary as they are typically reported to be.
    c. both a and b above
    d. neither a nor b above

Answer: d
What is intelligence? beyond IQ
p. 653

115. Standard intelligence tests have limitations when applied to members of other cultures. As your text notes:
    a. American tests emphasize speed of response, whereas other cultures may emphasize careful, deliberate thought.
    b. American tests reward guessing, but in some cultures guessing is discouraged.
    c. American tests include questions that Western schooling has led us to expect and understand.
    d. all of the above

116. Intelligence research findings were used by Congress in 1924 to justify quotas on immigration from eastern and southern Europe. This evidence actually reflected:
    a. false reporting of these immigrants' intelligence scores.
    b. the misapplication of norms to populations different from the standardization population.
    c. a hereditary difference in intelligence between western and eastern Europeans.
    d. the greater impact of nature than nurture in determining intelligence.

117. The Immigration act of 1924 justified quotas on immigration from eastern and southern Europe based on the low intelligence test scores of immigrants from these regions. As your text notes:
    a. these low test scores resulted from the restricted gene pool in rural areas of Southern and Eastern Europe.
    b. the intelligence test scores of immigrants increased the longer they remained in the United States, though they always remained statistically lower than scores of native-born Americans.
    c. the intelligence test scores of immigrants increased the longer they remained in the United States, reaching the same level as native-born Americans after about twenty years.
    d. none of the above

118. The term *phenotype* refers to an organism's:
    a. recessive genes.
    b. visible structure and behavior.
    c. genetic blueprint.
    d. shared characteristics with offspring.

119. What are the observable characteristics for an individual?
    a. phenotype.
    b. genotype.
    c. PKU.
    d. recessive genes.
    e. none of the above

120. An organism's genetic blueprint is called its:
    a. expression.
    b. dominant gene.
    c. genotype.
    d. phenotype.

121. An individual's phenotype:
    a. is a direct expression of his or her genotype.
    b. is different from, and independent of, his or her genotype.
    c. depends on the interaction between an individual's genotype and his or her environment.
    d. none of the above

Answer: c
Nature, nurture, and intelligence
p. 656

122. Which of the following causes of mental retardation does not belong with the others?
    a. PKU
    b. fragile-X syndrome
    c. fetal alcohol syndrome
    d. Down's syndrome

Answer: c
Nature, nurture, and intelligence
p. 656

123. In discussing the disease phenylketonuria (PKU), your textbook authors point out that:
    a. it is caused by the interaction of a number of different genes, illustrating the importance of polygenic models of inheritance.
    b. it only arises in certain intrauterine environments, indicating the importance of gene-environment interactions in determining an individual's phenotype.
    c. it can be controlled through appropriate diet, indicating that what is genetic is not necessarily fixed and unchangeable.
    d. all of the above

Answer: c
Nature, nurture, and intelligence
p. 656

124. The significance of the disease phenylketonuria (PKU) is that it:
    a. shows that recessive genes will sometimes be expressed.
    b. is a genetically inherited disorder.
    c. is a genetically inherited disorder affected by environmental influences.
    d. is an example of polygenic inheritance.

Answer: c
Nature, nurture, and intelligence
p. 656

125. The high correlations between IQ scores for close biological relatives canbe interpreted as evidence that:
    a. mental ability is affected by genetic inheritance.
    b. similar environments produce similar abilities.
    c. both a and b
    d. neither a nor b

Answer: d
Nature, nurture, and intelligence
p. 656

126. Intelligence scores across childhood are generally fairly stable. As your text notes:
    a. this is evidence that genetic inheritance affects intelligence.
    b. this only shows that, over time, a child maintains the same relative standing among his or her age mates.
    c. this may occur because the child's environment is also likely to be constant over this time period.
    d. all of the above

Answer: a
Nature, nurture, and intelligence
p. 657

127. Members of a pair of identical and fraternal co-twins can have different:
    a. phenotypes.
    b. sexes.
    c. eye color.
    d. genotypes.

128. If we compare the genetic similarity of twins and their non-twin siblings, we find that:
    a. identical twins always have exactly the same genotype.
    b. fraternal twins have different genotypes and they may be different sexes.
    c. fraternal twins have different genotypes, and they are no more genetically similar than non-twin siblings.
    d. all of the above

129. Identical co-twins:
    a. can differ in genotype.
    b. can differ in phenotype.
    c. can differ in both genotype and phenotype.
    d. arise from the simultaneous fertilization of two ova by two different sperm cells.

130. Studies comparing identical and fraternal co-twins reveal that:
    a. identical co-twins have more highly correlated intelligence scores.
    b. identical co-twins are generally better in verbal tasks than fraternal twins.
    c. identical co-twins have higher IQ scores than fraternal twins.
    d. blood tests are usually poor indicators of whether two people are identical or fraternal twins.

131. Some twins perceive themselves to be identical even when blood typing indicates that they are not. A study comparing the similarity of identical and fraternal twins indicated that perceived identity was:
    a. a better predictor of phenotypic similarity than actual genotypic identity.
    b. as strong a predictor of phenotypic similarity as actual genotypic identity.
    c. a poor predictor of phenotypic similarity compared to actual genotypic identity.
    d. was a good predictor of genotypic identity in male twins, but a poor predictor in female twins.
    e. none of the above

132. Which of the following is the best evidence for a genetic contribution to intelligence?
    a. the high correlation between intelligence scores of close biological relatives
    b. the constancy of an individual's intelligence score over time
    c. the fact that intelligence scores of identical co-twins tend to be more similar than those of fraternal co-twins
    d. the fact that intelligence scores of fraternal co-twins tend to be more similar than those of non-twin siblings

Answer: d
Nature, nurture, and intelligence
p. 658

133. Comparisons between the correlations of intelligence scores in identical and fraternal co-twins is often regarded as evidence for the role of genetic factors in the development of intelligence. This argument is based on the assumption that:
    a. intelligence is a valid measure of cognitive abilities.
    b. identical twins have the same phenotype.
    c. fraternal twins have the same genotype and different phenotypes.
    d. the environments of identical twins are no more similar than those of fraternal twins.

Answer: b
Nature, nurture, and intelligence
p. 658

134. When we compare the similarity in intelligence scores for identical twins reared together with identical twins reared apart, we find that identical twins reared apart are:
    a. significantly less similar than are identical twins reared together.
    b. nearly as similar as identical twins reared together.
    c. as similar as identical twins reared together in mathematical skills, but significantly different in verbal abilities.
    d. none of the above

Answer: a
Nature, nurture, and intelligence
p. 658

135. Which of the following pairs of correlations coefficients below most closely corresponds to the observed correlations between the intelligence scores of adopted children, and those of their adoptive or biological parents?
    a. child-adoptive: 0.15; child-biological: 0.28
    b. child-adoptive: 0.28; child-biological: 0.15
    c. child-adoptive: 0.90; child-biological: 0.10
    d. child-adoptive: 0.10; child-biological: 0.90

Answer: a
Nature, nurture, and intelligence
p. 658

136. If we compare the correlation between adopted children's intelligence scores and those of their biological and adoptive mothers, we find that:
    a. in both childhood and adolescence, children's intelligence scores are more highly correlated with those of their biological mothers than with those of their adoptive mothers.
    b. in both childhood and adolescence, children's intelligence scores are more highly correlated with those of their adoptive mothers than with those of their biological mothers.
    c. in childhood, children's intelligence scores are more highly correlated with those of their biological mothers, while in adolescence children's intelligence scores are more highly correlated with those of their adoptive mothers.
    d. in childhood, children's intelligence scores are more highly correlated with those of their biological mothers, while in adolescence, their scores are equally correlated with those of their biological and adoptive mothers.
    e. none of the above

137. Which of the following is inconsistent with the idea that there is a hereditary component in the development of intelligence?
   a. more highly correlated intelligence scores for identical than fraternal twins
   b. greater similarity of intelligence scores between adopted children and their biological parents than with their adoptive parents
   c. more highly correlated intelligence scores for full siblings than half-siblings who share only one parent
   d. a positive correlation between intelligence scores of adopted children and their adoptive parents

138. The importance of environmental factors in the development of intelligence is illustrated by the fact that:
   a. the intelligence scores of adopted children are correlated with the intelligence scores of their adoptive mothers.
   b. the intelligence scores of fraternal co-twins are more highly correlated than those of non-twin siblings.
   c. the longer children are in impoverished environments the lower their intelligence scores are likely to be.
   d. all of the above

139. Which of the following sources of evidence supports the idea that the environment plays an important role in determining intelligence scores?
   a. Spending a longer time in an impoverished environment leads to a lower IQ score.
   b. Spending a longer time in an enriched environment leads to a higher IQ score.
   c. Children raised in more enriched environments than those of their biological parents have higher intelligence scores than would be predicted based on the scores of their biological parents.
   d. all of the above

140. What is the Flynn effect?
   a. the role of genetic inheritance in the development of intelligence
   b. the effects of cultural expectations on intelligence scores
   c. the high correlation between multiple intelligences
   d. the recent worldwide improvement in intelligence scores

141. Which of the following is not a potential explanation of the Flynn effect?
   a. the increased sophistication of shared cultures
   b. widespread improvements in nutrition
   c. genetic inheritance within cultures
   d. increased exposure to wider sets of perspectives

142. The heritability ratio (H) of a given trait represents:
   a. the amount of a trait for an individual that is due to genetic inheritance.
   b. the proportion of the total population variance that is due to genetic differences.
   c. the variance within an individual produced by genetic differences.
   d. the total variance for a population minus the variance produced by different environments.

143. Which of the following traits should you expect to show the lowest heritability?
    a. eye color
    b. height
    c. length of hair
    d. visual acuity

144. If all of the children born this year were raised in absolutely identical environments, the heritability coefficient for intelligence measures would eventually be:
    a. close to 0.
    b. close to 1.00.
    c. close to 0.50
    d. unaffected, since it is a measure of the direct contribution of the genotype to intelligence.

145. If all of the children born this year could be raised in absolutely identical environments, the variability in their intelligence scores in ten years' time would probably:
    a. equal 0.
    b. be considerably reduced.
    c. be considerably increased.
    d. not be affected.

146. Comparative studies of intelligence scores of black versus white populations indicate that:
    a. there are no overlaps between the intelligence score distributions of these populations.
    b. variations of scores within groups are greater than those between groups.
    c. both a and b
    d. neither a nor b

147. In discussing the issue of whether intelligence tests are culturally biased, your text notes that:
    a. members of different cultures may have different degrees of exposure to the information relevant to answering questions on an intelligence test.
    b. members of different cultures may have different motivations in a test-taking situation.
    c. members of different cultures may have different vocabularies for routine use.
    d. all of the above
    e. a and b only

148. The example of mixed seeds growing in different soils illustrates the fact that:
    a. within-group differences in intelligence can be attributed to genetic factors.
    b. between-group differences in intelligence can be attributed to genetic factors.
    c. within-group differences in intelligence can be attributed to environmental factors.
    d. between-group differences in intelligence can all be attributed to environmental factors.

149. One sample of mixed varieties of seed is planted in barren soil; another sample from the same seed package is planted in soil that is extremely fertile. When the plants are fully grown, there are differences in height, both within each group of plants and between the two groups. Which differences can be regarded as genetic in origin?
    a. the within-group differences
    b. the between-group differences
    c. both a and b
    d. neither a nor b

150. The textbook illustration of mixed seeds growing in different soils illustrated that:
    a. genetic differences between groups can be directly assessed.
    b. high within-group heritability shows that between-group differences are also genetically determined.
    c. within-group differences and between-group differences may be caused by separate factors.
    d. different environments tend to produce the same amount of within-group variability.

151. When the out-of-wedlock offspring of U.S. servicemen stationed in Germany after World War II were given intelligence tests, the results showed that:
    a. their intelligence scores were higher if the father was white rather than black.
    b. their intelligence scores were higher if the father was black rather than white.
    c. their intelligence scores were the same regardless of whether the father was black or white.
    d. their intelligence scores depended on the mother's ethnicity, and were higher when she was white than when she was black.

152. The average intelligence for a sample of black children raised by white, middle-class parents was _____ that of the national average for black children.
    a. well above
    b. the same as
    c. only slightly below
    d. still considerably lower than

Answer: d
Nature, nurture, and intelligence
p. 664

153. Scarr and Weinberg examined the intelligence scores of 99 black childrenraised by white, middle-class parents. They found that the mean intelligence score of these children was about:
    a. 90 points higher than the intelligence score for black children but lower than the average for white children.
    b. 100 points higher than the intelligence score for black children and the same as the average of white children.
    c. 115 points higher than the intelligence score for black children and higher than the average for white children.
    d. none of the above

Answer: d
Nature, nurture, and intelligence
p. 665

154. In their discussion of differences in intelligence scores between American ethnic groups, your textbook authors conclude that:
    a. at least part of these differences are environmental in origin.
    b. these differences should not be viewed as inevitable or immutable.
    c. within group variability tends to be greater than between groups variability.
    d. all of the above

Answer: b
Taking stock
p. 665

155. Which of the following is not a conclusion of your textbook authors in their chapter on the nature and measurement of intelligence?
    a. Individual differences in intelligence are the products of environment, inheritance, and interactions between these factors.
    b. Performance on intelligence tests has little predictive validity in the context of academic performance and therefore has little practical significance.
    c. While there is strong evidence that within group variability in intelligence scores is influenced by genetic inheritance, there is little evidence for a genetic basis for between-groups differences.
    d. Psychologists today do not have a single accepted definition of intelligence, nor is intelligence investigated by means of a single theoretical approach.

CHAPTER 16

Personality I: Assessment, Trait Theory, and the Behavioral-Cognitive Approach

Answer: a
Personality I
p. 669

1. The notion that individuals differ in characteristic personality traits:
   a. is found in the writings of ancient Greece.
   b. developed during the Renaissance.
   c. was first advanced by Freud.
   d. is a byproduct of the intelligence-testing movement.

Answer: c
Personality I
p. 667

2. The following are all theoretical approaches for understanding personality except the:
   a. humanistic approach.
   b. psychodynamic approach.
   c. environmental approach.
   d. behavioral approach.

Answer: d
Methods of assessment
p. 678

3. The first personality inventory was designed to:
   a. identify mentally retarded children.
   b. investigate the nature of personality traits.
   c. diagnose different categories of psychiatric patients.
   d. identify emotionally disturbed army recruits.

Answer: c
Methods of assessment
p. 672

4. Which of the following is the most commonly used objective personality test administered in professional settings today?
   a. the Thematic Apperception test
   b. the Rorschach test
   c. the MMPI and MMPI-2
   d. the CPI and CPI-2

Answer: b
Methods of assessment
p. 672

5. The Minnesota Multiphasic Personality Inventory (MMPI) is called *multiphasic* because:
   a. it was developed in stages over a period of several years.
   b. it was developed to simultaneously assess several different psychiatric patterns.
   c. it must be administered in more than one setting to achieve validity.
   d. it is available in a number of alternative forms.

Answer: a
Methods of assessment
p. 672

6. In the design of the MMPI, an item would be eliminated if:
   a. the item failed to distinguish between psychiatric patients and normal subjects.
   b. the responses of the different diagnostic groups to that item made no sense to the authors of the test.
   c. the item failed to correlate with any checkup scale.
   d. the item failed to have construct validity.

Answer: c
Methods of assessment
p. 673

7. The revised MMPI-2 differs from the original MMPI because the second version:
   a. contains fewer than half the number of questions that were on the original MMPI.
   b. no longer describes personality in terms of scores on a set of scales.
   c. was standardized with a much larger and more diverse sample.
   d. all of the above

Answer: b
Methods of assessment
p. 673

8. Which of the following is true regarding interpretation of MMPI results?
   a. Clinicians make judgments about individuals based on subjective impressions and clinical expertise.
   b. Clinicians examine score profiles for individuals considering each scale value in relation to others.
   c. Clinicians interpret each individual's overall score, so that 100 points is average and the standard deviation is 15 points.
   d. none of the above

Answer: b
Methods of assessment
p. 674

9. The MMPI contains a series of questions that are designed to detect if an individual is lying or responding carelessly. These are best referred to as:
   a. deviance scales.
   b. validity scales.
   c. reliability scales.
   d. antisocial scales.

Answer: c
Methods of assessment
p. 674

10. If a research participant answers *true* to a large proportion of MMPI items like "My soul sometimes leaves my body," it is likely that he or she:
    a. is deeply depressed and should receive therapy.
    b. is acutely psychotic and is a good candidate for drug treatment.
    c. has misunderstood the instructions, responded carelessly, or is lying.
    d. is a highly creative person who will perform well on other tests of creativity.

Answer: b
Methods of assessment
p. 674

11. One limitation of the MMPI is that it is not very useful for:
    a. distinguishing normal research participants from psychiatric patients.
    b. measuring personality traits within the normal range.
    c. discriminating among different types of psychiatric illness.
    d. diagnosing individual personality problems.

12. The California Psychological Inventory (CPI), unlike the MMPI, is:
    a. designed to be administered to young children.
    b. composed of items with uniformly high construct validity.
    c. a reliable index of psychiatric symptoms.
    d. a measure of normal personality traits.

13. According to your textbook the California Psychological Inventory (CPI) is:
    a. a test like the MMPI, but designed to assess the personality of normal rather than pathological populations.
    b. a test like the MMPI, but designed to assess both personal adjustment and lifestyle congruity.
    c. a personality test in the form of an adjective checklist that is designed to assess anxiety and need achievement.
    d. a test designed to assess anxiety and need achievement.
    e. none of the above

14. How is the CPI different from the MMPI?
    a. The MMPI has validity scales and the CPI does not.
    b. The MMPI was developed for psychiatric patients and the CPI for normal research participants.
    c. The MMPI includes items that criterion groups answered differently; the CPI was constructed on a theoretical basis.
    d. none of the above

15. The California Psychological Inventory assesses for personality traits such as:
    a. dominance.
    b. sociability.
    c. responsibility.
    d. all of the above

16. The predictive validity of personality inventories (i.e., the correlation between inventory scores and real-world events) is:
    a. less than +0.10.
    b. +0.30.
    c. +0.50.
    d. +0.70.
    e. none of the above

17. The best available predictor of future behavior in a particular situation is:
    a. the Minnesota Multiphasic Personality Inventory.
    b. the Wechsler Adult Intelligence Test.
    c. the California Psychological Inventory.
    d. past behavior in similar situations.

Answer: d
Methods of assessment
p. 675

Answer: a
Methods of assessment
p. 675

Answer: c
Methods of assessment
p. 675

Answer: b
Methods of assessment
p. 675

Answer: b
Methods of assessment
p. 675

Answer: d
Methods of assessment
p. 675

Answer: a
Methods of assessment
p. 676

18. Which of the following is probably the best predictor of a mental patient's rehospitalization following his release?
    a. subscores on the MMPI
    b. interpretations based on both the TAT and the Rorschach test
    c. the patient's income and education level
    d. the thickness of the patient's medical file folder

19. Based on what you know about the published research, what would be the best predictor for whether a given person will commit theft?
    a. how often she or he has stolen things in the past
    b. the psychopathic deviance score on the MMPI-2
    c. ratings and predictions about the individual's behavior from peers
    d. self-predictions derived from a confidential questionnaire

20. _____ involves formulating and testing hypotheses about the relationships between a hypothesized personality trait and various overt behaviors.
    a. Predictive validation
    b. Reliability estimation
    c. Construct validation
    d. A checkup scale

21. Validating hypotheses and theoretical formulations of proposed personality traits using a number of different behaviors is called:
    a. predictive validation.
    b. construct validation.
    c. internal validation.
    d. reliability validation.

22. Which of the following groups is least likely to have high average scores on the psychopathic deviance scale of the MMPI?
    a. careless hunters
    b. good-natured nurses
    c. professional actors
    d. high school dropouts

23. The personality trait of psychopathic deviance is characterized in its extreme form by:
    a. shallow social and emotional ties.
    b. disregard of social mores and conventions.
    c. failure to consider potential dangers.
    d. all of the above

24. According to many authors (e.g., Cronbach), even a perfect measure of personality structure would not allow us to predict behavior with absolute accuracy because:
    a. personality only provides a disposition; circumstances determine how that disposition will be expressed.
    b. personality structure is unstable and changes from moment to moment.
    c. personality traits are only theoretical constructs.
    d. personality structures change just because of the testing experiences.

25. The Barnum effect refers to our tendency to:
    a. accept a very general personality description as accurate description of ourselves.
    b. believe the descriptions of ourselves that others tell us, even when our behavior is inconsistent with that description.
    c. exaggerate the positive traits of our personalities, downplaying the negative traits.
    d. none of the above

26. Which of the following brief personality sketches would be unlikely to produce a Barnum effect?
    a. There are times when you feel generous and other times when you are unable to part with things easily. You tend to be hard on yourself in many situations.
    b. You are outgoing in some situations and shy in others. You often "fly off the handle" at others when they irritate you.
    c. You feel that you have talents that have not been recognized yet. You are generally able to compensate for your personality weaknesses.
    d. You want others to respect you. You are confident in some situations and insecure in others.

27. _____ are devices for assessing personality by presenting unstructured stimuli that elicit responses of many kinds.
    a. Personality inventories
    b. Projective techniques
    c. Taxonomies
    d. Stimulus inventories

28. Tests containing ambiguous stimuli that can be interpreted in different ways by different research participants are:
    a. measures with high validity.
    b. objective tests.
    c. projective tests.
    d. none of the above

29. Users of projective techniques criticize paper-and-pencil tests such as the MMPI because:
    a. participants can easily lie to the test administrator.
    b. such tests are too loosely structured, and questionnaire items mean different things to different people.
    c. the questionnaire items can only address those aspects of personality of which the participant is consciously aware.
    d. correlations between scores on the MMPI and criterion measures are unacceptably low.

30. Which of the following is not a projective technique?
    a. sentence completion
    b. the Thematic Apperception Test
    c. the California Psychological Inventory
    d. the Rorschach inkblots

31. When taking the Rorschach inkblot test, the research participant is asked to:
    a. look at each inkblot and say what it might be.
    b. sort the inkblots into three piles, using a freely chosen criterion.
    c. write a story about each inkblot picture.
    d. choose the inkblot that looks most like a sample item.

32. In general, repeated Rorschach responding that involve the entire inkblot is interpreted as indicating:
    a. emotionality and impulsivity.
    b. negativism and rebelliousness.
    c. rich imagination and creative impulses.
    d. integrative, conceptual thinking.

33. Rorschach experts tend to interpret the frequent use of small details in the cards as a sign of:
    a. compulsive rigidity.
    b. rebelliousness and negativism.
    c. imagination and a rich inner life.
    d. emotionality and impulsivity.

34. Rorschach experts tend to interpret a relatively frequent use of the white spaces on the cards (which then serve as figure rather than as ground) as a sign of:
    a. compulsive rigidity.
    b. rebelliousness and negativism.
    c. imagination and a rich inner life.
    d. emotionality and impulsivity.

35. In traditional approaches to Rorschach interpretation, _____ is/are less important than the other major scoring categories.
    a. determinants
    b. shape
    c. content
    d. location

36. TAT interpretation is primarily based on:
    a. determinants.
    b. style.
    c. content.
    d. location.

37. _____ are/is to _____ as _____ are/is to _____.
    a. Determinants, TAT; content, Rorschach
    b. Determinants, Rorschach; content, TAT
    c. Content, CPI; psychopathology, MMPI
    d. Psychopathology, CPI; content, MMPI

Answer: d
Methods of assessment
p. 679

38. When taking the Thematic Apperception Test (TAT), the research participant's task is to:
    a. respond to a word with the first thing that comes to mind.
    b. discover the underlying theme in a set of brief descriptions.
    c. choose the picture that best fits a given story.
    d. construct a story about each of a set of ambiguous pictures.

Answer: b
Methods of assessment
p. 679

39. In clinical practice, TAT interpretations:
    a. are usually checked against MMPI scores.
    b. are usually impressionistic and global.
    c. employ a three-category scoring system.
    d. are systematic and structured.

Answer: e
Methods of assessment
p. 680

40. In discussing the validity of Rorschach indices, your textbbok authors note that:
    a. indices that do not refer to content are moderately correlated (0.35–0.50) with later psychiatric diagnoses.
    b. indices that are said to relate to creativity correlate modestly (0.25–0.40) with actual artistic creativity.
    c. indices that refer to content analyses are modestly (0.35–0.40) correlated with normal or pathological personality variables.
    d. none of the above

Answer: c
Methods of assessment
p. 680

41. Expert Rorschach predictions based on the entire verbatim record from testing with psychiatrists' judgments have a correlation coefficient of about
    a. $r = 0.00$.
    b. $r = +0.05$.
    c. $r = +0.21$.
    d. $r = +0.45$.

Answer: d
Methods of assessment
p. 680

42. In their discussion of the validity of the TAT, your textbook authors note that:
    a. scores on the TAT do not predict psychiatric diagnosis, but they are moderately correlated with normal personality traits.
    b. TAT scores are better predictors of psychiatric diagnosis than scores or indices on the Rorschach.
    c. TAT scores are correlated with differences in emotional states, but not with differences in cognitive functioning.
    d. none of the above

Answer: b
Methods of assessment
p. 681

43. A number of studies have shown that the TAT can be useful:
    a. in distinguishing psychiatric from normal populations.
    b. in detecting the presence of certain motives.
    c. in predicting likely future occupations.
    d. in distinguishing between different psychiatric groups.

44. In discussing the incremental validity of the Rorschach test and the TAT, your text notes that psychologists:
    a. make more accurate inferences about an individual's personality characteristics if they have Rorschach records as well as the individual's case history.
    b. make more accurate inferences about an individual's personality characteristics if they have TAT records as well as the individual's case history.
    c. are no more accurate in making inferences about an individual's personality characteristics if they have Rorschach and TAT records in addition to the individual's case history.
    d. are more accurate in making inferences about an individual's personality characteristics if they have Rorschach and TAT records in addition to the individual's case history.

45. The criticism that the Rorschach test and the TAT have little or no "incremental validity" in clinical practice means that the results of these tests:
    a. add little, if any, significant information to what is known from case histories.
    b. do not improve with increased expertise of the administrator.
    c. do not distinguish between major diagnostic groups.
    d. are scored differently by different clinicians.

46. Studies of the validity of the Rorschach test and the TAT indicate that these tests:
    a. are very good predictors of clinical psychiatric diagnoses.
    b. are poor predictors of psychiatric disorders, but provide considerable information about normal individuals.
    c. have minimal predictive validity, but may be useful in conjunction with clinical interviews.
    d. none of the above

47. According to your textbook authors, studies of the validity of the Rorshach test and the TAT reveal that:
    a. both the Rorschach test and TAT have limited validity.
    b. the predictive validity of the Rorschach test is low, while the predictive validity of the TAT is higher than that of most personality tests.
    c. the predictive validity of the TAT is low, while the predictive validity of the Rorschach test is higher than that of most personality tests.
    d. the predictive validity of both the Rorschach test and the TAT tends to be higher than that of most personality tests.
    e. the predictive validity of Rorschach test is low, but its incremental validity is high.

48. Your textbook authors discuss whether the Rorschach test and the TAT provide useful information beyond that available in a research participant's case history. They conclude that:
    a. the incremental validity of both the Rorschach test and the TAT is high.
    b. the incremental validity of the Rorschach test is low, while the incremental validity of the TAT is very high.
    c. the incremental validity of the TAT is low, while the incremental validity of the Rorschach test is high.
    d. the incremental validity of both the Rorschach test and TAT tends to be low.

49. *Energetic*, *lazy*, *meticulous*, and *conscientious* are attributes called:
    a. projective deviations.
    b. personality inventories.
    c. personality traits.
    d. projective characteristics.

50. In general, trait theories involve the idea that:
    a. different situations produce entirely different behaviors.
    b. a person's behavior is rarely consistent across time and situations.
    c. people can be grouped according to their basic underlying personality characteristics.
    d. the search for patterns in personality is misguided.

51. Raymond Cattell's personality inventory:
    a. was derived from a factor analysis of 171 trait names based on the thousands of words used to describe personality attributes.
    b. assesses 16 primary dimensions of personality.
    c. both a and b
    d. neither a nor b

52. Which of the following is not one of the Big Five personality factors identified by Warren Norman (1963)?
    a. extroversion
    b. emotional stability
    c. agreeableness
    d. concentration
    e. conscientiousness

53. "*My Very Elderly Mother Just Sold Uncle Nick's Puppy*" is an acronym or memory aid for remembering the names of the planets in our solar system (i. e., *Mercury, Venus, Earth, Mars, Jupiter, Saturn, Uranus, Neptune, Pluto*). Which of the following is an acronym that will help you remember the "Big Five" dimensions of personality?
    a. TRIPE
    b. WAGON
    c. OCEAN
    d. PORCH

Answer: c
The trait approach
p. 684

54. Hans Eysenck has attempted to encompass personality differences in a space defined by two dimensions, specifically _____ and _____.
    a. submissive-dominant; good-bad
    b. sociability-unsociability; activity level-inactivity level
    c. neuroticism-stability; introversion-extroversion
    d. conscientiousness; aggression

Answer: b
The trait approach
p. 685

55. Which of the values below is the one that Hans Eysenck would regard as the most likely correlation between introversion and neuroticism?
    a. $r = -0.20$
    b. $r = 0.00$
    c. $r = +0.20$
    d. $r = +0.40$

Answer: a
The trait approach
p. 685

56. A person is extremely aggressive, excitable, changeable, and impulsive. On the scales employed by Hans Eysenck, how do you think this individual would be categorized?
    a. neurotic extrovert
    b. non-neurotic extrovert
    c. neurotic introvert
    d. non-neurotic introvert

Answer: b
The trait approach
p. 685

57. Hans Eysenck has pointed out that his personality theory encompasses the four personality types proposed by Hippocrates. Specifically, Eysenck believes that Hippocrates' _____ type is equivalent to his own _____ character.
    a. choleric; stable extrovert
    b. melancholic; neurotic introvert
    c. sanguine; stable introvert
    d. phlegmatic; neurotic extrovert
    e. all of the above

Answer: d
The trait approach
p. 643

58. In discussing Hans Eysenck's third dimension of personality (i.e., psychoticism), your textbook authors note that psychoticism:
    a. is independent of both neuroticism and extroversion/introversion.
    b. is related to aggressive, impulsive, and self-centered attributes.
    c. encompasses the Big Five dimensions of agreeableness and conscientiousness.
    d. all of the above

Answer: c
The trait approach
p. 687

59. According to your textbook, Walter Mischel has criticized trait theories of personality on the basis of evidence that:
    a. different observers tend to describe a single individual in terms of different traits.
    b. personality is based on more fluid cognitive structures rather than systems of traits.
    c. people behave much less consistently across situations than trait theory would predict.
    d. all of the above

Answer: a
The trait approach
p. 687

60. Your textbook authors note that Walter Mischel criticized trait theory on the grounds that:
    a. people seem to behave much less consistently across situations than trait theory predicts.
    b. people seem to behave much more consistently across situations than trait theory would predict.
    c. people's behavior is no more consistent in similar situations than it is in very different situations.
    d. none of the above

Answer: b
The trait approach
p. 688

61. Walter Mischel described research on trait consistency showing that children who cheat on a test in school are most likely to be equally dishonest:
    a. at home.
    b. on another classroom test.
    c. in an athletic competition.
    d. all of the above

Answer: d
The trait approach
p. 688

62. Walter Mischel reported that children are _____ in their behavior in different circumstances. He saw this as evidence _____ the validity of personality traits.
    a. consistent; supporting
    b. inconsistent; supporting
    c. consistent; against
    d. inconsistent; against

Answer: b
The trait approach
p. 688

63. Walter Mischel has argued that personality tests have low predictive validities because:
    a. these tests were designed to yield construct validity rather than predictive validity.
    b. these tests are based on the assumption that behavior is consistent across situations.
    c. these test scores contain numerous errors of measurement.
    d. research participants try to hide personality flaws when taking the tests.

Answer: c
The trait approach
p. 688

64. Situationism is the idea that:
    a. it is important to measure traits in the situation in which they are most likely to appear or be relevant.
    b. personality traits manifest themselves differently in different situations.
    c. it is the characteristics of a situation rather than one's personality traits that determine how one behaves.
    d. none of the above

Answer: a
The trait approach
p. 688

65. In discussing consistencies in personality, your textbook authors describe, situationism which is:
    a. the idea that a person's behavior is more strongly determined by the situation than by internal traits.
    b. the observation that people are more consistent in their behavior in the same situation than in different situations.
    c. the observation the people are no more consistent in their behavior in similar situations than in different situations.
    d. the idea that personality consistency between situations is the most valid test of a personality theory.
    e. none of the above

Answer: d
The trait approach
p. 689

66. Critics of trait theory argue that:
    a. people's personalities seem stable because we repeatedly see them in the same social settings.
    b. our belief that there are consistent personality traits is an error of inference.
    c. traits are in the eye of the beholder rather than in the personality of the individual beheld.
    d. all of the above

Answer: d
The trait approach
p. 689

67. Longitudinal studies of personality traits indicate that:
    a. traits are no more consistent across time than they are across situations.
    b. the dependability of high-school males was only weakly correlated with their same trait ten years later.
    c. both a and b
    d. none of the above

Answer: d
The trait approach
p. 689

68. What were the conclusions of Seymour Epstein, who studied the cross-situational consistency of behavior?
    a. He argued that studies showing low cross-situational consistency employed only small samples of behaviors.
    b. He argued that determinations of cross-situational consistency require that behavior be measured on a number of occasions.
    c. He found that the correlations between mood and behavior across time increased with increasing numbers of observations.
    d. all of the above

Answer: d
The trait approach
p. 690

69. Walter Mischel has argued that human behavior is far less consistent than many personality theories suggest. Critics of Mischel's viewpoint present the counter-argument that:
    a. if properly assessed an individual's traits show considerable consistency over time.
    b. studies showing low cross-situational consistency assess too few behaviors to provide reliable measurements of traits.
    c. behaviors that appear to be different may actually be manifestations of the same trait.
    d. all of the above

Answer: d
The trait approach
p. 690

70. An eight-year-old boy is rated as highly aggressive because he fights with his peers a great deal. Results from longitudinal studies of traits suggest that:
    a. he will show the same overt behavior as an adult.
    b. his adult level of aggressiveness cannot be predicted.
    c. his aggressiveness will decrease significantly over the years.
    d. he will remain more aggressive than average, but exhibit it in different ways.

Answer: c
The trait approach
p. 691

71. Jamal and Liz are each given two tests of fearfulness, both rated on a 10-point scale in which zero means *no fear* and 10 means *maximum fear*. In the first test, both Jamal and Liz are confronted with a vicious dog. Here, Jamal's fear rating is 9 points and Liz's is 5. In the second test, both are about to take a difficult examination. Here, Jamal's rating is 5 points and Liz's is 9. These results illustrate:
    a. situational effects.
    b. differences in personal traits.
    c. person-by-situation interactions.
    d. none of the above.

Answer: c
The trait approach
p. 692

72. "Some people are more anxious than others; some situations evoke more fear than others." This statement refers to:
    a. the role of genetic inheritance in determining personality.
    b. the role of environment determining personality.
    c. the idea that personality is the result of an interaction between person and situation.
    d. the idea that anxiety develops in fearful situations.

Answer: b
The trait approach
p. 692

73. Mahalia and Martin, are each given two tests of fearfulness, both rated on a 10-point scale in which zero means *no fear* and 10 means *maximum fear*. In the first tests, both Mahalia and Martin are confronted with a vicious dog. Here, Mahalia's fear rating is 4 points while Martin's is 8 points. In the second test, both Mahalia and Martin are about to take a difficult examination. Here, Mahalia's rating is 4 points while Martin's is 8 points. The results illustrate:
    a. situational effects.
    b. differences in personal traits.
    c. a person-by-situation interactions.
    d. none of the above

Answer: a
The trait approach
p. 692

74. Jerome and Jenny are each given two tests of fearfulness, both rated on a 10-point scale in which zero means *no fear* and 10 means *maximum fear*. In the first test, both Jerome and Jenny are confronted with a vicious dog. Here, Jerome's fear-rating is 9 points and Jenny's is 9 points. In the second test, both are about to take a difficult examination. Now, Jerome's rating is 3 points and Jenny's rating is 3 points. These results illustrate:
    a. situational effects.
    b. differences in personal traits.
    c. a person-by-situation interactions.
    d. none of the above

75. The demonstration of person-by-situation interactions challenges:
    a. the existence of personality traits.
    b. the usefulness of general traits.
    c. the reality of *person constancy.*
    d. the assumption of situational influence.

76. Which of the following probably involves a person-by-situation interaction?
    a. Each of three research participants shows the same overall amount of aggressiveness, averaged across three different situations.
    b. Each of three participants produces the same overall amount of aggressiveness, averaged across three different participants.
    c. Each of three participants responds with a different amounts of aggression to the same situation.
    d. all of the above

77. Which of the following scenarios best illustrates a reciprocal interaction between person and situation, according to a social learning perspective?
    a. Herman examined the university course listing and then selected his fall courses, foreseeing the day he would be a well-trained, practicing psychologist.
    b. Belinda earned $1,500 by mowing lawns and doing yard work last summer.
    c. Mortimer dreamed about a large white rabbit wearing argyle socks and he wondered whether it could be a symbolic representation of his father.
    d. Euphemia is a self-actualizing individual who often has what she calls "peak experiences."

78. Which of the following is most likely to result in high levels of behavioral consistency for members of a group?
    a. interacting with family and friends.
    b. selecting a new vacation spot
    c. deciding to make a doctor's appointment
    d. attending a wedding ceremony

79. The self-monitoring scale developed by Mark Snyder:
    a. assesses person-by-situation interactions.
    b. assesses how consistent one's behavior is across different situations.
    c. uses factor analysis to assess personality traits.
    d. assesses the extent to which people try to control the impressions they make on others.
    e. none of the above

80. An individual who is high in self-monitoring:
    a. cares very much about the impression others have of him or her.
    b. is likely to be much more consistent in behavior from situation to situation than a low self-monitoring person.
    c. is extremely likely to be stubborn and rigid in behavior.
    d. all of the above

81. If people behave consistently from time to time and from situation to situation, this provides evidence for:
    a. person constancy.
    b. the adequacy of trait theory.
    c. an adequate taxonomy of personality traits.
    d. all of the above

82. A kindergarten pupil's report card bears the teacher's comment that she is "very easygoing, good-humored, and affable." Given only this information, which of the following predictions would you most confidently make?
    a. Her parents are overindulgent.
    b. She is much more troublesome at home.
    c. She was a good-humored, affable baby.
    d. Her siblings are equally easygoing.

83. According to Buss and Plomin, the two major dimensions of temperament are:
    a. sociability and emotionality.
    b. activity and emotionality.
    c. inhibition and excitation.
    d. none of the above

84. Buss and Plomin argued that emotionality and sociability are the two major dimensions of temperament. They also suggested that:
    a. the adult trait dimension of extroversion is represented in children by the trait of sociability.
    b. the adult trait dimension of neuroticism/stability is represented in children by the trait of emotionality.
    c. both sociability and emotionality are fairly stable over the first twenty years of life.
    d. all of the above

85. The claim that genetic factors contribute to personality is best supported by the fact that:
    a. different people have different reactions to the same situation.
    b. some traits seem to be related to somatotypes.
    c. an aggressive child is likely to become an aggressive adult.
    d. identical twins are more alike than fraternal twins on some personality measures.

86. The California Psychological Inventory scores of 850 pairs of twins were examined in an attempt to determine the heritability of personality traits. The results showed that:
    a. fraternal twins' scores were as similar as those of identical twins.
    b. identical twins were more alike than fraternal twins on every scale of the test.
    c. identical twins were more alike in personality than intelligence.
    d. fraternal twins were more alike on some scales of the test than identical twins.

87. Studies of the heritability of traits suggest that:
    a. almost all personality traits are equally heritable.
    b. most heritable personality traits seem to be related to Eysenck's supertraits of extroversion and neuroticism.
    c. both factor analytic studies of personality and studies of temperament reveal the importance of extroversion and neuroticism as foundations for personality traits.
    d. all of the above

Answer: d
The trait approach
p. 698

88. Which of the following is probably not a between-family difference in environment?
    a. child-rearing attitudes
    b. birth order and spacing of children
    c. socioeconomic status of parents
    d. parental religion

Answer: b
The trait approach
p. 698

89. Which of the following is evidence that it is between-family differences, rather than within-family differences, that operate to produce variations in personality?
    a. The correlation between the personality traits of adopted children and their adoptive siblings is essentially zero.
    b. The correlation between the personality traits of adopted children and their adoptive parents is essentially zero.
    c. The correlation between the traits of identical twins raised together and those reared apart is basically the same.
    d. none of the above

Answer: d
The trait approach
p. 699

90. Studies of how between-family differences and personality development suggest that:
    a. the average correlations between adopted children and their adoptive siblings is very low.
    b. the similarity of identical twins reared apart is greater than the similarity for identical twins reared together.
    c. neuroticism, but not extroversion, seems more affected by between-family than by within-family variables.
    d. all of the above

Answer: a
The trait approach
p. 699

91. Which of the following is not a within-family difference in environment?
    a. child-rearing attitudes in parents.
    b. birth order and spacing of children.
    c. accidents, injuries, and diseases that affect only a single child.
    d. differences in friends, teachers, and peers.

Answer: a
The trait approach
p. 699

92. In discussing how within-family differences arise, your textbook authors suggest that some within-family differences occur:
    a. by chance.
    b. because genetic differences lead siblings to create different environments for themselves.
    c. both a and b
    d. neither a nor b

Answer: c
The trait approach
p. 700

Answer: d
The trait approach
p. 700

93. In discussing the relative importance of within- and between-family differences, your textbook authors suggest that:
    a. in general, within-family differences are more important than between-family differences.
    b. between-family differences are fairly important in the development of intelligence.
    c. between-family differences may be more important when we consider families from a wider range of socioeconomic classes, and from different cultures.
    d. all of the above

Answer: b
The trait approach
p. 701

94. According to Hans Eysenck, introversion corresponds to:
    a. low levels of central nervous system arousal.
    b. high levels of central nervous system arousal.
    c. low levels of social neuroticism.
    d. high levels of social neuroticism.

Answer: d
The trait approach
p. 701

95. According to Hans Eysenck, introverts have:
    a. higher basic alertness than extroverts.
    b. lower basic alertness than extroverts.
    c. higher pain thresholds than extroverts.
    d. lower pain thresholds than extroverts.

Answer: d
The trait approach
p. 701

96. According to Hans Eysenck, introverts:
    a. have a higher pain tolerance than extroverts.
    b. prefer lower noise levels when studying than extroverts.
    c. are less active sexually than extroverts.
    d. all of the above

Answer: b
The trait approach
p. 701

97. According to Zuckerman, sensation-seeking:
    a. is related to, even identical to, extroversion.
    b. focuses on liveliness and intolerance for boredom, but has little to do with sociability.
    c. both a and b
    d. neither a nor b

Answer: b
The trait approach
p. 701

98. According to Zuckerman, what neurotransmitter is present in low levels in the brains of sensation seekers?
    a. acetylcholine
    b. norepinephrine
    c. dopamine
    d. serotonin

Answer: a
The behavioral-cognitive approach
p. 702

99. According to the theatrical metaphor developed in your textbook, which of the following is most important to the behavioral actor?
    a. overt behavior that others can see
    b. the emotions associated with actions
    c. unconscious conflicts that affect behavior
    d. events that occurred during childhood

Answer: a
The behavioral-cognitive approach
p. 703

100. B. F. Skinner's radical behaviorism included the idea that:
  a. the most appropriate subject matter of psychology is overt behavior.
  b. emotions and thoughts play a causal role in determining behavior.
  c. behavior is the result of interactions between internal, biological factors and the individual's environment.
  d. all of the above

Answer: d
The behavioral-cognitive approach
p. 703

101. B. F. Skinner believed that humans behave the way they do because of:
  a. internal mechanisms.
  b. their wishes and dreams.
  c. their genetic makeup.
  d. their external environment.

Answer: a
The behavioral-cognitive approach
p. 703

102. Dr. Know believes that people do what they do because of the situation they are in now or have been in previously. Dr. Know is a proponent of the:
  a. behavioral approach.
  b. psychodynamic approach.
  c. humanistic approach.
  d. trait approach.

Answer: c
The behavioral-cognitive approach
p. 703

103. Dr. Brown tells her friend, "I think that humans, like animals, need to be studied objectively." Dr. Brown is most likely a:
  a. neo-Freudian.
  b. psychoanalyst.
  c. behaviorist.
  d. psychiatrist.

Answer: a
The behavioral-cognitive approach
p. 704

104. How do behaviorists explain human behavior that continues to occur even when reinforcement is not present?
  a. Behavior patterns persist because they have been rewarded some of the time.
  b. Humans seek and need attention so they persist in these behaviors.
  c. These behaviors are embedded in personality and cannot be extinguished.
  d. Radical behaviorists do not attempt to explain this phenomenon.

Answer: b
The behavioral-cognitive approach
p. 704

105. Sally is rewarded every time she picks up her toys. Much to her parents' dismay, Sally suddenly stops engaging in this desirable activity. Sally's parents should probably use _____ to maintain Sally's good behavior.
  a. operant conditioning
  b. partial reinforcement
  c. classical conditioning
  d. negative reinforcement

Answer: d
The behavioral-cognitive approach
p. 704

106. People will often spend hundreds of dollars playing the slot machines at a casino. Slot machines typically operate based on which of the following?
  a. continuous reinforcement
  b. negative reinforcement
  c. behavioral contrast
  d. none of the above

107. Behaviorists argue that classically-conditioned fear reactions are very persistent because:
    a. we tend to avoid the feared object or situation, and so the fear can never be extinguished.
    b. for evolutionary reasons, fear is a stronger motivator than desire.
    c. human classical conditioning is partly determined by conscious cognitions, which are more difficult to change than reflexive conditioned responses.
    d. all of the above

108. Albert Bandura and Walter Mischel are best referred to as:
    a. radical behaviorists.
    b. neo-Freudians.
    c. social learning theorists.
    d. cognitive behavioralists.

109. In Walter Mischel's view of personality, competencies:
    a. are what a person knows and is capable of doing.
    b. are the individual's ways of interpreting the world.
    c. are the ways in which the individual regulates his or her behavior.
    d. are the individual's personal value structures.
    e. none of the above

110. What term below refers to the ways in which individuals tend to interpret situations?
    a. competencies
    b. subjective values
    c. self-regulatory systems
    d. encoding strategies

111. While Abdul assumes that others are basically honest and friendly, his sister Jill assumes that every behavior of others has some ulterior motive and that people cannot be trusted. Mischel would say that Abdul and Jill have very different:
    a. subjective values.
    b. self-regulatory systems.
    c. expectancies.
    d. encoding strategies.

112. Both Ralph and Harold want to ask Chris out to the movies. Ralph believes that Chris will turn down his invitation, while Harold believes that Chris will accept his. In terms of Mischel's model, we would say that Ralph and Harold have very different:
    a. expectancies.
    b. self-regulatory systems.
    c. subjective values.
    d. encoding strategies.
    e. none of the above

Answer: c
The behavioral-cognitive approach
p. 705

113. Ralph and Rebecca have just received their M.D. degrees and they are now deciding on their fields of specialization. Ralph entered medicine primarily because he wanted to make a positive difference in the lives of others: He opts for family medicine, which is emotionally rewarding. Rebecca entered medicine because of the status and income associated with it: She opts for surgery, which is much more lucrative. In terms of Mischel's model, these choices most clearly reflect differences between Ralph and Rebecca in their:
    a. self-regulatory systems.
    b. perceived competencies.
    c. subjective values.
    d. expectancies.
    e. none of the above

Answer: c
The behavioral-cognitive approach
p. 705

114. Competencies, encoding strategies, expectancies, and subjective values are all hallmarks of:
    a. Freud's psychosexual stages.
    b. Skinner's radical behaviorism.
    c. Mischel's social learning theory.
    d. Rotter's internal/external scale.

Answer: a
The behavioral-cognitive approach
p. 705

115. Penelope plans to become a Nobel-Prize-winning physicist. She studies hard in college and spends many hours preparing for her entrance exams. Mischel would label these behaviors part of Penelope's:
    a. self-regulatory system.
    b. encoding strategies.
    c. expectancies.
    d. internal locus of control.

Answer: d
The behavioral-cognitive approach
p. 706

116. In discussing people's feelings about control, your textbook authors suggest that:
    a. most people prefer to have control over their environments.
    b. babies are happier if an overhead mobile turns because of their actions compared to when it turns automatically.
    c. nursing home patients who had more control over their environments were more active and felt better than patients who lacked this control.
    d. all of the above

Answer: b
The behavioral-cognitive approach
p. 706

117. Attributional style is used to predict which of the following?
    a. how people will react in stressful situations
    b. if a person is likely to suffer from depression
    c. how a person identifies the causes of events in her life
    d. the nature of a person's perceived locus of control

Answer: a
The behavioral-cognitive approach
p. 706

118. Depression is related to the attribution of bad events to causes that are:
    a. internal, global, and stable.
    b. external, local, and stable.
    c. internal, local, and unstable.
    d. external, global, and stable.
    e. none of the above

Answer: b
The behavioral-cognitive approach
p. 706

119. Depression is related to the attribution of bad events as "internal, global, and stable." Which of the following people exhibits this attributional style?
    a. Jennie: "I'm depressed because my parents are getting a divorce."
    b. Terrence: "I'm depressed because I'm stupid and ugly."
    c. Moisha: "I'm depressed because I've always succeeded and I've just recently failed with a major project at work."
    d. Pete: "I'm depressed because I've deeply hurt a person that I care about."

Answer: b
The behavioral-cognitive approach
p. 707

120. Control is to _____ as self-control is to _____.
    a. delay of gratification; immediate satisfaction
    b. overcoming external obstacles; overcoming internal obstacles
    c. internal locus; external locus
    d. external locus; internal locus

Answer: b
The behavioral-cognitive approach
p. 707

121. When Jenny was six, she would wake her parents up at 4:00 AM on her birthday to open her presents. Now that she is fifteen, she waits until everyone is up and has eaten breakfast before opening her presents. Jenny has developed:
    a. a tolerance for frustration.
    b. self-control.
    c. delay mechanisms.
    d. control over her life.

Answer: d
The behavioral-cognitive approach
p. 707

122. People in some societies feel that couples should wait until they are married before engaging in sexual behavior. This is an example of which of the following?
    a. self-control
    b. locus of control
    c. group pressure
    d. delay of gratification

Answer: c
The behavioral-cognitive approach
p. 707

123. In his studies of delay of gratification in children, Mischel found that:
    a. the length of time that children could delay a desired reward did not depend on whether the reward was visible while the child was waiting.
    b. children delayed gratification longer if they spent the time imagining the pleasures they would get from the reward.
    c. children delayed gratification longer if they distracted themselves from thinking about the reward.
    d. children's ability to delay gratification was not related to thoughts or behaviors during the delay interval, but was highly correlated with personality characteristics such as introversion and responsibility.

124. Walter Mischel found which of the following to be true about human "will power"?
    a. It is a very rare, heroic quality.
    b. It does not exist in young children.
    c. It merely involves tolerating what cannot be avoided.
    d. none of the above

125. In examining the relationship between delay of gratification at age four and later adolescent behavior, Mischel found that the childhood ability to delay gratification was positively correlated with _____ in adolescence.
    a. academic and social competence
    b. attentiveness and verbal fluency
    c. general coping ability
    d. self-reliance
    e. all of the above

126. Children who can delay gratification in early childhood generally:
    a. lose this ability as they grow older.
    b. are more self-reliant and perform better under stress as adolescents and adults.
    c. feel as if they have been cheated out of many things and develop negative characteristics, such as impatience, as adults.
    d. make friends more quickly in social settings.

127. In comparing the views of contemporary social learning theorists with those of behaviorists and trait theorists, your textbook authors suggest that social learning theorists:
    a. are much more interested in cognitive processes than behaviorists or trait theorists.
    b. are like behaviorists, in that they emphasize the role of situational factors in behavior.
    c. are unlike trait theorists, in that they do not assume that personality attributes are built-in or genetic.
    d. all of the above

128. In their discussion of psychological approaches to understanding human personality, your textbook authors conclude that:
    a. psychologists today agree that an objective, scientific approach is the only useful perspective in this field.
    b. together, trait and behavioral-cognitive approaches provide a full understanding of human behavior and motivation.
    c. each perspective has its own validity, allowing subject matter in personality to be studied from different viewpoints.
    d. none of the above

CHAPTER 17

Personality II: Psychodynamic, Humanistic, and Sociocultural Approaches

Answer: b

The psychodynamic approach: Freud
and psychoanalysis
p. 713

1. Dr. York feels that people's motives and desires are derived from early childhood experiences and generally lie hidden in the unconscious. Dr. York adheres to the:
    a. humanistic approach.
    b. psychodynamic approach.
    c. behavioral approach.
    d. Freudian approach.

Answer: b

The psychodynamic approach: Freud
and psychoanalysis
p. 713

2. The dynamics in the psychoanalytic term *psychodynamics* most clearly refers to the:
    a. inevitable conflict between different family members during a child's first 5 to 6 years of life.
    b. relations among the various psychological forces hidden within the individual.
    c. differences in temperament among individuals.
    d. observations that the behavior of normal people is filled with meaningful activities, whereas that of people with major problems seems to be less active and meaningful.

Answer: c

The psychodynamic approach: Freud
and psychoanalysis
p. 713

3. In a Theatrical sense, the psychodynamic approach:
    a. closely follows the script written for each person.
    b. suggests that others often write a person's script.
    c. involves deviations away from a script to a subtext.
    d. emphasizes that we are deeply affected by other actors.

Answer: d

The psychodynamic approach: Freud
and psychoanalysis
p. 714

4. Sigmund Freud can be regarded as a modern Hobbesian since he, like Hobbes, believed that:
    a. man is inherently social.
    b. man's baser instincts are brought under control by the fear of external sanctions.
    c. human selfishness is caused by ignorance and superstition.
    d. humans will be savage and brutish unless tamed by civilization.

Answer: b
The psychodynamic approach: Freud
   and psychoanalysis
p. 714

Answer: b
The psychodynamic approach: Freud
   and psychoanalysis
p. 715

Answer: b
The psychodynamic approach: Freud
   and psychoanalysis
p. 715

Answer: c
The psychodynamic approach: Freud
   and psychoanalysis
p. 715

Answer: b
The psychodynamic approach: Freud
   and psychoanalysis
p. 715

Answer: b
The psychodynamic approach: Freud
   and psychoanalysis
p. 715

Answer: d
The psychodynamic approach: Freud
   and psychoanalysis
p. 715

5. At first, a child's behavior is based on a fear of direct social consequences. Later, he will avoid certain behaviors even when there is no obvious chance of punishment. Sigmund Freud would say that the control put on the child by society is then:
   a. eliminated.
   b. internalized.
   c. externalized.
   d. repressed.

6. Sigmund Freud began his medical practice by studying and treating:
   a. schizophrenia.
   b. hysteria.
   c. psychotics.
   d. mania.

7. Deafness or blindness, paralysis of parts of the body, uncontrollable trembling, and gaps in memory were the symptoms of _____, from which many of Sigmund Freud's patients suffered.
   a. amnesia
   b. hysteria
   c. psychosis
   d. schizophrenia

8. Symptoms are _____ when their cause is psychological rather than the result of organic damage to the nervous system.
   a. irrational
   b. internalized
   c. psychogenic
   d. unconscious

9. Hysterical symptoms are psychogenic, which means that:
   a. the cause of the disorder can be eliminated through hypnosis.
   b. they are a product of psychological rather than organic damage.
   c. they are a type of psychosis.
   d. they are a result of cultural values.

10. Which of the following is evidence that the patient suffers from a psychogenic disorder?
   a. One of his symptoms is paralysis of the legs.
   b. One of his symptoms is glove anesthesia.
   c. After he is hypnotized, he shows posthypnotic amnesia.
   d. He is extremely suggestible under hypnosis.

11. According to Breuer and Freud, the explosive release of dammed-up emotions is called:
   a. resistance.
   b. repression.
   c. aggression.
   d. catharsis.

12. A method used in psychoanalysis in which the patient is to say anything
    that comes into her mind, no matter how trivial, unrelated, or
    embarrassing, is called:
    a. free association.
    b. symbolism.
    c. reaction formation.
    d. wish fulfillment.

13. Sigmund Freud's patients often did something that alerted him to the
    existence of an unconscious conflict. What was it?
    a. They exhibited paranoia.
    b. They showed signs of resistance.
    c. They showed signs of transference.
    d. They described their latent dreams.

14. Sigmund Freud believed that the intensity of resistance on the part of a
    patient:
    a. reflected the degree to which the patient would be hypnotizable.
    b. was a reflection of the way in which the patient was socialized to
       inhibit emotional responses.
    c. indicated that the patient was close to retrieving an emotionally
       charged memory.
    d. was indicative of how much the patient liked the therapist.

15. All of the following statements made by a patient during free association
    are examples of resistance except:
    a. "I really can't think of anything to say right now."
    b. "I just forgot what I was about to say."
    c. "I'm thinking of something that has nothing to do with my prob-
       lem."
    d. "I just remembered a terrible experience from my childhood."

16. In Freud's view, resistance is the product of:
    a. anal fixation.
    b. transference.
    c. the forces of repression.
    d. none of the above

17. According to psychoanalytic theory, _____ is occurring when
    memories or impulses that give rise to anxiety are pushed out of
    consciousness.
    a. rationalization
    b. repression
    c. aggression
    d. catharsis

Answer: d

The psychodynamic approach: Freud
and psychoanalysis

p. 716

18. Anna, a late-19th-century unmarried woman, unconsciously desired to be sexually active, but her upbringing never allowed these feelings to surface, and she died a virgin when she was 70 years old. A psychodynamically oriented theorist would say that Anna _____ her wishes.
    a. suppressed
    b. inhibited
    c. sublimated
    d. repressed

Answer: d

The psychodynamic approach: Freud
and psychoanalysis

p. 716

19. Unlike some some of his followers, Sigmund Freud regarded the theory of unconscious conflict as applicable to the behavior of:
    a. hysterics.
    b. all neurotics.
    c. all psychiatric patients.
    d. everyone.

Answer: b

The psychodynamic approach; Freud
and psychoanalysis

p. 717

20. The id, ego, and superego are best regarded as a theory about:
    a. three separate personalities inhabiting one body.
    b. three different sets of reaction patterns within each personality.
    c. three separate stages in personality development.
    d. three distinct types of unconscious conflict.

Answer: d

The psych odynamic approach: Freud
and psychoanalysis

p. 717

21. Sigmund Freud viewed adult human personality as composed of which of the following subsystems?
    a. id
    b. ego
    c. superego
    d. all of the above

Answer: c

The psychodynamic approach: Freud
and psychoanalysis

p. 717

22. According to Sigmund Freud, _____ is the most primitive part of the human personality.
    a. the ego
    b. repression
    c. the id
    d. the unconscious

Answer: a

The psychodynamic approach: Freud
and psychoanalysis

p. 717

23. The id is governed by:
    a. the pleasure principle.
    b. the reality principle.
    c. the rational principle.
    d. the psychoanalytic principle.

Answer: b

The psychodynamic approach: Freud
and psychoanalysis

p. 717

24. Newborn babies scream for attention whenever they are hungry or wet. In Freudian terms, the behavior of a newborn is governed by:
    a. the superego.
    b. the id.
    c. the ego.
    d. sublimation.

Answer: c

The psychodynamic approach: Freud
and psychoanalysis
p. 717

25. According to Freudian theory, the _____ is said to be governed by the _____ principle.
    a. id; reality
    b. superego; pleasure
    c. ego; reality
    d. superego; pleasure

Answer: a

The psychodynamic approach: Freud
and psychoanalysis
p. 718

26. Id is to _____ as superego is to _____.
    a. immediate satisfaction; internal prohibitions
    b. conscious reaction; immediate satisfaction
    c. internal prohibitions; conscious reactions
    d. internal prohibitions; immediate satisfaction

Answer: a

The psychodynamic approach: Freud
and psychoanalysis
p. 718

27. Freud theorized that society's values are internalized as the:
    a. superego.
    b. ego.
    c. libido.
    d. id.

Answer: d

The psychodynamic approach: Freud
and psychoanalysis
p. 718

28. A three-year-old child who slaps her own hand to punish herself is showing signs of:
    a. sublimation.
    b. the reality principle.
    c. resistance.
    d. superego development.

Answer: c

The psychodynamic approach: Freud
and psychoanalysis
p. 718

29. In Sigmund Freud's view, the demands of _____ are essentially infantile, unconscious, and irrational.
    a. the id
    b. the superego
    c. both a and b
    d. none of the above

Answer: a

The psychodynamic approach: Freud
and psychoanalysis
p. 719

30. According to Sigmund Freud, forbidden acts become associated with anxiety:
    a. when a child is scolded or disciplined for engaging in them.
    b. when they are repressed into the unconscious.
    c. when the child associates them with Oedipal conflicts.
    d. none of the above

Answer: d

The psychodynamic approach: Freud
and psychoanalysis
p. 719

31. Why are thoughts and memories repressed, as well as actions?
    a. Children don't realize that thoughts are private.
    b. Thinking about an act is similar to performing it.
    c. Young children cannot distinguish between thought and action.
    d. all of the above

Answer: d

The psychodynamic approach: Freud
and psychoanalysis
p. 719

32. What did Sigmund Freud believe was the underlying principle of unconscious conflicts?
    a. protection from impure thoughts and actions
    b. escape from society's restraints
    c. fuel for the id
    d. defense against anxiety

Answer: d

The psychodynamic approach: Freud
  and psychoanalysis

p. 719

33. Sigmund Freud believed that unconscious conflict arises from:
    a. latent and manifest dreams.
    b. the pleasure principle and wish fulfillment.
    c. hypnosis and free association.
    d. anxiety and repression.

Answer: b

The psychodynamic approach: Freud
  and psychoanalysis

p. 719

34. What is the purpose of a defense mechanism?
    a. It keeps the id from dominating people's thoughts.
    b. It defends the consciousness against anxiety.
    c. It keeps the superego happy.
    d. It allows for positive coping in society.

Answer: d

The psychodynamic approach: Freud
  and psychoanalysis

p. 719

35. A child is punished by a parent. He then hits his brother. This is an example of:
    a. repression.
    b. transference.
    c. misplaced hysteria.
    d. displaced aggression.

Answer: b

The psychodynamic approach: Freud
  and psychoanalysis

p. 719

36. In a reaction formation:
    a. a mental urge manifests itself in a physical manner.
    b. a forbidden impulse is pushed out of the conscious by an opposite impulse.
    c. a person becomes fixated on a single pleasurable object or event.
    d. an unconscious impulse is manifested in a socially appropriate way.

Answer: a

The psychodynamic approach: Freud
  and psychoanalysis

p. 719

37. In _____, a repressed wish is warded off by diametrically opposed thoughts or behavior.
    a. reaction formation
    b. projection
    c. rationalization
    d. repression

Answer: b

The psychodynamic approach: Freud
  and psychoanalysis

p. 719

38. A child has deeply hidden feelings of hostility toward a younger sibling. However, the child treats her sibling with apparent love. This is an example of the defense mechanism known as:
    a. projection.
    b. reaction formation.
    c. rationalization.
    d. transference.

Answer: a

The psychodynamic approach: Freud
  and psychoanalysis

p. 720

39. After failing to receive a good job, the applicant decides that she wouldn't have liked the job anyway. This person is displaying a defense mechanism called:
    a. rationalization.
    b. projection.
    c. reaction formation.
    d. paranoia.

Answer: c
The psychodynamic approach: Freud
    and psychoanalysis
p. 720

40. When unacceptable behaviors are reinterpreted in more acceptable terms, the defense mechanism at work is:
    a. reaction formation.
    b. projection.
    c. rationalization.
    d. repression.

Answer: b
The psychodynamic approach: Freud
    and psychoanalysis
p. 720

41. The defense mechanism whereby a person attributes his own forbidden urges to others is called:
    a. reaction formation.
    b. projection.
    c. rationalization.
    d. repression.

Answer: d
The psychodynamic approach: Freud
    and psychoanalysis
p. 720

42. Edward, who often feels attracted to men, ridicules others for being homosexual. Sigmund Freud would say Edward's sexual impulses have been repressed through a defense mechanism known as:
    a. projection.
    b. displacement.
    c. rationalization.
    d. reaction formation.

Answer: a
The psychodynamic approach: Freud
    and psychoanalysis
p. 720

43. In the defense mechanism of isolation:
    a. anxiety-producing memories enter consciousness without the feelings that were originally associated with them.
    b. anxiety-producing memories are dissociated into a new, alternate personality.
    c. situations or stimuli that are associated with anxiety-producing events are avoided.
    d. none of the above

Answer: c
The psychodynamic approach: Freud
    and psychoanalysis
p. 720

44. Which of the following is not a defense mechanism according to Freud?
    a. repression
    b. projection
    c. induction
    d. reaction formation

Answer: d
The psychodynamic approach: Freud
    and psychoanalysis
p. 720

45. Which of the following is a psychoanalytic mechanism of defense?
    a. reaction formation
    b. rationalization
    c. projection
    d. all of the above

Answer: d
The psychodynamic approach: Freud
    and psychoanalysis
p. 720

46. According to Sigmund Freud, personality development occurs in a series of _____ stages.
    a. psychosocial.
    b. psychoanalytical.
    c. psychocultural.
    d. psychosexual.

47. For one-year-olds, most pleasure seeking is through which erogenous zone?
    a. the anus
    b. the genitals
    c. the mouth
    d. the fingers

Answer: c
The psychodynamic approach: Freud
  and psychoanalysis
p. 721

48. Which of the following presents Sigmund Freud's psychosexual stages inthe correct order?
    a. phallic, anal, oral, genital
    b. oral, anal, phallic, genital
    c. anal, oral, phallic, genital
    d. oral, genital, phallic, anal

Answer: b
The psychodynamic approach: Freud
  and psychoanalysis
p. 721

49. Which of the following is not one of Freud's stages of psychosexual development?
    a. the copulatory stage
    b. the phallic stage
    c. the anal stage
    d. the genital stage

Answer: a
The psychodynamic approach: Freud
  and psychoanalysis
p. 721

50. According to Freud, the process that moves a child from one psychosexual stage to the next:
    a. is based partly on physical maturation.
    b. involves changes in what parents allow, prohibit, or demand as the child grows older.
    c. both a and b
    d. none of the above

Answer: c
The psychodynamic approach: Freud
  and psychoanalysis
p. 721

51. Little Tommy is three years old and he still sucks his thumb. According to Sigmund Freud, this behavior is called:
    a. fixation.
    b. reaction formation.
    c. a latency period.
    d. none of the above

Answer: a
The psychodynamic approach: Freud
  and psychoanalysis
p. 721

52. Carl is very dependent on other people, especially the women that he dates. Sigmund Freud would describe Carl as a(n):
    a. anal character.
    b. phallic character.
    c. oral character.
    d. passive character.

Answer: c
The psychodynamic approach: Freud
  and psychoanalysis
p. 722

53. The obstinate "No!" of a child during the terrible twos would, within a Freudian framework, be related to:
    a. the reaction formations that develop following weaning.
    b. the discovery that parents can be manipulated by words alone.
    c. toilet training.
    d. a kind of "warming up" in preparation for the Oedipal conflict.

Answer: c
The psychodynamic approach: Freud
  and psychoanalysis
p. 722

Answer: d
The psychodynamic approach: Freud
and psychoanalysis
p. 722

54. Barbara is compulsively neat. She also hates to be told that she is wrong and she never budges from her own views. Sigmund Freud and Karl Abraham would characterize Barbara as:
    a. an oral character.
    b. a phallic character.
    c. a genital character.
    d. an anal character.

Answer: a
The psychodynamic approach: Freud
and psychoanalysis
p. 723

55. According to Sigmund Freud, the Oedipus complex develops during which psychosexual stage?
    a. phallic
    b. anal
    c. genital
    d. oral

Answer: c
The psychodynamic approach: Freud
and psychoanalysis
p. 723

56. According to Sigmund Freud, which of the following mechanisms of defense explains a little boy's castration anxiety?
    a. reaction formation
    b. displaced aggression
    c. projection
    d. regression

Answer: c
The psychodynamic approach: Freud
and psychoanalysis
p. 723

57. According to Sigmund Freud, which of the following is not characteristic of boys during the so-called "latency period?"
    a. a preference for being with other boys
    b. a high level of interest in physical activities
    c. fear of the father
    d. little overt interest in sexual matters

Answer: b
The psychodynamic approach: Freud
and psychoanalysis
p. 723

58. Freud thought that much of the emotional turbulence of adolescence was due to _____ during this period.
    a. the beginnings of phallic sexuality
    b. the revival of Oedipal conflicts
    c. the repression of sexual thoughts and impulses
    d. identification with the opposite sex

Answer: b
The psychodynamic approach: Freud
and psychoanalysis
p. 723

59. In Freud's theory of psychosexual development, the latency period occurs between the _____ and _____ stages.
    a. oral; anal
    b. phallic; genital
    c. phallic; anal
    d. genital; anal

Answer: c
The psychodynamic approach: Freud
and psychoanalysis
p. 724

60. The female equivalent of the Oedipus complex is known as the:
    a. Oedipa complex.
    b. Phoebe complex.
    c. Electra complex.
    d. Paternal complex.

Answer: c
The psychodynamic approach: Freud
   and psychoanalysis
p. 724

61. According to Sigmund Freud's theory of female psychosexual development, a little girl:
   a. becomes morally superior to males due to lack of a penis.
   b. develops greater castration fear than boys during the Electra complex.
   c. withdraws her love from her mother when she discovers that the mother has no penis.
   d. chooses the father as her sexual object because she envies the various social benefits of the male role in our culture.

Answer: d
The psychodynamic approach: Freud
   and psychoanalysis
p. 724

62. Freud's account of female psychosexual development is:
   a. counted among his most valuable contributions.
   b. confirmed by recent biological evidence.
   c. both a and b
   d. none of the above

Answer: d
The psychodynamic approach: Freud
   and psychoanalysis
p. 724

63. According to Sigmund Freud, slips of the tongue and dream interpretations reveal _____ processes
   a. personality
   b. attribution
   c. conscious
   d. unconscious

Answer: c
The psychodynamic approach: Freud
   and psychoanalysis
p. 725

64. Which of the following is not a Freudian interpretation of the fact that you have accidentally referred to your romantic partner by your parent's name?
   a. You unconsciously wish that your parent was your romantic partner.
   b. You feel guilty because you haven't called your parent recently.
   c. You just returned from visiting your parent and this occurred as a result of habit.
   d. You are angry with your romantic partner for going on a date with someone older than you.

Answer: b

The psychodynamic approach: Freud
   and psychoanalysis
p. 725

65. What did Sigmund Freud call the dreams that seem to recount life events?
   a. wish involvement
   b. day residue
   c. Freudian slips
   d. none of the above

Answer: d
The psychodynamic approach: Freud
   and psychoanalysis
p. 726

66. According to Freud, the actual events in our dreams are best referred to as _____ context.
   a. manifest
   b. sexual
   c. latent
   d. none of the above

Answer: a

The psychodynamic approach: Freud
  and psychoanalysis
p. 726

67. According to Sigmund Freud, neurotic symptoms most closely resemble:
   a. manifest dream content.
   b. the hypnotic state.
   c. daydreams.
   d. latent dream content.

Answer: d

The psychodynamic approach: Freud
  and psychoanalysis
p. 726

68. With respect to dreams, Freud argued that:
   a. every dream presents unfulfilled id impulses in disguised form.
   b. a dream is a compromise between forbidden urges and the repression that keeps them unconscious.
   c. the latent dream is modified to produce the manifest dream.
   d. all of the above

Answer: d

The psychodynamic approach: Freud
  and psychoanalysis
p. 726

69. According to Sigmund Freud, dreams of long or box-like objects were typically symbolic of male or female genitals, respectively. What else is true regarding Freud's views on dreams?
   a. Individualistic symbolism is based on life experience and can be understood through free association.
   b. Some dreams are merely a recounting of daily events, but most involve wish fulfillment.
   c. "Sometimes a cigar is just a cigar."
   d. all of the above

Answer: c

The psychodynamic approach: Freud
  and psychoanalysis
p. 727

70. Which of the following is inconsistent with a psychoanalytic interpretation of the fairy tale, *Snow White and the Seven Dwarfs*?
   a. Snow White's escape from the wicked queen by going underground is representative of a young girl's latency period.
   b. Snow White's evil stepmother is the target of hate and hostility arising from the Electra conflict.
   c. The seven dwarves represent the seven deadly sins, including lust and greed.
   d. The prince's awakening touch with his sword represents the release of Snow White's previously dormant sexual urges.

Answer: a

The psychodynamic approach: Freud
  and psychoanalysis
p. 727

71. From the psychoanalytic perspective, the tale of Snow White:
   a. is an allegory of a girl's passage through the Electra conflict.
   b. symbolically represents the interaction between id, ego, and superego.
   c. describes in personified terms, the operation of several important defense mechanisms.
   d. none of the above

Answer: a

The psychodynamic approach: Freud
  and psychoanalysis
p. 727

72. In your textbook authors' discussion of psychoanalytic interpretations of fairy tales, such as Snow White, each of the following comments was presented, except:
   a. "The psychoanalytic view sheds little, if any, light on individual development, and even less on our cultural heritage."
   b. "It is hard to know by what ground rules validity can be judged."
   c. "Death and resurrection are old themes in mythology..."
   d. "... myths may also embody dim folk memories of long-past wars, dynastic conflicts, previously held religions, and various catastrophes."

Answer: b

The psychodynamic approach: Freud
and psychoanalysis
p. 728

73. According to Ernest Jones's psychoanalytic interpretation of Hamlet, Hamlet's long delay in killing his uncle to avenge his father's death:
    a. grows out of anxiety over his own sibling rivalries.
    b. is an expression of the unconscious conflicts rooted in the Oedipus complex.
    c. is caused by fear of his own unconscious homosexual longings.
    d. is based on a reaction formation against his unconscious wishes to replace his uncle as king.

Answer: d

The psychodynamic approach: Freud
and psychoanalysis
p. 729

74. Which of the following types of evidence was not used by Freud to test psychoanalytic theory?
    a. slips of the tongue
    b. dreams
    c. free associations
    d. experimental data

Answer: d

The psychodynamic approach: Freud
and psychoanalysis
p. 729

75. Clinical evidence alone cannot test the validity of Freud's ideas because:
    a. the analyst's training may determine what he notices.
    b. the analyst's behavior may affect the patient's behavior.
    c. the analyst can explain the past but cannot predict the future.
    d. all of the above

Answer: d

The psychodynamic approach: Freud
and psychoanalysis
p. 730

76. In their critical evaluation of Freudian theory, your textbook authors note that:
    a. evidence from clinical practice cannot be totally objective.
    b. Freud's theory makes few specific predictions and it is very difficult to refute.
    c. a patient's statements can be interpreted to mean what they say, or the opposite, depending on the analyst's interpretation.
    d. all of the above

Answer: b

The psychodynamic approach: Freud
and psychoanalysis
p. 730

77. Which of the psychologists should not be referred to as a psychoanalytic theorist?
    a. Carl Jung
    b. Abraham Maslow
    c. Alfred Adler
    d. Karen Horney

Answer: c

The psychodynamic approach: Freud
and psychoanalysis
p. 730

78. According to neo-Freudians such as Karen Horney and H.S. Sullivan, a psychologically unhealthy individual is likely to show sexual symptoms because:
    a. our cultural restrictions on expressing sexuality cause us to repress socially unacceptable sexual desires.
    b. our psychological reactions to sexual stimulation inevitably result in guilt and embarrassment.
    c. our sexuality is a highly sensitive barometer of our interpersonal attitudes.
    d. our psychosexual conflicts are deeply rooted in our biology and are universal for our species.

Answer: e

The psychodynamic approach: Freud
   and psychoanalysis
p. 730

79. Which one of the following individuals is not considered a neo-
    Freudian?
    a. H. S. Sullivan
    b. Alfred Adler
    c. Erich Fromm
    d. Karen Horney
    e. A. A. Brill

Answer: a

The psychodynamic approach: Freud
   and psychoanalysis
p. 730

80. Compared with classical Freudian theory, neo-Freudians:
    a. describe inner conflicts in social and interpersonal terms.
    b. describe conflicts in biological terms.
    c. do not put as much emphasis on childhood.
    d. suggest that the Oedipal/Electra complex does not occur.

Answer: c

The psychodynamic approach: Freud
   and psychoanalysis
p. 731

81. The main argument of the neo-Freudians was that Sigmund Freud
    overemphasized:
    a. early social experience.
    b. internal conflicts.
    c. biological determination.
    d. individual differences.

Answer: a

The psychodynamic approach: Freud
   and psychoanalysis
p. 731

82. Neo-Freudians depart from Sigmund Freud's psychoanalytic theory in
    that they place greater emphasis on:
    a. the role of social factors in developing inner conflicts.
    b. the biological sources of childhood frustrations.
    c. the importance of sexual repression in creating neuroses.
    d. the universal nature of the Oedipal conflict.

Answer: d

The psychodynamic approach: Freud
   and psychoanalysis
p. 731

83. Research on the oral character indicates that:
    a. events associated with breast-feeding and weaning appear to be
       important in personality development.
    b. events associated with breast-feeding, but not those connected
       with weaning, appear to be important in personality development.
    c. breast-fed infants appear to be more emotionally dependent in
       later life than bottle-fed infants.
    d. none of the above

Answer: a

The psychodynamic approach: Freud
   and psychoanalysis
p. 732

84. Research on the anal character indicates that:
    a. the anal traits of neatness, obstinacy, and stinginess tend to be
       correlated.
    b. individuals with anal traits tend not to have mothers with the
       same characteristics.
    c. cultures in which toilet training is later or stricter tend to be
       higher in economic competitiveness and hoarding.
    d. all of the above

Answer: d

The psychodynamic approach: Freud
  and psychoanalysis
p. 732

85. The three anal traits seem to be clustered together in parents and children. According to your textbook authors, what is the best guess as to why this occurs?
    a. Parents want their children to be just like them.
    b. Children use their parents as primary role models.
    c. Young children are exposed to their parents' traits more often than those of others.
    d. They are a part of a general middle-class value and attitude system.

Answer: a

The psychodynamic approach: Freud
  and psychoanalysis
p. 732

86. The cross-cultural studies of anthropologists like Bronislaw Malinowski have yielded evidence to support:
    a. neo-Freudian criticism.
    b. cultural absolutism.
    c. genetically based sex differences.
    d. the universality of the Oedipus complex.

Answer: b

The psychodynamic approach: Freud
  and psychoanalysis
p. 732

87. In the Trobriand Islands, a male child is raised and disciplined by his maternal uncle rather than by his biological father. Evidence concerning the nature of Oedipal conflict in this culture suggests that:
    a. there is more friction between boys and their biological fathers than between boys and their maternal uncles.
    b. Trobrianders often have prophetic dreams of the death of maternal uncles.
    c. many Trobriand myths and legends involve evil fathers or stepfathers, but not evil maternal uncles.
    d. all of the above

Answer: a

The psychodynamic approach: Freud
  and psychoanalysis
p. 732

88. Among the Trobriand Islanders, where a mother's lover is her son's disciplinarian, young boys tend to resent and fear:
    a. the disciplinarian.
    b. their mother's lover.
    c. aunts and sisters
    d. all adult males.

Answer: d

The psychodynamic approach: Freud
  and psychoanalysis
p. 734

89. According to one hypothesis discussed in your textbook, dreams are expressive rather than a means of disguise. Evidence for this view comes from the fact that:
    a. there is a difference between latent and manifest dreams.
    b. only some dreams represent wish fulfillments.
    c. dogs have been shown to have undisguised dreams about desired objects.
    d. dreams about a forbidden urges are only sometimes disguised.

Answer: c

The psychodynamic approach: Freud
  and psychoanalysis
p. 734

90. Modern studies of dream content do not support Freud's view that:
    a. dreams often involve current emotional problems.
    b. dreams can employ condensed, symbolic imagery.
    c. dreams represent disguised wish fulfillments.
    d. all of the above

Answer: b

The psychodynamic approach: Freud
   and psychoanalysis
p. 734

91. In a memory task, anxiety-provoking words are recalled _____ neutral words.
   a. more readily than
   b. less readily than
   c. as readily as
   d. instead of

Answer: a

The psychodynamic approach:
   personality differences
p. 734

92. In considering a cognitive interpretation of repression, some psychologists suggest that repression:
   a. may be a case of retrieval failure due to poor retrieval cues.
   b. may result from failure to store memories, due to the distraction caused by anxiety.
   c. may result from lack of reinforcement for recalling the relevant information.
   d. all of the above

Answer: d

The psychodynamic approach:
   personality differences
p. 736

93. In evaluating Sigmund Freud's contribution to psychology, your textbook authors note that:
   a. although many of his ideas were flawed or disproven, they have had an enormous impact on the field of psychology.
   b. many of Freud's ideas are not supported by empirical evidence.
   c. the clinical method of psychoanalysis is not a good way of generating objective facts about personality and behavior.
   d. it is well-accepted that we experience internal conflicts of which we are consciously unaware.
   e. all of the above

Answer: c

The psychodynamic approach:
   personality differences
p. 737

94. What did Karen Horney believe was the cause of basic anxiety?
   a. childhood struggles with sexual urges
   b. reprimands by parents at vulnerable ages
   c. the culture's incompatible demands on a person
   d. the lack of stability and roots in modern society

Answer: b

The psychodynamic approach:
   personality differences
p. 737

95. Tabetha wants to be loved, but every time she starts dating someone new she smothers him with affection and he leaves her. Karen Horney would say that Tabetha is:
   a. an oral character.
   b. creating a vicious circle.
   c. displaying reaction formation.
   d. using a coping mechanism.

Answer: b

The psychodynamic approach:
   personality differences
p. 737

96. Pat drinks excessively. He knows that it is destroying his life, but this realization makes him scared and anxious, so he just drinks more. According to Karen Horney, Pat:
   a. has basic anxiety.
   b. is caught in a vicious circle.
   c. probably had overdemanding parents.
   d. is controlled by his id.

Answer: d

The psychodynamic approach: personality differences

p. 738

97. Emphasis on the ways we cope with the world rather than hiding from it or distorting it is a major element of:
    a. classical Freudian theory.
    b. behaviorism.
    c. humanism.
    d. ego psychology.

Answer: a

The psychodynamic approach: personality differences

p. 738

98. An ego psychologist would agree with which of the following statements?
    a. People try to deal with the realities of the world rather than hide from them.
    b. Behavior can be understood only if you examine past experiences.
    c. Normal and abnormal behavior is the sum total of what people have learned over the years.
    d. Freudian defense mechanisms allow effective coping strategies.

Answer: d

The psychodynamic approach: personality differences

p. 738

99. A longitudinal study:
    a. can be completed in a matter of weeks.
    b. provides information about many different people.
    c. is useful only if one develops a complete psychological history of the individual.
    d. involves studying the same group of people at various stages of development.

Answer: d

The psychodynamic approach: personality differences

p. 739

100. In his longitudinal study of coping mechanisms, George Vaillant classified defense mechanisms according to their level of maturity. For example:
    a. he considered denial to be less mature than projection.
    b. he classified repression and reaction formation as normal adult mechanisms.
    c. he considered suppression to be healthier and more mature than repression.
    d. all of the above

Answer: a

The psychodynamic approach: personality differences

p. 739

101. George Vaillant conducted a longitudinal study of coping patterns in male college graduates over a 30-year period. Vaillant found that:
    a. as participants grew older, their coping mechanisms became more mature.
    b. at both 31 and 47 years of age, participants tended to use the same defense mechanisms that they used at age 19.
    c. participants who had mature coping patterns at age 19 were no more likely to have gratifying jobs or better physical health later in life.
    d. all of the above

Answer: d
The psychodynamic approach:
  personality differences
p. 739

102. Jack Block conducted a longitudinal study of personality in 250 men and women from junior high school age, examining them again when they were in their thirties. He found that:
    a. well-adjusted adults were likely to come from psychologically healthy families.
    b. there was considerable continuity across the years in characteristics such as self-assurance and desire for achievement.
    c. there was a general improvement with age in overall personal adjustment.
    d. all of the above

Answer: c
The psychodynamic approach:
  personality differences
p. 739

103. What did Jack Block's longitudinal study reveal?
    a. poorer overall personal adjustment with age
    b. greater variablility in early history for well-adjusted participants than for those judged to be less psychologically healthy
    c. continuity in certain characteristics like self-assurance
    d. none of the above

Answer: a
The psychodynamic approach:
  personality differences
p. 739

104. In their longitudinal studies, both Vaillant and Block found that:
    a. personal adjustment improves with age.
    b. parents play a minor role in a child's personal adjustment.
    c. the nature of coping mechanisms varies throughout life.
    d. genetic inheritance plays an important role in adjustment.

Answer: c
The psychodynamic approach:
  personality differences
p. 740

105. How do some modern psychologists explain Freud's unconscious coping mechanisms?
    a. They appear only in neurotic people.
    b. They are a sign of mental breakdown.
    c. They provide a means of not attending to something stressful.
    d. They decrease intrapsychic conflict due to the trauma associated with birth.

Answer: b
The humanistic approach
p. 740

106. Freedom of choice is a hallmark of which of the following?
    a. behaviorism
    b. humanism
    c. social learning
    d. psychodynamic theory

Answer: a
The humanistic approach
p. 741

107. Humanistic psychologists believe people strive to:
    a. become self-actualizing.
    b. behave in ways dictated by outside forces.
    c. need to be told what is the matter with them and what they can do about it.
    d. focus on only the basic needs of life—food, sex, and safety.

Answer: c
The humanistic approach
p. 741

108. In theatrical terms, the humanistic approach emphasizes:
    a. a good script with which to deal with one's problems.
    b. glitzy scenery with which to impress people.
    c. spontaneity and improvisation from the script.
    d. good acting techniques in the face of life's trials.

Answer: a
The humanistic approach
p. 741

109. According to Abraham Maslow, the humanistic movement is one of the three forces of American psychology. The other two are:
    a. psychoanalysis and behaviorism.
    b. Gestalt psychology and cognitivism.
    c. behaviorism and cognitive psychology.
    d. none of the above

Answer: d
The humanistic approach
p. 741

110. The three forces of American psychology, according to Abraham Maslow, are the humanistic movement, behaviorism, and:
    a. classical conditioning.
    b. drug therapy.
    c. learning theory.
    d. psychoanalysis.

Answer: d
The humanistic approach
p. 741

111. Maslow referred to hunger, thirst, and sex as:
    a. animal needs.
    b. internal needs.
    c. external needs.
    d. deficiency needs.

Answer: b
The humanistic approach
p. 741

112. "People need more than food and sex. Sometimes the joy of doing something is reward enough." The person who says this is probably:
    a. a behaviorist.
    b. a humanist.
    c. a psychoanalyst.
    d. a neo-Freudian.

Answer: c
The humanistic approach
p. 742

113. Which of the following is the correct order in Abraham Maslow's hierarchy?
    a. safety, physiological, esteem, belongingness, self-actualization
    b. physiological, safety, esteem, belongingness, self-actualization
    c. physiological, safety, belongingness, esteem, self-actualization
    d. belongingness, physiological, safety, esteem, self-actualization

Answer: c
The humanistic approach
p. 742

114. Realizing one's potential to the fullest:
    a. requires abstinence from food and sexual gratification.
    b. requires little work—if it's going to happen it just does.
    c. is the pinnacle of Maslow's hierarchy of needs.
    d. is a major tenet of behaviorist theory.

Answer: a
The humanistic approach
p. 742

115. According to Abraham Maslow a major prerequisite for becoming self-actualizing is:
    a. having all of one's lower-order needs fulfilled.
    b. having a major altruistic streak.
    c. having a very selfless nature.
    d. having suffered in the past so you can truly appreciate the good aspects of life.

Answer: a
The humanistic approach
p. 742

116. According to Carl Rogers, our self-concept:
    a. is develops in early childhood.
    b. does not develop until we have become self-actualizing.
    c. is the combined effect of our id, ego, and superego.
    d. none of the above

Answer: a
The humanistic approach
p. 743

117. Jimmy sees himself as a person who takes action and makes decisions. In Rogerian, terms, Jimmy has a strong sense of:
    a. "I."
    b. "me."
    c. "you."
    d. others.

Answer: c
The humanistic approach
p. 743

118. Which of the following best describes the Rogerian concept of self?
    a. how other people feel about and view me
    b. an agent who takes or doesn't take action
    c. both a and b
    d. none of the above

Answer: b
The humanistic approach
p. 743

119. Carl Rogers believed that unconditional positive regard was important:
    a. for achieving full independence from parents and other adults.
    b. for developing a strong sense of personal self-worth.
    c. for internalizing moral values.
    d. for acquiring a self-concept.
    e. all of the above

Answer: b
The humanistic approach
p. 743

120. Unconditional positive regard is:
    a. the state of loving and approving of others.
    b. the sense of being loved and accepted without reserve.
    c. an achievement of those who self-actualize.
    d. an internal state facilitated by proper parenting procedures.

Answer: d
The humanistic approach
p. 743

121. Little Rodney spills a milkshake all over the velour seat of his parents' new car. "Do you hate me?" he asks. "No, we just wish you would be more careful. We still love you." According to Carl Rogers, Rodney's parents are providing:
    a. positive reinforcement.
    b. unconditional love.
    c. subtle conditioning.
    d. unconditional positive regard.
    e. tough love.

Answer: c
The humanistic approach
p. 743

122. For humanists such as Abraham Maslow and Carl Rogers, self-actualization is defined as:
    a. the final integration of personality traits and habits into a fully unified self.
    b. the achievement of happiness and personal contentment.
    c. fulfilling oneself and realizing one's full potential.
    d. becoming fully and consciously aware of all one's internal doubts and conflicts.
    e. none of the above

Answer: c
The humanistic approach
p. 743

123. Sonya is very accepting of herself. She sets realistic goals and sees her problems through to their conclusion. She has a satisfying relationship with her husband and several close friends. From Maslow's point of view, Sonya could best be described as:
    a. being self-directed and strong.
    b. having a positive self-image.
    c. being self-actualizing.
    d. having a strong sense of self-worth.

Answer: d
The humanistic approach
p. 743

124. Which of the following characteristics is not part of Abraham Maslow's description of the self-actualizing individual?
    a. She is realistically oriented.
    b. She accepts herself and others.
    c. She has intimate relationships with only a few people.
    d. She is orderly and methodical.

Answer: a
The humanist approach
p. 744

125. Peak experiences:
    a. are profound moments in a person's life.
    b. occur in the middle of Maslow's hierarchy of needs.
    c. only occur in self-actualizing people.
    d. occur only in the presence of other people.
    e. all of the above

Answer: b
The humanist approach
p. 744

126. An event that has important and lasting effects and causes a new view of life is called:
    a. self-actualization.
    b. a peak experience.
    c. a restored sense of self-worth.
    d. unconditional positive regard.

Answer: c
The humanist approach
p. 744

127. According to Carl Rogers, people with low self-regard:
    a. can never become self-actualizing.
    b. can only reach a certain level in his hierarchy of needs.
    c. can be healed if the person has an important growth experience.
    d. tend to view the world in a negative, apathetic way.

Answer: a
The humanist approach
p. 744

128. Unlike Sigmund Freud, Maslow and Rogers believed that:
    a. if given the appropriate conditions, people will grow to realize their inherent potentials.
    b. people have an innate potential for evil that must be restrained by society.
    c. people respond only mechanistically to environmental events.
    d. none of the above.

Answer: a
The humanist approach
p. 744

129. Someone with empathic understanding:
    a. genuinely understands what a person feels and feels it with him.
    b. tends to view others positively.
    c. is sympathetic only with regard to specific experiences.
    d. all of the above

Answer: c
The humanist approach
p. 745

130. According to your textbook authors which of the following is not a major criticism of the humanistic approach?
    a. It is difficult to draw conclusions about the effects of different parenting styles.
    b. Self-actualizing individuals may not be exactly as Maslow describes.
    c. There are so many prerequisites for being self-actualizing that it is very difficult to achieve.
    d. Many of the terms, like self-actualization and peak experiences, are vaguely defined.

Answer: b
The humanist approach
p. 745

131. According to your textbook authors, the humanistic approach can best be regarded as:
    a. a twentieth-century historical movement.
    b. a protest movement against psychoanalysis and behaviorism.
    c. an offshoot of psychoanalysis.
    d. a positive movement toward the realization of self.

Answer: d
The humanist approach
p. 745

132. The humanistic approach is similar to which of the following literary movements?
    a. classicism
    b. Shakespearean
    c. neo-classical
    d. Romanticism

Answer: b
The humanist approach
p. 747

133. Some critics argue that humanists tell us what personality _____ rather than what _____.
    a. is; it should be
    b. should be; it is
    c. is; causes it to be that way
    d. does; it could be

Answer: d
The humanist approach
p. 747

134. Despite many criticisms, the humanistic approach is credited with:
    a. inspiring the behaviorist approach to personality.
    b. clarifying biological and environmental factors in personality development.
    c. explaining innate animal actions.
    d. reminding us of the many phenomena other theories ignore.

Answer: b
The sociocultural perspective
p. 747

135. Modern critics of personality psychology often point out that the various theoretical perspectives (e.g., trait, psychoanalytic, behaviorist theories) all tend to omit a single important factor. What is it?
    a. individual behavior
    b. culture
    c. intrapsychic conflict
    d. nature

Answer: b
The sociocultural perspective
p. 748

136. In discussing the cross-cultural studies conducted by Ruth Benedict and Margaret Mead, your text notes that:
   a. Benedict's studies of three preliterate cultures revealed striking similarities in basic personality patterns.
   b. Mead's studies of preliterate New Guinea tribes found marked differences in male and female sex roles and personality.
   c. both Mead and Benedict argued that culture has only a minor effect on innate foundations of human personality.
   d. all of the above

Answer: d
The sociocultural perspective
p. 749

137. Critics of Margaret Mead's cross-cultural studies of personality argue that:
   a. despite cultural differences, there are probably some universal sex roles.
   b. the dimensions along which personality varies may be identical in all cultures, even if the specific patterns of personality differ.
   c. despite cross-cultural differences in gender roles, it is generally the males of a culture that engage in warfare.
   d. all of the above

Answer: c
The sociocultural perspective
p. 750

138. In discussing cross-cultural studies of child-rearing patterns, your text notes that:
   a. agricultural societies tend to stress conformity and responsibility in their child-rearing practices.
   b. in American society, child-rearing practices seem to vary as a function of social class.
   c. both a and b
   d. none of the above

Answer: d
The sociocultural perspective
p. 750

139. Your textbook authors suggest several sources for modern American concept of individualism. Which of the following is not one of these sources?
   a. the frontier life in 18th- and 19th- century America
   b. the Protestant Reformation with its idea of individual relationships with God
   c. the Italian Reformation when artists first began to sign their works
   d. the Greek city-state with its democratic ideals

Answer: a
The sociocultural perspective
p. 751

140. Different cultures and ethnic groups can be viewed as occurring along a individualism-collectivism dimension. In discussing this dimension, your textbook notes that:
   a. collectivist societies emphasize the needs and values of the family and community over those of the individual.
   b. collectivist societies are less likely to emphasize dependency and obedience in their child rearing practices.
   c. individualist societies are more likely to hold children to adult standards of morality than collectivist societies.
   d. none of the above

141. Members of collectivist societies are most likely to agree with which of the following statements?
    a. "Only those who depend on themselves get ahead in life."
    b. "It is important to be independent and self-reliant."
    c. "I feel I must subordinate my own wishes to the demands and needs of my family."
    d. "The best way to help one's family is to cease being a burden to them."

142. Compared with members of individualist societies, members of collectivist societies:
    a. are more affected by pressures from both their in-groups, and from out-groups.
    b. have stronger bonds with their in-group.
    c. tend to define their in-groups more broadly, including a wider range of individuals.
    d. all of the above

143. Many authors believe that the Western concept of self and personality cannot be applied to other cultures. For example:
    a. compared with Americans, people from India are more likely to describe acquaintances in terms of their social behavior rather than their personality traits.
    b. in several New Guinea languages, there are no first-person pronouns corresponding to the English "I" or "me."
    c. both a and b
    d. none of the above

144. Which of the following statements is false regarding theoretical emphases in psychological attempts to explain individual personality differences?
    a. Humanists focus on, and even exalt, individual uniqueness.
    b. Social-learning theorists focus on biologically inherited predispositions.
    c. Psychoanalysts focus on differences in unconscious motivations.
    d. Trait theorists focus on characteristics that can be psychometrically assessed.

145. Which of the following is an important lesson to be learned from the sociocultural view of human personality?
    a. Western conceptions of human individuality and the self may not apply to people from other cultures.
    b. Intrapsychic conflict in personality development is inevitable and universal as evidenced by the results of numerous cross-cultural studies.
    c. A Freudian slip is indicative of psychic conflict, regardless of the language in which it occurs.
    d. all of the above.

CHAPTER 18 | Psychopathology

Answer: d
Psychopathology
p. 757

1. The study of psychological disorders is called:
   a. psychophysiology.
   b. psychopathy.
   c. psychopharmacology.
   d. psychopathology.

Answer: d
Different conceptions of madness
p. 758

2. Fossil evidence suggests that prehistoric man may have made some attempts to treat mental disorders. This conclusion is based upon examination of:
   a. burn marks on prehistoric skulls.
   b. prehistoric skulls buried in elaborate enclosures.
   c. partial skeletons buried in sacred sites.
   d. holes chipped in prehistoric skulls.

Answer: c
Different conceptions of madness
p. 758

3. According to your textbook authors, the practice of cutting holes in the skull (i.e., trephining):
   a. may have been based on a primitive understanding that the source of mental disorder lies in the brain.
   b. may have been designed to relieve the pressure caused by brain swelling during infection or disease.
   c. may have been an attempt to allow evil spirits or devils a way out of the patient's body.
   d. none of the above

Answer: c
Different conceptions of madness
p. 760

4. Phillipe Pinel, an eighteenth-century French physician, is often credited with:
   a. the invention of the straitjacket.
   b. the discovery of the causes of paresis.
   c. major reforms in mental hospital practices.
   d. introducing tax laws for public support of asylums.

Answer: b
Different conceptions of madness
p. 760

Answer: c
Different conceptions of madness
p. 760

Answer: d
Different conceptions of madness
p. 760

Answer: d
Different conceptions of madness
p. 760

Answer: e
Different conceptions of madness
p. 761

Answer: b
Different conceptions of madness
p. 761

Answer: b
Different conceptions of madness
p. 761

5. Phillipe Pinel viewed abnormal behavior as symptoms of illness. Before Pinel's reform efforts, abnormal persons were viewed as:
   a. frauds.
   b. possessed by demons.
   c. psychologically stressed.
   d. all of the above

6. A somatogenic mental disorder is one that:
   a. results from conflict between the parents.
   b. has a psychological origin.
   c. has an organic origin.
   d. results from a psychologically traumatic event.

7. An example of a somatogenic mental disorder is:
   a. multiple personality disorder.
   b. hysterical paralysis.
   c. phobia.
   d. general paresis.

8. General paresis is an example of a(n):
   a. psychogenic disorder.
   b. hysteria.
   c. paranoia.
   d. somatogenic disorder.

9. General paresis once accounted for the occupancy of 10 percent of all beds in psychiatric hospitals. It is now known to be caused by:
   a. alcohol.
   b. hereditary factors.
   c. axonal degeneration.
   d. iron deficiency.
   e. syphilis.

10. The first clear demonstration of the causes of general paresis came from a study:
    a. that showed that the disorder was extremely common in prostitutes.
    b. in which several patients were innoculated with fluids taken from syphilitic sores.
    c. testing the effects of penicillin as a cure and preventive treatment for the disorder.
    d. on the effects of cerebral stroke in impairments of speech and mental functioning.

11. The discovery of a causal link between syphilis and general paresis:
    a. followed the discovery of penicillin.
    b. strengthened the somatogenic position.
    c. led to the discovery of the causes of depression.
    d. occurred in America in 1926.

12. Critics of the same somatogenic approach to understanding psychopathology pointed out that paralysis can be displayed by:
    a. alcoholics.
    b. tumor victims.
    c. hysterics.
    d. syphilitics.

13. Suppose a certain mental disorder is believed to be caused by severe fear reactions suffered in childhood. A new discovery shows that the disorder is really caused by the lack of a specific enzyme. The disorder will now change in classification from what to what?
    a. somatogenic to psychogenic.
    b. hysterical to psychoanalytic.
    c. psychoanalytic to pathological
    d. psychogenic to somatogenic

14. A psychogenic disorder is one that:
    a. has a physical cause.
    b. is organic in origin.
    c. is psychological in origin.
    d. has no cure.

15. The first major impetus for the idea that at least some mental disorders are psychogenic came from cases of:
    a. psychopathic personality.
    b. general paresis.
    c. schizophrenia.
    d. hysteria.

16. Your textbook authors note that the distinction between psychogenic and somatogenic disorders:
    a. will ultimately be a moot issue because all psychological events are based on neurophysiological processes.
    b. will remain with us until the discovery of the neurophysiological basis of learning and memory.
    c. is actually based on the differences between conditions with a known organic basis and those for which causes are as yet unknown.
    d. really amounts to saying that the most direct explanation of some disorders is at the psychological level, while for others it is at the organic level.

17. According to the DSM-IV, mental disorders:
    a. are clinically significant behavioral or psychological syndromes.
    b. may be associated with distressing symptoms or functional impairments.
    c. may be associated with significantly increased risks of suffering, disability, or loss of freedom.
    d. all of the above

18. Which of the following is false regarding the DSM-IV?
    a. It provides specific criteria for diagnosing illnesses and diseases of both psychological and physiological origin.
    b. It makes no reference to normality or abnormality because certain patterns of behavior qualify as mental disorders no matter how commonly they occur.
    c. It has undergone several revisions or refinements and is now published by the American Psychiatric Association in a 4th edition.
    d. It categorizes as a mental disorder any clinically significant condition that is associated with present distress, disability, or increased risk of suffering death, pain, disability, or important loss of freedom.

Answer: a
Different conceptions of madness
p. 763

19. The pathology model of mental disorders is based on the idea that:
    a. symptoms of mental disorders are produced by an underlying pathology.
    b. the underlying causes of all mental disorders are ultimately organic.
    c. the condition can be treated by members of the medical profession, especially by means of psychoactive drugs.
    d. all of the above

Answer: a
The underlying pathology model
p. 764

20. The "pathology model" of mental disorder involves the idea that:
    a. all mental disorders have physical causes.
    b. observable symptoms constitute the disease.
    c. treatment attempts should be aimed at overt symptoms.
    d. symptoms are caused by some underlying pathology.

Answer: d
The underlying pathology model
p. 764

21. Which of the following statements is consistent with the pathology model of mental disorders?
    a. there is no distinction between symptoms and causes.
    b. the underlying cause of a mental disorder can be regarded as a pathology.
    c. the causes of a disorder are somatogenic, rather than psychogenic.
    d. all of the above

Answer: b
The underlying pathology model
p. 764

22. The pathology model of mental disorders is based on the idea that:
    a. mental disorders are physical in origin.
    b. treatment should involve the identification and removal of underlying causes.
    c. effective treatment merely involves eliminating overt symptoms.
    d. psychoanalysis is inappropriate to treat mental patients.

Answer: b
The underlying pathology model
p. 764

23. The pathology model of mental disorders is based on the assumption that:
    a. symptoms are caused by some underlying pathology.
    b. the underlying cause of a disorder may be psychogenic.
    c. the underlying cause of a disorder may be somatogenic.
    d. all of the above

Answer: d
The underlying pathology model
p. 764

24. The biomedical model of mental disorders is based on the idea that:
    a. all mental disorders can be cured with drugs.
    b. only the symptoms need to be eliminated.
    c. mental illness can be an organic dysfunction or deficiency.
    d. all of the above

25. According to the psychoanalytic model, mental disorders are the end products _____ that generally originate in _____.
    a. maladaptive learning; physiological changes associated with conditioning
    b. somatogenic processes; genetic inheritance
    c. familial and other social conflicts; society and culture
    d. internal psychological conflicts; childhood experience

26. Which of the following models is not a subcategory of the pathology model?
    a. the psychiatric model
    b. the medical model
    c. the psychoanalytic model
    d. the learning model

27. An example of the pathology model is:
    a. the medical model.
    b. the psychoanalytic model.
    c. the learning model.
    d. all of the above

28. Dr. Pratt is currently treating a patient for depression. In her therapeutic approach, she pays special attention to the patient's inactivity and poor social interactions. She focuses on the development of a reinforcement schedule to change these behaviors. Which model of psychopathology does Dr. Pratt most likely subscribe to?
    a. a self-efficacy model
    b. a medical model
    c. a learning model
    d. a cognitive model
    e. a directive model

29. Dr. Leroy is currently treating a patient for depression. In his therapeutic approach, he pays special attention to the patient's maladaptive thinking processes. He focuses on changing the ways in which the patient interprets environmental events. Which model of psychopathology does Dr. Leroy most likely subscribe to?
    a. self-efficacy model
    b. medical model
    c. learning model
    d. cognitive model
    e. directive model

30. In making psychiatric diagnoses, the distinction between symptoms and signs is that:
    a. symptoms are complaints by the patient, while signs are behaviors or physiological measures that accompany the symptoms.
    b. signs are complaints by the patient, and symptoms are behaviors or physiological measures that accompany the signs.
    c. signs are complaints by the patient, while a symptom is a recurring pattern of signs.
    d. none of the above

31. In psychiatric classifications, a "syndrome" is:
    a. a pattern of signs and symptoms that usually occur together.
    b. a form of disorganized thinking associated with schizophrenia.
    c. the key symptom for identifying each psychiatric disorder.
    d. a mental disorder that causes physical damage.

32. Until about twenty-five years ago, it was believed that most mental disorders could be subsumed under three very broad categories: neuroses, psychoses, and:
    a. personality disorders.
    b. organic brain syndromes.
    c. psychophysiological disorders.
    d. functional disorders.
    e. none of the above

33. Why are the terms neurosis and psychosis less used today?
    a. Psychiatrists can't agree on suitable definitions of these terms.
    b. Research has shown that there is no difference between these types of disorders.
    c. Psychiatrists want to classify conditions according to observable symptoms.
    d. These terms are not widely understood by the public and they often lead to confusion.

34. Diagnostic criteria in the DSM-IV emphasize:
    a. the underlying causes of the disorder, like the defense mechanisms used to ward off anxiety.
    b. the remote causes of the disorder, like genetic predispositions.
    c. descriptions of the specific, observable symptoms of various disorders.
    d. psychoanalytic underpinnings of various disorders.

35. The DSM-IV currently lists and describes _____ disorders in _____ categories, including Alzheimer's disease, schizophrenia, the mood disorders, and substance abuse.
    a. 100; 12
    b. 400; 17
    c. 10,000; 50
    d. 10; 3

Answer: b
The underlying pathology model
p. 767

36. The proper diagnosis of a disease (e.g., diabetes) includes the analysis of the overt symptoms, the underlying pathology, and:
    a. the syndrome involved.
    b. the remote causes.
    c. the traditional treatments.
    d. the organic basis.

Answer: c
The underlying pathology model
p. 767

37. In diabetes, as in many other disorders, the remote causes are:
    a. hereditary factors.
    b. precipitating factors, like obesity.
    c. both a and b
    d. none of the above

Answer: c
The underlying pathology model

p. 768

38. The diathesis-stress model has been a useful way of conceptualizing a number of mental disorders. What does "diathesis" refer to in this model?
    a. economic pressures
    b. environmental conditions
    c. predispositions
    d. defense mechanisms to reduce anxiety
    e. age at onset and the related prognosis

Answer: d
The underlying pathology model
p. 768

39. Historically, mental illness has been described as:
    a. demonic possession.
    b. overt symptoms caused by underlying diseases.
    c. susceptibilities to illness triggered by environmental stress.
    d. all of the above

Answer: c
Schizophrenia
p. 768

40. Schizophrenia, literally translated, means:
    a. multiple personality.
    b. cleft mind.
    c. split mind.
    d. mixed brain.

Answer: b
Schizophrenia
p. 769

41. The Swiss psychiatrist Eugen Bleuler coined the term *schizophrenia* to capture the essence of a disorder involving:
    a. multiple or split personalities.
    b. abnormal disintegration of mental functions.
    c. a "Jekyll-Hyde" division between good and bad selves.
    d. a marked difference between present and past behavior.

Answer: b
Schizophrenia
p. 769

42. According to one estimate, _____ of Americans will be treated for schizophrenia at some time in their lives.
    a. between 10 and 20 percent
    b. between 0.01 and 0.02 percent
    c. between 1 and 2 percent
    d. between 0.001 and 0.002 percent

Answer: d
Schizophrenia
p. 770

43. The cognitive symptoms of schizophrenia include impairments in:
    a. the ability to ignore irrelevant ideas.
    b. selective attention to external stimuli.
    c. the capacity to maintain a unified purpose or theme.
    d. all of the above

Answer: c
Schizophrenia
p. 770

44. The schizophrenic's withdrawal from social contacts:
    a. may save him from further cognitive decline.
    b. is often recognized as a cry for help.
    c. results in increased idiosyncrasy of ideas.
    d. allows more objective reality testing.

Answer: b
Schizophrenia
p. 771

45. What Bleuler called restitutional symptoms in schizophrenia:
    a. included delusions and hallucinations.
    b. involved disturbances of emotional affect.
    c. involved withdrawal from an increasingly confusing and over-whelming external world.
    d. all of the above

Answer: a
Schizophrenia
p. 771

46. The strong conviction that television commercials contain a coded message especially for you is an example of a(n):
    a. idea of reference.
    b. hallucination.
    c. disturbance of attention.
    d. word salad.

Answer: d
Schizophrenia
p. 771

47. Elaborate delusional systems are especially common in persons diagnosed with:
    a. manic depression.
    b. multiple personalities.
    c. catatonic schizophrenia.
    d. paranoid schizophrenia.

Answer: c
Schizophrenia
p. 771

48. Strange beliefs that typically involve misinterpretations of real events are called:
    a. compulsions.
    b. hallucinations.
    c. delusions.
    d. obsessions.
    e. none of the above

Answer: b
Schizophrenia
p. 771

49. Sam hears the voice of Satan telling him what to do. This symptom of schizophrenia is called a(n):
    a. schizoid break.
    b. hallucination.
    c. disturbance of attention.
    d. delusion.
    e. negative symptom.

50. A perceptual experience that is not mased on appropriate external stimuli
    is called a(n):
    a. delusion.
    b. illusion.
    c. hallucination.
    d. none of the above

51. The hallucinations that occur in schizophrenia:
    a. are generally auditory rather than visual.
    b. usually involve voices speaking to and/or about the individual.
    c. may reflect an inability to distinguish between one's own
       thoughts and external stimuli.
    d. all of the above

52. _____ are misinterpretations of real events, while _____ are
    experiences with no real basis in external sensory stimulation.
    a. Disturbances of thought; hallucinations
    b. Hallucinations; ideas of reference
    c. Delusions; hallucinations
    d. Ideas of reference; delusions

53. The emotional reactions of schizophrenic patients are often found to be:
    a. exaggerated.
    b. blunted.
    c. inappropriate to the situation.
    d. all of the above

54. In diagnoses of _____, an individual remains virtually motionless
    for long periods of time.
    a. manic depression
    b. paranoid schizophrenia
    c. catatonic schizophrenia
    d. disorganized schizophrenia

55. After several months of repeatedly standing on one leg, Mr. Bates told
    his psychiatrist that he needed to remain absolutely still to keep from
    flying apart into the expanding universe. Mr. Bates is best described as:
    a. having manic episodes.
    b. having delusions of grandeur.
    c. catatonic.
    d. showing negative symptoms.
    e. all of the above

56. Mark often exhibits bizarre behavior. He talks in a strange language that
    only he can understand. He goes up to total strangers and smiles and
    laughs loudly at them. Sometimes he does not bathe for weeks. What
    subcategory of schizophrenia does Mark best fit into?
    a. disorganized
    b. paranoid
    c. delusional
    d. referential
    e. catatonic

Answer: a
Schizophrenia
p. 772

57. According to many researchers, the primary psychological deficit in schizophrenia is an inability:
    a. to maintain one line of thought or action without distraction.
    b. to adopt the point of view of another person.
    c. to benefit from reality testing.
    d. to establish and maintain contact with other people.

Answer: b
Schizophrenia
p. 773

58. The dopamine hypothesis is based on the idea that schizophrenia results from:
    a. the production of an abnormal brain chemical called dopamine.
    b. the overactivity of neurons sensitive to the neurotransmitter dopamine.
    c. an inability to produce enough of the neurotransmitter dopamine.
    d. the inhibition of brain activity caused by dopamine.

Answer: a
Schizophrenia
p. 773

59. Drugs that are particularly effective in the treatment of schizophrenia include a class of drugs called:
    a. major tranquilizers.
    b. sedatives.
    c. MAO inhibitors.
    d. opiates.

Answer: c
Schizophrenia
p. 773

60. If schizophrenic individuals are injected with a drug that increases dopamine activity:
    a. their symptoms disappear.
    b. their symptoms become milder and less extreme.
    c. their symptoms become wilder and more extreme.
    d. they fall asleep.

Answer: d
Schizophrenia
p. 773

61. Evidence for the dopamine hypothesis includes the fact(s) that:
    a. amphetamines, which enhance dopamine activity, can produce temporary psychosis.
    b. drugs that block the action of dopamine also alleviate the symptoms of schizophrenia.
    c. the same drugs alleviate both schizophrenia and amphetamine psychosis.
    d. all of the above

Answer: a
Schizophrenia
p. 773

62. When certain dopamine-releasing neurons in the brain are destroyed, animals:
    a. ignore sensory stimulation.
    b. become overreactive to sensory stimulation.
    c. assume bizarre postures.
    d. become ravenously hungry.

Answer: a
Schizophrenia
p. 773

63. Your textbook authors suggest that oversensitivity to dopamine may produce schizophrenia because:
    a. it results in chronic overstimulation of the brain, leading to cognitive overload.
    b. it interferes with perceptual integration, leading to hallucinations and delusions.
    c. it inhibits emotional responsiveness, leading to blunted affect and subsequent social withdrawal.
    d. none of the above

Answer: d
Schizophrenia
p. 774

64. Studies of brain structure indicate that some individuals diagnosed with schizophrenia:
    a. show cellular abnormalities in the frontal and temporal lobes.
    b. have enlarged ventricles, suggesting a loss of brain tissue.
    c. show low levels of brain metabolism and blood flow in the temporal and frontal lobes.
    d. all of the above

Answer: b
Schizophrenia
p. 774

65. A counterargument for the idea that schizophrenia involves overactive dopamine systems is that:
    a. some schizophrenic individuals have enlarged cerebral ventricles.
    b. some schizophrenic individuals do not respond to dopamine-blocking medications.
    c. schizophrenia can be related to environmental stressors.
    d. cerebral atrophy selectively destroys dopamine neurons.

Answer: a
Schizophrenia
p. 774

66. A schizophrenic symptom is called a positive symptom if:
    a. it involves behaviors not observed in nonschizophrenic individuals.
    b. it is associated with a good prognosis for recovery.
    c. it is considered to be an attempt to deal with other symptoms.
    d. it is part of the stress, rather than of the diathesis.
    e. none of the above

Answer: a
Schizophrenia
p. 774

67. Which of the following is not one of the positive symptoms of schizophrenia?
    a. emotional blunting
    b. hallucinations
    c. delusions
    d. bizarre behaviors

Answer: c
Schizophrenia
p. 774

68. A symptom of schizophrenia is called a negative symptom if:
    a. it involves behaviors not observed in nonschizophrenic individuals.
    b. it is associated with a poor prognosis for recovery.
    c. it involves a deficiency in normal functioning.
    d. it involves a loss of contact with reality.
    e. none of the above

Answer: b
Schizophrenia
p. 774

69. Which of the following is not one of the negative symptoms of schizophrenia?
    a. emotional blunting
    b. hallucinations
    c. poverty of speech
    d. apathy

Answer: b
Schizophrenia
p. 774

70. Emotional blunting, apathy, lack of speech, and the inability to experience pleasure are:
    a. positive symptoms of schizophrenia.
    b. negative symptoms of schizophrenia.
    c. not often seen in schizophrenics.
    d. characteristic of those suffering from paranoia.

Answer: c
Schizophrenia
p. 774

71. According to Timothy Crow's two-syndrome hypothesis of schizophrenia:
    a. schizophrenia is caused by two types of neurotransmitter deficiencies.
    b. schizophrenics suffer from both environmental and mental deficiencies.
    c. schizophrenia is caused by two pathologies that correspond to the positive and negative symptoms.
    d. schizophrenics have two enlarged ventricles in the brain.

Answer: d
Schizophrenia
p. 775

72. According to Timothy Crow's two syndrome hypothesis, Type I schizophrenia:
    a. is caused by a malfunction of specific neurotransmitters.
    b. produces positive rather than negative symptoms.
    c. responds well to antipsychotic medications.
    d. all of the above

Answer: d
Schizophrenia
p. 775

73. According to Timothy Crow's two-syndrome hypothesis, Type II schizophrenia:
    a. is caused by cerebral damage and atrophy.
    b. produces negative rather than positive symptoms.
    c. does not respond well to antipsychotic medications.
    d. all of the above

Answer: b
Schizophrenia
p. 775

74. Your textbook notes several problems with the dopamine hypothesis of schizophrenia. For example:
    a. antipsychotics block dopamine receptors within weeks, but alleviation of symptoms only takes hours.
    b. some schizophrenic individuals do not respond to dopamine-blocking medications.
    c. some schizophrenics have lowered rather than elevated levels of dopamine in the cerebrospinal fluid.
    d. all of the above

Answer: c
Schizophrenia
p. 776

75. The chances that a sibling of a schizophrenic individual will also be schizophrenic are fairly high, about 8/100. This does not show that schizophrenia is inherited because:
    a. if it were, the risk would be much closer to 100 percent.
    b. the level of risk is about the same in the general population.
    c. siblings usually grow up in the same environments.
    d. all of the above

Answer: b
Schizophrenia
p. 776

76. Studies with schizophrenic twins show that:
    a. genetic factors play a minor role in schizophrenia.
    b. identical twins have a higher concordance rate for schizophrenia than do fraternal twins.
    c. identical twins are more likely to become schizophrenic than fraternal twins.
    d. none of the above

Answer: d
Schizophrenia
p. 776

77. The concordance rate for schizophrenia among identical twins is 55 percent, while the comparable figure for fraternal twins is 9 percent. These results suggest that:
    a. genetic factors predominate in the etiology of schizophrenia.
    b. there is a very weak genetic component in the development of schizophrenia.
    c. schizophrenia is essentially caused by environmental factors.
    d. both genetic and environmental factors play important roles in the development of schizophrenia.

Answer: d
Schizophrenia
p. 776

78. Research regarding the possible genetic bases of schizophrenia reveal that:
    a. the concordance rate for identical twins is higher than for fraternal twins.
    b. children born of schizophrenic mothers and adopted by nonschizophrenic mothers are more likely to be schizophrenic than adopted children of nonschizophrenic mothers.
    c. the incidence of schizophrenia increases the more closely one is related to a schizophrenic individual.
    d. all of the above

Answer: a
Schizophrenia
p. 776

79. Some investigators believe that schizophrenia may be a neurodevelopmental disorder. According to this hypothesis:
    a. pathological genes produce brain abnormalities during fetal development.
    b. poor nutrition and lack of prenatal care produce retarded neuronal development during gestation.
    c. a lack of parental attention and sensory stimulation produce abnormal development of attentional and perceptual mechanisms.
    d. none of the above

80. Evidence consistent with the hypothesis that schizophrenia is a neurodevelopmental disorder comes from the observation that:
    a. there seems to be a strong genetic basis for schizophrenia.
    b. many cases of schizophrenia have childhood preludes or precursors.
    c. both a and b
    d. none of the above

Answer: c
Schizophrenia
p. 776

81. Your textbook notes that children who will later develop positive symptoms of schizophrenia:
    a. tend to be passive and socially unresponsive.
    b. tend to be aggressive and irritable.
    c. tend to be withdrawn and emotionally dependent.
    d. all of the above

Answer: b
Schizophrenia
p. 776

82. Your textbook notes that children who will later develop negative symptoms of schizophrenia:
    a. tend to be passive and socially unresponsive.
    b. tend to be aggressive and irritable.
    c. tend to be distractible and emotionally dependent.
    d. all of the above

Answer: a
Schizophrenia
p. 776

83. Environmental factors must play a role in causing schizophrenia because:
    a. some cultures produce no schizophrenics.
    b. concordance among identical twins is far from 100 percent.
    c. adopted children can become psychotic.
    d. none of the above.

Answer: b
Schizophrenia
p. 777

84. Sociological studies in many countries have found that the incidence of schizophrenia is:
    a. greatest in the upper classes.
    b. greatest in the middle classes.
    c. greatest in the lower classes.
    d. the same in every socioeconomic class.

Answer: c
Schizophrenia
p. 777

85. According to one study discussed in your textbook, there are _____ times as many persons with schizophrenia from poor socioeconomic areas as from high socioeconomic areas.
    a. 15
    b. 9
    c. 5
    d. 20

Answer: b
Schizophrenia
p. 777

86. Studies of the families of schizophrenics have shown that:
    a. poor parental care causes schizophrenia.
    b. schizophrenic children may produce pathological reactions in family members.
    c. fathers of schizophrenic individuals are usually very aggressive and violent.
    d. eventually all siblings show signs of the disease.

Answer: b
Schizophrenia
p. 778

Answer: a
Schizophrenia
p. 778

87. Investigations of the families of schizophrenics have often found:
    a. a high degree of instability and conflict.
    b. a cruel, demanding father who dominated the household.
    c. parents who were overly affectionate and permissive.
    d. no consistent differences compared to other families.

Answer: d
Schizophrenia
p. 778

88. The correlation between schizophrenia and certain family characteristics is probably due to the fact that:
    a. schizophrenics are disturbing to their families.
    b. schizophrenics share pathological genes with other family members.
    c. disturbed family systems can precipitate schizophrenia.
    d. all of the above

Answer: a
Schizophrenia
p. 778

89. Research findings suggest that family relations may determine how well a schizophrenic individual copes with the illness. Specifically:
    a. families with high levels of negative expressed emotions are associated with relapse and readmission.
    b. conflicts between parents, but not conflicts between siblings, are associated with relapse and readmission.
    c. families that provide emotional "crutches" and overattention are associated with relapse and readmission.
    d. all of the above

Answer: b
Schizophrenia
p. 779

90. In terms of the "pathology model," the ultimate causes of schizophrenia are likely to be:
    a. an inability to focus in time and space.
    b. heredity and environmental stress.
    c. social withdrawal and blunted emotions.
    d. biochemical defects in the brain.

Answer: d
Schizophrenia
p. 779

91. Which of the following is a contributing factor in the development of schizophrenia?
    a. stress
    b. low socioeconomic status
    c. family interactions
    d. all of the above

Answer: d
Schizophrenia
p. 779

92. Your textbook authors describe a study examining the outcomes for 200 patients who had been diagnosed with schizophrenia 30 years earlier. The study found that:
    a. the majority were married, working, and largely free of symptoms.
    b. the majority had never married and more han half had never worked.
    c. full-blown schizophrenic symptoms were present early throughout the lifespan.
    d. negative symptoms were associated with a better prognosis than positive symptoms.

93. In bipolar disorder, an individual's mood periodically alternates between:
    a. mania and normalcy.
    b. depression and normalcy.
    c. depression, mania, and normalcy.
    d. aggression and mania.

94. Which of the following is an example of a mood disorder?
    a. hysterical conversion
    b. phobia
    c. schizophrenia
    d. major depression

95. Most patients with unipolar disorder:
    a. remain either manic or depressed throughout the lifespan.
    b. suffer periods of deep depression.
    c. experience mood swings every few hours.
    d. experience only one manic episode in their lives.

96. In discussing the prevalence of mood disorders, your textbook authors note that:
    a. bipolar disorder occurs in about 0.5 to 1 percent of the population.
    b. between 10 and 20 percent of all Americans will experience a major depressive episode at some time in their lives.
    c. bipolar disorder is more frequently diagnosed in women than in men.
    d. all of the above

97. Robert has repeatedly missed work during the last year. A year ago he became hyperactive, staying up for numerous nights working on projects that caught his interest. He gradually became quiet and withdrawn. Recently, Robert swallowed a large quantity of sedatives. He is probably suffering from:
    a. bipolar disorder.
    b. schizophrenia.
    c. obsessive-compulsive disorder.
    d. conversion disorder.
    e. none of the above

98. In his autobiography, Clifford Beers recalls writing letters from twenty to thirty feet long, at the rate of twelve feet per hour, during an episode of:
    a. hypomania.
    b. schizophrenia.
    c. mania.
    d. depression.

Answer: c
Mood disorders
p. 781

99. Which of the following is not a symptom of a manic state?
    a. very lively and infectiously merry
    b. extremely talkative and on the go
    c. able to handle frustration easily
    d. very self-confident

Answer: a
Mood disorders
p. 782

100. Depressed individuals often exhibit vegetative symptoms. These include:
    a. weakness, loss of appetite, and sleep disorders.
    b. disrupted attention and poor short-term memory.
    c. social withdrawal, anxiety, and delusions of worthlessness.
    d. agitation, anxiety, and cognitive impairment.
    e. none of the above

Answer: d
Mood disorders
p. 782

101. Some of the symptoms that may occur in cases of major depression include:
    a. delusions or hallucinations.
    b. disrupted attention and short-term memory.
    c. fatigue, weakness, and sleep disorders.
    d. all of the above

Answer: c
Mood disorders
p. 782

102. Which one of the following people is most likely to successfully commit suicide?
    a. John: deep in his depression, doesn't care about anyone or anything.
    b. Sissy: still in a hospital setting seems to be on the road to recovery.
    c. Bart: having had several good therapy sessions, seems to be re-gaining some control of his life.
    d. Karyn: extremely depressed, and will not leave her apartment or see anyone.

Answer: c
Mood disorders
p. 782

103. A depressed individual is most likely to commit suicide:
    a. at the onset of a depressive episode.
    b. at the point of deepest despair.
    c. with recovery from a depressive episode.
    d. between depressive episodes.

Answer: c
Mood disorders
p. 782

104. Compared to men, why are women less likely to die as a result of a suicide attempt?
    a. Fewer women than men attempt to kill themselves.
    b. Women are not, on average, as seriously depressed as men.
    c. Women use methods that are less likely to be fatal compared to methods used by men.
    d. all of the above

Answer: c
Mood disorders
p. 783

105. Based on what you know about seasonal affective disorders, you should be able to predict that they would be most common in:
    a. modern, technologically advanced cultures.
    b. cultures that depend mainly on agriculture.
    c. nonacclimated persons living in polar regions like Alaska.
    d. equatorial regions like Zaire or Ecuador.

Answer: b
Mood disorders
p. 783

106. Seasonal affective disorders are linked to:
     a. the typical weather for each season.
     b. the amount of sunlight to which people are exposed.
     c. the specific holidays that occur during a season.
     d. the extremes in temperature that accompany seasonal changes.

Answer: b
Mood disorders
p. 783

107. In discussing the relationship between light and seasonal affective disorder, your textbook authors suggest that it may have something to do with _____, which is modulated by light.
     a. increased dopaminergic transmission in the brain
     b. the release of melatonin by the pineal gland
     c. stimulation of the cortex via the optic nerve
     d. all of the above

Answer: b
Mood disorders
p. 784

108. With respect to the genetic components of mood disorders, it has been shown that:
     a. concordance rates for both identical and fraternal twins are the same.
     b. genetic factors play a stronger role in bipolar than unipolar disorder.
     c. mood disorders are generally inherited through matrilinear descent.
     d. the same genetic factors give rise to both uni- and bipolar disorders.

Answer: a
Mood disorders
p. 784

109. In discussing the possible genetic basis of mood disorders, your textbook notes that:
     a. for bipolar, but not unipolar, mood disorders, the concordance rate for identical twins is much higher than the concordance rate for fraternal twins.
     b. unipolar, but not bipolar, mood disorders have been linked to a particular enzyme deficiency and to a form of color blindness.
     c. mood disorders do not tend to "breed true": people with unipolar or bipolar depression do not tend to have relatives with the same type of disorder.
     d. all of the above

Answer: d
Mood disorders
p. 784

110. The evidence that unipolar and bipolar disorders may actually be genetically separate disorders comes from the observation that:
     a. in bipolar, more than unipolar mood disorders, the concordance rate for identical twins is higher than that for fraternal twins.
     b. bipolar, but not unipolar, mood disorders have been linked to a particular enzyme deficiency and to a form of color blindness.
     c. mood disorders tend to "breed true," people with unipolar or bipolar depression tend to have relatives with the same type of disorder.
     d. all of the above

Answer: c
Mood disorders
p. 785

111. As your textbook notes, there are several biochemical hypotheses about the causes of mood disorders. One of these is that mood disorders result from:
    a. a shortage of dopamine at critical sites in the brain.
    b. enlarged ventricles and other structural abnormalities in the brain.
    c. a shortage of norepinephrine and serotonin in specific locations in the brain.
    d. all of the above

Answer: a
Mood disorders
p. 785

112. Reduced levels of norepinephrine has been linked to:
    a. depression.
    b. mania.
    c. schizophrenia.
    d. multiple personality disorder.

Answer: a
Mood disorders
p. 785

113. Abnormal levels of what neurotransmitters are involved in mania and depression?
    a. norepinephrine, serotonin
    b. serotonin, tricyclics
    c. norepinephrine, MAO inhibitors
    d. norepinephrine, tricyclics

Answer: a
Mood disorders
p.785

114. Antidepressant medications typically:
    a. elevate levels of both norepinephrine and serotonin.
    b. elevate levels of norepinephrine and suppress levels of serotonin.
    c. suppress levels of norepinephrine and elevate levels of serotonin.
    d. suppress levels of both norepinephrine and serotonin.

Answer: a
Mood disorders
p. 785

115. In discussing possible organic factors in the development of mood disorders, your textbook authors note that:
    a. norepinephrine levels are low during depressive episodes, and increase during manic episodes.
    b. depressed individuals show increased levels of biogenic amines in the bloodstream.
    c. drugs that decrease the amount of MAO in the blood tend to relieve depression.
    d. antidepressant drugs tend to decrease the amount of norepinephrine and serotonin available for synaptic transmission.

Answer: d
Mood disorders
p. 785

116. In discussing the evidence that norepinephrine and serotonin may be involved in mood disorders, your textbook notes that:
    a. metabolic byproducts of these neurotransmitters are lower in the spinal fluid and urine of depressed patients than in nondepressed individuals.
    b. antidepressant medications increase the amounts of serotonin and norepinephrine available for synaptic transmission.
    c. although antidepressants can immediately change the levels of these neurotransmitters symptoms of depression are not affected for several weeks.
    d. all of the above

117. The psychogenic view of mood disorders is based on the idea that:
   a. what the patient thinks is a result of his mood.
   b. what the patient thinks precipitates his mood.
   c. both a or b
   d. none of the above

118. Mood or cognition? According to the psychogenic view of depression:
   a. bleak thoughts cause depression.
   b. depression causes bleak thoughts.
   c. a bleak future causes depression.
   d. depression makes the future seem bleak.

119. According to Aaron Beck, depression is caused by three types of irrational beliefs. Which of the following is not one of these beliefs?
   a. "I am worthless."
   b. "My future is bleak."
   c. "Whatever happens around me is surely going to turn out badly for me."
   d. "No one truly loves me."

120. Bill views himself as worthless. Even when he does a good job, he insists that he is stupid and that he "lucked out" this time. He says that nexttime he will surely fail. Which of the following theories best describes Bill's state?
   a. Seligman's learned helplessness theory
   b. Freud's psychosexual theory
   c. Beck's cognitive theory
   d. Murphy's labeling theory

121. One group of dogs was exposed to a series of painful shocks about which they could do nothing. These animals were then placed in a shuttlebox in which they had to learn to jump from one compartment to another in order to avoid an electric shock. Their performance in the shuttle box was compared to that of another group of dogs who had no prior experience with shock. The results showed that:
   a. the first group learned the shuttle box task while the second group did not.
   b. the second group learned the shuttle box task while the first group did not.
   c. both groups learnedto perform the task about equally well.
   d. neither group learned to perform the task.

122. Learned helplessness in humans is very similar to learned helplessness in animals in that:
   a. both act as if nothing can be done to change unpleasant events in their lives.
   b. both humans and animals tend to respond favorably to antidepressant medications.
   c. both a and b.
   d. none of the above

Answer: a
Mood disorders
p. 787

123. As your textbook notes, one problem with the learned helplessness interpretation of depression is that it does not explain:
    a. why helplessness doesn't always lead to depression.
    b. why the depressive has depressed relatives.
    c. why drugs alleviate the symptoms of depression.
    d. all of the above

Answer: a
Mood disorders
p. 787

124. A revised learned helplessness model attributes depression to an attributional style that attributes negative events to:
    a. stable, global, and internal causes.
    b. unstable, local, and internal causes.
    c. stable, local, and external causes.
    d. stable, global, and external causes.
    e. none of the above

Answer: c
Mood disorders
p. 787

125. Depressive explanatory styles have been shown to predict depressive symptoms in:
    a. college students who learned that they performed badly on an exam.
    b. women in the second trimester of pregnancy.
    c. both a and b
    d. none of the above

Answer: a
Mood disorders
p. 788

126. Which of the following statements about sex differences in the prevalence of mood disorders is incorrect?
    a. Unlike bipolar disorder, major depression may be the result of predisposing genes that are located on the X chromosome.
    b. Men may be underrepresented in diagnoses of major depression because they are more likely than women to get drunk or get high than get therapy.
    c. Women are more likely than men to be diagnosed with mood disorders such as bipolar disorder and major depression.
    d. Cyclic hormonal changes and hormonal changes associated with postpartum and menopause may make women more vulnerable to mood disorders than men.

Answer: e
Mood disorders
p. 789

127. Your textbook authors suggest that more women than men are diagnosed with depression because:
    a. hormonal changes occur cyclically, after birth and at menopause.
    b. women may dwell more on their moods and try to figure out why they feel depressed.
    c. due to cultural conditioning, women may feel themselves to be less in control of their own fate.
    d. depression in men may be masked by use of drugs or alcohol.
    e. all of the above

Answer: a
Anxiety disorders
p. 789

128. The primary symptoms of anxiety disorders are:
    a. anxiety and defenses against anxiety.
    b. withdrawal and loss of contact with reality.
    c. unconscious conflicts.
    d. mania and/or depression.

Answer: b
Anxiety disorders
p. 790

129. Unlike many other types of other fears, a phobia is:
    a. persistent.
    b. irrational.
    c. unconscious.
    d. all of the above

Answer: d
Anxiety disorders
p. 790

130. An intense and irrational fear of some object or situation is called a(n):
    a. hysteria.
    b. obsession.
    c. compulsion.
    d. phobia.

Answer: b
Anxiety disorders
p. 790

131. Social phobia:
    a. is categorized as a specific phobia.
    b. involves the fear of embarrassment or humiliation in front of others.
    c. appears to arise from early unsatisfactory or traumatic experiences in relationships with others.
    d. all of the above

Answer: d
Anxiety disorders
p. 790

132. Which of the folllowing is true regarding specific phobias?
    a. Phobic individuals typically know that their fears are irrational.
    b. An individual who is afraid of cats and the number 13 would be described as both ailurophobic and triskaidekophobic.
    c. Although a phobic individual may not be incapacitated by avoidance of a feared object, the individual is at risk because fear can generalize to other objects.
    d. all of the above

Answer: a
Anxiety disorders
p. 791

133. According to a conditioning account of phobias, the feared object acts as a(n):
    a. conditioned stimulus.
    b. unconditioned stimulus.
    c. conditioned response.
    d. unconditioned response.

Answer: a
Anxiety disorders
p. 791

134. According to your textbook, phobic disorders may develop:
    a. as a result of classical conditioning.
    b. because the feared object is symbolic of some repressed event.
    c. as a means of avoiding dangerous or anxiety producing impulses.
    d. all of the above

Answer: b
Anxiety disorders
p. 791

135. How does the preparedness theory of phobias explain the high incidence of some types of phobias?
    a. People don't prepare themselves properly when faced with something that frightens them.
    b. Evolution favors those creatures with a built-in fear of dangerous things, like snakes or spiders.
    c. Society prepares people to be afraid of dangerous things like snakes.
    d. none of the above

Answer: c
Anxiety disorders
p. 791

136. Your textbook authors present several research findings that remain unexplained by a simple conditioning account of the development of phobias. Which of the following is not one of these research findings?
    a. Some specific phobias seem to arise in the absence of a relevant learning experience.
    b. Not everyone who has a fearful encounter with objects such as snakes or spiders develops phobias.
    c. Specific phobias tend to originate in childhood, affecting males more often than females.
    d. Phobias tend to run in families so that more than one member experiences fear of the same object or event.

Answer: a
Anxiety disorders
p. 792

137. Which of the following is an example of an obsession?
    a. persistent thoughts of murder
    b. incessant counting and recounting
    c. ritualistic, repetitive handwashing
    d. all of the above

Answer: a
Anxiety disorders
p. 792

138. The television commercial that keeps running through your mind is an example of a mild:
    a. obsession.
    b. compulsion.
    c. conversion reaction.
    d. none of the above

Answer: b
Anxiety disorders
p. 792

139. If your roommate suddenly begins to wash her hands every fifteen minutes, you might suspect she has developed:
    a. an obsession.
    b. a compulsion.
    c. a conversion reaction.
    d. none of the above

Answer: d
Anxiety disorders
p. 792

140. Which of the following is not a characteristic of obsessive-compulsive disorder?
    a. ritualistic acts
    b. persistent thoughts and wishes
    c. doing and undoing
    d. conversion

Answer: b
Anxiety disorders
p. 792

141. Nemi has a long-standing fear of contamination which compels her to carry out numerous cleansing activities each day. If she notices any dirt on her person, she thoroughly washes her hands and arms. Nemi is probably suffering from:
    a. schizophrenia.
    b. obsessive-compulsive disorder.
    c. conversion disorder.
    d. bipolar disorder.
    e. none of the above

Answer: a
Anxiety disorders
p. 792

142. According to one interpretation, incessant washing is an example of:
    a. a compulsion to undo the impulse that underlies the obsessive thought.
    b. an obsession to undo the impulse that underlies the compulsive thought.
    c. a compulsion to express the impulse that underlies the obsessive thought.
    d. an obsession to express the impulse that underlies the compulsive thought.

Answer: c
Anxiety disorders
p. 793

143. Generalized anxiety disorders, unlike phobias, characteristically involve:
    a. episodes of irrational panic.
    b. displacement.
    c. constant and pervasive anxiety.
    d. unpleasant physiological arousal.

Answer: d
Anxiety disorders
p. 793

144. Whereas _____ is related to a specific object, _____ is not.
    a. anxiety; fear
    b. anxiety; a phobia
    c. fear; a phobia
    d. a phobia; generalized anxiety

Answer: c
Anxiety disorders
p. 793

145. Which of the following is not a symptom of generalized anxiety disorders?
    a. oversensitivity
    b. inability to concentrate
    c. fear of a particular object or situation
    d. insomnia

Answer: d
Anxiety disorders
p. 793

146. A person tells you that she is constantly tense and has difficulty concentrating. She frequently suffers from insomnia and a rapid heartbeat. You suspect that:
    a. she has a panic disorder.
    b. she has a phobia of some sort.
    c. she has a conversion disorder.
    d. she has a generalized anxiety disorder.

Answer: c
Anxiety disorder
p. 793

147. The most common anxiety disorder is:
    a. panic disorder, occurring in about 5 percent of the population in any one year.
    b. phobia, occurring in about 7 percent of the population in any one year.
    c. generalized anxiety disorder, occurring in about 6 percent of the population in any one year.
    d. post-traumatic stress disorder, occurring in about 3 percent of the population in any one year.
    e. none of the above

148. In discussing the causes of generalized anxiety disorder, your textbook author points out that:
    a. it is unclear if there is a genetic predisposition for this disorder.
    b. it may be linked to abnormalities in levels of the neurotransmitter GABA.
    c. the psychoanalytic interpretation is that it occurs when unacceptable impulses enter consciousness.
    d. all of the above

149. What is the main difference between generalized anxiety disorder and panic disorder?
    a. Panic disorder involves specific objects or events while generalized anxiety disorder does not.
    b. Panic disorder is chronic while generalized anxiety disorder is not.
    c. Generalized anxiety disorder is brought on by stress while panic disorder is not.
    d. Panic disorder is intermittent while generalized anxiety disorder is not.

150. Agoraphobia is a:
    a. fear of heights.
    b. fear of being alone outside the home.
    c. fear of driving.
    d. fear of closed spaces.

151. Fear of a panic attack involves an autonomic process that leads to even more fear of an attack. This can cause a full-blown panic attack. What does this process best exemplify?
    a. a vicious cycle
    b. the start of a psychosis
    c. opponent processes
    d. negative feedback

152. An individual is diagnosed with post-traumatic stress disorder (PSTD) rather than acute stress disorder if:
    a. the reaction to the stressful event is dissociation.
    b. the post-traumatic symptoms include waking flashbacks to the stressful event.
    c. the reaction to the stressful event persists for at least one month.
    d. all of the above

153. Which of the following is not one of the symptoms of post-traumatic stress disorder?
    a. a period of numbness or dissociation immediately after the trauma.
    b. recurrent nightmares and flashbacks of the trauma.
    c. survival guilt, if friends or relatives were harmed or killed.
    d. periods of intense anxiety, for which the individual is later amnesic.
    e. sleep disturbances.

Answer: a
Dissociative disorders
p. 797

154. In dissociative fugue, the individual:
    a. experiences amnesia and wanders away from home.
    b. shows inappropriate emotional responses, but cannot remember doing so.
    c. acts aggressively towards others, but cannot remember having done so.
    d. behaves aggressively toward others, but cannot remember doing so.
    e. none of the above

Answer: a
Dissociative disorders
p. 797

155. Which of the following is not an example of dissociative disorder?
    a. schizophrenia
    b. amnesia
    c. multiple personality
    d. fugue state

Answer: d
Dissociative disorders
p. 797

156. An example of a dissociative disorder is:
    a. amnesia.
    b. identity disorder.
    c. fugue.
    d. all of the above

Answer: e
Dissociative disorders
p. 798

157. In discussing dissociative identity disorder, your textbook notes that:
    a. until twenty years ago, this disorder was considered very rare.
    b. critics believe that some apparent cases are inadvertently produced, by the suggestions of therapists.
    c. each auxiliary personality seems to be built on a nucleus of particular memories.
    d. auxiliary personalities may differ in mood, attitudes, and skills.
    e. all of the above

Answer: d
Dissociative disorders
p. 798

158. In discussing the possible mechanisms underlying dissociative disorders, your textbook authors suggest that:
    a. the development of auxiliary personalities may be a form of unconscious self-dramatization.
    b. it may be an attempt to defend the individual against something that he or she is unwilling to face.
    c. it may involve the implicit memories studied by information-procesing theorists.
    d. all of the above

Answer: d
Dissociative disorders
p. 799

159. In discussing the diathesis-stress model and dissociative disorders, your text notes that:
    a. people with dissociative disorders are more easily hypnotized than others.
    b. most cases of psychogenic amnesia and psychogenic fugue occur after major stresses.
    c. dissociative identity disorder seems to be closely associated with physical and/or sexual abuse in childhood.
    d. all of the above

160. What all somatoform disorders have in common is the fact that they involve:
    a. changes in mood, or in the expression of emotion.
    b. the experience of sensations or perceptions in the absence of any corresponding external stimuli.
    c. complaints about bodily functions in the absence of any known organic causes.
    d. loss of access to some or all of one's previous memories.
    e. none of the above

161. In hypochondriasis, the individual may:
    a. experience a loss of physical functioning, without any organic basis.
    b. believe that he or she has some specific disease.
    c. suddenly develop a sensory impairment.
    d. dissociate into two or more separate and distinct personalities.
    e. all of the above

162. In somatization disorder, the individual may:
    a. experience a loss of physical functioning, without any organic basis.
    b. believe that he or she has some specific disease.
    c. complain of a large number of miscellaneous aches and pains.
    d. experience chronic pain for which no physical basis can be found.
    e. all of the above

163. Which of the following is not a somatoform disorders?
    a. conversion disorder
    b. hypochondriasis
    c. somatization disorder
    d. dystonia

164. According to the psychoanalytic perspective, people suffering from conversion disorders resolve internal conflict by seeming:
    a. depressed.
    b. fatigued.
    c. incapable of handling the problem.
    d. sick.

165. Paralysis of a limb with no organic causes is symptomatic of:
    a. fugue states.
    b. dissociative reactions.
    c. anxiety neurosis.
    d. conversion disorders.

166. According to Sigmund Freud, people with conversion disorders resolve internal conflict by:
    a. sliping into a fugue state.
    b. developing multiple personalities.
    c. developing essential hypertension.
    d. developing a hysterical ailment.

Answer: b
Somatoform and psychophysiological
    disorders
p. 800

167. A gifted pianist who develops hand paralysis with no apparent
    biological cause might be suspected of having:
    a. an obsessive-compulsive disorder.
    b. a conversion disorder.
    c. a psychogenic disorder.
    d. major depression.

Answer: c
Somatoform and psychophysiological
    disorders
p. 800

168. A man witnesses his son's murder and immediately becomes blind
    and deaf. This man's problem could best be classified as a(n)
    _____ disorder.
    a. dissociative
    b. anxiety
    c. somatoform
    d. psychophysiological
    e. mood

Answer: d
Somatoform and psychophysiological
    disorders
p. 800

169. Conversion disorder is diagnosed much less frequently today than it was
    a century ago. In discussing this fact, your textbook authors note that:
    a. it may be due to more permissive child rearing, especially in the
        area of sexual behavior.
    b. it may be due to a general increase in medical sophistication in
        the lay population.
    c. chronic fatigue and somatoform pain disorder may have replaced
        conversion disorder in modern society.
    d. all of the above

Answer: d
Somatoform and psychophysiological
    disorders
p. 800

170. Conversion disorder is diagnosed much less frequently today than it was
    a century ago. Your textbook notes that this may be due to:
    a. more permissive child rearing, especially in the area of sexual
        behavior.
    b. a general increase in medical sophistication in the lay population.
    c. an increase in our ability to correctly detect and diagnose physi-
        cal and neurological disorders.
    d. all of the above

Answer: c
Somatoform and psychophysiological
    disorders
p. 800

171. Unlike organic disorders, psychophysiological conditions:
    a. will disappear in a real emergency.
    b. involve no actual physical damage.
    c. are produced or aggravated by emotional factors.
    d. all of the above

Answer: b
Somatoform and psychophysiological
    disorders
p. 800

172. People suffering from psychophysiological disorders tend to:
    a. complain of physical symptoms that have no underlying
        physiological bases.
    b. suffer actual physiological malfunctions caused or aggravated by
        emotional factors.
    c. react to physiological problems with neurotic or psychotic be
        havior.
    d. none of the above

<table>
<tr><td>

Answer: c
Somatoform and psychophysiological
  disorders
p. 801

</td><td>

173. "I can't stand wasting this much time on lunch!" says Donna only five minutes after placing her order in a restaurant. "Relax, enjoy your time away from the office," her friend Bill replies. How would you best characterize Donna's and Bill's personality types?
   a. Donna is a chronic worrier, while Bill is overly optimistic.
   b. Donna is a aggressive and hostile, while Bill is relaxed and adjusted.
   c. Donna is a Type A personality, while Bill is a Type B personality.
   d. Donna is a Type B personality, while Bill is a Type A personality.

</td></tr>
<tr><td>

Answer: b
Somatoform and psychophysiological
  disorders
p. 801

</td><td>

174. In discussing the link between Type A personality and coronary heart disease, your textbook authors note that:
   a. Type A people are more at risk because they smoke more and have higher blood pressure.
   b. like Type A men, Type A women are more prone to coronary heart disease than are Type B women.
   c. both Type A women and Type A men are more prone to kidney dysfunction and peptic ulcers than are their Type B counterparts.
   d. all of the above

</td></tr>
<tr><td>

Answer: a
Somatoform and psychophysiological
  disorders
p. 802

</td><td>

175. What personality type is most likely to make the following statement? "Sure, I think my co-workers are honest, but only because they are afraid of getting caught. If they thought they could get away with it, I'm sure they would steal from the company."
   a. a Type A personality
   b. a Type B personality
   c. a hypertensive personality
   d. a paranoid personality

</td></tr>
<tr><td>

Answer: a
Somatoform and psychophysiological
  disorders
p. 802

</td><td>

176. In discussing the aspects of Type A behavior patterns responsible for the link with coronary heart disease, your text notes that it is probably:
   a. continual hostility manifested as anger, cynicism, and distrust.
   b. competitiveness and constant striving to be better than others.
   c. the individual's inability to relax and enjoy his or her life.
   d. none of the above

</td></tr>
<tr><td>

Answer: a
Somatoform and psychophysiological
  disorders
p. 802

</td><td>

177. In discussing the mechanisms that produce narrowing of the coronary arteries in Type A individuals, your textbook authors suggests it may result from:
   a. the continual release of steroids and epinephrine that stimulates the formation of cholesterol deposits on artery walls.
   b. constant muscle tension that compresses artery walls and leads to hypertension.
   c. the effects of stress-related hormones on the immune system, leading to damage of the artery walls.
   d. none of the above

</td></tr>
</table>

178. Joe preys on elderly people, convincing them to buy phony health insurance from him. He assures them that this insurance will cover any and all medical treatment they may need and that it will save their families thousands of dollars. After taking their money Joe leaves town and moves on to a different place where he can repeat this scam. In psychological terms, Joe is:
    a. a victim of multiple personalities.
    b. an antisocial personality.
    c. suffering from obsessive-compulsive disorder.
    d. schizophrenic.

179. Which of the following is NoT a characteristic of antisocial personality?
    a. a lack of genuine love or loyalty
    b. high levels of fear and anxiety
    c. well-developed social skills
    d. little remorse about past misdeeds

180. Research regarding the possible biological bases of antisocial personality indicates that:
    a. the chemical composition of the blood of antisocial personality types is different from that of normal individuals.
    b. antisocial personalities seem to be highly reactive to physiological stress, but show few signs of anxiety.
    c. antisocial personalities appear to show little physiological response to stress compared to other individuals.
    d. none of the above

181. There is some evidence that antisocial personalities are:
    a. cortically overaroused and easily conditioned autonomically.
    b. cortically overaroused and difficult to condition autonomically.
    c. cortically underaroused and easily conditioned autonomically.
    d. cortically underaroused and difficult to condition autonomically.

182. Research supports which of the following statements about antisocial personalities?
    a. They experience consistent and strict discipline in childhood.
    b. They are cortically overaroused.
    c. They have abnormal EEG recordings.
    d. They are more likely to have alcoholic mothers than other individuals.
    e. none of the above

183. Data concerning the possible etiology of the sociopathic personality shows that:
    a. a high proportion of sociopaths have abnormal EEG patterns that resemble those of children.
    b. the sociopath is cortically underaroused, and seeks stimulation through thrills and danger.
    c. identical twins have higher concordance rates for sociopathy than fraternal twins.
    d. all of the above

Answer: d
Social deviance
p. 806

184. Data concerning the possible etiology of the sociopathic personality shows that:
    a. inconsistent childhood discipline is related to sociopathy in adulthood.
    b. sociopaths are more likely to have sociopathic or alcoholic fathers than normal individuals.
    c. a high proportion of sociopaths have abnormal EEG patterns that resemble those of children.
    d. all of the above

Answer: b
The scope of psychology
p. 806

185. In their concluding statements about the diagnosis of mental disorders, your textbook authors suggest that:
    a. psychiatrists should be more aggressive in their efforts to change society's views of criminal behavior.
    b. a tendency to be too inclusive in designating behavioral problems as mental disorders could be dangerous.
    c. the fourth edition of the DSM has proven to be extremely useful and it is unlikely to undergo further revisions.
    d. diagnosing maladaptive behavioral patterns as mental disorders if a good first step to understanding and treating the problem.

| Treatment of Psychopathology

Answer: c
Biological therapies
p. 811

1. Which of the following is not a biological therapy for mental illness?
   a. the use of drugs
   b. electroconvulsive shock
   c. psychoanalysis
   d. brain surgery

Answer: b
Biological therapies
p. 811

2. Treatment through manipulation of the body is called:
   a. drug therapy.
   b. biological therapy.
   c. cognitive therapy.
   d. psychotherapy.

Answer: a
Biological therapies
p. 811

3. The first major mental disorder to be conquered by biological therapy was:
   a. general paresis.
   b. schizophrenia.
   c. bipolar disorder.
   d. hysteria.

Answer: c
Biological therapies
p. 811

4. Psychotropic medications are least effective in the treatment of:
   a. schizophrenia.
   b. mood disorders.
   c. dissociative disorders.
   d. anxiety disorders.

Answer: c
Biological therapies
p. 812

5. Thorazine and Haldol are:
   a. antidepressants
   b. anxiolytics
   c. antipsychotics
   d. sedatives
   e. none of the above

Answer: a
Biological therapies
p. 812

6. You would be most likely to receive a prescription for Thorazine or Haldol if your psychiatric diagnosis was:
   a. schizophrenia.
   b. generalized anxiety disorder.
   c. bipolar mood disorder.
   d. unipolar depression.
   e. none of the above

Answer: c
Biological therapies
p. 812

7. Which of the following findings suggests that antipsychotic drugs like Thorazine and Haldol are more than just high-powered tranquilizers?
   a. These drugs do not relieve anxiety or depression.
   b. Powerful sedatives like phenobarbital have no effect on schizophrenic symptoms.
   c. both a and b
   d. none of the above

Answer: d
Biological therapies
p. 813

8. Prior to the development of drugs to treat schizophrenia, most people suffering from this disorder:
   a. could not be treated in hospitals.
   b. spent most of their lives either in a catatonic state or in a highly agitated state.
   c. were abandoned by their family and friends.
   d. spent most of their lives in mental hospitals.
   e. all of the above

Answer: d
Biological therapies
p. 813

9. In discussing the deinstitutionalization of psychiatric patients between 1950 and 1980, your textbook authors note that:
   a. before antipsychotic drugs were available, the majority of schizophrenic patients spent most of their lives in institutions.
   b. the number of hospitalized patients dropped from 600,000 in the 1950s to about 125,000 in the 1980s.
   c. in the 1980s, the average hospital stay for schizophrenics was about two months.
   d. all of the above

Answer: d
Biological therapies
p. 813

10. Antipsychotic drugs have drawbacks as well as advantages when they are used to treat schizophrenia. As your text notes, these drugs:
    a. only relieve symptoms while they are being taken.
    b. are more effective for positive than for negative symptoms.
    c. have a number of fairly serious side effects.
    d. all of the above
    e. a and c only

Answer: e
Biological therapies
· p. 813

11. According to your textbook, antipsychotic drugs have a number of side effects. Which of the following is not one of these side effects?
    a. cardiac irregularities
    b. tremors and muscle spasms
    c. restlessness and a shuffling gait
    d. constipation and difficulty in urination
    e. susceptibility to liver or kidney infections

Answer: e
Biological therapies
p. 814

12. In discussing Clozaril, a new antipsychotic drug for schizophrenia, your textbook notes that:
    a. Clozaril seems to work on some negative as well as positive symptoms.
    b. the drug may affect serotonin, as well as dopamine.
    c. a small proportion of patients develop a potentially fatal blood disorder.
    d. it is much more expensive than the older antipsychotics.
    e. all of the above

Answer: a
Biological therapies
p. 814

13. Antipsychotic drugs are not the perfect treatment for schizophrenia. For example:
    a. because of their side effects, many patients do not reliably take their medications.
    b. about 97 percent of patients taking medication regularly have further outbreaks of the illness requiring hospitalization.
    c. antipsychotics are ineffective in about 82 percent of schizophrenic patients.
    d. all of the above

Answer: d
Biological therapies
p. 814

14. When schizophrenic individuals are discharged from the hospital:
    a. some are cared for by their parents.
    b. some become homeless drifters.
    c. some live in less than ideal board-and-care homes.
    d. all of the above

Answer: b
Biological therapies
p. 814

15. Tricyclic antidepressants:
    a. seem to work by decreasing the amount of norepinephrine and serotonin available for synaptic transmission.
    b. block the reuptake of neurotransmitters from the synapse.
    c. increase the number or capacity of receptor sites.
    d. reduce levels of dopamine in certain locations in the brain.

Answer: d
Biological therapies
p. 814

16. Which of the following is used as a drug treatment for affective disorders?
    a. insulin
    b. phenothiazine
    c. chlorpromazine
    d. tricyclics

Answer: a
Biological therapies
p. 814

17. MAO inhibitors:
    a. seem to work by increasing the amount of norepinephrine and serotonin available for synaptic transmission.
    b. increase the reuptake of neurotransmitters, thereby increasing syntheis of the substances.
    c. both a and b
    d. none of the above

Answer: d
Biological therapies
p. 814

18. In comparing MAO inhibitors and tricyclic antidepressants, your textbook authors note that:
    a. both increase the amounts of norepinephrine and serotonin available for synaptic transmission.
    b. MAO inhibitors are prescribed less than tricyclics because they require dietary restrictions.
    c. these drugs are effective treatments for about 65 percent of depressed patients.
    d. all of the above

Answer: a
Biological therapies
p. 815

19. Which of the following would probably not help a depressed person?
    a. Haldol
    b. MAO inhibitors
    c. tricyclics
    d. Prozac

Answer: e
Biological therapies
p. 815

20. According to your textbook authors, Prozac:
    a. was designed to act primarily on serotonin and minimally on norepinephrine.
    b. is a selective serotonin reuptake inhibitor.
    c. is just as effective against symptoms of depression as the tricyclics and MAO inhibitors.
    d. has fewer side effects than the tricyclics and MAO inhibitors.
    e. all of the above

Answer: a
Biological therapies
p. 815

21. A common side effect of Prozac is:
    a. loss of sexual desire.
    b. muscle tremors and spasms.
    c. reduced blood clotting.
    d. throat irritations and susceptibility to bronchial infections.

Answer: b
Biological therapies
p. 815

22. When antidepressant drugs are given to nondepressed participants, these individuals experience:
    a. depression.
    b. little or no change in mood.
    c. euphoria.
    d. heightened levels of energy.

Answer: d
Biological therapies
p. 815

23. According to your textbook authors, antidepressants are not merely stimulants because they:
    a. do not produce any signs of euphoria in nondepressed individuals.
    b. do not elevate mood in individuals who are not depressed.
    c. are useful in treating panic disorder, eating disorders, and obsessive-compulsive disorder.
    d. all of the above

Answer: b
Biological therapies
p. 815

24. Lithium carbonate is used to treat:
    a. depression.
    b. bipolar disorders.
    c. dissociative disorders.
    d. schizophrenia.

25. Lithium carbonate is often used as a treatment for:
    a. general paresis.
    b. senility.
    c. manic episodes.
    d. schizophrenia.

26. A drug used in the treatment of mania is:
    a. imipramine.
    b. lithium carbonate.
    c. chlorpromazine.
    d. dopamine.

27. Which of the following is false regarding medications used to treat bipolar disorder?
    a. Although lithium carbonate is often an effective drug treatment, blood levels must be monitored closely due to potential toxicity effects.
    b. Two drug treatment alternatives to lithium carbonate, Tegretol and Depakote, achieve the same beneficial effects with no side effects.
    c. Tegretol and Depakote, once used to treat epilepsy, are more effective than lithium carbonate when mood cycles are frequent and rapid.
    d. Lithium carbonate is called an antimanic drug, although it also helps forestall depressive episodes in bipolar disorder.

28. Which of the following statements about anxiolytics is false?
    a. They usually work by increasing neurotransmission at synapses containing GABA.
    b. They are particularly useful for long-term treatment.
    c. They tend to be highly addictive.
    d. They interact dangerously with alcohol.

29. A simple "before and after" test of a new drug is inadequate because:
    a. people differ in the ways they respond to drugs.
    b. mentally ill participants may forget to take their medication unless supervised.
    c. spontaneous improvements may be attributed to the drug.
    d. improvements might not occur until after the second testing.

30. A researcher finds that after drinking nothing but milk for 3 months, 3 patients (out of 9) report that they no longer suffer from migraine headaches. The researcher proclaims the curative powers of milk. What critical question cannot be answered due to the absence of a control group that is standard in studies of therapeutic effectiveness?
    a. What is the spontaneous recovery rate without treatment?
    b. How did the milk cure the headaches?
    c. Why were only 1/3 of the patients cured?
    d. Can this finding be repeated?

Answer: c
Biological therapies
p. 816

31. In evaluating drug therapies, a method of controlling for spontaneous improvements might be:
    a. to carry out a longitudinal study on all of the participants.
    b. to administer before and after tests with many participants.
    c. to use a comparison group of untreated participants that has the same diagnosis.
    d. to simultaneously give each subject a placebo along with the medication.

Answer: a
Biological therapies
p. 817

32. Which of the following can be referred to as a placebo effect?
    a. improvement following treatment with a medically neutral substance.
    b. a drug-induced change in specific "target" symptoms.
    c. spontaneous improvement in the absence of any therapy.
    d. the ability of a drug to prevent a disease.

Answer: d
Biological therapies
p. 818

33. In evaluating the effectiveness of a drug therapy, one must be careful to control the potential effects of:
    a. spontaneous improvement.
    b. a placebo effect.
    c. the doctor's expectations.
    d. all of the above

Answer: a
Biological therapies
p. 818

34. To guard against the potential effects of a patient's or a doctor's expectations on treatment, investigators use:
    a. a double-blind technique.
    b. matching.
    c. prefrontal lobotomy.
    d. transference.

Answer: c
Biological therapies
p. 818

35. The double-blind experimental technique is used as a means of avoiding:
    a. placebo effects.
    b. negative therapeutic reactions.
    c. the effects of experimenter expectations.
    d. spontaneous improvements.

Answer: d
Biological therapies
p. 818

36. Which of the following is true about the use of placebos in double-blind studies of drug effectiveness?
    a. It may be unethical to give a placebo and withhold an accepted treatment.
    b. Because of characteristic side effects, it is sometimes easy to tell who has taken the medication and who has taken the placebo.
    c. It is more useful to test the effectiveness of a new drug against the best alternative treatment, rather than against a placebo.
    d. all of the above

37. As your textbook notes, a new medication is usually tested against the best current treatment, rather than against a placebo. One advantage of this approach is that:
    a. no patient is deprived of actual treatment.
    b. placebo effects should be about the same in both groups.
    c. differences in side effects between groups are less obvious.
    d. all of the above

38. According to your textbook authors, outcome measures for drug evaluation studies have recently shifted their focus from _____ to _____.
    a. duration or intensity of treatment; mood and behavioral improvements
    b. mood and behavioral improvements; duration or intensity of treatment
    c. self- or staff reports of improvement; cost-effectiveness
    d. cost-effectiveness; self- or staff reports of improvement

39. In weighing the benefits and costs of drug treatments, your textbook authors note that:
    a. drugs do not help every patient and they often have unpleasant side effects.
    b. drugs have completely changed the atmosphere of mental hospitals.
    c. antidepressants and anxiolytics generally do a fine job of controlling mood and anxiety disorders.
    d. all of the above

40. How have modern drug therapies changed the environments of mental hospitals?
    a. They keep the patients in a stupor-like state thus eliminating the need for restraints.
    b. They've greatly reduced the number of staff members needed to run a hospital.
    c. They've reduced the number of therapy sessions needed before release.
    d. They allow hospitals to function as therapeutic centers.

41. Modern drug therapies have changed the functioning of the mental hospital because:
    a. many individuals are restored to normal functioning, thereby reducing the number of inpatients.
    b. disruptive symptoms are reduced, so mental facilities can serve as a center for social and psychological services.
    c. mental hospitals resort to the use of restraints much less frequently than in the past.
    d. all of the above

42. The technique of prefrontal lobotomy largely has been abandoned because the surgery:
    a. disconnected the patients' thoughts from their emotions.
    b. impaired some higher cognitive functions.
    c. was to be reversible in far too many cases.
    d. produced inexpressive, mask-like faces.

43. Psychosurgery is much different today than in the past. For example:
    a. today, surgery is much more precise and localized than in the past.
    b. it is reserved for severely disabled patients who have shown no improvement with other treatments.
    c. both a and b
    d. none of the above

44. Which of the following disorders is least likely to be treated by psychosurgery?
    a. chronic pain
    b. obsessive-compulsive disorder
    c. severe depression
    d. panic disorder
    e. all of the above

45. Electroconvulsive shock therapy (ECT) is most effective in the treatment of:
    a. depression.
    b. epilepsy.
    c. schizophrenia.
    d. mania.

46. Which of the following statements about ECT is false?
    a. ECT was originally used as a treatment for schizophrenia.
    b. It is more effective for some individuals than antidepressants.
    c. Patients who are unresponsive to antidepressants generally do not respond well to ECT.
    d. The therapeutic effects of ECT occur more quickly than those of antidepressants.

47. Electroconvulsive shock therapy can result in:
    a. convulsions.
    b. memory impairment.
    c. relief from depression.
    d. all of the above

48. Electroconvulsive shock therapy was used quite frequently in past decades. Now it is used quite infrequently because of all the possible damage it can do. In what situation(s) is it still used?
    a. when drug therapy does not work
    b. when the patient is suicidal
    c. both a and b
    d. none of the above

Answer: b
Biological therapies
p. 820

49. One advantage of electroconvulsive shock treatment that makes it the treatment of choice in some special cases is that:
    a. it has no adverse side effects.
    b. it is very fast acting.
    c. it alleviates both schizophrenic and depressive symptoms.
    d. it rarely requires more than one or two administrations.

Answer: c
Psychotherapy
p. 821

50. According to your textbook, *psychotherapy* refers to:
    a. all attempts to treat mental disorders.
    b. all treatment aimed at exposing unconscious conflicts.
    c. treatment using psychological rather than biological methods.
    d. treatment of symptoms rather than of causes.

Answer: a
Psychotherapy
p. 822

51. Classical psychoanalysis is based on the idea that neurotic symptoms will disappear when:
    a. long-buried conflicts are uncovered and resolved.
    b. new adaptive behaviors are learned.
    c. childhood events prior to ages three to four are remembered.
    d. the patient learns to view his impulses as unacceptable.

Answer: c
Psychotherapy
p. 822

52. When a client in psychotherapy is asked to say whatever comes into his mind, it is believed that sooner or later the memory relevant to the disorder should be revealed. This technique is known as:
    a. resistance.
    b. repression.
    c. free association.
    d. role playing.

Answer: d
Psychotherapy
p. 822

53. A psychoanalyst tries to gain information about unconscious conflict from:
    a. dreams.
    b. resistances.
    c. slips of the tongue.
    d. all of the above

Answer: b
Psychotherapy
p. 823

54. What did Sigmund Freud call the relationship that develops between a patient and an analyst?
    a. catharsis
    b. transference
    c. resistance
    d. none of the above

Answer: b
Psychotherapy
p. 823

55. The psychoanalytic term *transference* refers to which of the following phenomena?
    a. one symptom disappears and is replaced by another
    b. the patient reacts to the analyst as though she were some other important person in his life
    c. previously unconscious wishes and fears shift to a conscious level
    d. the analyst tries to behave like a parent to the patient

56. The phenomenon of transference occurs during psychoanalysis when the patient:

    a. resists bringing unconscious feelings into consciousness.

    b. experiences an explosive release of repressed emotions.

    c. treats the therapist as the patient once treated a significant figure in his personal life.

    d. shifts formerly unconscious wishes and impulses into consciousness in order to deal with them.

    e. none of the above

57. According to classical and neo-Freudian psychoanalysts, what is the key to a neurosis?

    a. the conflict between the patient and her parents

    b. the hidden sexual desires of the patient

    c. unconscious conflicts

    d. a struggle between the id and the ego

58. Modern forms of psychodynamic therapy share with traditional psychoanalysis an emphasis upon:

    a. a detailed exploration of the client's early past.

    b. problems in the client's psychosexual development.

    c. emotional insight into unconscious conflicts.

    d. a long-term, intensive commitment to therapy.

59. Dr. Kore is a psychotherapist who stresses the influence of interpersonal and cultural factors in psychotherapy. She also emphasizes the current situation facing her client rather than the past. Dr. Kore believes that understanding comes through insight into unconscious processes. From this description, what type of therapy does Dr. Kore seem to practice?

    a. classical psychoanalytic

    b. neo-Freudian

    c. existential

    d. cognitive

    e. client-centered

60. Why do many modern therapists see their clients much less frequently than those who use classical psychoanalysis?

    a. The patient is often unwilling to reveal much about himself if he is forced to come in every day.

    b. Fewer sessions help keep therapy from becoming the focus of an individual's life, rather than making beneficial changes.

    c. Modern therapists have many more patients to see and can't afford to spend too much time on one patient.

    d. There is a social stigma attached to frequent sessions with a therapist.

61. Alternatives to classical psychoanalysis are:

    a. neo-Freudian psychoanalysis.

    b. behavior therapy.

    c. humanistic therapy.

    d. all of the above

Answer: b
Psychotherapy
p. 825

62. Behavior therapy is largely based upon the principle(s) of:
    a. Freudian psychoanalysis.
    b. operant and classical conditioning.
    c. humanistic philosophy and practice.
    d. psychopharmacology.

Answer: c
Psychotherapy
p. 825

63. Psychoanalytically oriented therapists focus on _____ , while behavior therapists focus on _____ .
    a. doing; understanding
    b. feeling; action
    c. understanding; doing
    d. present; past

Answer: c
Psychotherapy
p. 825

64. Which of the following is of least interest to a behavior therapist?
    a. past history
    b. current circumstances
    c. unconscious thoughts
    d. overt behavior

Answer: c
Psychotherapy
p. 825

65. Why is extinction difficult to use in the treatment of irrational fears?
    a. It merely treats the fear and does not reveal the underlying cause(s).
    b. Extinction is only effective with less intelligent organisms such as rats or pigeons.
    c. People tend to avoid fear-arousing situations, and therefore extinction is unlikely to occur.
    d. all of the above

Answer: d
Psychotherapy
p. 826

66. Systematic desensitization is most useful in treating:
    a. mania.
    b. free-floating anxiety.
    c. depression.
    d. phobias.

Answer: d
Psychotherapy
p. 826

67. Systematic desensitization:
    a. is a therapy derived from encounter group or sensitivity training techniques.
    b. is a humanistically oriented modification of psychoanalysis.
    c. is a major goal of rational-emotive therapy.
    d. none of the above

Answer: a
Psychotherapy
p. 826

68. Jennifer is terrified of insects. She won't even walk on grass or go into any areas with trees. If Dr. Joseph Wolpe, the well known behavioral therapist, were treating this phobia, which technique would he most likely use?
    a. systematic desensitization
    b. flooding
    c. aversion therapy
    d. modeling
    e. extinction

Answer: b
Psychotherapy
p. 826

69. What is the basic goal of systematic desensitization?
    a. The client learns to face his fear regardless of how scared it makes him feel.
    b. The client associates a state of relaxation with fear-evoking stimuli.
    c. The client systematically overcomes a fear by coming in contact with it every day.
    d. The client forms a series of visual images that can be used during a fear-evoking situation.

Answer: c
Psychotherapy
p. 826

70. In systematic desensitization, fear-producing stimuli are associated with:
    a. learned helplessness.
    b. increased motor activity.
    c. muscular relaxation.
    d. aggressive responses.

Answer: b
Psychotherapy
p. 826

71. Which of the following is not a feature of systematic desensitization?
    a. muscular relaxation
    b. free association
    c. a list of anxiety-provoking stimuli
    d. counterconditioning

Answer: d
Psychotherapy
p. 826

72. Bob is so afraid of cars he cannot go out of his home. If a therapist who ascribed to the therapeutic techniques of Dr. Joseph Wolpe were treating Bob, what would she most likely recommend as a first step in treatment?
    a. Expose the client to a busy downtown area.
    b. Ask the client to report any cognitions he has about cars.
    c. Try to determine what cars might symbolize to the client.
    d. Construct an anxiety hierarchy of feared situations.
    e. Ask Bob to describe his negative past experiences with cars.

Answer: c
Psychotherapy
p. 826

73. Joseph Wolpe typically constructed a(n) _____ to help clients deal with a fear gradually.
    a. cognitive schema
    b. relaxation chamber
    c. anxiety hierarchy
    d. panic scale

Answer: c
Psychotherapy
p. 827

74. Which of the following is a behavior therapy?
    a. client-centered therapy
    b. psychoanalysis
    c. aversive therapy
    d. rational-emotive therapy

Answer: b
Psychotherapy
p. 827

75. Both _____ are therapies that are based on classical conditioning.
    a. transference and resistance
    b. aversion therapy and systematic desensitization
    c. applied tolerance therapy and free association
    d. none of the above

Answer: d
Psychotherapy
p. 827

76. Dr. Ahman is a behavior therapist who has a client who cannot stop chewing gum. Which behavior therapy technique would Dr. Becker most likely use to get his client to stop this constant gum chewing?
    a. flooding
    b. modeling
    c. extinction
    d. aversion therapy
    e. systematic desensitization

Answer: a
Psychotherapy
p. 828

77. In discussing the effectiveness of aversion therapy, your textbook authors note that:
    a. the procedure may not always be effective outside the environment in which therapy took place.
    b. in cases of alcohol aversion therapy, clients often revert to their earlier level of alcohol intake only a month after ending therapy.
    c. in cases of cigarette aversion training, there does seem to be some reduction in smoking as long as six months after therapy.
    d. all of the above

Answer: b
Psychotherapy
p. 828

78. In some hospital wards, *token economies* are used with clients who are apathetic toward life. A token economy is a therapeutic technique based on:
    a. classical conditioning.
    b. operant conditioning.
    c. aversion techniques.
    d. cognitive therapy.

Answer: a
Psychotherapy
p. 828

79. Contingency management is a _____ therapeutic technique that teaches an individual that _____.
    a. behavioral; certain behaviors have predictable consequences
    b. cognitive; certain thoughts result in depression
    c. psychoanalytic; certain insights reduce anxiety
    d. humanistic; certain feelings are unique, yet universal

Answer: d
Psychotherapy
p. 829

80. Cognitive therapy was originally developed by _____ as a treatment for _____.
    a. Pavlov; habituation
    b. Skinner; neurosis
    c. Freud; sexual dysfunction
    d. Beck; depression

Answer: b
Psychotherapy
p. 829

81. Cognitive therapy is related to behavior therapy because:
    a. classical conditioning is used extensively to change cognitions.
    b. the therapist is extremely directive in her attempts to change the client's thinking.
    c. elaborate client histories allow insight into childhood events.
    d. all of the above

82. What role does the therapist play in cognitive therapy?
    a. The therapist is merely a sounding board for the client who is provided a safe means of confronting sensitive issues.
    b. The therapist attempts to cause the client to have an anxiety attack in a setting where it can be controlled and studied.
    c. The therapist plays the role of a sympathetic listener who asks questions to show the client that certain thoughts are irrational.
    d. The therapist asks a series of very personal questions to desensitize the client and facilitate discussion of sometimes embarrassing problems.

Answer: c
Psychotherapy
p. 829

83. Cognitive therapists typically attempt to change their clients':
    a. unconscious motives.
    b. overt behaviors.
    c. maladaptive beliefs.
    d. unpleasant emotions.

Answer: c
Psychotherapy
p. 829

84. Cognitive therapy deals primarily with:
    a. teaching the client to recall traumatic events from childhood.
    b. teaching the mind to react positively to stressful situations.
    c. teaching mind and body relaxation techniques.
    d. teaching the client to identify and change maladaptive patterns of thinking.

Answer: d
Psychotherapy
p. 829

85. How does cognitive therapy help people suffering from panic disorders?
    a. It teaches the client to relax her body at the onset of a panic attack.
    b. It teaches the client to achieve a more realistic interpretation of her bodily sensations.
    c. It teaches the client how to use positive thinking and imagery to alleviate panic attacks.
    d. It teaches the client how to use biofeedback to control panic attacks.

Answer: b
Psychotherapy
p. 829

86. "Dizziness occurs when there is a sudden drop in blood pressure and the shortness of breath you feel is the result of a slight biochemical change in your body. These physical changes occur when you overemphasize the importance of making a good impression." This therapist seems to be using _____ to explain a panic attack to client.
    a. the medical model
    b. systematic desensitization
    c. a biological therapy
    d. cognitive therapy
    e. none of the above

Answer: d
Psychotherapy
p. 829

87. What do therapists who use social education hope to do for a client?
    a. attempt to teach the client new skills for employment purposes
    b. attempt to help the client find new and more appropriate behavior patterns
    c. attempt to help the client accept the fact that there is a problem but it can be solved
    d. attempt to help the client admit that there is a problem and that it is not all his or her fault

Answer: b
Psychotherapy
p. 830

Answer: c
Psychotherapy
p. 830

88. Which of the following is not a therapy technique used in social education?
    a. modeling
    b. role playing
    c. flooding
    d. graded task assignments

Answer: a
Psychotherapy
p. 831

89. Which of the following is an example of a humanistic therapy?
    a. client-centered therapy
    b. catharsis
    c. free-association
    d. all of the above

Answer: d
Psychotherapy
p. 831

90. Client-centered therapy was developed by:
    a. Sigmund Freud.
    b. Abraham Maslow.
    c. Robert Yerkes.
    d. Carl Rogers.

Answer: c
Psychotherapy
p. 831

91. Carl Rogers is associated with which school of therapy?
    a. behavior
    b. drug
    c. humanistic
    d. biological

Answer: d
Psychotherapy
p. 831

92. Rogers's approach to therapy is based upon the belief that:
    a. all persons naturally strive to realize their human potential.
    b. human nature is inherently good.
    c. mental disorders result when personal growth is blocked.
    d. all of the above

Answer: a
Psychotherapy
p. 831

93. The use of expressions like "human nature is inherently good" are most likely to be used by:
    a. client-centered therapists.
    b. psychoanalysts.
    c. behavior therapists.
    d. psychiatrists.

Answer: a
Psychotherapy
p. 831

94 What are nondirective techniques?
    a. echoing or restating what a client seems to say or feel
    b. avoiding personal involvement with a client
    c. giving advice only when directly asked for it by the client
    d. using techniques that are not directed at any single specific goal

Answer: a
Psychotherapy
p. 831

95. Cognitive therapists focus on _____ , while humanist therapists focus on _____ .
    a. thinking; feeling
    b. feeling; thinking
    c. emotions; interpersonal relationships
    d. understanding; feeling

96. Therapists with a humanistic orientation try to identify _____ in each client:
    a. a set of conditioned fear responses
    b. a whole, unique, and complex person
    c. a level of unconscious conflicts
    d. a system of unrealistic beliefs

97. Psychoanalysis can be summarized by the word *unconscious* in the same way that behavior therapy can be represented by *conditioning*. What two words best summarize humanistic therapy?
    a. cause and effect
    b. empathy and acceptance
    c. directive and interpretive
    d. rational and emotive

98. In Carl Rogers's client-centered therapy, the most important function of the therapist is to provide:
    a. unconditional acceptance and regard.
    b. practice in exercising interpersonal skills.
    c. a structure for the patient's confused thoughts.
    d. a model for effective ways of handling situations.

99. According to existentialists, what is the cause of our inability to endow life with meaning?
    a. our obsession with money and material things
    b. the restless, anonymous nature of life in the twentieth century
    c. the lack of religion in many people's lives
    d. the changing roles of men and women in modern society

100. "I am nothing but a small wheel in a huge machine. If I disappeared tomorrow, nobody would even notice." This statement would be most meaningful to what type of therapist?
    a. neurotic
    b. psychotic
    c. manic-depressive
    d. existentialist
    e. humanist

101. The ultimate goal of existential therapy is to:
    a. reconcile the client to the emptiness of life.
    b. eliminate the symptoms of neurosis.
    c. help clients to find meaning in their lives.
    d. lead clients to rediscover traditional religious values.

102. Existential therapists are characterized by:
    a. the use of a couch and free association.
    b. the philosophy that life is meaningless.
    c. optimistic faith in the individual's capacity for growth.
    d. a belief in the importance of responsible, free choice.

Answer: b
Psychotherapy
p. 832

103. As an approach to psychotherapy, technical eclecticism involves:
   a. focusing on specific techniques, rather than achieving any particular of therapeutic result.
   b. combining techniques from a variety of different approaches.
   c. using conditioning techniques to achieve insight into unconscious processes.
   d. none of the above

Answer: d
Psychotherapy
p. 833

104. _____ helps most clients in psychotherapy realize that they really can conquer their problems and, according to some researchers, it may be the single most important ingredient in successful psychotherapy.
   a. Accurate diagnosis
   b. Insightful analysis
   c. A transference relationship
   d. Therapeutic alliance

Answer: c
Psychotherapy
p. 834

105. Which of the following is not a common purpose of all of the psychotherapies discussed?
   a. interpersonal learning
   b. greater self-knowledge
   c. insight into the past
   d. emotional reeducation

Answer: d
Psychotherapy
p. 834

106. Most psychotherapies aim to achieve:
   a. emotional defusing.
   b. interpersonal learning.
   c. self-knowledge.
   d. all of the above

Answer: c
Psychotherapy
p. 834

107. Which of the following is not a characteristic of most psychotherapies?
   a. emotional reeducation
   b. step-by-step progress in therapy
   c. diagnostic testing
   d. an intimate and confiding relationship between client and therapist

Answer: d
Psychotherapy
p. 834

108. Which of the following is not a common theme of the many schools of therapy?
   a. self-knowledge
   b. interpersonal learning
   c. emotional defusing
   d. use of drugs
   e. use of a step-by-step process

Answer: d
Psychotherapy
p. 834

109. In Sigmund Freud's time, psychotherapists did not:
   a. treat highly educated, adults.
   b. focus on the causes of psychopathology.
   c. attempt to alleviate their patient's distress.
   d. treat patients in group or family contexts.

110. Alcoholics Anonymous is an example of:
    a. family therapy.
    b. behavior therapy.
    c. individual therapy.
    d. group therapy.

111. The purpose of shared-problem groups like Alcoholics Anonymous is to:
    a. manage the problem that all members share.
    b. uncover each individual's emotional problems.
    c. allow emotional release within the group.
    d. none of the above

112. One of the major benefits of group therapy is that it provides opportunities for:
    a. interpersonal relations.
    b. role playing.
    c. flooding.
    d. free association.

113. Advocates of group therapy claim that group experience is more effective than individual therapy because:
    a. the individual client gets much more personalized attention.
    b. the group provides on-the-spot practice in interpersonal skills.
    c. group therapists typically use a client-centered approach.
    d. each patient learns that she is special and unique.

114. The growth of marital and family therapy has paralleled which of the following in America?
    a. the declining socioeconomic status of many Americans
    b. the increasing divorce rate and single parent households
    c. the increasing number of teenage pregnancies
    d. the rapidly changing roles of men and women in society

115. According to your textbook, the key to family and marital distress is to understand:
    a. the differences between man and woman, parent and child
    b. the lack of communication between family members
    c. the relationships within the family system
    d. the problems of each individual family member

116. What do many marital and family therapists see as their primary task in providing therapy?
    a. They want to help the family readjust their interpersonal relationships.
    b. They want to make each member recognize each others' individuality.
    c. They want to open the lines of effective communication.
    d. They want to encourage personal growth for each member.

117. Why do family therapists prefer to meet with the family as a group rather than with each family member individually?
     a. The therapist can act as a translator who helps each member better understand the other members.
     b. Family therapy is such a growing field that therapists don't have time to meet with each family member individually.
     c. Being part of a group often puts the clients more at ease.
     d. all of the above

118. In their discussion of the treatment of _____, your textbook authors point out that psychotherapy is now available for "shopping addicts," people suffering from an "excessive need for love," and even those who wish to "achieve their full human potential."
     a. subsyndromal conditions
     b. nondisorders
     c. OCD
     d. neuroses

119. The goals of many modern (e.g., humanistic, existential) therapies are broader than those of traditional psychoanalysis. As a result:
     a. therapists are no longer concerned about alleviating symptoms.
     b. therapy seems appropriate for a larger proportion of the population.
     c. clients remain in therapy for longer periods of time.
     d. therapeutic success is more easily demonstrated.

120. A subsyndromal condition is best described as:
     a. a nondisorder.
     b. a biomedical condition for which there is no available drug therapy.
     c. a mild version of a mental disorder.
     d. a diagnosable disorder without overt symptoms.

121. In discussing psychotherapy for different cultural groups, your text notes that:
     a. modern therapeutic approaches are general enough to meet the needs of members of most cultural communities.
     b. the goals of therapy must often be modified to conform to the patient's cultural values.
     c. many cultural groups have developed unique therapeutic approaches of their own, some of which are being adopted by mainstream therapists.
     d. all of the above

Answer: b
Evaluating therapeutic outcome
p. 839

122. A major critique of psychotherapy was published by the British psychologist Hans Eysenck in 1961. Eysenck's main argument against the effectiveness of psychoanalysis and related psychotherapies was that:
    a. these therapies are not based on scientific theories of human behavior.
    b. the rate of improvement after therapy is no greater than the spontaneous recovery rate.
    c. the client's symptoms are only the overt signs of an underlying psychopathology.
    d. improvement must be evaluated by an independent observer, rather than by a psychiatrist.

Answer: d
Evaluating therapeutic outcome
p. 839

123. With respect to Eysenck's critique of psychotherapy, which of the following statements is false?
    a. Eysenck estimated that 60 percent of neurotic clients improve following psychotherapy.
    b. Eysenck estimated that 70 percent of neurotic clients improve without therapy.
    c. Eysenck probably underestimated the number of clients who improve following therapy.
    d. Eysenck's critique was proably unduly harsh.

Answer: a
Evaluating therapeutic outcome
p. 839

124. Meta-analysis is a method that is convenient for assessing the effectiveness of psychotherapy because:
    a. it allows the results of many different studies to be combined.
    b. it allows for a finer, more detailed statistical study.
    c. it is much simpler than most other statistical methods.
    d. it provides more accurate results than other methods.

Answer: d
Evaluating therapeutic outcome
p. 839

125. According to a meta-analytic investigation of therapy outcomes described in your textbook, a review of 475 studies revealed that the average person who receives therapy is better off at the end of it than _____ of persons who do not receive therapy.
    a. 10 percent
    b. 25 percent
    c. 50 percent
    d. 80 percent

Answer: d
Evaluating therapeutic outcome
p. 840

126. What is the deterioration effect?
    a. a client deteriorates as soon as therapy stops
    b. the ever-decreasing effectiveness of drugs as a function of time
    c. the ever-decreasing effectiveness of psychotherapy as a function of time
    d. some clients get worse instead of better due to therapy

Answer: b
Evaluating therapeutic outcome
p. 840

127. According to your textbook, one possible cause of the deterioration effect is that:
    a. therapy raises hopes in the client that are not always realized.
    b. therapy disrupts what is stable in the client's life without providing a substitute.
    c. for some clients, therapy slows, but does not stop, a decline in adaptation that began before therapy started.
    d. all of the above

Answer: c
Evaluating therapeutic outcome
p. 840

128. Which of the following is presented in your textbook as a possible cause of the deterioration effect?
    a. Some people just become immune to a drug's effect.
    b. Some people are just not open to therapy.
    c. Appropriate substitutes are not provided when psychotherapy disrupts stability.
    d. A client is not taught effective ways of dealing with psychological problems.

Answer: c
Evaluating therapeutic outcome
p. 841

129. Which of the following best describes the Dodo Bird verdict?
    a. Only therapies that deal with the underlying cause of the problem can be effective.
    b. Clients who come to a therapist with a hostile attitude are less likely to be helped than those who come with a positive attitude.
    c. The differences between various psychotherapies and their effectiveness is very slight or nonexistent.
    d. Therapies that force the client to confront personal problems are the most effective.

Answer: d
Evaluating therapeutic outcome
p. 841

130. The study conducted by Gordon Paul showed that what a person believes can have as much of an effect on well-being as treatment. This study demonstrated the:
    a. Dodo bird effect.
    b. affirmation effect.
    c. false belief effect.
    d. placebo effect.

Answer: d
Evaluating therapeutic outcome
p. 841

131. A client is asked to perform a phony breathing exercise and is then exposed to a supposedly stressful situation. The client is not stressed and believes the breathing exercise to be responsible for this benefit. This client has demonstrated the:
    a. carryover effect.
    b. expectation effect.
    c. false information effect.
    d. placebo effect.
    e. none of the above

Answer: b
Evaluating therapeutic outcome
p. 842

132. According to your textbook, Gordon Paul's study regarding the effectiveness of psychotherapy in the treatment of anxiety revealed that:
    a. groups receiving treatment were no more improved than groups left untreated.
    b. a placebo-treated group improved more than a no-treatment control group.
    c. desensitization therapy was more effective than insight therapy or placebo therapy.
    e. none of the above

Answer: d
Evaluating therapeutic outcome
p. 842

133. In Gordon Paul's study with students afraid of public speaking, the placebo control group:
    a. experienced increased levels of anxiety due to treatment.
    b. improved less than a no-treatment group.
    c. showed no improvement at all.
    d. none of the above

Answer: a
Evaluating therapeutic outcome
p. 842

134. Genuine psychotherapy typically leads to _____ improvement compared to placebo treatments.
    a. more
    b. less
    c. the same
    d. an undetermined amount of

Answer: b
Evaluating therapeutic outcome
p. 843

135. With respect to psychotherapies, prescriptionism refers to:
    a. the tendency of therapists to use the same therapeutic approach for all patients.
    b. the belief that specific therapies should be used to treat specific mental disorders.
    c. the tendency of patients to get better just because they have been given treatment.
    d. none of the above

Answer: b
Evaluating therapeutic outcome
p. 843

136. According to your textbook, which of the following would probably be the most effective treatment for panic disorder?
    a. behavioral therapies
    b. cognitive therapy together with antidepressants
    c. psychodynamic therapy together with antidepressants
    d. humanistic therapy
    e. none of the above

Answer: d
Evaluating therapeutic outcome
p. 843

137. Your textbook authors suggest that some therapies work better than others for specific disorders. For example:
    a. anxiety disorders are best treated using behavior therapies.
    b. cognitive therapy is more effective than behavior therapy for panic disorder.
    c. psychotherapy is of little use in bipolar disorders.
    d. all of the above

Answer: d
Evaluating therapeutic outcome
p. 843

138. Which of the following was not mentioned in your textbook as an effective treatment for depression?
    a. antidepressant medication
    b. electroconvulsive treatment
    c. cognitive therapy
    d. humanistic therapy

Answer: c
Evaluating therapeutic outcome
p. 844

139. In a recent court case, a client suffering from depression received compensation from the hospital that provided treatment. The grounds for the suit were that:
    a. in order to make more money, they had kept him in treatment long after he was well enough to leave the hospital.
    b. they used controversial biological treatments without his informed consent.
    c. the client's condition worsened because the hospital had used intensive psychotherapy rather than antidepressants.
    d. the client's condition worsened because he was refused access to the therapist of his choice.
    e. none of the above

Answer: b
Evaluating therapeutic outcome
p. 844

140. Legal and economic concerns have changed the way psychotherapists work. According to your textbook, therapists are now more likely to:
    a. continue therapy longer in order to minimize the risks of relapse.
    b. use briefer problem-focused therapies.
    c. focus on prosocial aspects of therapy, such as insight and emotional control.
    d. none of the above

Answer: c
A century of therapy
p. 845

141. Which of the following is not a sentiment expressed by your textbook authors as they summarize a century of psychotherapy?
    a. There is little doubt that psychotherapy produces some nonspecific benefits.
    b. Psychotherapy fills a social vacuum.
    c. There are genuine creative benefits to psychotherapy.
    d. Progress relating to biological therapies has been dramatic.

Methods of Scientific Research

Answer: b
Introduction
p. A1

1. In their discussion of research methods, your textbook authors emphasized:
   a. what psychologists know about psychology.
   b. how psychologists learned what they know about psychology.
   c. what topics are studied by psychologists.
   d. how psychologists decide to become psychologists.

Answer: d
Why science?
p. A1

2. According to your textbook authors, how does the psychological approach differ from philosophical and theological approaches to understanding human thoughts, feelings, and behavior?
   a. Psychologists avoid theorizing and speculation.
   b. Psychologists avoid hypothetical thinking.
   c. Psychologists use logic and reasoning.
   d. Psychologists use the scientific method.

Answer: a
Why science?
p. A2

3. Which of the following is an aspect of the scientific method that is necessary for the development of reliable and useful claims about psychological events?
   a. systematic and objective testing of ideas
   b. the use of psychophysical measures
   c. an avoidance of hypothetical thinking
   d. all of the above

Answer: c
Why science?
p. A2

4. According to your textbook discussion of the scientific method, a hypothesis is a prediction that is:
   a. credible.
   b. valid.
   c. testable.
   d. unique.

Answer: d
Why science?
p. A3

5. If the results of a psychological study are consistent with a scientist's predictions, then the hypothesis is:
   a. proven.
   b. replicable.
   c. useful.
   d. confirmed.

Answer: b
Why science?
p. A3

6. Imagine that you have just completed a psychological investigation demonstrating that social praise improves academic performance in young children. You are pleased that your findings confirmed your hypothesis. As a scientist, how should you view this situation?
   a. Your study provided definitive proof that social praise has this benefit.
   b. Your investigation provided evidence that should be supported by replication.
   c. Your techniques should be immediately implemented in the educational system.
   d. Your procedure should be viewed as the most appropriate means of teaching.

Answer: a
Designing a persuasive experiment
p. A3

7. What scientific procedure involves manipulating a single factor to be studied, while holding all other factors constant?
   a. an experiment
   b. behavioral observation
   c. correlational studies
   d. all of the above

Answer: c
Designing a persuasive experiment
pp. A3–A4

8. Penny wants to design a study to determine if physical attractiveness affects hiring decisions in the workplace. As she plans this study, Penny predicts that a job candidate is likely to be eliminated if he has too high a level or too low a level of attractiveness. At this stage of her research, Penny should be most concerned about:
   a. systematic data collection.
   b. replication of her findings.
   c. generating a testable hypothesis.
   d. using a large sample population.

Answer: d
Designing a persuasive experiment
p. A4

9. According to your textbook authors, what must you do to scientifically test the superstition that "bad things come in threes"?
   a. define "bad things"
   b. specify the time interval in which these events must occur
   c. identify an end period in which no such events occur
   d. all of the above

Answer: d
Designing a persuasive experiment
p. A4

10. Anecdotal evidence should be viewed skeptically because it does NOT involve:
    a. appropriate sample sizes.
    b. credible eyewitnesses.
    c. testable ideas about behavior.
    d. systematic data collection.

Answer: b
Designing a persuasive experiment
p. A4

11. _____ evidence tends to be dismissed by psychological scientists because it involves information that is acquired through informal or unsystematic methods.
    a. Correlational
    b. Anecdotal
    c. Experimental
    d. none of the above

Answer: a
Designing a persuasive experiment
p. A5

12. What is the "file-drawer problem"?
    a. the tendency for studies with encouraging results to be published, while those with ambiguous or less-interesting results go unreported
    b. the tendency for studies involving massive amounts of data to go unreported, while those that require simpler statistical analyses get published
    c. the tendency for studies by well-known scientists to be published, while those of less-famous researchers go unreported
    d. none of the above

Answer: c
Designing a persuasive experiment
p. A5

13. As you informally consider your friends' testimonies about the effectiveness of a new headache remedy, _____ is likely to occur due to selective memory and other types of memory errors.
    a. the file-drawer problem
    b. a false rejection
    c. a confirmation bias
    d. none of the above

Answer: d
Designing a persuasive experiment
p. A5

14. According to your textbook authors, informal and unsystematic data collection is problematic because it can be biased by:
    a. the file-drawer problem.
    b. memory errors.
    c. a confirmation bias.
    d. all of the above

Answer: b
Designing a persuasive experiment
pp. A5–A6

15. A psychologist plans to investigate the effects of room lighting on mood in high school students. In this study, what is the dependent variable?
    a. the room lighting
    b. mood
    c. the age of the participants
    d. the sample size of the participants

Answer: a
Designing a persuasive experiment
p. A6

16. Clarissa is conducting research to determine if physical punishment affects moral competency in three-year-old male children. In this study, _____ is the dependent variable.
    a. moral competancy
    b. physical punishment
    c. the age of the children
    d. the gender of the children

17. Clarissa is conducting research to determine if physical punishment affects moral competancy in three-year-old male children. In this study, _____ is the independent variable.
    a. moral competancy
    b. physical punishment
    c. the age of the children
    d. the gender of the children

18. A psychologist plans to investigate the effects of room lighting on mood in high-school students. In this study, what is the independent variable?
    a. the room lighting
    b. mood
    c. the age of the participants
    d. the sample size of the participants

19. Which of the following is most useful in psychological studies that involve variables such as attractiveness that cannot be directly assessed?
    a. informal and subjective assessments
    b. good experimenter intuition
    c. multivariate analyses of data
    d. interrater reliability measures

20. A psychologist plans to investigate the effectiveness of a new psychoactive drug designed to treat schizophrenia. To do this, the psychologist randomly divides participants into two groups, and only one group is given the new drug. Why?
    a. A control group provides information about levels of schizophrenic symptoms in the absence of drug treatment.
    b. An experimental group provides information about levels of schizophrenic symptoms in the absence of drug treatment.
    c. An independent group provides information about levels of schizophrenic symptoms in the absence of drug treatment.
    d. A dependent group provides information about levels of schizophrenic symptoms in the absence of drug treatment.

21. Jamal conducts a research study to investigate the effects of cigarette smoking on attentiveness to a problem-solving task in habitual cigarette smokers. In this study, what is the experimental manipulation?
    a. the problem-solving task
    b. cigarette smoking
    c. measurement of attentiveness
    d. none of the above

22. What is the minimal number of groups of participants necessary to conduct a well-designed multi-participant experiment to test the effects of chocolate ingestion on memory?
    a. 1
    b. 2
    c. 3
    d. 4

Answer: c
Designing a persuasive experiment
p. A7

23. A psychologist plans to investigate the effectiveness of a new psychoactive drug designed to treat schizophrenia. To do this, the psychologist randomly divides the participants into two groups, of which only one group is given the new drug. What should the researcher give to the participants who do not receive this drug treatment?
    a. monetary compensation for the delay of treatment
    b. a full explanation of the drug's potential treatment effects
    c. a placebo that is physically similar to the drug being tested
    d. a list of the potential side effects related to this drug treatment

Answer: d
Designing a persuasive experiment
p. A7

24. A psychologist plans to investigate the effects of exposure to violent cartoons on aggressive behavior in young children. To do this, the psychologist randomly divides the participants into two groups, of which only one group is shown violent cartoons. How should the researcher treat the participants who do not view these violent cartoons?
    a. They should be placed in the situation in which aggression is assessed without any form of preliminary treatment.
    b. They should be placed in the situation in which aggression is assessed after playing alone for the duration of the cartoons.
    c. They should be placed in the situation in which aggression is assessed after playing in a group for the duration of the cartoons.
    d. They should be placed in the situation in which aggression is assessed after watching nonviolent cartoons.

Answer: c
Designing a persuasive experiment
p. A7

25. In an experiment, _____ can be reduced or eliminated when the researcher treats participants in the experimental and control groups similarly.
    a. file-drawer problems
    b. confirmation biases
    c. demand characteristics
    d. all of the above

Answer: b
Designing a persuasive experiment
p. A8

26. In a _____ experiment, neither the participants nor the investigator knows who is in the experimental group or who is in the control group.
    a. single-blind
    b. double-blind
    c. univariate
    d. multivariate

Answer: d
Designing a persuasive experiment
p. A8

27. What do scientists call the uncontrolled factors that could influence the results of a research study?
    a. experimental variables
    b. control variables
    c. placebos
    d. confounds

Answer: b
Designing a persuasive experiment
p. A8

28. Jeffrey conducted a study to investigate the effects of room color on mood in the elderly. However, he did not take into consideration the possibility that some of his research participants were using medications that influenced their moods. In Jeffrey's study, this uncontrolled factor is best referred to as a:
    a. placebo effect.
    b. confound.
    c. controlling variable.
    d. none of the above

Answer: d
Designing a persuasive experiment
p. A8

29. If a psychological researcher concludes that an experiment was conducted properly and her results were not affected by confounds, then the experiment can be said to be:
    a. externally reliable.
    b. internally reliable.
    c. externally valid.
    d. internally valid.

Answer: d
Designing a persuasive experiment
pp. A8–A9

30. In a well-designed experiment:
    a. experimental and control groups are treated identically, except for the experimental manipulation.
    b. the research begins with a clearly stated and testable hypothesis.
    c. dependent variables are clearly defined so that the results can be measured accurately and reliably.
    d. all of the above

Answer: a
Observational studies
pp. A10–A11

31. Kurt wants to investigate whether people with large hands also tend to have large feet. Which of the following is true regarding the procedures that Kurt should use to conduct this research?
    a. Kurt must conduct an observational study, rather than an experiment.
    b. Kurt must divide the research participants into two matched groups.
    c. Kurt must administer a placebo to the comparison group.
    d. all of the above

Answer: b
Observational studies
p. A11

32. It is unethical to directly manipulate an independent variable such as physical abuse in children. Therefore, researchers often rely on _____ to investigate these and other similar issues.
    a. experimental methods
    b. observational methods
    c. case studies
    d. library research

Answer: c
Observational studies
p. A11

33. _____ studies assess the degree of relatedness between two variables.
    a. Experimental
    b. Observational
    c. Correlational
    d. none of the above

34. Unlike the results of most experiments, correlational studies tend to have:
    a. interrater reliability.
    b. internal validity.
    c. confounds.
    d. causal ambiguity.

35. Which of the following can resolve causal ambiguity in a correlational study?
    a. elimination of potential confounds
    b. a specific time-order relationship between variables
    c. an increase in external validity
    d. reduction in the number of participants
    e. both a and b

36. Charlene conducted a correlational study and discovered that there was a strong relationship between the frequency with which students conversed with other students in class and the frequency that students attended weekend parties. Charlene is cautious about interpreting her findings. Why?
    a. Correlational studies can have directionality problems, so Charlene does not know whether students had more conversations because they met other students at parties or if students were invited to more parties because they took part in more classroom conversations.
    b. Correlational studies can have third-variable problems, so Charlene does not know if some other variable, such as sociability, directly affected whether students engaged in more classroom conversations and whether they attended more parties.
    c. both a and b
    d. none of the above

37. When considering the costs and benefits of the various research methods discussed in your textbook, it is important to remember that:
    a. correlation does not imply causation.
    b. experimentation does not imply manipulation.
    c. observation does not imply theorization.
    d. all of the above

38. According to your textbook authors, what is the essential difference between experimental and correlational research designs?
    a. the amount of external validity
    b. elimination of confounds
    c. random assignment to groups
    d. the use of interrater reliability measures

39. A case study usually involves _____ research participant(s).
    a. 1
    b. 10 to 50
    c. 50 to 100
    d. more than 100

Answer: b
Observational studies
p. A14

40. Using case studies to investigate a psychological phenomenon can be problematic because:
    a. it is difficult to collect the large amount of data required to fully understand a single individual.
    b. an individual participant may be unique and the findings of the case study may not be applicable to other people.
    c. acceptable interrater reliability measures are difficult to achieve when only a single individual is studied.
    d. all of the above

Answer: c
Observational studies
p. A15

41. Single-case experiments typically involve:
    a. systematic assessment of the effects of manipulating an independent variable.
    b. investigation of the behavior of a single research participant.
    c. both a and b
    d. neither a nor b

Answer: a
The importance of multiple methods
p. A15

42. Which of the following is a conclusion presented by your textbook authors as they discuss the use of various psychological research methods, including experimentation, correlation, and single-case designs?
    a. ". . . psychologists often use them all, even when pursuing a single question."
    b. ". . . psychologists typically become expert in using a single method and they tend to use it exclusively."
    c. ". . . psychologists generally agree that correlational studies have more advantages than other research techniques."
    d. none of the above

Answer: b
Generalizing from research
p. A17

43. What can you say about a research study in which the participants are representative of a larger population of people and the research stimuli are representative of those encountered in the real world?
    a. The research study is internally valid.
    b. The research study is externally valid.
    c. both a and b
    d. none of the above

Answer: c
Generalizing from research
p. A17

44. Benny conducted an undergraduate research study using only a few participants consisting of his closest friends. Benny's research can be said to have:
    a. low internal validity.
    b. high external validity.
    c. low external validity.
    d. high internal validity.

Answer: d
Generalizing from research
p. A17

45. Toby is interested in whether persons diagnosed with schizophrenia are helped by behavioral therapies. Because Toby cannot study every schizophrenic individual in the entire world, he must select a smaller group of participants who will be representative of the others. What is the correct term for this carefully selected group of research participants that Toby will study?
    a. the experimental group
    b. the control group
    c. a population
    d. a sample

Answer: b
Generalizing from research
p. A18

46. In a _____ sample, every individual has an equal opportunity for selection to participate in a research study, compared to any other individual.
    a. matched
    b. random
    c. population
    d. planned
    e. stratified

Answer: a
Generalizing from research
p. A18

47. In a _____ sample, subgroups are represented in proportions equal to their occurrence in a larger, naturally occurring, group of people.
    a. stratified
    b. matched
    c. random
    d. planned

Answer: c
Generalizing from research
p. A18

48. Laboratory studies sometimes lack external validity because participants are tested under artificial conditions. Which of the following research topics is most likely to have high external validity when studied in a laboratory environment?
    a. courtship activities in humans
    b. maternal behavior in chimpanzees
    c. visual perception in rodents
    d. cheating behavior in students

Answer: b
Research ethics
p. A19

49. Research ethics are a serious consideration in psychology. In the United States, what professional organization has established the ethical guidelines for conducting psychological research?
    a. the National Science Foundation
    b. the American Psychological Association
    c. the National Institute of Mental Health
    d. the American Psychological Society

Answer: d
Research ethics
pp. A20–A21

50. Which of the following is not part of the guidelines for the ethical conduct of psychological research, published by the American Psychological Association?
    a. Nonhuman animals should be provided adequate housing and nutrition.
    b. Human participants should be informed about research procedures prior to their participation.
    c. The privacy and autonomy of human participants should be protected.
    d. Monetary compensation for participation is required for human participants.

Answer: a
Research ethics
p. A20

51. Based on what you know about the benefits of double-blind studies, which of the following ethical principles for the conduct of psychological research is most likely to conflict with a researcher's desire to conduct an internally valid research study?
    a. informed consent
    b. confidentiality
    c. avoidance of coercion
    d. the right to cease participation

Answer: b
Research ethics
p. A20

52. According to the American Psychological Association's guidelines for the ethical conduct of psychological research, what should occur at the end of every psychological research study?
    a. informed consent
    b. debriefing of participants
    c. elimination of confidentiality
    d. all of the above

Answer: c
Research ethics
p. A21

53. In their concluding remarks about psychological research methods, your textbook authors suggest that, as we move into the next millenium, we will need a science that is as _____ as it is _____.
    a. flexible; unique
    b. valid; interesting
    c. humane; rigorous
    d. all of the above

APPENDIX 2

Statistics: The Description, Organization, and Interpretation of Data

Answer: a
Describing the data
p. B2

1. A researcher asks people their opinions on gun control and then codes their responses from 1 (strongly opposed) to 7 (strongly in favor). This coding is a way of:
    a. scaling the data.
    b. accounting for variability in the data.
    c. eliminating variability in the data.
    d. correlating the data.

Answer: a
Describing the data
p. B2

2. On a certain questionnaire the sex of a subject is indicated as *1* if female and *2* if male. These numbers are an example of a(n):
    a. nominal scale.
    b. ordinal scale.
    c. interval scale.
    d. ratio scale.

Answer: a
Describing the data
p. B2

3. A researcher chooses 20 works of art and randomly numbers them from 1 to 20. She then asks people to write down the numbers assigned to the three works they like the most out of the 20. The numbers they write down form a(n):
    a. categorical scale.
    b. ordinal scale.
    c. ratio scale.
    d. interval scale.

Answer: b
Describing the data
p. B2

4. A researcher asks people to look at 20 works of art and assign each a number from 1 (most preferred) to 20 (least preferred). These numbers form a(n):
    a. interval scale.
    b. ordinal scale.
    c. ratio scale.
    d. categorical scale.

5. With an ordinal scale:
   a. numbers are assigned arbitrarily, rather than meaningfully.
   b. scores cannot be added or subtracted.
   c. the difference between a score of 2 and a score of 4 is equal to the difference between a score of 8 and a score of 10.
   d. a and b

6. With an interval scale:
   a. numbers are assigned arbitrarily rather than meaningfully.
   b. the difference between a score of 2 and a score of 4 is equal to the difference between a score of 8 and a score of 10.
   c. scores cannot be added or subtracted.
   d. a and c

7. Subjects are asked, according to their opinion, to rank the top ten hockey players. One subject, *A*, lists Bobby Orr as fourth on his list. Another subject, B, lists Bobby Orr as eighth. An appropriate conclusion is that:
   a. subject *A* thinks that Bobby Orr is twice as good a player as subject *B* does.
   b. subject *B* thinks that Bobby Orr is only half as good as subject *A* does.
   c. subject *A* thinks there are only 3 players better than Orr, while *B* thinks there are 7.
   d. all of the above.

8. An experimenter determines the time it takes each of 20 runners to run a mile. These numbers make up a(n):
   a. nominal scale.
   b. interval scale.
   c. ratio scale.
   d. ordinal scale.

9. Saying that SPF (sun protection factor) uses a ratio scale means that:
   a. an SPF of 30 is twice as strong as an SPF of 15.
   b. the difference between an SPF of 5 and of 10 is equal to the difference between an SPF of 15 and of 20.
   c. there is a true zero point for SPF.
   d. all of the above

10. A histogram:
    a. is a graphic presentation of a frequency distribution.
    b. cannot be created when the dependent variable has many possible values.
    c. can only be created after the mean has been calculated.
    d. always results in a normal distribution.

11. A histogram can be used to read off the _____ of the sample directly.
    a. mode
    b. mean
    c. standard deviation
    d. variance

Answer: d
Organizing the data
p. B5

12. A measure of central tendency:
    a. reflects the variability of a distribution.
    b. is used to calculate the range of a distribution.
    c. provides the same score for central tendency regardless of the procedure used to calculate that central tendency.
    d. is one way of summarizing a set of data.

Answer: d
Organizing the data
p. B5

13. In the distribution, 1 1 2 2 3 3 3 4 4 5 5, number 3 is the:
    a. mode.
    b. median.
    c. mean.
    d. all of the above

Answer: d
Organizing the data
p. B5

14. In the distribution, 1 2 5 7 7 9 10 10 10 12, the mode is:
    a. 7.
    b. 7.3.
    c. 8.
    d. 10.

Answer: d
Organizing the data
p. B5

15. In the distribution: 1, 2, 5, 7, 7, 9, 10, 10, 10, 12, the median is:
    a. 7.3.
    b. 7.
    c. 10.
    d. 8.

Answer: d
Organizing the data
p. B5

16. The median:
    a. is a measure of central tendency.
    b. divides a distribution into two equal halves.
    c. allows for a calculation of variability in a distribution.
    d. a and b

Answer: b
Organizing the data
p. B5

17. The mean of a distribution:
    a. divides the distribution into two equal halves.
    b. is the arithmetic average of the scores.
    c. is the same as the median.
    d. can be read directly off of a histogram.

Answer: b
Organizing the data
p. B5

18. The least useful measure of central tendency is the:
    a. mean.
    b. mode.
    c. median.
    d. All of the above are equally useful.

Answer: b
Organizing the data
p. B5

19. An experimenter collects reaction time data and notices that the participants' scores are quite variable. Most of them are extremely fast reaction times (in the order of milliseconds), while a few are extremely slow times (in the order of seconds). The best measure of central tendency for these data is provided by the:
    a. mode.
    b. median.
    c. mean.
    d. range.

Answer: c
Organizing the data
p. B5

20. A teacher gives a test to 50 students and the mean of the resulting distribution is 80. She discovers that she made a mistake in grading, and that she has to give an additional 5 points to every student in the class. When she calculates the new mean, the result is:
    a. 80.0.
    b. 80.1.
    c. 85.0.
    d. 90.0.

Answer: b
Organizing the data
pp. B5–B6

21. In a skewed distribution:
    a. scores are symmetrically arranged around the mean.
    b. the mean is not equal to the median.
    c. there is very little variability.
    d. there is no mode.

Answer: d
Organizing the data
p. B6

22. If a distribution of scores is symmetrical, then:
    a. there are as many scores below the mean as above it.
    b. the mean equals the median.
    c. the variability equals zero.
    d. a and b

Answer: d
Organizing the data
pp. B6–B7

23. If a distribution has zero variability, then:
    a. the mean equals the median.
    b. the mode equals the mean.
    c. all of the scores are identical.
    d. all of the above

Answer: c
Organizing the data
p. B6

24. In the following sample — 18, 22, 17, 17, 16, 14, 20, 15 — the range is:
    a. 2.
    b. 4.
    c. 8.
    d. 18.

Answer: c
Organizing the data
pp. B7–B8

25. Which of the following is a measure of variability?
    a. mean
    b. median
    c. standard deviation
    d. mode

Answer: a
Organizing the data
pp. B6–B8

26. Which of the following is not a measure of variability in a sample?
    a. median
    b. range
    c. variance
    d. standard deviation

Answer: d
Organizing the data
p. B7

27. The variance is:
    a. the square root of the standard deviation.
    b. the square of the mean.
    c. the square of the median.
    d. the square of the standard deviation.

Answer: d
Organizing the data
p. B7

28. The variance:
    a. can never be smaller than the mean.
    b. can be positive or negative in sign.
    c. is equal to the square of the range.
    d. can only be zero when the range of the distribution is zero.

Answer: e
Organizing the data
p. B7

29. In order to calculate variance, you need:
    a. the values of all the scores in the sample.
    b. the mean of the sample.
    c. the values of just the highest and lowest scores in the sample.
    d. the median of the sample.
    e. a and b

Answer: b
Organizing the data
p. B8

30. The standard deviation of a sample is:
    a. the square of the variance of that sample.
    b. the square root of the variance of that sample.
    c. equal to the variance of a sample if the distribution is symmetrical.
    d. the square root of the range of the sample.

Answer: b
Organizing the data
p. B8

31. The standard deviation of the following sample—4, 7, 10—is equal to:
    a. the square root of 3.
    b. the square root of 6.
    c. the square root of 7.
    d. 3.

Answer: c
Organizing the data
p. B8

32. A teacher gives a test to 50 students. The resulting mean of the distribution is 100, and the standard deviation is 9. He now discovers he has made a mistake in grading and that he has to give an additional 5 points to every student in the class. When he calculates the new frequency distribution, its standard deviation is:
    a. the square root of 104.
    b. 14.
    c. 9.
    d. 5.

Answer: b
Organizing the data
p. B8

33. Joe has a percentile score of 64 percent on some test. This means that:
    a. 64 percent of people score higher than Joe.
    b. 64 percent of people score lower than Joe.
    c. the z-score associated with that score is negative.
    d. the distribution of the test has a standard deviation of 8.

Answer: c
Organizing the data
p. B8

34. Jane gets a score of 70 on an arithmetic test. The mean of the scores on the test was 60; the standard deviation was 5. What is Jane's z-score on that test?
    a. +30
    b. +10
    c. +2
    d. +5

35. A z-score:
    a. allows for comparison of scores obtained from different distributions.
    b. evaluates a particular score relative to the median and range of the distribution.
    c. is a measure of central tendency of a distribution.
    d. is a measure of variability within a distribution.

36. Jerry's baseball team has averaged about 5 runs per game all season. His sister Judy's basketball team has averaged about 35 points per game. The siblings want to decide which team has had a better season, and they have the scoring averages of each team in both leagues. To make this comparison they should:
    a. calculate the median score in each league.
    b. calculate the modal score in each league.
    c. simply decide that Judy's 35 indicates better performance than Jerry's 5.
    d. convert scores in each league to z-scores or percentile ranks.
    e. calculate the correlation between the teams.

37. To convert a score to a z-score, you need:
    a. the distribution's standard deviation and mean.
    b. the distribution's standard deviation and median.
    c. the distribution's mean and number of scores.
    d. the distribution's range and mean.

38. To evaluate her baseball ability relative to the other members of her team, Jill and the other team members take a baseball skills test. After taking the test, Jill calculates her z-score and finds that it equals zero. Therefore:
    a. Jill is the worst player on her team.
    b. Jill is the best player on her team.
    c. Jill is average in ability relative to her teammates.
    d. Jill's ability cannot be determined from the above data.

39. The normal curve:
    a. has a mode that equals its median.
    b. is a special case of a histogram.
    c. has an equal number of scores above and below the mean.
    d. all of the above

40. In a normal curve the percentage of scores that lie between minus-one standard deviation and plus-one standard deviation is:
    a. approximately 68 percent.
    b. equal to the percentage lying between the mean and one standard deviation.
    c. equal to the mean times its frequency.
    d. approximately 50 percent.

Answer: b
Organizing the data
pp. B9–B10

41. A professor finds that scores on her recent exam in a large class are normally distributed. She decides to standardize the scores and assign grades to the resulting z-scores as follows: F for $z \leq -2$; D for $-2 < z \leq -1$; C for $-1 < z < 1$; B for $1 \leq z < 2$; and A for $z \geq 2$. Which of the following statements is false?
    a. Students will need to score in at least the 84th percentile to receive a B.
    b. How many students are assigned each grade will depend on what the mean score was.
    c. As many As will be assigned as Fs.
    d. Students whose score equals the class mean will receive a C.

Answer: b
Organizing the data
p. B10

42. If a coin is tossed many times, the distribution of the number of times the coin comes up tails:
    a. cannot be predicted.
    b. will be a normal curve.
    c. will be skewed.
    d. will have a different mean, median, and mode.
    e. c and d

Answer: c
Describing the relation between
    two variables
p. B11

43. A correlation refers to:
    a. the degree of variability in a set of numbers.
    b. the central tendency of a set of numbers.
    c. the relationship between two variables.
    d. the relationship between the variability and the central tendency of a distribution.

Answer: a
Describing the relation between
    two variables
p. B11

44. In golf the better one's ability, the lower are one's golf scores. Golfing ability and golf scores are:
    a. negatively correlated.
    b. positively correlated.
    c. related according to their square roots.
    d. too variable to be correlated.

Answer: a
Describing the relation between
    two variables
p. B11

45. If two variables are positively correlated, then:
    a. increasing values of one variable are associated with increasing values of the other variable.
    b. increasing values of one variable are associated with decreasing values of the other variable.
    c. each value of one variable is identical to each value of the second variable.
    d. their line of best fit slips downward.

Answer: d
Describing the relation between
    two variables
pp. B11–B12

46. If two variables are correlated perfectly in a negative way, then:
    a. all the data points in a scatter plot will lie on the line of best fit.
    b. the line of best fit will slope downward.
    c. the scatter plot will reveal points scattered about the line of best fit but the general trend will be a downward slope.
    d. a and b

47. A scatter diagram of two variable shows that the line of best fit slopes downward. This tells us that the correlation between the two variables is:
    a. sizable.
    b. negligible.
    c. positive.
    d. negative.

48. When two variables are perfectly correlated:
    a. all points on a scatter plot will lie on the line of best fit.
    b. if one variable increases, the other does as well.
    c. each score on one variable is identical to its related score on the other variable.
    d. all of the above

49. If the line of best fit in a scatter plot is horizontal:
    a. the relation between the variables cannot be determined.
    b. the variables are negatively correlated.
    c. the variables are perfectly positively correlated.
    d. the variables are unrelated.

50. A teacher gives her students a test in arithmetic and another test in vocabulary. She computes the correlation between the tests and finds that it is +0.50. Afterward, she finds she has made a mistake in grading. To correct it, she adds 5 points to every arithmetic score and 2 points to every vocabulary score. She then recomputes the correlation coefficient. What can we say about the recomputed correlation coefficient?
    a. It will be less than +0.50.
    b. It will be more than +0.50.
    c. It will be +0.50.
    d. There is no way of telling what it will be without knowing the means and standard deviations of the two tests.

51. The correlation coefficient between two sets of randomly generated numbers is:
    a. +1.0.
    b. 0.
    c. positive but not exactly +1.0.
    d. negative but not exactly −1.0.

52. To calculate the correlation coefficient, you need:
    a. the ranges of the two variables.
    b. the medians of the two variables.
    c. the z-scores for each value in each variable.
    d. all of the above

Answer: a
Describing the relation between
    two variables
p. B13

53. Which of the following statements is false?
    a. With a correlation of 0, one variable can be predicted from another better than with a correlation of –0.5.
    b. With a correlation of –0.8, one variable can be predicted from another better than with a correlation of –0.3.
    c. With a correlation of –0.6, one variable can be predicted from another better than with a correlation of +0.4.
    d. b and c

Answer: b
Describing the relation between
    two variables
p. B14

54. An investigator finds a positive correlation between years of schooling and later adult income. Why can't we infer from this evidence that length in school is a cause of later earnings?
    a. because there are many millionaires who never finished high school
    b. because both variables may be positively correlated with yet a third variable that causes the other two
    c. because the correlation is not perfect
    d. a and c

Answer: a
Describing the relation between
    two variables
p. B14

55. If we found that time spent watching *Baywatch* was positively correlated with swimming ability, it would mean that:
    a. on average, better swimmers spend more time watching *Baywatch* than do poorer swimmers.
    b. people learn to swim better from watching *Baywatch*.
    c. people who spend a lot of time practicing swimming are often too tired for anything other than watching mindless TV when they get home, so they watch a lot of *Baywatch*.
    d. a and b

Answer: a
Interpreting data
pp. B15–B16

56. An experimenter tests a certain variable by running an experimental and a control group. He knows that the variable has an effect if:
    a. the variance within the experimental and the control groups is substantially less than the overall variance.
    b. the variance within the experimental and the control groups is substantially more than the overall variance.
    c. if the variance within the experimental group is substantially more than the variance within the control group.
    d. if the variance within the experimental group is substantially less than the variance within the control group.

Answer: d
Interpreting data
p. B17

57. An experimenter devises a test which she feels will predict hitting ability in baseball. The experimenter administers the test to a random sample of major league baseball players at the beginning of the season and then correlates their scores with their batting average at the end of the season. The correlation coefficient is +0.50. One can say that:
    a. taking the test has improved the players' batting ability by an average of 50 percent.
    b. the score on the test explains 50 percent of the variance in batting ability.
    c. approximately half of the players improve their batting skills as a result of taking the test.
    d. less than half of the variance in batting ability can be explained by the batting test scores.

58. The correlation coefficient between two variables is minus 0.50. The percentage of the variance in one variable that can be accounted for by the variance in the other variable is:
    a. more than 50 percent.
    b. 50 percent.
    c. 25 percent.
    d. less than 25 percent.

59. *X* and *Y* are correlated, with a correlation coefficient of *r*. What is the proportion of the variance of *Y* that can be accounted for by variable *X*?
    a. *r*
    b. the square of *r*
    c. the square root of *r*
    d. the variance of *X* times *r*

60. A critical ratio is:
    a. a measure of variability in sample means.
    b. generally larger than 2.
    c. a *z*-score.
    d. a measure of central tendency

61. If one obtains a critical ratio of 5, then:
    a. one can be absolutely confident in rejecting the null hypothesis.
    b. one should accept the null hypothesis.
    c. one should accept the alternative hypothesis.
    d. the difference between means was less than the standard error.

62. Behavioral scientists generally regard a score as "statistically reliable" if:
    a. it is less than two standard deviations away from the mean.
    b. it is at least two standard deviations away from the mean.
    c. it is above 70.
    d. it is between one and two standard deviations away from the mean.

63. In testing a hypothesis about a single score:
    a. the researcher is choosing between the null hypothesis and an alternative hypothesis.
    b. a researcher who chooses the critical value carefully will always be correct.
    c. the researcher compares the score to the median of the population.
    d. the researcher must convert the score to a *z*-score.
    e. a and d

Answer: d
Interpreting data
p. B18

64. A teacher grades an examination and finds 1 test paper with an extremely low score. That score is so low that the teacher wonders whether the paper really belonged to one of his own students or whether it somehow accidentally slipped in from another class. As a first check, the teacher looks at the class mean and the class standard deviation which are 100 and 5 respectively. Using the standard critical ratio, what is the highest score that probably came from another class?
   a. 105
   b. 50
   c. 95
   d. 90

Answer: a
Interpreting data
p. B18

65. A distribution has a mean of 105 and a standard deviation of 20. Which of the following scores probably comes from a different distribution?
   a. 60
   b. 90
   c. 100
   d. 135

Answer: c
Interpreting data
p. B18

66. An experimenter tests the ability of drug *X* to improve memory by testing memory capacity of research participants after giving them that drug. She compares their performance to a test she administered to the same participants when they were not drugged. In this experiment the null hypothesis predicts that memory capacity during the drug state will be:
   a. significantly greater than that during the nondrug state.
   b. significantly poorer than that during the nondrug state.
   c. not significantly different from that during the nondrug state.
   d. indeterminate, for the null hypothesis allows no prediction.

Answer: d
Interpreting the data
p. B18

67. The null hypothesis states that:
   a. an obtained score, although different in magnitude from the mean, is not significantly different from the mean.
   b. all scores must fall within two standard deviations about the mean.
   c. an obtained score falls within the normally expected variability about a mean.
   d. a and c

Answer: c
Interpreting the data
p. B21

68. A standard error is the:
   a. variance of a distribution of sample means.
   b. variance of a distribution of population means.
   c. standard deviation of a distribution of sample means.
   d. standard deviation of a distribution of population means.

Answer: c
Interpreting the data
p. B21

69. The standard error:
   a. equals the variance divided by the number of scores.
   b. is equal to the standard deviation in the case of symmetrical distributions.
   c. is inversely related to the sample size.
   d. equals the critical ratio divided by the difference between the means.

70. A distribution of 6 scores has a standard deviation of 100. The standard error of this distribution is:
    a. 4.
    b. 5.
    c. 10.
    d. 20.

71. An experimenter is designing an experiment. She desires to maximize the accuracy of the sample mean which she will obtain. The experimenter should be advised to:
    a. use a large sample size.
    b. measure a normally distributed variable.
    c. select a greater critical ratio.
    d. all of the above

72. A confidence interval:
    a. is another term for the range of the data.
    b. is the range in which the population mean is highly likely to fall.
    c. is the sample mean plus or minus one standard deviation.
    d. is the sample mean plus or minus 3 percent.

73. Imagine that we found that people scored higher on a reading comprehension test after eating a bowl of chocolate ice cream than after eating a bowl of vanilla ice cream, and that this difference was statistically reliable. It would be appropriate to infer that:
    a. the difference is probably not due to chance.
    b. every member of the chocolate group scored at least as high as every member of the vanilla group.
    c. our sample size was fairly small.
    d. the difference is definitely not due to chance.
    e. b and d

74. To say that a difference is *statistically reliable* means that:
    a. it has important implications.
    b. it is very unlikely to be due to chance.
    c. it is definitely not due to chance.
    d. we cannot reject the null hypothesis.
    e. a and b